Official
XTREE
MS-DOS, Windows, & Hard Disk Management Companion 3rd Edition

Official
XTREE®
MS-DOS, Windows, & Hard Disk Management Companion 3rd Edition

By Beth Slick

IDG BOOKS

IDG Books Worldwide, Inc.
An International Data Group Company
San Mateo, California 94402

The Official XTree MS-DOS, Windows, & Hard Disk Management Companion, 3rd Edition

Published by
IDG Books Worldwide, Inc.
An International Data Group Company
155 Bovet Road, Suite 610
San Mateo, CA 94402
415-312-0650

Copyright © 1992 by IDG Books Worldwide, Inc. All rights reserved. No part of this book, including interior design, cover design, and icons, may be reproduced or transmitted in any form, by any means (electronic, photocopying, recording, or otherwise) without the prior written permission of the publisher.

Library of Congress Catalog Card No.: 92-72197

ISBN 1-878058-57-6

Printed in the United States of America

10 9 8 7 6 5 4 3 2 1

Distributed in the United States by IDG Books Worldwide, Inc.

Distributed in Canada by Macmillan of Canada, a Division of Canada Publishing Corporation; by Woodslane Pty. Ltd. in Australia and New Zealand; and by Computer Bookshops in the U.K and Ireland.

For information on translations and availability in other countries, contact Marc Jeffrey Mikulich, Foreign Rights Manager, at IDG Books Worldwide. Fax: 415-358-1260.

For sales inquiries and special prices for bulk quantities, write to the address above or call IDG Books Worldwide at 415-312-0650.

Trademarks: XTree is a registered trademark, and XTreePro, XTreePro Gold, XTree Easy, XTreeNet, 1Word, XTree for Windows, and XTree Company are trademarks of Executive Systems, Inc. Windows is a trademark of Microsoft Corporation. All other brand names and product names used in this book are trademarks, registered trademarks, or trade names of their respective holders. IDG Books Worldwide is not associated with XTree Company or any other product or vendor mentioned in this book.

Limits of Liability/Disclaimer of Warranty: The author and publisher of this book have used their best efforts in preparing this book. IDG Books Worldwide, Inc., International Data Group, Inc., and the author make no representation or warranties with respect to the accuracy or completeness of the contents of this book, and specifically disclaim any implied warranties or merchantability or fitness for any particular purpose, and shall in no event be liable for any loss of profit or any other commercial damage, including but not limited to special, incidental, consequential, or other damages.

Acknowledgments

We would like to thank Chris Williams, Rick James, Chris Clancy, Joe Raftery, Janna Custer, Michael McCarthy, Bob Kimball, Todd Walker (for the Q&A's from the tech department), Therese Solimeno, Michael Chuises, Tracey Immel, and Carey Williams Cahlin.

                                      Beth Slick
                                      Michael Cahlin

(The publisher would like to give special thanks to Patrick J. McGovern, without whom this book would not have been possible.)

About IDG Books Worldwide

Welcome to the world of IDG Books Worldwide.

IDG Books Worldwide, Inc., is a division of International Data Group (IDG), the world's largest publisher of computer-related information and the leading global provider of information services on information technology. IDG publishes over 185 computer publications in 60 countries. Thirty million people read one or more IDG publications each month.

If you use personal computers, IDG Books is committed to publishing quality books that meet your needs. We rely on our extensive network of publications, including such leading periodicals as *InfoWorld, PC World, Computerworld, Macworld, Publish, Network World,* and *SunWorld,* to help us make informed and timely decisions in creating useful computer books that meet your needs.

Every IDG book strives to bring extra value and skill-building instruction to the reader. Our books are written by experts, with the backing of IDG periodicals, and with careful thought devoted to issues such as audience, interior design, use of icons, and illustrations. Our editorial staff is a careful mix of high-tech journalists and experienced book people. Our close contact with the makers of computer products helps ensure accuracy and thorough coverage. Our heavy use of personal computers at every step in production means we can deliver books in the most timely manner.

We are delivering books of high quality at competitive prices on topics customers want. At IDG, we believe in quality, and we have been delivering quality for over 25 years. You'll find no better book on a subject than an IDG book.

John Kilcullen
President and Publisher
IDG Books Worldwide, Inc.

IDG Books Worldwide, Inc. is a division of International Data Group. The officers are Patrick J. McGovern, Founder and Board Chairman; Walter Boyd, President; Robert A. Farmer, Vice Chairman. International Data Group's publications include: **ARGENTINA's** Computerworld Argentina, InfoWorld Argentina; **ASIA's** Computerworld Hong Kong, PC World Hong Kong, Computerworld Southeast Asia, PC World Singapore, Computerworld Malaysia, PC World Malaysia; **AUSTRALIA's** Computerworld Australia, Australian PC World, Australian Macworld; **AUSTRIA's** Computerwelt Oesterreich, PC Test; **BRAZIL's** DataNews, Mundo IBM, Mundo Unix, PC World, Publish; **BULGARIA's** Computerworld Bulgaria, Ediworld, PC World Express; **CANADA's** ComputerData, Direct Access, Graduate Computerworld, InfoCanada, Network World Canada; **CHILE's** Computerworld, Informatica; **COLUMBIA's** Computerworld Columbia; **CZECHOSLOVAKIA's** Computerworld Czechoslovakia, PC World Czechoslovakia; **DENMARK's** CAD/CAM WORLD, Communications World, Computerworld Danmark, Computerworld Focus, Computerworld Uddannelse, LAN World, Lotus World, Macintosh Produktkatalog, Macworld Danmark, PC World Danmark, PC World Produktguide, Windows World; **EQUADOR's** PC World; **EGYPT's** PC World Middle East; **FINLAND's** Mikro PC, Tietoviikko, Tietoverkko; **FRANCE's** Distributique, GOLDEN MAC, InfoPC, Languages & Systems, Le Guide du Monde Informatique, Le Monde Informatique, Telecoms & Reseaux; **GERMANY's** Computerwoche, Computerwoche Focus, Computerwoche Extra, Computerwoche Karriere, edv aspekte, Information Management, Macwelt, Netzwelt, PC Welt, PC Woche, Publish, Unit; **HUNGARY's** Computerworld SZT, PC World; **INDIA's** Computers & Communications; **ISRAEL's** Computerworld Israel, PC World Israel; **ITALY's** Computerworld Italia, Lotus Magazine, Macworld Italia, Networking Italia, PC World Italia; **JAPAN's** Computerworld Japan, Macworld Japan, SunWorld Japan; **KOREA's** Computerworld Korea, Macworld Korea, PC World Korea; **MEXICO's** Compu Edicion, Compu Manufactura, Computacion/Punto de Venta, Computerworld Mexico, MacWorld, Mundo Unix, PC World, Windows; **THE NETHERLANDS'** Computer! Totaal, LAN Magazine, Lotus World, MacWorld Magazine; **NEW ZEALAND's** Computerworld New Zealand, New Zealand PC World; **NIGERIA's** PC World Africa; **NORWAY's** Computerworld Norge, C/world, Lotusworld Norge, Macworld Norge, Networld, PC World Ekspress, PC World Norge, PC World's Product Guide, Publish World, Student Guiden, Unix World, Windowsworld, IDG Direct Response; **PERU's** PC World; **PEOPLES REPUBLIC OF CHINA's** China Computerworld, PC World China, Electronics International; **IDG HIGH TECH** Newproductworld, Consumer Electronics New Product World; **PHILLIPPINES'** Computerworld, PC World; **POLAND's** Computerworld Poland, PC World/Komputer; **ROMANIA's** InfoClub Magazine; **RUSSIA's** Computerworld-Moscow, Networks, PC World; **SOUTH AFRICA's** Computing S.A.; **SPAIN's** Amiga World, Autoedicion, Communicaciones World, Computerworld Espana, Macworld Espana, Network World, PC World Espana, Publish, Sunworld; **SWEDEN's** Attack, CAD/CAM World, ComputerSweden, Corporate Computing, Lokala Natverk/LAN, Lotus World, MAC&PC, Macworld, Mikrodatorn, PC World, Publishing & Design (CAP), Datalngenjoren, Maxi Data, Windows World; **SWITZERLAND's** Computerworld Schweiz, Corporate Computing, Macworld Schweiz, PC & Workstation; **TAIWAN's** Computerworld Taiwan, Global Computer Express, PC World Taiwan; **THAILAND's** Thai Computerworld; **TURKEY's** Computerworld Monitor, Macworld Turkiye, PC World Turkiye; **UNITED KINGDOM's** Lotus Magazine, Macworld, Sunworld; **UNITED STATES'** AmigaWorld, Cable in the Classroom, CIO, Computerworld, DOS Resource Guide, Electronic News, Federal Computer Week, GamePro, inCider/A+, IDG Books, InfoWorld, InfoWorld Direct, Macworld, Multimedia World, Network World, NeXTWORLD, PC Games, PC World, PC Letter, Publish, RUN, SunWorld, SWATPro; **VENEZUELA's** Computerworld Venezuela, MicroComputerworld Venezuela; **YUGOSLAVIA's** Moj Mikro.

The text in this book is printed on recycled paper.

About the Author

Beth Slick bought a computer in 1983 for word processing and a few months later ended up working for the store where she bought it. During her seven-year tenure at the computer store, which catered to writers, she not only ended up managing the place, but provided six hours of training each to most of the clients, including Carol Burnett, Gene Roddenberry, John Lithgow, and Larry Gelbart. Also during that time, she sold several television scripts (including two for "Star Trek: The Next Generation") and wrote for *PC Magazine* and *PC Today*. Now a freelance writer, Beth Slick has continued selling scripts as well as designing and conducting seminars in DOS, hard disk survival, and other topics.

Credits

President and Publisher
John J. Kilcullen

Publishing Director
David Solomon

Project Editor
Janna Custer

Managing Editor
Mary Bednarek

Production Director
Lana J. Olson

Acquisitions Editor
Terrie Lynn Solomon

Copy Editor
Megg Bonar

Technical Reviewer
Gina Hara, XTree Company

Text Preparation
Mary Ann Cordova
Dana Bryant Sadoff

Proofreader
Tema Goodwin

Indexer
Ty Koontz

Book Design and Production
Peppy White
Francette M. Ytsma
Kathy Smith
Tracy Strub
(University Graphics, Palo Alto, California)

XTree at a Glance

XTree for DOS
Applications Menu 38
Attributes (File) 41
Avail..44
Batch Files 44
Branch 49
Cancel...49
Command Shell 51
Compare 55
Configuration Options 58
Copy 65
Date and Time Stamp 76
Delete 78
Directory Management 84
Edit 94
Execute 100
File Display 103
Filespec 106
Find...112
Formatting Floppy Disks 116
Global 119
Graft..121
Help 121
Hide/Unhide 126
History 126
Invert 128
Log 129
Memory Management 134
Mouse Commands 136
Move...138
Oops!..145
Open (and Associate) 147
Print..148
Pull-Down Menus 152
Quit...156
Rename 157
Securing Files and Directories 160
Sort Criteria 166
Split/Unsplit..169

Statistics	171
Substituting with SUBST	174
Tag/Untag	177
View	184

XTree for Novell Networks

Attach/Detach	206
Attributes (Directory)	206
Attributes (File)	207
Tag/Untag a Branch	208
Tag/Untag by Attributes	209
Map	209
Volume	210

XTree for Windows

Arranging Your Windows	234
Attributes (File)	236
Auto Directory	237
Auto View	238
Close	238
Configuration Options	239
Copy	239
Date and Time Stamp	244
Delete	244
Detail Box	245
Directory Window	245
Exit	252
Expand/Collapse Tree	252
Find/Find Again	254
Formatting Floppy Disks	255
Launch	257
Log	257
Mark and Unmark	258
Move	260
Move-Up Button	263
Open	264
Preferences	265
Rename	267
Run	268
Selecting and Deselecting	268
Sort Order	271
Statistics	272
Tool Palette	272
Unknown and ?	275
View Window	275

Table of Contents

Acknowledgments v
XTree at a Glance ix
Foreword xxvi
Introduction 1

Part I: XTree for DOS 7

Chapter 1: MS-DOS Concepts 9
In This Chapter 9
What is MS-DOS? 10
   Operating system 10
   A place on the hard disk 10
   You are not in a program 11
Understanding Drives 11
   Drive names 11
   Current drives 12
Examining Directories 12
   Understanding the tree structure 12
   Understanding the directory system 13
   Creating directories 14
Understanding System Prompts 14
Understanding Files 15
   Naming files 16
   Making filenames unique 17
Examining Extensions 17
   Common extensions 17
   Guidelines for extensions 18
Using Wildcards 18
   The asterisk wildcard 19
      Correct asterisk uses 19
      Incorrect asterisk uses 19
   The question mark wildcard 20

Understanding File Attributes 20
Revealing Special Files 21
    Operating system files 21
    CONFIG.SYS file 21
    AUTOEXEC.BAT file 22
Copying Files 22
The End . . . Or Is It? 23
Summary 23

Chapter 2: XTree for DOS Basics 25

In This Chapter 25
Introducing the Family XTree 25
Getting Started 25
Examining XTree Screen Elements 26
    On-screen windows 26
        Directory window 27
        Small file window 27
        Expanded file window 27
        Disk and Disk Statistics windows 28
    Other on-screen elements 28
        Directory and file commands 28
        The ^ symbol 28
Operating in XTree 28
    Moving between windows 29
    Highlighting the current directory 29
    Highlighting the current file 29
    Tagging files and directories 30
    Untagging files and directories 31
    Using the Filespec command 31
    Getting Help 32
    Using the Command shell 32
Using The XTree for DOS Quick Reference Guide 33
Summary 33

Chapter 3: XTree for DOS Quick Reference Guide 35

In This Chapter 35
All Versions of XTree for DOS? 35
    How the side-by-side comparison works 36
    Using a Mouse 37
    Where to Start 37
The Application Menu 38
    Introducing XTreePro Gold's Application Menu 38

Table of Contents

Editing the Application Menu 39
Using the Application Menu for system management 41
Attributes (File) 41
Displaying a file's attributes 41
Changing a file's attributes 42
AutoView 43
Avail 44
Batch Files 44
What is a batch file? 44
Making a batch file 45
Using DOS's batch file variables 46
Using XTree batch file variables 48
Branch 49
Cancel 49
Canceling a command with XTree 49
Canceling a command with XTreePro, XTreePro Gold,
XTree Easy, and XTreeGold 50
The Command Shell 51
What is the Command shell? 51
Activating the Command shell 51
Using the Command shell with XTree 52
Using the Command shell with XTreePro, XTreePro Gold,
XTree Easy, and XTreeGold 52
The History command and XTreePro 53
The History command and XTree Easy, XTreePro Gold, and
XTreeGold 54
Compare 55
Comparing directories from a Directory window 56
Comparing directories from a File window 57
Configuration Options 58
Configuring XTree 59
Configuring XTreePro 60
Configuring XTree Easy, XTreePro Gold, and XTreeGold 61
Copy 65
Copying a file to another drive (including a floppy drive) 66
Replacing a file in XTree 67
Replacing a file in XTreePro, XTreePro Gold, XTree Easy, and
XTreeGold 68
Copying a file to another directory 68
Copying multiple files 69
Copying files and directory structures 70
Using Graft to copy one directory to another 73
Using the Destination window to simplify copying 74

The Date and Time Stamp	76
Using XTreePro Gold and XTreeGold's Newdate command	76
Delete	78
Deleting a file	78
Deleting a file from a floppy drive	78
Deleting more than one file	79
Deleting a directory	80
Using Prune with XTreePro Gold and XTreeGold	81
Using Wash Disk with XTreePro Gold and XTreeGold	81
DIR Empty/DIR Not Logged	82
Directory Management	84
Using Make to create a directory	84
Using Rename to change a directory's name	85
Using Delete to remove a directory	86
Using Copy to duplicate directory structures (and files)	87
Using Prune with XTreePro Gold and XTreeGold	88
Using Graft to move a directory with XTreeGold and XTreePro Gold	89
Collapsing the directory display with XTreePro Gold and XTreeGold	90
Using F5 to collapse two levels in a directory	91
Using F6 to collapse all levels in a directory	92
Hiding and unhiding a directory	93
The Directory Window	94
Editing with 1Word	94
Using 1Word Commands	95
Editing a file with 1Word	95
Creating a new file with 1Word	99
Making Edit launch your word processor	99
Execute	100
Using Execute with all versions of XTree	100
File Display	103
The File Window	105
Filespec	106
Understanding Filespec basics	106
Using multiple filespecs	108
XTreePro and multiple filespecs	108
XTree Easy, XTreePro Gold, and XTreeGold and multiple filespecs	108
Using the Filespec History feature	110
Using the Global file window with XTreePro Gold and XTreeGold	110
Using Invert with XTreePro Gold and XTreeGold	111
Finding Words, Files, and Directories	112
Finding a directory	112

Table of Contents

    Finding a file on the currently logged disk(s) 112
    Finding a file on floppies 113
        Using XTree to find files on floppy disks 113
        Using XTreePro to find files on floppy disks 113
        Using XTree Easy, XTreePro Gold, and XTreeGold to
        find files on floppy disks 114
    Finding text with XTreePro Gold and XTreeGold.......................................114
    Finding text over several logged drives 115
Formatting Floppy Disks...116
    How can you tell if it's formatted?...116
    The difference between high-density and low-density floppies 116
    Formatting floppies with XTree and XTreePro..117
    Formatting floppies with XTree Easy, XTreePro Gold,
    and XTreeGold 117
Function Keys 119
Global 119
Graft..121
Help 121
    Using the Help command in XTree..121
    Using the Help command in XTreePro, XTreePro Gold,
    XTree Easy, and XTreeGold...122
    Using XTreePro Gold's Quick Reference 124
Hide/Unhide 126
History 126
    Creating a permanent history 127
    Using labels to name entries 128
Invert 128
    Using Invert with XTreePro Gold and XTreeGold.......................................129
Log...129
    Logging cumulatively with XTreePro, XTreePro Gold,
    and XTreeGold 130
        Moving among logged drives with XTreePro and
        XTreePro Gold 130
        Moving among logged drives with XTreeGold 2.5 130
    Releasing logged disks from memory 130
    Releasing logged disks with XTreePro and XTreePro Gold 130
    Logging directories with XTreePro Gold 131
    Logging directories with XTreeGold 131
    Using Instant Log 132
    Configuring XTreeGold's logging instructions 133
    Command line switches for logging in XTreeGold 2.5 133
        Preselecting your filespecs 133
        Logging more than one drive..134
        Logging only a specific directory 134

Managing Memory 134
    Adjusting memory in XTreePro 135
    Adjusting memory in XTreePro Gold and XTreeGold 135
XTree Menus 136
Mouse Commands 136
    Using the mouse in the command menu 136
    Using the mouse in the Directory window 137
    Using the mouse in the File window 137
Move 138
    Moving a file 138
    Moving more than one file 140
    Using Graft to move a directory 141
    Using the Destination window to simplify moving 142
    Using the History command to simplify moving 143
No Files! 143
Oops! 145
Open (and Associate) 147
        Creating an association 147
Print 148
    Printing a list of files and directories 148
    Printing files 149
    Printing with XTree 150
    Printing with XTreePro, XTree Easy, XTreePro Gold
    and XTreeGold 150
        Printing headers with XTreeGold 2.5 151
    Printing with 1Word 151
Pull-Down Menus 152
Quit 156
    Quitting XTree 156
    Quitting XTreePro, XTreePro Gold, XTree Easy,
    and XTreeGold 156
        Quitting to another directory 156
    Making a Zippy exit 156
Rename 157
    Renaming a file 157
    Renaming a directory 158
    Renaming a volume label 159
    Using History while renaming 160
Securing Files and Directories 160
    Hiding and unhiding files 161
        Hiding hidden files 162
        Hiding and unhiding tagged files 162

Table of Contents

Hiding and Unhiding directories	162
Using Wash Disk for security	164
The Showall File Window	165
Using Showall to view all files on the current drive	165
Using Showall with Filespec	165
Viewing tagged files with Showall	165
Sort Criteria	166
Sort Criteria commands for XTree	167
Sort Criteria commands for XTreePro, XTree Easy, XTreePro Gold, and XTreeGold	167
Split/Unsplit	169
File and Directory Statistics	171
DISK Statistics window	171
DIRECTORY Stats window	172
SHOWALL (and GLOBAL) Statistics window	172
Extended statistics window	172
Substituting with SUBST	174
SUBST and XTree and XTreePro	176
SUBST and XTreePro Gold	177
Tag/Untag	177
Tagging and untagging a file	178
Tagging and untagging all files in a directory	178
Tagging and untagging the whole disk	179
Tagging and untagging with filespecs	179
Tagging by attributes	180
Using Showall to view tagged files	181
Inverting tags	181
Partially untagging files	182
View	184
Viewing a document file	184
Viewing files in XTree	184
Viewing files in XTreePro	185
Viewing in XTree Easy	186
Viewing files in XTreePro Gold and XTreeGold	186
Searching for text in a viewed file	188
Saving a viewed file to disk with XTreePro Gold and XTreeGold	188
Printing a viewed file with XTreePro Gold and XTreeGold	189
Viewing tagged files with XTreePro Gold and XTreeGold	189
Using AutoView with XTreePro Gold and XTreeGold	190
Using AutoView with XTreeGold 2.5	190
The XTreeMenu	191
Accessing the XTreeMenu	192
Changing XTreeMenu's display	193

Editing the XTreeMenu 193
Editing XTreeMenu's instructions 196

Part II: XTree for Novell Networks 199

Chapter 4: XTreeNet — Network File Management Made Easy 201

In This Chapter 201
Introducing XTreeNet 201
    Who this chapter is for 201
    What's so special about a LAN? 202
Understanding XTreeNet Concepts 203
    Peer-to-peer file management 203
    Peer-to-peer remote control 204
    Directory information 205
    Pick list 205
Using XTreeNet Commands 205
    Attach/Detach 206
    Attributes (Directory) 206
    Attributes (File) 207
        Dates 207
        Flags 207
    Tag or untag a Branch 208
    Tag or untag by attributes 209
    Map 209
    Volume 210
Summary 210

Part III: XTree for Windows 211

Chapter 5: Windows Concepts 213

In This Chapter 213
Using Windows 213
    On-screen elements 213
    Mouse moves 215
    Keyboard tactics 215
Discovering Windows Wonders 216
    Active and inactive windows 216

Table of Contents

Closing a window 216
Moving a window 217
Changing a window's size 217
Minimized programs on the desktop 218
Main menu and pull-down menus..218
Dialog boxes 219
Summary..220

Chapter 6: XTree for Windows Basics..221

In This Chapter 221
Welcome to XTree for Windows..221
Getting Started 221
Understanding the Windows in XTree for Windows.................................222
The Active Window..224
Tree and Directory window basics...224
Expanding the tree structure...224
Traveling the directory tree...224
Traveling in the Directory window 225
Working with Files, Directories, and Disks...225
Using the Tool Palette...227
Going from XTree for DOS to XTree for Windows 227
New Terms in XTree for Windows 228
A window by any other name 228
New ways of doing things 229
Navigating directories with the mouse 230
Navigating directories with the keyboard 230
Some things never change..230
Missing: The Commands that Didn't Make it 230
Summary..231

Chapter 7: XTree for Windows Quick Reference Guide 233

In This Chapter 233
Mouse and Keyboard Deliberations..233
Arranging Your Windows 234
The Standard Region Layout...234
The Auto Viewer Region Layout 234
Window Layout options...235
The Auto Arrange option 235
The Arrange Now option...236
Attributes (File) 236
Making attributes visible 236
Changing a file's attributes 237

The Auto Directory Window	237
The Auto View Window	238
Close	238
Configuration Options	239
Copy	239
Using the Copy dialog box options	240
Selecting a destination	240
Renaming while copying	240
Replacing exiting files	241
Selecting directory options	241
Selecting File Options	241
Saving your selections	242
Using the Preferences dialog box options	242
Getting messages from XTree	243
The Date and Time Stamp	244
Delete	244
The Detail Box	245
The Directory Window	245
Opening a Directory window	246
Opening a custom Directory window	247
Opening an Auto Directory window	248
Navigating a Directory window	248
Set Scope	248
Using the Move Up button	249
Moving down to a subdirectory	249
Modifying your directory display	249
Directory Format	249
Directory Filter	250
Directory Sort Order	251
The Edit Menu	251
Execute	251
Exit	252
Expand/Collapse Tree	252
Using the level expansion buttons	252
Using the + or - icons	252
Using the View menu	253
The File Menu	254
Find/Find Again	254
Finding files and directories	254
Finding text in a View window	255
Formatting Floppy Disks	255
How can you tell if it's formatted?	256

Table of Contents

The difference between high-density and low-density floppies 256
Formatting a floppy disk 256
Function Keys 257
Launch 257
Logging Files and Directories 257
    Setting logging options 257
    Refreshing your display 258
Mark and Unmark 258
    Marking files and directories 259
    Unmarking files and directories 260
Move 260
    Choosing Move options 261
        Selecting a destination 261
        Renaming while moving 262
        Replacing files with the same name 262
        Selecting Directory Options 262
        Setting defaults 262
    Getting messages from XTree 263
The Move Up Button 263
    Moving up in a Tree window 263
    Moving up in a Directory window 264
Open 264
    Activating a new window 264
    Launching a program 265
The Preferences Dialog Box 265
    Disk Logging 266
    Copying and Moving Operations 266
        The Save Defaults and Window Arrangements on Application Exit option 266
Rename 267
    Rename while copying 267
    Renaming with care 267
    Rename a disk's volume label 267
Run 268
Selecting and Deselecting 268
    Personal visit selection techniques 269
        Highlighting objects with a mouse 269
        Highlighting objects with a keyboard 269
    Long distance selection techniques 269
        Highlighting objects with the Tool Palette 269
        Highlighting objects from the Edit menu 269
        Using the Select/Deselect dialog box 270
    Keeping objects selected while moving between windows 271

Sort Order 271
Statistics 272
The Tool Palette 272
The Tools Menu 273
The Tree Window 273
    Opening a tree 274
    Opening combination trees 274
    Using Set Scope 274
Unknown and ? 275
The View Menu 275
The View Window 275
    Viewing files 275
    Viewing graphics files 276
    Viewing text files 276
The Volume Menu 278
The Window Menu 278

Part IV: XTree Extras 279

Chapter 8: Hard Disk Management in a Nutshell 281

In This Chapter 281
Hard Disk Optimization 282
    Taking advantage of free options 282
        Using CHKDSK 282
        Using efficient directory strategies 283
    Configuring your system properly 284
        A sample CONFIG.SYS file 284
        A sample AUTOEXEC.BAT file 284
    Shelling out cash for optimization 285
        Other backup programs 285
        Disk defraggers 285
        Disk scrubbers 286
        Cache programs 286
        Unerase and disaster recovery 286
        The ideal wish list 287
        Your version of DOS 287
Step-by-Step Hard Disk Maintenance 288
    Backing up your hard disk 288
        The daily backup 288
        The system backup 289
        The incremental backups 289

Table of Contents

Prepare your floppies 289
Deleting obsolete files 290
Hard Disk Maintenance with XTree for DOS 290
  Keeping track of your backups 290
  Making incremental backups 291
  Backing up by date 291
  Removing duplicate files 292
  Removing BAK and TMP files 292
  Retiring old files 293
Hard Disk Maintenance with XTree for Windows 294
  Making incremental backups and backing up by date 294
  Removing duplicate files 294
  Removing BAK and TMP files 295
  Retiring old files 296
Summary 296

Chapter 9: Archiving with XTreePro Gold, XTreeGold, and XTree for Windows 297

Archiving Basics 297
Deciding When to Archive 298
Archiving with XTreePro Gold 299
  Creating an archive file 299
    Selecting an archive format 300
    Applying data encryption 301
  Opening an archive 302
  Extracting a file from an archive 303
  Modifying an existing Arc file 304
Archiving with XTreeGold 305
  Creating a Zip (or Arc) file 305
    Paths 307
    Encryption 307
    Method 308
    Speed/size 308
  Opening an archived file 309
    Extracting a file from an archive 310
  Modifying an existing compressed file 311
Archiving with XTree For Windows 312
  Using the shortcut 312
  Zipping the long way 313
  Amending Zip file properties 315
  When is a Zip file like a drive? 315

Using File ⇨ Open to view Zip files 315
Mounting Zip files..316
Summary..316

Chapter 10: Linking Computers with XTreeLink........................317

In This Chapter 317
Preparing Computers for Linking 318
Preparing the XTreeLink Installation 319
Counting your drives...319
Modifying CONFIG.SYS with XTreeGold 319
Modifying CONFIG.SYS with XTree for Windows...................320
Installing XTreeLink 320
Running XTreeLink...321
Activating the remote computer...321
Activating the local computer..322
Using XTreeLink..323
Running XTreeGold with XTreeLink..323
Running XTree for Windows with XTreeLink..........................323
Using XTreeLink option switches 325
Exiting XTreeLink 325
Summary..326

Part V: Appendixes 327

Appendix A: Shortcuts: Command Keys and Function Keys 329

XTree Shortcuts..330
XTreePro Shortcuts..331
XTreePro Gold Shortcuts 333
XTree Easy Shortcuts...335
XTreeGold Shortcuts..337
XTreeNet Shortcuts..340
XTree for Windows Shortcuts..343

Appendix B: Laptop Configuration 345

XTree Modules 345
XTreePro Modules..346
XTreePro Gold Modules 346
XTree Easy Modules...348
XTreeGold Modules..350
XTree for Windows Modules..352

Appendix C: Insider Info from XTree Tech Support 355
The Most Commonly Asked Questions about XTree for DOS 355
XTree Questions 355
XTreePro Questions 356
XTreePro Gold Questions..357
XTreeGold 2.0 Questions...360
XTreeGold 2.5 Questions...361
Questions for All Versions...363
XTreeNet Questions 364

Appendix D: Where to Go from Here 367
The XTree Company 367
Mailing Address for XTree..368
Technical Support for XTree...368
Recommended Software..368
Books on MS-DOS, Windows, Hard Disks, and PC Systems 369

Appendix E: An Unapologetic History of XTree 370

Appendix F: Pop Quiz Answers...375

Index 378

Reader Response Survey ....End of Book

Foreword

There are, I imagine, several reasons I was asked to write this foreword.

First, I'm not a computer professional, but a comic book writer who uses a computer daily. *The Official XTree Companion, 3rd Edition* was written primarily for people like me — and probably you.

Secondly, I created a character called "Howard the Duck," so I suppose I've got some minor name-recognition value for the cover. For all I know, all fifteen people who went to see the movie are XTree users and will snap up this book instantly on that basis alone.

Anyway, I hope they, along with thousands of others, will do so because — third and most importantly — I've known the author, Beth Slick, for eight years and can vouch for her ability to turn a bewildered, terrified, first-time computer user into a competent, confident one.

Beth taught me how to use my first computer, a hoary Kaypro 10 machine, back in 1984. As she waltzed me through the twisted, Yoda-like command syntax of CP/M ("Rename to this, that.") and the basics of an antediluvian version of WordStar, I came to realize that her ability to explain the goings-on inside the box in terms of tactile, real-world analogies was a special kind of talent.

Ask most computer instructors to explain Zip files, for example, and you'll get a jargon-laden discussion of data compression, archiving systems, and so on.

Ask Beth, and she'll tell you: "A Zip file is like a suitcase. You fold up files like clothes and pack them tightly inside the Zip file, so you can carry them around together and store them in a minimum of space."

Gee. Even a comic book writer can understand *that*.

The most remarkable thing about *The Official XTree Companion, 3rd Edition* isn't the motherlode of information it contains, but that it's actually fun to read. As you'll discover, Beth manages to turn the learning curve into a waterslide. She writes the way she teaches in person, in a witty, irreverent style that utterly undermines a student's best efforts to remain intimidated. Whatever you need to know about XTree, you'll absorb it painlessly and with a laugh or two.

Foreword

After reading the first edition of *The Official XTree MS-DOS and Hard Disk Companion*, I told Beth that I hoped she had launched a new trend — the entertaining computer book. Judging from the success of both earlier editions and the release of this, the third one, she has. If you've ever slogged your way through a software manual written with all the flair of a government pamphlet on mulching — and what computer user hasn't? — you'll appreciate the public service Ms. Slick has performed.

More than that, you'll *enjoy* this book, and enjoy using XTree more productively as a result.

Steve Gerber
Burbank, California

The 5th Wave **By Rich Tennant**

"IT'S XTREE PRO GOLD AND QUICKLY VIEWS FILES ON YOUR HARDDISK FOR EASY MAINTENANCE. I CALL IT 'X-PRO-VISION.' THEN AGAIN, I CALL MYSELF 'XTREE-MAN' AND RUN AROUND IN A CAPE AND BLUE TIGHTS."

Introduction
3rd Edition

MS-DOS, Windows, and Hard Disk Management — Are We Having Fun Yet?

Granted, on the "fun meter," MS-DOS, Windows, and hard disk management generally register somewhere below flossing your teeth and remembering to put more fiber in your diet.

A lot less fun, however, is wasting your time with arcane MS-DOS commands or struggling with File Manager when you could be taking full advantage of the terrific tools contained in the XTree product line.

The bad news

Unfortunately, every version of XTree (including XTree for Windows) has presented a bizarre paradox: XTree encourages you to forget about MS-DOS commands — yet you need a decent working knowledge of MS-DOS to get the most out of it. In other words, to figure out how to use XTree, you have to know how to get along without it!

The good news

The good news is that you don't have to earn a black belt in MS-DOS or Windows to use XTree. Far from it. You are actually only a few concepts away from doing power-user stuff with XTree.

The solution

The Official XTree MS-DOS, Windows, and Hard Disk Management Companion, 3rd Edition bridges the gap between the desire and the power. By giving you only the information you need (and in a task-oriented way that can be put to immediate use), this book is a valuable ally in taking control of your computer.

How To Use This Book

Begin at the very beginning. No matter what version of XTree you're using, start with Chapter 1, "MS-DOS Concepts." Be brave, there are only a few things you really need to know to use XTree to its fullest.

Next, if you're an XTree for DOS user, continue with the rest of Part I. If you're an XTreeNet user, jump to Part II. XTree for Windows types should please proceed directly to Part III (do not disembark until told to do so).

All users of XTree (both XTree for DOS and XTree for Windows) will find helpful the "Quick Reference Guide" for each platform. Chapter 3, in Part I, covers all versions of XTree for DOS; Chapter 7, in Part III, covers XTree for Windows.

Part IV, of interest to everyone, contains tips and tricks on hard disk management, archiving files, and linking computers.

And if that isn't enough, look to the Appendixes for a wide variety of useful information, ranging from how you can get "help" directly from the XTree Company's wild and crazy technical support staff, to a "Where to Go from Here" section that directs you to additional resources for hard disk maintenance.

Part I: XTree for DOS

If you own XTree, XTreePro, XTreePro Gold, XTree Easy, or XTree Gold, you'll spend most of your time with the chapters in this part.

Chapter 1, MS-DOS Concepts, covers the basics you need to know about DOS in order to use XTree.

Chapter 2, XTree for DOS Basics, presents the concepts that each XTree for DOS product has in common, as well as some they don't share.

Chapter 3, XTree for DOS Quick Reference Guide, is a handy reference for the five XTree for DOS products. The "Reference Guide," which is organized by task, shows you how to effortlessly copy files, create directories, format disks, and back up whenever the mood — and the need — should strike. You'll also learn

Introduction

(depending on which version of XTree you have) how to search through your whole hard disk for a "lost" file or a file that contains a certain piece of text. You can create a menu system to automate frequently used commands and learn lots of other timesaving, power-user tricks.

Be sure to read the introduction to this chapter because it provides information on how to best make use of the chapter as reference.

Part II: XTree for Novell Networks

There is only one chapter in this part since XTreeNet is basically XTreePro Gold with network capabilities.

Chapter 4, XTreeNet: Network File Management Made Easy, explains how XTreeNet makes using a Novell NetWare system easier than ever.

Part III: XTree for Windows

If you own XTree for Windows, you'll spend most of your time with the chapters in this part.

Chapter 5, Windows Concepts, covers the basics you need to know about Windows in order to use XTree for Windows.

Chapter 6, XTree for Windows Basics, tells you how to get around the XTree for Windows desktop.

Chapter 7, XTree for Windows Quick Reference Guide, covers the commands and concepts you'll frequently (or infrequently, in some cases) use in your daily XTree for Windows routines. Like the "Reference Guide" in Chapter 3, this chapter is organized by task. You learn how to copy files, create directories, format disks, and back up your files in XTree for Windows. You also learn how to search for lost or hidden files.

Part IV: XTree Extras

The chapters in this part apply to all XTree users because they cover handy XTree features that can help make your life easier.

Chapter 8, Hard Disk Management in a Nutshell, explains how you can use all versions of XTree to keep your hard disk healthy (and in good shape to boot). Included in this chapter is a section that answers the important question, "What's the least amount of maintenance I can get by with?" You also learn how to use XTree to back up your files for a rainy day.

Chapter 9, Archiving with XTreePro Gold, XTreeGold, and XTree for Windows, shows you how easy it is to make more space on your hard drive by using XTree's handy archiving feature.

Chapter 10, Linking Computers with XTreeLink, tells you how you can use XTreeLink, which comes with XTreeGold and XTree for Windows, to connect two computers and exchange information.

Part V: Appendixes

Several appendixes contain vital information you'll want to know.

Appendix A, Shortcuts: Command Keys and Function Keys, covers the keyboard shortcuts available for every version of XTree.

Appendix B, Laptop Configuration, is basically a list of modules that you can leave off your laptop, saving valuable hard disk space.

Appendix C, Insider Info from XTree Tech Support, contains real questions that people like you have and call XTree with. Before you touch that dial, check out this appendix.

Appendix D, Where to Go from Here, lists various resources you may call on for help in your computing travails.

Appendix E, An Unapologetic History of XTree, is for you computer history buffs who want to know what started where and how.

Appendix F, Answers to Pop Quizzes, contains the answers to pop quizzes presented in Chapters 1 and 9.

Conventions Used in This Book

Certain features used in this book are intended to help you navigate the material and use any DOS or Windows commands properly.

Icons

This book features a variety of icons, which are located in the margins. The icons are intended to alert you to information you can keep in mind as you learn about XTree. Here is what to look for:

The cross reference icon points to a more complete discussion in another chapter or section.

The note icon highlights a special point of interest about the topic under discussion.

The warning icon alerts you to potential problems and pitfalls.

The tip icon accompanies information you should keep in mind when performing various XTree tasks.

Commands and keystrokes

The following is a list of special conventions for keystrokes and commands.

- Key combinations for versions of XTree for DOS, in which you hold down one key and press another, are shown in hyphenated format (Ctrl-F10, for example). This indicates that you hold down the Ctrl key while you press F10. In Windows, the keys are separated by a plus sign (+), as in Ctrl+F10.
- *Italic* type is used for new terms or emphasis.
- Commands you are to type appear in a **bold** typeface.
- For commands selected from a Windows menu, an underline is used to indicate the letter the user presses to choose the command (File ➪ Save As).
- On-screen information and code listings appear in `a special typeface`.

- DOS and Windows commands and filenames appear in uppercase letters and in a special typeface:

    ```
    COPY MYFILE HISFILE
    ```

    When such commands and filenames are embedded in a paragraph, they appear in uppercase letters.

Closing Remarks

The purpose of *The Official XTree MS-DOS, Windows, and Hard Disk Management Companion, 3rd Edition* is to help you harness the power of XTree to make hard disk main-tenance simple and, perhaps, even fun. The idea is to always be prepared for the inevitable hard disk crash.

The inevitable hard disk crash? Of course, inevitable. Remember, a hard disk is nothing more than an ordinary piece of machinery assembled by human beings right here on good ol' planet Earth. Hard disks are subject to the same laws of Murphy and entropy as refrigerators, cars, and marriages. In other words, you should live like there's no tomorrow when it comes to the life of your hard disk — because it may be gone tomorrow.

Which brings us to the most important XTree benefit . . . peace of mind.

Ladies and Gentlemen, start your engines.

Part I
XTree for DOS

Chapter 1 9
MS-DOS Concepts

Chapter 2 25
XTree for DOS Basics

Chapter 3 35
XTree for DOS Quick
Reference Guide

The 5th Wave   By Rich Tennant

"OUR XTREE HANDBOOK HAS US MAINTAINING OUR HARD DISK THROUGH A MORE COMPREHENSIVE DOS SHELL, AND YOU ASK WHY WE'RE DANCING?"

Chapter 1
MS-DOS Concepts

In This Chapter
- What DOS is and why you need an operating system anyway
- Where you are when you're *in* DOS
- The difference between a hard drive and a floppy drive
- How to set up directories on your hard disk
- What the components of a system prompt are
- How to (and how not to) name your files
- What an extension on a filename means
- How to use DOS wildcards
- DOS file attributes and why they are important

To be sure, this chapter is *not* a comprehensive course in DOS, but it is intended to get you comfortable with the few DOS principles you have to know in order to tap into XTree's power. XTree takes care of the boring details of issuing properly phrased commands to DOS. By the way, what you learn here about DOS may be surprisingly useful when you're using other programs. Even you Windows users should hang around; these DOS concepts can be a big help to you, too.

If you already know DOS, you can skim (or skip) this section. The margin headings denote the major points, and the pop quizzes along the way help guarantee you're getting the point.

NOTE Any DOS command may be entered in either upper- or lowercase letters; it doesn't make a difference.

What Is MS-DOS?

Basically, MS-DOS (an acronym for **M**icro**s**oft **D**isk **O**perating **S**ystem) is a software program entrusted with the critical task of telling your computer how to behave like a proper computer.

You may have assumed that when you bought your computer, it already knew how to be a computer. In fact, it didn't. Without MS-DOS (or "DOS" for short), a computer is as useful as a tape player without a tape. (When you bought your computer, what you actually got was a box with tremendous potential.)

Operating system

What your computer *does* know how to do, every time you turn it on, is to seek out the *operating system.* Within a few seconds of gearing up, your computer automatically finds DOS (right there on your hard disk where you or your dealer put it) and transforms itself into a fully functional computer, eagerly awaiting your commands.

A major part of what an operating system does takes place invisibly. Behind the scene, DOS quietly processes dozens of functions to keep the computer running — much like the autonomic part of your body's own operating system, which pumps blood, breathes, grows toenails, and so on, all without any conscious effort on your part.

In addition to the invisible DOS activities, there's another level of DOS that requires a *conscious* effort on your part (much like jogging requires conscious will). When you want to delete files, format a disk, and so forth, you have to make your desires known to DOS by way of typed commands.

These typed commands, DOS commands, must be entered using a particular set of words in a precise order. Most people get frustrated with DOS because they don't speak the language very well (or at all) and don't care (or have the time) to learn.

In general, then, the term DOS refers to both the behind-the-scenes and conscious portions of the computer's disk operating system. The term DOS is also used to refer to a couple of other things, such as the place on the hard disk where DOS is stored.

A place on the hard disk

Most people give the name DOS to the *place* on their hard disk where the DOS accessory programs are stored. This method is a convenient way to keep DOS files separate from other program files. We'll learn more about this in the section on directories.

You are not in a program

Being in DOS means you are *not in a program*. When you're finished working with a particular software application and you press the quit command, you may be questioned whether you really want to exit to DOS. (The reason you're asked if you're *sure* you want to exit is not because the program feels you should rethink your decision. Rather, it's just double checking that you didn't hit the quit command by accident.) Once you confirm your decision to exit, you're dumped out of your program and you're back at the disk operating system level. You're not in a program, you're *in DOS*.

> **POP QUIZ #1**
>
> What are the three things DOS can mean?
>
> For the answer, go to Appendix F.

Being in DOS is not the same thing as being in the place (directory area) on your hard disk named DOS where all your DOS files are stored, as described previously. In this case, in DOS simply means *not in a program*.

Understanding Drives

A *drive* in a computer is a device that records and plays back information. A *hard disk drive* stores information on a special piece of metal (hence, hard). A *floppy disk drive* stores information on something like videotape (which would be very floppy if it weren't in its special plastic jacket). Both hard and floppy disk drives work a lot like a VCR or tape player that uses heads to record (save) and play back.

The hard disk, which can store a tremendous amount of information, is where DOS, your programs, and your work are kept. By comparison, a floppy disk can really hold only a small amount of information. The main job of the floppy disk is to act as your hard disk's link to the outside world. You can copy *from* the hard disk to a floppy or *from* a floppy to the hard disk.

Drive names

When it's time to copy something to or from a hard disk, you can't just ask DOS to copy a file to "that drive that's over there on the top." You have to specify where the information is located and where it should be copied to (the name or *address* for the drive).

The address for the first floppy drive is A:; if you have two floppy drives, the second drive is B:. The address for the hard disk is C:. Some hard disks are *partitioned* into more than one drive — such hard disks may also have a D:, E:, and F: drive. Don't forget the colon. That little colon (:) tells DOS you're talking about a *drive* named A rather than a file named A. (If you forget the colon, you could find the files you want to copy mushed together in a giant file called A!)

> **POP QUIZ #2**
>
> What does the colon (:) mean when you see A: and C:?
>
> For the answer, go to Appendix F.

Current drives

As you work on your computer, one of your drives is the designated, or *current*, drive. The current drive is where DOS expects to find the next program you want to use. Usually the current drive is your hard drive (C:). If you want to make a different drive into the current drive, you type the drive's name and press the Enter key on your keyboard. For example, type **A:** and press Enter to make drive A: the current drive. You'll see how this works later when the issue of the *current drive* comes up.

Examining Directories

When hard disks that could hold thousands of files were invented, the inventors probably realized that dumping all sorts of files onto one hard disk would soon create chaos. (Imagine trying to find one specific file in a directory list of a thousand different files!) Clearly, a method was needed for organizing files on a hard disk. Thus, the venerable Inverted Tree Hierarchical Structure was born.

Understanding the tree structure

You may ask, "What is an Inverted Tree Hierarchical Structure anyway and why do I have to know about it?" You have to know about the tree structure because it's the backbone of your computer system. Broken down into comfortable bite-size pieces, the hierarchical tree is easy to understand.

First, an *inverted tree* structure is nothing more than an upside-down tree. If you visualize a tree turned upside down, you'll see that the *root* becomes the top of the tree. Beneath the root are several main branches. Each of the main branches may host several smaller branches. Each of those subbranches may also have a number of sub-subbranches, and so on.

Chapter 1: MS-DOS Concepts

A *hierarchical* structure means that all the branches and subbranches do not have equal status. The highest branches are the parents of the next generation of (child) lower branches. The child branches can be parents to another set of branches below them, and so on.

On a hard disk, the branches are called *directories.* The purpose of each directory is to provide a storage area for your files and programs. The system of directories is generally referred to as the *tree structure* or *directory system*.

Understanding the directory system

One way to look at this directory system is to imagine your hard disk as a house. An expensive house.

As you enter your expensive home you find yourself in the entryway. This is equivalent to the what is called the root of the hard disk (the top of your inverted tree). Once you are in the root/entryway, you can see several doors leading to other rooms/branches.

In your home, if you want to watch TV, for instance, you first must go to the room where the TV is located. In a computer, if you want to use your word processor, you first must go into the directory where your word processor is stored. Once you are in the TV room, you can turn on the TV. Similarly, once you are in the word processing directory, you can activate your word processing program.

When you conclude a work session and you'd like to work in another program, you must exit the current program (turn off the TV in your house) and go back to the root (exit the TV room and go back to the entryway). The root (entryway) is the place where you can then access the other directories (doors) leading to the other parts of the hard disk (house). You must travel in this way through your directories to get to specific programs or data. After all, you cannot just walk through the walls of your expensive house!

You use a statement called the *path* to tell the computer which route to take to get to a particular directory. (The path statement plays an important role in the setup of your system, which I'll discuss in Chapter 9, "Hard Disk Management in a Nutshell.")

You may wonder where all these directories and branches come from. Well, they come from you. You are the architect of your hard disk; you make and delete directories as the need arises.

Creating directories

Your hard disk may come with two or three directories (for example, a directory named DOS in which you store your DOS files, and a directory for each of the software programs you have). As time goes by, you'll want to create additional directories to accommodate new software or to reduce overcrowding.

Too many files in one directory can seriously slow down file retrieval and degrade hard disk performance. Exactly what constitutes *too many* files depends on what book or manual you're reading. Some books recommend no more than 50 files in a directory, but most agree on a top figure of 100. If you've got more than 200 files in one directory, it's *definitely* time to split things up into separate areas.

> **POP QUIZ #3**
>
> What is the purpose of directories?
>
> For the answer, go to Appendix F.

On the other end of the spectrum, it's not wise to go overboard in creating directories and making lots of new ones. Every directory, by virtue of being created, eats up disk space and takes up memory.

The simple rule is to make a place for everything and keep everything in its place. You'll save wear and tear not only on your hardware, but also on your wetware (aka your brain). How to create new directories for your files is explained under "Directory Management" in Chapter 3 for XTree for DOS users and "The Directory Window" in Chapter 7 for XTree for Windows users.

Understanding System Prompts

When you're not in one of your software programs, the computer displays a *system prompt* on-screen, which usually tells you two things:

- The computer is ready for a command (it's prompting, or asking, you to do something).
- What drive and directory you are currently in (just like the red arrow on the map at the mall that says "You are here").

You get to the system prompt either by turning on your computer or by exiting a program. When you first turn on your computer, the system prompt (also just called the *prompt*) probably looks something like this:

```
       C:\LETTERS
       |        |
  current drive  current directory
```

Chapter 1: MS-DOS Concepts

The reason I say that your prompt *probably* looks like this example is because the "look" of the system prompt is determined by you or your computer dealer (or your best friend who knows about computers). A fancy system prompt can have the date and time, happy faces, and a lot of other junk. However, most people have the typical plain system prompt — C:\>.

The first item in the prompt is the name of the current drive (with that infamous colon). The second item in the prompt shows the directory you are in: the backslash (\) is DOS's symbol for the root directory. Basically, a system prompt like this tells you that you're on the C: drive in the root directory (the root part denoted by that backslash). The greater-than symbol (>) is always located at the end of the prompt (just to tell you "That's all, folks"). Here are two more system prompts:

```
C:\WP>
```

This first example tells you you're on the C: drive, in the WP directory.

```
C:\WP\LETTERS>
```

This second example tells you you're still on the C: drive, but now you're in a *subdirectory* of WP called LETTERS that is situated one level of branches down from the WP directory.

POP QUIZ #4

The system prompt tells you what two things?

For the answer, go to Appendix F.

If your system prompt doesn't change when you go to different directories — if it always looks like this: C> — then a simple adjustment to your AUTOEXEC.BAT file is in order. I'll show you how to go about this in "Editing with 1Word," in Chapter 3. Then your system prompt will behave as just described!

Understanding Files

The computer, the operating system, and the disk, with its structure of directories, all exist for the purpose of housing *files*. What, exactly, are files?

A file may be a program or it may be data. A program file is a file that *does* something. A data file, on the other hand, simply *holds information.* A data file is something you create using a specific software program. Your word processor is an example of a software program and the documents you create using the word processor are data files.

Although there are many different kinds of program and data files, the differences between them are not worth dwelling on right now (or ever, probably).

Naming files

Although there are many kinds of files with many different purposes, they all have one thing in common: the style of their names. Knowing how to work that style is key to using all versions of XTree and can be a tremendous help, as well as a time-saver, when using DOS commands.

To start at the beginning, all filenames must be *at least* one character long but no longer than eight characters. If you want more than eight characters in your filename, you can add a period (.) to the end of the filename; DOS then generously allows you up to three more characters. That's it. Some typical filenames are:

```
REPORT.DOC
C
BILLING.WK1
RECIPES
#566.REP
```

> **POP QUIZ #5**
>
> A filename can be up to eight characters long and optionally followed by a period with up to three more letters. Which of the following filenames are valid and which are invalid?
>
> 1. MARY
> 2. LETTER#1.DOC
> 3. BIG LAKE.TXT
> 4. BOB_LET
> 5. A.OV
> 6. JIMMY.OLSEN
>
> **Answers:** The invalid filenames are number 3 (which contains an illegal space in the name) and number 6 (which has more than three letters after the period).
>
> The remaining valid filenames illustrate acceptable variations in the file-naming rules. Number 1 illustrates that a filename can be shorter than eight letters long. Number 2 shows the longest filename possible and contains examples of allowable punctuation and number use, here the pound sign and the numeral one.
>
> Number 4 has a legal punctuation mark in it. Number 5 illustrates a filename that has only one character before the period, then only two letters after. (After the period you can have *up to three* characters, but you don't have to use all three characters.)

Chapter 1: MS-DOS Concepts

A *character,* by the way, can be a letter or a number, as well as some (but not all) punctuation marks. For instance, underlines, hyphens, and pound signs (#) are okay, but question marks (?), asterisks (*), and spaces are forbidden, for reasons that are explained shortly.

If it seems there are a lot of little rules to remember when naming a file, take comfort in the fact that the computer does not allow you to save a file with an *invalid* filename. So you really can't give a file a wrong name.

Making filenames unique

One last rule about file naming is that, like snowflakes, no two can be exactly alike. You can't have two files in the same directory with the same name. If you try to do this (either on purpose or accidentally), DOS may, without warning or asking permission, simply delete the oldest of the two files (the oldest file being the one that was there first).

Examining Extensions

Another subtlety about filenames is the *extension,* those last three letters after the period. You must always use a period between filenames and their extensions. Here are some examples:

```
        WORD.EXE     SCRIPT.BAK    AUTOEXEC.BAT
                         extensions
```

Extensions works a bit like a person's last name — they can identify which group a file belongs to. A file's extension may reveal to the semicasual observer what type of file it is.

Common extensions

For instance, in the previous example, the EXE extension tells you that you've got a program file. (Program files can also have a COM extension.) The BAK extension indicates that the file was an automatically created word processing backup file. The file ending in BAT is a batch file — a kind of little program that you can (and will) write to simplify your chores.

There are lots of extensions in general use, but the most common are EXE, COM, BAK, and BAT. Two other commonly used extensions are DOC, which indicates that the file was created by a word processor, and TXT, which usually means that the file is an ASCII file. (ASCII stands for the American Standard Code for Information Interchange. An ASCII file contains only letters and numbers. If you're wondering what *else* can be in a file other than letters and numbers, wait till you get to the View command in XTree, and you'll find out.)

Guidelines for extensions

Unless you're a programmer, you can use the last three characters of a filename for whatever you want. The important thing about naming files is to use a name that means something to *you,* so when you look at the filename a few days after you have created it, you'll remember just what's in the file by its name. Sometimes people put their initials, the date, or a condensed description of the contents of the file in those last three characters.

Using Wildcards

Now that you're a file-naming expert, let's pretend you have a hard disk with a directory containing your word processing program and four data files. The four data files are:

```
DAFFY.DOC
DATA.DOC
DONALD.DOC
PAPA.DOC
```

These four filenames all have one thing in common. Can you spot it? (Come on, take a second and give it a shot.)

Right, they *all* have the same DOC extension!

Because these four filenames have the same extension, we can separate them from other files on the disk. If we wanted to copy only these files to another location, for instance, we could tell DOS, "Copy everything that ends in DOC."

Of course, DOS has its own way of phrasing such a statement; DOS uses *wildcards* for this sort of thing. Just like in poker, you have one card (or symbol) that can mean anything. Unlike poker, however, the DOS wildcard symbols are not one-eyed jacks. In DOS, wildcards are the asterisk (*) and the question mark (?).

Chapter 1: MS-DOS Concepts

The asterisk wildcard

The purpose of the asterisk, when searching for files, is to replace characters that are not common in each filename. To specify "all files that end in DOC," substitute an asterisk for the characters in the filename that come before the DOC, as in this example:

```
*.DOC
```

Let's try another example. You might notice that three of our four files begin with the letter *D*. We can carve those three files away from the pack by typing: **D*.DOC.** (The filenames all start with a D, and the asterisk stands for any number or combination of letters that come after the D and before the period. DOC after the period means we specifically want files that end with the DOC extension.)

What if we wanted to single out the first two files in our example? Do they have anything in common? Sure they do. You could type **DA*.DOC** since both the first and second files begin with the letters DA. Some things to keep in mind when using the asterisk wildcard:

- The asterisk can be used only once *before* the period in the filename and once *after* the period.
- Although you can specify characters *before* the placement of the asterisk, you cannot specify letters *after* the asterisk, unless it's after the period.

Some of this may seem confusing, so the following sections provide examples that should clear things up.

Correct asterisk uses

CHAP*.DOC   This indicates any file starting with CHAP and ending with DOC. This could mean CHAPTER.DOC, CHAPS.DOC, and even CHAPEAU.DOC.

T*.*   This indicates any file starting with T, upper- or lowercase, no matter what the ending or extension is.

.   This indicates every file, regardless of its name.

Incorrect asterisk uses

D*SO.DOC   This is incorrect because you cannot specify any letters after the asterisk (unless the letters come after the period).

D*.DOC*   Only three letters are allowed in the extension; the wildcard is considered to be a character. DOS would ignore this wildcard.

The question mark wildcard

The question mark (?) can also be used to single out files. As you might expect, it works a bit differently than the asterisk. The question mark takes the place of one *single* character in a filename, whereas the asterisk takes the place of any and *all* characters — no matter the number. Let's see how this works.

To match the pattern ????.DOC, a file would have to be *up to four* characters long, have a period, and end with DOC.

Back to our previous example: the letter *A* was the second letter in three of the files listed. To indicate just those three files, ?A*.DOC would do the trick. This combination says that we don't care what the first letter of the file is, but the second letter must be an *A*. The wildcard after the *A* stands for any number of letters after the *A*, up to that eight-character total. Finally, the files must end in DOC.

> **POP QUIZ #6**
>
> What do these filenames mean?
>
> *.TXT
> L*.DOC
> CHAP?.DOC
> *.*
>
> For the answer, go Appendix F.

Using wildcards makes it easy to differentiate a certain set of files from the rest of the files in a directory. Keep this in mind when naming files you may want to later group together.

Understanding File Attributes

Just when you think there's nothing more that could possibly be said about a file, we're going to trot out one more concept: *file attributes*.

You may already know that when you save a file, DOS simultaneously records the date and time. In addition to this, DOS also secretly maintains additional information on each file. This additional information, which remains hidden to the naked eye unless you have a program like XTree, is known as the file's attributes. As you might guess, these attributes have nothing to do with being thrifty, reverent, or on time for supper. These are computer attributes. They are read-only, archive, system, and hidden.

Read-only The read-only attribute means you can open the file (call it up), but you can't change it in *any* way. If you've ever tried to delete a file but it just wouldn't go away, it was probably because the file was marked read-only.

Archive The archive attribute keeps track of whether the file has been backed up since the last time it was saved. This attribute is used by some of the programs that back up your hard disk.

System The system attribute tells the computer that the file is really important to DOS. You might correctly guess that this implies you should never delete a system file.

Hidden The hidden attribute renders files invisible to the un-XTree'd eye. Why have an invisible file? Basically, because if you don't know a file is there, you're less likely to delete it. Usually only system files are hidden.

Revealing Special Files

Let's bring system files and hidden files out of the realm of the esoteric and into the real world. At this very moment you have system and hidden files sitting on *your* hard disk (if you didn't, your computer wouldn't work). Descriptions of some of these files follow.

Operating system files

Remember that when the computer is booted up, its first job is to find DOS. DOS can be found in three files: COMMAND.COM, IO.SYS, and MSDOS.SYS. (Versions of DOS before version 5.0 used files named COMMAND.COM, IBMBIO.COM, and IBMDOS.COM.)

Of these three files, you have direct access only to COMMAND.COM. Direct access means you have the power to see it and to delete it, but *do not delete* COMMAND.COM, ever. No COMMAND.COM, no working computer. Got it?

The other two files (IO.SYS and MSDOS.SYS) are protected as read-only, system, and hidden files. That means you can't delete them, they are part of the system, and you won't even see them listed when you ask DOS for a list of files (except in XTree).

CONFIG.SYS file

After DOS finds COMMAND.COM, IO.SYS, and MSDOS.SYS and the computer starts up, the next job on the computer's agenda is to find the CONFIG.SYS file. CONFIG.SYS tells the computer about how to handle memory, whether you've got a mouse or any other special devices attached, and so on. CONFIG.SYS tells your operating system about *your* personal computer. Though all computers should have a CONFIG.SYS file, the contents of your CONFIG.SYS are unique to your computer.

> **POP QUIZ #7**
>
> Here are still more questions about files:
>
> 1. If you can't delete a file, what does that tell you about the file's attributes?
> 2. Is it OK to delete system files?
> 3. Which one of the file attributes tells you whether you've backed up a file or not?
> 4. Do all computers have the same CONFIG.SYS and AUTOEXEC.BAT files?
>
> For the answers, go to Appendix F.

AUTOEXEC.BAT file

After DOS finishes with CONFIG.SYS, it looks for the AUTOEXEC.BAT file. AUTOEXEC.BAT contains a series of commands that the computer performs every time you turn it on. The contents of the AUTOEXEC.BAT file are also unique to your computer. After the computer finishes executing the commands in your AUTOEXEC.BAT file, you get a system prompt.

Copying Files

The concept of copying, or duplicating, a file is so straightforward that you can read about it in two short paragraphs (and without a quiz!).

Unlike copying a videotape, nothing is lost in the process of copying a file. The twentieth copy of a copy is exactly the same as the first. That's why, instead of using the terms *original* and *duplicate*, DOS prefers to use the terms *source* (original) and *target* (duplicate) during the copying process.

While copying a file, you can give the copy a new name. You give a duplicate a new name if you intend to alter the file and want to keep a copy of the original on hand. In addition to copying one or more files, you can copy a whole disk or a bunch of files *and* their associated directories. You'll get the "how to's" on copying in Chapters 3 and 8 (Quick Reference Guides for XTree for DOS and XTree for Windows).

Chapter 1: MS-DOS Concepts

The End . . . Or Is It?

Well, believe it or not, that's it. Those are the only MS-DOS concepts you *really* need to understand in order to successfully operate XTree. All of these ideas are used (repeatedly) throughout Chapter 3, "XTree for DOS Quick Reference Guide," and Chapter 8, "XTree for Windows Quick Reference Guide." The commands and concepts are listed in alphabetical order in these two chapters.

Although the DOS concepts presented here *are* all the DOS you need to know to run XTree, they're not all the DOS you may need to know to run your computer. Some other important DOS commands that are covered elsewhere in the book include:

FORMAT   This command is for *formatting* floppy disks. Floppy disks must be formatted before you can use them, unless you purchase pre-formatted floppies (see Chapter 3).

CHKDSK   This command helps keep your disk fit (see Chapter 9).

BACKUP   This command makes sure you've got a duplicate copy of your hard disk on a set of floppies (see Chapter 9).

VER   This command tells you what version of DOS you own. For more detail on VER, see Chapter 9.

Summary

▶ MS-DOS is a software program that functions *invisibly* (performing tasks that keep your computer running) and *actively* (carrying out commands that you type to start other software programs, copy and move files, and organize information).

▶ DOS resides on your hard drive and responds to commands that you enter in a very specific format.

▶ Your hard drive is organized in a treelike structure, with branches called *directories*, that accommodates vast amounts of information. You set up the directories and decide what goes where.

▶ You may give a file a name that is up to eight characters long, with an optional three-character extension following a period. No two filenames can be exactly alike and reside in the same directory.

▶ DOS recognizes two different wildcards that can be used to make document manipulation easier: the asterisk and the question mark.

▶ File attributes are aspects of files that DOS uses to maintain additional information about files. This information includes the date and time the file was saved, whether the file is a system file needed by DOS, and so on.

The 5th Wave **By Rich Tennant**

"OOO-KAY, LET'S SEE. IF WE CAN ALL REMAIN CALM AND STOP ACTING CRAZY, I'M SURE I'LL EVENTUALLY REMEMBER WHAT NAME I FILED THE ANTIDOTE UNDER."

Chapter 2
XTree for DOS Basics

In This Chapter
- The concepts and commands common to all versions of XTree for DOS
- The basic components of the initial XTree display screens and how to move among them
- The process of tagging and untagging files
- How file specifications can make your work easier
- The XTree command shell and its advantages

Now that you're familiar with the MS-DOS concepts introduced in Chapter 1, you're ready to move on to the basics of XTree for DOS. (XTree for Windows users can jump to Part III where the XTree for Windows stuff kicks in.) Chapter 3, "XTree for DOS Quick Reference Guide," covers specific XTree commands for various tasks.

Introducing the Family XTree

XTree has evolved from the simple (but revolutionary) file-maintenance program that debuted in 1985 to the comprehensive hard disk management application it is today. The original hard disk maintenance software package has been updated a number of times to include several more sophisticated features.

Currently, two versions of XTree for DOS are available: XTree Easy and XTreeGold 2.5. Because all previous versions of the program (XTree, XTreePro, and XTreePro Gold) are still useful and fully functional, I'll discuss all versions in this book.

Getting Started

When you first activate XTree, the blank DOS screen is replaced by a large rectangle that contains several smaller rectangles. XTree starts reading (or logging) the current disk drive (for example, if the system prompt is C:\>, XTree logs, or reads, the C: drive). As XTree scans the disk, a file count is displayed on

```
       Path: \CHECK
                                                     FILE: *.*
             ┌─AB
             ├─BLOCK                                 DISK: C: POWER USER
             ├─CCPLUS                                   Available
Directory ───├─CHECK                                       Bytes: 3,522,560
window       ├─COLLAB
             ├─DOS                                   DISK Statistics
             │  └─VIRUS                                 Total
             ├─DS                                          Files:      2,438
             ├─DU                                          Bytes:63,348,916
             ├─EXCEL                                    Matching
             │  └─BETH                                     Files:      2,438
             ├─FAX                                         Bytes:63,348,916
             │  ├─IMG                                   Tagged
                                                           Files:          0
             BOFA89  .ACT    BOFA89  .DTA    BOFA90  .ACT  Bytes:          0
Small file ──BOFA89  .BGT    BOFA89  .GRP    BOFA90  .BGT  Current Directory
window       BOFA89  .CHK    BOFA89  .SOR    BOFA90  .DEF  CHECK
             BOFA89  .DEF    BOFA89  .ZIP    BOFA90  .DTA  Bytes:    786,291

       DIR      Available  Delete  Filespec  Log disk  Makedir  Print  Rename
       COMMANDS  ^Showall  ^Tag  ^Untag  Volume  eXecute
       ↑↓  scroll  RETURN  file commands    ALT menu         F1 quit F2 help
```

(annotations: DISK and DISK Statistics window)

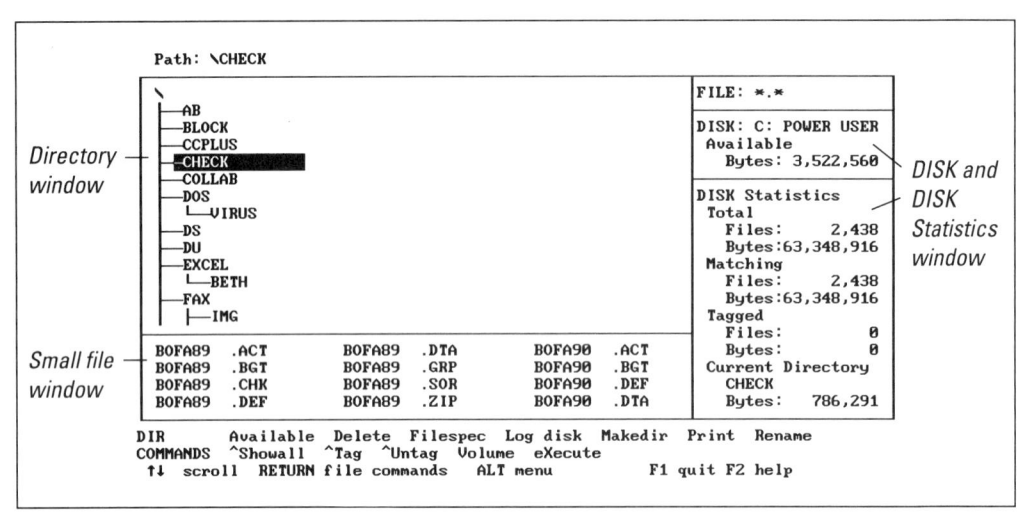

Figure 2-1: The display screen of the original XTree program.

the right side of the screen. Once XTree has finished logging the disk, the visual display changes to look something like Figure 2-1.

Figure 2-1 shows the display screen of the original XTree program; other versions of XTree have similar displays (remember, each program builds on the previous one). At this point we're dealing only with the elements all XTree for DOS programs have in common — no matter which version you own. The commands and displays specific to each version of XTree are covered in Chapter 3.

Examining XTree Screen Elements

The XTree display screen is composed of several rectangular "windows" (not to be confused with Microsoft Windows) and commands.

On-screen windows

The main windows on-screen are the Directory window, the Small file window, and the DISK and DISK Statistics windows. The Small file window expands into the Expanded file window. Each window provides different kinds of information about your hard disk.

Chapter 2: XTree for DOS Basics

Directory window

The Directory window in the upper-left corner is the biggest window. It provides a visual representation of your disk's directory structure (ye olde inverted tree hierarchical structure). You can use the up- and down-arrow keys (cursor keys) to move through the directory structure.

Small file window

The Small file window directly below the Directory window reveals some (or all) of the files contained in a highlighted Directory window. As you move your cursor up and down through the tree structure in the Directory window, the file display in the Small file window changes to reflect the contents of directories highlighted by the cursor.

Expanded file window

The Small file window may not be large enough to show all the files in a directory that contains a lot of files. When this is the case, you can use the Expanded file window to get a better view. See the section "Moving between windows," later in this chapter for instructions on how to expand your file display. An expanded display is shown in Figure 2-2.

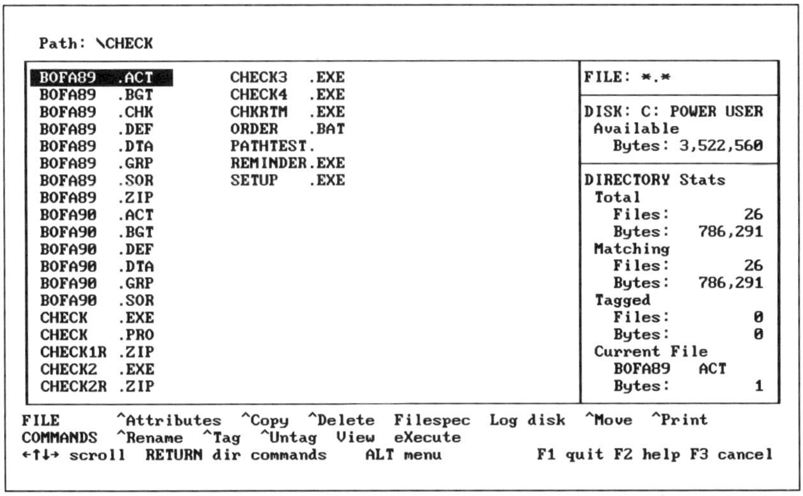

```
Path: \CHECK

BOFA89   .ACT      CHECK3    .EXE        FILE: *.*
BOFA89   .BGT      CHECK4    .EXE
BOFA89   .CHK      CHKRTM    .EXE        DISK: C: POWER USER
BOFA89   .DEF      ORDER     .BAT         Available
BOFA89   .DTA      PATHTEST.                Bytes: 3,522,560
BOFA89   .GRP      REMINDER.EXE
BOFA89   .SOR      SETUP     .EXE        DIRECTORY Stats
BOFA89   .ZIP                             Total
BOFA90   .ACT                              Files:           26
BOFA90   .BGT                              Bytes:      786,291
BOFA90   .DEF                             Matching
BOFA90   .DTA                              Files:           26
BOFA90   .GRP                              Bytes:      786,291
BOFA90   .SOR                             Tagged
CHECK    .EXE                              Files:            0
CHECK    .PRO                              Bytes:            0
CHECK1R  .ZIP                             Current File
CHECK2   .EXE                              BOFA89    ACT
CHECK2R  .ZIP                              Bytes:            1

FILE         ^Attributes  ^Copy  ^Delete  Filespec  Log disk  ^Move  ^Print
COMMANDS     ^Rename  ^Tag  ^Untag  View  eXecute
←↑↓→ scroll   RETURN dir commands    ALT menu        F1 quit F2 help F3 cancel
```

Figure 2-2: The Expanded file window shows more files in crowded directories.

DISK and DISK Statistics windows

On the right, the DISK and DISK Statistics windows show the current bottom-line data for your disk — how much space remains on the drive, how many directories you have, how many files you've got, and that sort of thing.

Other on-screen elements

In addition to the on-screen windows, there are a few (and only a few) additional items you need to know about in order to decipher XTree screens.

Directory and file commands

Commands you perform on directories and files are located at the bottom of the XTree screen. When your cursor is active in the Directory window, commands specific to directories are available. When your cursor is in the Small file window, commands for performing file operations are available. (See "Moving between windows" later in this chapter for navigating instructions.) You activate commands by typing the first letter (or the boldfaced letter) of the action you want to carry out.

The ^ symbol

You may notice the mysterious ^ symbol in the command area. This symbol is shorthand for "Hold down the Ctrl key." When you see, for example, ^C, you are to hold down both the Ctrl key and the letter C at the same time. The ^ in front of a letter usually orders XTree to perform the *bigger* version of a command (see "Tagging files and directories" later in this chapter).

Operating in XTree

Whenever you want to perform operations on files or directories, your cursor needs to be in the File or Directory window, respectively. You then maneuver the cursor with the directional keys on your keyboard until it highlights the file or directory you want to manipulate.

If you are running XTreePro Gold, XTreeGold, or XTree Easy, you can use your mouse to maneuver about the screen. The following methods of operation apply if you do not have a mouse or if you prefer to use the keyboard to navigate.

Moving between windows

When your cursor is in the Directory window, you'll see the phrase RETURN file commands at the bottom of the screen where the commands are displayed. "Return" translates into "Enter" on your keyboard (a throwback to the carriage-return days of the typewriter). If you press Enter repeatedly, the cursor moves in a round-robin fashion between the Directory window, the Small file window, and the Expanded file window and rotates the commands at the bottom of the screen from those that apply to directories to those that apply to files.

When your cursor is in the Small file window, RETURN expanded display becomes the current phrase at the bottom of the screen; pressing Enter from here expands the Small file window into the Expanded file window for viewing contents of larger directories (the commands at the bottom of the screen remain file-specific). You can see approximately five times more files in the Expanded file window. Pressing Enter when you are in the Expanded file window returns you to the Directory window.

> **TIP** Pressing Esc or Backspace always bring you back to the Directory window, no matter where your cursor is.

Highlighting the current directory

You use your up-, down-, left-, and right-arrow keys or your mouse to *highlight* files and directories. Take a look back at Figure 2-1: The cursor is in the Directory window and highlights the CHECK directory. Highlighting a directory makes it the *current* directory. (If you have any doubt about which directory is current, sneak a peek at the top of the display screen for the *path,* which includes the current directory.)

You can now perform directory operations on the highlighted directory. The available commands are listed at the bottom of the screen. Any command you invoke at this point affects the current directory; for this example, pressing R (for Rename) allows you to rename the highlighted CHECK directory.

To the left of the current commands, the legend DIR COMMANDS reminds you that your cursor is in the Directory window.

Highlighting the current file

Files in the current directory are listed in the Small file window just below the Directory window. If you are in the Directory window and want to operate on a file in the current directory, press Enter; the cursor jumps down to the Small file window and XTree presents the file commands at the bottom of the screen.

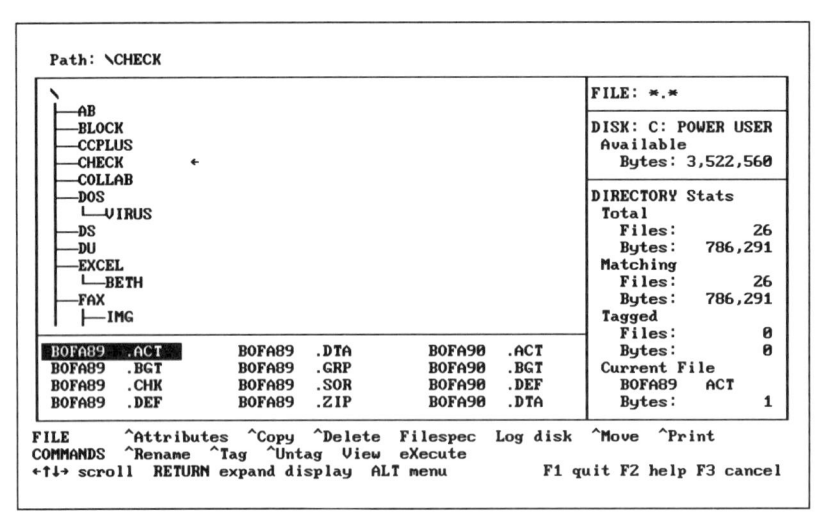

```
Path: \CHECK
                                              ┌──────────────────────────┐
 \                                             │FILE: *.*                 │
   ├─AB                                        │                          │
   ├─BLOCK                                     │DISK: C: POWER USER       │
   ├─CCPLUS                                    │ Available                │
   ├─CHECK       ←                             │   Bytes:       3,522,560 │
   ├─COLLAB                                    │                          │
   ├─DOS                                       │DIRECTORY Stats           │
   │  └─VIRUS                                  │ Total                    │
   ├─DS                                        │   Files:              26 │
   ├─DU                                        │   Bytes:         786,291 │
   ├─EXCEL                                     │ Matching                 │
   │  └─BETH                                   │   Files:              26 │
   ├─FAX                                       │   Bytes:         786,291 │
   │  ├─IMG                                    │ Tagged                   │
                                               │   Files:               0 │
 ┌─────────────┐                               │   Bytes:               0 │
 │BOFA89   .ACT│  BOFA89   .DTA   BOFA90  .ACT │ Current File             │
 └─────────────┘                               │   BOFA89     ACT         │
  BOFA89   .BGT   BOFA89   .GRP   BOFA90  .BGT │   Bytes:               1 │
  BOFA89   .CHK   BOFA89   .SOR   BOFA90  .DEF │                          │
  BOFA89   .DEF   BOFA89   .ZIP   BOFA90  .DTA │                          │
                                               └──────────────────────────┘
 FILE         ^Attributes  ^Copy  ^Delete  Filespec  Log disk  ^Move  ^Print
 COMMANDS     ^Rename  ^Tag  ^Untag  View  eXecute
 ←↑↓→ scroll  RETURN expand display   ALT menu        F1 quit F2 help F3 cancel
```

Figure 2-3: BOFA89.ACT is the highlighted file in the Small file window.

These commands are specific to file operations. (Depending on which window you're in, the available commands at the bottom of the screen are specific to that window.)

When you highlight a file with your cursor or mouse, any command you select affects that highlighted file. So pressing R for Rename allows you to rename the highlighted file. Figure 2-3 shows a highlighted file in the current file list.

Tagging files and directories

You perform operations on files and directories by highlighting them with the cursor or mouse and pressing the boldfaced letter that corresponds to the command you wish to carry out. You can command each file and directory in this way, but it's a tedious process if you want to perform an operation on a dozen or more; the best way to manipulate a number of files and directories is to first indicate to XTree the ones you wish to work on and then execute a command once. The process of selecting numerous files and directories for operation is known as *tagging*.

To tag a file or directory, highlight it with your cursor or mouse and then press T for tag. A diamond appears to the right of the filename or directory, indicating its tagged status. When your cursor is in one of the file windows, pressing Ctrl-T tags all the files in the current directory. (I mentioned earlier that a ^ in front of a command tells XTree to perform the bigger version of the command. Ctrl-T in

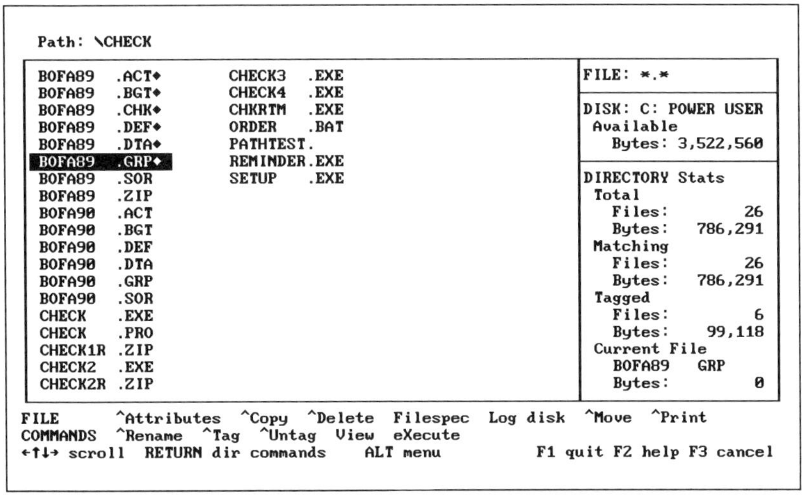

Chapter 2: XTree for DOS Basics

```
Path: \CHECK
 BOFA89   .ACT♦    CHECK3   .EXE         FILE: *.*
 BOFA89   .BGT♦    CHECK4   .EXE
 BOFA89   .CHK♦    CHKRTM   .EXE         DISK: C: POWER USER
 BOFA89   .DEF♦    ORDER    .BAT         Available
 BOFA89   .DTA♦    PATHTEST.                 Bytes:  3,522,560
 BOFA89   .GRP♦    REMINDER.EXE
 BOFA89   .SOR     SETUP    .EXE         DIRECTORY Stats
 BOFA89   .ZIP                           Total
 BOFA90   .ACT                               Files:          26
 BOFA90   .BGT                               Bytes:     786,291
 BOFA90   .DEF                           Matching
 BOFA90   .DTA                               Files:          26
 BOFA90   .GRP                               Bytes:     786,291
 BOFA90   .SOR                           Tagged
 CHECK    .EXE                               Files:           6
 CHECK    .PRO                               Bytes:      99,118
 CHECK1R  .ZIP                           Current File
 CHECK2   .EXE                               BOFA89      GRP
 CHECK2R  .ZIP                               Bytes:           0

 FILE          ^Attributes  ^Copy  ^Delete  Filespec  Log disk  ^Move  ^Print
 COMMANDS      ^Rename  ^Tag  ^Untag  View  eXecute
 ←↑↓→ scroll   RETURN dir commands    ALT menu      F1 quit F2 help F3 cancel
```

Figure 2-4: The six files at the top of the screen have all been tagged.

this case means "Tag all the files.") Several files are tagged in Figure 2-4. Once all files to be operated on are tagged, press the letter for the command you wish to carry out.

When the cursor is in the Directory window, commands take place on the directory level. So when your cursor is active in this window, pressing T tags the highlighted directory and Ctrl-T tags all directories.

Untagging files and directories

If you accidentally tag a file or directory you don't want to operate on, simply press U for untag. If you wanted to untag all tagged files, pressing Ctrl-U can fix your wagon.

Using the FILESPEC command

One of the most powerful tools in XTree is the Filespec command. This is where you get to use all the wildcard stuff I discussed in Chapter 1.

If you want to find all the files on your hard disk with a BAK extension, for example, you don't have to manually search through all your files to find them. All you have to do is change the file specification (called the *filespec*) to *.BAK, and then only those files meeting that criterion (those ending in BAK) will be displayed in the window. Of course, this also works with *.WK1 files, *.DOC files, or any sort of filename you care to specify.

A directory that doesn't have any files that meet the current filespec displays a "No Files!" message. This doesn't mean there are no files at all in that directory, merely that no files in that directory match the current file specification.

In the upper-right corner of the XTree screen is the FILE: window, where the current filespec is displayed. Unless you've changed it, the filespec is *.*. This filespec is pronounced *star-dot-star* in computer lingo and includes all files everywhere.

Getting Help

XTree's online Help is always available. Whenever you're using the program and need a hint, you are just a function key (F2 in XTree and F1 in Easy, Pro, ProGold, and Gold) away from a helpful screen and index. Don't forget that Help is there when you're in a jam.

Using the Command shell

XTree has a feature called the *Command shell,* which is also known as a *DOS shell.* Unlike your other software programs, XTree is designed not only to manage your files, but to actually *start* other programs. While another program is running, XTree remains active in the background, ready to appear the moment you quit out of that other program.

The command to start another program begins with X, for Execute. When you press X, the XTree display completely disappears and you're in a state that is *almost* like being at the system prompt. In fact, everything works as though you are at the system prompt. XTree remains in your computer's memory, and when you quit the program you're using, you'll automatically end up back in XTree. XTree becomes your *command central.*

Using The XTree for DOS Quick Reference Guide

Now that you know about the basic concepts of XTree for DOS, you're equipped to perform most of the maintenance tasks of XTree. You may be thinking, "Yeah, I get this stuff so far, but how *exactly* do I copy a directory, how do I delete all my BAK files, how do I change file attributes?"

Relax. Answers to these questions (and more) are in the Quick Reference Guide in Chapter 3. This guide is a combination of XTree commands and computer stuff in general. Important concepts like batch files are in this chapter, so don't miss out.

Summary

▶ The location of the cursor determines which file, directory, or window is current.

▶ Tagging files and directories is a way to select more than one file or directory for action.

▶ File specifications enable you to trim the number of files displayed to match a specific set of criteria. This makes it easier to find and tag the files you need.

▶ Use the XTree command shell to start other software programs; XTree remains active in the background, ready for action when you quit those programs.

The 5th Wave
By Rich Tennant
TARZAN VIEWS THE XTREE PRO GOLD PROGRAM IN ACTION.
©RICH TENNANT
HMM - NICE TREE STRUCTURE.

Chapter 3
XTree for DOS Quick Reference Guide

In This Chapter

▶ Task-oriented topics for all versions of XTree for DOS

▶ Step-by-step instructions for each topic

▶ XTree commands and how to use them in all versions of XTree for DOS

All Versions of XTree for DOS?

For many years, three versions of XTree — XTree, XTreePro, and XTreePro Gold — lived in peaceful coexistence, each one fitting perfectly into its own niche. In fact, when the first edition of this book appeared in 1990, it covered only those three programs.

A lot has happened since then.

Basically, XTree Company staged a revolution. Rather than continue their policy of adding new versions with new names in endless ranks, they stopped making XTree and XTreePro (though there are still plenty of copies around), gave XTreePro Gold new features, and capped it off by giving it an easier-to-pronounce name: XTreeGold. Next, they created a petite version of XTreeGold and dubbed it XTree Easy. Then they developed XTreeNet for local area networks (covered in Part II of this book) and XTree for Windows (see Part III of this book).

Suddenly, things got a whole lot more complex. Undaunted, however, I'm still covering *all* versions of XTree in this book; in this chapter, the XTree for DOS programs are detailed side by side.

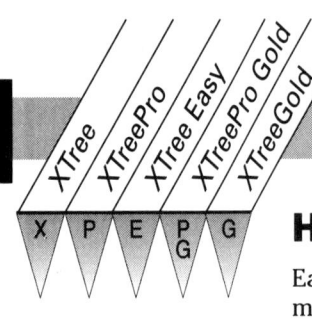

How the side-by-side comparison works

Each section in Chapter 3 begins with an explanation of the command or concept. Within each section are topic headings; to the left of the topic headings are icons that inform you if this section is relevant to your version of the program.

It works like this:

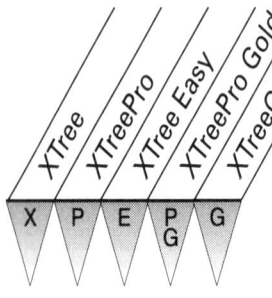

These instructions apply to XTree, XTreePro, XTree Easy, XTreePro Gold, and XTreeGold.

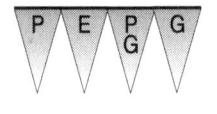

These instructions work in XTreePro, XTree Easy, XTreePro Gold, and XTreeGold.

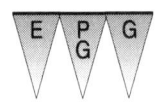

These instructions apply to XTree Easy, XTreePro Gold, and XTreeGold.

These instructions apply to XTreePro Gold and XTreeGold.

These instructions work in XTreeGold only.

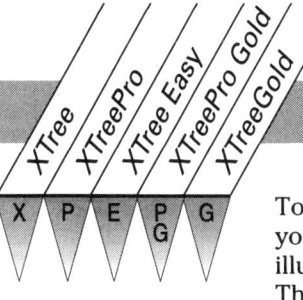

Chapter 3: XTree for DOS Quick Reference Guide

To use this chapter most effectively, find the name of the program you own, locate the icon associated with that program (as just illustrated), and read the selections appropriate to your software. The icons are your sign posts to all the instructions for your particular software.

In some cases one version of XTree can perform a particular task using several techniques. For instance, you can use XTreeGold to delete a directory by following the same steps specific to the original XTree, or you can use the new and improved method, which will be explained later in that section. So be sure to scan the whole section for your software icon!

Finally, to keep things jumping, the figures are a mix of all versions of XTree. If you own XTreeGold, and a particular figure illustrates the original XTree, the figure may still apply to your situation. Remember to use the icons as your road map to what is relevant to your software package.

This all sounds more complicated than it really is (trust me). I'm using this side-by-side approach in order to avoid repeating (five times!) the many commands all versions have in common. You'll see that 75 percent of each section are shared commands and techniques, with each program branching off here and there with new tips and tricks. Besides, this side-by-side system lets you see how the versions stack up — more advanced features may tempt you to upgrade, and if you do upgrade to another version, you won't have to buy another XTree book. (Such a deal!)

Using a Mouse

You can use a mouse with XTreePro Gold, XTreeGold, and XTree Easy. All you have to do is position the mouse pointer on the command you wish to use and click the button. This action replaces typing the command from the keyboard. Some additional things you can do with a mouse are noted as the chapter progresses.

Where to Start

Again, this chapter is task oriented. So you may read the whole chapter, skim through it (looking for new stuff), or just jump to a particular task. (Don't forget the Index — it can help guide you to the right place.) If you're starting from scratch, a good place to begin is with the Tag/Untag and Filespec sections, since so many XTree operations are made easier by mastering those two features. (Also, if you didn't read Chapter 1, "MS-DOS Concepts," you may want to review it now.)

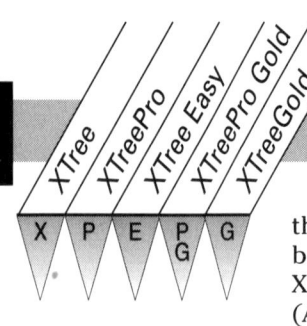

The Application Menu

See The Command Shell, Execute, and Batch Files

Introducing XTreePro Gold's Application Menu

If you wanted to, you could get into XTreePro Gold the moment you turn your computer on and stay in XTreePro Gold without ever quitting — and still use all your software — thanks to the Application Menu.

So what the heck is an Application Menu?

First of all, *application* means programs. Software. Stuff like WordPerfect, Lotus 1-2-3, Microsoft Word, Quicken, and so on. A *menu,* of course, is a list of available options.

You can set up your Application Menu to list your applications as well as any DOS commands you find yourself using over and over. Then, when you want to carry out a command on the menu, just highlight the appropriate menu item and press Enter. This shortcut releases brain cells devoted to remembering DOS commands for activities that are more profitable (or fun).

To activate the Application Menu, press the F9 function key. Although the sample menu shown in Figure 3-1 contains four items, the first time *you* press F9 you'll be greeted with a blank menu you can fill with up to thirteen items.

To activate a menu item, use the up- and down-arrow keys to highlight your choice. In the Application Menu shown in Figure 3-1, the procedure FULL BACKUP is highlighted. Simply pressing Enter at this point is all it takes to back up the hard disk. You, too, can create menu items like this. Just wait.

Chapter 3: XTree for DOS Quick Reference Guide

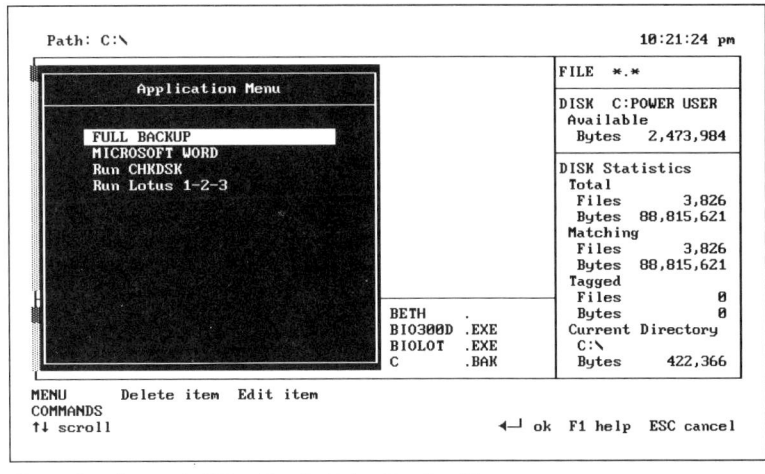

```
Path: C:\                                    10:21:24 pm
                                    ┌─────────────────────────┐
        ┌──────────────────────┐    │ FILE    *.*             │
        │   Application Menu   │    │ DISK  C:POWER USER      │
        │                      │    │ Available               │
        │ FULL BACKUP          │    │   Bytes      2,473,984  │
        │ MICROSOFT WORD       │    │                         │
        │ Run CHKDSK           │    │ DISK Statistics         │
        │ Run Lotus 1-2-3      │    │ Total                   │
        │                      │    │   Files          3,826  │
        │                      │    │   Bytes     88,815,621  │
        │                      │    │ Matching                │
        │                      │    │   Files          3,826  │
        │                      │    │   Bytes     88,815,621  │
        │                      │    │ Tagged                  │
        │                      │    │   Files              0  │
        │                      │    │ BETH    .   │   Bytes              0  │
        │                      │    │ BIO300D .EXE│ Current Directory     │
        │                      │    │ BIOLOT  .EXE│  C:\                  │
        │                      │    │ C       .BAK│  Bytes         422,366│
        └──────────────────────┘    └─────────────────────────┘
 MENU       Delete item   Edit item
 COMMANDS
 ↑↓ scroll                              ← ok   F1 help   ESC cancel
```

Figure 3-1: A sample XTreePro Gold Application Menu.

Editing the Application Menu

When you want to add something to the Application Menu, position the highlight on an empty space and press E (for Edit item). At the bottom of the screen you'll see a prompt for an item name; this is the name that will appear on the menu, so type in what you want and then press Enter.

```
 XTreeGOLD (tm) Application Menu                       10:23:16 pm
┌─────────────────────────────────────────────────────────────────┐
│ Item name: FULL BACKUP                                          │
├─────────────────────────────────────────────────────────────────┤
│ 01> backup c:\ A:/S                                             │
│ 02>                                                             │
│ 03>                                                             │
│ 04>                                                             │
│ 05>                                                             │
│ 06>                                                             │
│ 07>                                                             │
│ 08>                                                             │
│ 09>                                                             │
│ 10>                                                             │
│ 11>                                                             │
│ 12>                                                             │
│ 13>                                                             │
│ 14>                                                             │
│ 15>                                                             │
│ 16>                                                             │
│ 17>                                                             │
└─────────────────────────────────────────────────────────────────┘
 EDIT       Copy  Delete  Edit  Insert  Move  edit Name  Undo
 COMMANDS
 ↑↓ scroll                                      F1 help   ESC menu
```

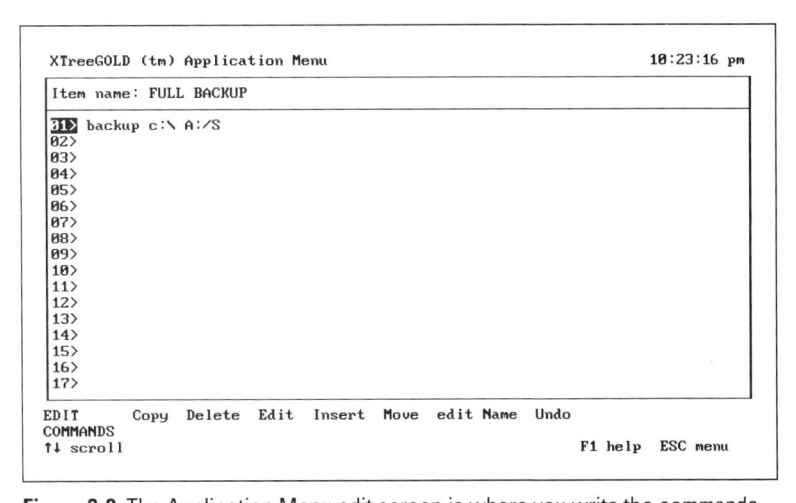

Figure 3-2: The Application Menu edit screen is where you write the commands you want XTreePro Gold to carry out for a menu item.

```
XTreeGOLD (tm) Application Menu                              12:38:06 pm
Item name: Run CHKDSK

01> CHKDSK %2:
02>
03>
04>
05>
06>
07>
08>
09>
10>
11>
12>
13>
14>
15>
16>
17>

EDIT          Copy   Delete   Edit   Insert   Move   edit Name   Undo
COMMANDS
↑↓ scroll                                              F1 help   ESC menu
```

Figure 3-3: Editing the Run CHKDSK menu item.

The next screen that appears is similar to that shown in Figure 3-2, which shows you what it takes to create the FULL BACKUP procedure (using DOS's BACKUP program). The Item name: category at the top of the screen reminds you which menu item you are currently editing.

In Figure 3-2, the cursor is highlighting line 01. To edit that line, just press E for Edit and then type the command you want to use. When you're finished with a line, press Enter to move the cursor to the next line (there's space for up to 17 lines of instructions).

Figure 3-3 illustrates the innards of the Run CHKDSK menu item — a little more fancy than FULL BACKUP. Please note the "%2:": When XTreePro Gold sees that %2, it knows it's supposed to put the letter of the current drive (in this case, C) in place of the %2 and then carry out the command. This means that you can select the Run CHKDSK menu item while in any drive and XTreePro Gold will automatically check out that drive, whatever it is. (Pretty clever.)

The Edit Commands at the bottom of the screen allow you to copy, delete, edit, insert, and move the line that the cursor is on. (You can even undo a change!) If you want to delete an entry from the Application Menu, for example, simply highlight that item and press D (for Delete Item).

When you're finished, move the cursor to a blank line and press Esc to return to the Application Menu.

Using the Application Menu for system management

The Application Menu can play a key role in managing your system in three situations:

- When you want an ultracustomized system that can perform repetitive tasks.
- When you need to design a system simple enough for computer novices. (If you do set up a system for someone else, consider configuring XTreePro Gold to prohibit others from changing what you've set up.)
- Although Open (see also the "Execute" section) *is* a great command, the Application Menu does a lot more than just start up a program.

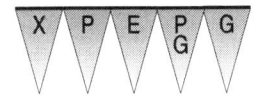

Attributes (File)

As you may recall from Chapter 1, "MS-DOS Concepts," there are four file attributes: Read-only, Archive, System, and Hidden. (If you don't remember what each means, you can go back to Chapter 1 and refresh your memory.)

If you attempt to copy, delete, move, or rename a file with a read-only attribute, XTree refuses to carry out your command. The only way you can force XTree to carry out your command is to first turn off the file's read-only attribute. Keep in mind, however, that the read-only parameter is usually set for a reason. Before you turn this attribute off, please be sure it's safe to do so.

Displaying a file's attributes

If you're considering tinkering with your file attributes, a first step (though not required) might be to change your file display to reveal the attributes for each file (just press Alt-F; see "File Display" for more details). Figure 3-4 shows an Expanded file window with file attributes divulged. Next to the filenames and

Attributes (File)

```
Path: \

ANSI        .RTF    4,403 ....      CONFIG   .OLD      128 ....     FILE: *.*
ANSI        .SCR    2,000 ....      CONFIG   .SYS      256 ....
ASCII       .DOC    3,584 ....      FRECOVER.BAK   78,336 ra..     DISK: C: POWER USER
ASCII       .RTF    4,403 ....      FRECOVER.DAT   78,336 ra..     Available
ASCII       .SCR    2,000 ....      FRECOVER.IDX       29 rash     Bytes: 2,686,976
AUTOEXEC.BAK         512 ....      HIMEM    .SYS   11,304 ....
AUTOEXEC.BAT         512 ....      IBMBIO   .COM   23,591 r.sh     DIRECTORY Stats
AUTOEXEC.DBK         512 ....      IBMBIO   .XUP      201 ....     Total
BETH        .         82 ....      IBMDOS   .COM   30,632 r.sh       Files:            34
BIO300D     .EXE   36,363 ....      IBMDOS   .XUP      255 ....       Bytes:       420,121
BIOLOT      .EXE   48,919 ....      OLDAUTO  .BAT      512 ....     Matching
C           .BAK      128 ....      PIX      .BAT       19 ....       Files:            34
C           .BAT      128 ....      VTECH    .CFG        8 ....       Bytes:       420,121
CAP         .BAT       20 ....      VTECH    .EXE   32,174 ....     Tagged
CHECKUP     .LOG   34,733 .a..      WED      .CHK       13 .a..       Files:             0
COMMAND     .COM   25,332 ....                                        Bytes:             0
COMMAND     .XUP      312 ....                                      Current File
CONFIG      .BAK      256 ....                                        ANSI       RTF
CONFIG      .DBK      128 ....                                        Bytes:         4,403

FILE          ^Attributes   ^Copy    ^Delete   Filespec   Log disk   ^Move   ^Print
COMMANDS      ^Rename   ^Tag   ^Untag   View   eXecute
←↑↓→ scroll   RETURN dir commands         ALT menu           F1 quit  F2 help  F3 cancel
```

Figure 3-4: An XTree Expanded file window shows each file's size (the number next to the filenames) and attributes (r, a, s, and h).

sizes are either four dots or one or more of the initials r, a, s, and h (signifying read-only, archive, system, and hidden, of course).

Changing a file's attributes

To change the attributes of a file, highlight the file and press A for attributes. The filename and the file's attributes appear at the bottom of the screen, as shown in Figure 3-5. The file CHECKUP.LOG is marked with the archive attribute and the file's attributes can now be changed.

Press the minus sign (–) key to turn an attribute off and the plus sign (+) key to turn an attribute on; then enter the letter of the attribute you want to change. Figure 3-6 shows the process of removing the archive attribute from CHECKUP.LOG. If, in the future, you forget what the attribute letters stand for, helpful definitions are only a keystroke away (Help is F2 in XTree and F1 in the other versions).

> You can also tag a bunch of files and then press Ctrl-A to change the attributes of all tagged files.

Chapter 3: XTree for DOS Quick Reference Guide

```
Path: \
ANSI     .RTF      CONFIG   .OLD         FILE: *.*
ANSI     .SCR      CONFIG   .SYS
ASCII    .DOC      FRECOVER.BAK          DISK: C: POWER USER
ASCII    .RTF      FRECOVER.DAT          Available
ASCII    .SCR      FRECOVER.IDX            Bytes: 2,695,168
AUTOEXEC.BAK      HIMEM    .SYS
AUTOEXEC.BAT      IBMBIO   .COM         DIRECTORY Stats
AUTOEXEC.DBK      IBMBIO   .XUP         Total
BETH     .        IBMDOS   .COM           Files:            34
BIO300D  .EXE     IBMDOS   .XUP           Bytes:       420,121
BIOLOT   .EXE     OLDAUTO  .BAT         Matching
C        .BAK     PIX      .BAT           Files:            34
C        .BAT     VTECH    .CFG           Bytes:       420,121
CAP      .BAT     VTECH    .EXE         Tagged
CHECKUP  .LOG     WED      .CHK           Files:             0
COMMAND  .COM                              Bytes:             0
COMMAND  .XUP                            Current File
CONFIG   .BAK                              CHECKUP   LOG
CONFIG   .DBK                              Bytes:        34,733

ATTRIBUTES for file: CHECKUP.LOG    .a..   6-27-90  10:44 am
            :
enter attribute changes (+/- R A S H)        F1 quit F2 help F3 cancel
```

Figure 3-5: Pressing A for Attributes in the XTree Expanded file window allows you to change the attributes of a file.

```
Path: \
ANSI     .RTF      CONFIG   .OLD         FILE: *.*
ANSI     .SCR      CONFIG   .SYS
ASCII    .DOC      FRECOVER.BAK          DISK: C: POWER USER
ASCII    .RTF      FRECOVER.DAT          Available
ASCII    .SCR      FRECOVER.IDX            Bytes: 2,695,168
AUTOEXEC.BAK      HIMEM    .SYS
AUTOEXEC.BAT      IBMBIO   .COM         DIRECTORY Stats
AUTOEXEC.DBK      IBMBIO   .XUP         Total
BETH     .        IBMDOS   .COM           Files:            34
BIO300D  .EXE     IBMDOS   .XUP           Bytes:       420,121
BIOLOT   .EXE     OLDAUTO  .BAT         Matching
C        .BAK     PIX      .BAT           Files:            34
C        .BAT     VTECH    .CFG           Bytes:       420,121
CAP      .BAT     VTECH    .EXE         Tagged
CHECKUP  .LOG     WED      .CHK           Files:             0
COMMAND  .COM                              Bytes:             0
COMMAND  .XUP                            Current File
CONFIG   .BAK                              CHECKUP   LOG
CONFIG   .DBK                              Bytes:        34,733

ATTRIBUTES for file: CHECKUP.LOG    .a..   6-27-90  10:44 am
            : -A
enter attribute changes (+/- R A S H)        F1 quit F2 help F3 cancel
```

Figure 3-6: Pressing –A and then Enter removes the archive attribute from CHECKUP.LOG.

AutoView — Command

See View

Avail, Batch Files

Avail — Command

The Avail command in XTreeGold tells you how much space is available on a disk drive. Generally, you can find out how much space is left on the current drive just by looking in the upper-right corner of your screen, where the `Available Bytes` are displayed.

Avail is helpful when you want to know how much free space is on another drive (a floppy disk, for instance) without going through the logging and relogging process, which on slower machines can be tedious.

Press A (for Avail) and, when prompted, type in the name of the disk drive in question (for example, A) and press Enter. In a flash, you have an answer.

Batch Files

See Execute and The Application Menu

What is a batch file?

A batch file is a file that contains a series (or a *batch*) of commands — the sort of commands that you normally type at the system prompt. Once the commands are gathered together in a batch file, merely typing the name of that file causes all the commands in the batch file to be executed as though they were being typed by you. (If you're familiar with macros, a batch file is like a DOS macro.) Once you get the hang of this you'll discover that they're as addictive as potato chips.

Here's how it works:

Say, for example, you use WordPerfect, and every time you turn on the computer you type **CD \WP** and press Enter to get to the directory where WordPerfect is stored. Then you type **WP** and press Enter to start WordPerfect.

You can put those two commands into a batch file and name the file W.BAT. (All batch files must have the BAT extension, like W.BAT and AUTOEXEC.BAT). Then, when you want to start

Chapter 3: XTree for DOS Quick Reference Guide

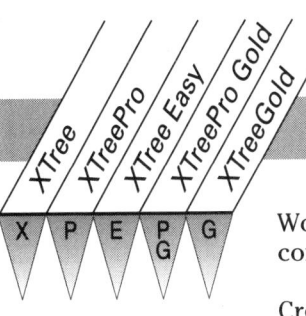

WordPerfect, all you have to do is press W and then Enter. The two commands in the W.BAT file are carried out.

Creating and using batch files is part of DOS's domain. While XTreePro Gold, XTree Easy, and XTreeGold may push the batch file envelope (as you'll see coming up) with some special batch file commands, you can make and use batch files whether you are using an XTree product or not.

Before getting into anything special, however, let's start at the beginning with the ordinary DOS batch files.

Making a batch file

There are dozens of ways to create batch files. One way is with XTreePro or XTreeGold's text editor, 1Word. (See "Editing with 1Word" for details.) However, you can create a simple batch file without using *any* text editor. The first step in creating a batch file is to get to the DOS prompt (which you can do by quitting whatever program you're in — if you're in XTree just press X to get to the Command shell).

Let's say you must frequently format floppy disks. You decide to reduce the number of keystrokes required to accomplish this task by creating a batch file. Because you're building a shorthand way to format disks in the A: drive, you decide that an easy-to-remember name for this batch file is FA.BAT (Format the disk in A:). Whenever you need to format a floppy disk in the A: drive, all you'll have to do is type **FA** and press Enter.

From the DOS prompt, type **COPY CON FA.BAT** and press Enter. This starts the batch file creation process and names the new batch file FA.BAT. When you create another batch file, substitute your *new* batch filename in the place of FA.BAT.

Now it's time to enter the commands you want FA.BAT to carry out (in this case, there's only one command): type **FORMAT A:** and press Enter. That's all FA.BAT needs to do. However, if in the future you want to create a more complex batch file, continue typing the necessary commands and press Enter at the end of each line.

You cannot edit a previous line with this method. If you realize you made a mistake, you must press Ctrl-C to void the entire batch file and start again.

```
C:\XTREE >copy con fa.bat
format a:
^Z
        1 File(s) copied

C:\XTREE >
```

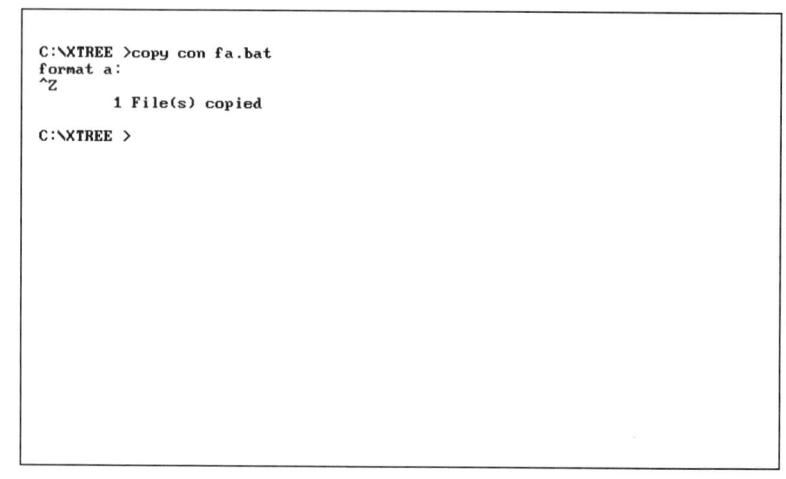

Figure 3-7: Creating a batch file (C:\XTREE> means the prompt is active in the XTree directory; your system prompt may vary).

When you are finished entering the commands, press Enter once again so you end on an empty line. Then, to finish the process, press the F6 function key (which displays a ^Z on-screen) and then press Enter. The computer then displays the message 1 File(s) copied. Figure 3-7 shows how this process looks on-screen.

From now on, whenever you type FA and press Enter, the computer responds with FORMAT A: (Enter), and DOS asks you to insert a new disk for drive A: and press Enter when ready — just as though you had typed FORMAT A: and pressed Enter yourself!

Batch files can be created for moving around directories, starting up programs, and accomplishing anything else possible from a DOS prompt. You can even do some tricky things that *can't* be done from a DOS prompt.

Using DOS's batch file variables

You could make a batch file that puts to use the fact that most word processing programs allow you to specify the name of the file you want to edit when you launch the program. If you type WP DAFFY.DOC and then press Enter, for instance, WordPerfect starts and automatically retrieves the DAFFY.DOC file for you.

Chapter 3: XTree for DOS Quick Reference Guide

You could even put the command to load DAFFY.DOC in a batch file. The drawback is that even though you're working on DAFFY.DOC today, tomorrow you might want the file WHATSUP.DOC. A batch file whose sole purpose is to call up any one file (unless you work on that file exclusively) has a limited utility.

To get around this, DOS has a way to make a batch file that can say "start WordPerfect and get a file to be named later." The file to be named later is called a *variable* because the name of the file will vary. Naturally, there's an arcane symbol that signifies a variable: the percent sign (%).

A batch file that starts WordPerfect and retrieves a file to be named later looks like this:

```
CD \WP\LETTERS
WP %1
```

As the batch file executes, the file to be named later is placed in the %1 spot. You specify the file to be named later by typing its name after the batch filename. In this case, assuming the batch file is still named W.BAT, you type W DAFFY.DOC and press Enter, and DOS puts DAFFY.DOC in the %1 spot and the computer acts as though the batch file actually reads:

```
CD \WP\LETTER
WP DAFFY.DOC
```

Or, if you type W BILLS.DOC and press Enter, the computer places BILLS.DOC in the %1 spot (and calls up the file BILLS.DOC). If you don't have a preference about which file you want to work on, you can still type plain old W, press Enter, and WordPerfect kicks into action, ignoring the %1.

You can have more than one % (variable) in a file (so you can specify a directory to be named later, for instance). Each variable is represented by a number. The first one is %1, the next one is %2, after that is %3, and so forth. Actually, you can have *lots* of variables, labels, If-Then and Goto statements, and well, let's just say there are books the size of Yuletide logs that cover the programming of batch files. Obviously, therefore, there's a lot more to say about batch files than what you'll find here, which is just a bare-bones course in batch files to get you started. (For more information about batch files, check out the books recommended in Appendix D, "Where to Go from Here.")

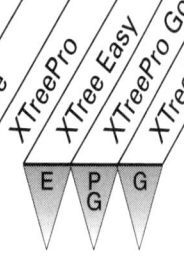

Using XTree batch file variables

One day, the gang at XTree decided to take some DOS variables and extend the concept. They realized that it would be really great if a file highlighted in XTree could be automatically passed on as a variable in a batch file.

The special variables described next work only in XTreePro Gold, XTree Easy, and XTreeGold. Furthermore, these special batch command variables are used exclusively by Application Menu (XTreePro Gold), the Open command, and XTreeMenu (XTreeGold).

The special, improved variables specific to these three XTree programs are as follows:

Variable	Action	Example
%1	the file's path & name	C:\WP\LETTERS\DAFFY.DOC
%2	the drive ID	C:
%3	the file's path	\WP\LETTERS
%4	the file's name	DAFFY
%5	the file's extension	DOC

Let's say you've created a batch file with one line:

```
C:\WP\WP.EXE %1
```

Now, imagine you've highlighted a file called REPORT.DOC using XTreePro Gold, XTree Easy, or XTreeGold. If you now invoke this batch file (using the Application Menu, XTreeMenu, or Open), XTree starts WordPerfect and calls up the highlighted file.

If you want to run the DOS program CHKDSK on the current drive, you could create a batch file (or menu command) that looks like this:

```
CHKDSK %2:
```

This command runs CHKDSK; XTree knows to insert the current drive in the %2 spot.

Branch — Command

A new command now appearing at the bottom of local XTreeGold screens everywhere is the Branch command. The Branch command is a local or mini Showall command. While Showall puts every file on your entire hard drive in one list, usually alphabetically, Branch shows only those files in the current directory and in all that directory's child directories that match the current filespec. Once you've used Branch to organize your files into an easy-to-handle list, you can carry out XTree commands, find duplicates, and so forth.

To use Branch, first move to a Directory window and then highlight a parent directory and press B. All files (matching the current file specification, of course) are listed as though they were in one megadirectory.

If you press Ctrl-B, only files currently tagged will be displayed.

Cancel — Command

Drat! You've changed your mind and don't want to carry out a particular command after all. To countermand any command, just select cancel, which appears in the lower-right corner of your XTree screen whenever you initiate any action that can be canceled. You can cancel a command at any time.

Quit is not the same as cancel. Quit is used to exit the XTree program itself.

Canceling a command with XTree

In the original XTree program, there are two ways to cancel file operations. In Figure 3-8, for example, the file BOFA89.ACT is in the process of being deleted. To cancel this activity, you can either press F3 (the hotkey for cancel) or N, which answers the question `delete this file (y/n)?` at the bottom of the screen.

```
                      Path: \CHECK

                      BOFA89   .ACT    CHECK3   .EXE           FILE: *.*
                      BOFA89   .BGT    CHECK4   .EXE
                      BOFA89   .CHK    CHKRTM   .EXE           DISK: C: POWER USER
                      BOFA89   .DEF    ORDER    .BAT           Available
                      BOFA89   .DTA    PATHTEST.                 Bytes: 3,276,800
                      BOFA89   .GRP    REMINDER.EXE
                      BOFA89   .SOR    SETUP    .EXE           DIRECTORY Stats
                      BOFA89   .ZIP                            Total
                      BOFA90   .ACT                              Files:             26
                      BOFA90   .BGT                              Bytes:        786,291
                      BOFA90   .DEF                            Matching
                      BOFA90   .DTA                              Files:             26
                      BOFA90   .GRP                              Bytes:        786,291
                      BOFA90   .SOR                            Tagged
                      CHECK    .EXE                              Files:              0
                      CHECK    .PRO                              Bytes:              0
                      CHECK1R  .ZIP                            Current File
                      CHECK2   .EXE                              BOFA89     ACT
                      CHECK2R  .ZIP                              Bytes:              1

                      DELETE file: BOFA89.ACT

                      delete this file (Y/N) ?                  F1 quit F2 help F3 cancel
```

Figure 3-8: In the original XTree, the cancel command, F3, appears when you're in the middle of an operation.

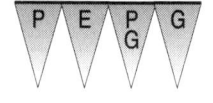

Canceling a command with XTreePro, XTreePro Gold, XTree Easy, and XTreeGold

The newer XTrees use Esc to cancel operations. In Figure 3-9, the file 3270.TXT has been selected for copying. To cancel the copying process, press Esc or click cancel. Even *after* the copying process begins, you can still select cancel to stop the command from being carried out any further.

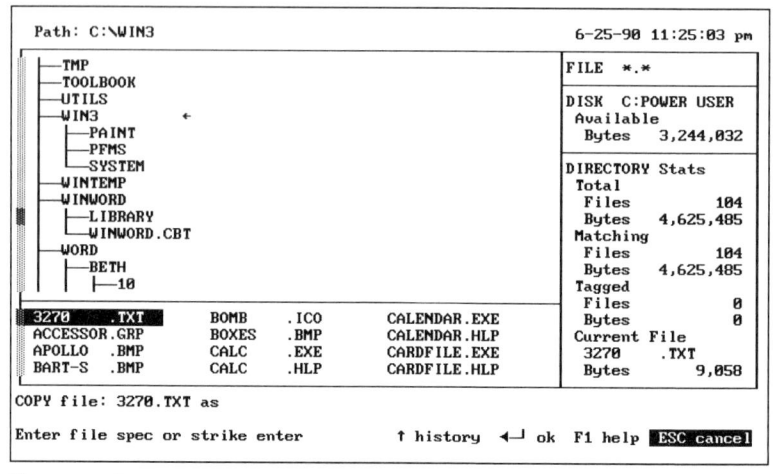

```
   Path: C:\WIN3                                    6-25-90 11:25:03 pm

   ├─TMP                                         FILE  *.*
   ├─TOOLBOOK
   ├─UTILS                                       DISK  C:POWER USER
   └WIN3              ←                          Available
      ├─PAINT                                      Bytes     3,244,032
      ├─PFMS
      └─SYSTEM                                   DIRECTORY Stats
   ├─WINTEMP                                     Total
   └WINWORD                                        Files           104
      ├─LIBRARY                                    Bytes     4,625,485
      └─WINWORD.CBT                              Matching
   └WORD                                           Files           104
      ├─BETH                                       Bytes     4,625,485
      └─10                                       Tagged
                                                   Files             0
   3270      .TXT    BOMB    .ICO   CALENDAR.EXE   Bytes             0
   ACCESSOR.GRP      BOXES   .BMP   CALENDAR.HLP Current File
   APOLLO   .BMP     CALC    .EXE   CARDFILE.EXE   3270       .TXT
   BART-S   .BMP     CALC    .HLP   CARDFILE.HLP   Bytes         9,058

   COPY file: 3270.TXT as

   Enter file spec or strike enter       ↑ history  ↵ ok  F1 help  ESC cancel
```

Figure 3-9: Pressing Esc stops commands from being carried out in XTreePro, XTreePro Gold, XTree Easy, and XTreeGold. (If you have a mouse, you can click cancel.)

Chapter 3: XTree for DOS Quick Reference Guide

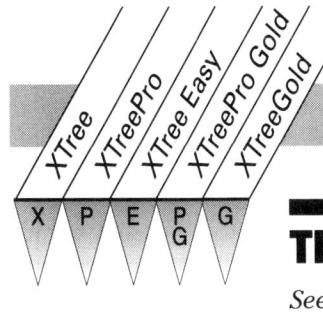

The Command Shell

See Execute, The Application Menu, and The XTreeMenu

What is the Command shell?

The purpose of a command shell is to let you work with DOS directly, without actually quitting XTree. There are several command shells available, one of which comes with DOS itself. All XTree products have command shells, too.

When you enter an XTree Command shell, it looks as though XTree has disappeared from your screen. Actually, it's waiting in background memory until you've finished your DOS business. The look of XTree's prompt, and what you can do when you're there, varies depending on what version of XTree you own.

Activating the Command shell

To activate the Command shell, merely press X for Execute. Depending on where your cursor is when you press X, one of two things happens:

- If you press X when a program's name is highlighted in the Small file or Expanded file window, that program's name is automatically entered for you at XTree's system prompt. (More about this in the "Execute" section.) Once a program name appears at XTree's prompt, you can press Enter to activate that program.

- If you press X while your cursor is in the Directory window, you'll find yourself at XTree's blank system prompt. You can now perform any DOS command or start any program.

If you happen to create or delete a file while using the Command shell, you must relog your drive (that is, "take an inventory" of the drive) before the changes will appear in the File window. Press L to relog your drive. (See "Log" for more details.)

Using the Command shell with XTree

Figure 3-10 shows what your XTree screen will look like when you invoke the Execute command from the Directory window. As you can see, the XTree system prompt is similar to the DOS prompt, except that no drive letter is specified. Also, at the top of the figure, XTree prompts you to enter a DOS command. This doesn't mean you can only perform DOS commands per se (such as FORMAT or DIR, for example). It means you can enter any command you might normally type at a system prompt, such as those that start applications like Microsoft Word or Lotus 1-2-3.

If you want to return to XTree after using a DOS command, press Enter at an empty system prompt and you'll bounce back to XTree. If you used an application, you'll be returned to the prompt when you exit the program. You can then just press Enter (or any key) to return to the XTree screen.

```
Current Path: C:\DOS
Enter a DOS command, or press RETURN on an empty line to return to XTREE.
>
```

Figure 3-10: XTree's Command shell.

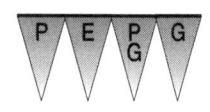

Using the Command shell with XTreePro, XTreePro Gold, XTree Easy, and XTreeGold

The Command shells in the later versions of XTree perform similarly to XTree's, but they are a bit more informative. The XTreePro Command shell is shown in Figure 3-11. At the top of the screen you get the date, time, free memory, and free disk space.

Chapter 3: XTree for DOS Quick Reference Guide 53

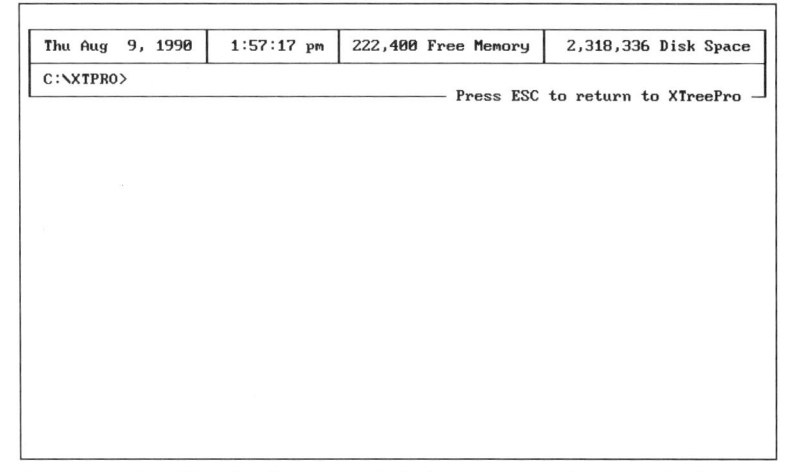

```
┌─────────────────────────────────────────────────────────────────────┐
│ Thu Aug  9, 1990 │ 1:57:17 pm │ 222,400 Free Memory │ 2,318,336 Disk Space │
│ C:\XTPRO>                                                           │
│                                          Press ESC to return to XTreePro │
│                                                                     │
│                                                                     │
│                                                                     │
│                                                                     │
│                                                                     │
│                                                                     │
│                                                                     │
└─────────────────────────────────────────────────────────────────────┘
```

Figure 3-11: The XTreePro Command shell gives you more than just a DOS prompt — you get the date, time, free memory, and free disk space.

You enter the Command shell in the same manner as with regular XTree: by pressing X. If you press X while your cursor is active in either the Small file window or the Expanded file window, the currently highlighted file will be executed (provided, of course that it is either a BAT, EXE, or COM file). Once you're in the Command shell you can enter any command you might normally enter at your system prompt. The procedure for exiting is different, however. As you can see in the figure, you only need press Esc to return to the "normal" screen.

Mousers can also execute a program by double-clicking the program's name. The program will start right up.

If you receive "insufficient memory" error messages when you invoke the Command shell, try using Alt-X instead of just X to start the Command shell. This makes XTreePro, XTreePro Gold, XTree Easy, and XTreeGold reduce themselves to the smallest size possible for carrying out your command.

The History command and XTreePro

XTreePro remembers the last 15 commands you invoked from the Command shell and, if you ask nicely, will show them to you. Just press the up- or down-arrow key, and your 15 most recently used

```
┌─────────────────────────────────────────────────────────────────────┐
│ Thu Aug  9, 1990 │ 1:55:07 pm │ 222,400 Free Memory │ XTreePro Disk Space │
│ C:\XTPRO>dir \dos\*.txt                                             │
│                                      ─ Press ESC to return to XTreePro ─│
│                                                                     │
│                                                                     │
│                                                                     │
│                                                                     │
│ dir b:                                                              │
│ dir /w                                                              │
│ cd \lotus                                                           │
│ cd\xtpro                                                            │
│ dir \dos\*.tx                                                       │
│                                                                     │
└─────────────────────────────────────────────────────────────────────┘
```

Figure 3-12: The command history, shown here at the bottom of the XTreePro Command shell screen, appears when you press the up- or down-arrow key.

commands appear at the bottom of the screen. Figure 3-12 shows a sample XTreePro command history.

As you move the cursor up and down the command history list, the currently highlighted command is automatically placed at the prompt; you can then edit the command or press Enter to carry out the command.

The History command and XTree Easy, XTreePro Gold, and XTreeGold

XTree Easy, XTreePro Gold, and XTreeGold remember the last 13 commands you invoked from the Command shell — even if you issued them several days ago.

When you're in the Command shell, the History command appears as an option at the bottom of the screen, as shown in Figure 3-13. If you have a mouse you can simply click on History to bring up the history of the last commands you used. Otherwise, just press the up-arrow key and the command history will appear. When you are highlighting the command you want to use, just press Enter to execute it.

Chapter 3: XTree for DOS Quick Reference Guide

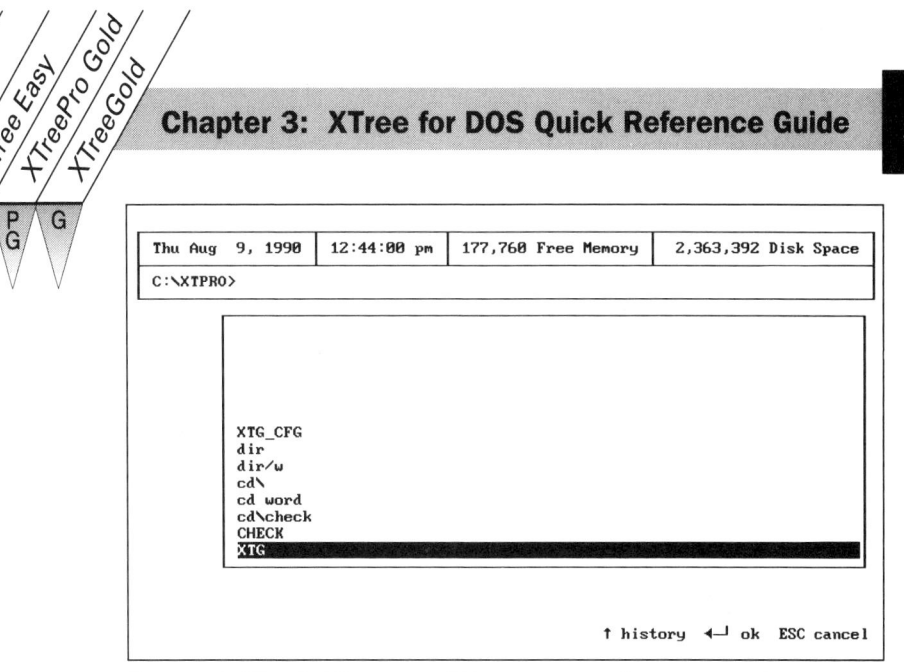

```
┌─────────────────────────────────────────────────────────────────────┐
│ Thu Aug  9, 1990  │ 12:44:00 pm │ 177,760 Free Memory │ 2,363,392 Disk Space │
│ C:\XTPRO>                                                           │
├─────────────────────────────────────────────────────────────────────┤
│                                                                     │
│                                                                     │
│     XTG_CFG                                                         │
│     dir                                                             │
│     dir/w                                                           │
│     cd\                                                             │
│     cd word                                                         │
│     cd\check                                                        │
│     CHECK                                                           │
│     XTG                                                             │
│                                                                     │
│                                                                     │
│                              ↑ history  ↵ ok  ESC cancel            │
└─────────────────────────────────────────────────────────────────────┘
```

Figure 3-13: XTreeGold's command history pops up when you press the up-arrow key, revealing previous commands.

> **TIP**: The History command is useful for editing typographical errors. For example, if you type a command, press Enter, and then get a BAD COMMAND OR FILENAME message, chances are you either used bad syntax or misspelled something. To avoid retyping the whole thing, just press the up-arrow key to access the command history, highlight the bad command, and press Enter. This brings the command back to the Command shell prompt, where you can correct the typo. Once the command is letter perfect, press Enter.

Compare   Command

A convenient feature that began in XTreePro Gold is the split window command. Two directories side by side — that's great! This feature opened new vistas along with new problems. Why does the directory on the left have more files than the one on the right? What is missing? Which one has the newest version? Now, the Compare command in XTreeGold can tag the matches and the mismatches for you. It compares not only two directories on one drive, but also two directories on different drives.

Comparing directories from a Directory window

To compare two directories, highlight the first (source) directory and then press C for Compare. You'll be asked to specify the name of the second (compare) directory; type in the second directory's name (or use Point or History) and press Enter. Figure 3-14 illustrates this process. After selecting the EXPRESS directory as the source, I pressed C for Compare and then entered C:\EXCEL as the directory to compare it to. As you can see at the bottom of the screen, XTreeGold has some further questions about which criteria to use for the comparison and will tag files that match the criteria. You may chose from among the following tagging options:

Identical	Tags files in the source directory with the same name, date, size, and attributes as identical files in the compare directory.
Unique	Tags files in the source directory that don't exist in the compare directory.
Newer	Tags files in the source directory that are newer (by date/time) than files in the compare directory.
Older	Tags files in the source directory that are older (by date/time) than files in the compare directory.

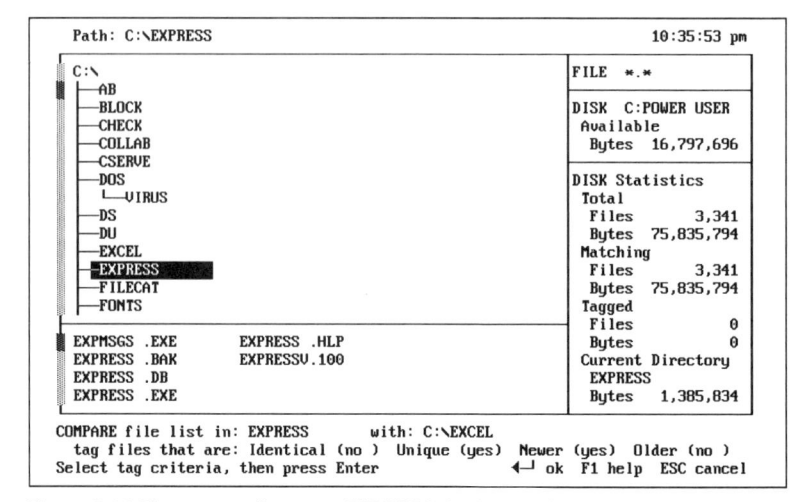

Figure 3-14: The source directory, EXPRESS, is about to be compared to the EXCEL directory.

Chapter 3: XTree for DOS Quick Reference Guide

Each of these options can be turned on and off by pressing the highlighted letter (I for Identical, for instance). The options are not mutually exclusive — mix and match to get what you want. In Figure 3-14, the options Unique and Newer are on, so files in the source directory that are not in the compare directory or that are newer will be tagged.

Once your options are set, press Enter to have XTreeGold tag the appropriate files in the source directory.

Comparing directories from a File window

Just because Compare appears as an option only when you're in a directory window doesn't mean you can't use it from the various file windows. You can use Alt-F4 to activate Compare from the file windows.

What's really fun (if you think you can handle it) is to invoke Compare from a Branch, Showall, or Global file window. This means you can compare files from more than one drive and more than one disk. Using Compare from these windows gives you a few extra options, as illustrated in Figure 3-15. The additional choices at the bottom of the screen are as follows:

Duplicate	Files with the same names
Unique	Files that are one-of-a-kind
Identical dates	Duplicate names and same dates
Newest dates	Newest version of files with the same name (if more than one file shares the same date, they are all listed)
Oldest dates	Oldest version of files with the same names (if more than one file shares the same date, they are all listed)
Scope	Used in the Global window. The three options for Scope are:

	All	Files with the same names
	Across drives	Files with same names on different drives
	Matching paths	Files with the same names and same paths but on different disks

```
Path: c:\word\docs\bbs\modem                              12:51:42 pm
 1      .TXT     GOLD1   .DOC              FILE   *.*
 10     .TXT     GOLD2   .DOC
 11     .TXT     GOLD2   .DOC              DISK  C:POWER USER
 12     .TXT     INDEX   .DOC              Available
 2      .TXT     INDEX   .DOC                Bytes    11,051,008
 3      .TXT     INST    .CAP
 4      .TXT     SLIDE   .BAT              BRANCH Statistics
 5      .TXT     THATSA  .EXE              Total
 6      .TXT                                 Files            27
 7      .TXT                                 Bytes     1,674,246
 8      .TXT                               Matching
 9      .TXT                                 Files            27
BBSTALK .DOC                                 Bytes     1,674,246
BBSWKSHT.DOC                               Tagged
BIGX    .BAK                                 Files             0
BIGX    .BAK                                 Bytes             0
BIGX    .DOC                               Current File
BIGX    .DOC                                 1       .TXT
GOLD1   .DOC                                 Bytes           274

Show files with:  Duplicate names   Unique names
                  duplicates with: Identical dates  Newest dates  Oldest dates
                  global Scope (n/a)                F1 help  ESC cancel
```

Figure 3-15: Alt-F4 invokes the Compare command from a Branch, Showall, or Global file window, offering extra tagging options.

Press the highlighted letter associated with these additional choices and XTreeGold redisplays the files.

Compare can be also be used in your backup scheme. Use the Compare command to compare the source directory to your backup disk and then copy only the tagged (unique and/or newer) files onto your backup disk.

Configuration Options

Configuration refers to the way things are set up. XTree, like most software programs, can be altered to behave in a certain fashion to accommodate your desires. Think of this as customization rather than configuration. Configuration is an aspect of XTree that you'll probably want to explore *after* you've been using the program for a little while; by then you'll have ideas about how things might suit you better. To reconfigure any XTree program, you simply use the Installation program in XTree and the Configuration program in the subsequent versions; these programs are installed onto your hard disk when you first install XTree.

Chapter 3: XTree for DOS Quick Reference Guide

Each of the XTree programs have features that can be changed. For instance, if you have a color monitor and you don't like how XTree looks, you can change the colors to something more pleasing. Although you can configure an XTree program while you're actually using it, the changes you make won't take effect until you exit the program and start again.

Configuring XTree

There are only two aspects of XTree that can be altered through the Installation program. One is to change the kind of computer and monitor you have, and the second is to change the color display.

To make one of these adjustments, go to the directory where XTree is stored, highlight the file XTREEINS.EXE, and press X; this loads the Command shell. XTREEINS.EXE appears on the command line, and you can press Enter to start the program. If you want to alter your configuration options from DOS, rather than from the Command shell, go to the directory where XTree is stored, type **XTREEINS**, and press Enter. Either way, you'll get the screen shown in Figure 3-16.

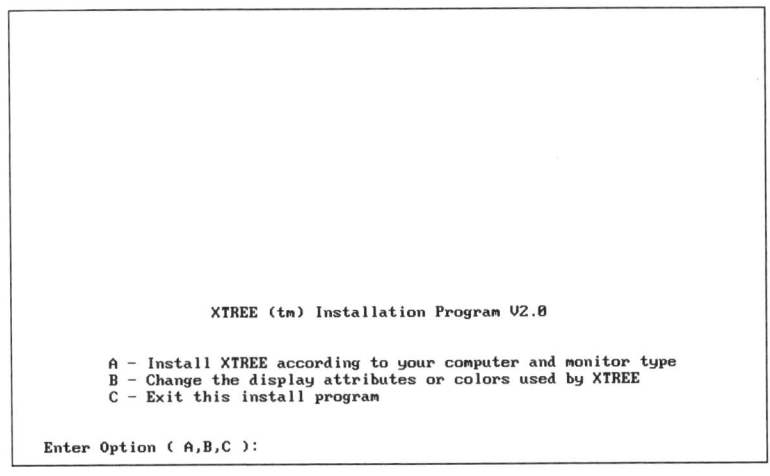

```
                    XTREE (tm) Installation Program V2.0

             A - Install XTREE according to your computer and monitor type
             B - Change the display attributes or colors used by XTREE
             C - Exit this install program

        Enter Option ( A,B,C ):
```

Figure 3-16: XTree's Installation program allows you to make limited adjustments, even after initial installation.

Choose option A or B from the screen shown in Figure 3-16 and another screen appears with more instructions. If you make a mistake, you can always go back to the way it was by *not saving your changes* when given the opportunity to do so. Not saving your changes puts you back at square one — no harm, no foul — and you can start again.

Configuring XTreePro

There are quite a few things that can be changed about XTreePro; let's take a peek at all the options.

In the directory where XTree is stored, highlight XTPROCFG.EXE, press X to start the Command shell, and then press Enter to start the XTreePro Configuration program. If you want to do this from DOS, go to the directory where XTreePro is stored, type **XTPROCFG**, and press Enter. Either action will bring up the main menu.

From this menu you can modify XTreePro configuration items, display color selection, restore default configuration (translation: put things back the way they were), save configuration and exit, or quit without saving changes. (You can always quit without saving your changes if you feel you have made some less-than-elegant choices.)

Most of the main menu choices are self-explanatory. We're going to look at Modifying Configuration Items for this example. Highlight that choice and press Enter, and your screen should resemble Figure 3-17.

As you move the highlight up and down the list of XTreePro Configuration Items, a definition for the currently highlighted item appears in the box at the bottom of the screen. If you want to change an item, highlight it and press Enter. At this point you may be prompted to fill in a blank with your new preference, or the item will toggle to a new choice automatically. Following are two examples of how this works:

- You can change the way Pro sorts files. Highlight the item Sort Order and press Enter; ASCENDING in the right-hand column then changes to DESCENDING. Press Enter and it's back to ASCENDING. Those are the only two acceptable responses, and pressing Enter toggles you back and forth between them.

Chapter 3: XTree for DOS Quick Reference Guide

```
                    XTreePro Configuration Items
  XTreePro Path                              C:\XTPRO
  File/Directory Limit                       10,000
  Disk Logging Method                        QUICK
  Display Type                               RGB/MONOCHROME
  Display is "flicker free"                  YES
  Audible Error Indicator                    ON
  Directory Display Highlight Bar            SCROLLING
  Keep Filespec                              NO
  File Display Format                        THREE COLUMNS
  Filename Separator                         "."
  Small File Window Access                   SELECTABLE
  System and Hidden File Access              YES
  Sort Criteria                              NAME
  Sort Order                                 ASCENDING
  Printer Redirection                        PRINTER
  Print Form Length                          55

  Return to Main Menu

     Set the maximum number of files and directories to hold in memory.

  ←↑↓→ Select Item    ENTER Change Item
```

Figure 3-17: To change an XTreePro configuration item, highlight the item and press Enter.

- You can change the File/Directory Limit (Pro assumes you'll be counting the maximum number of files). If you don't have that many files on your system, you can reduce the amount of memory Pro uses by reducing the limit. Highlight File Directory Limit and press Enter. You'll be prompted to type in a new limit; when you've finished, simply press Enter.

Once you have finished exploring the configuration items, highlight Return To Main Menu at the bottom of the screen and press Enter. Once you have returned to the main menu, you can save your modifications or exit without saving them. Make your decision and press Enter.

Remember, if you started the Configuration program from the Command shell, the changes won't take effect until *after* you quit and restart XTreePro.

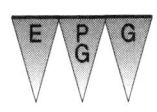

Configuring XTree Easy, XTreePro Gold, and XTreeGold

For XTreePro Gold, XTreeGold, and XTree Easy, there is a virtual cornucopia of configuration options available. If you're a control freak, you'll love this!

Configuration Options

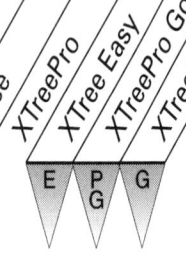

To start the Configuration program, the easiest thing to do is to press Alt-F10. To activate the program through DOS, go to the directory where your version of XTree is stored and type the appropriate command:

- For XTreeGold or XTreePro Gold, type **XTG_CFG** and press Enter

- For XTree Easy, type **XTR_CFG** and press Enter

Once you get a main menu (like XTree Easy's menu, shown in Figure 3-18), you have the following options:

```
Modify configuration items

Display color selection

Read permanent settings from disk
```
(put things back the way you had them)
```
Restore factory default settings
```
(put things back the way they were when you got the program out of the box)
```
Save configuration and quit

Quit configuration program
```

```
XTree Easy - Configuration                                    Main Menu


                         1 Modify configuration items

                         2 Display color selection

                         3 Read permanent settings from disk

                         4 Restore factory default settings


                         S Save configuration and quit

                         Q Quit configuration program




   ↑↓ Select function   ENTER Execute                          ESC quit
```

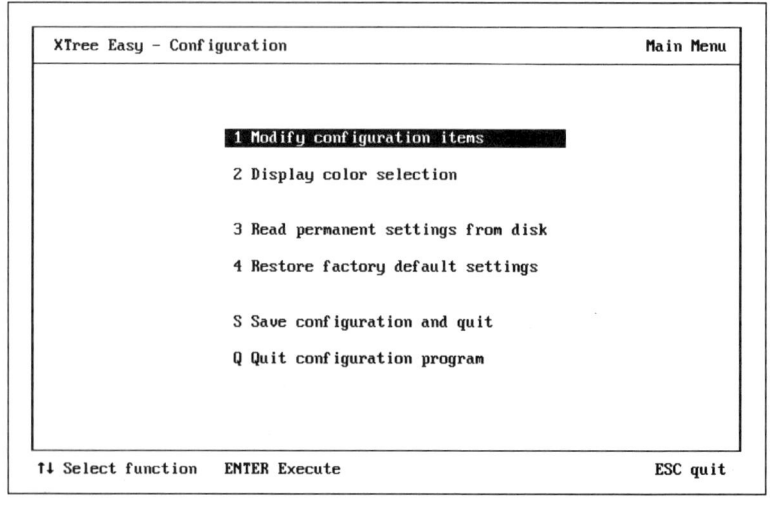

Figure 3-18: The XTree Easy Configuration Main Menu is much like the one in XTreePro Gold and XTreeGold.

Chapter 3: XTree for DOS Quick Reference Guide

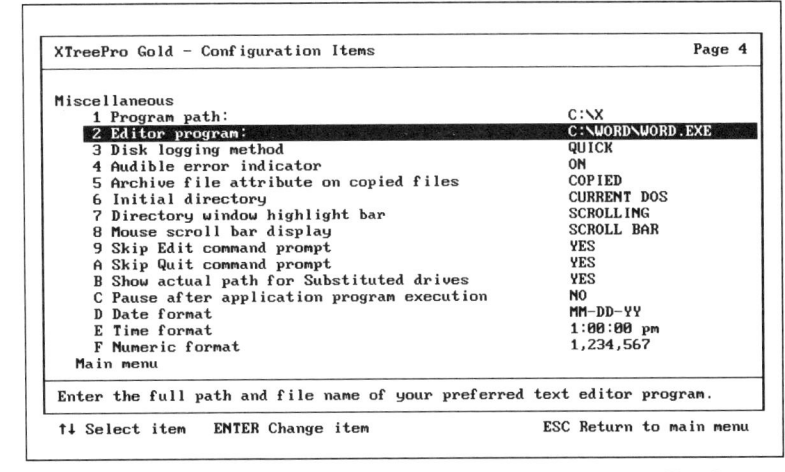

```
XTreePro Gold - Configuration Items                        Page 4

Miscellaneous
    1 Program path:                                C:\X
    2 Editor program:                              C:\WORD\WORD.EXE
    3 Disk logging method                          QUICK
    4 Audible error indicator                      ON
    5 Archive file attribute on copied files       COPIED
    6 Initial directory                            CURRENT DOS
    7 Directory window highlight bar               SCROLLING
    8 Mouse scroll bar display                     SCROLL BAR
    9 Skip Edit command prompt                     YES
    A Skip Quit command prompt                     YES
    B Show actual path for Substituted drives      YES
    C Pause after application program execution    NO
    D Date format                                  MM-DD-YY
    E Time format                                  1:00:00 pm
    F Numeric format                               1,234,567
Main menu

Enter the full path and file name of your preferred text editor program.

↑↓ Select item    ENTER Change item         ESC Return to main menu
```

Figure 3-19: This is only one page of many configuration options for XTreePro Gold.

If you select the first item (Modify configuration items), you'll be able to sift through a number of screens of configuration items by highlighting a word and pressing Enter. See Figure 3-19 for an XTreePro Gold configuration screen example. If you highlight the item Main Menu at the bottom of the list and then press Enter, you'll go back to the beginning of this process.

While you view the configuration items, moving the highlight up and down the list, definitions for the currently highlighted item appear in the box at the bottom of the screen. If you want to change a highlighted item, press Enter. The Configuration program will either ask you to fill in a choice, or you'll toggle between the available choices. XTreePro Gold and XTreeGold have the most configuration options. XTree Easy, naturally, has a bit less to choose from. (Figure 3-20 shows an XTreeGold Configuration Items list, and Figure 3-21 shows an XTree Easy Configuration Items list.)

Some configuration options you may want to change are as follows:

    Initial directory   This option allows you to have either the root or the current directory as your initial directory.

Configuration Options

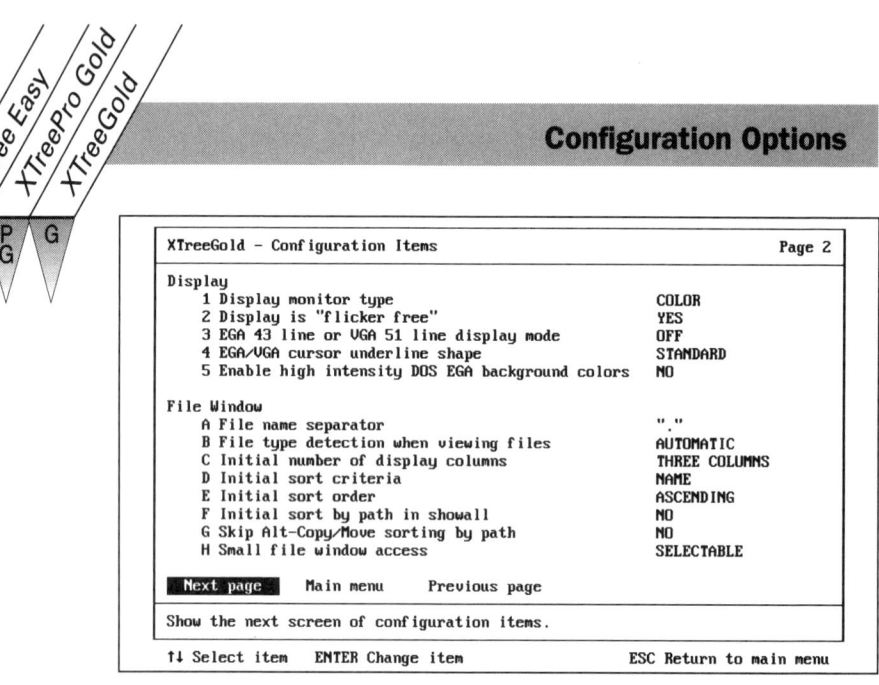

```
XTreeGold - Configuration Items                          Page 2
Display
    1 Display monitor type                               COLOR
    2 Display is "flicker free"                          YES
    3 EGA 43 line or VGA 51 line display mode            OFF
    4 EGA/VGA cursor underline shape                     STANDARD
    5 Enable high intensity DOS EGA background colors    NO

File Window
    A File name separator                                "."
    B File type detection when viewing files             AUTOMATIC
    C Initial number of display columns                  THREE COLUMNS
    D Initial sort criteria                              NAME
    E Initial sort order                                 ASCENDING
    F Initial sort by path in showall                    NO
    G Skip Alt-Copy/Move sorting by path                 NO
    H Small file window access                           SELECTABLE

   Next page    Main menu    Previous page

Show the next screen of configuration items.

↑↓ Select item    ENTER Change item         ESC Return to main menu
```

Figure 3-20: XTreeGold Configuration Items (Page 2) offer many customization choices.

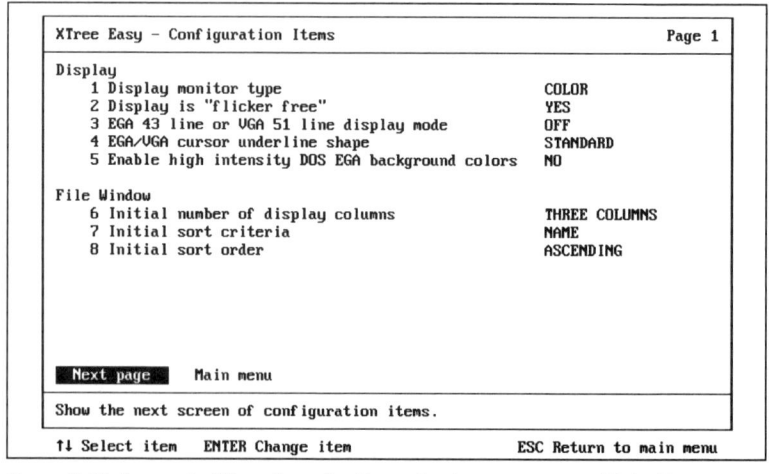

```
XTree Easy - Configuration Items                         Page 1
Display
    1 Display monitor type                               COLOR
    2 Display is "flicker free"                          YES
    3 EGA 43 line or VGA 51 line display mode            OFF
    4 EGA/VGA cursor underline shape                     STANDARD
    5 Enable high intensity DOS EGA background colors    NO

File Window
    6 Initial number of display columns                  THREE COLUMNS
    7 Initial sort criteria                              NAME
    8 Initial sort order                                 ASCENDING




   Next page    Main menu

Show the next screen of configuration items.

↑↓ Select item    ENTER Change item         ESC Return to main menu
```

Figure 3-21: A sample XTree Easy Configuration Items screen, which allows some, but not many, changes to the system.

Chapter 3: XTree for DOS Quick Reference Guide

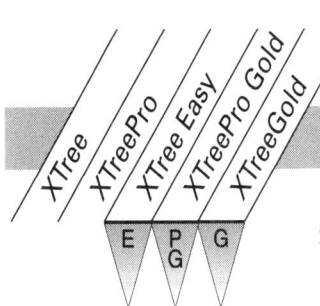

Skip Quit command	This option turns off that QUIT XTREEGOLD AND RETURN TO DOS? invective.
Audible error indicator	This option can be turned off so you won't get beeped at when you make a mistake.
EGA and VGA	To see even more files and more of your directory tree at one time, you can set the screen to 43 lines (EGA) or 51 lines (VGA). (Note, however, that using this extended display may cause some systems to slow down.) You don't have to be in the Configuration section to *temporarily* change the display. You may toggle between normal and extended display by using the key combination Alt-F9.

Let your fingers do the walking through the configuration pages. You may find something that will make life a little easier (or, at least, more attractive).

Copy   Command

The Copy command allows you to copy something (usually a file), which results in two of the original item. Most people use the Copy command primarily to make safety copies of files (known as *backups*). You may also want to copy a file and give it to a co-worker (or copy something from a co-worker onto your hard disk) and so forth.

Sometimes, however, what you *really* want to do is move something to a new location, so you end up with one copy in a new place. In this case, see the Move command. (Unless you have XTreeGold, you cannot move something to another *disk* — you still have to use Copy).

The one important rule for copying is that you can't have two files with the same name in the same place. If you want to have two versions of the same file in the same place, one of them has to have a different name. Having said all that, let's jump into the wacky world of the Copy command.

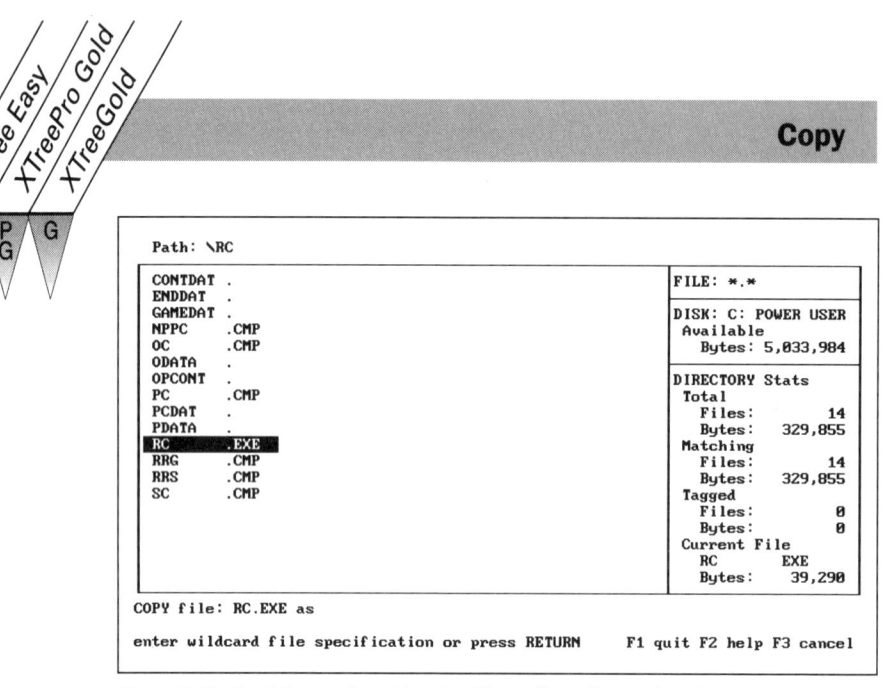

```
Path: \RC

CONTDAT   .                                FILE: *.*
ENDDAT    .
GAMEDAT   .                                DISK: C: POWER USER
NPPC      .CMP                             Available
OC        .CMP                               Bytes: 5,033,984
ODATA     .
OPCONT    .                                DIRECTORY Stats
PC        .CMP                             Total
PCDAT     .                                  Files:           14
PDATA     .                                  Bytes:      329,855
RC        .EXE                             Matching
RRG       .CMP                               Files:           14
RRS       .CMP                               Bytes:      329,855
SC        .CMP                             Tagged
                                             Files:            0
                                             Bytes:            0
                                           Current File
                                             RC       EXE
                                             Bytes:       39,290

COPY file: RC.EXE as

enter wildcard file specification or press RETURN    F1 quit F2 help F3 cancel
```

Figure 3-22: Don't be confused by the "Copy file as" question that appears when you press C for Copy. Press Enter to leave the filename as is.

Copying a file to another drive (including a floppy drive)

To copy a file, highlight the file to be copied and press C for Copy. At the bottom of the screen, XTree raises the question of what to name the copy of the file. Figure 3-22 shows XTree asking `Copy file: RC.EXE as`. Basically, this question — which you'll see every single time you want to copy something — gives you the option to rename a file when you copy it. Usually, you don't want to change the name; so just press Enter and the filename will remain the same.

If you do want to give the copy a new name, do so before pressing Enter. One reason you might want to give the copy a new name is if you want to keep different versions of the same file. Once the name issue is settled, the next question is where to put the copy. In this case, let's copy it to a floppy disk. As you can see in Figure 3-23, after you specify the filename, the next question is `enter destination for copy ([d:] [path])`. To copy the file to the A: drive, simply type **A:** and press Enter. The file is copied to the A: drive and that's that! (Break out the champagne.) If you want to copy the file to the B: drive, type **B:** instead. And if you copy a file to another directory on your hard disk, you must include the `[path]` along with the drive.

Chapter 3: XTree for DOS Quick Reference Guide

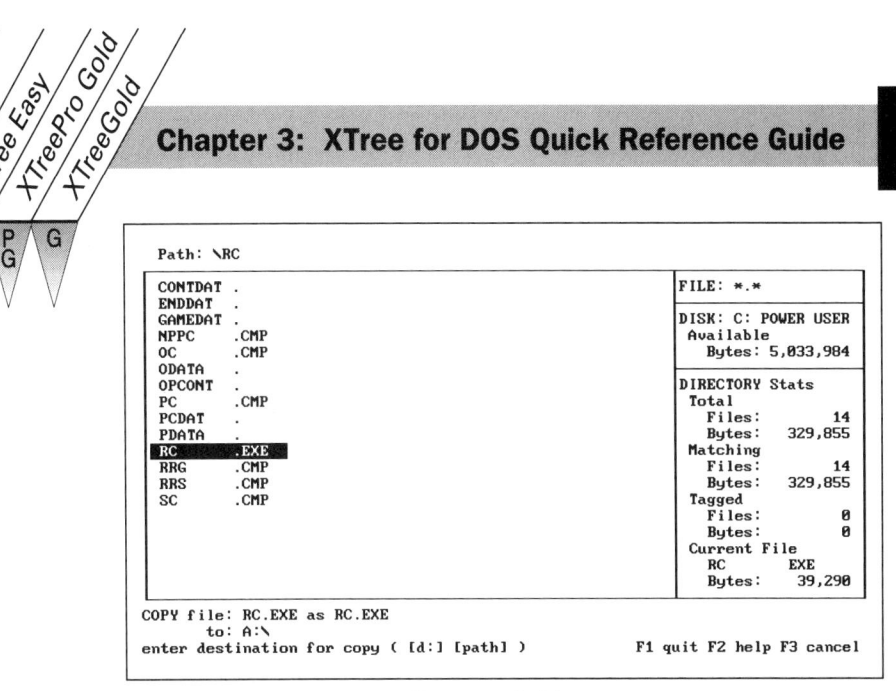

```
Path: \RC

CONTDAT  .                              FILE: *.*
ENDDAT   .
GAMEDAT  .                              DISK: C: POWER USER
NPPC     .CMP                           Available
OC       .CMP                             Bytes: 5,033,984
ODATA    .
OPCONT   .                              DIRECTORY Stats
PC       .CMP                           Total
PCDAT    .                                Files:            14
PDATA    .                                Bytes:       329,855
RC       .EXE                           Matching
RRG      .CMP                             Files:            14
RRS      .CMP                             Bytes:       329,855
SC       .CMP                           Tagged
                                          Files:             0
                                          Bytes:             0
                                        Current File
                                          RC        EXE
                                          Bytes:        39,290

COPY file: RC.EXE as RC.EXE
      to: A:\
enter destination for copy ( [d:] [path] )      F1 quit F2 help F3 cancel
```

Figure 3-23: Type A: to copy a file to your A: drive.

However (there's always something), let's say there's *already* another file on A: with the same name. If a file with the same name already exists on A:, you'll be asked if you want to replace it.

Replacing a file in XTree

When you want to replace a file with another of the same name, XTree simply asks you if you want to replace the file, as shown in Figure 3-24. You may reply with a Y (for yes), in which case the old file will be erased in favor of the new file; or an N (for No), which cancels the operation without copying or erasing anything.

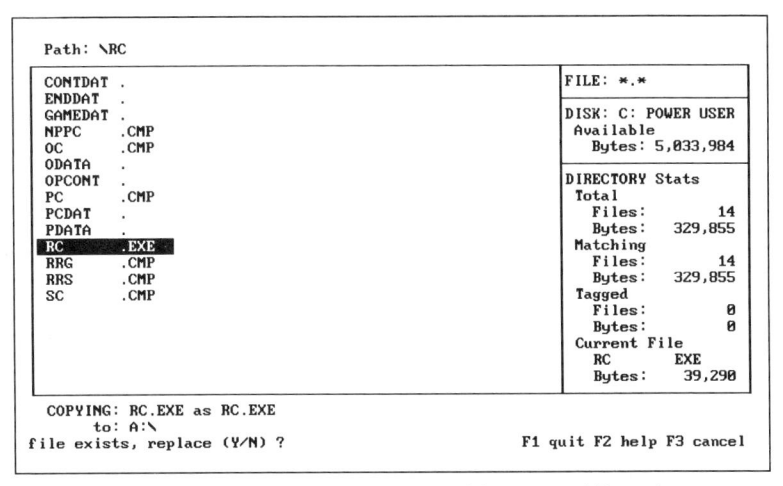

```
Path: \RC

CONTDAT  .                              FILE: *.*
ENDDAT   .
GAMEDAT  .                              DISK: C: POWER USER
NPPC     .CMP                           Available
OC       .CMP                             Bytes: 5,033,984
ODATA    .
OPCONT   .                              DIRECTORY Stats
PC       .CMP                           Total
PCDAT    .                                Files:            14
PDATA    .                                Bytes:       329,855
RC       .EXE                           Matching
RRG      .CMP                             Files:            14
RRS      .CMP                             Bytes:       329,855
SC       .CMP                           Tagged
                                          Files:             0
                                          Bytes:             0
                                        Current File
                                          RC        EXE
                                          Bytes:        39,290

COPYING: RC.EXE as RC.EXE
     to: A:\
file exists, replace (Y/N) ?                    F1 quit F2 help F3 cancel
```

Figure 3-24: Watch for questions at the bottom of the screen. XTree gives a warning that a file already exists on A: named RC.EXE.

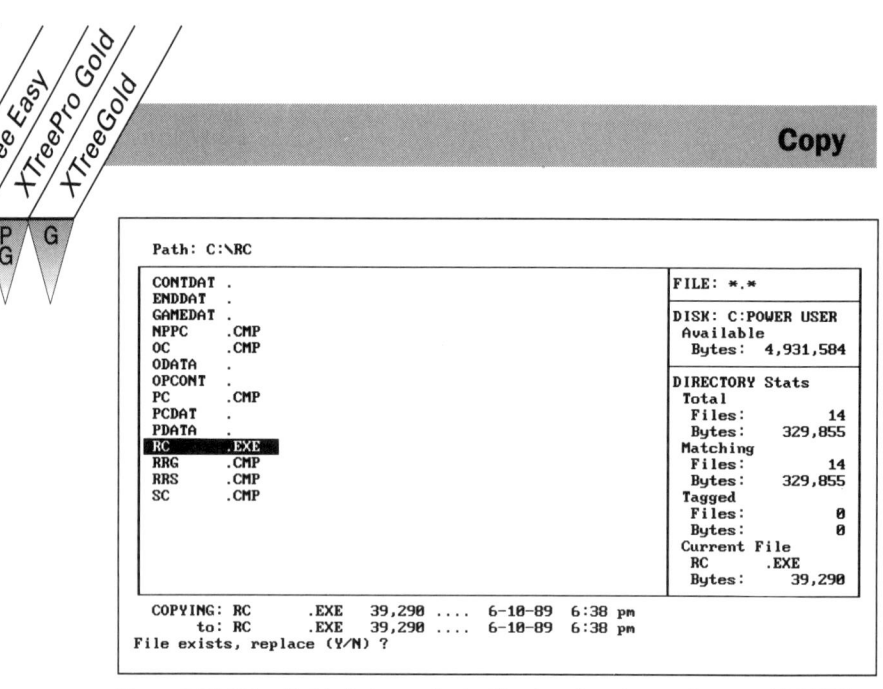

```
Path: C:\RC                                    FILE: *.*
CONTDAT  .
ENDDAT   .                                     DISK: C:POWER USER
GAMEDAT  .                                       Available
NPPC     .CMP                                    Bytes:    4,931,584
OC       .CMP
ODATA    .                                     DIRECTORY Stats
OPCONT   .                                       Total
PC       .CMP                                      Files:           14
PCDAT    .                                         Bytes:      329,855
PDATA    .                                       Matching
RC       .EXE                                      Files:           14
RRG      .CMP                                      Bytes:      329,855
RRS      .CMP                                    Tagged
SC       .CMP                                      Files:            0
                                                   Bytes:            0
                                                 Current File
                                                   RC       .EXE
                                                   Bytes:       39,290

COPYING: RC     .EXE   39,290  ....  6-10-89  6:38 pm
    to:  RC     .EXE   39,290  ....  6-10-89  6:38 pm
File exists, replace (Y/N) ?
```

Figure 3-25: XTreeGold alerts you that a file already exists on A: named RC.EXE, and offers statistics about the date, time, size, and attributes of the two files.

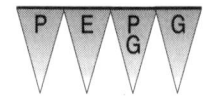

Replacing a file in XTreePro, XTreePro Gold, XTree Easy, and XTreeGold

When the advanced XTree versions ask if you want to copy a file of the same name into another drive or directory (File exists, replace (Y/N) ?), these versions also show you the statistics of both files so you can compare the date, time, size, and attributes, as shown in Figure 3-25.

Most likely, the newer or bigger file will be the one you want to keep, although not always. You may reply with a Y (for yes), in which case the old file will be erased in favor of the new file; or an N (for No), which cancels the operation without copying or erasing anything.

Copying a file to another directory

The process of copying a file to another directory is virtually identical to copying a file to a floppy disk. The only difference is the destination. Begin the process by highlighting the file to be copied and pressing C for Copy. When asked what to name the file, press Enter to keep the same filename. The last step is to enter a destination.

Chapter 3: XTree for DOS Quick Reference Guide

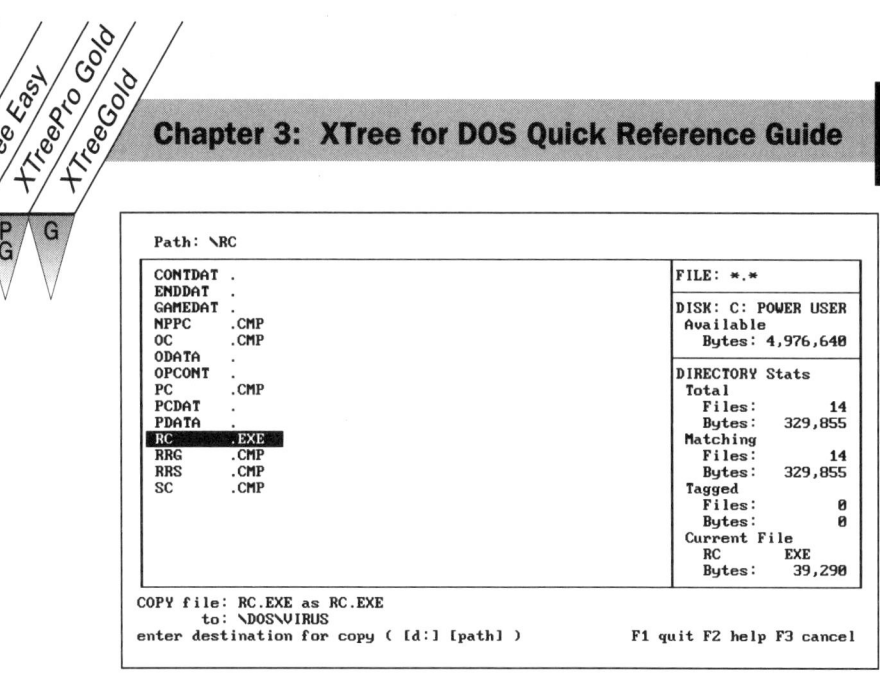

```
Path: \RC
CONTDAT  .                           FILE: *.*
ENDDAT   .
GAMEDAT  .                           DISK: C: POWER USER
NPPC     .CMP                        Available
OC       .CMP                           Bytes: 4,976,640
ODATA    .
OPCONT   .                           DIRECTORY Stats
PC       .CMP                        Total
PCDAT    .                              Files:            14
PDATA    .                              Bytes:       329,855
RC       .EXE                        Matching
RRG      .CMP                           Files:            14
RRS      .CMP                           Bytes:       329,855
SC       .CMP                        Tagged
                                        Files:             0
                                        Bytes:             0
                                     Current File
                                        RC        EXE
                                        Bytes:        39,290

COPY file: RC.EXE as RC.EXE
       to: \DOS\VIRUS
enter destination for copy ( [d:] [path] )       F1 quit F2 help F3 cancel
```

Figure 3-26: XTree reminds you to type the destination drive (if you're copying a file to another drive) and pathname before pressing Enter.

Type in the destination path, as shown in Figure 3-26. In this example, the file is to be copied to the \DOS\VIRUS directory. Once you've typed in the destination, press Enter and the file will be copied.

In the original XTree, it's a good idea to know where you want to send your file before you invoke the Copy command, because you can't examine the directory tree once the copying process has started.

Later versions of XTree offer the Destination window as a method for pointing to and selecting a destination directory. (See "Using the Destination window to simplify copying," coming up shortly.)

Copying multiple files

The process of copying lots of files is very similar to copying just one file. However, instead of starting out by highlighting a single file to be copied, you must first *tag* all the files you want to copy. Once you've rounded up a bunch of tagged files, press Ctrl-C to copy the tagged files. (Notice the difference between pressing plain old C to copy one currently highlighted file vs. Ctrl-C, which copies all tagged files.)

Copy

X P E P G
  G

It's best to start this procedure from the Expanded file window of the directory containing the files you want to copy. (Highlight the directory you want to copy from and then press Enter twice.)

NOTE: If you are unfamiliar with the Tag/Untag or Filespec commands, now's a good time to flip to those sections and read about them. However, to save you the bother of wading through several sections of this book just find out how to copy a bunch of files, let's go through an example of the process right now. (Then, be sure to read through "Tag/Untag" and "Filespec" for additional details.)

Say, for example, you want to copy all the files that end in DOC to a floppy disk (to back up your word processing work). Once all the files in the directory are displayed, you can proceed in one of two ways:

- The first approach is to highlight each file you wish to copy, one at a time, and press T for Tag until all files to be copied are tagged.

- The second approach is to use the Filespec command to ask XTree to show only the DOC files. To do this, just press F for Filespec, and you'll see the message at the bottom of the screen in Figure 3-27.

```
Path: \KEYS

 2KEYS    .DTX     DIALPNT .DTX    SKLASJET.DTX    FILE: *.*
 89       .DTX     DOSEDIT .COM    SKSETUP .COM
 ASCII    .DTX     DOSEDIT .DOC    SKWINDOW.EXE    DISK: C: POWER USER
 BARMENU  .DTX     DVORAK  .DOC    SMARTKEY.EXE    Available
 CLICK    .COM     DVORAK17.COM    STUFF   .DTX      Bytes: 4,919,296
 COMMANDS .DTX     DVORAK20.COM    SUNBOW  .DTX
 COMMCMD1 .DTX     LOTUS   .DTX    TEST    .DTX    DIRECTORY Stats
 COMMCMD2 .DTX     MENU    .DTX    TREK    .DTX    Total
 COMMDEFN .DTX     MENUDEMO.DTX    TUNE    .DTX      Files:         49
 COMMFILE .DTX     PCKEY17 .COM    WORDPERF.DTX      Bytes:    330,365
 COMMMODI .DTX     PCKEY20 .COM    WORDSTAR.DTX    Matching
 COMMOPT  .DTX     README  .1ST                      Files:         49
 COMMSYS  .DTX     README  .COM                      Bytes:    330,365
 CRYPTOR  .COM     SAMPLE  .DTX                    Tagged
 D        .COM     SKBATCH .COM                      Files:          0
 DATASCRN .DTX     SKBLANK .COM                      Bytes:          0
 DBASE    .DTX     SKBLANK .DOC                    Current File
 DIALER   .DTX     SKEPSON .DTX                      2KEYS     DTX
 DIALPAUS .DTX     SKIBMPRO.DTX                      Bytes:      1,152

FILE specification:
enter a file spec or press RETURN for *.*        F1 quit F2 help F3 cancel
```

Figure 3-27: After you press F for Filespec, you can use wildcards to narrow the focus of the files displayed and then copy files by group.

Chapter 3: XTree for DOS Quick Reference Guide

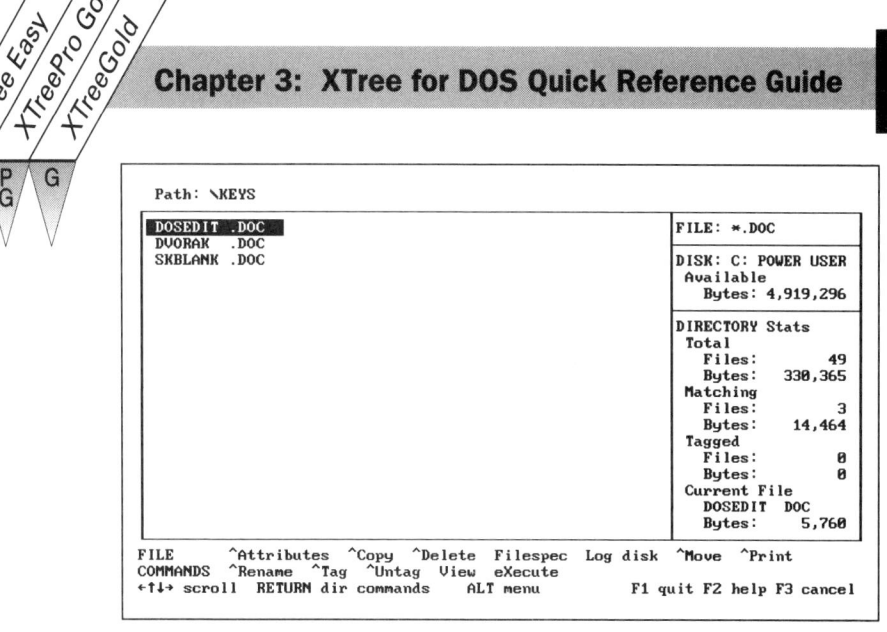

```
Path: \KEYS
 DOSEDIT  .DOC                         FILE: *.DOC
 DVORAK   .DOC
 SKBLANK  .DOC                         DISK: C: POWER USER
                                       Available
                                          Bytes: 4,919,296

                                       DIRECTORY Stats
                                       Total
                                          Files:            49
                                          Bytes:       330,365
                                       Matching
                                          Files:             3
                                          Bytes:        14,464
                                       Tagged
                                          Files:             0
                                          Bytes:             0
                                       Current File
                                          DOSEDIT   DOC
                                          Bytes:         5,760

FILE        ^Attributes  ^Copy  ^Delete  Filespec  Log disk  ^Move  ^Print
COMMANDS    ^Rename  ^Tag  ^Untag  View  eXecute
←↑↓→ scroll  RETURN dir commands     ALT menu         F1 quit F2 help F3 cancel
```

Figure 3-28: Files with the DOC extension can be isolated by using the *.DOC filespec.

Filespec is the command that let's you exercise what you learned about wildcards to filter in (or out) particular files from the display. (If you don't quite remember learning about wildcards, slide on over to Chapter 1, "MS-DOS Concepts.") In this case I want all files that end in DOC, so I type the filespec ***.DOC** and press Enter. Now the File window in Figure 3-28 displays only those files with the DOC extension. The upper-right corner of the screen reminds you of the current file specifications.

Now that the only visible files on-screen are the files to be copied, simply pressing Ctrl-T tags all displayed files. (T tags one file and Ctrl-T tags all files.) Next, press Ctrl-C to copy all of the tagged files. Press Enter so the files can keep their original names, as shown in Figure 3-29.

All that's left is to supply a scenic destination for those DOC files. For this example, let's send them to the A: drive by typing **A:** and pressing Enter. You'll be asked if you want to automatically replace the files on drive A: with the same name. Reply Y for yes to send the files on their way. (By the way, if you don't want to automatically replace existing files with the same name, press N and XTree will ask for a new name, one file at a time, every time it locates a file with the same name as the one being copied. This way, you can make a case-by-case decision.)

Whenever you finish an operation like this, be sure to put the filespec back to *.* or you'll freak yourself out later on when it seems as though some of your files are missing.

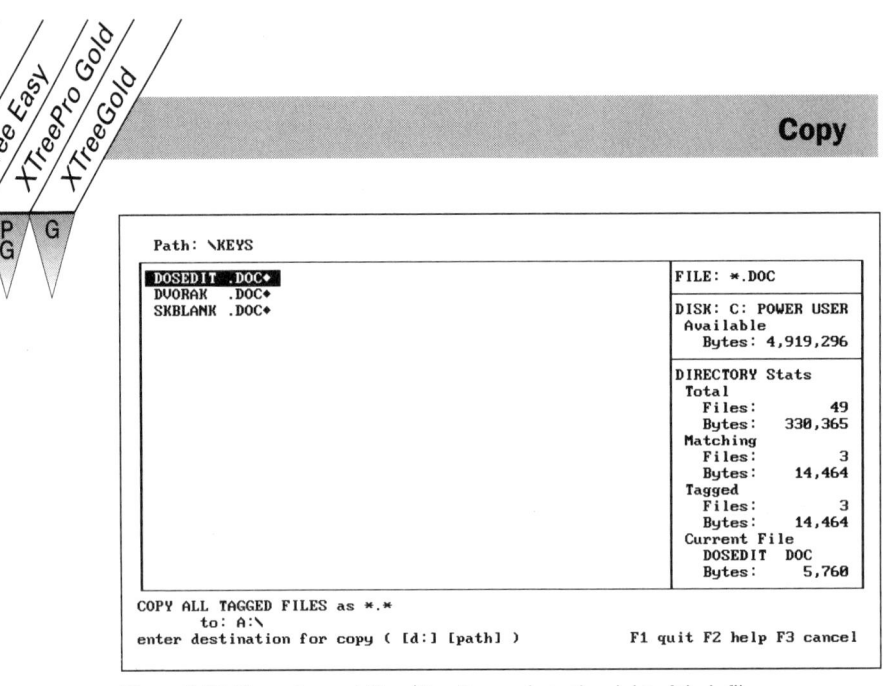

```
Path: \KEYS
    DOSEDIT  .DOC♦                          FILE: *.DOC
    DVORAK   .DOC♦
    SKBLANK  .DOC♦                          DISK: C: POWER USER
                                            Available
                                              Bytes:   4,919,296

                                            DIRECTORY Stats
                                            Total
                                              Files:          49
                                              Bytes:     330,365
                                            Matching
                                              Files:           3
                                              Bytes:      14,464
                                            Tagged
                                              Files:           3
                                              Bytes:      14,464
                                            Current File
                                              DOSEDIT   DOC
                                              Bytes:       5,760

COPY ALL TAGGED FILES as *.*
         to: A:\
enter destination for copy ( [d:] [path] )     F1 quit F2 help F3 cancel
```

Figure 3-29: These tagged files (the diamonds to the right of their filenames indicate they are tagged) are about to be copied to the A: drive.

Copying files and directory structures

In addition to duplicating a file (or files), XTree can also duplicate the file's directory structure. Having your hard disk's directory structure backed up to a floppy disk is extremely helpful if you ever need to resurrect a crashed hard disk.

The first step is to tag the files you want to copy. (See "Tag/Untag" if you don't yet know how to tag.) From a File window, press Alt-C to Copy and duplicate the file's path.

At the bottom of the screen you'll be given the opportunity to rename your files as you copy them (press Enter to decline that option). Next you'll be prompted to choose a destination drive. Let's say the A: drive is your destination. Type **A** (the colon and backslash will be put in for you) and then press Enter.

▽ G

XTreeGold 2.5, only, also allows you to specify a directory as a destination (rather than another disk, as in the other versions). The source directory structure is duplicated underneath the destination directory. You choose to either duplicate the full source pathname or just the portion of the pathname where the files are actually stored. You'll be asked whether you want to `replace existing files?`. In other words, if there are already files on the disk with the same name, do you *really* want to replace them with the files you are copying now? Generally, you do, so press Y. At this point the copying commences and the files and their directories are copied to the drive.

Chapter 3: XTree for DOS Quick Reference Guide

```
Path: C:\WORD\BETH\SCRIPTS

HORTNOTE.DOC♦                          FILE: *.*
HORTON  .DOC♦
LIVEAC  .STY♦                          DISK: C:POWER USER
LIVEOUT .STY♦                          Available
LIVOUTSS.STY♦                            Bytes:     4,497,408
MENQUIZ .DOC♦
OUTDFT  .STY♦                          DIRECTORY Stats
SCRIPTOR.STY♦                          Total
SMOU    .DOC♦                            Files:            10
SMOUBEAT.DOC♦                            Bytes:        31,232
                                       Matching
                                         Files:            10
                                         Bytes:        31,232
                                       Tagged
                                         Files:            10
                                         Bytes:        31,232
                                       Current File
                                         HORTNOTE.DOC
                                         Bytes:         1,920

DUPLICATE PATHS ON ANOTHER DISK AND COPY ALL TAGGED FILES as *.*
    to: A:\
Enter destination disk for alt copy                    ESC cancel
```

Figure 3-30: Press Alt-C to copy tagged files and their directory structure.

Using Graft to copy one directory to another

XTreeProGold and XTreeGold allow you to *graft* a directory. This means you can take a directory (and its contents) and attach it to another directory, a sort of "cut and paste" for your directory tree. This is not, actually, *copying* a directory (it's *moving* a directory), but this command seemed to fit into this section anyway.

To graft a directory, highlight the directory to be moved and press Alt-G for Graft. At the bottom of the screen you'll be asked *where* you want to move your directory to, and you're automatically given the Destination window so you can highlight the directory you want to move to (though you can still type in the path, manually, if you're the old-fashioned sort.)

In Figure 3-31 I'm moving the directory CHECK90 so that it will appear *under* the directory CHEKBOOK. When you're ready to graft, press Enter. As a precaution, you'll be asked one more time if you're sure you want to do this. Just press Y if you are, and Pro Gold and Gold will carry out the command.

> **NOTE:** If, instead of grafting, you receive a Can't Update Parent Directory error message, you have an older version of XTreeGold that does not get along with your version of DOS. An upgrade is available to fix this problem. (See Appendix D, "Where to Go from Here.")

> **NOTE:** After you graft a directory, press L to relog the drive so the grafted directory will appear in alphabetical order on the tree.

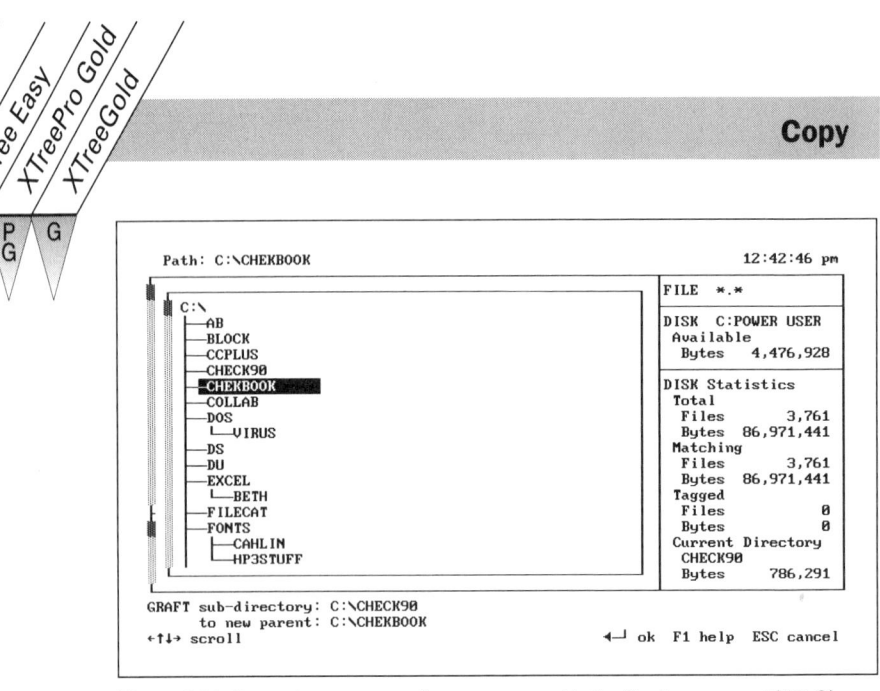

```
Path: C:\CHEKBOOK                                      12:42:46 pm
                                              ┌─────────────────────┐
  C:\                                         │ FILE  *.*           │
   ├─AB                                       │ DISK C:POWER USER   │
   ├─BLOCK                                    │ Available           │
   ├─CCPLUS                                   │   Bytes    4,476,928│
   ├─CHECK90                                  │                     │
   ├─CHEKBOOK                                 │ DISK Statistics     │
   ├─COLLAB                                   │ Total               │
   ├─DOS                                      │   Files        3,761│
   │  └─VIRUS                                 │   Bytes   86,971,441│
   ├─DS                                       │ Matching            │
   ├─DU                                       │   Files        3,761│
   ├─EXCEL                                    │   Bytes   86,971,441│
   │  └─BETH                                  │ Tagged              │
   ├─FILECAT                                  │   Files            0│
   ├─FONTS                                    │   Bytes            0│
   │  ├─CAHLIN                                │ Current Directory   │
   │  └─HP3STUFF                              │ CHECK90             │
                                              │   Bytes      786,291│
GRAFT sub-directory: C:\CHECK90
       to new parent: C:\CHEKBOOK
 ←↑↓→ scroll                                  ↵ ok  F1 help  ESC cancel
```

Figure 3-31: Cut and paste your directory tree with the Graft command (Alt-G).

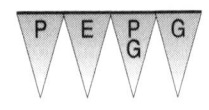

Using the Destination window to simplify copying

XTreePro, XTree Easy, XTreePro Gold, and XTreeGold make it easier for you to specify a destination. These programs feature the `F2 select path` (or `F2 point` in XTreeGold) option. When you want to copy a file to some weird directory, F2 is a très handy item, as we'll see momentarily.

Start the copy procedure by highlighting the name of the file to be copied, pressing C to Copy, and then pressing Enter to keep the same filename. At this point, as shown in Figure 3-32, XTree asks you to specify an exotic destination for your file.

As always, you can type in the drive and pathname to receive the copy of the selected file. However, as an exciting alternative to typing in a lengthy (and boring) destination pathname, press the F2 function key and the Destination window (a version of the directory tree) pops up over what you're doing, as shown in Figure 3-33.

Now it's just a simple matter of highlighting the correct destination directory and then pressing Enter. By the way, once the Destination window is visible, you can also press L to log onto

Chapter 3: XTree for DOS Quick Reference Guide

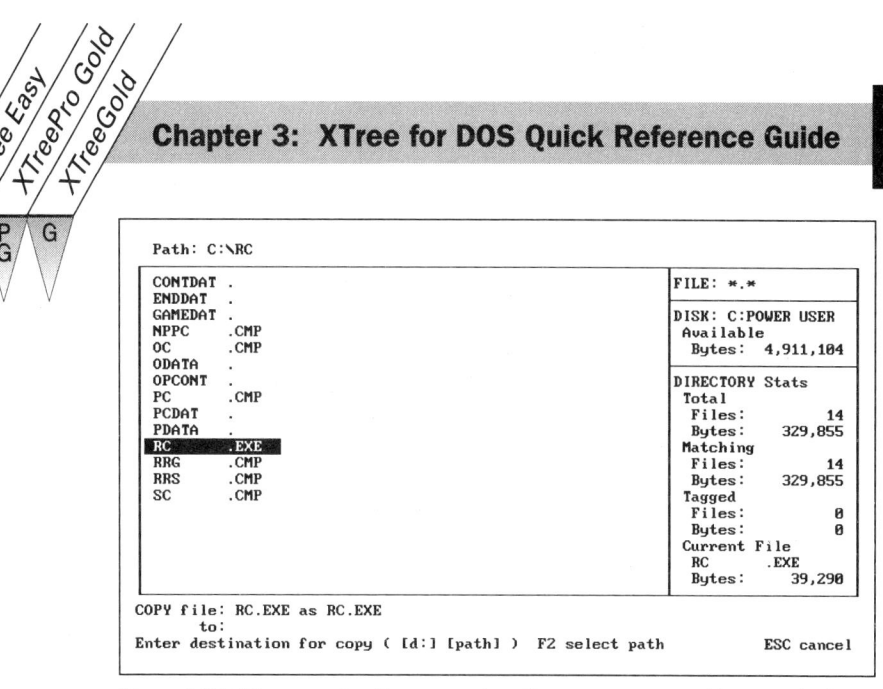

```
Path: C:\RC

CONTDAT   .                                    FILE: *.*
ENDDAT    .
GAMEDAT   .                                    DISK: C:POWER USER
NPPC      .CMP                                 Available
OC        .CMP                                   Bytes:    4,911,104
ODATA     .
OPCONT    .                                    DIRECTORY Stats
PC        .CMP                                 Total
PCDAT     .                                      Files:            14
PDATA     .                                      Bytes:       329,855
RC        .EXE                                 Matching
RRG       .CMP                                   Files:            14
RRS       .CMP                                   Bytes:       329,855
SC        .CMP                                 Tagged
                                                 Files:             0
                                                 Bytes:             0
                                               Current File
                                                 RC        .EXE
                                                 Bytes:        39,290

COPY file: RC.EXE as RC.EXE
        to:
Enter destination for copy ( [d:] [path] )  F2 select path      ESC cancel
```

Figure 3-32: When copying files to another directory, you may either type in the destination or press F2 to pop up the Destination window.

```
Path: C:\RC

        ┌─PCLFONTS                              FILE: *.*
        ├─PCPLUS
        ├─PD                                    DISK: C:POWER USER
        ├─PM                                    Available
        ├─QA                                      Bytes:    4,911,104
        ├─QM
        │  ├─DOWNLOAD                           DIRECTORY Stats
        │  │   ├─COMP                           Total
        │  │   └─MAC                              Files:            14
        │  ├─MSG                                  Bytes:       329,855
        │  └─SCRIPTS                            Matching
        ├─RC                                      Files:            14
        ├─RCOURIER                                Bytes:       329,855
        ├─SPELL                                 Tagged
        ├─SPINRITE                                Files:             0
        ├─TAPCIS                                  Bytes:             0
        │  └─CATSCAN                            Current File
                                                  RC        .EXE
                                                  Bytes:        39,290

COPY file: RC.EXE as RC.EXE
        to: C:\PD
←↑↓→ scroll   Log disk drive         F2 select path  F1 help  ESC cancel
```

Destination window →

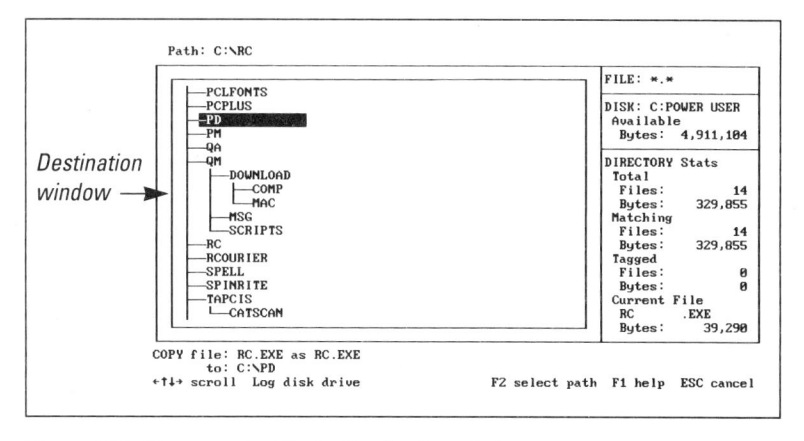

Figure 3-33: After pressing F2, the Destination window appears, allowing you to point or highlight a destination, rather than having to type it.

another drive and then peruse its tree for the proper repository of your file.

> **NOTE:** XTree Easy, XTreePro Gold, and XTreeGold users can also use the History command to specify a previously selected destination. When you finally select your destination, press Enter and the file will be copied.

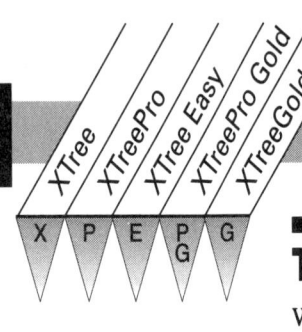

The Date and Time Stamp

When you save a file, DOS records the date and time the file was saved. If the clock inside your computer works, the date and time will be accurate. If you don't have a clock, DOS assigns *some* date and *some* time to the file when its saved. (That's why you may find that you have some files dated *before* personal computers were even invented.) Anyway, this is called the *date and time stamp*.

Even if your computer doesn't have a clock, it can still keep time for you, *as long as the computer remains turned on.* To have the computer keep time for you, type **DATE**, press Enter at the system prompt, type the correct date, and press Enter again. Now type **TIME**, press Enter, type the correct time, and press Enter again. (Remember, most computers are on a 24-hour clock — 1 p.m. is 13:00 to the computer.)

Using XTreePro Gold and XTreeGold's Newdate command

You can alter the date and time information DOS assigns to your files only with XTreePro Gold and XTreeGold's Newdate command. Wanting to change the date and time stamp on a file is not necessarily a red flag for having too much time on your hands. Rather, it's a way to correct date and time data on files transferred from another computer. Or, since XTree can display files sorted by date and time, it's a way to group files together for some sort of action.

To change the date and time stamp on a file, just highlight the file (or tag a group of files if you want to change the date and time on more than one at a time) and press N. At the bottom of the screen the highlighted filename (or first tagged filename), its attributes, and the current date and time stamp appear. Pro Gold and Gold suggest using the *current* date and time as the new date and time stamp, as shown in Figure 3-34.

If the current date and time is what you want, press **Enter.** If you want to use another date and time, change the date and time offered. Backspacing erases the current date and time. The arrow keys allow you to move *over* the time and date without deleting anything so you may make discrete changes.

If you want to see a file's date and time *before* you press N to change it, press Alt-F twice to change the file display. If you want to have the files displayed by date and time, press Alt-S (to Sort) and

Chapter 3: XTree for DOS Quick Reference Guide

```
Path: C:\CHECK                                              11:54:48 am
  BOFA89   .ACT       CHECK3   .EXE           FILE   *.*
  BOFA89   .BGT       CHECK4   .EXE
  BOFA89   .CHK       CHKRTM   .EXE           DISK  C:POWER USER
  BOFA89   .DEF       ORDER    .BAT           Available
  BOFA89   .DTA       PATHTEST.                 Bytes     2,437,120
  BOFA89   .GRP       REMINDER.EXE
  BOFA89   .SOR       SETUP    .EXE           DIRECTORY Stats
  BOFA89   .ZIP                                Total
  BOFA90   .ACT                                  Files            26
  BOFA90   .BGT                                  Bytes       786,291
  BOFA90   .DEF                                Matching
  BOFA90   .DTA                                  Files            26
  BOFA90   .GRP                                  Bytes       786,291
  BOFA90   .SOR                                Tagged
  CHECK    .EXE                                  Files             0
  CHECK    .PRO                                  Bytes             0
  CHECK1R  .ZIP                                Current File
  CHECK2   .EXE                                  BOFA89   .ACT
  CHECK2R  .ZIP                                  Bytes             1

STAMP file: BOFA89   .ACT      1 ....  4-19-90  3:40:20 pm
       to:  6-27-90 11:54:30 am
Enter date and time                  ↑ history  ⏎ ok  F1 help  ESC cancel
```

Figure 3-34: Pressing N in XTreePro Gold and XTreeGold lets you change the date and time stamp on a file or group of tagged files.

D (to sort by Date). (See "File Display" and "Sort Criteria" for details on these commands.) Figure 3-35 shows files sorted by date; older files come first in the list.

> If you just want to know the current date and time, Pro Gold and Gold display this information in the upper-right corner of the screen at all times.

```
Path: C:\CHECK                                              12:49:35 pm
  BOFA89   .CHK        52 .... 10-04-89  8:24:08 am    FILE   *.*
  BOFA89   .BGT     2,162 .... 12-31-89 12:53:54 pm
  BOFA89   .SOR     1,334 .... 12-31-89  1:37:18 pm    DISK  C:POWER USER
  BOFA89   .ZIP    18,206 .... 12-31-89  2:59:34 pm    Available
  ORDER    .BAT       514 ....  1-08-90  4:00:42 am      Bytes     2,363,392
  BOFA90   .DEF        43 ....  1-09-90  8:26:42 am
  PATHTEST.             1 ....  1-09-90  8:49:38 am    DIRECTORY Stats
  BOFA90   .GRP       506 ....  1-09-90  8:50:02 am    Total
  CHECK    .PRO     1,216 ....  1-09-90  8:56:00 am      Files            26
  BOFA89   .DEF        43 ....  1-14-90 12:16:46 pm     Bytes       813,291
  BOFA89   .GRP         0 ....  1-14-90 12:16:48 pm   Matching
  CHECK    .EXE    21,313 ....  4-02-90  4:03:00 am     Files            26
  CHECK2   .EXE   129,953 ....  4-02-90  4:03:00 am     Bytes       813,291
  CHECK3   .EXE    10,769 ....  4-02-90  4:03:00 am   Tagged
  CHECK4   .EXE    48,721 ....  4-02-90  4:03:00 am     Files             0
  CHKRTM   .EXE    70,680 ....  4-02-90  4:03:00 am     Bytes             0
  REMINDER.EXE      6,001 ....  4-02-90  4:03:00 am   Current File
  SETUP    .EXE    31,057 ....  4-02-90  4:03:00 am     BOFA89   .CHK
  CHECK2R  .ZIP    78,334 ....  4-10-90  5:06:04 pm     Bytes            52

FILE       Attributes  Copy   Delete  Edit   Filespec  Invert  Log disk  Move
COMMANDS   New date    Open   Print   Rename Tag       Untag   View  eXecute  Quit
 ⏎ tree   F7 autoview  F8 split      F9 menu  F10 commands    F1 help   ESC cancel
```

Figure 3-35: Pressing Alt-F twice changes the file display to show the date and time each file was saved.

Part III: XTree for Dos

Delete   Command

Deleting obsolete files from your hard disk is essential to maintain a healthy drive. It's not just a matter of being neurotic about neatness, either. Extra files actually slow down computer performance, shorten hard disk life, and make it more difficult to find what you're looking for. Any version of XTree makes file deletion painless: the trick is to make hard disk housekeeping a part of your normal routine.

Deleting a file

To delete a file, simply go to a File window, highlight the file you want to delete, and press D for Delete. XTree will ask if you really want to delete the file, as shown in Figure 3-36. When XTree receives your affirmative acknowledgment (Y), it deletes the file. (Press N to cancel the process.)

Deleting a file from a floppy drive

To delete a file from a floppy drive, the first step is to go to the floppy drive containing the file you want to delete. To do this, press L for Log, press A for the A: drive, and then press Enter

```
Path: \QM\DOWNLOAD

251-WARN.DOC    F10       .ARC    MW5ART    .ZIP    FILE: *.*
387      .ZIP   FFM10     .ZIP    NAMER     .ZIP
ADD-MACH.ZIP    FM        .EXE    NEWDOS    .ZIP    DISK: C: POWER USER
ALTZ     .ZIP   FONTS     .ZIP    NOJTY     .ZIP      Available
ART-XMAS.ZIP    GRAB51    .ZIP    NOPMBU    .TXT        Bytes: 4,837,376
CHEDRR   .ZIP   GRIDMAKR  .ZIP    NOTOLLS   .ZIP
CHEKKERS.ZIP    HISCORES.         NPAD      .ZIP    DIRECTORY Stats
CHKUP    .EXE   HP3-MS    .ZIP    OCR-A     .ZIP     Total
DBOOT1   .ZIP   L3HPGL    .ZIP    PILOT90   .ZIP      Files:           77
DE10     .ZIP   LHC15     .EXE    PKZ110    .EXE      Bytes:    2,972,016
DESKDLL  .EXE   LJTODJ    .ZIP    POST61    .ARC    Matching
DIALOGUE.GLY    LZESHL    .ZIP    POSTBINS  .ZIP      Files:           77
DISKBUFF .ZIP   MAKEBA    .ZIP    PRN2FILE  .ZIP      Bytes:    2,972,016
DLR      .EXE   MOREMAC   .ZIP    PSDR32    .ARC    Tagged
DMVTEST  .ZIP   MOUSE624  .ZIP    PUMA100   .ZIP      Files:            0
DT       .EXE   MOVIE1    .EXE    QUICTY    .ARC      Bytes:            0
E-ICON   .ARC   MSAPP21   .ZIP    README    .DOC    Current File
EDIAL12  .ZIP   MSMOUSE7  .ZIP    RECONFIG  .ZIP      251-WARN DOC
ENVMACRO.ZIP    MSWITCH   .ZIP    RECYCL    .HP       Bytes:        21,571

DELETE file: 251-WARN.DOC

delete this file (Y/N) ?                            F1 quit F2 help F3 cancel
```

Figure 3-36: Whenever you give the Delete command (D for Delete), you'll be asked to confirm (by pressing Y for Yes) that you really want to delete that file.

Chapter 3: XTree for DOS Quick Reference Guide

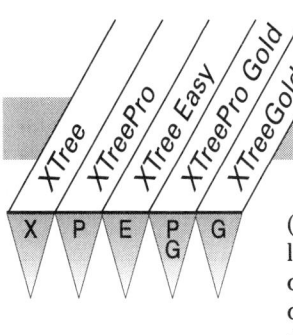

(substitute B if your want to log onto the B: drive). Once you've logged onto the floppy drive, find and highlight the file you want to delete and then press D. You will be asked to confirm your decision to delete, naturally, and after you press Y for Yes, XTree deletes the file. (You can then log back onto the hard disk.)

Deleting more than one file

Sometimes you want to delete a whole slew of files. (Confidentially, it can be quite a rush to wipe out a flock of files.) When it comes time to delete BAK files or get rid of unneeded programs, it is easier to tag (select) the files to be nuked and then give one delete command than it is to individually delete all those files.

First, tag the files for deletion by highlighting each file and pressing T (for tag). A diamond appears on-screen confirming that the file is tagged. (For the full story on this process, check out "Filespec" and "Tag/Untag"). Once you've tagged the files, press Ctrl-D to delete all tagged files. (Note that pressing D deletes the current file and Ctrl-D deletes all tagged files.) Before the files are actually deleted, however, XTree asks if you want to confirm the deletion of each file, as shown in Figure 3-37.

```
Path: C:\RC

CONTDAT   .  ◆               FILE: *.*
ENDDAT    .  ◆
GAMEDAT   .  ◆               DISK: C:POWER USER
MPPC     .CMP◆                 Available
OC       .CMP◆                   Bytes:   4,763,648
ODATA     .  ◆
OPCONT    .  ◆               DIRECTORY Stats
PC       .CMP◆                 Total
PCDAT     .  ◆                   Files:           14
PDATA     .  ◆                   Bytes:      329,855
RC       .EXE◆                 Matching
RRG      .CMP◆                   Files:           14
RRS      .CMP◆                   Bytes:      329,855
SC       .CMP◆                 Tagged
                                 Files:           14
                                 Bytes:      329,855
                               Current File
                                 CONTDAT    .
                                 Bytes:       38,097

DELETE all tagged files

Confirm delete for each file (Y/N) ?
```

Figure 3-37: Before XTree carries out the Ctrl-D command to delete all tagged files, it asks whether you want to confirm the deletion on a file-by-file basis.

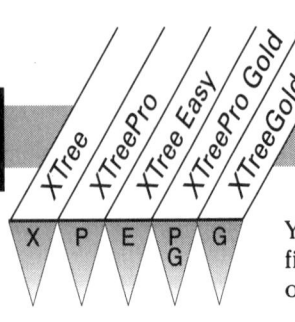

You can either press N to give XTree permission to delete all the files in one fell swoop or press Y to have XTree stop at each file one at a time, begging for your permission.

Deleting a directory

Before you can delete a directory you must delete any files in it or any subdirectories under it. To delete all the files in a directory, go to a File window and press Ctrl-T to tag all files. Then press Ctrl-D to delete the tagged files. (Then confirm that you wish to delete all the files.)

If you find that XTree won't delete one (or more files), it's probably because the files have been set to read-only, system, or hidden. See "Attributes (File)" to learn how to remove these attributes so you can delete the files.

Once all files are deleted, go back to the Directory window, put your cursor on the directory you want to delete, and press D to delete the now-empty directory. Finally, of course, XTree asks if you really want to delete the directory. Enter either Y for yes (or N for no if you've changed your mind) to wind up the operation. Figure 3-38 shows this final confirmation process.

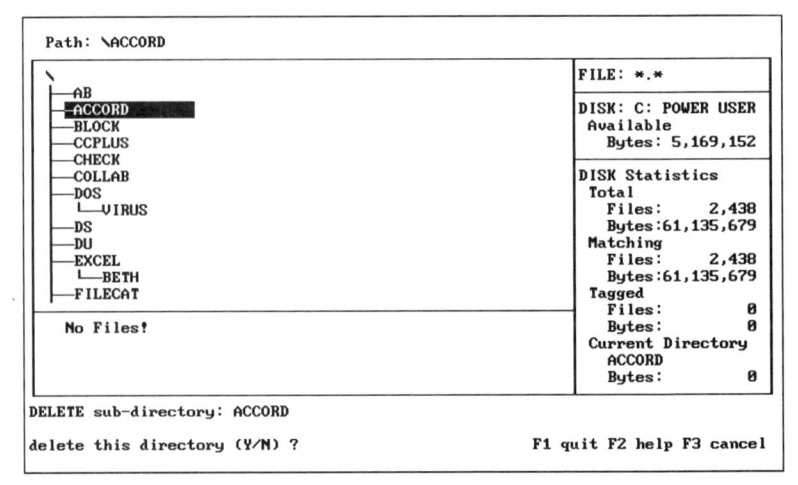

```
Path: \ACCORD

  ├─AB                              FILE: *.*
  ├─ACCORD
  ├─BLOCK                           DISK: C: POWER USER
  ├─CCPLUS                          Available
  ├─CHECK                             Bytes: 5,169,152
  ├─COLLAB
  ├─DOS                             DISK Statistics
  │ └─VIRUS                         Total
  ├─DS                                Files:       2,438
  ├─DU                                Bytes:  61,135,679
  ├─EXCEL                           Matching
  │ └─BETH                            Files:       2,438
  └─FILECAT                           Bytes:  61,135,679
                                    Tagged
                                      Files:           0
  No Files!                           Bytes:           0
                                    Current Directory
                                      ACCORD
                                      Bytes:           0

DELETE sub-directory: ACCORD
delete this directory (Y/N) ?              F1 quit F2 help F3 cancel
```

Figure 3-38: Pressing D on a highlighted directory name deletes an empty directory.

Using Prune with XTreePro Gold and XTreeGold

With XTreePro Gold and XTreeGold, you can delete a directory, any subdirectories underneath it, and any files in those directories or subdirectories with one powerful command: Prune.

Pruning is simple: just highlight the directory to be deleted and press Alt-P for Prune. Because a misplaced Prune command could have dire consequences, you are asked to verify your command by typing **PRUNE** and pressing Enter, as shown in Figure 3-39.

Using Wash Disk with XTreePro Gold and XTreeGold

There are special programs on the market that can *unerase* deleted files and directories. The fact that deleted material can be retrieved is great news if you've accidentally deleted something, and terrible news if you thought deleting a file *guaranteed* that no one would ever see it (just ask Oliver North). If you've got confidential material on your drive that you *really* want to delete, XTreePro Gold and XTree Gold's Wash Disk command can make all deleted files unrecoverable. No matter what.

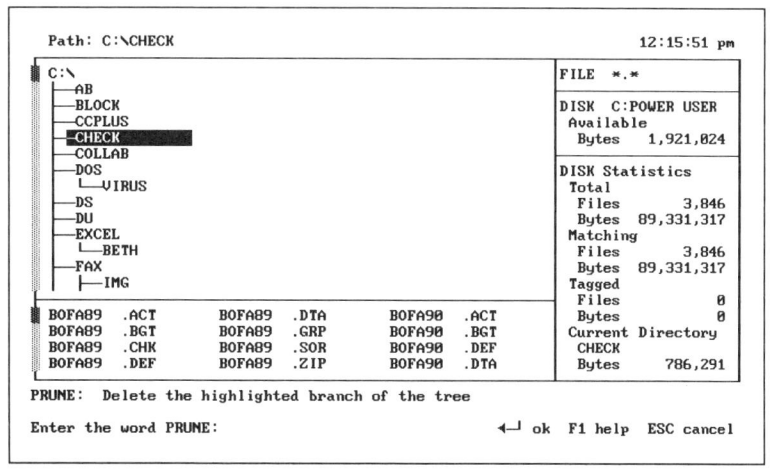

```
Path: C:\CHECK                                              12:15:51 pm
 C:\                                          FILE  *.*
  ├─AB
  ├─BLOCK                                     DISK  C:POWER USER
  ├─CCPLUS                                    Available
  ├─CHECK                                       Bytes      1,921,024
  ├─COLLAB
  ├─DOS                                       DISK Statistics
  │ └─VIRUS                                   Total
  ├─DS                                          Files          3,846
  ├─DU                                          Bytes     89,331,317
  ├─EXCEL                                     Matching
  │ └─BETH                                      Files          3,846
  ├─FAX                                         Bytes     89,331,317
  │ ├─IMG                                     Tagged
                                                Files              0
 BOFA89   .ACT    BOFA89   .DTA   BOFA90  .ACT  Bytes              0
 BOFA89   .BGT    BOFA89   .GRP   BOFA90  .BGT Current Directory
 BOFA89   .CHK    BOFA89   .SOR   BOFA90  .DEF  CHECK
 BOFA89   .DEF    BOFA89   .ZIP   BOFA90  .DTA  Bytes        786,291

 PRUNE:  Delete the highlighted branch of the tree
 Enter the word PRUNE:                     ↵ ok  F1 help  ESC cancel
```

Figure 3-39: After pressing Alt-P, XTreePro Gold and XTreeGold ask you to type the word PRUNE to verify that you really want to delete a directory and all of its files and subdirectories.

Delete, DIR Empty

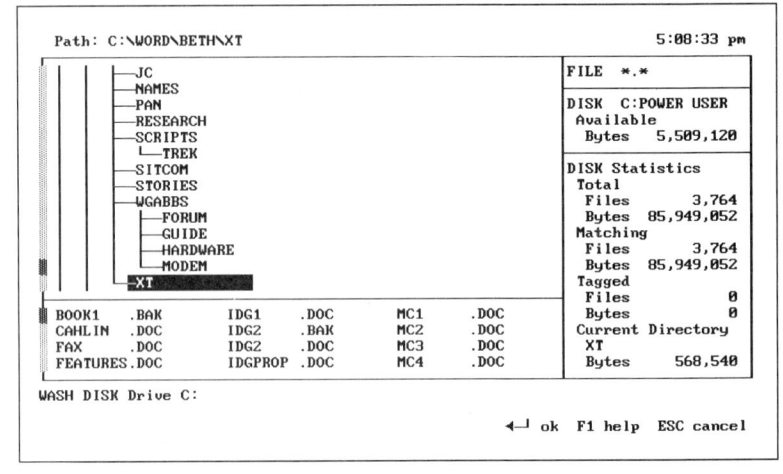

Figure 3-40: XTreePro Gold and Gold can make deleted files unrecoverable with the Wash Disk command (Alt-W).

To wash your hard disk, go to the Directory window and press Alt-W for Wash. XTree asks you to confirm with an Enter your desire to Wash your disk, as shown in Figure 3-40.

After you press Enter, have a cup of coffee (decaf, of course); all deleted files and directories on the hard disk will be truly deleted.

XTreeGold version 2.5 users are given an additional choice. Pressing the F2 function key toggles between Six passes (XTree will scrub over the deleted files six times) and DoD (washing per Department of Defense specifications DOD 5220.22-M). Once you've selected your choice (and one certainly hopes that the Department of Defense technique is the most thorough and takes the longest), press Enter.

DIR Empty/ DIR Not Logged

Error message

In XTreeGold, the infamous No Files! error message has finally been eliminated and replaced by three more reassuring, and meaningful, messages:

Chapter 3: XTree for DOSQuick Reference Guide   83

DIR EMPTY — This message means there are no files in the current directory at all.

NO FILES MATCH — This message means that there are files in the current directory but none of them meet the current File Specification. In Figure 3-41, notice the File Specification (in the upper-right corner) is set to show *.DOC (files ending in DOC). There are no DOC files in the PLOTS directory, hence the NO FILES MATCH warning. The File Specification must be set to *.* to see all files.

DIR NOT LOGGED — This message means that, for some reason, the directory you're pointing at has, well, not been logged. A directory doesn't get logged for one of two reasons: either you told XTree not to log that directory, or the computer ran out of memory before the hard disk was finished logging.

All things being equal, you won't run out of memory unless you're logging a bunch of floppies or you have a CD-ROM or something with so many files on it that it demands a lot of memory. One way to get XTree to log the directory is to tell XTree to forget all the other disks you've logged so far (use the Release command, Alt-R, for this) and then log the directory with the plus key (or the whole drive with the Log command, L).

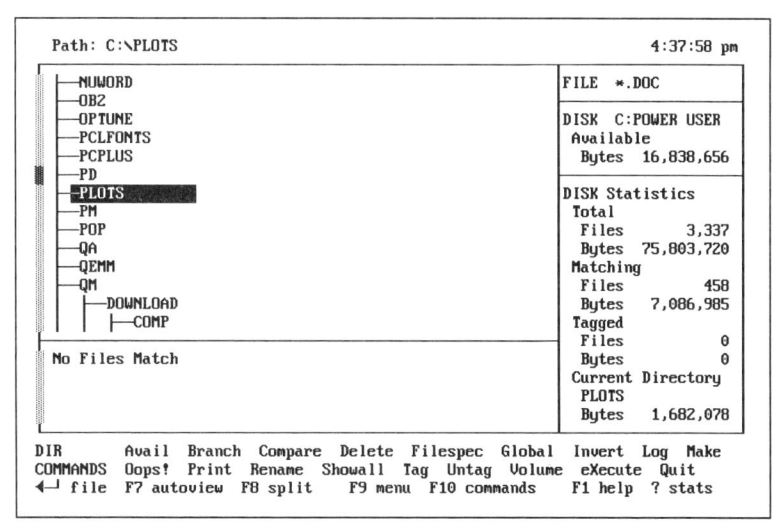

```
Path: C:\PLOTS                                         4:37:58 pm
  ─NUWORD                                    FILE  *.DOC
  ─OB2
  ─OPTUNE                                    DISK  C:POWER USER
  ─PCLFONTS                                  Available
  ─PCPLUS                                      Bytes    16,838,656
  ─PD
  ─PLOTS                                     DISK Statistics
  ─PM                                        Total
  ─POP                                         Files         3,337
  ─QA                                          Bytes    75,803,720
  ─QEMM                                      Matching
  ─QM                                          Files           458
    ─DOWNLOAD                                  Bytes     7,086,985
      ─COMP                                  Tagged
                                               Files             0
No Files Match                                 Bytes             0
                                             Current Directory
                                             PLOTS
                                               Bytes     1,682,078

DIR      Avail  Branch  Compare Delete Filespec Global Invert Log Make
COMMANDS Oops!  Print   Rename  Showall Tag   Untag Volume eXecute Quit
←┘ file   F7 autoview  F8 split   F9 menu  F10 commands  F1 help ? stats
```

Figure 3-41: XTreeGold reflects that there are no files in the current directory that match the file specifications.

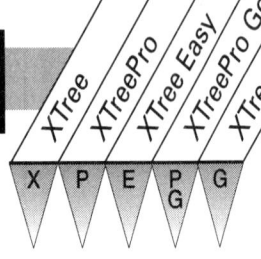

Directory Management

The commands discussed in the following sections are for creating, deleting, moving, and viewing your directories. (See Chapter 1, "MS-DOS Concepts," for more details about directory strategies.)

Using Make to create a directory

You use the Make command to create a new directory. The first step is to place the cursor in the Directory window and then position it on the directory under which you want your new directory to appear.

If you want to make a new directory under the root, for instance, position the cursor on the root directory (\). Or, if you want to make a subdirectory under WP, put your cursor on the WP directory.

When the cursor is positioned properly, press M for Make to create the directory. In Figure 3-42, a new directory will be created within the CHECK directory as soon as XTree knows what to name the new directory.

To name the new directory 1990, for example, just type in **1990** and press Enter. And voilà! Figure 3-43 shows the new 1990 subdirectory under the CHECK directory. That's all there is to it.

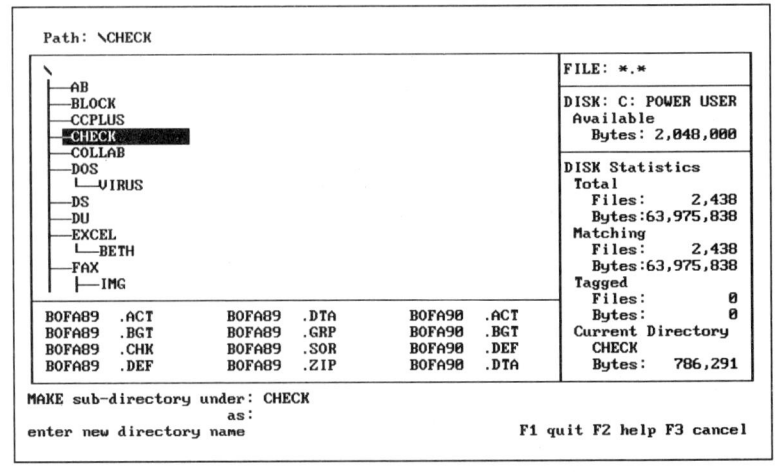

```
Path: \CHECK

         ─AB                                                  FILE: *.*
         ─BLOCK
         ─CCPLUS                                              DISK: C: POWER USER
         ─CHECK                                               Available
         ─COLLAB                                                Bytes: 2,048,000
         ─DOS
         │  └─VIRUS                                           DISK Statistics
         ─DS                                                  Total
         ─DU                                                    Files:      2,438
         ─EXCEL                                                 Bytes:63,975,838
         │  └─BETH                                            Matching
         ─FAX                                                   Files:      2,438
         ├─IMG                                                  Bytes:63,975,838
                                                              Tagged
                                                                Files:          0
BOFA89   .ACT    BOFA89   .DTA    BOFA90   .ACT                 Bytes:          0
BOFA89   .BGT    BOFA89   .GRP    BOFA90   .BGT              Current Directory
BOFA89   .CHK    BOFA89   .SOR    BOFA90   .DEF                CHECK
BOFA89   .DEF    BOFA89   .ZIP    BOFA90   .DTA                Bytes:    786,291

MAKE sub-directory under: CHECK
                      as:
enter new directory name                         F1 quit F2 help F3 cancel
```

Figure 3-42: Press M to make a directory, type in the new directory name, and you're ready to cook.

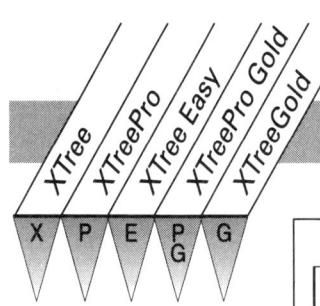

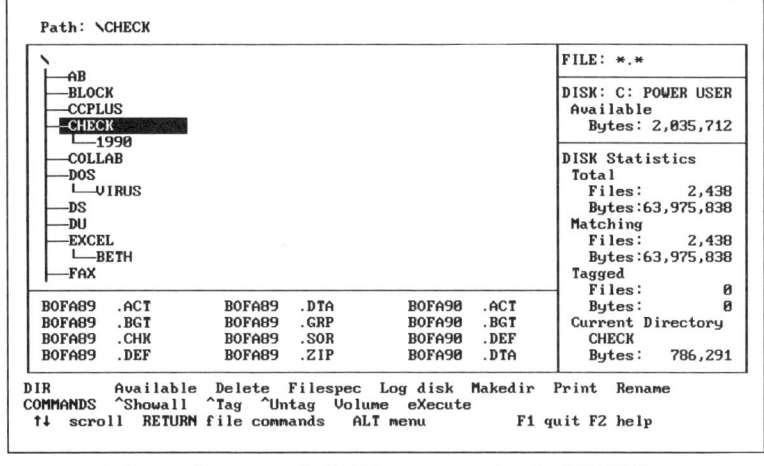

Chapter 3: XTree for DOS Quick Reference Guide 85

Figure 3-43: A new directory called 1990 appears under the CHECK directory.

Using Rename to change a directory's name

Say, for example, you realize that you need a directory called 1991, not 1990. To change the 1990 directory's name, highlight the directory and press R for Rename. As you might expect, a prompt appears at the bottom of the screen (shown in Figure 3-44), asking for the name of the new directory (which, in this case, is 1991).

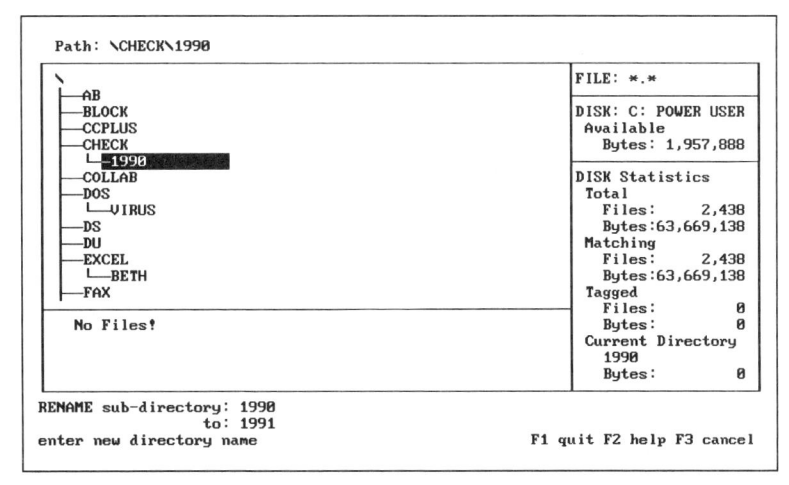

Figure 3-44: You can rename any directory by highlighting it, pressing R (for Rename), and entering a new name.

Directory Management

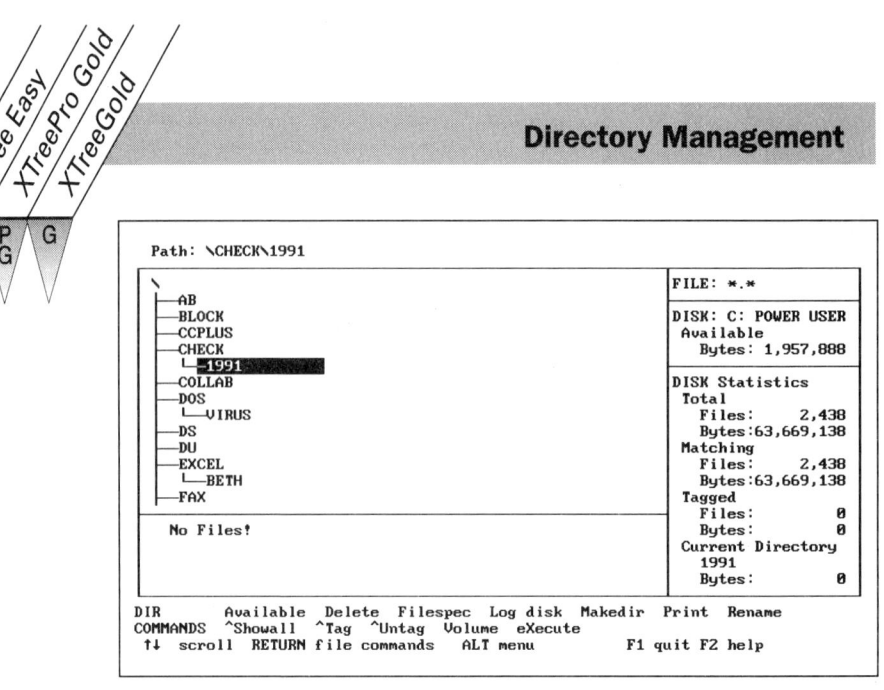

```
Path: \CHECK\1991
                                              FILE: *.*
  \
  ├─AB                                        DISK: C: POWER USER
  ├─BLOCK                                        Available
  ├─CCPLUS                                          Bytes: 1,957,888
  ├─CHECK
  │  └─1991                                   DISK Statistics
  ├─COLLAB                                       Total
  ├─DOS                                             Files:       2,438
  │  └─VIRUS                                        Bytes:  63,669,138
  ├─DS                                           Matching
  ├─DU                                              Files:       2,438
  ├─EXCEL                                           Bytes:  63,669,138
  │  └─BETH                                      Tagged
  ├─FAX                                             Files:           0
                                                    Bytes:           0
  No Files!                                     Current Directory
                                                  1991
                                                    Bytes:           0

DIR        Available  Delete  Filespec  Log disk  Makedir  Print  Rename
COMMANDS   ^Showall   ^Tag    ^Untag    Volume    eXecute
↑↓  scroll  RETURN file commands    ALT menu       F1 quit F2 help
```

Figure 3-45: The 1990 directory from Figure 3-43 is renamed to 1991.

Once you press Enter, you'll see that the 1990 directory has been renamed 1991. The newly renamed directory is shown in Figure 3-45.

> **NOTE:** If you change a directory name that contains a program, you may also have to adjust the path statement in your AUTOEXEC.BAT file. See Chapter 8, "Hard Disk Management in a Nutshell," for details on changing this file.

Using Delete to remove a directory

The first step in deleting a directory is to delete any files or subdirectories in that directory. To delete all the files in a directory, go to a File window and press Ctrl-T to tag all files. Then press Ctrl-D to delete the tagged files. (Then confirm that you wish to delete all the files.)

> **NOTE:** If you find that XTree won't delete one (or more files), it's probably because the files have been set to read-only, system, or hidden. See "Attributes (File)" to learn how to remove such attributes so you can delete the files.

Chapter 3: XTree for DOS Quick Reference Guide

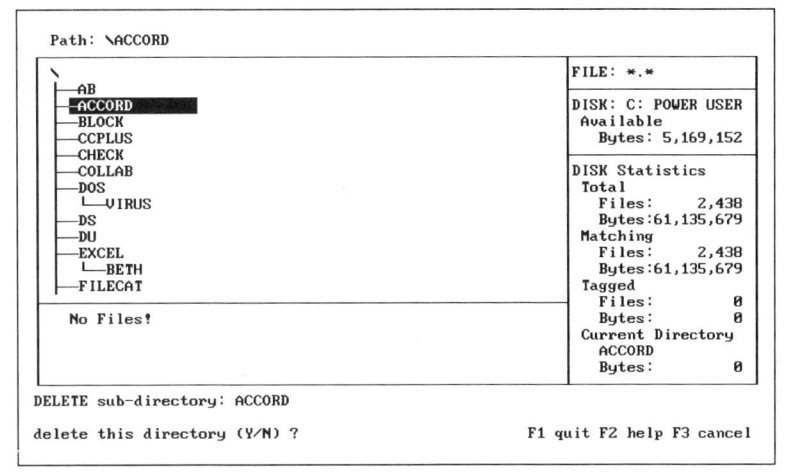

Figure 3-46: Pressing D on a directory name deletes an empty directory.

Once all files are deleted, go back to the Directory window, put your cursor on the directory to be deleted, and press D to delete the now-empty directory. Finally, of course, XTree asks if you really want to delete the directory. Enter either Y for yes (or N for no if you've changed your mind) to wind up the operation. Figure 3-46 shows this final confirmation process.

Using Copy to duplicate directory structures (and files)

If you wish, you can copy a directory structure (and its files) to another location. Having your hard disk's directory structure backed up to a floppy disk is extremely helpful if you ever need to resurrect a crashed hard disk.

The first step is to tag the files you want to copy. (See "Tag/Untag" if you don't yet know how to tag files.) From a File window, press Alt-C to Copy and duplicate the file's path.

At the bottom of the screen you'll be given the opportunity to rename your files as you copy them (press Enter to decline that option). Next you'll be prompted to choose a destination drive, as shown in Figure 3-47. Say, for example, the A: drive is your destination. Type **A** (the colon and backslash will be put in for you) and then press Enter.

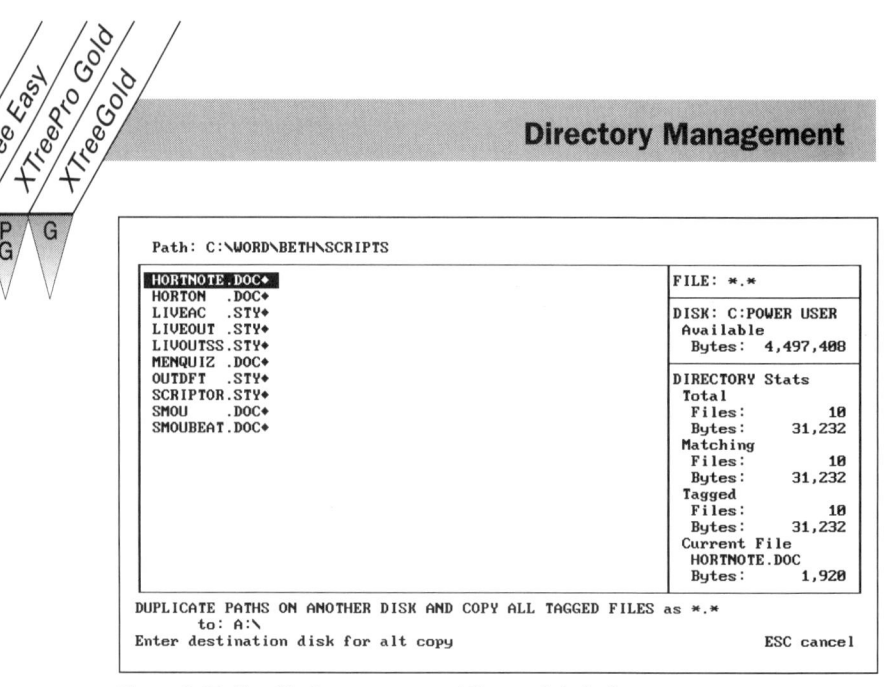

```
Path: C:\WORD\BETH\SCRIPTS
HORTNOTE.DOC♦                           FILE: *.*
HORTON   .DOC♦
LIVEAC   .STY♦                          DISK: C:POWER USER
LIVEOUT  .STY♦                          Available
LIVOUTSS .STY♦                            Bytes:    4,497,408
MENQUIZ  .DOC♦
OUTDFT   .STY♦                          DIRECTORY Stats
SCRIPTOR .STY♦                          Total
SMOU     .DOC♦                            Files:          10
SMOUBEAT .DOC♦                            Bytes:      31,232
                                        Matching
                                          Files:          10
                                          Bytes:      31,232
                                        Tagged
                                          Files:          10
                                          Bytes:      31,232
                                        Current File
                                          HORTNOTE.DOC
                                          Bytes:       1,920

DUPLICATE PATHS ON ANOTHER DISK AND COPY ALL TAGGED FILES as *.*
     to: A:\
Enter destination disk for alt copy                    ESC cancel
```

Figure 3-47: Use Alt-C to copy tagged files and their directory structure.

XTreeGold 2.5 also allows you to specify a directory as a destination (rather than another disk, as in the other versions). The source directory structure is duplicated underneath the destination directory. You choose to either duplicate the full source pathname or just the portion of the pathname where the files are actually stored. You'll be asked whether you want to `Replace existing files?`. In other words, if there are already files on the disk with the same name, do you *really* want to replace them with the files you are copying now? Generally, you do. So, press Y. At this point the copying commences and the files and their directories are copied to the disk.

Using Prune with XTreePro Gold and XTreeGold

With XTreePro Gold and XTreeGold, you can delete a directory, any subdirectories underneath it, and any files in those directories or subdirectories with one powerful command: Prune.

Pruning is simple: just highlight the directory to be deleted and press Alt-P for Prune. Because a misplaced Prune command could have dire consequences, you are asked to verify your command by typing **PRUNE** and pressing Enter, as shown in Figure 3-48.

Chapter 3: XTree for DOS Quick Reference Guide

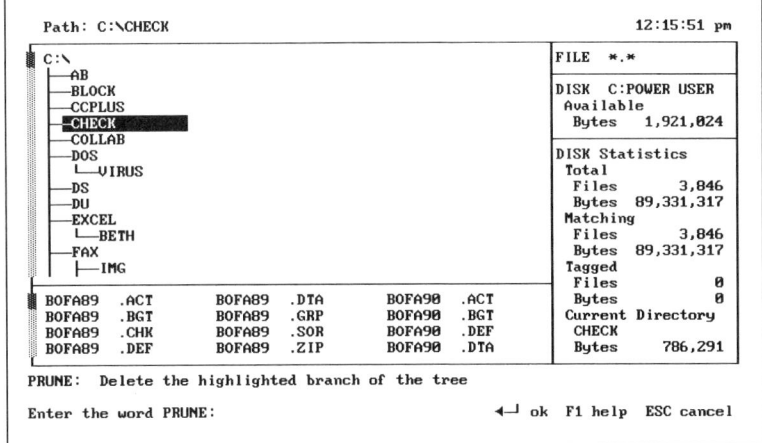

```
Path: C:\CHECK                                          12:15:51 pm
┌──────────────────────────────────────────────┬──────────────────┐
│ C:\                                          │ FILE   *.*       │
│  ├─AB                                        │                  │
│  ├─BLOCK                                     │ DISK  C:POWER USER│
│  ├─CCPLUS                                    │ Available        │
│  ├─CHECK                                     │  Bytes   1,921,024│
│  ├─COLLAB                                    │                  │
│  ├─DOS                                       │ DISK Statistics  │
│  │  └─VIRUS                                  │ Total            │
│  ├─DS                                        │  Files     3,846 │
│  ├─DU                                        │  Bytes 89,331,317│
│  ├─EXCEL                                     │ Matching         │
│  │  └─BETH                                   │  Files     3,846 │
│  ├─FAX                                       │  Bytes 89,331,317│
│  │  ├─IMG                                    │ Tagged           │
│                                              │  Files         0 │
│ BOFA89  .ACT   BOFA89  .DTA   BOFA90  .ACT   │  Bytes         0 │
│ BOFA89  .BGT   BOFA89  .GRP   BOFA90  .BGT   │ Current Directory│
│ BOFA89  .CHK   BOFA89  .SOR   BOFA90  .DEF   │ CHECK            │
│ BOFA89  .DEF   BOFA89  .ZIP   BOFA90  .DTA   │  Bytes     786,291│
├──────────────────────────────────────────────┴──────────────────┤
│ PRUNE:  Delete the highlighted branch of the tree               │
│ Enter the word PRUNE:              ⏎ ok  F1 help  ESC cancel    │
└─────────────────────────────────────────────────────────────────┘
```

Figure 3-48: XTreePro Gold and XTreeGold ask you to type the word PRUNE to verify that you really want to delete a directory and all of its files and subdirectories.

Using Graft to move a directory with XTreePro Gold and XTree Gold

Ever want to pick up a directory (files and all) and attach it to another directory? That's what the Graft command is used for. To graft a directory, highlight the directory you want to move and press Alt-G, for Graft.

At the bottom of the screen you'll be asked *where* you want to move your directory to; the Destination window appears automatically, so you can highlight the directory you want to move to (though you can still type in the path, manually, if you're the old-fashioned sort).

Figure 3-49 shows the directory CHECK90 being moved *under* the CHEKBOOK directory. When you're ready to graft, press Enter. As a precaution, you'll be asked one more time if you're sure you want to do this. Just press Y if you're sure, and Pro Gold and Gold will carry out the command.

> **NOTE:** If, instead of grafting, you receive a Can't Update Parent Directory error message, you have an older version of XTreeGold that does not get along with your version of DOS. An upgrade is available to fix this problem. (See Appendix D, "Where to Go from Here.")

> **NOTE:** After you graft a directory, press L to relog the drive so the grafted directory appears in alphabetical order on the tree.

Directory Management

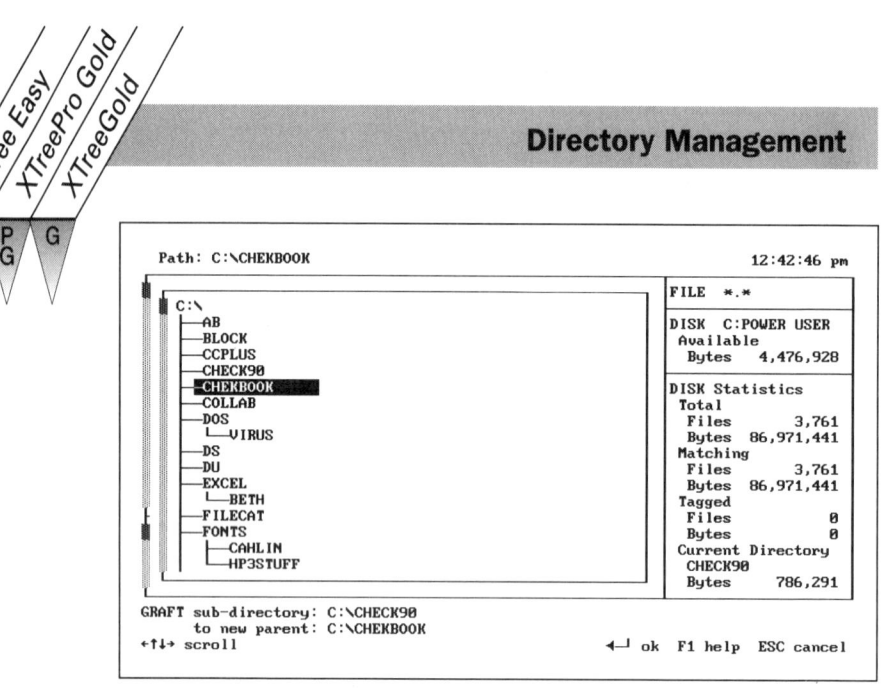

```
Path: C:\CHEKBOOK                                       12:42:46 pm
┌─────────────────────────────────────────┬──────────────────────┐
│   C:\                                   │ FILE  *.*            │
│    ├─AB                                 │                      │
│    ├─BLOCK                              │ DISK  C:POWER USER   │
│    ├─CCPLUS                             │ Available            │
│    ├─CHECK90                            │   Bytes    4,476,928 │
│    ├─CHEKBOOK                           │                      │
│    ├─COLLAB                             │ DISK Statistics      │
│    ├─DOS                                │ Total                │
│    │  └─VIRUS                           │   Files        3,761 │
│    ├─DS                                 │   Bytes   86,971,441 │
│    ├─DU                                 │ Matching             │
│    ├─EXCEL                              │   Files        3,761 │
│    │  └─BETH                            │   Bytes   86,971,441 │
│    ├─FILECAT                            │ Tagged               │
│    ├─FONTS                              │   Files            0 │
│       ├─CAHLIN                          │   Bytes            0 │
│       └─HP3STUFF                        │ Current Directory    │
│                                         │   CHECK90            │
│                                         │   Bytes      786,291 │
└─────────────────────────────────────────┴──────────────────────┘
GRAFT sub-directory: C:\CHECK90
         to new parent: C:\CHEKBOOK
 ←↑↓→ scroll                            ↵ ok  F1 help  ESC cancel
```

Figure 3-49: You can cut and paste your directory tree with the Graft (Alt-G) command.

Collapsing the directory display with XTreePro Gold and XTreeGold

If you have a large hard disk with a long and involved directory tree, you may find yourself wishing for a less-complete view of your directory structure. When you collapse your directory tree, selected portions of the directory structure disappear from view until you either quit XTree or restore the view to normal. (If you're familiar with outline programs, then you've got an idea of how this works.) The

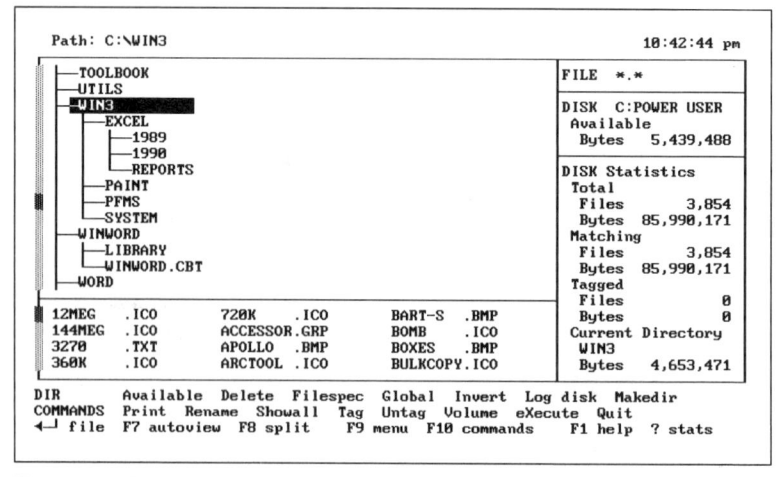

```
Path: C:\WIN3                                           10:42:44 pm
┌─────────────────────────────────────────┬──────────────────────┐
│  ├─TOOLBOOK                             │ FILE  *.*            │
│  ├─UTILS                                │                      │
│  ├─WIN3                                 │ DISK  C:POWER USER   │
│  │  ├─EXCEL                             │ Available            │
│  │  │  ├─1989                           │   Bytes    5,439,488 │
│  │  │  ├─1990                           │                      │
│  │  │  └─REPORTS                        │ DISK Statistics      │
│  │  ├─PAINT                             │ Total                │
│  │  ├─PFMS                              │   Files        3,854 │
│  │  └─SYSTEM                            │   Bytes   85,990,171 │
│  ├─WINWORD                              │ Matching             │
│  │  ├─LIBRARY                           │   Files        3,854 │
│  │  └─WINWORD.CBT                       │   Bytes   85,990,171 │
│  └─WORD                                 │ Tagged               │
│                                         │   Files            0 │
│ 12MEG   .ICO   720K    .ICO  BART-S .BMP│   Bytes            0 │
│ 144MEG  .ICO   ACCESSOR.GRP  BOMB   .ICO│ Current Directory    │
│ 3270    .TXT   APOLLO  .BMP  BOXES  .BMP│   WIN3               │
│ 360K    .ICO   ARCTOOL .ICO  BULKCOPY.ICO│  Bytes    4,653,471 │
└─────────────────────────────────────────┴──────────────────────┘
DIR        Available  Delete  Filespec  Global  Invert  Log disk  Makedir
COMMANDS   Print  Rename  Showall  Tag  Untag  Volume  eXecute  Quit
  ↵ file  F7 autoview  F8 split    F9 menu  F10 commands   F1 help  ? stats
```

Figure 3-50: The "before" picture for the following examples. The WIN3 directory and its subdirectories.

benefit of collapsing a directory tree is that when you travel up and down through your directory tree, you don't have to travel through a bunch of subdirectories you're not planning to work with anyway.

Collapsing a directory tree makes no changes to your hard disk — you just collapse the *view* of the hard disk. There are two directory-collapsing function keys, F5 and F6. To illustrate how to use these keys, the next two sections are based on the example in Figure 3-50, which shows a directory called WIN3 and seven subdirectories.

Using F5 to collapse two levels in a directory

To collapse two levels of only the WIN3 directory, press F5; all directories in the current branch more than one level below the cursor then disappear from view. Yes, this explanation is very tongue-tied, but this is what the command does. Take a look at Figure 3-51: notice that 1989, 1990, and REPORTS (the directories two levels down from WIN3 in Figure 3-50) have disappeared from view. The little plus (+) sign next to the EXCEL directory is a visual clue that tells you there are other, hidden directories under the EXCEL directory. Pressing F5 (with WIN3 highlighted) a second time will restore the view back to normal (as in Figure 3-50).

If you put your cursor on the root directory and press F5, the first level of directories on the hard disk will be displayed, as shown in Figure 3-52. Again, pressing F5 a second time at the root level toggles between the collapsed and normal view.

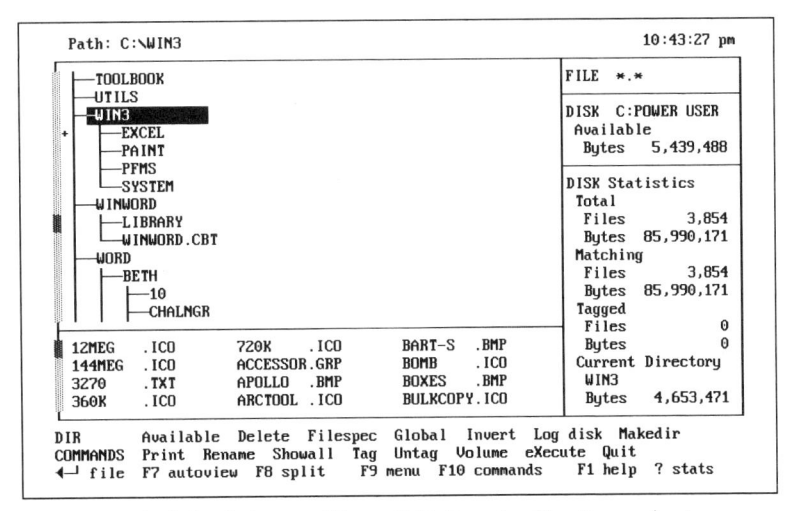

```
Path: C:\WIN3                                              10:43:27 pm
    ┌─TOOLBOOK                              FILE  *.*
    ├─UTILS
    ├─WIN3                                  DISK  C:POWER USER
  + │  ├─EXCEL                              Available
    │  ├─PAINT                                Bytes     5,439,488
    │  ├─PFMS
    │  └─SYSTEM                             DISK Statistics
    ├─WINWORD                               Total
    │  ├─LIBRARY                              Files         3,854
    │  └─WINWORD.CBT                          Bytes    85,990,171
    └─WORD                                  Matching
       ├─BETH                                 Files         3,854
       ├─10                                   Bytes    85,990,171
       └─CHALNGR                            Tagged
                                              Files             0
  12MEG   .ICO    720K    .ICO   BART-S  .BMP  Bytes             0
  144MEG  .ICO    ACCESSOR.GRP   BOMB    .ICO Current Directory
  3270    .TXT    APOLLO  .BMP   BOXES   .BMP WIN3
  360K    .ICO    ARCTOOL .ICO   BULKCOPY.ICO  Bytes     4,653,471

  DIR       Available  Delete   Filespec  Global  Invert  Log disk  Makedir
  COMMANDS  Print  Rename  Showall  Tag  Untag  Volume  eXecute  Quit
  ←┘ file   F7 autoview  F8 split    F9 menu  F10 commands    F1 help   ? stats
```

Figure 3-51: An "after" picture of Figure 3-50. Pressing F5 collapses (and uncollapses) the directories two levels below the cursor on the current branch.

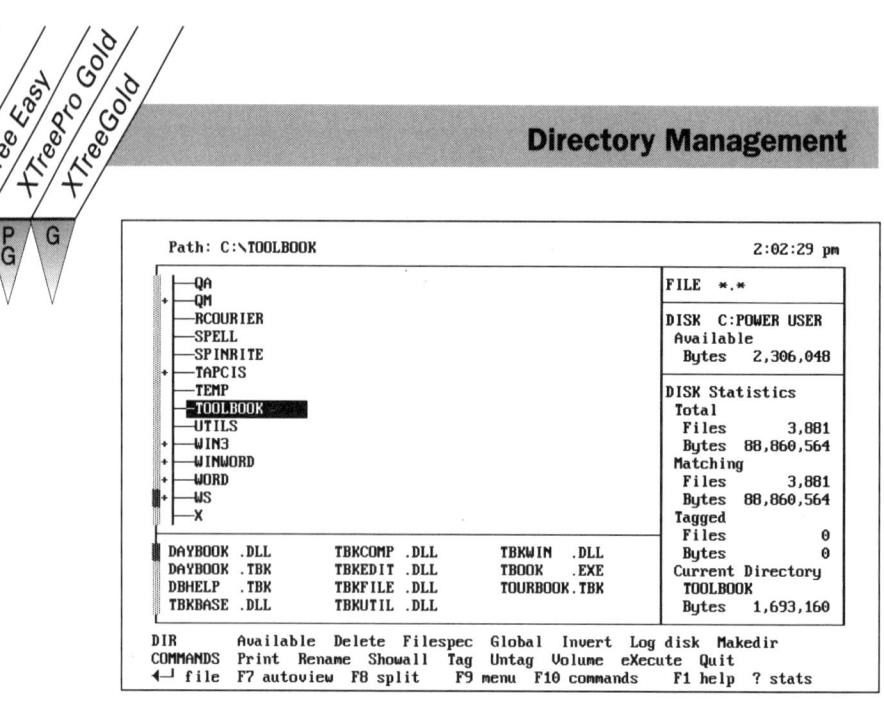

Figure 3-52: A reduction program that would put Jenny Craig to shame. Pressing F5 at the root changes the display so that only the "top" levels are visible.

Using F6 to collapse all levels in a directory

To collapse all subdirectories beneath the WIN3 directory, press F6 (the tell-tale plus sign next to the directory indicates it is collapsed). For example, in Figure 3-53 the plus sign adjacent to WIN3 indicates that WIN3 contains subdirectories that are hidden from view. Press F6 again (on the highlighted WIN3 directory) to return the view back to normal (Figure 3-50).

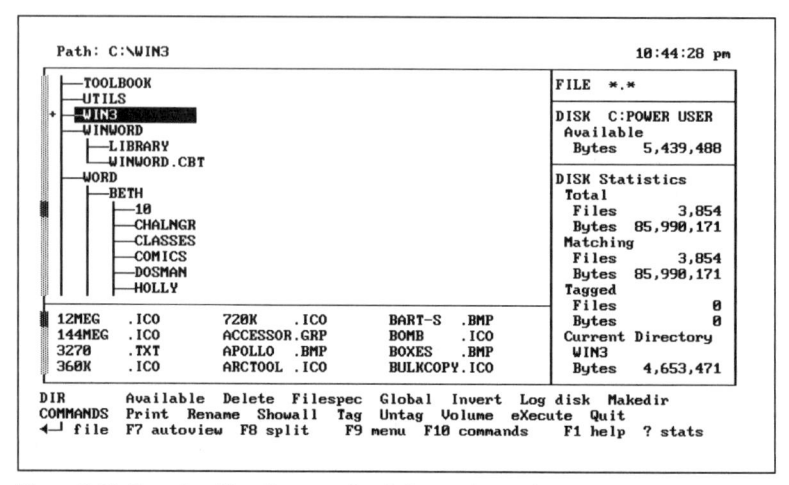

Figure 3-53: Pressing F6 collapses all subdirectories under the current, highlighted directory.

Chapter 3: XTree for DOS Quick Reference Guide

Hiding and unhiding a directory

XTreePro Gold and XTreeGold allow you to hide a directory (and its files) from view. These directories remain hidden not only while you are using Gold, but even after you've quit Gold and are using *other* programs. Even DOS's DIR command won't give away a directory's hiding place.

Why hide a directory? Is this someone's idea of a sick joke? Maybe. However, hiding a directory is one way to provide a measure of control over who accesses that directory. If you know a hidden directory's name, you can access the programs or data contained in that directory. Hiding a directory doesn't prevent unauthorized access, it just limits access to those who know the directory name.

Let's say you've put your personal checkbook on your office computer. (Naturally you're spending time on your personal checkbook *only* during your lunch hour or after work.) However, you don't want the Big Boss (or even your secretary) to have access to your personal finances. So you decide to hide the directory.

The first step is to highlight the directory to be hidden. Press Alt-H, and you'll be presented with messages similar to those at the bottom of Figure 3-54.

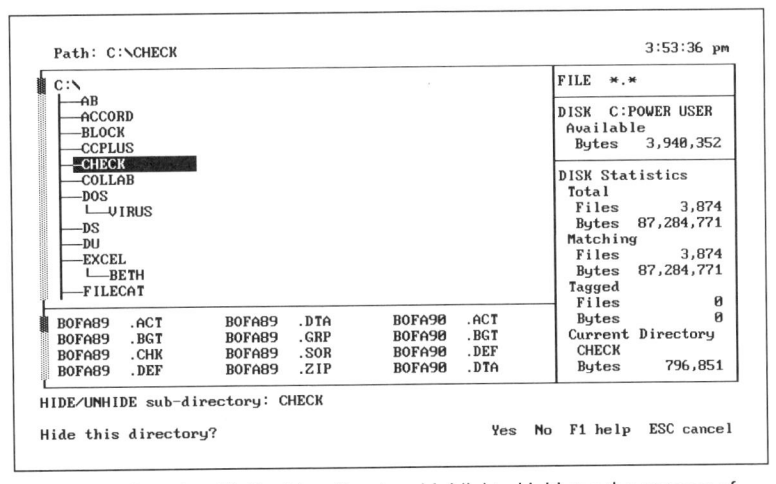

```
Path: C:\CHECK                                          3:53:36 pm
 C:\                                          FILE   *.*
   ─AB
   ─ACCORD                                    DISK   C:POWER USER
   ─BLOCK                                     Available
   ─CCPLUS                                      Bytes      3,940,352
   ─CHECK
   ─COLLAB                                    DISK Statistics
   ─DOS                                       Total
     └─VIRUS                                    Files          3,874
   ─DS                                          Bytes     87,284,771
   ─DU                                        Matching
   ─EXCEL                                       Files          3,874
     └─BETH                                     Bytes     87,284,771
   ─FILECAT                                   Tagged
                                                Files              0
   BOFA89  .ACT   BOFA89  .DTA   BOFA90  .ACT   Bytes              0
   BOFA89  .BGT   BOFA89  .GRP   BOFA90  .BGT Current Directory
   BOFA89  .CHK   BOFA89  .SOR   BOFA90  .DEF  CHECK
   BOFA89  .DEF   BOFA89  .ZIP   BOFA90  .DTA   Bytes        796,851

HIDE/UNHIDE sub-directory: CHECK

Hide this directory?                    Yes  No  F1 help  ESC cancel
```

Figure 3-54: Pressing Alt-H with a directory highlighted initiates the process of hiding that directory in XTreePro Gold and XTreeGold. Answer Y for Yes to complete the process.

At the bottom of the screen you're asked to confirm this action with Y or cancel with N. Press Y to hide the CHECK directory. At this point the directory name will still be visible on-screen, though in lowercase letters (`check` instead of `CHECK`), indicating that the directory is not visible in DOS. If you want the hidden directory to disappear even from Gold's Directory window, you'll have go to Page 3 of Gold's Configuration program and change the `System/Hidden file and directory access` option to `No`.

For details on Gold's Configuration program, see "Configuration Options," earlier in this chapter. One important note, however, is that in order to make this particular change, you must first exit Gold and run XTG_CFG from DOS. You will not have access to the `System/Hidden file and directory access` option if you use Alt-F10 to enter the Configuration program. This is part of Gold's security system.

Later, if *you* forget the names of the directories you've hidden, just go back into the Configuration program and change the `System/Hidden file and directory access` option back to `Yes`, and all will be revealed.

The Directory Window

The Directory window is where the directory tree is displayed. It's what you see when you first enter XTree. When the cursor highlight is in the tree, you're in XTree's Directory window.

At any time (unless you're in the middle of doing something else with XTree) you may get to the Directory window by pressing Esc or Backspace. Or, if you are in one of the two file windows (the Small or the Expanded), just cycle through the three windows by pressing Enter a few times, and you'll get back to the Directory window.

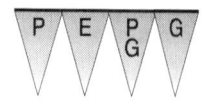

Editing with 1Word

All versions of XTree, except the original, have a built-in *text editor* called *1Word*. Although 1Word comes with its own manual and is capable of a lot of things, don't race to delete WordPerfect or Microsoft Word from your hard disk quite yet. First of all, 1Word won't underline or boldface characters, much less have anything to do with fonts or graphics. Second, you can't use 1Word to edit a file any longer than thirty pages (more or less).

Why bother with 1Word at all? Well, batch files (and ASCII files) are simple files that are not allowed to use fonts or underlines or import graphics, anyway. Batch files and ASCII files contain *only* simple, unformatted letters and numbers. A text editor, like 1Word, keeps batch files simple and clean. Full-fledged word processing programs such as WordPerfect, Microsoft Word, and others normally create files with a lot more than just letters and numbers in them — they've got hidden codes and symbols and a truck-load of gobbledygook that you can't normally see. When you need a quick, simple way to edit a four-line batch file, 1Word is handy and gobbledygook-free.

I'm assuming that you would prefer not to learn a jillion 1Word commands, so this section covers only a few elementary commands (just what you need to get by). If you're familiar with WordStar 3.3, then you'll be astonished to learn that by a bizarre coincidence, both programs' commands are virtually identical! However, if you do want to learn more about 1Word, take a look at the six pages of help screens available from inside the program or (ahem) read the manual.

Important reminder: You should not use 1Word to edit files created by your word processor nor should you use your word processor to edit files created by 1Word. Either process could trash either type of file.

Using 1Word commands

Before you can edit a file in 1Word, you'll need to know these seven basic keyboard commands (which will probably be all you'll ever need):

Backspace	Deletes the character to the left of the cursor.
Del	Deletes a highlighted character.
Ctrl-Y	Deletes the line the cursor is on.
Esc	For exiting 1Word. If you're in the process of editing a file, pressing Esc pops up the Quit Commands, and highlights Save file and quit

Esc Esc	Pressing Esc twice activates 1Word's Main menu, where more advanced commands are available.
Esc	Pressing Esc from the Main menu returns you to edit mode.
F1	Pressing this function key activates 1Word's Help feature, where you can get advice on 1Word commands.
Up- and down-arrow keys	Use these keys to move the cursor within the body of the text.

Editing a file with 1Word

Let's start out with something really fun: editing the AUTOEXEC.BAT file. In Chapter 8, "Hard Disk Management in a Nutshell," elements of your computer system setup are discussed. Two key parts of your system setup are your AUTOEXEC.BAT and CONFIG.SYS files. Samples in Chapter 8 of these two files are offered as standard setups. Let's see how yours compares.

Before changing your AUTOEXEC.BAT file, make a backup copy *first!* The importance of doing so cannot be overly stressed.

Okay, assuming you're all backed up, move your cursor up the directory tree to the root (\) directory and press Enter twice. (The AUTOEXEC.BAT and CONFIG.SYS files reside in the root directory of your hard disk.) Figure 3-55 shows how your screen should look at this point.

Once you find your AUTOEXEC.BAT file, highlight it and press E for edit. When you press Enter again, 1Word appears on-screen with the AUTOEXEC.BAT file loaded, similar to that shown in Figure 3-56; the contents of the AUTOEXEC.BAT file appear on-screen, along with the file's statistics. The AUTOEXEC.BAT in this figure is probably very simple in comparison to yours.

For this editing example, I'll assume that your AUTOEXEC.BAT doesn't include a path statement for XTree and I'll show you how to add such a statement: use the arrow keys to move to the end of the existing path statement and type **;C:\XTGOLD**. (This

Chapter 3: XTree for DOS Quick Reference Guide

```
Path: A:\
   AUTOEXEC.BAT                           FILE: *.*
   COMMAND  .COM
   CONFIG   .SYS                          DISK: A:
                                          Available
                                            Bytes:      799,744

                                          DIRECTORY Stats
                                          Total
                                            Files:            3
                                            Bytes:       25,946
                                          Matching
                                            Files:            3
                                            Bytes:       25,946
                                          Tagged
                                            Files:            0
                                            Bytes:            0
                                          Current File
                                            AUTOEXEC.BAT
                                            Bytes:          512

EDIT file: AUTOEXEC.BAT
Enter file specification or press ENTER              F1 help  ESC cancel
```

Figure 3-55: Use XTree's built-in text editor, 1Word, to edit your AUTOEXEC.BAT or CONFIG.SYS. Highlight the file you want to edit, press E for Edit, and then press Enter.

discussion assumes, of course, that you've got a C: drive as well as XTreeGold in a directory named XTGOLD. If you have another version of XTree, substitute the directory name for that program for XTGOLD in this example.) This statement appears in Figure 3-57, before the last item, ;C:\WORD.

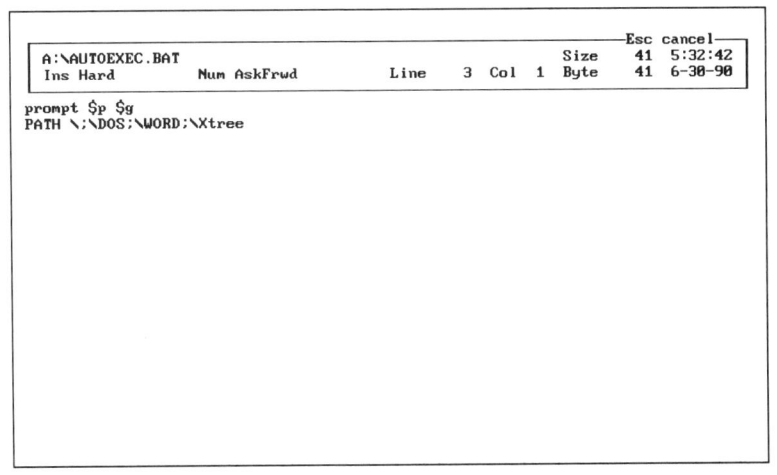

```
                                                 ┌─Esc cancel─┐
 A:\AUTOEXEC.BAT                          Size    41  5:32:42
   Ins Hard       Num AskFrwd    Line  3  Col  1  Byte    41  6-30-90
prompt $p $g
PATH \;\DOS;\WORD;\Xtree
```

Figure 3-56: An AUTOEXEC.BAT file loaded into 1Word, XTree's built-in text editor.

Editing with 1Word

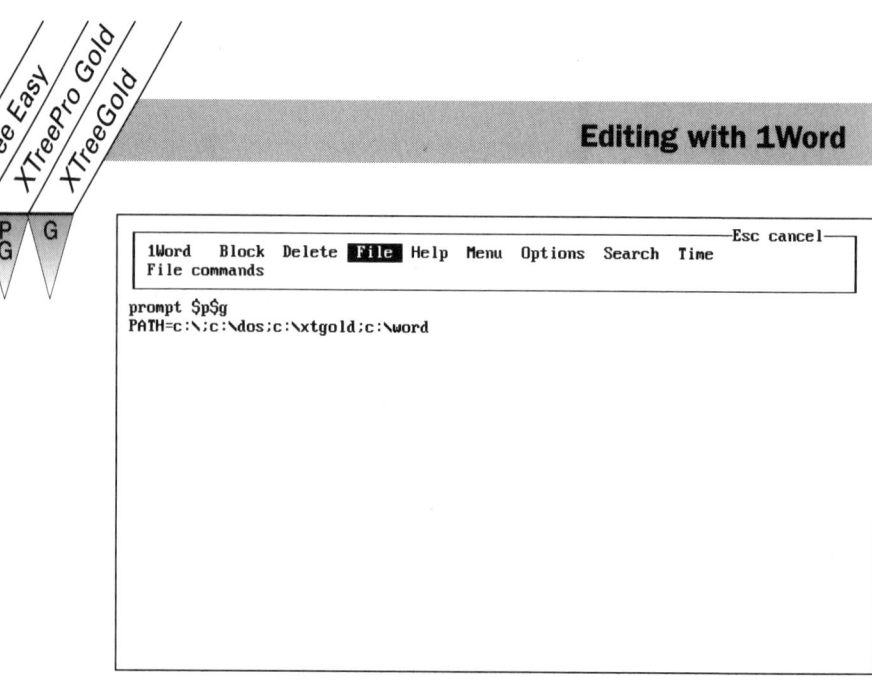

```
┌─                                                       ─Esc cancel─┐
│ 1Word    Block   Delete  File  Help  Menu  Options  Search  Time   │
│ File commands                                                      │
prompt $p$g
PATH=c:\;c:\dos;c:\xtgold;c:\word
```

Figure 3-57: Pressing Esc twice while in edit mode reveals the additional editing and file commands at the top of the screen.

If you press Esc twice while in edit mode, some additional editing and file commands appear at the top of the screen, as shown in Figure 3-57. When you're finished editing, press Esc once and the Quit Commands window, shown in Figure 3-58, pops up. You can either quit and save or quit without saving. Highlight whichever option you prefer and press Enter; you'll be out of 1Word and back where you started from.

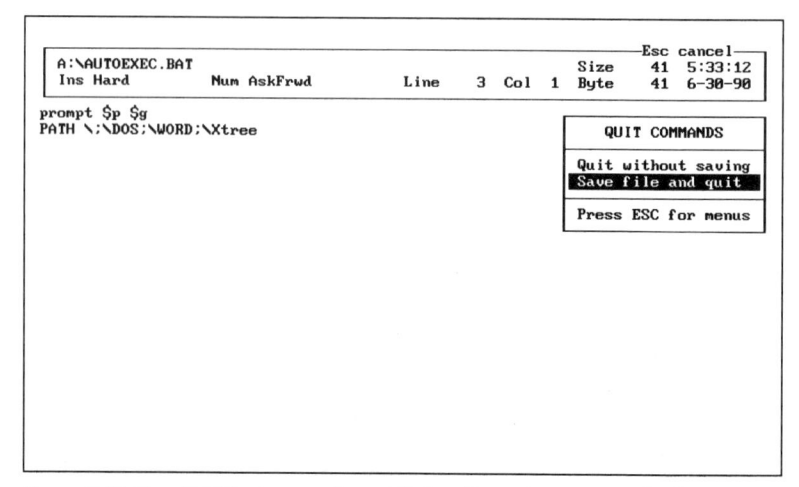

```
┌─                                                            ─Esc cancel─┐
│ A:\AUTOEXEC.BAT                                  Size   41   5:33:12    │
│ Ins Hard         Num AskFrwd       Line  3  Col 1  Byte   41   6-30-90  │
prompt $p $g
PATH \;\DOS;\WORD;\Xtree                          ┌─ QUIT COMMANDS ──────┐
                                                  │ Quit without saving  │
                                                  │ Save file and quit   │
                                                  ├──────────────────────┤
                                                  │ Press ESC for menus  │
                                                  └──────────────────────┘
```

Figure 3-58: To exit 1Word, press Esc while in edit mode to pop up the Quit Commands window, and press Enter while `Save file and quit` is highlighted.

Creating a new file with 1Word

To create a new text file in Pro Gold or Gold, put your cursor on the directory where you want the new file to appear and press E for Edit. Give the new file a name by typing it and pressing Enter. 1Word appears and you can go ahead and create your document. When you have finished writing and editing your file, press Esc once, highlight Save and Exit on your screen and press Enter.

If you want to save a file under a different name, press Ctrl-K-A and modify the name shown on-screen.

Making Edit launch your word processor

You can use XTreePro Gold and XTree Gold's Configuration program (see "Configuration Options," earlier in this chapter) to designate *any* word processing program to be the one that launches with the Edit command (it doesn't have to be 1Word). To swap your favorite word processor with 1Word, go into Gold's Configuration program (press Alt-F10). Once inside the Configuration program, take the following steps.

Steps: Configuring Edit to launch your word processor

Step 1. Press 1 to Modify configuration items.

Step 2. Press Enter three times to skip to Page 4.

Step 3. Press 2 to select the Editor program.

Step 4. At the bottom of the screen, type in the full pathname and program name of your word processor, for instance C:\WORD5\WORD.EXE or C:\WP\WP.EXE.

Step 5. Press Esc to return to the main menu.

Step 6. Choose S and Y to save your changes and exit.

Before you decide to make the swap, however, remember that most full-featured word processor programs embed non-ASCII characters in your batch files that can prevent them from working. If you want to use your word processor to edit or create batch files, you must remember to save such files in text or ASCII mode. In any case, you can always go back into the Configuration program and swap 1Word back in!

Execute   Command

See The Application Menu, The Command Shell, and Open (and Associate).

In computer terminology, the word *execute* means to carry out or perform a task or command (as in execute orders). You can execute programs and batch files and DOS commands.

XTree's Execute command gives you the ability to execute programs, batch files, and DOS commands from *inside* XTree. Even when you activate other programs from inside XTree and XTree disappears from the screen, its not really *entirely* gone. While you work on your application, a kernel of XTree is, like an attentive servant, waiting silently in the background until it's called upon. Once you exit your application, XTree automatically pops up again, ready to escort you to your next destination. Using XTree as a DOS shell in this way means that you can use XTree as your command center.

Using Execute with all versions of XTree

Executing programs from within XTree is simple: just highlight the program's name in a File window, press X, and then press Enter. In the example shown in Figure 3-59, CHECK.EXE is highlighted. (You'll have to find the program name for the program you want to launch — WORD.EXE for Microsoft Word or WP.EXE for WordPerfect, for example.)

Once you press X (to Execute), XTree delivers you to its Command shell, with the program's name typed in on the command line for you. In the example in Figure 3-60, the CHECK.EXE program highlighted in Figure 3-59 has been placed on the command line in the XTree Command shell. All that's necessary for running CHECK.EXE at this point is to press Enter.

When you finish using a program you launch in this manner, you will be delivered back to XTree's Command shell. Figure 3-61 shows the Command shell for XTreePro, and Figure 3-62 shows the Command shell for XTreePro Gold and XTreeGold. At this point you can either type in another command or, to get back into XTree, press Enter without specifying a command.

Chapter 3: XTree for DOS Quick Reference Guide

```
Path: \CHECK
 BOFA89   .ACT     CHECK3   .EXE           FILE: *.*
 BOFA89   .BGT     CHECK4   .EXE
 BOFA89   .CHK     CHKRTM   .EXE           DISK: C: POWER USER
 BOFA89   .DEF     ORDER    .BAT           Available
 BOFA89   .DTA     PATHTEST.                   Bytes: 2,158,592
 BOFA89   .GRP     REMINDER.EXE
 BOFA89   .SOR     SETUP    .EXE           DIRECTORY Stats
 BOFA89   .ZIP                              Total
 BOFA90   .ACT                                Files:           26
 BOFA90   .BGT                                Bytes:      786,291
 BOFA90   .DEF                              Matching
 BOFA90   .DTA                                Files:           26
 BOFA90   .GRP                                Bytes:      786,291
 BOFA90   .SOR                              Tagged
▌CHECK    .EXE▐                               Files:            0
 CHECK    .PRO                                Bytes:            0
 CHECK1R  .ZIP                              Current File
 CHECK2   .EXE                                CHECK       EXE
 CHECK2R  .ZIP                                Bytes:       21,313

FILE       ^Attributes  ^Copy   ^Delete  Filespec  Log disk  ^Move  ^Print
COMMANDS   ^Rename      ^Tag    ^Untag   View      eXecute
←↑↓→ scroll   RETURN dir commands         ALT menu          F1 quit F2 help F3 cancel
```

Figure 3-59: One way to start a program from within XTree is to highlight the program's name and then press X to start the program.

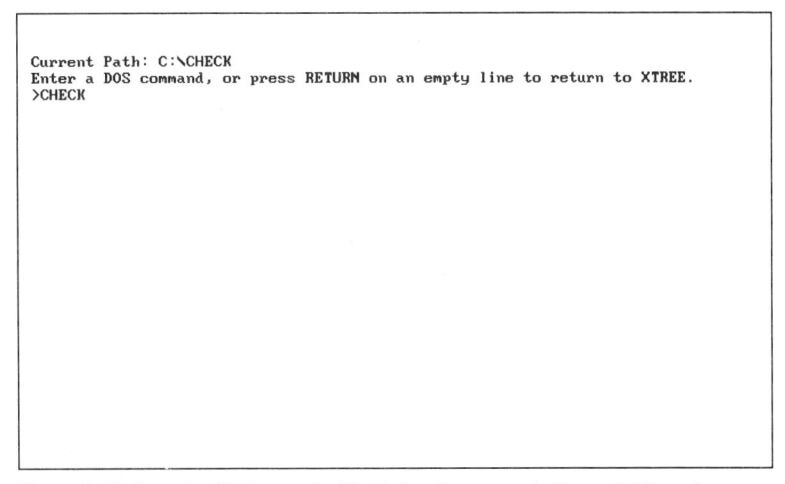

```
Current Path: C:\CHECK
Enter a DOS command, or press RETURN on an empty line to return to XTREE.
>CHECK
```

Figure 3-60: Pressing X places the highlighted program in Figure 3-59 on the command line in XTree's Command shell (your Command shell may vary depending on which version of XTree you own, but it works just the same).

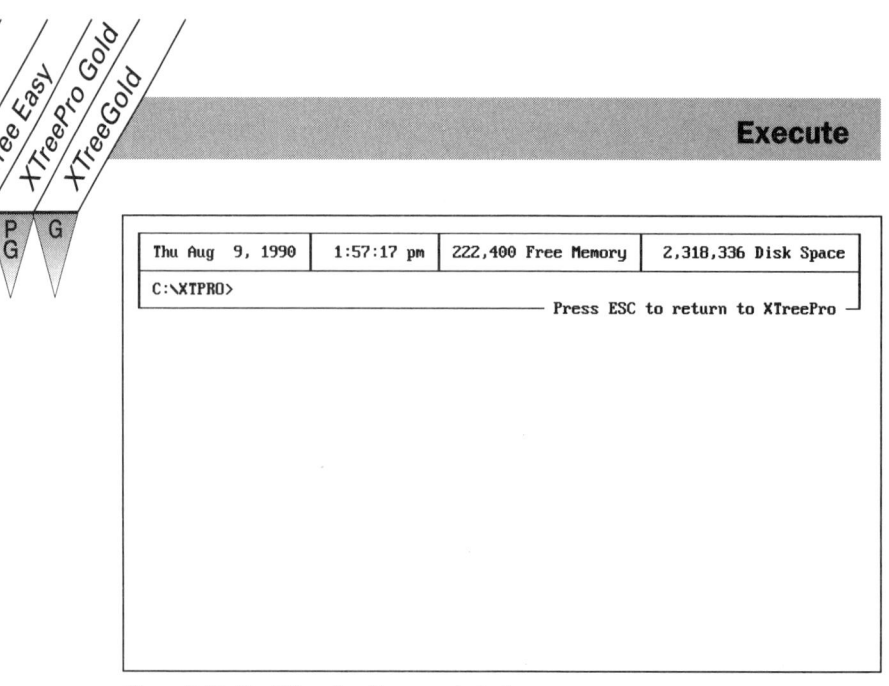

```
┌─────────────────────────────────────────────────────────────────────────┐
│  Thu Aug  9, 1990  │  1:57:17 pm  │  222,400 Free Memory │ 2,318,336 Disk Space │
├─────────────────────────────────────────────────────────────────────────┤
│  C:\XTPRO>                                                              │
│                                          ─ Press ESC to return to XTreePro ─│
│                                                                         │
│                                                                         │
│                                                                         │
│                                                                         │
│                                                                         │
│                                                                         │
│                                                                         │
└─────────────────────────────────────────────────────────────────────────┘
```

Figure 3-61: The XTreePro Command shell.

> If you receive `insufficient memory` error messages when you invoke the Command shell, enter the shell by using Alt-X instead of just X. This makes XTreePro, XTreePro Gold, XTree Easy, and XTreeGold reduce to the smallest size possible for carrying out your command.

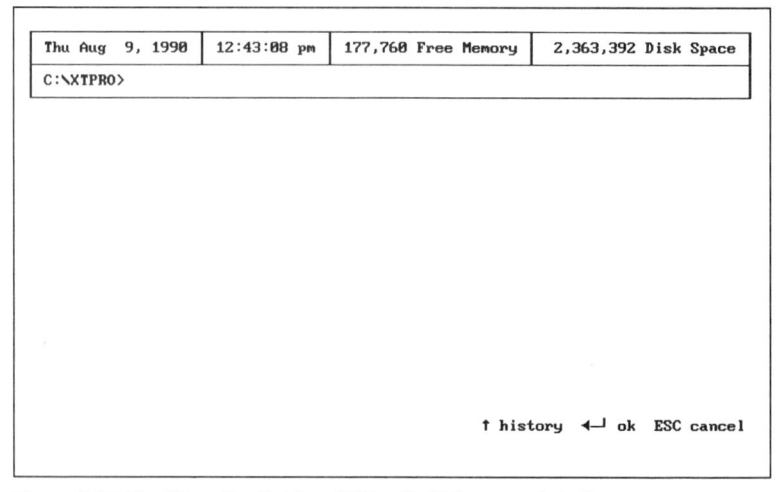

```
┌─────────────────────────────────────────────────────────────────────────┐
│  Thu Aug  9, 1990  │ 12:43:08 pm  │  177,760 Free Memory │ 2,363,392 Disk Space │
├─────────────────────────────────────────────────────────────────────────┤
│  C:\XTPRO>                                                              │
│                                                                         │
│                                                                         │
│                                                                         │
│                                                                         │
│                                                                         │
│                                                                         │
│                                          ↑ history  ←┘ ok  ESC cancel   │
└─────────────────────────────────────────────────────────────────────────┘
```

Figure 3-62: The XTreePro Gold and XTreeGold Command shell.

Chapter 3: XTree for DOS Quick Reference Guide

File Display   Command

When you view files in XTree's file windows, normally only the names are shown. However, XTree can display more information on each file, such as attributes, size, and date and time saved, via the File Display command. Figure 3-63 shows a normal file display. Filenames are listed in a three-column format. No information other than the filename appears for each file.

If you hold down the Alt key, however, the legend at the bottom of the screen changes to ALT FILE COMMANDS. Pressing F for File Display (Alt-F, for short) changes the file display to a two-column listing of files and their attributes, similar to what is shown in Figure 3-64.

If you press Alt-F once again, you get even more information than you thought possible. Take a look at Figure 3-65. Although only one column of files is displayed at this point, all sorts of other data is now available for those files (size, attributes, and date and time saved). Press Alt-F one last time to restore the file display back to the original three-column motif.

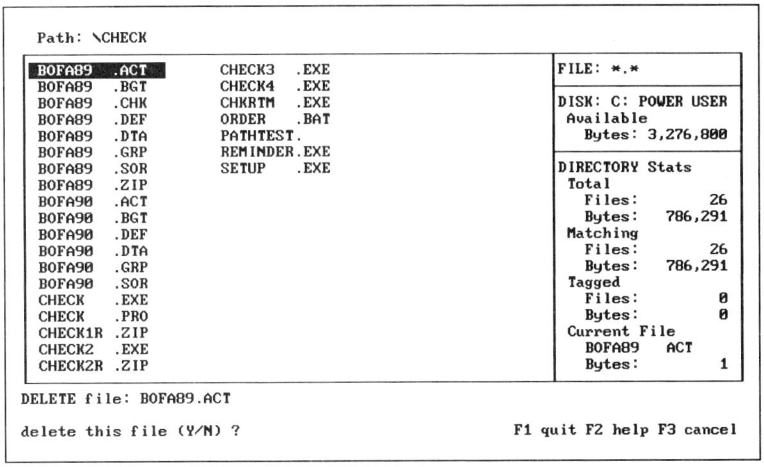

```
Path: \CHECK
┌─────────────────┬──────────────────┬──────────────────────┐
│ BOFA89    .ACT  │ CHECK3    .EXE   │ FILE: *.*            │
│ BOFA89    .BGT  │ CHECK4    .EXE   │                      │
│ BOFA89    .CHK  │ CHKRTM    .EXE   │ DISK: C: POWER USER  │
│ BOFA89    .DEF  │ ORDER     .BAT   │ Available            │
│ BOFA89    .DTA  │ PATHTEST.        │   Bytes: 3,276,800   │
│ BOFA89    .GRP  │ REMINDER.EXE     │                      │
│ BOFA89    .SOR  │ SETUP     .EXE   │ DIRECTORY Stats      │
│ BOFA89    .ZIP  │                  │ Total                │
│ BOFA90    .ACT  │                  │   Files:          26 │
│ BOFA90    .BGT  │                  │   Bytes:     786,291 │
│ BOFA90    .DEF  │                  │ Matching             │
│ BOFA90    .DTA  │                  │   Files:          26 │
│ BOFA90    .GRP  │                  │   Bytes:     786,291 │
│ BOFA90    .SOR  │                  │ Tagged               │
│ CHECK     .EXE  │                  │   Files:           0 │
│ CHECK     .PRO  │                  │   Bytes:           0 │
│ CHECK1R   .ZIP  │                  │ Current File         │
│ CHECK2    .EXE  │                  │   BOFA89      ACT    │
│ CHECK2R   .ZIP  │                  │   Bytes:           1 │
├─────────────────┴──────────────────┴──────────────────────┤
│ DELETE file: BOFA89.ACT                                   │
│ delete this file (Y/N) ?         F1 quit F2 help F3 cancel│
└───────────────────────────────────────────────────────────┘
```

Figure 3-63: A normal file display shows the filename and extension of each file in a three-column format.

File Display

```
Path: \CHECK
 BOFA89   .ACT        1   ....   CHECK3   .EXE   10,769 ....   FILE: *.*
 BOFA89   .BGT    2,162   ....   CHECK4   .EXE   48,721 ....
 BOFA89   .CHK       52   ....   CHKRTM   .EXE   70,680 ....   DISK: C: POWER USER
 BOFA89   .DEF       43   ....   ORDER    .BAT      514 ....   Available
 BOFA89   .DTA   96,860   ....   PATHTEST.              1 ....    Bytes: 2,560,000
 BOFA89   .GRP        0   ....   REMINDER .EXE    6,001 ....
 BOFA89   .SOR    1,334   ....   SETUP    .EXE   31,057 ....   DIRECTORY Stats
 BOFA89   .ZIP   18,206♦ .a..                                   Total
 BOFA90   .ACT    2,101   ....                                    Files:          26
 BOFA90   .BGT    1,973   ....                                    Bytes:     813,291
 BOFA90   .DEF       43   ....                                   Matching
 BOFA90   .DTA  106,420   ....                                    Files:          26
 BOFA90   .GRP      506   ....                                    Bytes:     813,291
 BOFA90   .SOR      678   ....                                   Tagged
 CHECK    .EXE   21,313   ....                                    Files:           3
 CHECK    .PRO    1,216   ....                                    Bytes:     280,893
 CHECK1R  .ZIP  184,353♦ .a..                                   Current File
 CHECK2   .EXE  129,953   ....                                    BOFA89    ACT
 CHECK2R  .ZIP   78,334♦ .a..                                     Bytes:           1

ALT FILE   Copy   File display   Sort criteria   Tag   Untag   eXecute
COMMANDS                                                          F1 quit
```

Figure 3-64: Alt-F changes the file display to include the size of files and their attributes.

If you have XTreePro, XTree Easy, XTreePro Gold, or XTreeGold, and you find yourself constantly changing the default file display to one of these other settings, you can change your configuration so that a one- or two-column setting is the norm. (See "Configuration Options," earlier in this chapter, to learn how to use the Configuration programs.)

```
Path: \CHECK
 BOFA89   .ACT        1   ....   4-19-90    3:40 pm   FILE: *.*
 BOFA89   .BGT    2,162   ....  12-31-89   12:53 pm
 BOFA89   .CHK       52   ....  10-04-89    8:24 am   DISK: C: POWER USER
 BOFA89   .DEF       43   ....   1-14-90   12:16 pm   Available
 BOFA89   .DTA   96,860   ....   4-19-90    3:40 pm      Bytes: 2,560,000
 BOFA89   .GRP        0   ....   1-14-90   12:16 pm
 BOFA89   .SOR    1,334   ....  12-31-89    1:37 pm   DIRECTORY Stats
 BOFA89   .ZIP   18,206♦ .a..  12-31-89    2:59 pm    Total
 BOFA90   .ACT    2,101   ....   8-06-90   11:22 am     Files:          26
 BOFA90   .BGT    1,973   ....   7-01-90    5:20 pm     Bytes:     813,291
 BOFA90   .DEF       43   ....   1-09-90    8:26 am   Matching
 BOFA90   .DTA  106,420   ....   8-06-90   11:22 am     Files:          26
 BOFA90   .GRP      506   ....   1-09-90    8:50 am     Bytes:     813,291
 BOFA90   .SOR      678   ....   8-06-90   11:22 am   Tagged
 CHECK    .EXE   21,313   ....   4-02-90    4:03 am     Files:           3
 CHECK    .PRO    1,216   ....   1-09-90    8:56 am     Bytes:     280,893
 CHECK1R  .ZIP  184,353♦ .a..   4-10-90    5:11 pm    Current File
 CHECK2   .EXE  129,953   ....   4-02-90    4:03 am     BOFA89    ACT
 CHECK2R  .ZIP   78,334♦ .a..   4-10-90    5:06 pm     Bytes:           1

ALT FILE   Copy   File display   Sort criteria   Tag   Untag   eXecute
COMMANDS                                                          F1 quit
```

Figure 3-65: Pressing Alt-F twice changes the file display to include the date and time stamp on each file.

The File Window

See Chapter 2, "XTree for DOS Basics"

Whenever your highlight rests on a filename, you are in a File window. File windows come in two sizes, Small and Expanded, and three forms, Global, Showall, and Branch. The Small file window is what you see underneath the Directory window. The Expanded file window, logically, is a larger version of the Small file window. To get to the Small file window from the Directory window, which is the default, press Enter. When you press Enter from the Small file window, you'll end up in the Expanded file window, an example of which is shown in Figure 3-66.

For more information on the Global, Showall, and Branch file windows, refer to those sections in this chapter.

Figure 3-66: An example of the Expanded file window.

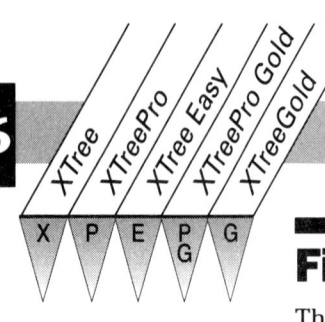

Filespec　　　　　　　　　　　　　　　　　Command

The Filespec command is for selecting a group or groups of files for display in a File window. The default file specification, which appears in the upper-right window in XTree, is the *.* wildcard. (See Chapter 1, under "Using Wildcards," for more on the asterisk and the question mark, which is the other wildcard.) Because *.* means all files, when this specification appears in the filespec window all files in a highlighted directory will appear in the File window. When you change the file specification with the Filespec command, only the files that match the file specification will appear in a File window. For example, if you set the filespec to be *.DOC, only files with the DOC extension will be visible. In addition, any file commands (Copy, Tag, Delete, and so on) you perform affect only the files currently displayed. The Filespec command can make it easier to work on a specific group of files.

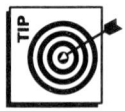

In XTree, XTreePro, and XTreePro Gold, a No Files! message appears in the file window of any directory that contains no files that meet current filespecs. Remember, No Files! doesn't mean no files at all. No Files! means there are no files in that directory which match the current file specifications. A filespec of *.* will display all files.

Understanding Filespec basics

You can use the Filespec command when you are either in the Directory window or a File window (which is 90 percent of the time). Just press F and you'll be asked to enter a filespec. In the example in Figure 3-67, *.ZIP is entered at the bottom of the screen. Pressing Enter after changing the filespec causes two things happen immediately: only files ending in ZIP are displayed in the File window, and the box in the upper-right corner of the screen now displays the new filespec, as shown in Figure 3-68.

When entering a filespec, you can use any legal combination of the asterisk (*) and question mark (?) wildcards to help single out the files you want to see. To return the filespec to normal (all files displayed), enter *.* as the filespec.

If you are looking for one particular file, type in its name and then go into a Showall file window by pressing S. (Showall reveals all the files on the entire hard drive that match the current filespec.)

Chapter 3: XTree for DOS Quick Reference Guide

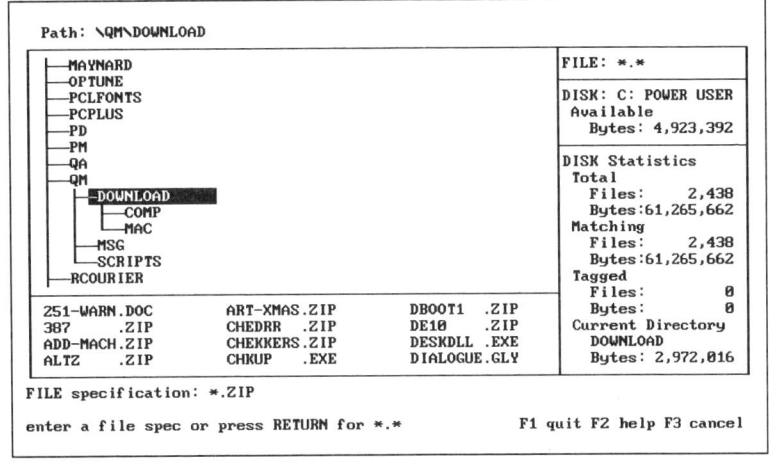

```
Path: \QM\DOWNLOAD
  ├─MAYNARD                                          FILE: *.*
  ├─OPTUNE
  ├─PCLFONTS                                         DISK: C: POWER USER
  ├─PCPLUS                                           Available
  ├─PD                                                 Bytes: 4,923,392
  ├─PM
  ├─QA                                               DISK Statistics
  └─QM                                                 Total
     ├─DOWNLOAD                                         Files:       2,438
     │   ├─COMP                                         Bytes:  61,265,662
     │   └─MAC                                        Matching
     ├─MSG                                              Files:       2,438
     └─SCRIPTS                                          Bytes:  61,265,662
  ├─RCOURIER                                         Tagged
                                                       Files:           0
 251-WARN.DOC    ART-XMAS.ZIP    DB00T1   .ZIP        Bytes:           0
 387     .ZIP    CHEDRR   .ZIP   DE10     .ZIP      Current Directory
 ADD-MACH.ZIP    CHEKKERS.ZIP    DESKDLL  .EXE        DOWNLOAD
 ALTZ    .ZIP    CHKUP    .EXE   DIALOGUE.GLY         Bytes:   2,972,016

FILE specification: *.ZIP
enter a file spec or press RETURN for *.*      F1 quit F2 help F3 cancel
```

Figure 3-67: Press F for Filespec and enter a new a file specification. In this example, the file specification is *.ZIP.

You'll immediately see the file's name and path displayed. In the example in Figure 3-69 the filespec *.BAK was entered and then the Showall command was issued. As you can see, all the BAK files stored on the hard disk now appear in the Showall file window. You can now perform file operations on all such files in this situation.

```
Path: \QM\DOWNLOAD
 387     .ZIP    LZESHL   .ZIP   REMOVE  .ZIP     FILE: *.ZIP
 ADD-MACH.ZIP    MAKEBA   .ZIP   SAYINV  .ZIP
 ALTZ    .ZIP    MOREMAC  .ZIP   SCRIPT  .ZIP     DISK: C: POWER USER
 ART-XMAS.ZIP    MOUSE624.ZIP    SERMON  .ZIP     Available
 CHEDRR   .ZIP   MSAPP21  .ZIP   SETENV  .ZIP       Bytes: 4,923,392
 CHEKKERS.ZIP    MSMOUSE7.ZIP    SETPTH14.ZIP
 DB00T1   .ZIP   MSWITCH  .ZIP   SHELLP  .ZIP     DIRECTORY Stats
 DE10    .ZIP    MW5ART   .ZIP   ST251ART.ZIP       Total
 DISKBUFF.ZIP    NAMER    .ZIP   STUFFKEY.ZIP         Files:          77
 DMVTEST .ZIP    NEWDOS   .ZIP   SUBMIT  .ZIP         Bytes:   2,972,016
 EDIAL12 .ZIP    NOJTY    .ZIP   TECHREF .ZIP     Matching
 ENVMACRO.ZIP    NOTOLLS  .ZIP   TURBOEMS.ZIP         Files:          51
 FFM10   .ZIP    NPAD     .ZIP   UXARC   .ZIP         Bytes:   1,909,212
 FONTS   .ZIP    OCR-A    .ZIP                     Tagged
 GRAB51  .ZIP    PILOT90  .ZIP                       Files:           0
 GRIDMAKR.ZIP    POSTBINS.ZIP                        Bytes:           0
 HP3-MS  .ZIP    PRN2FILE.ZIP                     Current File
 L3HPGL  .ZIP    PUMA100  .ZIP                       387        ZIP
 LJTODJ  .ZIP    RECONFIG.ZIP                        Bytes:      24,472

FILE         ^Attributes  ^Copy   ^Delete  Filespec  Log disk  ^Move  ^Print
COMMANDS     ^Rename  ^Tag   ^Untag  View  eXecute
 ←↑↓ scroll   RETURN dir commands   ALT menu        F1 quit F2 help F3 cancel
```

Figure 3-68: What do these files have in common? They all end in ZIP! The FILE: window in the upper-right corner shows that the filespec was set to *.ZIP.

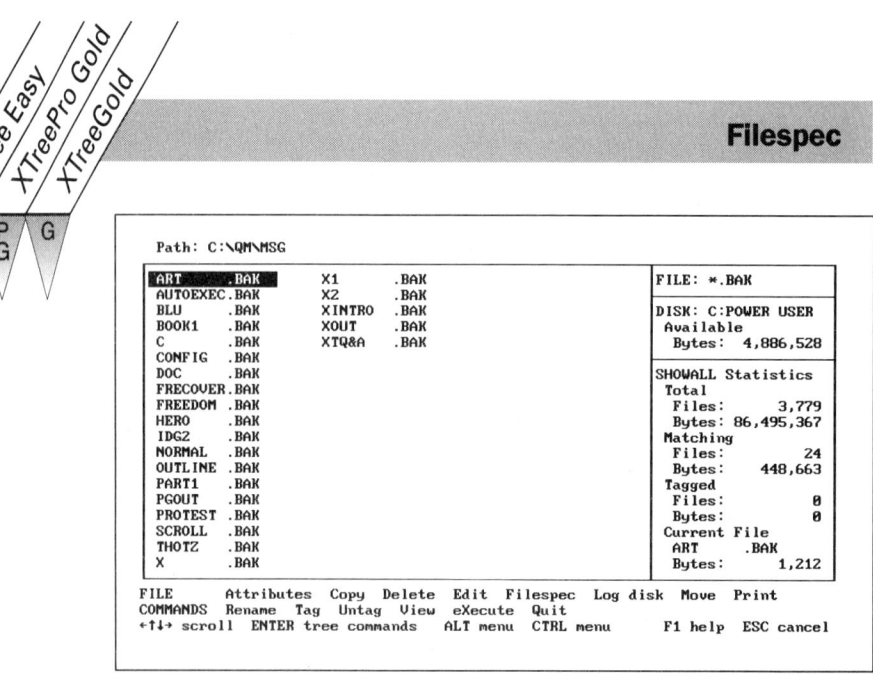

Figure 3-69: Find any file on your hard disk by using the Filespec and Showall commands.

Using multiple filespecs

Although you'll usually need to enter only one filespec at a time, some versions of XTree let you enter more than one filespec. This feature allows you to specify that more than one kind of file will be displayed. For example, you may want to see all DOC files and their corresponding BAK files.

XTreePro and multiple filespecs

XTreePro allows you to enter not just one, but up to *four* different filespecs (separated by commas). Figure 3-70 shows an XTreePro screen. The four filespecs, DOC, CMP, MSS, and TXT, shown at the bottom of the screen, limit the display in the File window to files with any of those four extensions. Be sure to separate the specs with commas.

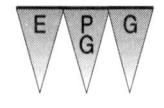

XTree Easy, XTreePro Gold, and XTreeGold and multiple filespecs

The advanced versions of XTree allow you to enter not just one, not just four, but up to *sixteen* different specifications. That means you could enter *.DOC *.BAK *.TXT A*.* (with these later versions, you can separate filespecs with either a space or a comma), press

Chapter 3: XTree for DOS Quick Reference Guide

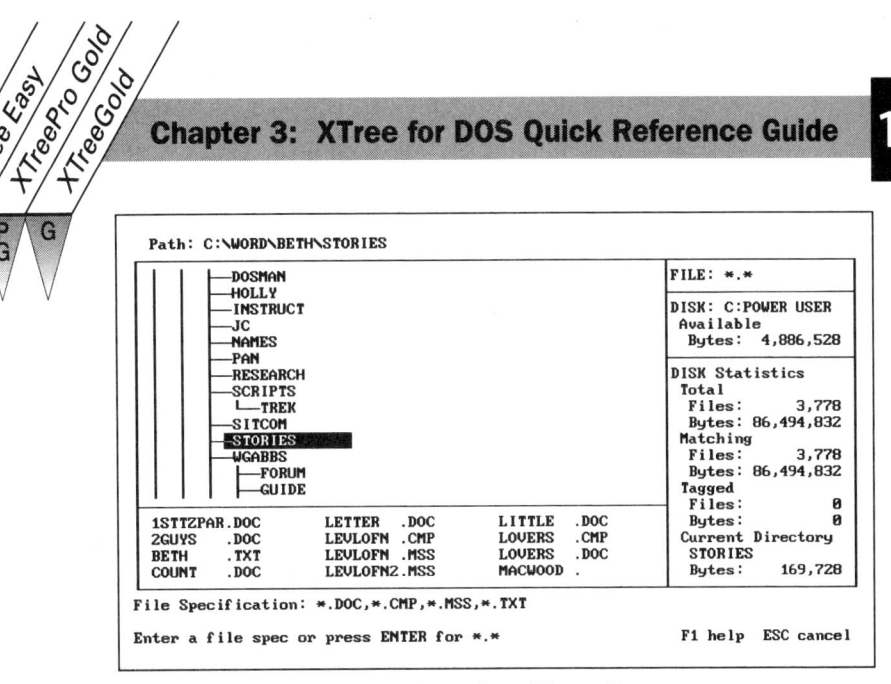

```
Path: C:\WORD\BETH\STORIES
        ├─DOSMAN                                FILE: *.*
        ├─HOLLY
        ├─INSTRUCT                              DISK: C:POWER USER
        ├─JC                                    Available
        ├─NAMES                                   Bytes:      4,886,528
        ├─PAN
        ├─RESEARCH                              DISK Statistics
        ├─SCRIPTS                               Total
        │  └─TREK                                 Files:          3,778
        ├─SITCOM                                  Bytes:     86,494,832
        ▓STORIES▓                               Matching
        └─WGABBS                                  Files:          3,778
           ├─FORUM                                Bytes:     86,494,832
           └─GUIDE                              Tagged
                                                  Files:              0
 1STTZPAR.DOC    LETTER  .DOC    LITTLE  .DOC     Bytes:              0
 2GUYS   .DOC    LEVLOFN .CMP    LOVERS  .CMP   Current Directory
 BETH    .TXT    LEVLOFN .MSS    LOVERS  .DOC   STORIES
 COUNT   .DOC    LEVLOFN2.MSS    MACWOOD .        Bytes:        169,728

 File Specification: *.DOC,*.CMP,*.MSS,*.TXT
 Enter a file spec or press ENTER for *.*          F1 help  ESC cancel
```

Figure 3-70: XTreePro is allowed up to four different filespecs.

Enter, and all files meeting at least one of those filespecs will be displayed.

It gets better. XTree Easy, XTreePro Gold, and XTreeGold also allow *Exclusionary specifications.* That means you can say "I want everything *except* . . .," and exclude certain file types from being displayed. This feature works just like a normal filespec: press F for filespec to start and then enter the filespecs. The only difference is that you type a minus sign (–) in front of the filespec(s) you want to exclude. For instance, –*.DOC displays all files *except* those ending in DOC.

WARNING: If you use an exclusionary filespec in a list of specifications, make sure the exclusionary specification is listed *first*. If not, it will be ignored.

Finally, lucky XTreeGold 2.5 users can also preselect filespecs when they activate the program. If you're starting XTreeGold 2.5 with a mission — to boldly seek out all DOC files — then just type **XTGOLD *.DOC**, press Enter, and the filespec *.DOC will be automatically fed into the program. Then, when you enter a File window, only those files ending in DOC will be visible.

You can save even more keystrokes (and isn't saving keystrokes the key to happiness?) by using the command **XTGOLD \WORD *.DOC** to start XTreeGold 2.5. This command logs only the Word directory (you don't have to wait for the whole drive to log) and displays only those files ending in DOC.

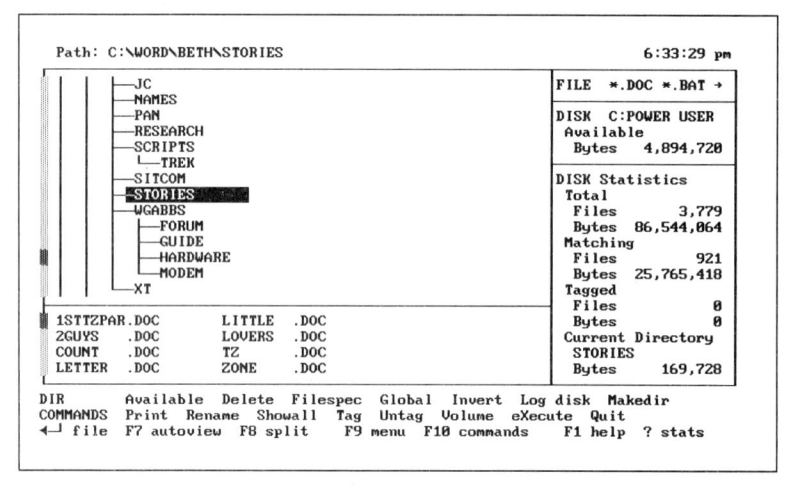

```
Path: C:\WORD\BETH\STORIES                                    6:33:29 pm
            ├─JC                               FILE   *.DOC *.BAT →
            ├─NAMES
            ├─PAN                              DISK   C:POWER USER
            ├─RESEARCH                         Available
            ├─SCRIPTS                              Bytes      4,894,720
            │ └─TREK
            ├─SITCOM                           DISK Statistics
            ├─STORIES                          Total
            ├─WGABBS                               Files          3,779
            │ ├─FORUM                              Bytes     86,544,064
            │ ├─GUIDE                          Matching
            │ ├─HARDWARE                           Files            921
            │ └─MODEM                              Bytes     25,765,418
            └─XT                               Tagged
                                                   Files              0
 1STTZPAR.DOC      LITTLE  .DOC                    Bytes              0
 2GUYS   .DOC      LOVERS  .DOC                Current Directory
 COUNT   .DOC      TZ      .DOC                    STORIES
 LETTER  .DOC      ZONE    .DOC                    Bytes        169,728

 DIR        Available Delete   Filespec  Global  Invert  Log disk Makedir
 COMMANDS   Print     Rename   Showall   Tag     Untag   Volume   eXecute Quit
 ←┘ file    F7 autoview  F8 split   F9 menu  F10 commands  F1 help  ? stats
```

Figure 3-71: The FILE: window sports a right arrow, indicating a long-winded file specification.

> **NOTE:** A lengthy file specification will not fit in the tiny filespec window. The little arrow shown in Figure 3-71 tells you there's more. If you forget what filespecs you've entered, press F (for filespecs) and they'll be listed at the bottom of the screen.

Using the Filespec History feature

In XTreePro, XTreePro Gold, XTree Easy, and XTreeGold, the History command (the ability to recall previous responses and enter them as your current response) is available for use with the Filespec command. Whenever you see History at the bottom of your screen, pressing the up-arrow key provides you with the display of previously entered filespecs, as shown in Figure 3-72.

Using the Global file window with XTreePro Gold and XTreeGold

Since XTreePro Gold and XTreeGold allow you to log multiple drives simultaneously (for example, drive A: and drive C: and drive D:), you can enter a filespec and then press G for Global. The Global file window now displays the files on all logged drives that match the current filespec. You can do some intense searching and comparing with this feature.

Chapter 3: XTree for DOS Quick Reference Guide

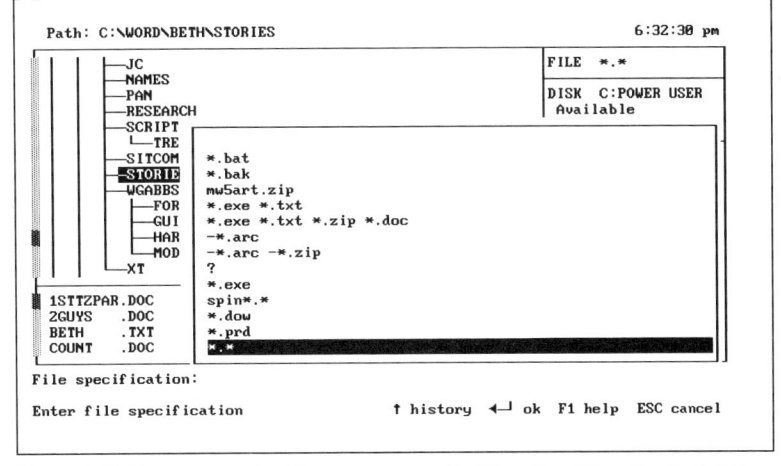

```
Path: C:\WORD\BETH\STORIES                              6:32:30 pm
        ─JC                                  ┌─────────────────────┐
        ─NAMES                               │ FILE  *.*           │
        ─PAN                                 ├─────────────────────┤
        ─RESEARCH                            │ DISK  C:POWER USER  │
        ─SCRIPT                              │       Available     │
         └─TRE                               └─────────────────────┘
        ─SITCOM    ┌──────────────────────────────┐
        ─STORIE    │ *.bat                        │
        ─WGABBS    │ *.bak                        │
         ├─FOR     │ mw5art.zip                   │
         ├─GUI     │ *.exe *.txt                  │
         ├─HAR     │ *.exe *.txt *.zip *.doc      │
         ├─MOD     │ -*.arc                       │
         └─XT      │ -*.arc -*.zip                │
                   │ ?                            │
                   │ *.exe                        │
  1STTZPAR.DOC     │ spin*.*                      │
  2GUYS   .DOC     │ *.dow                        │
  BETH    .TXT     │ *.prd                        │
  COUNT   .DOC     │ *.*                          │
                   └──────────────────────────────┘
  File specification:
  Enter file specification              ↑ history  ↵ ok  F1 help  ESC cancel
```

Figure 3-72: You can use the History command in XTreePro, XTreePro Gold, XTree Easy, and XTreeGold to select previously used filespecs.

Using Invert with XTreePro Gold and XTreeGold

You can *invert* an existing filespec by using the Invert command. Press I for Invert; all the files that *don't* match the filespec will be displayed in a File window. Take a look at Figure 3-73; in this figure, *.DOC is the specified filespec. After pressing I to activate Invert, a choice between inverting filespecs or tags is offered. Choose F for File Specifications to reveal the files that do *not* end in DOC. When you select the Invert command, your display switches to reverse

```
Path: C:\WORD\BETH\XT                                     7:38:45 pm
 13260957.                              ┌─────────────────────────┐
 BOOK1    .BAK                          │ FILE  *.DOC             │
 IDG2     .BAK                          ├─────────────────────────┤
 MC4      .TXT                          │ DISK  C:POWER USER      │
 NORMAL   .BAK                          │       Available         │
 NORMAL   .GLY                          │       Bytes  4,882,432  │
 OUTLINE  .BAK                          ├─────────────────────────┤
 OUTLINE  .STY                          │ DIRECTORY Stats         │
 PART1    .BAK                          │ Total                   │
 TEST     .BAT                          │   Files           42    │
 THOTZ    .BAK                          │   Bytes      958,703    │
 X        .BAK                          │ Matching                │
 X        .STY                          │   Files           19    │
 X1       .BAK                          │   Bytes      698,095    │
 X2       .BAK                          │ Tagged                  │
 XINTRO   .BAK                          │   Files            0    │
 XOUT     .BAK                          │   Bytes            0    │
 XTQ8A    .BAK                          │ Current File            │
 XTREE    .CMP                          │   13260957.             │
                                        │   Bytes      360,979    │
                                        └─────────────────────────┘
 FILE       Attributes  Copy  Delete  Edit  Filespec  Invert  Log disk  Move
 COMMANDS   New date  Open  Print  Rename  Tag  Untag  View  eXecute  Quit
 ↵ tree      F7 autoview  F8 split    F9 menu  F10 commands    F1 help  ESC cancel
```

Figure 3-73: Use Invert to display all files that don't match the filespecs.

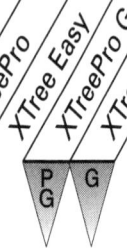

video to remind you that you're in Invert mode. To return to normal mode, just press I-F again (the Invert command is a toggle switch).

Finding Words, Files, and Directories

Locating something on a hard disk can make finding the proverbial needle in a haystack seem simple by comparison. Nothing is more frustrating than being under a deadline and not being able to remember which one of REPORT1 though REPORT24 files has that legal phrasing everyone liked. But of course, XTree has ways to find words, files, and anything else you may want to track down.

Finding a directory

To find a particular directory, move the cursor up or down the Directory tree. The directories are listed in alphabetical order. Pressing the Home key on your keyboard moves your cursor to the top of the list; pressing the End key scoots you to the bottom. You can use the PgUp and PgDn keys to move you up and down the list a screenful at a time.

XTreeGold 2.5 users can jump straight to a directory, rather than scrolling, scrolling, scrolling. If you're looking for the WINDOWS directory, press Shift-W (the first letter of the WINDOWS directory) and you'll be transported to the first directory that starts with that letter. You may have to repeat the Shift-*letter* combination a couple of times until you land on the directory of your desires.

Finding a file on the currently logged disk(s)

To find a file on the currently logged drive, use the Filespec command (press F) and enter the name of the file you want to find. Press S for Showall, and all the files on the current drive that match your filespec will be displayed. The file's location, or path, will also be displayed at the top of the screen. This method is a quick and easy way to find duplicate files.

Since XTreePro Gold and XTreeGold allow you to log onto more than one drive at a time, you can also search for a file in all of your drives. Just press F, enter the name of the file you want to find, and then press G for Global; all the files (on all the logged drives) matching your filespec will be displayed, including their drives and pathnames.

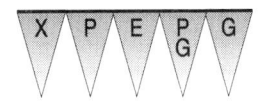

Finding a file on floppies

Here's the scenario: you need to find a file that is somewhere on one of several floppy disks. The easiest way to find a file is to enter the filespecs of the long-lost file and then keep logging new disks until the file appears in the window. The easiest way, however, isn't always the easiest thing to accomplish. The method is different with each subsequent release of XTree, as you'll see in the following sections.

Using XTree to find files on floppy disks

First, use the Filespec command to enter the filespec of the filename you want to find, and then press F5 (XTree's undocumented Keep Filespec function key). You have to ask for the filespec to stay the same, because XTree normally defaults the filespec to *.* whenever you log another drive. Put your first floppy in the A: drive and log it with the L command. If the file is on that floppy, you'll see it displayed on-screen (and `Matching File Statistics`, in the window on the right, will change from zero). If the file isn't on that floppy, take it out, put the next one in, and log it, Danno.

Using XTreePro to find files on floppy disks

If you know in advance, before you start XTreePro, that you're on a file-hunting mission, then you can invoke XTreePro by typing **XTPRO /K+**. The /K+ option tells Pro to keep the filespec you specify even when you log a new drive. After you start Pro with the /K+ option, enter the filespec you are looking for. Then put the first floppy drive you want to search on into the A: drive and log it. When `Matching File Statistics` is no longer zero, you've found your file.

Finding Words, Files, and Directories

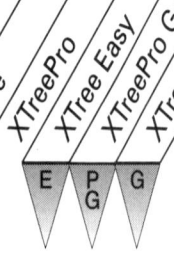

Using XTree Easy, XTreePro Gold, and XTreeGold to find files on floppy disks

Finally, in the advanced versions, XTree automatically keeps a filespec until you change it, even when you log a new drive. Get out your pile of floppies and keep logging them until `Matching File Statistics` changes from zero.

Finding text with XTreePro Gold and XTreeGold

XTreePro Gold and XTreeGold can sweep through the files on your hard disk looking for a particular word or phrase. These are the only XTree products that have a text search feature.

The first step is to tag all the files you suspect contain the word or phrase you're looking for. Or, if you don't have a clue where the text is, you can tag all files. (The more files you have tagged, however, the longer the search will take.) To tag all of your files, press S to go into a Showall file window and then press Ctrl-T to tag all files. After the suspect files are tagged, press Ctrl-S to search all tagged files. XTree then asks you to enter the text you want to find, as shown in Figure 3-74.

Figure 3-74: A Showall file window with all files tagged for searching. Ctrl-S (search) brings up the pertinent question of what word or phrase you are looking for.

Chapter 3: XTree for DOS Quick Reference Guide

Type in the word (or words) you're looking for and then press Enter. Pro Gold and Gold then search through each tagged file and untag any that do *not* contain your search phrase. When Pro Gold and Gold are finished searching, press Esc and then Ctrl-S; only the remaining tagged files (those that contain the text you're searching for) will be displayed.

If you have a number of remaining tagged files, you can highlight each file, one by one, and press V for View. The contents of the highlighted file will be displayed, with the search phrase highlighted, as shown in Figure 3-75. (See "View" for more about this command.)

Finding text over several logged drives

With XTreePro Gold and XTreeGold, you can find text over several logged drives. Use the same sequence of steps just discussed, but instead of using the Showall file window, use the Global file window.

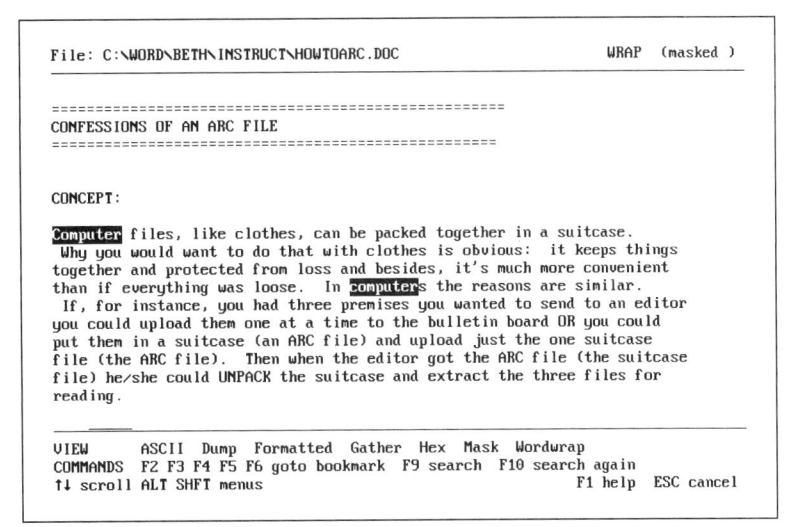

```
File: C:\WORD\BETH\INSTRUCT\HOWTOARC.DOC                    WRAP   (masked )


===========================================================
CONFESSIONS OF AN ARC FILE
===========================================================


CONCEPT:

  Computer files, like clothes, can be packed together in a suitcase.
   Why you would want to do that with clothes is obvious:  it keeps things
  together and protected from loss and besides, it's much more convenient
  than if everything was loose.  In computers the reasons are similar.
   If, for instance, you had three premises you wanted to send to an editor
  you could upload them one at a time to the bulletin board OR you could
  put them in a suitcase (an ARC file) and upload just the one suitcase
  file (the ARC file).  Then when the editor got the ARC file (the suitcase
  file) he/she could UNPACK the suitcase and extract the three files for
  reading.


VIEW       ASCII  Dump  Formatted  Gather  Hex  Mask  Wordwrap
COMMANDS   F2 F3 F4 F5 F6 goto bookmark   F9 search  F10 search again
↑↓ scroll ALT SHFT menus                             F1 help  ESC cancel
```

Figure 3-75: The text searched for is highlighted when you View a file that has gone through the search process.

Formatting Floppy Disks

Floppy disks must be *formatted* before you can use them. Formatting allows DOS to lay down a magnetic system for recording and retrieving information — sort of like an "electronic honeycomb." These days, you can buy disks that have been preformatted. If you find formatting disks a chore, you can spend a little extra to have someone else do it for you.

How can you tell if it's formatted?

From the outside, an unformatted disk looks exactly like a formatted one. When you format an already formatted disk (called *reformatting*), you erase anything that might be stored on it. You can see why it's a good idea, if you're not sure, to verify that a floppy disk isn't already formatted and storing valuable information before you give that format command. To determine whether the disk is or isn't formatted, you can use XTree's Log command.

To do this, put the suspect floppy in the drive and press L for Log. When XTree asks you for the drive to log onto, type **A** (or **B**, as the case may be). After you type A, there will be a pause and one of two things will happen:

- You'll get an error message, which you can interpret to mean that the disk is *not* formatted and you should cancel the Log command.

- The disk will log normally, indicating that the disk is *already* formatted.

The difference between high-density and low-density floppies

Both 5 ¼- and 3 ½-inch floppy drives come in either low-density (also known as double-density) or high-density flavors. Density refers to, basically, how much information can be stored on the disk.

A low-density drive can format only low-density disks. A high-density drive can, theoretically, format both high- and low-density disks. A word of caution: some computers (mostly older

Chapter 3: XTree for DOS Quick Reference Guide

computers) with high-density drives cannot format low-density disks very well — the low density disk may work fine in *your* high-density drive computer, but not on any other machine. You can experiment to see if a low-density disk you format on your high-density drive can be read in another machine, but you'd better keep copies of important files you transfer to low-density disks until you know the target computer can read them. The newer the computer, the better the chances are the low-density disk can be read by other high-density machines.

Formatting floppies with XTree and XTreePro

Neither XTree nor XTreePro have a format disk feature built in; you have to do it the old-fashioned way, via DOS.

To format a disk using DOS, press X to get to the Command shell prompt (see "The Command Shell," earlier in this chapter). Then, type FORMAT A: and press Enter (or FORMAT B: and press Enter if you want to format a floppy in drive B:). These commands assume that you've got a low-density disk in a low-density drive or a high-density disk in a high-density drive. There is a different DOS command for formatting a low-density disk in a high-density drive.

After you've entered the FORMAT command, DOS instructs you to put a disk in the drive (whether there's one already in the drive or not) and press any key (or press Enter). After you do this, the formatting process commences. You'll thrill to the visual feedback of heads and cylinders being counted. When the formatting concludes, you'll be given the chance to format another disk. If this is what you want, press Y, insert another floppy, and press Enter; if you're already bored with the project, press N to end the process.

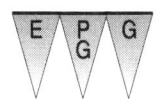

Formatting floppies with XTree Easy, XTreePro Gold, and XTreeGold

If you have a later version of XTree, there's a wonderfully convenient way to format disks — just press Alt-F2. If you've got more than one floppy drive, the program asks which drive you want to format. Once you've selected your drive, you'll be asked to select your media, as shown in Figure 3-76.

Formatting Floppy Disks

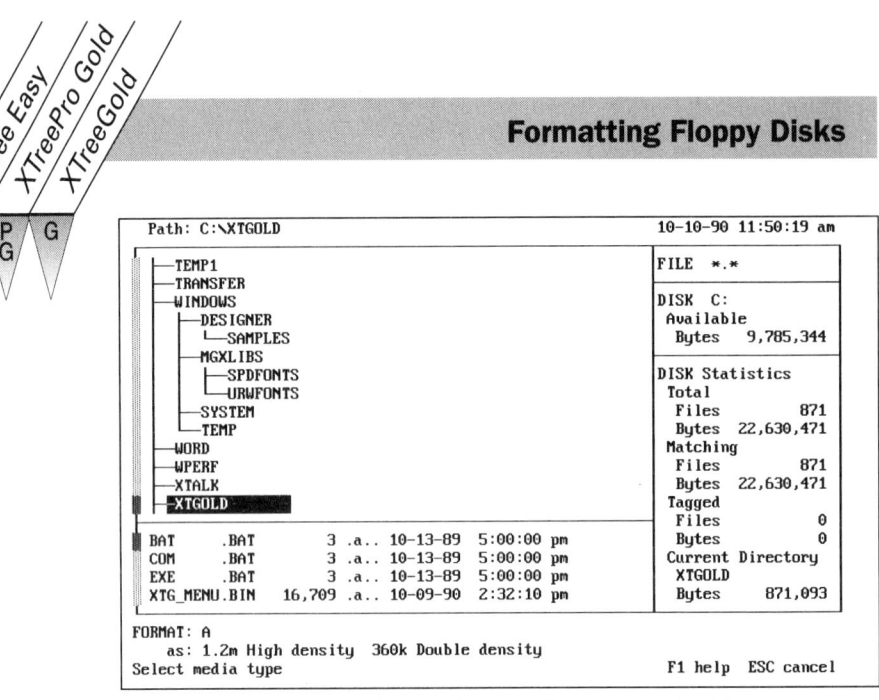

```
Path: C:\XTGOLD                                    10-10-90 11:50:19 am
   ├─TEMP1                                    FILE  *.*
   ├─TRANSFER
   ├─WINDOWS                                  DISK  C:
   │   ├─DESIGNER                             Available
   │   │   └─SAMPLES                             Bytes      9,785,344
   │   ├─MGXLIBS
   │   │   ├─SPDFONTS                         DISK Statistics
   │   │   └─URWFONTS                         Total
   │   ├─SYSTEM                                  Files             871
   │   └─TEMP                                    Bytes      22,630,471
   ├─WORD                                     Matching
   ├─WPERF                                       Files             871
   ├─XTALK                                       Bytes      22,630,471
   ├─XTGOLD                                   Tagged
                                                 Files               0
 BAT       .BAT       3 .a.. 10-13-89 5:00:00 pm  Bytes               0
 COM       .BAT       3 .a.. 10-13-89 5:00:00 pm Current Directory
 EXE       .BAT       3 .a.. 10-13-89 5:00:00 pm  XTGOLD
 XTG_MENU.BIN    16,709 .a.. 10-09-90 2:32:10 pm  Bytes         871,093

FORMAT: A
     as: 1.2m High density   360k Double density
Select media type                                     F1 help  ESC cancel
```

Figure 3-76: After pressing Alt-F2 to format a disk, you must decide whether you're formatting a high-density or low-density disk.

What the heck is *media*? Media is simply a fancy way of referring to your floppy disk. XTree wants to know whether your floppy disk is high density or low density (also known as double density). After you respond appropriately, the formatting process begins. You'll see the cylinders, sides, and sectors being counted, as shown in Figure 3-77, so you know that things are moving forward.

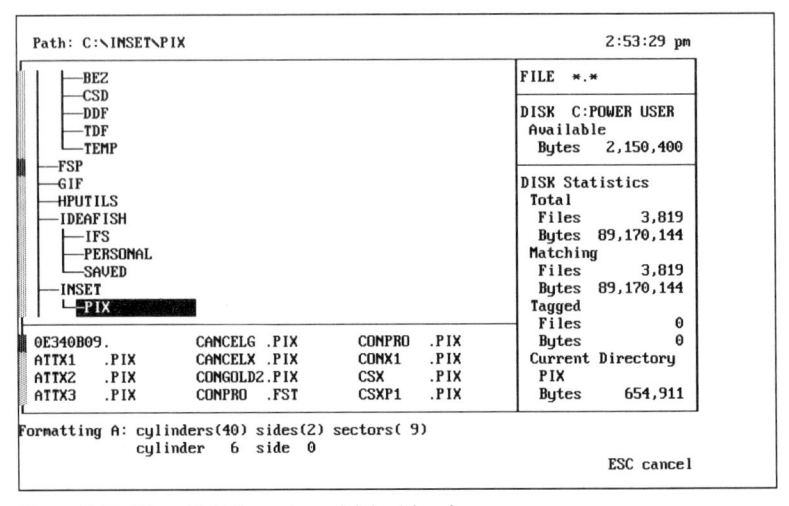

```
Path: C:\INSET\PIX                                         2:53:29 pm
      ├─BEZ
      ├─CSD                                    FILE  *.*
      ├─DDF
      ├─TDF                                    DISK  C:POWER USER
      └─TEMP                                   Available
   ├─FSP                                          Bytes      2,150,400
   ├─GIF
   ├─HPUTILS                                   DISK Statistics
   ├─IDEAFISH                                  Total
   │   ├─IFS                                      Files          3,819
   │   ├─PERSONAL                                 Bytes     89,170,144
   │   └─SAVED                                 Matching
   ├─INSET                                        Files          3,819
       └─PIX                                      Bytes     89,170,144
                                               Tagged
 0E340B09.        CANCELG .PIX    CONPRO  .PIX    Files              0
 ATTX1    .PIX    CANCELX .PIX    CONX1   .PIX    Bytes              0
 ATTX2    .PIX    CONGOLD2.PIX    CSX     .PIX Current Directory
 ATTX3    .PIX    CONPRO  .FST    CSXP1   .PIX  PIX
                                                  Bytes        654,911

Formatting A: cylinders(40) sides(2) sectors( 9)
             cylinder   6  side  0
                                                             ESC cancel
```

Figure 3-77: XTreeGold formats a disk in drive A:.

When the formatting process is finished, you'll be asked whether you want to format another disk. Press Enter to repeat the process or Esc to cancel any further disk formatting.

Function Keys

Function keys (those keys on your keyboard labeled "F-something") are used by many software programs to abbreviate important commands to the fewest number of keystrokes. Since XTree is basically a simple program, the need for shortcuts isn't exactly pressing (if you'll pardon the pun). In other words, XTree doesn't make much use of function keys.

Of the function key commands that XTree does use, you'll find that sometimes they work and sometimes they don't. It's not that XTree is "buggy," it's just that some of XTree's function keys have a function *only* under certain circumstances. For instance, if you're traveling up and down your directory tree, the Cancel command doesn't appear at the bottom of the screen. Why? Simply because there's no operation to cancel.

If, on the other hand, you're about to copy a bunch of files, Cancel appears as a choice at the bottom of the screen, reminding you that the operation can be canceled. As you get yourself in and out of different situations with XTree, applicable function keys appear and disappear at the bottom of the screen. So pay attention to the command menu, it is your friend. Which, if you think about it, is kind of cool.

A few function key commands — such as the Alt-Lock and Ctrl-Lock commands — are never listed as an option at the bottom of the screen. You just have to know they're there. A couple of function keys aren't even listed in the manual. A complete list of function key commands appears in Appendix A, "Shortcuts: Command Keys and Function Keys."

Global   Command

See File Display and Sort Criteria

When you issue the Global command, the file display changes to the Global file window, where you can work with files from more than one disk drive (actually, up to twenty-six) simultaneously. Think of the Global file window as a Showall file window for several drives. In a Global file window, all the files on the currently logged disks are displayed in alphabetical order. (If you prefer the files to be sorted and displayed by size or date, you can change the sort criteria to accommodate your desires. Press Alt-S to access the Sort command. (See "Sort Criteria" for details.)

Global requires that at least two drives are logged in order to work, so to use it you must log another drive (such as drive A: or drive B:) in addition to the currently logged C: drive. To log drive A:, press L and then enter the drive letter. This second drive and the previously logged one are now both in memory. After you've logged at least two drives, go to the Directory window and press G for Global, and *bingo!* All the files from the currently logged drives are displayed in alphabetical order.

In the example in Figure 3-78, the current drive is C:; however, the B: drive is also logged. The highlighted file in the figure, CONFIG.SYS, is actually located in the root of the B: drive, which is noted by the path designation at the top of the screen (Path: B:\).

You can press G to enter the Global file window from any of the currently logged drives. Once you're in the Global file window, you

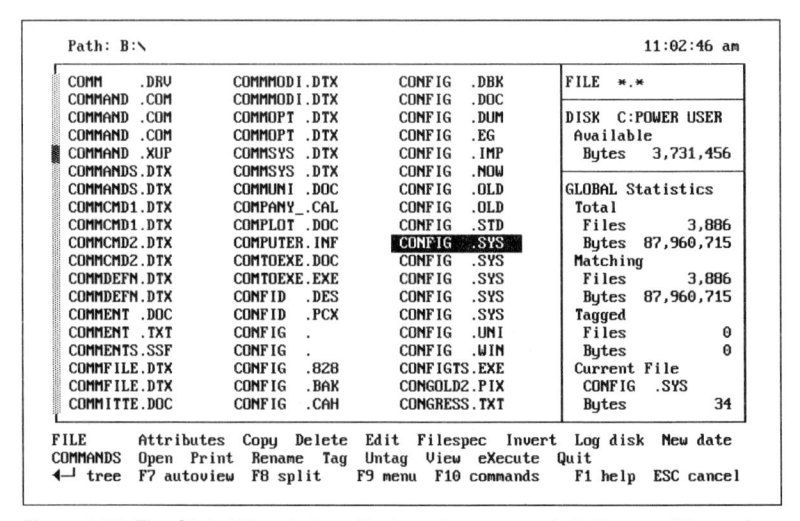

Figure 3-78: The Global file window displays the names of all files on all logged drives.

Chapter 3: XTree for DOS Quick Reference Guide

can perform any sort of function you want — delete, copy, sort, and so on. You can also can enter a filespec before or after you press G (such as *.WK1 to see all the WK1 files on all the logged drives). This method is useful when checking for duplicate filenames on different drives.

Another variation of the Global command is the Ctrl-G command. You can tag various files on each of the logged drives and press Ctrl-G to see the tagged files, only, side by side. Once the files are in view simultaneously, you can compare file attributes, copy files, delete files, or do whatever else you like.

Graft   Command

See "Directory Management" and Copy

The Graft command enables you to move a directory (and its files and subdirectories) to a new location on the directory tree. Specific instructions on using Graft are located in "Directory Management" and "Copy."

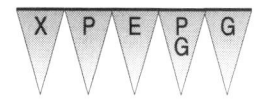

Help   Command

Each version of XTree offers some form of online help. This means that while you are using XTree, you can press the Help function key and up pops Help to come to your assistance. When you've finished using Help, you'll be returned to whatever view you were in (though, hopefully, with more smarts) before you invoked Help.

Using the Help command in XTree

XTree's help is accessed by pressing the F2 function key. When you press F2 you'll see something like what is shown in Figure 3-79, which is sort of a map of where to go for help. Pressing the up- or down-arrow key pages you through Help's contents. If you have a question about the command line, you can tell from the maplike diagram shown on-screen that the information is found on pages 6 through 9. Just press the down-arrow key until you get to page 6 and start reading. Once you're finished with Help, press Enter to return to the program — exactly where you were before you asked for Help.

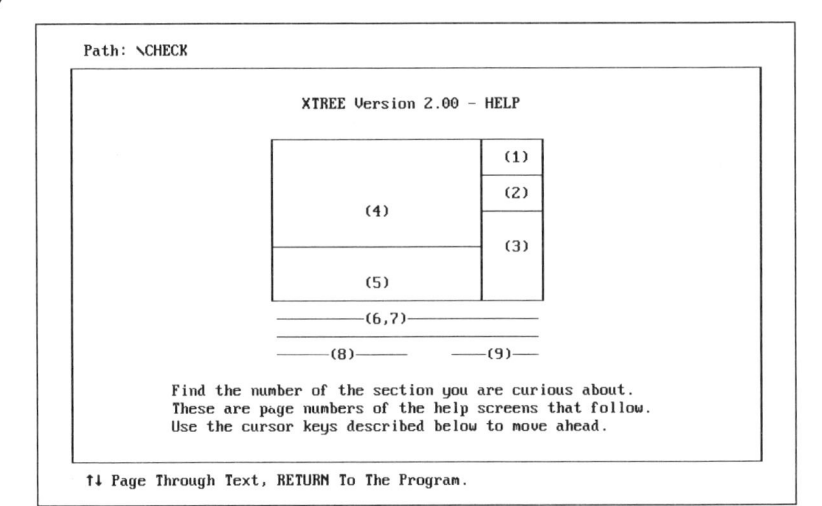

Figure 3-79: XTree's opening Help screen and map of contents.

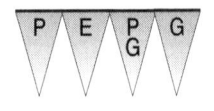

Using the Help command in XTreePro, XTreePro Gold, XTree Easy, and XTreeGold

In XTreePro, XTreePro Gold, XTree Easy, and XTreeGold, F1 is the function key for accessing Help (just like almost every other DOS program). When you press F1, you'll see something like that shown in Figure 3-80 (for XTreePro) or Figure 3-81 (for XTreeGold). The

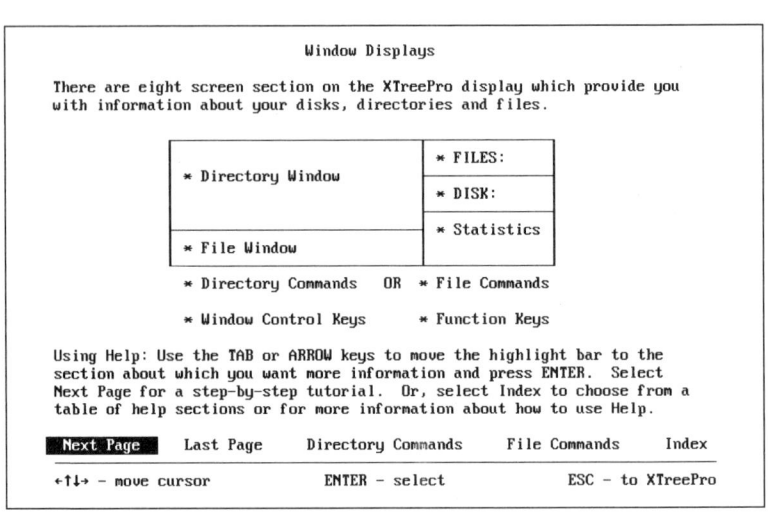

Figure 3-80: XTreePro's Help screen and map of contents.

Chapter 3: XTree for DOS Quick Reference Guide

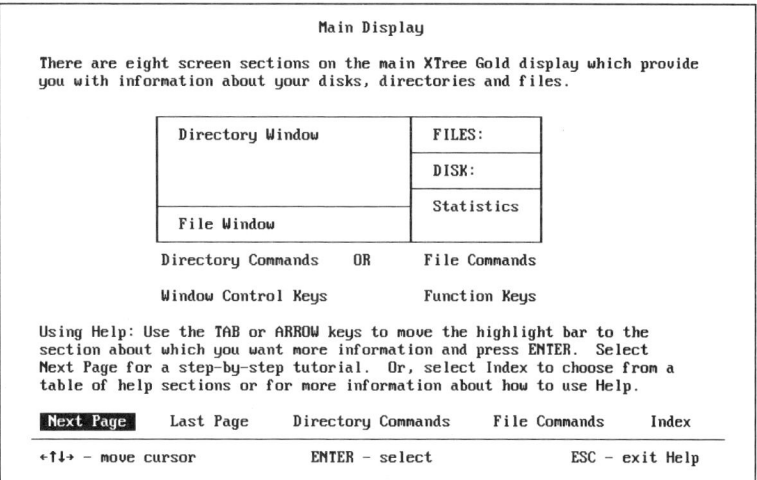

```
                          Main Display
  There are eight screen sections on the main XTree Gold display which provide
  you with information about your disks, directories and files.

         ┌─────────────────────────┬──────────────────┐
         │   Directory Window      │  FILES:          │
         │                         ├──────────────────┤
         │                         │  DISK:           │
         │                         ├──────────────────┤
         │                         │  Statistics      │
         │   File Window           │                  │
         └─────────────────────────┴──────────────────┘

         Directory Commands     OR      File Commands

         Window Control Keys            Function Keys

  Using Help: Use the TAB or ARROW keys to move the highlight bar to the
  section about which you want more information and press ENTER. Select
  Next Page for a step-by-step tutorial. Or, select Index to choose from a
  table of help sections or for more information about how to use Help.

  ▌Next Page▐   Last Page    Directory Commands    File Commands    Index

  ←↑↓→ - move cursor           ENTER - select           ESC - exit Help
```

Figure 3-81: XTreeGold's Help screen and map of contents.

Help screens function nearly identically for XTreePro Gold and XTree Easy, so if one of these two is your XTree program, you can follow along in this discussion with no problem.

Figures 3-80 and 3-81 show that you can choose from a dizzying, though helpful, array of topics. While the cursor is positioned on "Next Page," pressing Enter brings up the next screenful of alphabetically listed information. Alternatively, pressing the up-arrow from here moves the highlight to "Window Control Keys." You can use the arrow keys to highlight any other subject you're interested in learning more about and press Enter to bring up a screen of information on that selected topic. Another approach is to manipulate the cursor on over to "Index" (or save yourself some keystrokes by just pressing I) and press Enter to access the Index. The Help Index (for XTreePro) is shown in Figure 3-82. XTreeGold's Help Index is shown in Figure 3-83. As usual, if your XTree program supports a mouse, you can simply click on a subject to bring up the corresponding help screen.

You can use the cursor to move to the topic you want help with and then press Enter to get to the page with information. A nice feature about Help is that if you happen to be in the middle of an operation (copying a file, for instance) when you press F1, XTree assumes you have a question about copying (because that's what you were doing) and jettisons you directly to the Help section on copying. This feature is called *context-sensitive help* and can be very time-saving.

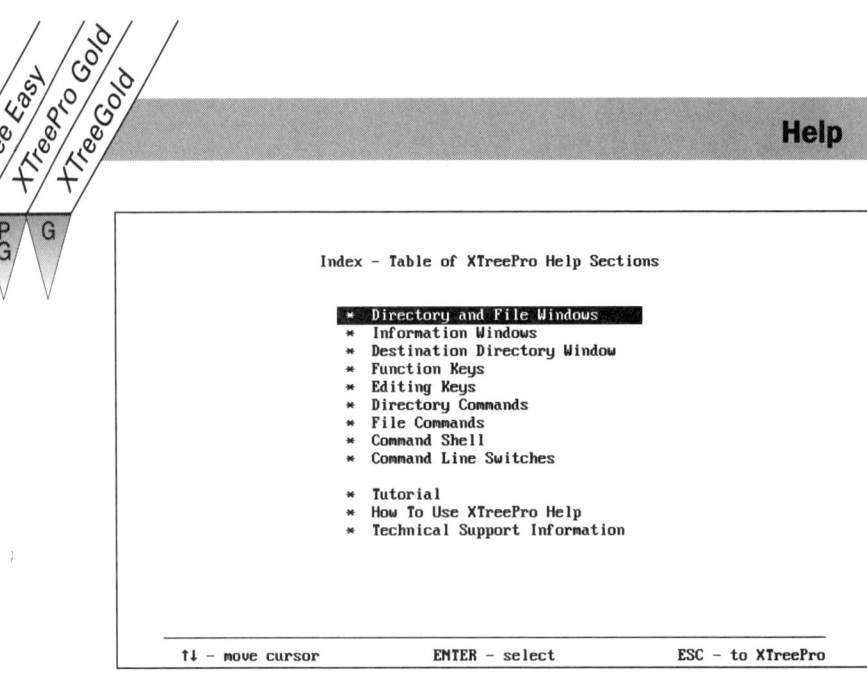

```
            Index - Table of XTreePro Help Sections

                    * Directory and File Windows
                    * Information Windows
                    * Destination Directory Window
                    * Function Keys
                    * Editing Keys
                    * Directory Commands
                    * File Commands
                    * Command Shell
                    * Command Line Switches

                    * Tutorial
                    * How To Use XTreePro Help
                    * Technical Support Information


   ↑↓ - move cursor        ENTER - select        ESC - to XTreePro
```

Figure 3-82: XTreePro's Help index.

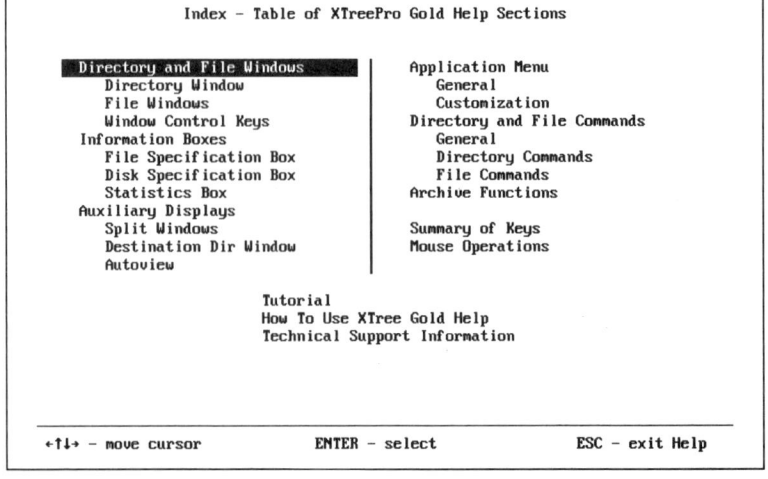

```
            Index - Table of XTreePro Gold Help Sections

       Directory and File Windows      Application Menu
           Directory Window                General
           File Windows                    Customization
           Window Control Keys         Directory and File Commands
       Information Boxes                   General
           File Specification Box          Directory Commands
           Disk Specification Box          File Commands
           Statistics Box              Archive Functions
       Auxiliary Displays
           Split Windows               Summary of Keys
           Destination Dir Window      Mouse Operations
           Autoview

                        Tutorial
                        How To Use XTree Gold Help
                        Technical Support Information


  ←↑↓→ - move cursor        ENTER - select        ESC - exit Help
```

Figure 3-83: XTreeGold's Help index.

Using XTreePro Gold's Quick Reference

XTreePro Gold is the only version of XTree that has a Quick Reference, which is a Helplike feature that provides information on all Directory and File commands. Pressing F10 from the Directory window pops up the screen shown in Figure 3-84, which details the shortcut keys that are available when you're in a Directory window. Pressing F10 from one of the File windows pops up the directory of File commands, as shown in Figure 3-85.

Chapter 3: XTree for DOS Quick Reference Guide

```
DIRECTORY COMMANDS Quick Reference          XTreePro Gold - Version 1.4

       ► WINDOW ◄              ► DISK ◄                  ► FILE ◄
File display cols ALT-F   Available space      A    Edit new file       ALT-E
Sort criteria      ALT-S  Format diskette   ALT-F2   Tag dir files            T
File spec              F  Log disk             L    Tag all files       CTRL-T
                          Print catalog        P    Tag by attribute    ALT-T
Split/close window    F8  Release disk      ALT-R   Untag dir files          U
Autoview window       F7  Volume name          V    Untag all files     CTRL-U
Extended stats window ?   Wash disk         ALT-W   Untag by attrib     ALT-U
                                                    Invert dir tags          I
Show all files         S      ► DIRECTORY ◄         Invert all tags     CTRL-I
Show all tagged   CTRL-S  Delete directory     D
Global files           G  Graft branch      ALT-G       ► SPECIAL ◄
Global tagged     CTRL-G  Hide/unhide dir   ALT-H   Application menu        F9
                          Make new dir         M    Configure          ALT-F10
                          Prune branch      ALT-P   eXecute                  X
                          Rename directory     R    eXecute             ALT-X
                          Relog directory  ALT-F3   Quit                     Q
                                                    Quit to dir         ALT-Q

Change the file window display format to 1, 2, or 3 columns
←↑↓→ point to command                                ←┘ ok    ESC cancel
```

Figure 3-84: XTreePro Gold's Directory commands in a nutshell.

In both cases, whenever you highlight a command, a quick explanation of that command is displayed at the bottom of the screen. In Figure 3-85, for instance, Alt-F, the File Display command, is highlighted. As you can see at the bottom of the screen, the explanation of how to use this key combination is displayed. To exit the Quick Reference, just press Esc and you'll go back to where you were in Pro Gold before you pressed F10.

```
FILE COMMANDS Quick Reference            XTreePro Gold - Version 1.4

       ► WINDOW ◄              ► FILE ◄                  ► FILE ◄
File display cols ALT-F   Copy tagged       CTRL-C   View tagged         CTRL-V
Sort criteria      ALT-S  Copy files/dirs   ALT-C    Tag file                 T
File spec              F  Delete file          D     Tag files           CTRL-T
Split/close window    F8  Delete tagged     CTRL-D   Tag by attribute    ALT-T
Autoview window       F7  Edit file            E     Untag file               U
Extended stats window ?   Move file            M     Untag files         CTRL-U
                          Move tagged       CTRL-M   Untag by attrib     ALT-U
         ► DISK ◄         New date             N     Invert file tag          I
Format diskette  ALT-F2   New date tagged   CTRL-N   Invert all tags     CTRL-I
Log disk              L   Open file            O     Merge tags          CTRL-F6
Release disk      ALT-R   Open file         ALT-O
                          Print file           P        ► SPECIAL ◄
         ► FILE ◄         Print tagged      CTRL-P   Application menu        F9
Attributes            A   Rename file          R     eXecute                  X
Attributes        CTRL-A  Rename tagged     CTRL-R   eXecute             ALT-X
Batch file        CTRL-B  Search tagged     CTRL-S   Quit                     Q
Copy file             C   View file            V     Quit to dir         ALT-Q

Change the file window display format to 1, 2, or 3 columns
←↑↓→ point to command                                ←┘ ok    ESC cancel
```

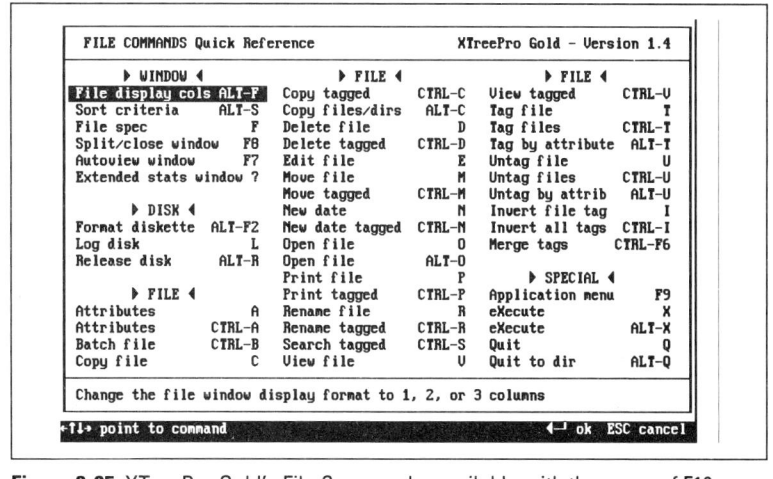

Figure 3-85: XTreePro Gold's File Commands, available with the press of F10.

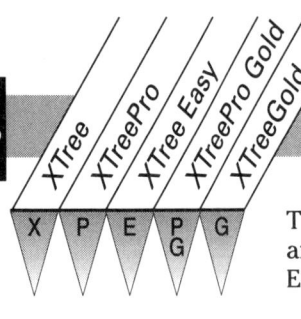

Hide/Unhide　　　　　　　　　　　　　　　　　Command

See Directory Management, The File Window, and Securing Files and Directories

History　　　　　　　　　　　　　　　　　　　Command

If you own a copy of XTree Easy, XTreePro Gold, and XTreeGold, you have access to the History command. Whenever you type an answer to an XTree prompt, your response is saved in what's called a *History file*. Separate histories are maintained for the Command shell, the Filespec command, and many other operations. You'll see history at the bottom of the screen as a reminder to use this *great* resource.

Let's see how this works in the real world. When you invoke the Filespec command (press F for filespec), for example, and XTree asks you to enter a File Specification, you can use the History command (just press the up-arrow key) to reveal your past entries (assuming you've made past entries). In the example in Figure 3-86, there are nine History entries shown in the History screen (XTreePro Gold stores up to 13; XTreeEasy and XTreeGold store up to 16). If you want use the filespec *.EXE at the top of the list, just press the up-arrow key until your cursor is positioned on that entry; once you're there, all you have to do is press Enter, and *.EXE is automatically entered as the new filespec. If you have a mouse, just click on history to reveal previous commands and then select a command from the list.

> **TIP:** If the highlight is at the top and you want the bottom entry, you don't have to down-arrow through the entire list — the cursor keys wrap from the top to the bottom and vice versa.

You can also use the History command to repeat commands you invoke from the Command shell prompt. Just press the up-arrow key and the command history will appear. When your cursor highlights the command you want to use, just press Enter to execute it.

Chapter 3: XTree for DOS Quick Reference Guide

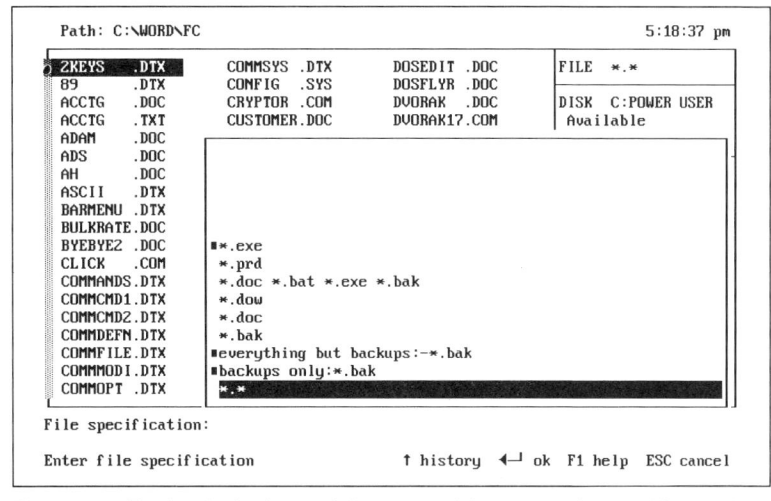

```
Path: C:\WORD\FC                                           5:18:37 pm

 2KEYS    .DTX     COMMSYS  .DTX    DOSEDIT  .DOC    FILE  *.*
 89       .DTX     CONFIG   .SYS    DOSFLYR  .DOC
 ACCTG    .DOC     CRYPTOR  .COM    DVORAK   .DOC    DISK  C:POWER USER
 ACCTG    .TXT     CUSTOMER .DOC    DVORAK17 .COM    Available
 ADAM     .DOC
 ADS      .DOC
 AH       .DOC
 ASCII    .DTX
 BARMENU  .DTX
 BULKRATE .DOC
 BYEBYE2  .DOC    ■*.exe
 CLICK    .COM     *.prd
 COMMANDS .DTX     *.doc *.bat *.exe *.bak
 COMMCMD1 .DTX     *.dow
 COMMCMD2 .DTX     *.doc
 COMMDEFN .DTX     *.bak
 COMMFILE .DTX    ■everything but backups:-*.bak
 COMMMODI .DTX    ■backups only:*.bak
 COMMOPT  .DTX     *.*

File specification:

Enter file specification          ↑ history  ←┘ ok  F1 help  ESC cancel
```

Figure 3-86: The box in the lower-right corner of the screen shows a history of filespecs to choose from again.

> **TIP:** The History command is useful for editing typographical errors. For example, if you type a command, press Enter, and then get a BAD COMMAND OR FILENAME message, chances are you either used bad syntax or misspelled something. To avoid retyping the whole thing, just press the up-arrow key to access the command history, highlight the bad command, and press Enter. This brings the command back to the Command shell prompt, where you can correct the typo. Once the command is letter-perfect, press Enter.

The advantage of using the History command is that it eliminates typos and brain-strain, and you don't have to remember what that command was you used *last* time. And, the contents of your History file are saved from day to day. Your History file stays put no matter how many times you start and quit the program. A command used a week ago could very well still be saved in the History file. Remember, only the last 16 (or 13) responses are saved — the oldest responses make way for new responses after the limit is reached. Which segues nicely into the next topic.

Creating a permanent history

You can *save* your favorite commands and filespecs — the ones you use all the time — so they'll never get the heave-ho. XTree calls these *permanent entries*. You can make any entry permanent by highlighting the entry and pressing Insert on your keyboard. A little square appears to the left of the item in your list of saved commands, indicating its permanent status. Back in Figure 3-86, the item at the top of the list (*.EXE) is a permanent entry. Make your permanent entries unpermanent by highlighting them and pressing Insert again.

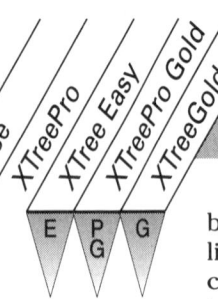

Using labels to name entries

You can also name your history entries with *labels*. In Figure 3-86 there are two entries with the labels, everything but backup and backups only. This way you can combine English words with your entries, making the task of remembering the significance of obscure commands much easier. You can also set things up to be simpler for others to use. To make a label, your cursor must be on the command line. You can type anything you want as long as it's followed by a colon (:). After the colon comes the actual response (no space in between). For example, the following entry reminds you that the *.DOC filespec is for viewing document files only:

DOCUMENTS ONLY:*.DOC

The colon before the filespec tells XTree to ignore your English explanation. Once you press Enter, your command line entry goes to the History file for use later on (be sure to make it permanent).

Although the Filespec and Command shell histories were used as examples in this section, History files are maintained on most commands (including Copy, Edit, Date, Print, and Execute, to name just a few).

Invert   Command

See Tag/Untag

Invert is the Gold command that allows you to reverse current filespecs or tags.

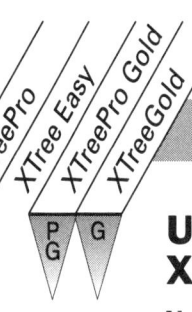

Using Invert with XTreePro Gold and XTreeGold

You can *invert* an existing filespec by using the Invert command. Press I for Invert; all the files that *don't* match the filespec will be displayed in a File window. Take a look back at Figure 3-73; in this figure, *.DOC is the specified filespec. After pressing I to activate Invert, a choice between inverting filespecs or tags is offered. Choose F for File Specifications to reveal the files that do *not* end in DOC. When you select the Invert command, your display switches to reverse video to remind you that you're in Invert mode. To return to normal mode, just press I-F again (the Invert command is a toggle switch).

Log   Command

When you call up any XTree program, it first takes inventory of the files and directories on your hard disk (or currently logged drive) and then displays them on your screen. This inventory process is called *logging*. The larger the disk and the number of files, the longer it takes to log. It only makes sense that XTree must log a disk before it can act upon it in any way.

In addition to your hard drive, you may also want to log a floppy disk or, if your hard disk is partitioned, your other hard drives (D:, E:, F:, and so on). XTree and XTree Easy can log only one disk at a time. The other versions of the program can, in their own ways, log up to 26 drives at a time (though each logged disk eats up computer memory).

Pressing L for Log (while in the Directory or File windows) prompts XTree to ask you which disk you want to log. You type in the drive letter, press Enter, and *boom*, you're logged onto that drive. Want to come back to C:? Type **L-C** and press Enter, and XTree forgets the currently logged drive and logs C:.

If you use Execute, the Command Shell, the Application Menu, Open, or the XTreeMenu to temporarily jump out of XTree, any changes you make to files and directories will not appear in XTree until you relog (or refresh) the disk. The reason this works this way is two-fold. First, XTree doesn't want to make you wait for relogging every time you pop in and out of XTree (this process can be tedious). Second, XTree assumes you're going to be making file and directory changes within XTree.

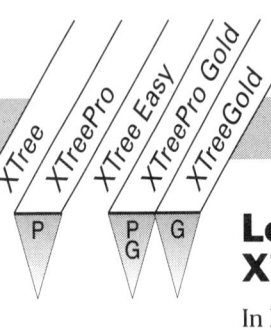

Logging cumulatively with XTreePro, XTreePro Gold, and XTreeGold

In XTreePro, XTreePro Gold, and XTreeGold, you can log drives cumulatively. That is, every time you log another drive, XTreePro, XTreePro Gold, and XTreeGold keep the drive's stats in memory. There is no command for this, it's just how these programs work. The advantage to this is that you can instantly switch to *previously* logged disks without having to wait for them to relog.

Moving among logged drives with XTreePro and XTreePro Gold

Once a drive is logged, you can cycle through your logged drives using the plus (+) or minus (–) keys to move you forward and backward, respectively.

Moving among logged drives with XTreeGold 2.5

Once a drive is logged, you can cycle through your logged drives using the greater-than (>) and less-than (<) keys to handle the task (these occupy the same keys as the comma and the period, but you don't have to use the Shift key to use them, thank goodness).

Releasing logged disks from memory

Every time you log another drive, XTree has to remember it. If you log drives often, XTree will eventually run out of memory. Or, sometimes, if you want to launch a program, you may find yourself short of memory. Releasing a drive's log stats from memory may give you back enough memory to solve your problems.

Since XTree and XTree Easy do not cumulatively log disks, there is no command for them to release a disk from memory.

Releasing logged disks with XTreePro and XTreePro Gold

If you want XTreePro and XTreePro Gold to forget the drives you've logged, press Alt-L to release the currently logged disks from memory and log the new drive. For example, if you have three disks logged, and you press Alt-L, all three logged disks will be

Chapter 3: XTree for DOS Quick Reference Guide

removed from memory. Once a disk is released from memory, the only way to access it is via the Log command.

Logging directories with XTreePro Gold

In XTreePro Gold, Alt-F3 allows you to relog the current *directory*. So if you've made some changes in a directory, you don't have to relog the whole drive, just the one directory. (Though it's not always listed, Alt-F3 is available from all windows.)

Logging directories with XTreeGold

In XTreeGold, you log a directory by highlighting the directory name and pressing the plus key (+). You can unlog a directory by highlighting it and pressing the minus key (–). Additional logging commands, of special interest to those with mega-hard disks, are available through the Alt-L (Log options) command, as shown in Figure 3-87. Before pressing Alt-L, be sure to highlight the directory you want to work with.

The bottom of the screen in Figure 3-87 shows the various options you can use to log: Branch, Disk drive, One level (of directories), Refresh (the current) directory, or Tree only.

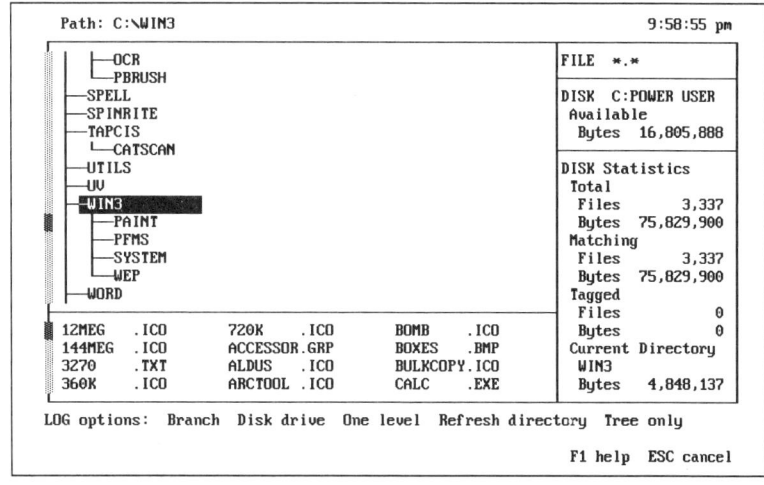

```
Path: C:\WIN3                                            9:58:55 pm
       ┌─OCR
       └─PBRUSH                              FILE  *.*
    ─SPELL
    ─SPINRITE                                DISK  C:POWER USER
    ─TAPCIS                                  Available
       └─CATSCAN                               Bytes  16,805,888
    ─UTILS
    ─UV                                      DISK Statistics
    ─WIN3                                    Total
       ─PAINT                                  Files       3,337
       ─PFMS                                   Bytes  75,829,900
       ─SYSTEM                               Matching
       └─WEP                                   Files       3,337
    ─WORD                                      Bytes  75,829,900
                                             Tagged
                                               Files           0
  12MEG   .ICO    720K     .ICO   BOMB    .ICO  Bytes           0
  144MEG  .ICO    ACCESSOR.GRP    BOXES   .BMP Current Directory
  3270    .TXT    ALDUS    .ICO   BULKCOPY.ICO  WIN3
  360K    .ICO    ARCTOOL  .ICO   CALC    .EXE  Bytes   4,848,137

LOG options:   Branch  Disk drive  One level  Refresh directory  Tree only
                                                  F1 help  ESC cancel
```

Figure 3-87: LOG options, shown here at the bottom of the screen, give you total control of what is and isn't logged.

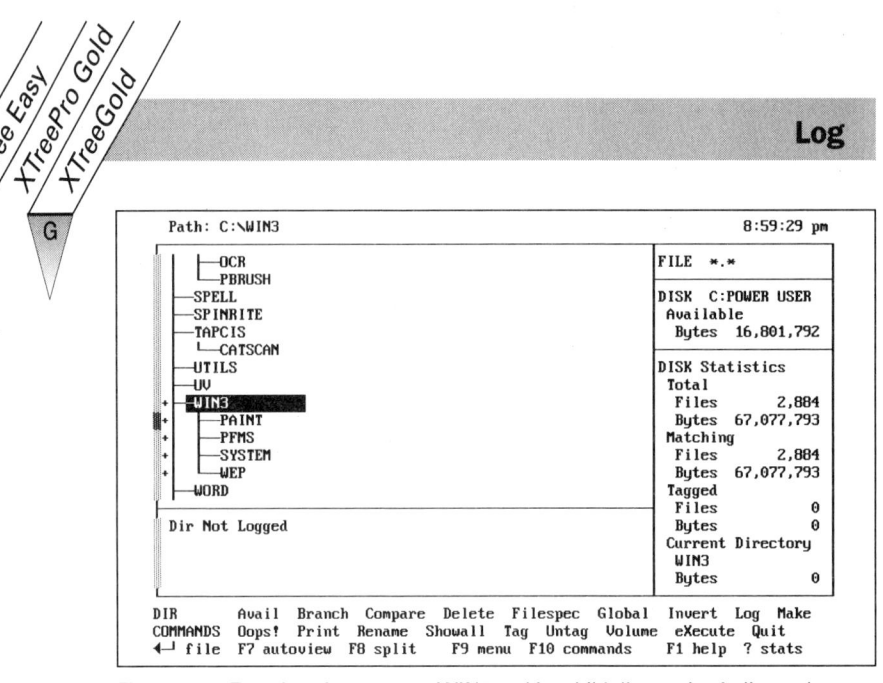

Figure 3-88: The plus signs next to WIN3 and its child directories indicate that these directories haven't been logged.

The last option, Tree only, logs only the tree structure (without the files) in the current directory and its child directories (subdirectories). In the example in Figure 3-88, the WIN3 directory was unlogged through the following process: I first highlighted the directory, then pressed Alt-L and T (for Tree only). As you can see in the figure, the message at the bottom of the screen is Dir Not Logged, even though the WIN3 directory is still highlighted. The plus signs next to WIN3 and its subdirectories indicate that the contents of these directories haven't been logged, though all other directories in the list have been logged. You can relog the unlogged directories using any of the techniques described previously.

Using Instant Log

The Instant Log command, available in XTreePro Gold and XTreeGold, allows you to bypass the logging process altogether. It requires some planning ahead, though. To use Instant Log, you have to quit XTree using the Alt-Z key combination. This method of exiting takes a "snapshot" of your currently tagged files, window status, everything. When you get into XTreePro Gold or XTreeGold again, the programs then use the snapshot instead of logging the drives. Naturally, if you delete some files before returning to Gold, the Instant Log record will not be totally accurate — it reflects the condition of your drive *when you quit.*

Chapter 3: XTree for DOS Quick Reference Guide

```
XTreeGold - Configuration Items                            Page 1

Application Menu
    1 Opening screen is the Application Menu          NO
    2 Pause after application program execution       NO

Directories
    3 Program path:                                   C:\X
    4 Editor program:

Disk logging
    5 Disk logging method                             QUICK
    6 Log disk commands only read the root directory  NO
    7 Log disk commands only read the directory tree  NO




  Next page     Main menu
Show the next screen of configuration items.

↑↓ Select item    ENTER Change item          ESC Return to main menu
```

Figure 3-89: XTreeGold's Configuration program allows you to limit how much of your hard disk is logged when the program is invoked.

Configuring XTreeGold's logging instructions

XTreeGold offers more features for controlling the logging process. If you've got a large hard disk, waiting for XTreeGold to log all the files and directories may be frustrating. One solution is to change the Configuration program so that XTreeGold logs only your disk's tree structure. Figure 3-89 shows the Disk logging items available from the Configuration program. You can select from among several options to control how XTreeGold logs your drives.

Command line switches for logging in XTreeGold 2.5

In XTreeGold 2.5 you can, on the spur of the moment, select precisely what, where, and when files will be logged, just by how you start the program from the DOS command line. The following sections detail your options.

Preselecting your filespecs

If you type **XTGOLD *.DOC** and press Enter, for example, when XTreeGold 2.5 loads, only those files ending in DOC will be visible in the File window. (If you aren't familiar with wildcards and filespecs, see "Using Wildcards," in Chapter 1, and "Filespec," earlier in this chapter.)

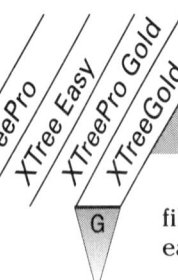

Logging more than one drive

If you want XTreeGold 2.5 to log more than one drive as it loads, type **XTGOLD C: D: E:**, for example, from the DOS command line and press Enter to log drives C:, D:, and E:.

Alternatively, when you start XTreeGold 2.5, you can place a period after the drive name to force XTreeGold 2.5 to log only the root directory and the drive's directory structure. For example, type **XTGOLD C:. D:. E:.** and press Enter to log the root directories of drives C:, D:, and E:.

Logging only a specific directory

You can also coerce XTreeGold to log a specific directory on start up. For example, type **XTGOLD \WINDOWS** and press Enter to log *only* the files in the WINDOWS directory. (To log additional directories once you're in XTreeGold 2.5, highlight those directories and press Enter.)

You can mix and match several commands at the same time. For example, type **XTGOLD \WORD *.DOC** and press Enter to log the WORD directory and display only the files ending in DOC.

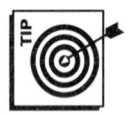

If you really want to impress yourself, put your favorite XTreeGold 2.5 logging commands in a batch file. (See "Batch Files," earlier in this chapter if you're unfamiliar with the concept.)

Managing Memory

One thing people run out of on a computer quicker than anything (besides patience) is *memory*. If you're trying to use XTree as your command central, you may from time to time run into `insufficient memory` error messages. If you ever get this kind of message, don't throw your hands up — yet. Try the solutions in the following sections first, before you despair. These suggestions apply only to XTreePro, XTreePro Gold, and XTreeGold.

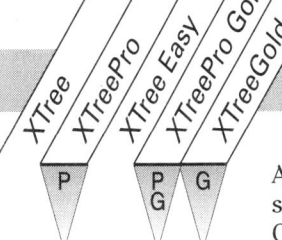

A good first place to start for *any* computer problem is to make sure your computer's CONFIG.SYS file is properly set up (see Chapter 8, "Hard Disk Management in a Nutshell," for more on this topic).

Adjusting memory in XTreePro

If you are running XTreePro, you can reduce the amount of memory needed to run XTreePro by reducing the File/Directory limit (see "Configuration Options," earlier in this chapter, for more on this item). When you execute a program from within XTreePro, be sure to use the Alt-X version of the Execute command so that XTreePro will reduce itself to the smallest size possible, releasing as much memory as possible to the program you're trying to run. That should take care of the problem.

Adjusting memory in XTreePro Gold and XTreeGold

XTreePro Gold and XTreeGold promise to reduce themselves to what is called a *7K Wedge*. But you have to follow three rules to make that happen:

- Make sure the program is configured properly. Specifically, set the `Memory utilization` option on page 3 of the Configuration program to `All Memory`.

- When invoking XTreeGold, type **XTGOLD** (rather than **XTG**) and then press Enter; this allows XTreeGold to collapse to its smallest size.

- Instead of using X (or O) to Execute (or Open) a program, use Alt-X (or Alt-O), or use the XTreeMenu (F9). This allows XTreeGold to release the maximum amount of memory to the program you're executing.

XTreeGold 2.5/DOS 5.0 users can load XTreeGold into high memory, if it is available, with the LH XTGOLD or LOADHIGH XTGOLD commands.

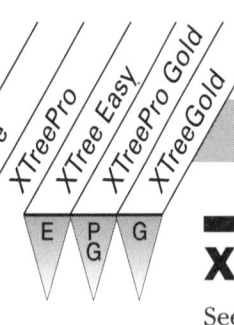

XTree Menus

See "Using the Application Menu" ("command central" in XTreePro Gold), "Using Pull-Down Menus" (the new XTreeGold and XTree Easy interface), or "Using the XTreeMenu" (the updated application menu in XTreeGold and XTree Easy.

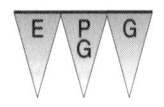

Mouse Commands

Although the original XTree (and XTreePro) debuted when mice were still only lab animals (computer research lab animals, of course), XTreePro Gold (and then XTreeGold and XTree Easy) seamlessly integrate mouse technology for those "mousers" who prefer to consolidate commands to a Morse-codelike series of clicks and double-clicks. (If you've got a three-button mouse, ignore the middle button while you're in XTree.)

This section is not going to contain any illustrations because showing how to delete a file with a *mouse* looks pretty much like deleting a file with the keyboard. In short, mouse commands don't do anything more (or less) than keyboard commands. It's a matter of convenience or preference.

XTree programs do not come with a mouse driver — the piece of software that makes the mouse functional. Don't worry, though, because if your mouse works with other programs, it'll work with XTree, too. Likewise, if your mouse isn't working, it's not XTree's fault.

Using the mouse in the command menu

To execute the commands at the bottom of the screen with a mouse, you just point to a command and click (either the left or right button). If you click a command that's associated with a History file, the history will automatically be displayed. If you want to use a History entry, just double-click the appropriate item. If you don't want to use a History item, you must enter a response the old-fashioned way — via the keyboard. However, once your entry is correct, you can choose OK.

To cancel a command, click Esc.

Chapter 3: XTree for DOS Quick Reference Guide

If you want to see the Alt menu, click on the word Alt. If you want to log a disk, click on the word Log. To see the FILE COMMANDS, just click on the words (this action replaces pressing Enter to toggle between File and Directory windows). In short, you can activate just about any command by clicking on it.

Using the mouse in the Directory window

To scroll through the directory tree, use the left-hand border of the screen, called the *scroll bar*. A scroll bar in XTree works just like all the other scroll bars on the planet. To travel up or down the directory tree with the scroll bar, position the mouse cursor on the scroll bar button, hold down the left button, and slide the mouse up or down. You can scroll in chunks similar to how PgUp and PgDn keys operate by moving the mouse cursor up or down the scroll bar and *then* clicking.

Once you arrive at a directory you wish to work with, there are several mouse options. Place the mouse cursor on a *directory name* and click the left mouse button to make that directory current, or click the right mouse button to tag and untag all files in the directory. To jump to the Expanded file window, double-click the left mouse button.

Using the mouse in the File window

Scrolling through the File window is just like scrolling through the Directory window. Just belly up to the scroll bar.

Once you arrive at a file that you wish to work with, you have several options. Place the mouse cursor on a *filename* and click the left mouse button to make a file the current file. Click the right mouse button to tag or untag the file (hold down the right mouse button and slide the mouse up or down to continue to tag and untag files).

Double-clicking the left mouse button on a filename opens that file (see "Open") and its associated application. Double-clicking the right mouse button on a filename puts the file in view mode (see "View").

Move   Command

Move is used to transport a file from one location to another. Until the arrival of XTreeGold (and XTree Easy), you could only move a file from one directory to another on the same disk. To move a file to another disk, you had to copy it first and then delete the original.

If you are familiar with the steps required to Copy a file, you're already 99 percent able to Move a file.

> **NOTE:** Only XTree Easy and XTreeGold let you move a file to another disk. Although the examples used below assume you want to move a file to another directory on the hard drive, you can also specify another disk drive by typing A: or B: (or whatever your disk drive is) if you have XTree Easy and XTreeGold.

Moving a file

To move a single file, highlight the file and press M for Move. XTree asks what name you want to give the file you are moving, as shown in Figure 3-90 by the statement MOVE file: AUTOEXEC.BAT as. XTree is asking what to call the AUTOEXEC.BAT file. The question — which you'll see every time you want to move something —

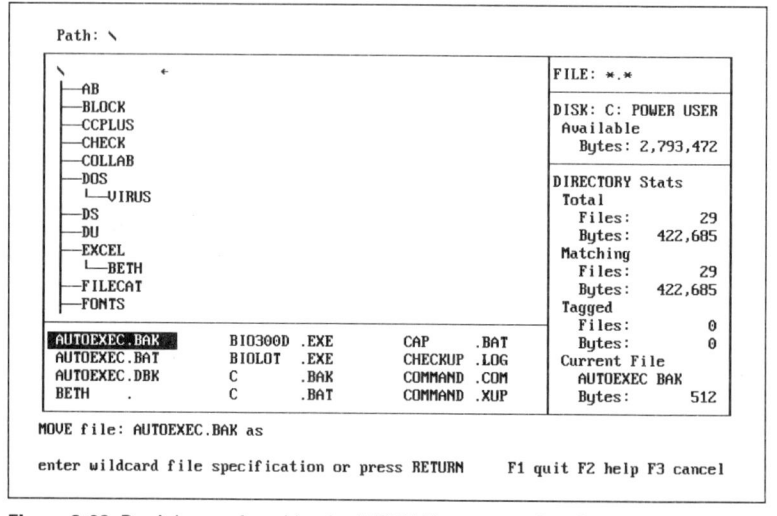

```
Path: \

                            ←                                    FILE: *.*
    ├─AB
    ├─BLOCK                                                       DISK: C: POWER USER
    ├─CCPLUS                                                        Available
    ├─CHECK                                                           Bytes: 2,793,472
    ├─COLLAB
    ├─DOS                                                         DIRECTORY Stats
    │  └─VIRUS                                                    Total
    ├─DS                                                            Files:           29
    ├─DU                                                            Bytes:      422,685
    ├─EXCEL                                                       Matching
    │  └─BETH                                                       Files:           29
    ├─FILECAT                                                       Bytes:      422,685
    ├─FONTS                                                       Tagged
                                                                    Files:            0
 AUTOEXEC.BAK     BIO300D  .EXE      CAP       .BAT               Bytes:            0
 AUTOEXEC.BAT     BIOLOT   .EXE      CHECKUP   .LOG               Current File
 AUTOEXEC.DBK     C        .BAK      COMMAND   .COM                 AUTOEXEC BAK
 BETH    .        C        .BAT      COMMAND   .XUP               Bytes:          512

MOVE file: AUTOEXEC.BAK as

enter wildcard file specification or press RETURN      F1 quit F2 help F3 cancel
```

Figure 3-90: Don't be confused by the MOVE file: as question. Press Enter to leave the filename unchanged.

Chapter 3: XTree for DOS Quick Reference Guide

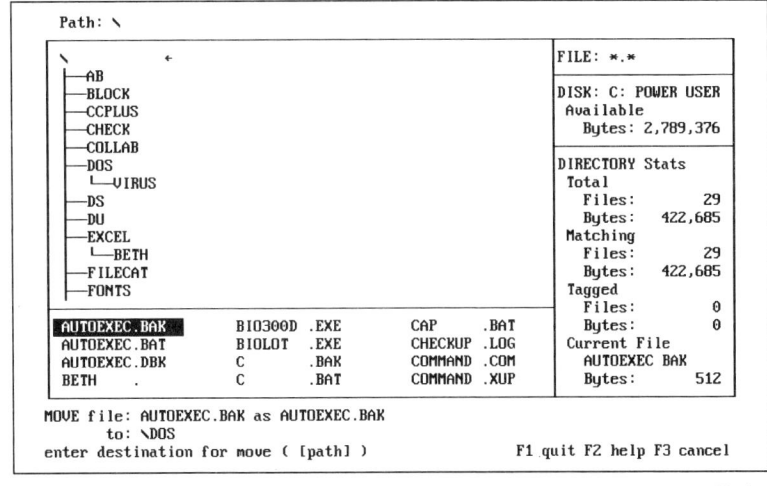

```
Path: \
                                              FILE: *.*
 \            ←
  ├─AB                                        DISK: C: POWER USER
  ├─BLOCK                                       Available
  ├─CCPLUS                                        Bytes: 2,789,376
  ├─CHECK
  ├─COLLAB                                    DIRECTORY Stats
  ├─DOS                                         Total
  │ └─VIRUS                                       Files:         29
  ├─DS                                            Bytes:    422,685
  ├─DU                                          Matching
  ├─EXCEL                                         Files:         29
  │ └─BETH                                        Bytes:    422,685
  ├─FILECAT                                     Tagged
  ├─FONTS                                         Files:          0
 AUTOEXEC.BAK    BIO300D .EXE   CAP     .BAT    Bytes:          0
 AUTOEXEC.BAT    BIOLOT  .EXE   CHECKUP .LOG  Current File
 AUTOEXEC.DBK    C       .BAK   COMMAND .COM    AUTOEXEC BAK
 BETH     .      C       .BAT   COMMAND .XUP    Bytes:        512

MOVE file: AUTOEXEC.BAK as AUTOEXEC.BAK
       to: \DOS
enter destination for move ( [path] )         F1 quit F2 help F3 cancel
```

Figure 3-91: XTree asks where to move AUTOEXEC.BAT to. In this case, the file is moving to the \DOS directory.

means "Do you want to rename the file when you move it?" If you don't want to change the name, press Enter and the filename will remain the same. If you do want to rename the file as you move it, type in the new name and then press Enter. This procedure lets you keep different versions of the same file.

Once the renaming issue is settled, you'll be asked for a destination (*where* do you want to move it to?). In the current example, the file is moving to the DOS directory, as illustrated in Figure 3-91. To indicate that the file should be moved to the DOS directory, just type **\DOS** and press Enter. The file moves to the DOS directory, unless that directory already has another file with the same name.

If there is already another file in the directory with the same name as the file you are moving, XTree handles the situation by asking if you want to replace the existing file, as shown in Figure 3-92. Press Y to replace the file, N not to replace it, or Esc to cancel.

The later versions of XTree ask if you wish to replace the existing file, but they also display the file's stats so you can compare date, time, size, and attributes to make an *informed* decision, as shown in Figure 3-93. If one file is newer or bigger, that one may be the version you want to keep (although not always). In any case, press Y to continue the moving process and press N to stop it.

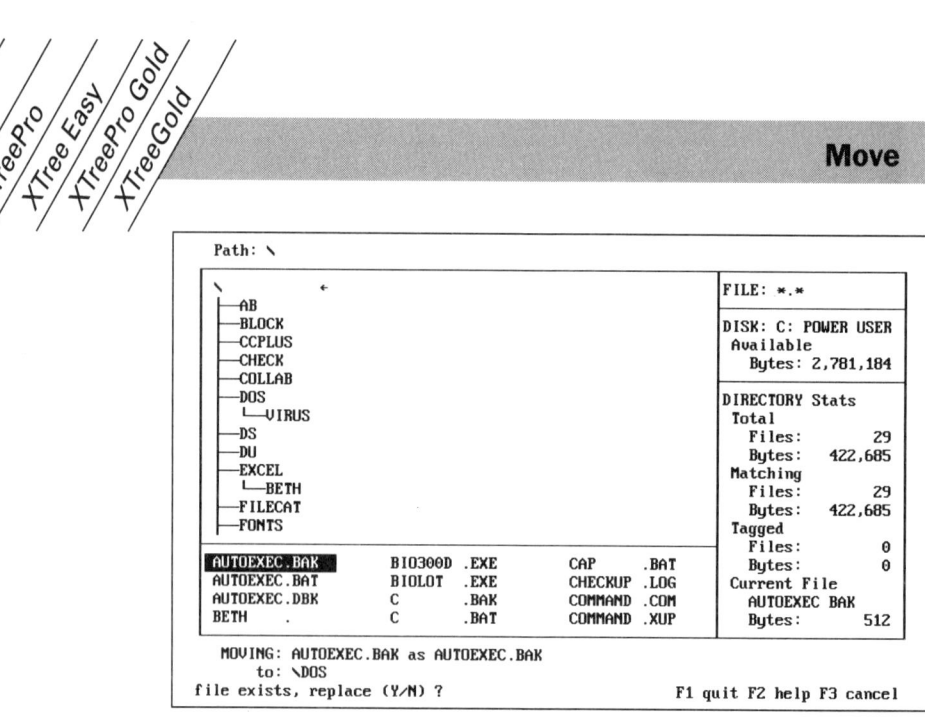

```
Path: \
                                              FILE: *.*
  ─AB
  ─BLOCK                                      DISK: C: POWER USER
  ─CCPLUS                                       Available
  ─CHECK                                          Bytes: 2,781,184
  ─COLLAB
  ─DOS                                        DIRECTORY Stats
    └─VIRUS                                     Total
  ─DS                                             Files:        29
  ─DU                                             Bytes:   422,685
  ─EXCEL                                        Matching
    └─BETH                                        Files:        29
  ─FILECAT                                        Bytes:   422,685
  ─FONTS                                        Tagged
                                                  Files:         0
  AUTOEXEC.BAK   BIO300D .EXE    CAP     .BAT     Bytes:         0
  AUTOEXEC.BAT   BIOLOT  .EXE    CHECKUP .LOG   Current File
  AUTOEXEC.DBK   C       .BAK    COMMAND .COM     AUTOEXEC BAK
  BETH     .     C       .BAT    COMMAND .XUP     Bytes:       512

MOVING: AUTOEXEC.BAK as AUTOEXEC.BAK
    to: \DOS
file exists, replace (Y/N) ?                  F1 quit F2 help F3 cancel
```

Figure 3-92: Watch for questions at the bottom of the screen. XTree warns that a file named AUTOEXEC.BAT already exists in the \DOS directory.

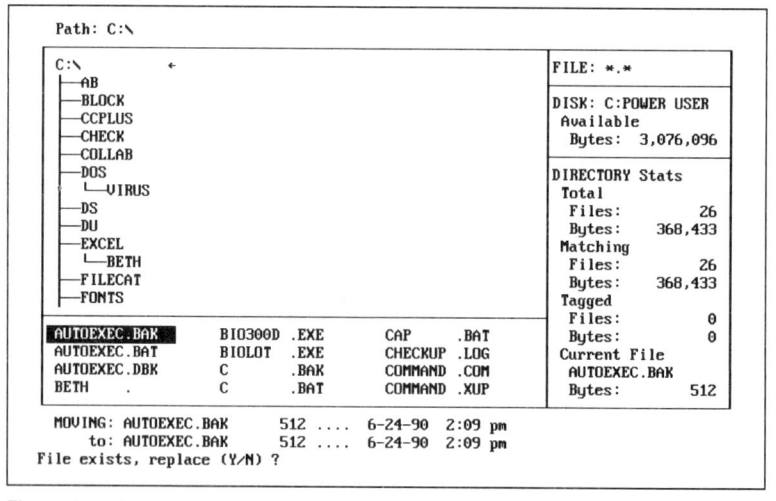

```
Path: C:\
                                              FILE: *.*
C:\
  ─AB
  ─BLOCK                                      DISK: C:POWER USER
  ─CCPLUS                                       Available
  ─CHECK                                          Bytes: 3,076,096
  ─COLLAB
  ─DOS                                        DIRECTORY Stats
    └─VIRUS                                     Total
  ─DS                                             Files:        26
  ─DU                                             Bytes:   368,433
  ─EXCEL                                        Matching
    └─BETH                                        Files:        26
  ─FILECAT                                        Bytes:   368,433
  ─FONTS                                        Tagged
                                                  Files:         0
  AUTOEXEC.BAK   BIO300D .EXE    CAP     .BAT     Bytes:         0
  AUTOEXEC.BAT   BIOLOT  .EXE    CHECKUP .LOG   Current File
  AUTOEXEC.DBK   C       .BAK    COMMAND .COM     AUTOEXEC.BAK
  BETH     .     C       .BAT    COMMAND .XUP     Bytes:       512

MOVING: AUTOEXEC.BAK       512 ....  6-24-90  2:09 pm
    to: AUTOEXEC.BAK       512 ....  6-24-90  2:09 pm
File exists, replace (Y/N) ?
```

Figure 3-93: Later versions of XTree give you more information about the files you are replacing.

Moving more than one file

The process of moving lots of files is very similar to moving just one file. However, instead of starting out by highlighting a single file to be moved, you must first *tag* all the files to be moved. Once you've rounded up a bunch of tagged files, press Ctrl-M to move all tagged files. (Remember, M moves a file, but Ctrl-M moves all tagged files.) Once you've pressed Ctrl-M, it's a matter of following the same procedures that were just described for moving a single file.

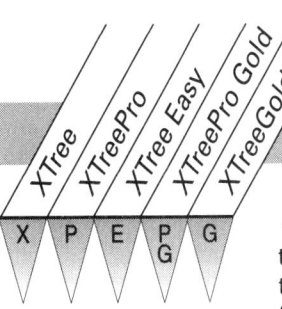

If you haven't perused the "Tag/Untag" and "Filespec" sections yet, now's a good time.

Using Graft to move a directory

XTreePro Gold and XTreeGold allow you to graft a directory. This means you can take a directory (and its contents) and attach it to another directory on the tree. To graft a directory, highlight the directory you want to move and press Alt-G for Graft, as shown in Figure 3-94.

As you can see in Figure 3-94, you're asked *where* you want to move your directory to, and you're shown the Destination window so you can highlight the directory you want to move to, instead of entering it from the keyboard. In this case, we're moving the directory CHECK90 so that it appears under the directory CHEKBOOK. Once you have highlighted the directory, issue the Graft command, highlight the directory you want to graft to, and then press Enter.

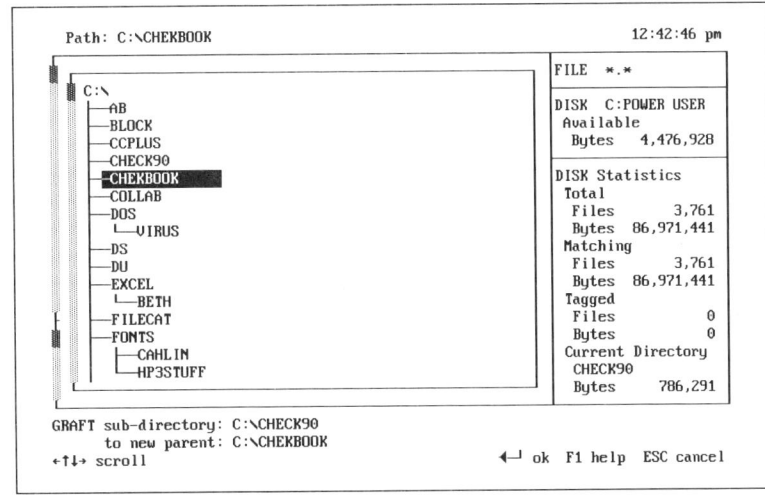

```
Path: C:\CHEKBOOK                                    12:42:46 pm
                                          ┌─────────────────────────┐
 ┌────────────────────────────────────────┤ FILE  *.*               │
 │ C:\                                    │                         │
 │   ├─AB                                 │ DISK  C:POWER USER      │
 │   ├─BLOCK                              │ Available               │
 │   ├─CCPLUS                             │   Bytes      4,476,928  │
 │   ├─CHECK90                            │                         │
 │   ├─CHEKBOOK                           │ DISK Statistics         │
 │   ├─COLLAB                             │ Total                   │
 │   ├─DOS                                │   Files         3,761   │
 │   │  └─VIRUS                           │   Bytes    86,971,441   │
 │   ├─DS                                 │ Matching                │
 │   ├─DU                                 │   Files         3,761   │
 │   ├─EXCEL                              │   Bytes    86,971,441   │
 │   │  └─BETH                            │ Tagged                  │
 │   ├─FILECAT                            │   Files             0   │
 │   ├─FONTS                              │   Bytes             0   │
 │   │  ├─CAHLIN                          │ Current Directory       │
 │   │  └─HP3STUFF                        │ CHECK90                 │
 │                                        │   Bytes       786,291   │
 └────────────────────────────────────────┴─────────────────────────┘
 GRAFT sub-directory: C:\CHECK90
       to new parent: C:\CHEKBOOK
 ←↑↓→ scroll                          ←┘ ok  F1 help  ESC cancel
```

Figure 3-94: Moving a directory and its contents with the Graft command.

Move

As a precaution, you'll be asked one more time if you're sure you want to do this. Just press Y if you are, and XTreePro Gold and XTreeGold will carry out the command. After you graft a directory, you will have to relog the drive (press L for Log) for the grafted directory to appear in alphabetical order on the tree.

> **NOTE:** If you receive a `CAN'T UPDATE PARENT DIRECTORY` error message, you have an older version of Gold that doesn't get along with your version of DOS. An upgrade is available to fix this problem. (See Appendix D, "Where to Go from Here.")

Using the Destination window to simplify moving

XTreePro, XTreePro Gold, XTree Easy, and XTreeGold make moving a file easier for you with the addition of the `F2 Select Path` (`F2 Point` in XTreeGold) option.

After highlighting the file you want to move, press M and then press Enter (so the filename remains the same). Now you're ready to specify the destination for that file. When you press F2, the Destination window, as shown in Figure 3-95, pops up over what you're doing. When you highlight the destination directory and press Enter, your path statement will automatically be entered for you. All that's left to do is press Enter and (barring any filename conflicts) the file will be moved.

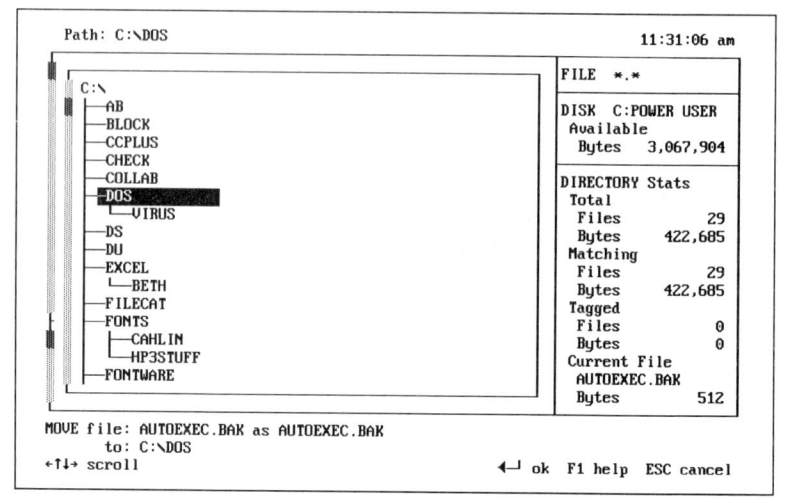

```
Path: C:\DOS                                        11:31:06 am
   C:\                                    FILE  *.*
   ├─AB
   ├─BLOCK                                DISK  C:POWER USER
   ├─CCPLUS                                 Available
   ├─CHECK                                    Bytes   3,067,904
   ├─COLLAB
   ├─DOS                                  DIRECTORY Stats
   │  └─VIRUS                               Total
   ├─DS                                       Files            29
   ├─DU                                       Bytes       422,685
   ├─EXCEL                                  Matching
   │  └─BETH                                  Files            29
   ├─FILECAT                                  Bytes       422,685
   ├─FONTS                                  Tagged
   │  ├─CAHLIN                                Files             0
   │  └─HP3STUFF                              Bytes             0
   └─FONTWARE                              Current File
                                            AUTOEXEC.BAK
                                             Bytes           512

MOVE file: AUTOEXEC.BAK as AUTOEXEC.BAK
       to: C:\DOS
←↑↓→ scroll                              ⏎ ok  F1 help  ESC cancel
```

Figure 3-95: You can move a file to a directory you select from the Destination window.

Chapter 3: XTree for DOS Quick Reference Guide

Figure 3-96: You can use the History command to select a directory for moving files to, provided you've recently done this.

Using the History command to simplify moving

With XTree Easy, XTreePro Gold, and XTreeGold you can also use the History command when moving files and so avoid typing any filenames or destination directories. Of course, this command is helpful only if you frequently move files into a particular directory. Highlight the file to be moved and press M. When you're asked `Move file as ?`, use the up- or down-arrow keys (or click on `history` with your mouse) to open the History window, where you can find a directory you've previously moved files into. In Figure 3-96, the History window shows several files and two directories, BONBOOK and T. Highlighting one of these two directories and pressing Enter twice moves AUTOEXEC.BAT (the name won't change) into the directory of choice.

When in the Destination window, XTree Easy and XTreeGold can also Log onto another drive, making it easier to move files to another drive and directory.

No Files! Error message

When you see the `No Files!` error message in XTree, XTreePro, XTreePro Gold, don't panic. `No files!` simply means that no files in the current directory *match* the filespec you have currently set.

No Files!

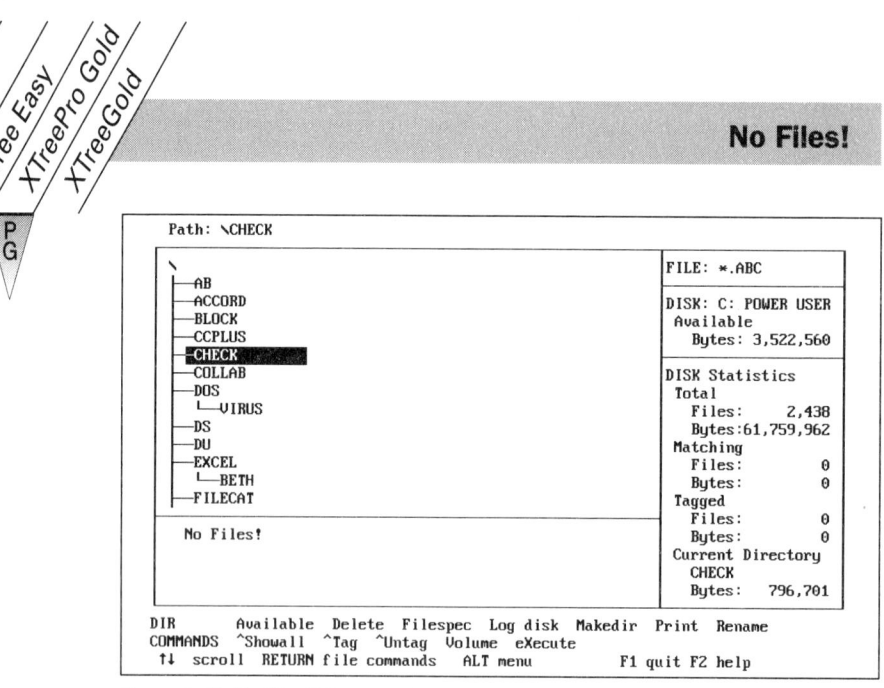

```
Path: \CHECK

                                            FILE: *.ABC
      ─AB
      ─ACCORD                               DISK: C: POWER USER
      ─BLOCK                                Available
      ─CCPLUS                                   Bytes: 3,522,560
      ─CHECK
      ─COLLAB                               DISK Statistics
      ─DOS                                  Total
         └─VIRUS                                Files:      2,438
      ─DS                                       Bytes:61,759,962
      ─DU                                   Matching
      ─EXCEL                                    Files:          0
         └─BETH                                 Bytes:          0
      ─FILECAT                              Tagged
                                                Files:          0
    No Files!                                   Bytes:          0
                                            Current Directory
                                              CHECK
                                              Bytes:    796,701

 DIR       Available  Delete  Filespec  Log disk  Makedir  Print  Rename
 COMMANDS  ^Showall  ^Tag  ^Untag  Volume  eXecute
   ↑↓  scroll  RETURN file commands    ALT menu       F1 quit F2 help
```

Figure 3-97: No files?! Lost data? Neither, actually. The CHECK directory contains no files that match the current file specification.

Figure 3-97 shows a No Files! message in the File window. In the File Specification window in the right-hand corner of the figure, the filespec is *.ABC. The No Files! message appears when the CHECK directory is highlighted, because there *are* no files with the ABC extension in the CHECK directory.

You can check that there really are files in that directory in one of two ways. Either press F for Filespec and then press Enter to reset the filespec to *.* (aka everything), or take a quick peek at the bottom of the Disk Statistics window, where the Current Directory is shown. As you can see in Figure 3-97, there are 796,701 bytes of files in the CHECK directory. Clearly there *are* files in there — just none with the extension of ABC.

You'll also get a No Files! message if you've got more files than XTree can count. XTree can log 2,500 files; XTreePro up to 16,000 (you may have to go into the Configuration program to set the File/Directory limit); XTreeGold can log up to 13,000 (fewer than XTreePro because it's a bigger program and takes up more memory, and so has less space for logging files.) If you have too many files for your version of XTree to count, when you start up the program, you'll get an error message saying there are too many files; and the extras will be ignored.

The average person on an average system won't run into capacity problems. However, if you start factoring in 200-megabyte hard drives and CD-ROMs, you can certainly push the envelope on XTree's capacity.

Oops! Command

There's nothing worse than the moment when you realize with horror that you've just deleted files you really didn't want to delete. Perhaps you even say something like "oops!" when you imagine the consequences of your error. Perhaps you say something worse. To the rescue is XTree Gold's new Oops! command, which enables you to bring your files back from the dead... sometimes.

The *sometimes* qualifier is necessary because of the way DOS saves and deletes files. A so-called "deleted" file can be recovered only because the computer doesn't erase the file when you order it to do so. Instead of actually exterminating the file, the computer reclassifies the space that the file occupied as *available* (rather than *reserved*). After the deleted file's space becomes available, it's only a matter of time before another file uses the space for itself (like a VCR recording over a previously used tape).

So, if you decide to undelete a file that you deleted a month ago, chances are high that the space has since been used by another file and your deleted file is lost. If, however, you want to undelete a file you deleted ten minutes ago, your chances for recovery are excellent.

NOTE: If you plan to undelete a file, do *not* use the Wash command (see "Securing Files and Directories" later in this chapter) or a disk defragger (see Chapter 8, "Hard Disk Management in a Nutshell") prior to undeleting. Running either of these types of programs will render all deleted files permanently unrecoverable (by recording over the deleted file's space). If your computer is set up to automatically run a disk defragger as part of its daily start-up activities, be sure to take care of your undeletes before turning your computer off (and on) again.

For now, let's assume that all aspects are favorable. The first step in retrieving a deleted file is to highlight the directory containing the file (or files) to be retrieved. Now press O (for Oops!) and Gold will list the files in the current directory that are recoverable, as shown in Figure 3-98. Three deleted Lotus 1-2-3 files can be recovered using the Oops! command (they all begin with a question mark, which indicates their deleted status). As you can see, to the right of ?AN92.WK1, the first file listed, are two asterisks (**). These asterisks indicate that this file should be undeleted before the others: if you undelete one of the other files first, that file will record over the first file's space, making it unretrievable. If you don't want the ** file, then go forth and undelete the other files.

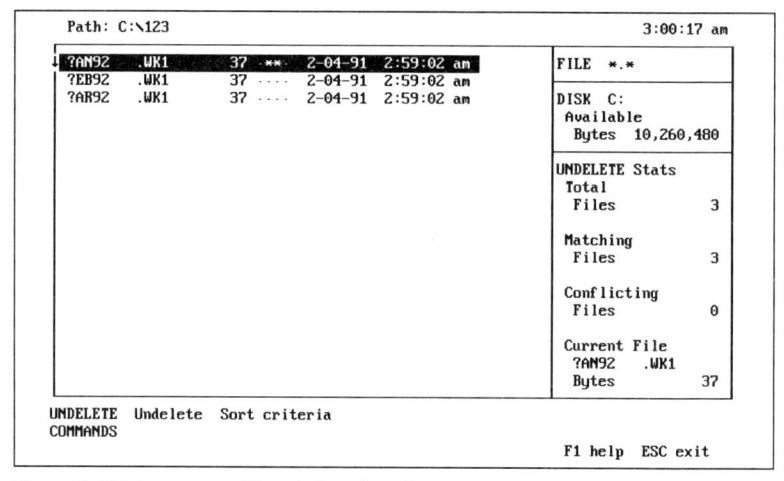

```
Path: C:\123                                          3:00:17 am
 ?AN92    .WK1    37 -**- 2-04-91  2:59:02 am    FILE  *.*
  ?EB92    .WK1    37 ---- 2-04-91  2:59:02 am
  ?AR92    .WK1    37 ---- 2-04-91  2:59:02 am    DISK  C:
                                                  Available
                                                   Bytes   10,260,480

                                                  UNDELETE Stats
                                                  Total
                                                    Files            3

                                                  Matching
                                                    Files            3

                                                  Conflicting
                                                    Files            0

                                                  Current File
                                                    ?AN92   .WK1
                                                    Bytes           37

UNDELETE    Undelete  Sort criteria
COMMANDS
                                                      F1 help  ESC exit
```

Figure 3-98: The current File window lists files in the 123 directory that XTreeGold can bring back from the dead (undelete).

To undelete a file, highlight it and press U (for undelete). Next, XTreeGold asks what to name the file to be undeleted. At this point you can do one of two things: simply type that missing first letter (such as J), or type in the whole filename, as shown in Figure 3-99, and then press Enter. XTreeGold undeletes the file and removes it from DOS's "undelete file list." After the last file in the list is undeleted, an error message appears, telling you there are no more files to undelete. Press Enter and you'll be conducted back to a Directory window.

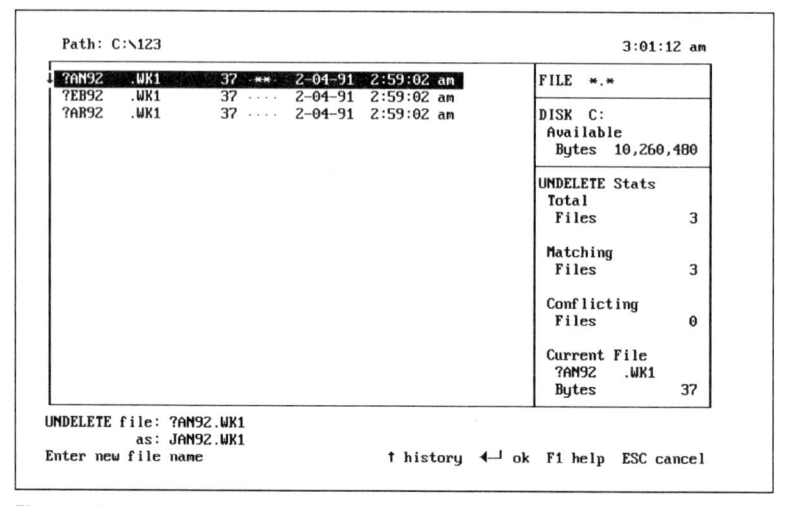

```
Path: C:\123                                          3:01:12 am
 ?AN92    .WK1    37 -**- 2-04-91  2:59:02 am    FILE  *.*
  ?EB92    .WK1    37 ---- 2-04-91  2:59:02 am
  ?AR92    .WK1    37 ---- 2-04-91  2:59:02 am    DISK  C:
                                                  Available
                                                   Bytes   10,260,480

                                                  UNDELETE Stats
                                                  Total
                                                    Files            3

                                                  Matching
                                                    Files            3

                                                  Conflicting
                                                    Files            0

                                                  Current File
                                                    ?AN92   .WK1
                                                    Bytes           37

UNDELETE file: ?AN92.WK1
          as: JAN92.WK1
Enter new file name              ↑ history  ↵ ok  F1 help  ESC cancel
```

Figure 3-99: After pressing U for Undelete, XTreeGold asks what to name the file to be recovered.

Open (and Associate)   Command   O

The Open command can mean two things in XTree: If you're looking to open an Arc or Zip file, see Chapter 9. To learn how to link a program to its data files — or find out what the heck that means — read on.

Although *Open and associate* may *sound* like some sort of New Wave singles scene, it isn't. It is a convenient feature in XTreePro Gold and XTreeGold that puts filename extensions to use in a unique way. You can use the Open command in a similar manner as the Execute command to launch programs and automatically open the file you want to work in.

Most programs give their data files a common extension. For instance, Microsoft Word files all end in DOC, Lotus 1-2-3 files end in WK1, and so forth. With XTreePro Gold and XTreeGold you can link (or associate) an extension with its program. In other words, you can tell XTree that all files ending with DOC are Microsoft Word files. Then, you can highlight a Word file (like REPORT.DOC) in a File window and press O (for Open); Pro Gold and Gold will know to automatically launch Word and load REPORT.DOC.

Creating an association

Extensions and programs become associated via a batch file that you write. (If you're not familiar with creating batch files, see "Batch Files," earlier in this chapter for details on this topic.) The key to creating an association is in naming the batch file. You must use the file extension as the first part of the filename, then add the extension BAT. For example, a Microsoft Word–associated batch file would be called DOC.BAT, a Lotus file would be called WK1.BAT.

The associated batch file must contain the name and location of the program you want to launch, followed by %1. The %1 variable means *use the currently highlighted file*. (Pro Gold and Gold have a number of variables you can use, all listed in "Batch Files.") The DOC.BAT (Microsoft Word) batch file would, therefore, contain this single command line:

```
C:\WORD5\WORD.EXE %1
```

After this association is made, you need only highlight a DOC file and press O (for Open) to activate DOC.BAT. DOC.BAT then finds and executes the Word program, replacing the currently highlighted DOC file for the %1 variable. Word then loads with the file open. Another example of an Associate batch file might be one named XLS.BAT that contains the line:

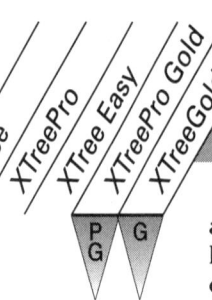

```
C:\EXCEL\EXCEL.EXE %1
```

Yes, you can start Excel from within Gold!

If a file refuses to open, you've either run out of memory or the Associate batch file can't be found. If you get an insufficient memory error message, try using the Alt-O key combination instead of just O to open a file. Using the Alt-O command ensures that as much memory as possible will be released to the program you're trying to use (similar to Alt-X and the Execute command). Also, make sure the Associate batch file is stored in the same directory as Pro Gold and Gold. (Of course it wouldn't hurt to double-check the commands in the batch file!)

Mousers can both Execute and Open files (you still have to set up an Associate batch file, though, just like the keyboarders) by double-clicking on the filename with the left mouse button.

Print Command

Sure, print. But print *what?* Well... how about your directory names, your directory tree, or whatever files you've tagged? How about printing out a copy of your AUTOEXEC.BAT and CONFIG.SYS files for future reference? How about a list of those files you just copied to a floppy disk? Yep. That's what XTree can print. And, of course, more.

Printing a list of files and directories

If you are in the directory display, press P to Print. Your options are to print out a catalog of tagged files, pathnames, or a tree, as shown at the bottom of Figure 3-100. Press the first letter of the option you want to print to set the process in motion (provided, of course, your printer is turned on).

Chapter 3: XTree for DOS Quick Reference Guide

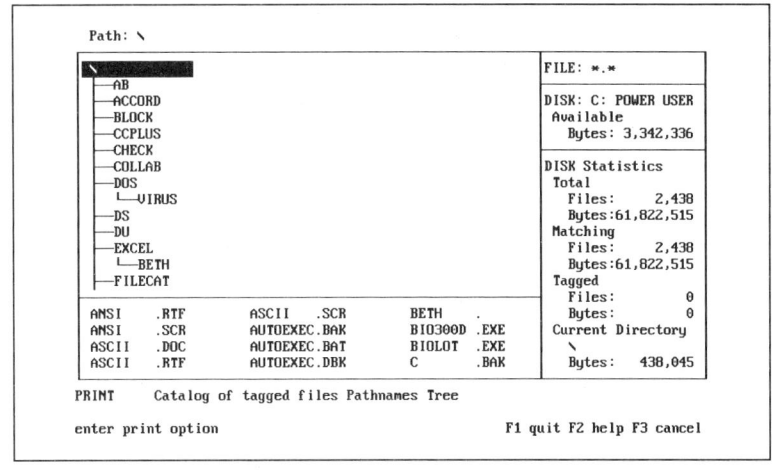

Figure 3-100: After you press P for Print, printing options appear at the bottom of the screen.

Printing files

Another thing that all versions of XTree can do is print files. Generally XTree doesn't do so well with files created by your word processor (oh, it'll try, but the result will probably be a mess). XTree can reliably print only simple ASCII files (see "View"). Even so, believe it or not, you do have some ASCII files that you may want to print. For instance, your AUTOEXEC.BAT and CONFIG.SYS files are ASCII files.

To print a file, highlight the file to be printed and press P. You'll be prompted to press any key when the printer is ready. (Alternatively, you can tag a bunch of files, then press Ctrl-P to print all the files you tagged.)

Another file you may want to print out is that little file that comes with every new program you buy. It's a file usually named READ.ME (or README, or README.1ST, or some variation). READ.ME files are generally ASCII files (unless the file came with your word processor), and they contain information and corrections that didn't make it into the program's manual. Even XTree came with a READ.ME file, so let's print it out for an exercise. Highlight the file and hit P to Print. The following sections discuss the differences in printing between the various XTree programs.

Printing with XTree

If you have XTree, all you need to do, as shown in Figure 3-101, is press any key and the file will print.

```
Path: \DOS

BLANKS   .COM    DISKCOPY.COM    KEYB    .COM    FILE: *.*
CACHE    .EXE    DISKINIT.EXE    KEYBDP  .COM
CACHE    .SCR    DISPLAY .SYS    KEYBDP  .SCR    DISK: C: POWER USER
CAPSRLSE.COM     DOS33   .PAT    KEYBOARD.SYS     Available
CAPSRLSE.DOC     DOS33A  .PAT    KP      .COM       Bytes: 3,383,296
CEMM     .COM    DRIVER  .SYS    LABEL   .COM
CEMM     .EXE    EDLIN   .COM    LIST    .COM    DIRECTORY Stats
CEMMC    .SCR    ENHDISK .SYS    MODE    .COM     Total
CEMME    .SCR    EXE2BIN .EXE    MODE    .SCR       Files:        86
CHECKUP  .EXE    FASTOPEN.EXE    MORE    .COM       Bytes: 1,288,460
CHECKUP  .OLD    FDISK   .COM    MOUSE   .SYS    Matching
CHECKUP  .REG    FIND    .EXE    OC      .EXE       Files:        86
CHKDSK   .COM    GRAPHICS.COM    PRINT   .COM       Bytes: 1,288,460
COMMAND  .COM    GRAPHICS.SCR    READ    .ME     Tagged
CPANEL   .COM    HELP    .COM    README  .CPQ       Files:         0
DAB      .EXE    HIMEM   .SYS    RECOVER .COM       Bytes:         0
DATECHEK.COM     HPDLBL  .EXE    REPLACE .EXE    Current File
DAYCHEK .BAT     INSTALL .EXE    RESTORE .COM      READ    ME
DEBUG    .COM    INSTALL .SCR    ROMREV  .COM      Bytes:     1,987

PRESS ANY KEY WHEN THE PRINTER IS READY

                                              F1 quit F2 help F3 cancel
```

Figure 3-101: XTree will print READ.ME when any key is pressed.

Printing with XTreePro, XTree Easy, XTreePro Gold and XTreeGold

In the advanced versions, you have more decisions to make. With XTreePro, XTree Easy, XTreePro Gold, and XTreeGold, press P for Print, and your screen should resemble that shown in Figure 3-102. These versions allow you to specify page length — in other words you can "pretty up" your printout with margins. If you don't care about top and bottom margins, and you don't want to specify the number of lines per page in the document you are printing, press 0 (that's a zero) when you are asked for page number value. If you want a specific number of lines per page, enter that number. Experiment to see what works for your printer and what is the best margin width for whatever document you're printing. Laser printers are *generally* set to produce a maximum of 62 lines per page.

Once you find the page length of your dreams, you can go into XTreePro, XTreePro Gold, or XTreeGold's Configuration program to

Chapter 3: XTree for DOS Quick Reference Guide 151

```
Path: C:\DOS

CEMM      .EXE    EDLIN    .COM    LIST     .COM    FILE: *.*
CEMMC     .SCR    EMMDISK  .SYS    MODE     .COM
CEMME     .SCR    EXE2BIN  .EXE    MODE     .SCR    DISK: C:POWER USER
CHECKUP   .EXE    FASTOPEN .EXE    MORE     .COM    Available
CHECKUP   .OLD    FDISK    .COM    MOUSE    .SYS      Bytes:    3,325,952
CHECKUP   .REG    FIND     .EXE    OC       .EXE
CHKDSK    .COM    GRAPHICS .COM    PRINT    .COM    DIRECTORY Stats
COMMAND   .COM    GRAPHICS .SCR    READ     .ME     Total
CPANEL    .COM    HELP     .COM    README   .CPQ      Files:          86
DAB       .EXE    HIMEM    .SYS    RECOVER  .COM      Bytes:   1,288,460
DATECHEK  .COM    HPDLBL   .EXE    REPLACE  .EXE    Matching
DAYCHEK   .BAT    INSTALL  .EXE    RESTORE  .COM      Files:          86
DEBUG     .COM    INSTALL  .SCR    ROMREV   .COM      Bytes:   1,288,460
DISKCOPY  .COM    KEYB     .COM    ROMREV   .SCR    Tagged
DISKINIT  .EXE    KEYBDP   .COM    SAVEDIR  .COM      Files:           0
DISPLAY   .SYS    KEYBDP   .SCR    SELECT   .COM      Bytes:           0
DOS33     .PAT    KEYBOARD .SYS    SETCLOCK .COM    Current File
DOS33A    .PAT    KP       .COM    SETUP    .EXE      READ    .ME
DRIVER    .SYS    LABEL    .COM    SETUP    .SCR      Bytes:       1,987

Printing file: READ.ME: Number of lines per page: 55
Enter new value, or 0 for no form feeds                         ESC cancel
```

Figure 3-102: Before printing a file in the advanced versions of XTree, you can select the number of lines per page you want to use.

change the default Print Form Length so that your page setup will always be the size you want (see "Configuration Options," earlier in this chapter).

> **NOTE:** In XTreePro Gold and XTree Gold, the History command can help you remember what page length you used last time. Remember, you can enter several frequently used page lengths, label them, and make them permanent (see "History").

Printing headers with XTreeGold 2.5

Users of XTreeGold 2.5 have an additional option available when printing ASCII files. You can add headers to the printout, using the F2 function key, as shown in Figure 3-103. The headers can include the current date and time, the file's name, directory, size, attributes, and page numbers. You get all that by just pressing F2!

Printing with 1Word

You can also print a file in XTreePro, XTreePro Gold, and XTreeGold, using 1Word (the built-in text editor). To print a file using 1Word, highlight the victim file, press E for Edit, then press Enter. Once you are inside 1Word, press Esc twice and then press F-P to print the file. As shown in Figure 3-104, that question about how many lines you want per page comes up again.

Print, Pull-Down Menus

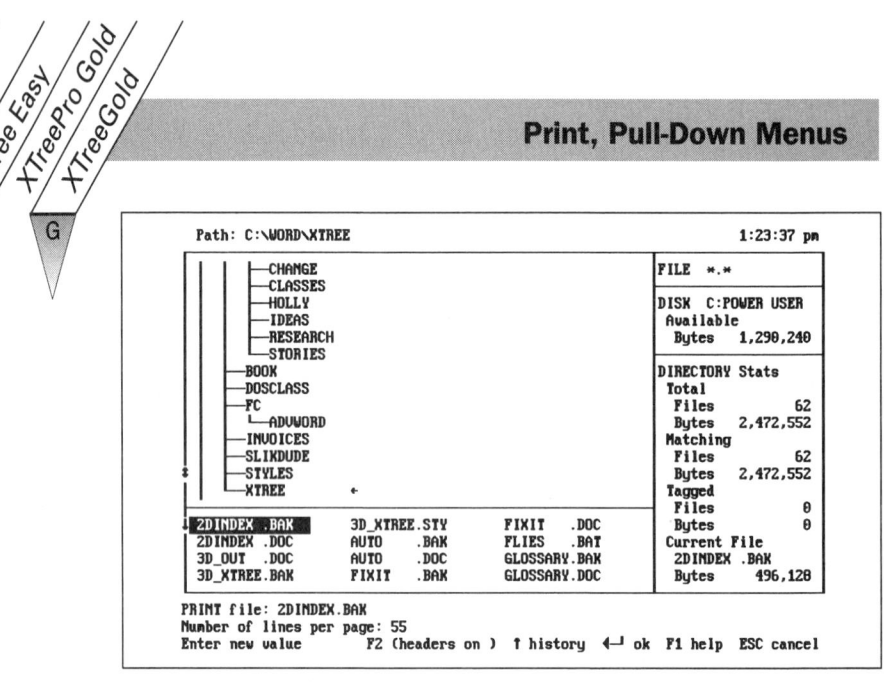

Figure 3-103: XTreeGold 2.5 allows you to add informational headers to your printouts.

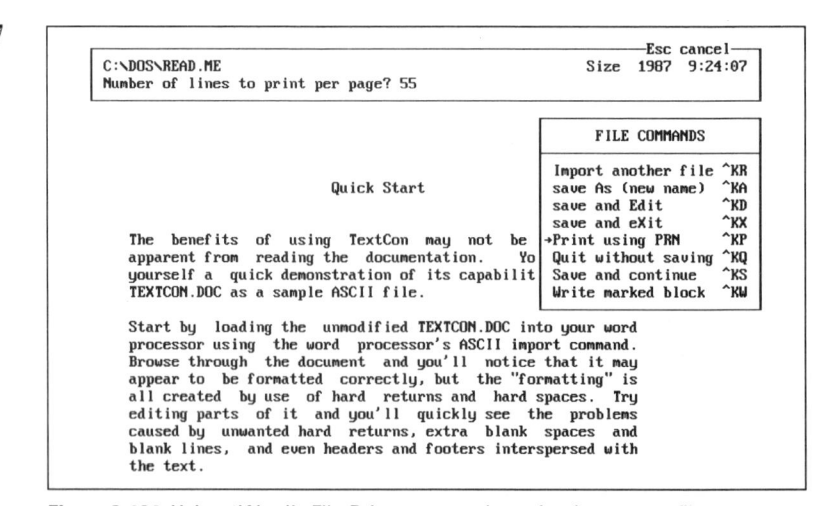

Figure 3-104: Using 1Word's File Print command to print the current file.

Pull-Down Menus

What's all the brouhaha about pull-down menus? Other than the fact that they're cute, pull-down menus present XTree Easy's and XTreeGold's command structure in a more logical way — by subject — and make files and directories easier to find. Say goodbye to searching for commands that use Ctrl to reveal the Ctrl

Chapter 3: XTree for DOS Quick Reference Guide

commands, Alt to reveal the Alt commands, and so forth. All the Ctrl and Alt commands are now organized by subject in the pull-down menus.

Whenever you see `F10 Commands` at the bottom of the screen, you can access the pull-down menus by pressing the F10 function key (or clicking the top line with the mouse). After you press F10, a menu bar at the top of the screen and several major topics, or menu names, will display. When you highlight a particular menu name, commands related to that menu are revealed on the list that drops down.

If you use F10 instead of a mouse, the first menu item on the menu bar automatically highlights and the available options drop down in a list. If you're in a Directory window when you press F10, you'll get the menu bar shown in Figure 3-105; the cursor is highlighting XTree, the first item on the menu bar. Below the first topic, the pertinent XTree command options are automatically disclosed.

`Application menu` is on the list of command options shown in Figure 3-105. To access the Application Menu, you either press A (the highlighted letter in `Application menu`), use the down-arrow key to move the cursor to that item, and then press Enter, or double-click the option with your mouse. Alternatively, you may simply press F9, as listed on the menu, at any time: this function key loads the Application Menu whether the pull-down menu is up or not (the Application Menu is called the XTreeMenu in Gold).

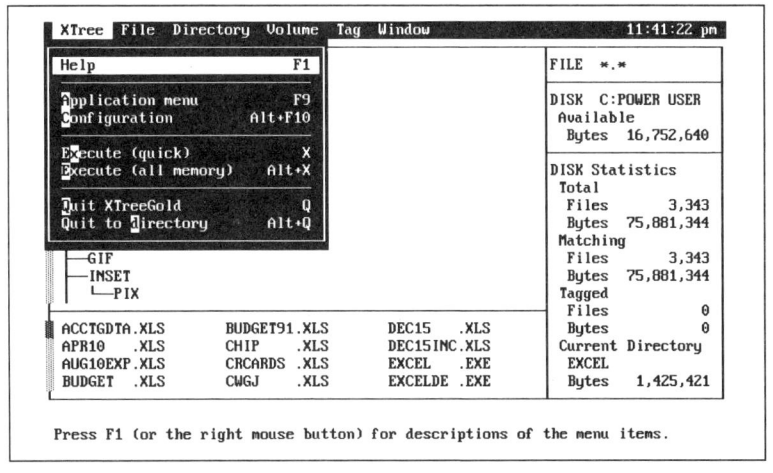

Figure 3-105: The first pull-down menu, XTree, appears when you press F10 in XTree Easy and XTreeGold.

Pull-Down Menus

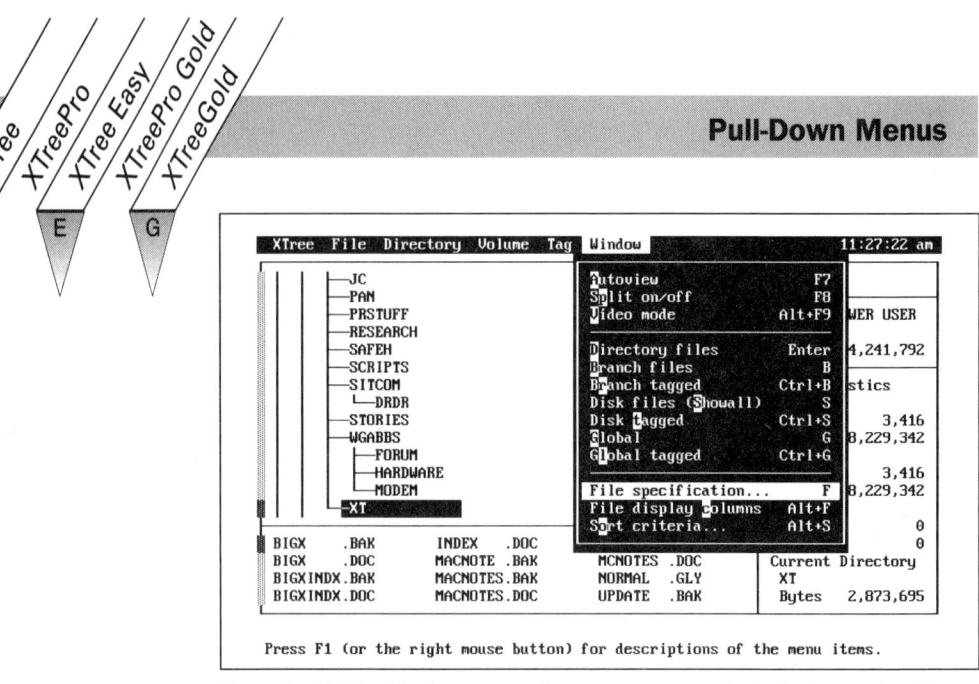

```
XTree  File  Directory  Volume  Tag  Window                       11:27:22 am
       ─JC                        Autoview              F7
       ─PAN                       Split on/off          F8
       ─PRSTUFF                   Video mode         Alt+F9    WER USER
       ─RESEARCH
       ─SAFEH                     Directory files    Enter     4,241,792
       ─SCRIPTS                   Branch files          B
       ─SITCOM                    Branch tagged      Ctrl+B    stics
        └─DRDR                    Disk files (Showall)  S
       ─STORIES                   Disk tagged        Ctrl+S        3,416
       ─WGABBS                    Global                G     8,229,342
         ├─FORUM                  Global tagged      Ctrl+G
         ├─HARDWARE                                                3,416
         └─MODEM                                              8,229,342
        ─XT                       File specification... F
                                  File display columns Alt+F
    BIGX      .BAK    INDEX    .DOC   Sort criteria... Alt+S          0
    BIGX      .DOC    MACNOTE  .BAK   MCNOTES  .DOC                   0
    BIGXINDX  .BAK    MACNOTES .BAK   NORMAL   .GLY    Current Directory
    BIGXINDX  .DOC    MACNOTES .DOC   UPDATE   .BAK    XT
                                                      Bytes   2,873,695

    Press F1 (or the right mouse button) for descriptions of the menu items.
```

Figure 3-106: The Window menu offers many commands, including setting file specifications.

To select another menu item, press the right-arrow key to move the highlight to another menu. When you highlight File, command options pertinent to file operations drop down from the File list. You may continue moving to the right, to reveal other commands.

You may have noticed that some of the commands have ellipses (you know, those three dots: . . .) next to them. When you select a menu option ending with an ellipsis, XTree will ask for additional information before performing that command. In Figure 3-106, for instance, File specification, an option on the Window menu, ends with an ellipses. If you highlight this option and press Enter, XTree asks for the file specification you want to specify.

On the other hand, the next command — File display columns — has no ellipsis after it. If you press Enter (or Alt-F) with this item highlighted, XTree proceeds to adjust the file display in the normal fashion (toggling between three columns, two columns, and one column).

Just as XTree's commands change depending on which window you're in, the pull-down menu also changes to match whatever window you're currently in. Figure 3-106 shows the pull-down menus available from the Directory window. In Figure 3-107, however, the pull-down menus are pertinent to the Small file window. Notice how the topics and commands change to fit the

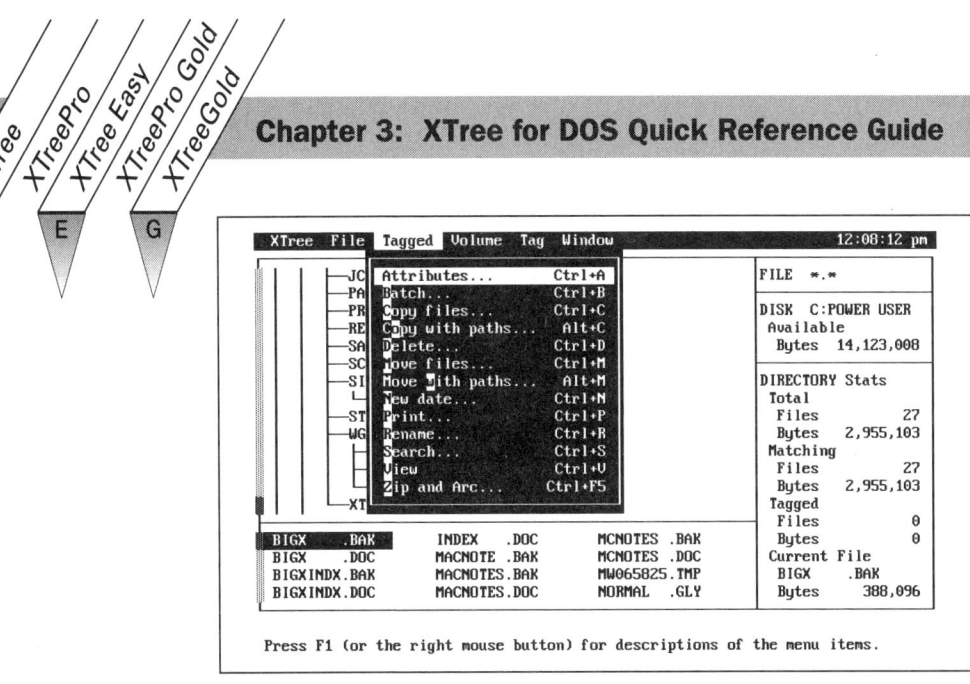

Chapter 3: XTree for DOS Quick Reference Guide 155

Figure 3-107: When you are working in a File window, the pull-down menus offer file-specific commands.

situation. In Figure 3-108, the highlighted file is a ZIP file, so menus on the menu bar contain commands that are specific to working with archived files.

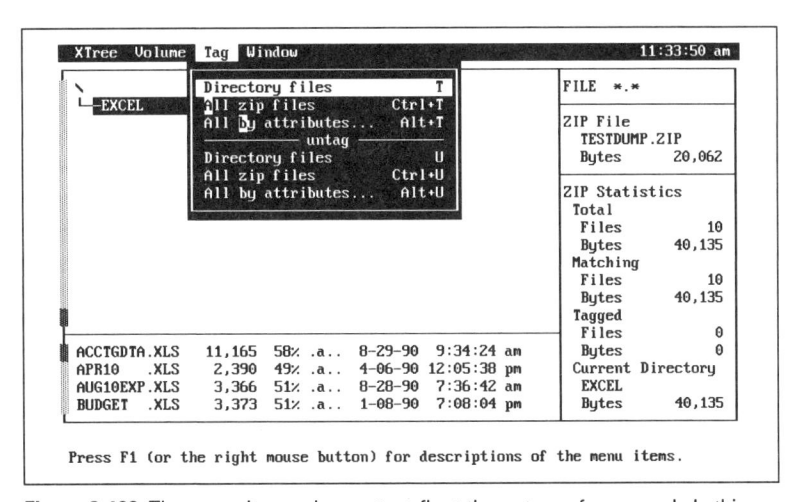

Figure 3-108: The menu items change to reflect the nature of your work. In this case, a ZIP file is highlighted, revealing commands specific to working with archived files.

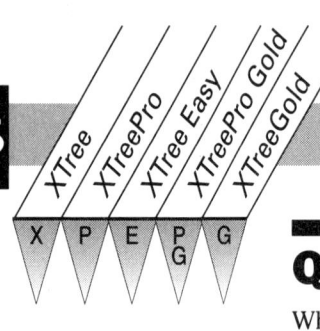

Quit Command

When you've finished using XTree, you can exit the various programs using the Quit command. As you can see in the following sections, the rules vary a bit between XTree and the later versions.

Quitting XTree

In XTree, use the F1 command to quit the program. You'll be asked if you're sure you want to return to DOS — just press Y for yes and you'll be returned to the directory you were in when you invoked XTree.

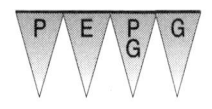

Quitting XTreePro, XTreePro Gold, XTree Easy and XTreeGold

The advanced versions use the Q command to quit the program. You'll be asked if you want to return to DOS; press Y for yes and you'll be returned to the directory you were in when you invoked the program.

Quitting to another directory

You can also use Alt-Q to exit, with slightly different results. If, for instance, you invoke XTreePro, XTreePro Gold, XTree Easy, or XTreeGold from the \WP directory, when you quit, you will normally be delivered back to that directory. You can, instead, highlight another directory and then press Alt-Q; upon exit you'll be in that highlighted directory.

Making a Zippy exit

You can also use the Alt-Z command (for Zip) to exit XTreePro Gold and XTreeGold. When you exit these two programs with Alt-Z, they take a snapshot of whatever is on-screen (whatever information is logged, for example) and *save* it. When you enter XTreePro Gold and XTreeGold again, the logging process is bypassed and that snapshot is used instead. You are returned to the exact place you were in when you pressed Alt-Z. This feature is particularly helpful when you're in the middle of some sort of intricate

Chapter 3: XTree for DOS Quick Reference Guide

operation and you're interrupted. (Say you're tagging a bunch of files to be copied to floppies when you realize you have no floppies left and you've got to go buy some.) If you were to exit XTree by pressing Q, you'd lose all your tags. However, Alt-Z saves your tags. You can go buy your floppies — or go on vacation for that matter!

When you exit with Alt-Z and then reenter the program, XTreePro Gold and XTreeGold bypass the logging procedure and merely reinstate the environment from its snapshot. Because of this, changes made to the disk in the interim will *not* be reflected. You must relog the drive to see any changes.

Rename   Command

The Rename command is useful for changing the names of files and directories. To rename a file or directory, highlight the item you want to change and then press R for Rename. You can instantly swap the offensive name for something more palatable — or meaningful. (You can rename a volume label with the V command.)

Renaming a file

To rename a file, highlight the filename in a File window and press R for Rename. XTree asks for a new name, as shown in Figure 3-109. You may use any filename as long as you follow the basic rules

```
Path: \WIN3

12MEG    .ICO    CDRIVE2  .ICO    FLOPPY   .ICO    FILE: *.*
144MEG   .ICO    CEO      .ICO    GAMES    .GRP
3270     .TXT    CEO2     .ICO    GCICON1  .WRI    DISK: C: POWER USER
360K     .ICO    CHART    .ICO    ICONDRAW.EXE       Available
720K     .ICO    CHESS    .BMP    LABELS   .ICO       Bytes: 3,502,080
ACCESSOR.GRP     CLIPBRD  .EXE    LOCK     .DOC
APOLLO   .BMP    CLIPBRD  .HLP    LOCK     .EXE    DIRECTORY Stats
ARCTOOL  .ICO    CLOCK    .EXE    MACRO    .ICO    Total
BART-S   .BMP    CONTROL  .EXE    MAIN     .GRP      Files:           136
BOMB     .ICO    CONTROL  .HLP    MARK30   .DOC      Bytes:     4,653,055
BOXES    .BMP    CONTROL  .INI    MARK30   .EXE    Matching
BULKCOPY.ICO     DIGITAL  .FON    MARK30   .ZIP      Files:           136
CALC     .EXE    DOS      .ICO    METZ     .ORD      Bytes:     4,653,055
CALC     .HLP    DT1      .BMP    MINIDISK.ICO     Tagged
CALENDAR.EXE     DT2      .BMP    MOUSE    .OLD      Files:             0
CALENDAR.HLP     DT3      .BMP    MOUSE    .SYS      Bytes:             0
CARDFILE.EXE     EMAIL    .ICO    MS       .EXE    Current File
CARDFILE.HLP     EMM386   .SYS    MSAVR1   .ZIP      MOUSE     OLD
CC       .ICO    ERASE    .ICO    MSDOS    .EXE      Bytes:        31,701

RENAME file: MOUSE.OLD
          to:
enter new file name                               F1 quit F2 help F3 cancel
```

Figure 3-109: Highlighting a file and pressing R starts the Rename process. Naturally, XTree waits for you to type in a new name.

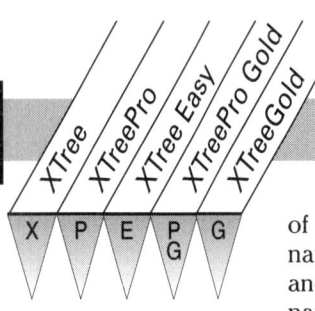

of filenames (see Chapter 1 for more details on the rules of file-naming). Once you've typed a new name for your file, press Enter and the file appears in the list, with its new name. (If you want the name to appear alphabetically, you must relog the directory.)

Renaming a directory

Use the same rules to rename a directory as for renaming a file. Highlight the directory name to be changed and press R to Rename. You'll be greeted with the message enter new directory name, as shown in Figure 3-110. Give the directory a new name and press Enter.

If you change a directory name that is part of any batch file — including your AUTOEXEC.BAT file — the batch file should be changed accordingly. If you decided, for instance, to change your WordPerfect directory name from WORD_PRF to WP, you'd find that WordPerfect would no longer work *unless* you also adjusted your path statement in your AUTOEXEC.BAT file to reflect the new directory name. If your old path statement was this:

PATH=C:\;C:\WORD_PERF;C:\DOS

then the new path statement that reflects the name change in your WordPerfect directory would be this:

PATH=C:\;C:\WP;C:\DOS

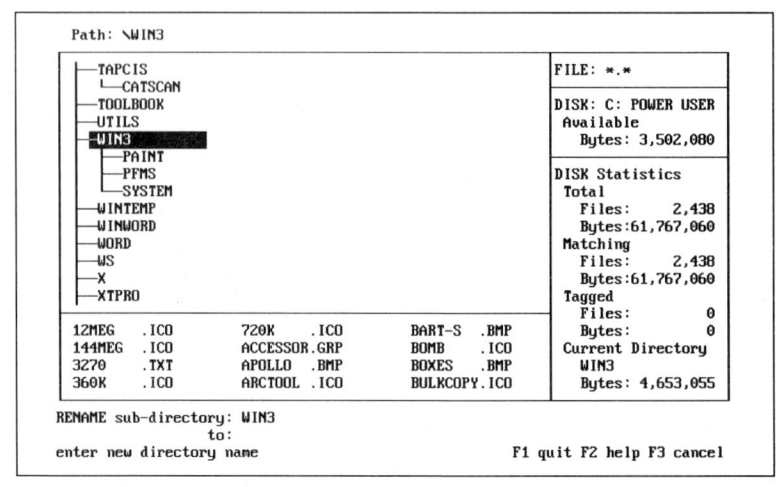

Figure 3-110: Renaming a directory is exactly the same as renaming a file; highlight the directory and press R for Rename.

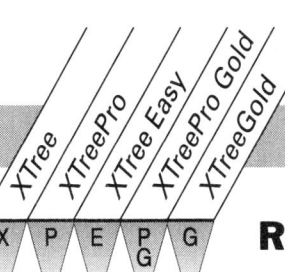

Renaming a volume label

Whenever you format a disk, you can give that disk a name. This name is called a *label*. A *volume* is simply a disk. You may have seen the VOLUME HAS NO LABEL message, which just means you didn't name the disk when you formatted it. This has nothing to do with whether or not you put a sticker on the disk.

Naming the volume is useful because when you log a disk in XTree, the volume name appears on the right in the DISK window. You can tell from the name if you're working with the right disk without taking the disk out of the drive to examine the sticker.

A lot of people don't bother putting labels on their volumes, but XTree provides a very simple process for doing so. Just log onto the disk (even a hard disk) whose label you want to change. From the Directory window, press V for Volume, and you'll be asked for a new volume name, as shown in Figure 3-111. In this example, the volume is labeled POWER USER. Look, ma — spaces! That's right; unlike filenames, volume names can include spaces. So, knock yourself out!

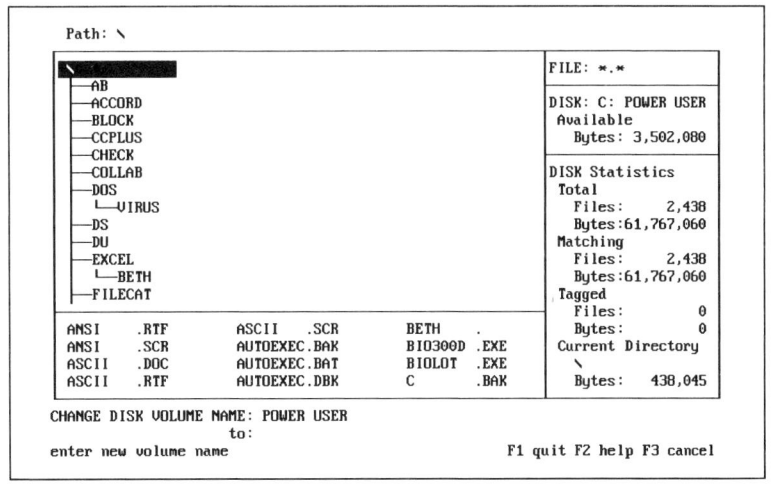

Figure 3-111: Press V for Volume to give a disk (even your hard disk) a new name.

```
Path: C:\WORD\BETH\XT                                          7:59:23 am
073A1C0C.            MC4          .DOC     X3        .DOC    FILE   *.*
BIGTEST .BAK         MC4          .TXT     XDUMP     .DOC
BIGTEST .DOC         MC5          .DOC     XINTRO    .BAK    DISK  C:POWER USER
BOOK1   .BAK         NORMAL       .BAK     XINTRO    .DOC    Available
CAHLIN                            .GLY     XOUT      .BAK      Bytes      3,457,024
FAX                               .DOC     XOUT      .DOC
FEATURES                    E    .BAK     XTG       .DOC    DIRECTORY Stats
IDG1                        E    .STY     XTP       .DOC    Total
IDG2                             .BAK     XTQ&A     .BAK      Files             51
IDG2                             .BAK     XTQ&A     .DOC      Bytes      1,302,550
IDG3                             .DOC     XTREE     .CMP    Matching
IDG3                             .BAK     XTREE     .DOC      Files             51
IDG4                             .STY     XTREE     .ZIP      Bytes      1,302,550
IDG4                             .BAK                       Tagged
IDGPROP     *.*                  .DOC                         Files              0
LET'S       BONBOOK              .BAK                         Bytes              0
MC1         BONBOOK.DOC          .DOC                       Current File
MC2         MWHELP.ORI           .RTF                         BIGTEST .DOC
MC3         CAHLIN.DOC           .BAK                         Bytes          1,024

RENAME file: BIGTEST.DOC
         to:
Enter file specification                  ↑ history  ⏎ ok  F1 help  ESC cancel
```

Figure 3-112: A History file is maintained, even for your responses to the Rename command. Use it to minimize typos and keep track of what you're doing.

Using History while renaming

A History file is maintained when you rename files, directories, and even volume labels, as shown in Figure 3-112 (see "History"). If you're naming a bunch of disks sequentially, using the History file to recall your previous responses could be very helpful for keeping things straight.

Securing Files and Directories

There are several features in all versions of XTree that can be used to help protect the data on your hard disk from prying eyes. Keep in mind, however, that someone with a lot of computer knowledge (or even *some* computer knowledge) who *really* wants to get at what you've got on hard disk, probably can. It's a lot like locking the front door to your house: no matter what, the best you can hope for is to slow the thief down.

If you're extremely concerned about security, you should investigate software that specializes in system protection. However, if you just want to keep your data hidden from co-workers, a few simple precautions on your part are enough to discourage browsing in your confidential files. Here are two simple non-XTree hints:

Chapter 3: XTree for DOS Quick Reference Guide

- Remember that most word processed files come in pairs: the original and the BAK version. If you delete one for security purposes, be sure to delete the other.

- Many computers come with keys to lock out keyboard input. If you have a key, use it.

Hiding and unhiding files

There is actually no "hide a file" command. But, remember all that stuff about attributes and hidden files? (If you don't, see "Attributes (File)," earlier in this chapter.) You can use the hidden attribute to render a file invisible. You can still call up the file, add to it, and save it, as long as *you* remember the filename.

To convert a file to hidden status, first highlight the file. Then press A for attributes, type **+H** (translation: add "hidden" to this file's attributes) and press Enter. This scenario is illustrated in Figure 3-113.

In all but the original version of XTree, once the file is hidden, its filename will still be displayed, but in lowercase letters; as shown in Figure 3-114, `bonnie.doc` is now in lowercase letters. This means that, in DOS, the file will not appear in its directory. However, anyone using XTree can still find the file. Read on for how to hide hidden files.

```
Path: C:\WORD\BETH\SITCOM

BAFA6    .DOC    FINALBF  .RTF    PROPOSAL.DOC    FILE: *.*
BF       .CMP    FINALPW  .DOC    PW4      .DOC
BF       .DOC    FINALPW  .RTF    REALWOM  .DOC    DISK: C:POWER USER
BINDING  .DOC    GOLDEN   .DOC    REVWOM1  .DOC    Available
BONNIE   .DOC    GOLDEN   .STY    RON      .DOC      Bytes:    3,538,944
BONNIE   .TXT    HP_REFIL .TXT    RON      .RTG
CAST     .DOC    LUTZ     .DOC    RWA      .DOC    DIRECTORY Stats
CHARS    .DOC    LUTZ     .STY    S1A      .DOC    Total
COMMENT  .DOC    NORMAL   .GLY    S1B      .DOC      Files:           59
COMMENT  .TXT    NPW      .DOC    S1C      .DOC      Bytes:    1,139,558
DAD56    .DOC    PITCH    .DOC    SGONE    .DOC    Matching
DADDY1   .DOC    PITCH2   .DOC    SGONE    .RGF      Files:           59
DADDY2   .DOC    PITCH6   .DOC    SGONEB   .DOC      Bytes:    1,139,558
DADEND   .DOC    PITCH6   .RTF    SHERIFF  .ZIP    Tagged
DADTIME  .DOC    PITCH7   .BAK    SING3    .DOC      Files:            0
DRDR     .DOC    PITCH7   .DOC    SITCOM   .STY      Bytes:            0
DUMP     .DOC    PITCH7   .RTF    TV       .DOC    Current File
FATHER   .DOC    PITCH7B  .RTF    TV       .STY    BONNIE   .DOC
FINALBF  .DOC    POP1     .DOC    TV5      .STY      Bytes:        1,536

ATTRIBUTES for file: BONNIE.DOC            1,536 ....  6-02-90  7:39 pm
                   : +H
Enter attribute changes (+/- R A S H)                 F1 help  ESC cancel
```

Figure 3-113: Adding the hidden attribute to BONNIE.DOC.

Securing Files and Directories

```
Path: C:\WORD\BETH\SITCOM

BAFA6      .DOC    FINALBF  .RTF    PROPOSAL .DOC    FILE: *.*
BF         .CMP    FINALPW  .DOC    PW4      .DOC
BF         .DOC    FINALPW  .RTF    REALWOM  .DOC    DISK: C:POWER USER
BINDING    .DOC    GOLDEN   .DOC    REWWOM1  .DOC     Available
bonnie     .doc    GOLDEN   .STY    RON      .DOC      Bytes:   3,538,944
BONNIE     .TXT    HP_REFIL .TXT    RON      .RTG
CAST       .DOC    LUTZ     .DOC    RWA      .DOC    DIRECTORY Stats
CHARS      .DOC    LUTZ     .STY    S1A      .DOC     Total
COMMENT    .DOC    NORMAL   .GLY    S1B      .DOC      Files:          59
COMMENT    .TXT    NPW      .DOC    S1C      .DOC      Bytes:   1,139,558
DAD56      .DOC    PITCH    .DOC    SGONE    .DOC     Matching
DADDY1     .DOC    PITCH2   .DOC    SGONE    .RGF      Files:          59
DADDY2     .DOC    PITCH6   .DOC    SGONEB   .DOC      Bytes:   1,139,558
DADEND     .DOC    PITCH6   .RTF    SHERIFF  .ZIP    Tagged
DADTIME    .DOC    PITCH7   .BAK    SING3    .DOC      Files:           0
DRDR       .DOC    PITCH7   .DOC    SITCOM   .STY      Bytes:           0
DUMP       .DOC    PITCH7   .RTF    TV       .DOC    Current File
FATHER     .DOC    PITCH7B  .RTF    TV       .STY     bonnie   .doc
FINALBF    .DOC    POP1     .DOC    TV5      .STY     Bytes:        1,536

FILE          Attributes  Copy  Delete  Edit  Filespec  Log disk  Move  Print
COMMANDS      Rename  Tag  Untag  View  eXecute  Quit
←↑↓→ scroll   ENTER tree commands     ALT menu    CTRL menu     F1 help  ESC cancel
```

Figure 3-114: A filename in lowercase letters is hidden to DOS.

Hiding hidden files

You can take these Mata Hari dealings one step further if you don't want XTreePro, XTreePro Gold, and XTreeGold to list the names of your hidden files at all. Go into the Configuration program and change the System and Hidden File Access option to No (see "Configuration Options," earlier in this chapter, for more on this program). Once you've changed this option, any hidden files will not be displayed in their respective directory lists.

Hiding and unhiding tagged files

To add the hidden attribute to several files at once, just tag the files to be hidden and then press Ctrl-A to change the attributes of all tagged files.

Hiding and Unhiding directories

While this feature may not impress magician David Copperfield, XTreePro Gold and XTreeGold can actually make whole *directories* disappear from view.

Once a directory is designated as *hidden*, the directory and its files are, theoretically, not visible from any program (including DOS) except XTreePro Gold and XTreeGold. Just keep in mind that there

Chapter 3: XTree for DOS Quick Reference Guide

are other utility programs with abilities similar to Pro Gold and Gold that allow you to view hidden directories anyway. The hidden attribute is not a fool-proof security system. Further, anyone (like you) who knows the name of a hidden directory can access it. Hiding does not prevent unauthorized access but just assumes that only those who *know* the directory name should have access to it.

Let's say you've put your personal checkbook on your office computer. (Naturally you're spending time on your personal checkbook only during your lunch hour or after work.) However, you don't want the Big Boss (or even your secretary) to have access to your personal finances. So you decide to hide the directory. The first step is to highlight the directory you want to hide and then press Alt-H for Hide. You'll be presented with something like that in Figure 3-115, where at the bottom of the screen, XTree asks you to confirm this action. Press Y to hide the directory or N to cancel the command.

Once a directory is officially hidden, the directory name is still visible on-screen in XTree, though it now appears in lowercase type. If you wish, you can make the directory name disappear from the XTree Directory window, but you must first go to the Configuration program to do this. Under Security, change the System/Hidden file and directory access option to No. If you should forget the names of the directories you've hidden later, just go back into the Configuration program and change the System/Hidden file and directory access option back to Yes, and all will be revealed.

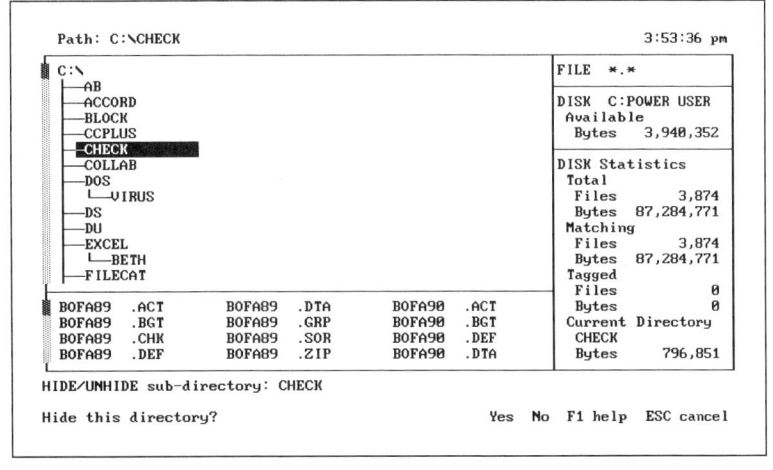

```
Path: C:\CHECK                                           3:53:36 pm
C:\                                         │FILE  *.*
 ├─AB                                       │
 ├─ACCORD                                   │DISK  C:POWER USER
 ├─BLOCK                                    │Available
 ├─CCPLUS                                   │  Bytes      3,940,352
 ├─CHECK
 ├─COLLAB                                   │DISK Statistics
 ├─DOS                                      │Total
 │ └─VIRUS                                  │  Files          3,874
 ├─DS                                       │  Bytes     87,284,771
 ├─DU                                       │Matching
 ├─EXCEL                                    │  Files          3,874
 │ └─BETH                                   │  Bytes     87,284,771
 ├─FILECAT                                  │Tagged
                                            │  Files              0
BOFA89  .ACT   BOFA89  .DTA   BOFA90  .ACT  │  Bytes              0
BOFA89  .BGT   BOFA89  .GRP   BOFA90  .BGT  │Current Directory
BOFA89  .CHK   BOFA89  .SOR   BOFA90  .DEF  │  CHECK
BOFA89  .DEF   BOFA89  .ZIP   BOFA90  .DTA  │  Bytes        796,851

HIDE/UNHIDE sub-directory: CHECK

Hide this directory?                     Yes  No  F1 help  ESC cancel
```

Figure 3-115: Highlight the directory you wish to hide and press Alt-H. Press Y to confirm your request.

Using Wash Disk for security

As you may have already read in the "Delete" section, deleting a file doesn't exactly remove it from your disk. Deleting a file tells DOS that the space on the disk previously used by the deleted file is now free for other files to use as needed. And as long as that space has not been put to use by another file, anyone can use one of many programs designed specifically to *undelete* files. The Wash Disk command visits all currently unused areas on the disk and makes sure that all deleted files are no longer recoverable. The Wash Disk command is simple to invoke. Press Alt-W and then press Enter when you are presented with the screen shown in Figure 3-116.

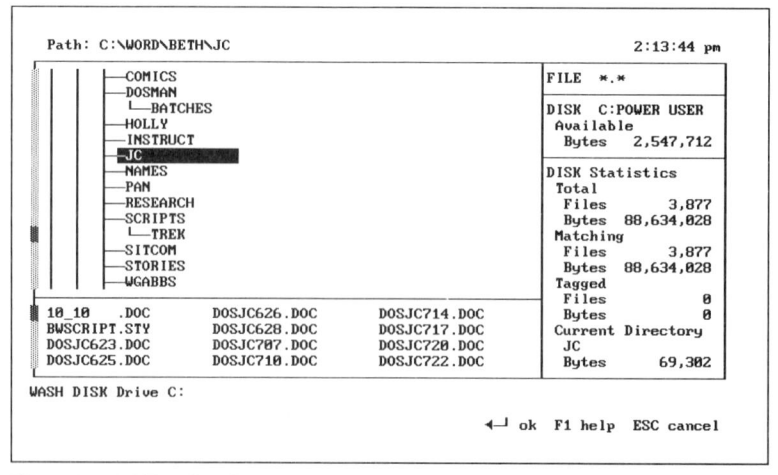

```
Path: C:\WORD\BETH\JC                                    2:13:44 pm

         ├─COMICS                          FILE  *.*
         ├─DOSMAN
         │  └─BATCHES                      DISK  C:POWER USER
         ├─HOLLY                           Available
         ├─INSTRUCT                         Bytes    2,547,712
         ├─JC
         ├─NAMES                           DISK Statistics
         ├─PAN                             Total
         ├─RESEARCH                         Files         3,877
         ├─SCRIPTS                          Bytes    88,634,028
         │  └─TREK                         Matching
         ├─SITCOM                           Files         3,877
         ├─STORIES                          Bytes    88,634,028
         └─WGABBS                          Tagged
 10_10   .DOC    DOSJC626.DOC   DOSJC714.DOC     Files            0
 BWSCRIPT.STY    DOSJC628.DOC   DOSJC717.DOC     Bytes            0
 DOSJC623.DOC    DOSJC707.DOC   DOSJC720.DOC   Current Directory
 DOSJC625.DOC    DOSJC710.DOC   DOSJC722.DOC    JC
                                                 Bytes       69,302
 WASH DISK Drive C:

                                          ↵ ok   F1 help   ESC cancel
```

Figure 3-116: XTreePro Gold and XTreeGold can make sure files cannot be undeleted. At this point, you need to hit Enter to start washing.

XTreeGold version 2.5 users are given an additional choice. Pressing the F2 function key toggles between Six passes (XTree will scrub over the deleted file six times) and DoD (washing per Department of Defense specifications DOD 5220.22-M). Once you've selected your choice (and one certainly hopes that the Department of Defense technique is the most thorough and takes the longest), press Enter and go read Dear Abby for a few minutes while Gold 2.5 goes to work: this could take a while.

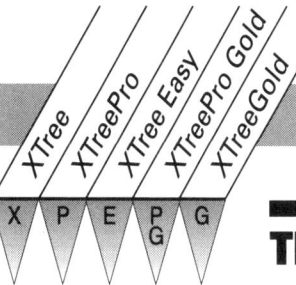

The Showall File Window

The Showall command asks XTree to show *all* the files on the current drive, regardless of directory, in alphabetical order in the Showall file window. Or, if you prefer the files to be sorted and displayed by size or date, press Alt-S and you can change the sort criteria to accommodate your desires. See "Sort Criteria," next, for details.

Using Showall to view all files on the current drive

To open the Showall file window, start from the Directory window and press S for Showall. The Directory and File windows will merge into one window, the entire screen will highlight, and all files on the disk will be listed in alphabetical order. When a filename is highlighted, its pathname is displayed above the Showall file window.

Using Showall with Filespec

The Showall command, like all file commands, works in conjunction with the Filespec command. So, if you are searching for certain files on the hard disk, use a file specification command before (or after) invoking Showall to filter out the files you don't care about. For instance, if you want to see your BAK files, press F for filespec and type ***.BAK** for the file specification. Then, from the Directory window, press S for Showall to see all files with the BAK extension in the Showall file window.

An example of this is shown in Figure 3-117. Right before your very eyes, all of the BAK files on your hard disk appear in one list. You could press Ctrl-T to tag all those files and Ctrl-D to delete them all — freeing up all that space on your disk!

Viewing tagged files with Showall

You can view any and all files you've tagged on your computer by pressing Ctrl-S rather than S.

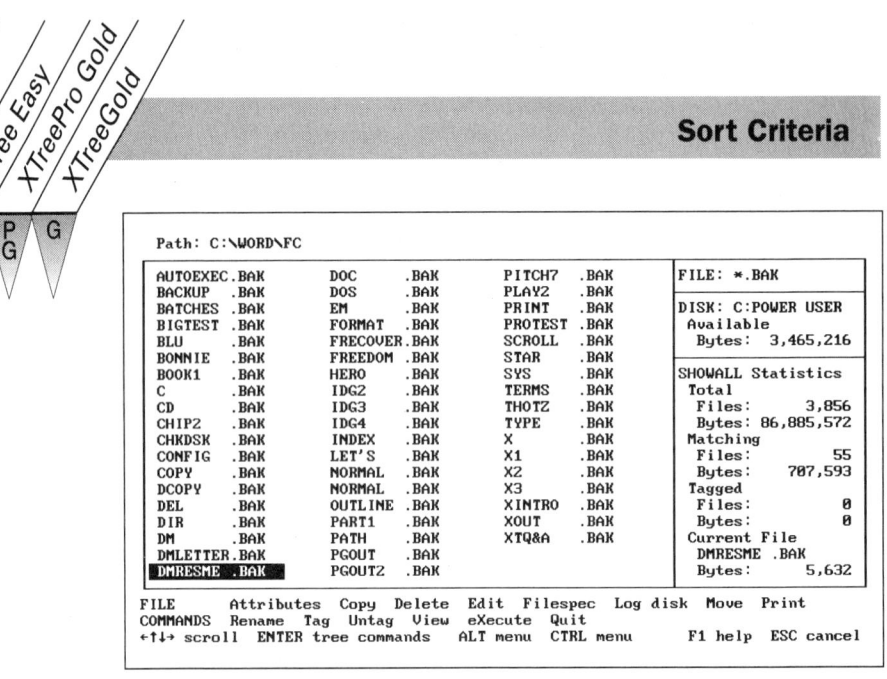

```
Path: C:\WORD\FC

AUTOEXEC .BAK    DOC       .BAK    PITCH7   .BAK    FILE: *.BAK
BACKUP   .BAK    DOS       .BAK    PLAY2    .BAK
BATCHES  .BAK    EM        .BAK    PRINT    .BAK    DISK: C:POWER USER
BIGTEST  .BAK    FORMAT    .BAK    PROTEST  .BAK    Available
BLU      .BAK    FRECOVER  .BAK    SCROLL   .BAK       Bytes:   3,465,216
BONNIE   .BAK    FREEDOM   .BAK    STAR     .BAK
BOOK1    .BAK    HERO      .BAK    SYS      .BAK    SHOWALL Statistics
C        .BAK    IDG2      .BAK    TERMS    .BAK    Total
CD       .BAK    IDG3      .BAK    THOTZ    .BAK       Files:       3,856
CHIP2    .BAK    IDG4      .BAK    TYPE     .BAK       Bytes: 86,885,572
CHKDSK   .BAK    INDEX     .BAK    X        .BAK    Matching
CONFIG   .BAK    LET'S     .BAK    X1       .BAK       Files:          55
COPY     .BAK    NORMAL    .BAK    X2       .BAK       Bytes:     707,593
DCOPY    .BAK    NORMAL    .BAK    X3       .BAK    Tagged
DEL      .BAK    OUTLINE   .BAK    XINTRO   .BAK       Files:           0
DIR      .BAK    PART1     .BAK    XOUT     .BAK       Bytes:           0
DM       .BAK    PATH      .BAK    XTQ&A    .BAK    Current File
DMLETTER .BAK    PGOUT     .BAK                        DMRESME   .BAK
DMRESME  .BAK    PGOUT2    .BAK                        Bytes:       5,632

FILE              Attributes  Copy  Delete  Edit  Filespec  Log disk  Move  Print
COMMANDS          Rename  Tag  Untag  View  eXecute  Quit
←↑↓→ scroll  ENTER tree commands     ALT menu   CTRL menu      F1 help  ESC cancel
```

Figure 3-117: Using Showall and specifying a *.BAK filespec causes all the BAK files on this hard disk to appear in one list.

In XTreeGold you can update the Ctrl/Showall file window if you've untagged some of your previously tagged files. Press F2 to filter out the newly untagged files from the Ctrl/Showall file window.

Sort Criteria   Command

One of the great things about XTree is that when you get a list of files, they are in alphabetical order. In other words, by default, the files are sorted alphabetically in ascending order, starting with A. Alphabetical order, however, is just the beginning when it comes to having it your way in XTree's file display. With files displayed in a certain order, you'll find it easier to tag, find, or compare files. There are a number of criteria by which files can be sorted.

Whether you are in the Directory window or a File window, you invoke the Sort Criteria command by pressing Alt-S. Then, select the criteria you want to use to sort your information and press the appropriate highlighted letter.

Sort Criteria commands for XTree

Pressing Alt-S in XTree gives you four options, as shown in Figure 3-118 and explained here:

Name — Lists files alphabetically by name. This is the default.

Ext — Groups files alphabetically by extension and then by name within each extension. All the BAKs, DOCs, WK1s, and so on are grouped together (in alphabetical order).

Date & time — Lists files sorted by date of creation and then by time. The newest files are at the head of the list.

Size — Lists files in order by size. The biggest files are listed first.

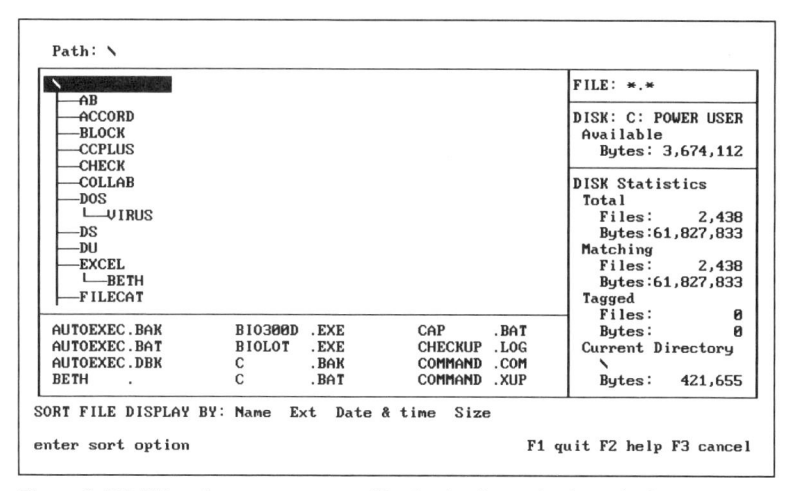

```
Path: \
       ┌─AB
       ├─ACCORD
       ├─BLOCK
       ├─CCPLUS
       ├─CHECK
       ├─COLLAB
       ├─DOS
       │  └─VIRUS
       ├─DS
       ├─DU
       ├─EXCEL
       │  └─BETH
       ├─FILECAT

AUTOEXEC.BAK     BIO300D .EXE     CAP      .BAT
AUTOEXEC.BAT     BIOLOT  .EXE     CHECKUP  .LOG
AUTOEXEC.DBK     C       .BAK     COMMAND  .COM
BETH    .        C       .BAT     COMMAND  .XUP

FILE: *.*

DISK: C: POWER USER
Available
   Bytes: 3,674,112

DISK Statistics
Total
   Files:      2,438
   Bytes:61,827,833
Matching
   Files:      2,438
   Bytes:61,827,833
Tagged
   Files:          0
   Bytes:          0
Current Directory
\
   Bytes:    421,655

SORT FILE DISPLAY BY: Name   Ext   Date & time   Size
enter sort option                          F1 quit F2 help F3 cancel
```

Figure 3-118: XTree lets you sort your files by the four criteria at the bottom of the screen (Name, Ext, Date & time, and Size).

Sort Criteria commands for XTreePro, XTree Easy, XTreePro Gold, and XTreeGold

When you use the Alt-S command in XTreePro, XTreePro Gold, XTree Easy, or XTreeGold, you'll see something like that in Figure 3-119. The Name, Ext, Date & time, and Size criteria can each be modified by the Order option. If the Order option specifies

Sort Criteria

ascending, sorting files by Date & time lists the oldest files first and the newest last. Similarly, specifying *ascending* for the Size option lists the smallest files first, and continues through the biggest. If the Order option is set to *descending*, the Name and Ext options will be in reverse alphabetical order; Date & time will start with the newest files and drop down to the oldest; Size will start with the biggest files and shrink down to the smallest. In addition to Order, you also have the following options:

Name	Lists files alphabetically by name. This is the default.
Ext	Groups files alphabetically by extension and then by name within each extension. All the BAKs, DOCs, WK1s, and so on are grouped together (in alphabetical order).
Date & time	Lists files sorted by date of creation and then by time. The newest files are at the head of the list.
Size	Lists files in order by size. The biggest files are listed first.
Unsorted	Lists files in the actual order DOS stores them in on the disk (what you see if you use DOS's DIR command).

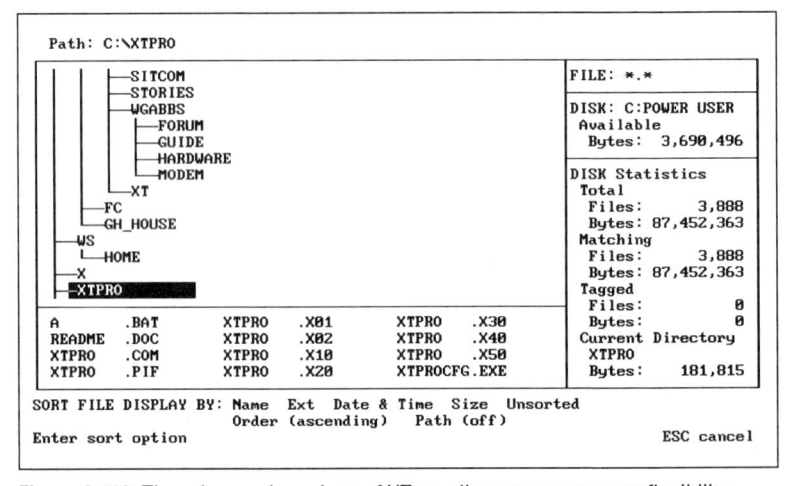

```
Path: C:\XTPRO
                                                          FILE: *.*
       ├─SITCOM
       ├─STORIES                                          DISK: C:POWER USER
       ├─WGABBS                                            Available
       │   ├─FORUM                                          Bytes:    3,690,496
       │   ├─GUIDE
       │   ├─HARDWARE                                     DISK Statistics
       │   └─MODEM                                         Total
       ├─XT                                                 Files:        3,888
       ├─FC                                                 Bytes:   87,452,363
       └─GH_HOUSE                                          Matching
 ├─WS                                                       Files:        3,888
 │  └─HOME                                                  Bytes:   87,452,363
 ├─X                                                       Tagged
 ├─XTPRO                                                    Files:            0
                                                            Bytes:            0
A        .BAT    XTPRO    .X01    XTPRO    .X30          Current Directory
README   .DOC    XTPRO    .X02    XTPRO    .X40           XTPRO
XTPRO    .COM    XTPRO    .X10    XTPRO    .X50            Bytes:      181,815
XTPRO    .PIF    XTPRO    .X20    XTPROCFG .EXE

SORT FILE DISPLAY BY: Name  Ext  Date & Time  Size  Unsorted
                     Order (ascending)  Path (off)
Enter sort option                                              ESC cancel
```

Figure 3-119: The advanced versions of XTree allow you even more flexibility when arranging your file display.

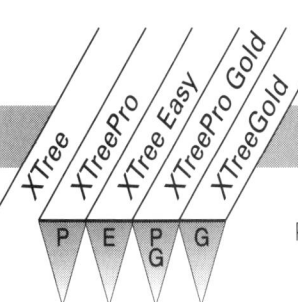

Chapter 3: XTree for DOS Quick Reference Guide 169

Path — When you're in a Showall or Global file window and path is turned on (default is off), the files will not be mushed together in a huge alphabetical listing. Instead the files will be grouped by directory area first and then by the specified option section.

Remember, some sort criteria defaults can be changed permanently via the Configuration program or specified at the command line when the program is invoked.

Split/Unsplit   Command

XTreePro Gold and XTreeGold let you double your fun and divide the screen into two windows, as shown in Figure 3-120, much as Moses parted the Red Sea. Whether you are in a File window or a Directory window, you can use the F8 function key (the Split command) to split the display into two independent windows. Each of the two split windows is capable of performing all of the normal XTreePro Gold and XTreeGold commands. However, only one window can function at a time.

Figure 3-121 shows another example of a split window. The *active window* in this figure is the one on the left, because that's where the highlight is. When you issue a command, it will affect only the

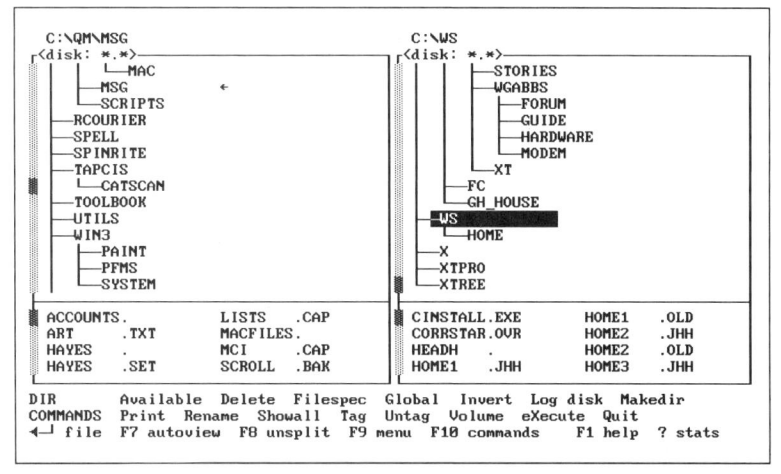

Figure 3-120: Compare two drives, two directories, two trees, two of anything with the Split (F8) command.

Split/Unsplit

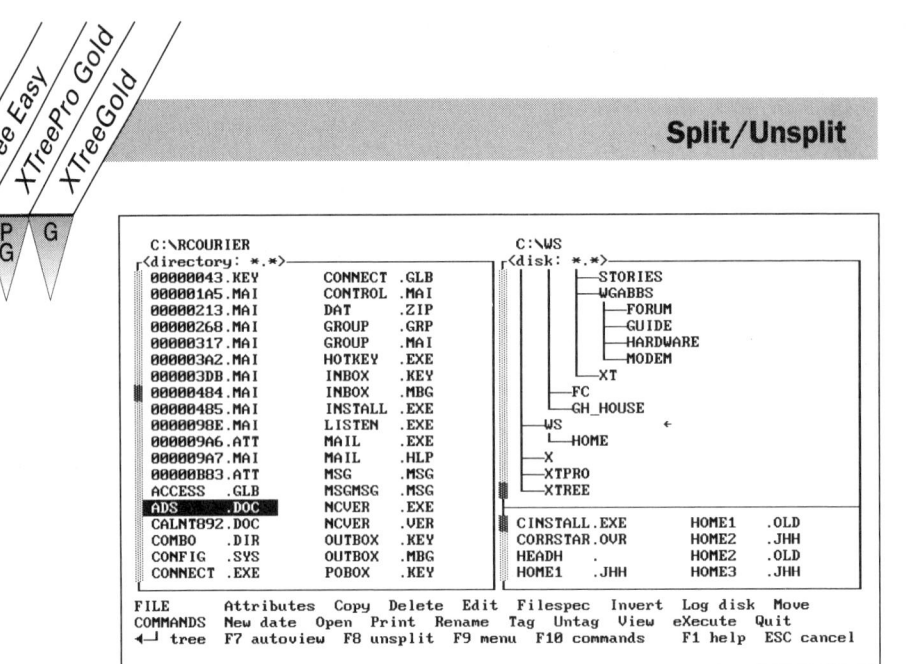

```
C:\RCOURIER                                    C:\WS
<directory: *.*>                               <disk: *.*>
 00000043.KEY    CONNECT .GLB                   ┌─STORIES
 000001A5.MAI    CONTROL .MAI                   ├─WGABBS
 00000213.MAI    DAT     .ZIP                   │  ├─FORUM
 00000268.MAI    GROUP   .GRP                   │  ├─GUIDE
 00000317.MAI    GROUP   .MAI                   │  ├─HARDWARE
 000003A2.MAI    HOTKEY  .EXE                   │  └─MODEM
 000003DB.MAI    INBOX   .KEY                   └─XT
 00000484.MAI    INBOX   .MBG                  ├─FC
 00000485.MAI    INSTALL .EXE                  └─GH_HOUSE
 0000098E.MAI    LISTEN  .EXE                 ─WS
 000009A6.ATT    MAIL    .EXE                   └─HOME
 000009A7.MAI    MAIL    .HLP                 ─X
 00000B83.ATT    MSG     .MSG                 ─XTPRO
 ACCESS  .GLB    MSGMSG  .MSG                 ─XTREE
▌ADS     .DOC    NCVER   .EXE
 CALNT892.DOC    NCVER   .VER                   CINSTALL.EXE    HOME1   .OLD
 COMBO   .DIR    OUTBOX  .KEY                   CORRSTAR.OUR    HOME2   .JHH
 CONFIG  .SYS    OUTBOX  .MBG                   HEADH   .       HOME2   .OLD
 CONNECT .EXE    POBOX   .KEY                   HOME1   .JHH    HOME3   .JHH

FILE       Attributes  Copy   Delete  Edit   Filespec  Invert  Log disk  Move
COMMANDS   New date    Open   Print   Rename Tag       Untag   View  eXecute  Quit
 ↵ tree   F7 autoview  F8 unsplit  F9 menu  F10 commands    F1 help  ESC cancel
```

Figure 3-121: When a window is split, the active window is the one with the cursor in it. Use Tab to travel back and forth between windows.

active window. Press the Tab key to move the highlight back and forth between the windows.

> The left side of Figure 3-121 shows an Expanded file window, and the right side shows a Directory window. You can log onto different drives, tag different files, or do whatever you wish in a split window. The main point of splitting the display into two windows is so you can compare directory trees on two different disks or compare files in two different directories. Which directory has more files? Which file is newer or bigger?

An important thing to realize is that if you delete a file on one side of the display, the inactive side will not reflect that change until it becomes the *active* window. For example, if both windows display the same list of files and you delete a file, only the *active* screen will no longer list the file. The inactive window will continue to list the file until you Tab over to that window and make it active; it then automatically updates itself (and the deleted file disappears).

When you want to restore the normal screen display, press the F8 function key again to make the inactive window disappear. In the example shown in Figure 3-121, pressing F8 makes \RCOURIER, the directory on the left, fill the screen.

Normally when you unsplit the windows, files you've tagged in the active window stay tagged and files tagged in the inactive window become untagged. As an alternative, you can use the Ctrl-F6 command (from a File window only) to transfer the tags from the active file window to an inactive file window so that both windows

Chapter 3: XTree for DOS Quick Reference Guide

have the same tags. To do this, press Ctrl-F6, then use the Tab key to move the highlight over to the other window to see the new, merged tagging take effect.

File and Directory Statistics

No one can deny that we live in a bottom-line kind of era. XTree accommodates type-A personalities by providing a box (window), on the right side of the screen, filled with your *current statistics*. That's why the window on the right is called the Statistics window.

As you travel up and down the directory tree, go into a directory, enter filespecs, tag files, and so forth, the Statistics window continually updates to reflect your actions. How many files are on this disk? How many are in this directory? How many are tagged? How many match the filespecs? How big is this file? This directory? How much space do the tagged files take up? Etc. All this stuff is right there on your screen. Pretty impressive, huh?

DISK Statistics window

If your cursor is active in the Directory window, the statistics window becomes the DISK Statistics window. The Total, Matching, and Tagged files and bytes reflect what's going on with the whole disk. An example of these statistics is shown in Figure 3-122.

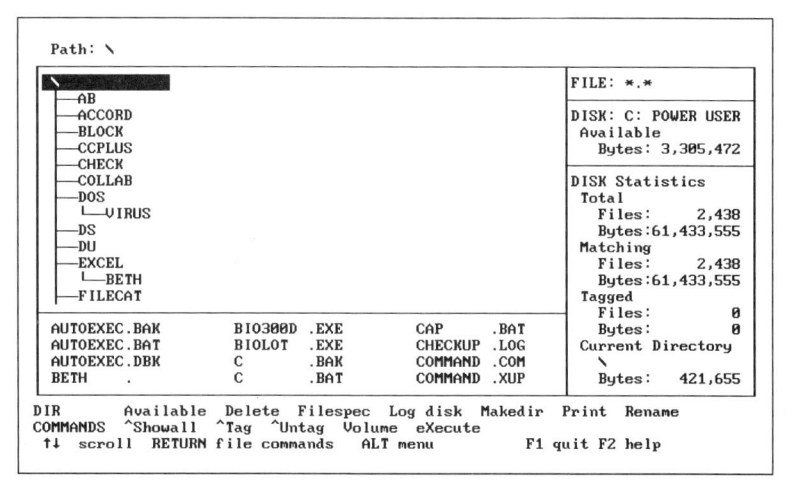

```
Path: \
            ─AB                                              FILE: *.*
            ─ACCORD
            ─BLOCK                                           DISK: C: POWER USER
            ─CCPLUS                                          Available
            ─CHECK                                             Bytes: 3,305,472
            ─COLLAB
            ─DOS                                             DISK Statistics
              └─VIRUS                                        Total
            ─DS                                                Files:       2,438
            ─DU                                                Bytes:  61,433,555
            ─EXCEL                                           Matching
              └─BETH                                           Files:       2,438
            ─FILECAT                                           Bytes:  61,433,555
                                                             Tagged
                                                               Files:           0
     AUTOEXEC.BAK    BIO300D .EXE     CAP     .BAT            Bytes:           0
     AUTOEXEC.BAT    BIOLOT  .EXE     CHECKUP .LOG          Current Directory
     AUTOEXEC.DBK    C       .BAK     COMMAND .COM          \
     BETH    .       C       .BAT     COMMAND .XUP            Bytes:     421,655

  DIR        Available  Delete  Filespec  Log disk  Makedir  Print  Rename
  COMMANDS   ^Showall  ^Tag  ^Untag  Volume  eXecute
      ↑↓ scroll  RETURN file commands    ALT menu        F1 quit F2 help
```

Figure 3-122: The DISK Statistics window, visible on the right as long as you're in the Directory window, is the fuel gauge for your hard disk.

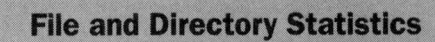

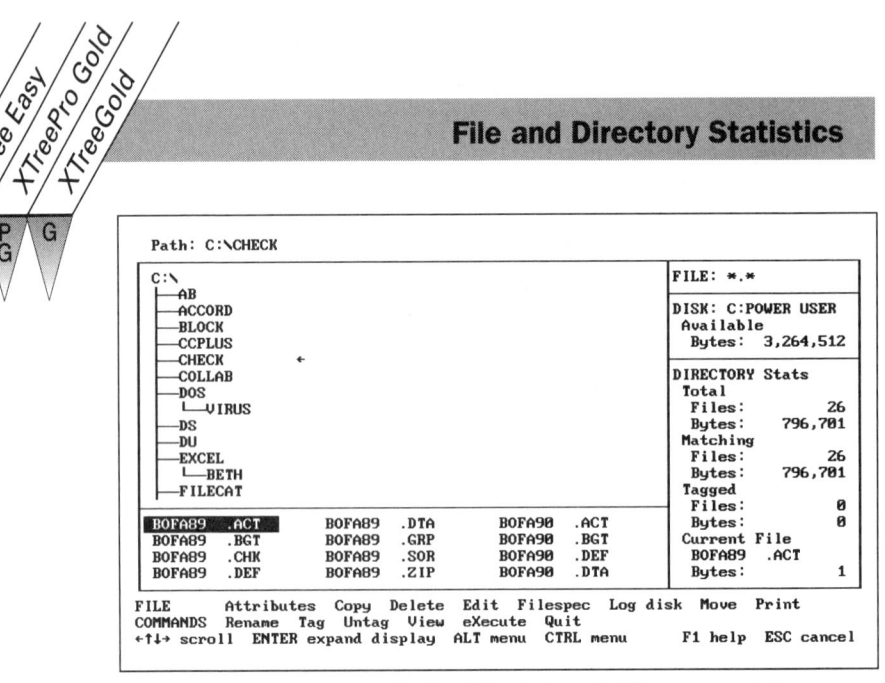

```
Path: C:\CHECK

C:\                                                        FILE: *.*
 ├─AB
 ├─ACCORD                                                  DISK: C:POWER USER
 ├─BLOCK                                                   Available
 ├─CCPLUS                                                    Bytes:    3,264,512
 ├─CHECK        ←
 ├─COLLAB                                                  DIRECTORY Stats
 ├─DOS                                                     Total
 │  └─VIRUS                                                  Files:           26
 ├─DS                                                        Bytes:      796,701
 ├─DU                                                      Matching
 ├─EXCEL                                                     Files:           26
 │  └─BETH                                                   Bytes:      796,701
 ├─FILECAT                                                 Tagged
                                                             Files:            0
BOFA89   .ACT    BOFA89   .DTA    BOFA90   .ACT             Bytes:            0
BOFA89   .BGT    BOFA89   .GRP    BOFA90   .BGT           Current File
BOFA89   .CHK    BOFA89   .SOR    BOFA90   .DEF             BOFA89   .ACT
BOFA89   .DEF    BOFA89   .ZIP    BOFA90   .DTA             Bytes:            1

FILE         Attributes  Copy  Delete  Edit  Filespec  Log disk  Move  Print
COMMANDS  Rename  Tag  Untag  View  eXecute  Quit
←↑↓→ scroll  ENTER expand display  ALT menu   CTRL menu       F1 help  ESC cancel
```

Figure 3-123: While you're active in a File window, the Directory statistics are continually updated.

DIRECTORY Stats window

When your cursor is positioned in a File window, the statistics window becomes the DIRECTORY Stats window and reflects the Total, Matching, and Tagged statistics of the *current directory* only, as shown in Figure 3-123.

SHOWALL (and GLOBAL) Statistics window

If you're in a Showall (or Global) file window, the statistics box transforms into a SHOWALL or GLOBAL Statistics window, revealing the statistics for the current drive, or all logged drives, as shown in Figure 3-124.

Extended statistics window

Just when you think it couldn't get any better, yet *another* group of statistics for you insatiable number-crunchers is available. The Extended Statistics window gives you even more detail about the files on your disk. (Bet you're dying to know the average file size on your hard disk, right?) From the Directory window, type a **?** (a question mark) and you'll get something like what is shown in Figure 3-125. Since some of this stuff is pretty technical (I doubt if you're interested in discussing sector and cluster sizes), I'm not

Chapter 3: XTree for DOS Quick Reference Guide

```
Path: C:\WORD\BETH
#1REC89D .ZIP      00000317.MAI    10_10      .DOC      FILE: *.*
$$$$$$$$ .F5       000003A2.MAI    11         .TXT
$DEFAULT .F1       000003DB.MAI    12         .TXT      DISK: C:POWER USER
$DEFAULT .F10      00000404.MAI    123SETUP.DOC          Available
$DEFAULT .F2       00000405.MAI    12MEG      .ICO       Bytes:    3,264,512
$DEFAULT .F3       0000009E.MAI    12_19ID    .DOC
$DEFAULT .F4       000009A6.ATT    12_22PRM.DOC         GLOBAL Statistics
$DEFAULT .F5       000009A7.MAI    144MEG     .ICO       Total
$DEFAULT .F6       00000B83.ATT    1STTZPAR.DOC           Files:         3,896
$DEFAULT .F7       0B340959.        1WORD1    .PIX        Bytes:    87,866,372
$DEFAULT .F8       1           .DOC 1WORD2    .PIX       Matching
$DEFAULT .F9       1           .TXT 1WORD3    .FST        Files:         3,896
$UPDATE  .IFS      10          .BAT 1WORD3    .PIX        Bytes:    87,866,372
(C)ALDUS .'88      10          .TXT 1WORD4    .PIX       Tagged
(C)BITS  .'89      10391438.        2         .TXT        Files:             0
00000043 .KEY      103B164D.       22BLOCKS.DOC           Bytes:             0
000001A5 .MAI      10MAN       .CMP 22BLOCKS.PM3         Current File
00000213 .MAI      10MAN       .DOC 251-WARN.DOC          #1REC89D.ZIP
00000268 .MAI      10MAN       .STY 2GUYS    .DOC         Bytes:       106,479

FILE         Attributes  Copy  Delete  Edit  Filespec  Log disk  Print
COMMANDS     Rename  Tag  Untag  View  eXecute  Quit
←↑↓→ scroll  ENTER tree display   ALT menu   CTRL menu      F1 help  ESC cancel
```

Figure 3-124: The GLOBAL Statistics window appears when you have logged more than one drive and are in a Global file window.

going to go through it here (read your operations manual if you're intrigued by this kind of information).

Normally, the ? in the lower-right corner of the screen reminds you that the Extended statistics window is available. In XTreePro Gold and XTreeGold, however, once you've logged more than one drive, the +/– prompt appears in that spot. Even though the question mark may not be visible on-screen, you can press it anyway to get access to the Extended statistics window.

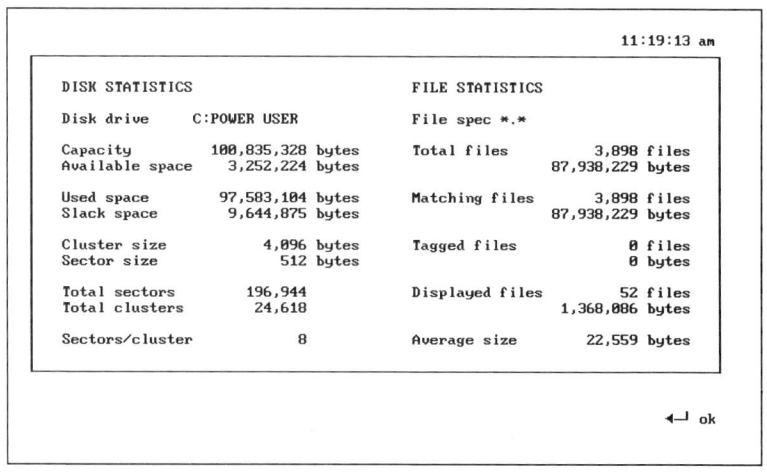

```
                                                              11:19:13 am
    DISK STATISTICS                   FILE STATISTICS

    Disk drive    C:POWER USER        File spec  *.*

    Capacity          100,835,328 bytes   Total files        3,898 files
    Available space     3,252,224 bytes                 87,938,229 bytes

    Used space         97,583,104 bytes   Matching files     3,898 files
    Slack space         9,644,875 bytes                 87,938,229 bytes

    Cluster size            4,096 bytes   Tagged files           0 files
    Sector size               512 bytes                          0 bytes

    Total sectors         196,944        Displayed files        52 files
    Total clusters         24,618                        1,368,086 bytes

    Sectors/cluster             8        Average size      22,559 bytes


                                                              ↵ ok
```

Figure 3-125: The Extended statistics window provides both DISK and FILE statistics for all you closet nerds.

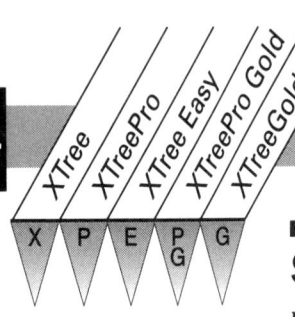

Substituting with SUBST

If you're envious of XTreeGold's ability to log just one directory (as described earlier in the "Log" section), you needn't suffer a moment longer. There is another way to force XTree to log just one directory: all you have to do is fool XTree into thinking that your favorite directory is actually a drive. That's where SUBST comes in. SUBST is not an XTree command, it's a DOS command. SUBST can tell DOS to pretend that a directory is actually a drive (for example, you could pretend that C:\EXCEL is a drive called G:), and then log only onto that "drive."

To log only to a directory that pretends to be a drive, however, requires that you have two things: DOS version 3.1 or higher, and a willingness to change your CONFIG.SYS file. (Be sure to *back up* your present CONFIG.SYS file before you make any changes to it.)

So, if you're determined to go forward, let's give it a shot. (This section is rated R and may be too intense for newer users. If the following material seems way over your head, skip it for now. However, it's quite a time-saver if you have a large, complex drive and you don't have XTreeGold.)

Provided you have the appropriate version of DOS (3.1 or higher), all you have to do now is edit your CONFIG.SYS file (be sure to back it up, first). The following is an example of a typical CONFIG.SYS file:

```
FILES=20
BUFFERS=30
DEVICE=\DOS\ANSI.SYS
```

Once you've backed up your CONFIG.SYS file, you can edit it. First, you need to determine two simple things:

- The name of the directory you want to be able to log onto (for this example, I'll use the WORD directory).

- The name of the *last* disk drive on your hard disk — C:, D:, or E:, most likely. For this example, the last drive is C:. Knowing which drive is the last drive is important, because the next alphabetical letter will be assigned to our directory. In this case, the WORD directory will become drive D:.

Chapter 3: XTree for DOS Quick Reference Guide

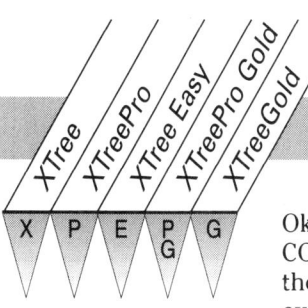

Okay, now you can edit your CONFIG.SYS file. To the sample CONFIG.SYS file just listed, you need to add a line telling DOS what the last hard drive on your system is. The CONFIG.SYS file in our example will end up looking like this:

```
FILES=20
BUFFERS=30
DEVICE=\DOS\ANSI.SYS
LASTDRIVE=F:
```

The only addition is the `LASTDRIVE=F:` line. If you already have a drive F:, your version should read `LASTDRIVE=G:`.

If you don't know how to enter and edit your CONFIG.SYS file, see "Editing with 1Word." Briefly, however, if you're using XTree Pro or XTree Gold, highlight the CONFIG.SYS file in the root (\) directory and press E for Edit. Add the `LASTDRIVE=` line to the file and then press Esc and save the file.

After you've edited the file, you need to reboot your computer and get to a system prompt. Now, when you type: **SUBST D: C:\WORD** and press Enter, you are telling DOS to pretend that C:\WORD is drive D:. You can now type **D:** and press Enter, and you'll be on your new D: drive, which is actually the WORD directory on drive C:. If you engage XTree from the D: prompt, it'll log only that drive. If you want to void the substitution, first quit XTree, go back to your *real* drive and type: **SUBST D: /D**, and press Enter. Translation: delete the D: drive substitution.

When you're in substitute mode, you *cannot* rename or delete a directory or subdirectory that is part of the substitution. Also, you cannot change the volume label.

If you just *love* substituting directories for drives, you may want to put the SUBST command and the directory you want to appear as a drive in your AUTOEXEC.BAT file so that it will take effect automatically when you turn on your computer. Once you've got your "fake drive" in place, log onto it and invoke XTree.

SUBST and XTree and XTreePro

Once you've invoked XTree and XTreePro, these programs are completely fooled by the substitution; they both think that drive D: now exists. See Figures 3-126 and 3-127, respectively.

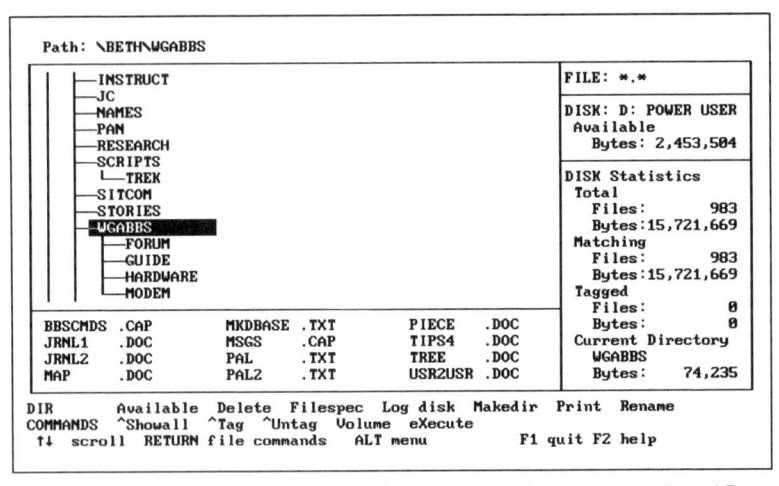

Figure 3-126: XTree's DISK box reports the fact that we're on the substituted D: drive.

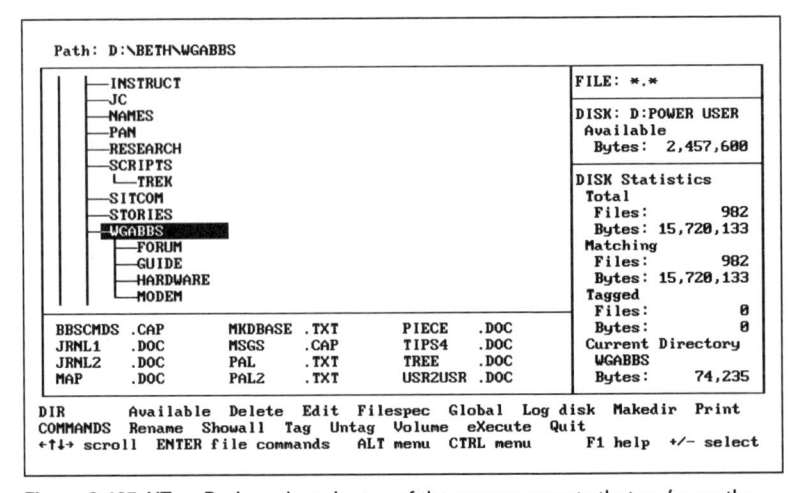

Figure 3-127: XTreePro's path at the top of the screen reports that we're on the substituted D: drive.

SUBST and XTreePro Gold

XTreePro Gold properly reports the actual drive you are on, as shown in Figure 3-128, where the path statement confesses in parentheses that the current directory is C:\WORD, even though it keeps statistics on D: as though it were a drive. Pretty smart, huh?

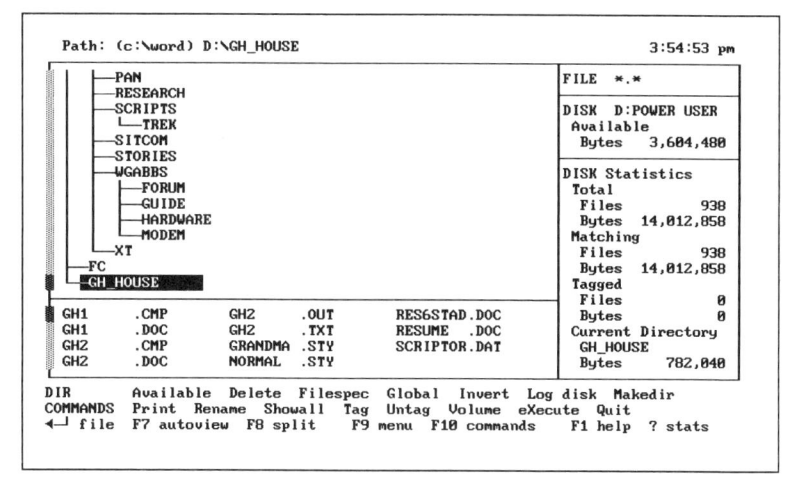

```
Path: (c:\word) D:\GH_HOUSE                              3:54:53 pm
     ├──PAN                              FILE   *.*
     ├──RESEARCH
     ├──SCRIPTS                          DISK  D:POWER USER
     │  └──TREK                          Available
     ├──SITCOM                             Bytes     3,604,480
     ├──STORIES
     ├──WGABBS                           DISK Statistics
     │  ├──FORUM                         Total
     │  ├──GUIDE                           Files            938
     │  ├──HARDWARE                        Bytes     14,012,858
     │  └──MODEM                         Matching
     └──XT                                 Files            938
  ├──FC                                    Bytes     14,012,858
  ├──GH_HOUSE                            Tagged
                                           Files              0
  GH1    .CMP    GH2    .OUT   RES6STAD.DOC  Bytes            0
  GH1    .DOC    GH2    .TXT   RESUME  .DOC  Current Directory
  GH2    .CMP    GRANDMA.STY   SCRIPTOR.DAT  GH_HOUSE
  GH2    .DOC    NORMAL .STY                 Bytes      782,040

  DIR       Available Delete  Filespec Global Invert Log disk Makedir
  COMMANDS  Print  Rename  Showall  Tag  Untag  Volume  eXecute  Quit
  ↵ file   F7 autoview  F8 split    F9 menu  F10 commands  F1 help  ? stats
```

Figure 3-128: At the top of the screen, XTreePro Gold proves it is not fooled by the DOS SUBST command.

Tag/Untag   Command

When you wish to perform an operation on a file (or files or directories), there are two ways to indicate to XTree which file to copy, delete, or whatever. One selection method is to simply highlight the file (or directory). However, if you wish to perform an operation on a group of files, you must use the second method, called *tagging*. There are two ways to tag files:

- Simply highlight the file and press T for tag.

- Use the Filespec command to display a set of files (like *.BAK to show all BAK files) and then press Ctrl-T to tag them all at once. (Notice that T tags the current file and Ctrl-T tags all files on display.)

Tag/Untag

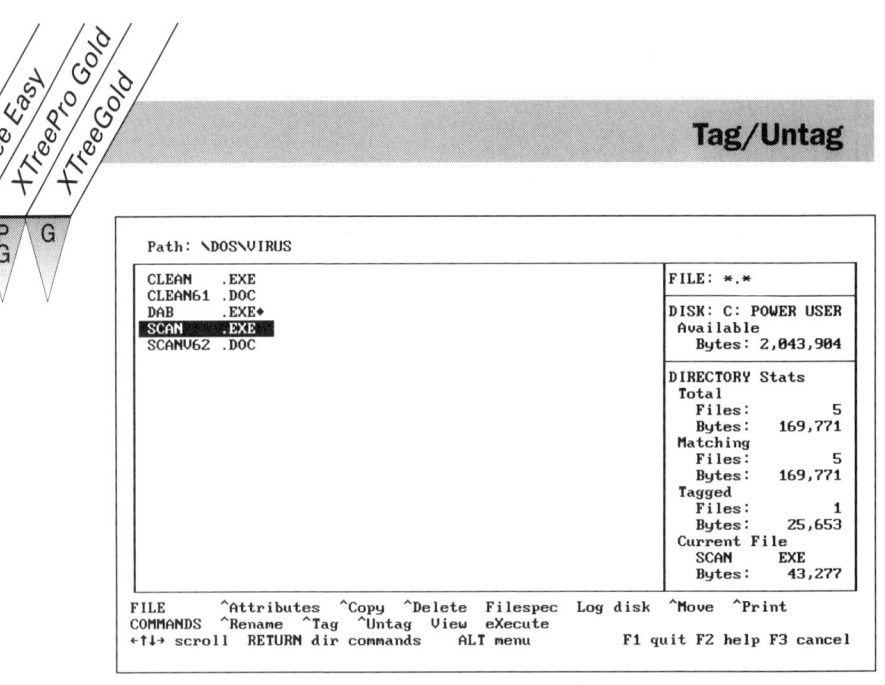

```
Path: \DOS\VIRUS

CLEAN    .EXE            FILE: *.*
CLEAN61  .DOC
DAB      .EXE♦           DISK: C: POWER USER
SCAN     .EXE            Available
SCANV62  .DOC              Bytes: 2,043,904

                         DIRECTORY Stats
                         Total
                           Files:         5
                           Bytes:   169,771
                         Matching
                           Files:         5
                           Bytes:   169,771
                         Tagged
                           Files:         1
                           Bytes:    25,653
                         Current File
                           SCAN     EXE
                           Bytes:    43,277

FILE        ^Attributes  ^Copy  ^Delete  Filespec  Log disk  ^Move  ^Print
COMMANDS    ^Rename  ^Tag  ^Untag  View  eXecute
←↑↓→ scroll  RETURN dir commands   ALT menu       F1 quit F2 help F3 cancel
```

Figure 3-129: In this example, DAB.EXE is tagged (the diamond to the right of the name confirms it), and SCAN.EXE is highlighted, but not tagged.

If you have tagged a file in error, highlight the file and press U for Untag. If you want to untag all the currently tagged files, Ctrl-U will do the job.

Tagging and untagging a file

To tag a file, highlight the file to be tagged and press T (for tag). A diamond appears next to the filename, indicating that the file is tagged. In Figure 3-129, DAB.EXE is tagged (see the little diamond to the right of the filename?) and SCAN.EXE is highlighted but not tagged (no diamond). Pressing T while the highlight is on SCAN.EXE tags it, also. To tag several files in a row, keep T pressed and don't let go. The cursor will automatically move to subsequent files and tag them until you let go. To untag DAB.EXE, just highlight it and press U.

Tagging and untagging all files in a directory

There are two approaches to tagging all files in a directory. First, from a Directory window, highlight a directory name and press T for Tag. Every file in that directory, as shown in the example in Figure 3-130, will be tagged. You can see some of the tagged files in

Chapter 3: XTree for DOS Quick Reference Guide

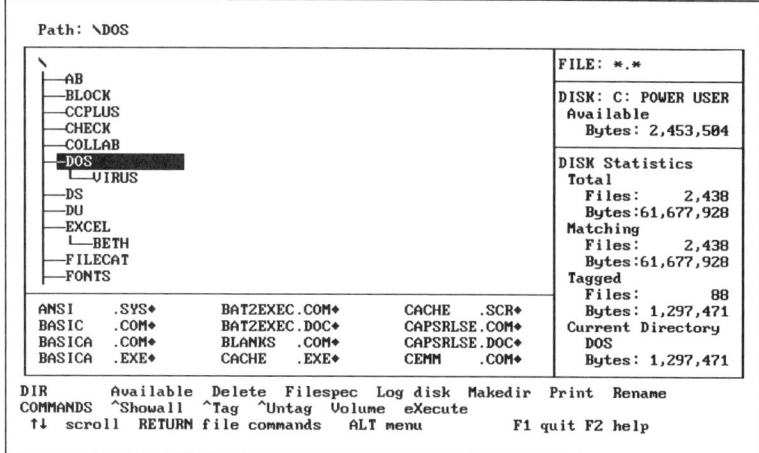

```
Path: \DOS
    ├─AB                              FILE: *.*
    ├─BLOCK
    ├─CCPLUS                          DISK: C: POWER USER
    ├─CHECK                           Available
    ├─COLLAB                             Bytes: 2,453,504
    ├─DOS
    │  └─VIRUS                        DISK Statistics
    ├─DS                              Total
    ├─DU                                 Files:      2,438
    ├─EXCEL                              Bytes:61,677,928
    │  └─BETH                         Matching
    ├─FILECAT                            Files:      2,438
    ├─FONTS                              Bytes:61,677,928
                                      Tagged
ANSI     .SYS♦   BAT2EXEC.COM♦   CACHE    .SCR♦      Files:         88
BASIC    .COM♦   BAT2EXEC.DOC♦   CAPSRLSE.COM♦       Bytes:  1,297,471
BASICA   .COM♦   BLANKS  .COM♦   CAPSRLSE.DOC♦   Current Directory
BASICA   .EXE♦   CACHE   .EXE♦   CEMM    .COM♦       DOS
                                                     Bytes:  1,297,471
DIR       Available Delete  Filespec Log disk Makedir Print Rename
COMMANDS  ^Showall  ^Tag    ^Untag   Volume   eXecute
↑↓  scroll  RETURN file commands   ALT menu         F1 quit F2 help
```

Figure 3-130: Highlight a directory name and then press T to tag all files in that directory.

the Small file window in this figure. To untag all the files in the directory, highlight the directory name and press U for Untag.

The second approach to tagging all files requires that you first get into the File window containing the files you want to tag. Then, press Ctrl-T to tag *all* files displayed in the current directory. Conversely, press Ctrl-U to untag all the tagged files.

Tagging and untagging the whole disk

You can tag all the files on your disk by pressing Ctrl-T from a Directory window. Press Ctrl-U to untag all tagged files.

Tagging and untagging with filespecs

Using Ctrl-T in conjunction with the filespec command is a powerful way to tag a particular group of files. In the example in Figure 3-131, the filespec *.BAK was entered, so XTree shows all files that match the filespec (in other words, only the files ending in BAK). Pressing Ctrl-T tags the currently displayed files, which can now be copied, deleted, or whatever.

For a different example, let's say you've got some DOC files along with other files in a directory. You want to keep all the DOC files

Tag/Untag

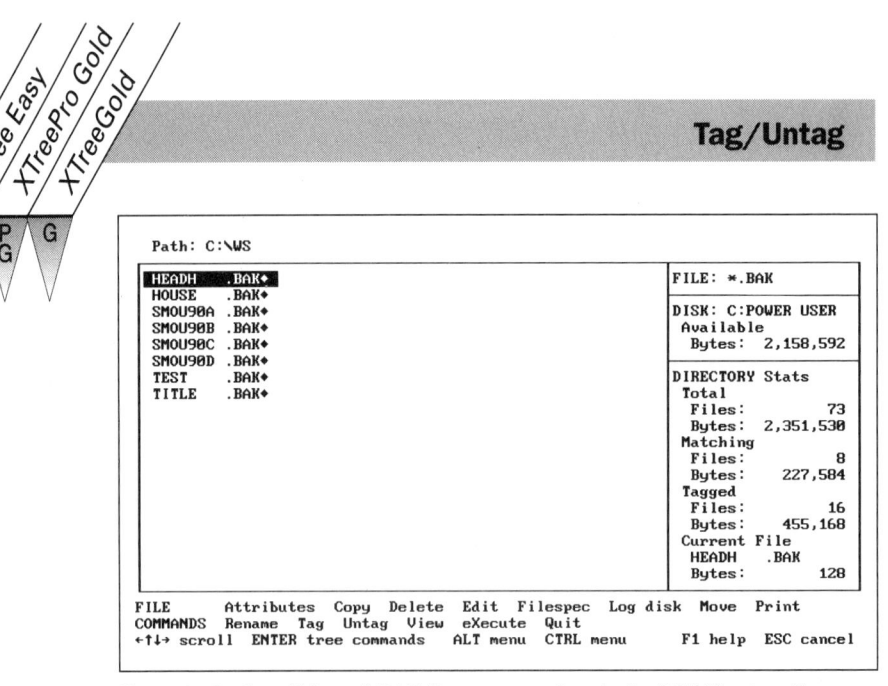

```
Path: C:\WS

HEADH    .BAK◆                          FILE: *.BAK
HOUSE    .BAK◆
SMOU90A  .BAK◆                          DISK: C:POWER USER
SMOU90B  .BAK◆                          Available
SMOU90C  .BAK◆                            Bytes:   2,158,592
SMOU90D  .BAK◆
TEST     .BAK◆                          DIRECTORY Stats
TITLE    .BAK◆                          Total
                                          Files:            73
                                          Bytes:     2,351,530
                                        Matching
                                          Files:             8
                                          Bytes:       227,584
                                        Tagged
                                          Files:            16
                                          Bytes:       455,168
                                        Current File
                                          HEADH    .BAK
                                          Bytes:           128

FILE       Attributes  Copy   Delete  Edit  Filespec  Log disk  Move  Print
COMMANDS   Rename   Tag    Untag   View   eXecute    Quit
←↑↓→ scroll   ENTER tree commands       ALT menu   CTRL menu     F1 help  ESC cancel
```

Figure 3-131: Specifying a *.BAK filespec reveals only the BAK files in a directory. They can be tagged simultaneously with Ctrl-T.

and delete the rest. First, go to the directory and use the Ctrl-T command to tag all the files (trust me on this). Then enter a filespec of ***.DOC**. Once you've got the DOC files on-screen, press Ctrl-U to untag the DOC files. Next, change your filespecs back to ***.*** and you'll see that all files *except* the DOC files are tagged! Now, you can use the Ctrl-D command to delete all tagged files. (If you can't "see" this in your brain, try it out on your computer.) Just remember, the art of this program is in the mixing and matching of all the tools (commands) you are given.

In XTreeGold and XTree Easy, you can do the same thing by typing the exclusionary filespec of **−*.DOC** to display all files but the DOC files. Then, using the simple Ctrl-T and Ctrl-D key combinations, tag and delete the files.

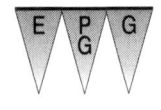

Tagging by attributes

In XTreePro Gold, XTreeGold, and XTree Easy you can tag files based on their attributes (remember those exciting read-only, archive, system, and hidden attributes?). In the following example, a new kind of T — Alt-T — tags all files in the current window with certain attributes. Naturally, XTree wants to know *which* attributes to use as criteria for tagging.

Chapter 3: XTree for DOS Quick Reference Guide

```
Path: C:\WS                                                    2:29:24 pm
┌─────────────────────────────────────────────────────────────────────────┐
│ CINSTALL.EXE    PERSONAL.DCT    SMOU90A  .        FILE    *.*           │
│ CORRSTAR.OUR    RESET   .PTR    SMOU90A  .BAK                           │
│ HEADH   .       SCRIPTOR.001    SMOU90A  .OLD     DISK   C:POWER USER   │
│ HEADH   .BAK    SCRIPTOR.002    SMOU90B  .           Available          │
│ HOME1   .JHH    SCRIPTOR.003    SMOU90B  .BAK        Bytes   2,117,632  │
│ HOME1   .OLD    SCRIPTOR.004    SMOU90B  .OLD                           │
│ HOME2   .JHH    SCRIPTOR.005    SMOU90C  .        DIRECTORY Stats       │
│ HOME2   .OLD    SCRIPTOR.DAT    SMOU90C  .BAK     Total                 │
│ HOME3   .JHH    SCRIPTOR.FMT    SMOU90C  .OLD        Files          73  │
│ HOME3   .OLD    SCRIPTOR.MSG    SMOU90D  .           Bytes   2,351,530  │
│ HOMETIT .DOC    SCRIPTOR.PRD    SMOU90D  .BAK     Matching              │
│ HOUSE   .       SKBATCH .COM    SMOU90D  .OLD        Files          73  │
│ HOUSE   .BAK    SMOU    .DOC    SMOU9_17.ZIP         Bytes   2,351,530  │
│ INSTALL .COM    SMOU    .DTX    SMOUH    .ZIP     Tagged                │
│ INTERNAL.DCT    SMOU    .ICF    SMOUOLD  .ZIP        Files           0  │
│ LASER   .EXE    SMOU    .ZIP    SMOUP    .DOC        Bytes           0  │
│ MAILMRGE.OUR    SMOU2   .DOC    SMOUTIT  .DOC     Current File          │
│ MAIN    .DCT    SMOU89  .ZIP    TEST     .           CINSTALL.EXE       │
│ MAKE-ICF.EXE    SMOU90  .ICF    TEST     .BAK        Bytes      16,384  │
│                                                                         │
│ TAG ALL MATCHING FILES BY ATTRIBUTES                                    │
│           : +A                                                          │
│ Enter attributes (+/- RASH)         ↑ history  ↵ ok  F1 help  ESC cancel│
└─────────────────────────────────────────────────────────────────────────┘
```

Figure 3-132: To tag all files by their attributes, use Alt-T.

In the example shown in Figure 3-132, all files that have their *archive attribute* turned on will be tagged. The +A that you see at the bottom of Figure 3-132 means the archive attribute is turned on, or *positive*. (See the section on attributes in Chapter 2 if you need a refresher on this topic.)

Using Showall to view tagged files

There may be times when you have files tagged in different directories, spread out over your hard disk, and you'd like to display them all. Type Ctrl-S from the Directory window to show all tagged files on the disk. The Showall file window operates just like the regular directory window, except the statistics box on the right reads SHOWALL Statistics.

Inverting tags

In example in Figure 3-131, a filespec of *.BAK causes XTree to display all files ending with the BAK extension. If you want to do something to the other files in that directory — those that *don't* end in BAK — you can just say "Reverse the tags" and everything that was tagged is now untagged and vice versa. To accomplish such a feat, use the Invert command.

With all the BAK files tagged, and the filespecs set to *.*, press Ctrl-I to invert all tagged files. When you use this command, you

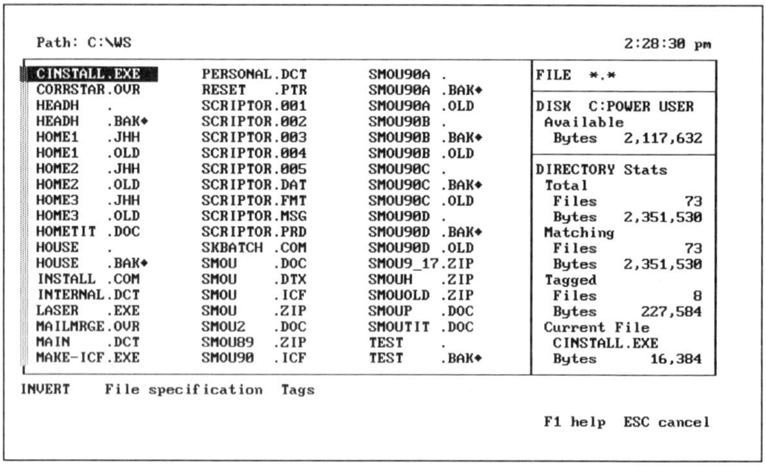

Tag/Untag

```
Path: C:\WS                                              2:28:30 pm
CINSTALL.EXE    PERSONAL.DCT    SMOU90A .       FILE  *.*
CORRSTAR.OVR    RESET   .PTR    SMOU90A .BAK♦
HEADH   .       SCRIPTOR.001    SMOU90A .OLD    DISK  C:POWER USER
HEADH   .BAK♦   SCRIPTOR.002    SMOU90B .         Available
HOME1   .JHH    SCRIPTOR.003    SMOU90B .BAK♦     Bytes   2,117,632
HOME1   .OLD    SCRIPTOR.004    SMOU90B .OLD
HOME2   .JHH    SCRIPTOR.005    SMOU90C .       DIRECTORY Stats
HOME2   .OLD    SCRIPTOR.DAT    SMOU90C .BAK♦    Total
HOME3   .JHH    SCRIPTOR.FMT    SMOU90C .OLD      Files              73
HOME3   .OLD    SCRIPTOR.MSG    SMOU90D .         Bytes       2,351,530
HOMETIT .DOC    SCRIPTOR.PRD    SMOU90D .BAK♦   Matching
HOUSE   .       SKBATCH .COM    SMOU90D .OLD      Files              73
HOUSE   .BAK♦   SMOU    .DOC    SMOU9_17.ZIP     Bytes       2,351,530
INSTALL .COM    SMOU    .DTX    SMOUH   .ZIP    Tagged
INTERNAL.DCT    SMOU    .ICF    SMOUOLD .ZIP     Files               8
LASER   .EXE    SMOU    .ZIP    SMOUP   .DOC     Bytes         227,584
MAILMRGE.OVR    SMOU2   .DOC    SMOUTIT .DOC    Current File
MAIN    .DCT    SMOU89  .ZIP    TEST    .        CINSTALL.EXE
MAKE-ICF.EXE    SMOU90  .ICF    TEST    .BAK♦    Bytes          16,384

INVERT     File specification    Tags

                                              F1 help  ESC cancel
```

Figure 3-133: To invert the file tags in a directory, press Ctrl-I.

must indicate which file specification tags you want to invert, as shown in Figure 3-133.

At the bottom of the screen in Figure 3-133, XTree is asking whether to invert the File Specification or the Tags. Inverting the File Specification affects which files are displayed, while inverting the Tags affects which files are tagged. In this case, pressing T causes the tags to invert, and instantly the files with the BAK are untagged and the other files are tagged.

Partially untagging files

Okay, here's the setting. You've tagged a slew of files and you're in the middle of copying them to another disk. You're halfway through when that familiar beep tells you the destination disk is full. A message appears at the bottom of the screen, as in Figure 3-134, confirming your suspicions. You have a few choices at this point: put another disk in the B: drive and press Enter to format a disk and continue copying, or press Alt-Z to exit and save your tags. However, let's say you decide to do something different; you want to put the rest of the files on a disk in the A: drive. The first step is to cancel the current operation.

At this point, all the files in the directory shown in Figure 3-134 up to LZESHELL.EXE have been copied. When the copy process starts again, LZESHELL.EXE should be the next file copied. Normally, if you press Ctrl-C to copy, XTreePro Gold and XTreeGold begin copying with the first tagged file. To pick up copying where you

Chapter 3: XTree for DOS Quick Reference Guide

```
Path: C:\UTILS                                              2:34:19 pm
10       .BAT♦   CONFIG   .    ♦   GLOBAL   .EXE♦   FILE  *.*
3D       .BAT♦   CONFIG   .828♦   GUIDE    .BAT♦
AUTOEXEC.IMP♦   CONFIG   .CAH♦   IN       .BAT♦   DISK  C:POWER USER
AUTOEXEC.MEM♦   CONFIG   .DUM♦   INSTRUCT.BAT♦   Available
AUTOEXEC.OLD♦   CONFIG   .EG ♦   JC       .BAT♦     Bytes    2,088,960
AUTOEXEC.SAV♦   CONFIG   .IMP♦   LJ2UP    .EXE♦
AUTOEXEC.STD♦   CONFIG   .NOW♦   LZESHELL.EXE♦   DIRECTORY Stats
AUTOEXEC.WIN♦   CONFIG   .OLD♦   LZEXE    .EXE♦   Total
BETH     .   ♦   CONFIG   .STD♦   MALE     .BAT♦     Files         107
BETH     .BAT♦   CONFIG   .UNI♦   MC       .BAT♦     Bytes     804,642
BLANKS   .COM♦   CONFIG   .WIN♦   MENU     .BAT♦   Matching
BLU      .BAT♦   CONFIGTS.EXE♦   MSG      .BAT♦     Files         107
BUFFERS  .RPT♦   DEF      .COM♦   MYMENU   .DAT♦     Bytes     804,642
BUFFERS1.RPT♦   DESET    .BAT♦   MYMENU   .EXE♦   Tagged
CAT      .BAT♦   DL       .BAT♦   NUKEBAK  .EXE♦     Files         107
CHECKS   .BAT♦   E        .BAT♦   OLDAUTO  .BAT♦     Bytes     804,642
CIM      .BAT♦   EXAMPLE  .BAT♦   OLDZIP   .EXE♦   Current File
CLASSES  .BAT♦   FC       .BAT♦   ORG      .BAT♦     LZESHELL.EXE
COMICS   .BAT♦   FFEED    .COM♦   PDAILY   .DAT♦     Bytes      18,746

COPYING: LZESHELL.EXE as LZESHELL.EXE
    to: B:\JUNK
DESTINATION DISK FULL:       F2 format diskette  ↵ continue copy  ESC cancel
```

Figure 3-134: Destination Disk Full needn't be on your suicide note; you can use Partial Untag and then Snapshot to save your status while you go buy another box of disks.

leave off, you have to go back and manually *untag* all the files up to LZESHELL.EXE. Fortunately, there's a way to automatically do this. The Alt-F8 key combination is the *partial untag* command. The Alt-F8 command tells XTreePro Gold and XTreeGold to untag all the files that have *already* been operated on and removes the small diamonds that indicated their tagged status, as shown in Figure 3-135. The partial untag command saves you the bother of untagging files one by one. (Neat, huh?)

```
Path: C:\UTILS                                              2:35:06 pm
10       .BAT    CONFIG   .       GLOBAL   .EXE    FILE  *.*
3D       .BAT    CONFIG   .828    GUIDE    .BAT
AUTOEXEC.IMP    CONFIG   .CAH    IN       .BAT    DISK  C:POWER USER
AUTOEXEC.MEM    CONFIG   .DUM    INSTRUCT.BAT    Available
AUTOEXEC.OLD    CONFIG   .EG     JC       .BAT      Bytes    2,080,768
AUTOEXEC.SAV    CONFIG   .IMP    LJ2UP    .EXE
AUTOEXEC.STD    CONFIG   .NOW    LZESHELL.EXE♦   DIRECTORY Stats
AUTOEXEC.WIN    CONFIG   .OLD    LZEXE    .EXE♦   Total
BETH     .      CONFIG   .STD    MALE     .BAT♦     Files         107
BETH     .BAT   CONFIG   .UNI    MC       .BAT♦     Bytes     804,642
BLANKS   .COM   CONFIG   .WIN    MENU     .BAT♦   Matching
BLU      .BAT   CONFIGTS.EXE    MSG      .BAT♦     Files         107
BUFFERS  .RPT   DEF      .COM    MYMENU   .DAT♦     Bytes     804,642
BUFFERS1.RPT   DESET    .BAT    MYMENU   .EXE♦   Tagged
CAT      .BAT   DL       .BAT    NUKEBAK  .EXE♦     Files          63
CHECKS   .BAT   E        .BAT    OLDAUTO  .BAT♦     Bytes     683,786
CIM      .BAT   EXAMPLE  .BAT    OLDZIP   .EXE♦   Current File
CLASSES  .BAT   FC       .BAT    ORG      .BAT♦     LZESHELL.EXE
COMICS   .BAT   FFEED    .COM    PDAILY   .DAT♦     Bytes      18,746

FILE        Attributes  Copy   Delete  Edit   Filespec  Invert  Log disk  Move
COMMANDS    New date    Open   Print   Rename  Tag   Untag  View  eXecute  Quit
↵ tree    F7 autoview  F8 split      F9 menu  F10 commands    F1 help  ESC cancel
```

Figure 3-135: Alt-F8 removes the tags (and diamonds) from the files that have already been copied. You can save this setup with Alt-Z, or continue copying on another floppy drive.

View   Command

Are you convinced that a gremlin of some sort gets into your computer at night and creates files with unrecognizable names? "Where did *that* file come from?" you wonder. "I didn't create that file! No siree!" Then you call the file up in your word processor or spreadsheet program and realize, "Oh yeah. . . I *need* this," and vow never to forget that filename again. Sound familiar?

XTree's incredible View command allows you to take a quick peek at files without leaving XTree and starting the corresponding program.

The View command works on any file, with varying results, depending on which version of XTree you own and what kind of file you're trying to view. While the original XTree can successfully view only those files containing text, XTreeGold 2.5 has the capacity to view just about any kind of file from databases and spreadsheets to word processing and graphics files (in color, no less!).

No matter what version you own, viewing program files — those files with EXE and COM extensions — will give you a screenful of unrecognizable characters. However, it doesn't hurt the file to try to view it, so if you're curious, go for it — get crazy!

Viewing a document file

The figures in the following sections show how to use the View command with the various versions of XTree.

Viewing files in XTree

For this example let's view a CONFIG.SYS file. After highlighting CONFIG.SYS and pressing V, the contents of CONFIG.SYS appear on-screen, as shown in Figure 3-136. As you can see at the top of the figure, other commands, such as PgUp, PgDn, and G)oto (which searches for specific text) are available for navigating in the exposed file. Because this file is so short, there's really nothing to page down or up to.

When you finish viewing a file in XTree, press Enter to return to a normal File window.

Chapter 3: XTree for DOS Quick Reference Guide

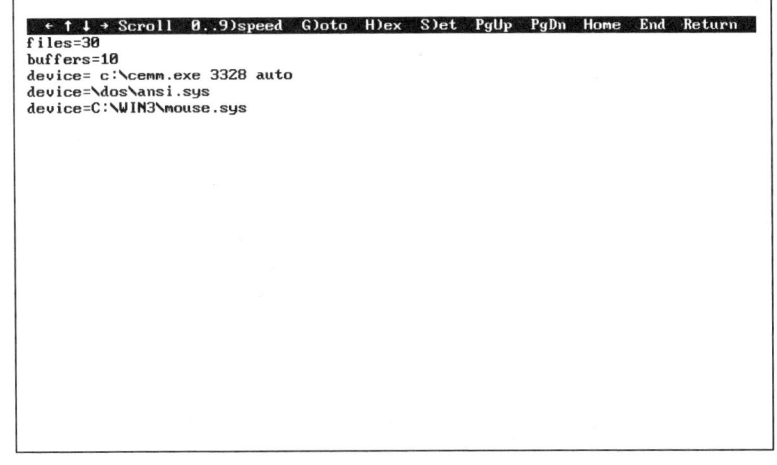

```
← ↑ ↓ → Scroll  0..9)speed  G)oto  H)ex  S)et  PgUp  PgDn  Home  End  Return
files=30
buffers=10
device= c:\cemm.exe 3328 auto
device=\dos\ansi.sys
device=C:\WIN3\mouse.sys
```

Figure 3-136: Viewing CONFIG.SYS with XTree's View command. View screen commands appear at the top of the screen.

Viewing files in XTreePro

For this example, let's look at a document file. After highlighting a file and pressing V for view, XTreePro's View screen appears, as shown in Figure 3-137. You can see at the top of the screen that XTreePro is civilized enough to let you know what file you're

```
File: C:\WS\HOME\HOME1
←↑↓→ Scroll  0..9)speed  G)oto  S)et  M)ask  D)isplay mode: NORMAL
trudges forward, only slightly revived by the cooling
evening air.
                    ANNA
              (to herself)
          This is it. I've got to get a car...
          no matter what...

Her thoughts are broken when she hears the excited
BARKS of a small, black COCKAPOO. Anna sees the dog
a short distance down the road, on the other side of
a small bridge over a now-dry creek. The dog is
running back and forth over the bridge barking down
at the creek bed and then stopping to stare and
listen, only to whimper and begin barking again
                    ANNA
          How'd you get out again, Muffin?
          They shouldn't let a little boy like
          you wander around out here...
          Whatcha doing? You smell something
          down there?
```

Figure 3-137: XTreePro's View screen includes the name of the file you are viewing.

```
File: A:\HOME1                                    ASCII (masked )
slightly revived by the cooling evening air.

                    ANNA
                (to herself)
           This is it.  I've got to get a
           car... no matter what...

Her thoughts are broken when she hears the excited BARKS of a
small, black COCKAPOO. Anna sees the dog a short distance down
the road, on the other side of a small bridge over a now-dry
creek.  The dog is running back and forth over the bridge
barking down at the creek bed and then stopping to stare and
listen, only to whimper and begin barking again

                    ANNA
           How'd you get out again, Muffin?
           they shouldn't let a little boy
           like you wander around out here...
           Whatcha doing? You smell

VIEW       ASCII  Hex   Mask
COMMANDS   F9 search  SPACE search again
↑↓ scroll                                F10 commands  F1 help  ESC cancel
```

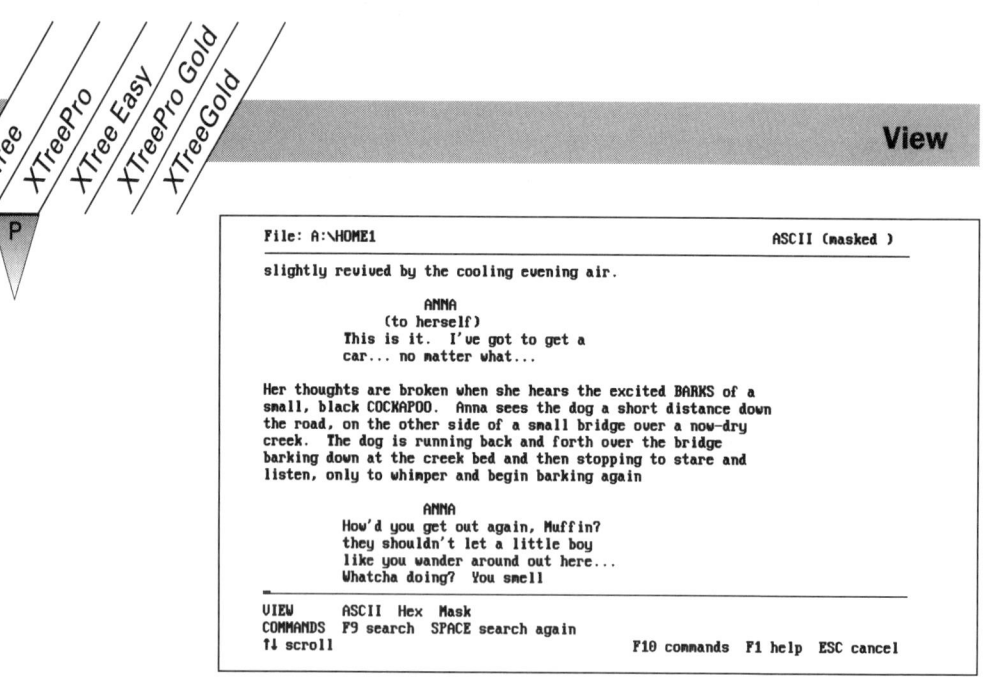

Figure 3-138: XTree Easy's view screen.

looking at. Use the commands at the top of the screen, such as PgUp, PgDn, and G)oto (which searches for specific text) to scroll through lengthy documents.

Viewing files in XTree Easy

XTree Easy's view screen, shown in Figure 3-138, is unique in that it offers access to the F10 commands (the pull-down menus).

Viewing files in XTreePro Gold and XTreeGold

Highlighting a file and using the View command in XTreePro Gold and XTreeGold gives you something like the Microsoft Word file shown in Figure 3-139. Note the extraneous characters in the upper-left corner. The reason for the odd characters is that we are viewing the file without benefit of XTreePro Gold and XTreeGold's Formatted mode.

XTreePro Gold and XTreeGold come with some file format *filters* so that you can see files in a way that more closely resembles how they appear in the program that created them.

When you enter XTreePro Gold and XTreeGold's view mode, these programs (usually) automatically recognize the file format and put in the proper mode. Sometimes, though, you have to prompt XTreePro Gold and XTreeGold by using the F command (for

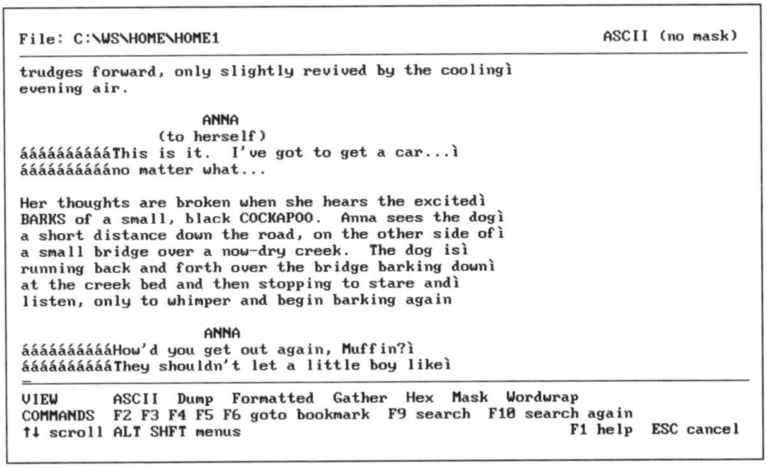

Chapter 3: XTree for DOS Quick Reference Guide

```
File: C:\WS\HOME\HOME1                                    ASCII (no mask)

trudges forward, only slightly revived by the cooling
evening air.
                         ANNA
                     (to herself)
ááááááááááThis is it.  I've got to get a car...
ááááááááááno matter what...

Her thoughts are broken when she hears the excited
BARKS of a small, black COCKAPOO.  Anna sees the dog
a short distance down the road, on the other side of
a small bridge over a now-dry creek.  The dog is
running back and forth over the bridge barking down
at the creek bed and then stopping to stare and
listen, only to whimper and begin barking again
                         ANNA
ááááááááááHow'd you get out again, Muffin?
ááááááááááThey shouldn't let a little boy like

VIEW       ASCII  Dump  Formatted  Gather  Hex  Mask  Wordwrap
COMMANDS   F2 F3 F4 F5 F6 goto bookmark  F9 search  F10 search again
↑↓ scroll  ALT SHFT menus                           F1 help  ESC cancel
```

Figure 3-139: Viewed files may contain weird characters, but that doesn't mean there is anything wrong with the file.

Formatted). Within seconds, your file appears in whatever format it was originally in.

Figure 3-140, for instance, shows a perfectly formatted Excel file. At the bottom of the view screen you'll see, as usual, the current options (including the F10 command that can be used to pop up the menu bar). When you're finished viewing a file, press Esc to take you back to the normal view.

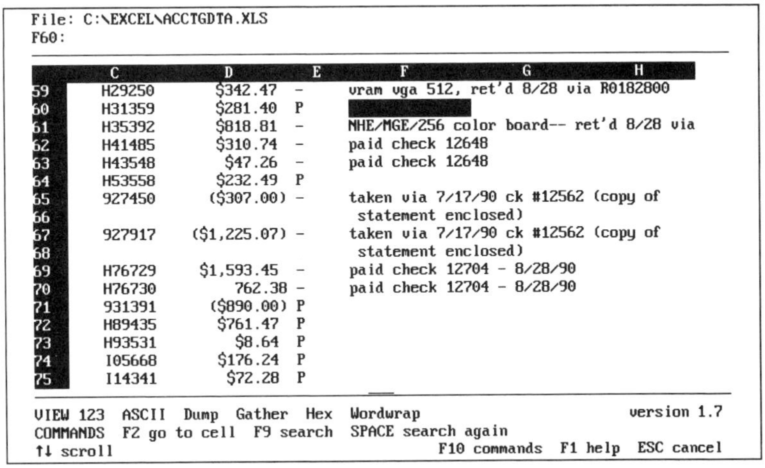

```
File: C:\EXCEL\ACCTGDTA.XLS
F60:
         C         D         E      F              G           H
   59  H29250    $342.47    -    vram vga 512, ret'd 8/28 via R0182800
   60  H31359    $281.40    P
   61  H35392    $818.81    -    NHE/MGE/256 color board-- ret'd 8/28 via
   62  H41485    $310.74    -    paid check 12648
   63  H43548     $47.26    -    paid check 12648
   64  H53558    $232.49    P
   65  927450   ($307.00)   -    taken via 7/17/90 ck #12562 (copy of
   66                              statement enclosed)
   67  927917  ($1,225.07)  -    taken via 7/17/90 ck #12562 (copy of
   68                              statement enclosed)
   69  H76729  $1,593.45    -    paid check 12704 - 8/28/90
   70  H76730    762.38     -    paid check 12704 - 8/28/90
   71  931391   ($890.00)   P
   72  H89435    $761.47    P
   73  H93531      $8.64    P
   74  I05668    $176.24    P
   75  I14341     $72.28    P

VIEW    123  ASCII  Dump  Gather  Hex  Wordwrap              version 1.7
COMMANDS  F2 go to cell  F9 search  SPACE search again
↑↓ scroll                                    F10 commands  F1 help  ESC cancel
```

Figure 3-140: You can view many kinds of files, even if you don't own the program that created them.

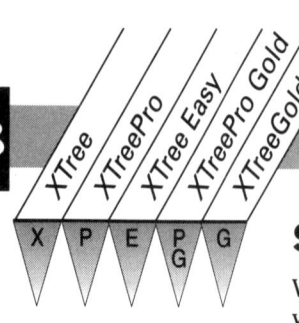

Searching for text in a viewed file

While viewing a file (regardless of format), you may search for text within the file (press G for Go to in XTree and XTreePro and press the F9 function key in XTree Easy, XTreePro Gold, and XTreeGold). You then enter the word or phrase you're looking for and press Enter. This technique can eliminate some PgUp and PgDn keystrokes if you're looking for something in particular.

Saving a viewed file to disk with XTreePro Gold and XTreeGold

If you have XTreePro Gold or XTreeGold, you can take advantage of another advanced feature. While viewing a file, you can save it as an ASCII file. The advantage of this is that you can take a file that was created in a program you don't have, save it as ASCII, and then open it on any word processor for editing or merging to another document.

The first thing you must do is *Gather* (XTree's word for highlight) the material to be saved. Press G for Gather, then position the cursor at the beginning of the material to be gathered and press Enter. Move the cursor to the end of the section you want to save and press Enter again. At this point you'll see the message `Append marked text to file:` appear at the bottom of the screen, as shown in Figure 3-141.

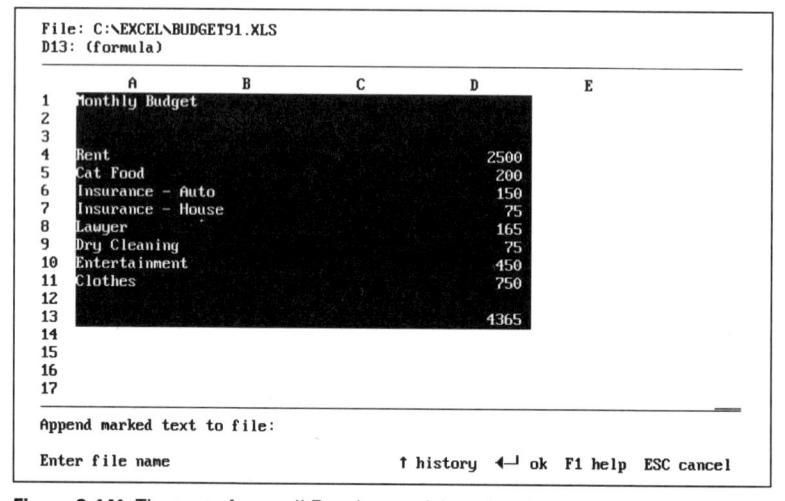

```
File: C:\EXCEL\BUDGET91.XLS
D13: (formula)

         A              B          C          D          E
1   Monthly Budget
2
3
4   Rent                                      2500
5   Cat Food                                   200
6   Insurance - Auto                           150
7   Insurance - House                           75
8   Lawyer                                     165
9   Dry Cleaning                                75
10  Entertainment                              450
11  Clothes                                    750
12
13                                            4365
14
15
16
17
Append marked text to file:

Enter file name                    ↑ history  ←┘ ok  F1 help  ESC cancel
```

Figure 3-141: The text of a small Excel spreadsheet has been gathered to be saved or printed.

To save the text as an ASCII file (which doesn't hurt the original file in any way), type a filename (something other than the file's current name) and Enter. In the blink of an eye, you'll have a file named whatever you just chose, sitting on your disk and ready for use in another program.

Printing a viewed file with XTreePro Gold and XTreeGold

XTreePro Gold and XTreeGold allow you to print the file you are viewing. The printout won't have fonts or anything fancy. In fact, it'll probably be downright ugly. However, the information you want will be there. The process is virtually identical to saving the file.

The first thing you must do is *Gather* (XTree's word for highlight) the material to be printed out. Press G for Gather, then position the cursor at the beginning of the material to be gathered and press Enter. Move the cursor to the end of the material and press Enter again. After you press Enter for the second time, you'll see the message `Append marked text to file:` appear at the bottom of the screen, as shown back in Figure 3-141.

If you want to print the file, type PRN — the computer's secret code for printer — and press Enter. (If you have a laser printer, and nothing seems to come out of the printer, take the printer off-line and press the form-feed button to retrieve your page.)

Viewing tagged files with XTreePro Gold and XTreeGold

If you wish to view a group of files, tag them and then press Ctrl-V (to view all tagged files). The first tagged file will appear in a view screen. When you're ready to view the next tagged file, press N. You can continue through the list, cycling back to the first file after viewing the last file in the group.

While using the Ctrl-V command, you can view only files in unformatted, or ASCII mode. You cannot invoke the format command.

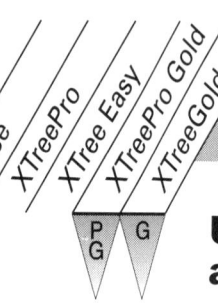

Using AutoView with XTreePro Gold and XTreeGold

AutoView allows you to travel up and down a file window on the left-hand side of the screen, while the contents of the highlighted file are automatically displayed on the right-hand side of the screen, as illustrated in Figure 3-142. To enter the AutoView mode, press F7.

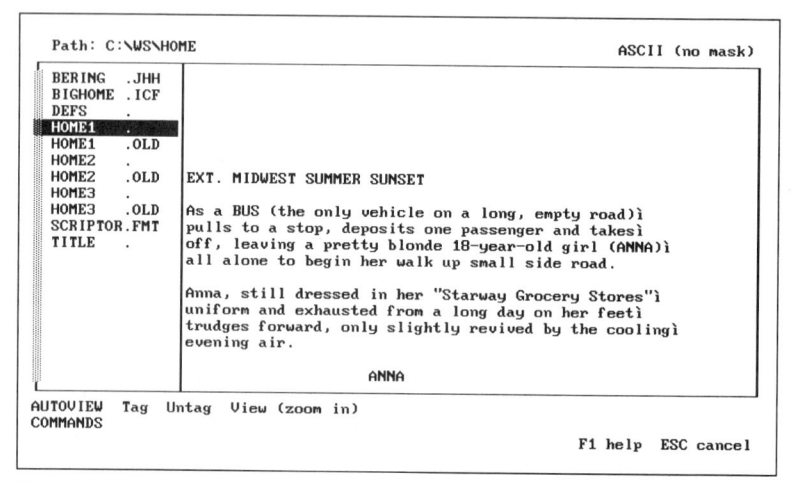

```
Path: C:\WS\HOME                                    ASCII (no mask)
 BERING   .JHH
 BIGHOME  .ICF
 DEFS     .
 HOME1    .
 HOME1    .OLD
 HOME2    .
 HOME2    .OLD    EXT. MIDWEST SUMMER SUNSET
 HOME3    .
 HOME3    .OLD    As a BUS (the only vehicle on a long, empty road)ì
 SCRIPTOR.FMT     pulls to a stop, deposits one passenger and takesì
 TITLE    .       off, leaving a pretty blonde 18-year-old girl (ANNA)ì
                  all alone to begin her walk up small side road.

                  Anna, still dressed in her "Starway Grocery Stores"ì
                  uniform and exhausted from a long day on her feetì
                  trudges forward, only slightly revived by the coolingì
                  evening air.

                                        ANNA

 AUTOVIEW   Tag  Untag  View (zoom in)
 COMMANDS
                                                  F1 help  ESC cancel
```

Figure 3-142: AutoView (F7) lets you view (and tag) files as you travel up and down a list of files.

Use your cursor to navigate up and down the list of files on the left; the currently highlighted file is automatically shown as a view file on the right. This procedure allows you to look at the contents of a file and then tag or untag the file.

Whenever you like, you can Zoom in on a file by pressing V. The View window will expand so you can get a better look at your file. When you're done zooming, press Enter or Esc and you'll return to AutoView. (If you want to see a formatted view of a file, you must first zoom in.) Press Enter (or Esc) when you're finished browsing in AutoView to go back to a File window.

Using AutoView with XTreeGold 2.5

XTreeGold 2.5 has a monster AutoView command with dozens of program and graphics filters, as shown in Figure 3-143. While you are in the AutoView mode, in addition to Tag, Untag, and Zoom, the

Chapter 3: XTree for DOS Quick Reference Guide 191

```
Path: C:\WORD\XTREE                                    ASCII (masked )

  2DINDEX .BAK
  2DINDEX .DOC
  3D_OUT  .DOC
  3D_XTREE.BAK
‡ 3D_XTREE.STY◆
  AUTO    .BAK
  AUTO    .DOC   EXT. MIDWEST SUMMER SUNSET
  FIXIT   .BAK
  FIXIT   .DOC   As a BUS (the only vehicle on a long, empty road) pulls to a
  FLIES   .BAT   stop, deposits one passenger and takes off again at a 90 degre
  GLOSSARY.BAK◆  angle to the road, leaving a pretty blonde 18-year-old girl
  GLOSSARY.DOC◆  (ANNA) all alone to begin her walk up the country road.
 ▌HOME1    . ▐
  IDG1    .DOC   Anna, still dressed in her "Starway Grocery Stores" uniform
  INDX_SPC.DOC◆  and exhausted from a long day on her feet trudges forward, onl
  KEYSX   .DOC   slightly revived by the cooling evening air.
  KINGLEE .DOC
  MASTER55.GLY                   ANNA
  MET     .DOC               (to herself)

AUTOVIEW  Attributes  Copy  Delete  Edit  Filespec  Invert  Move
COMMANDS  New date  Open  Print  Rename  Tag  Untag  View  eXecute
          F9 menu  F10 commands                       F1 help  ESC cancel
```

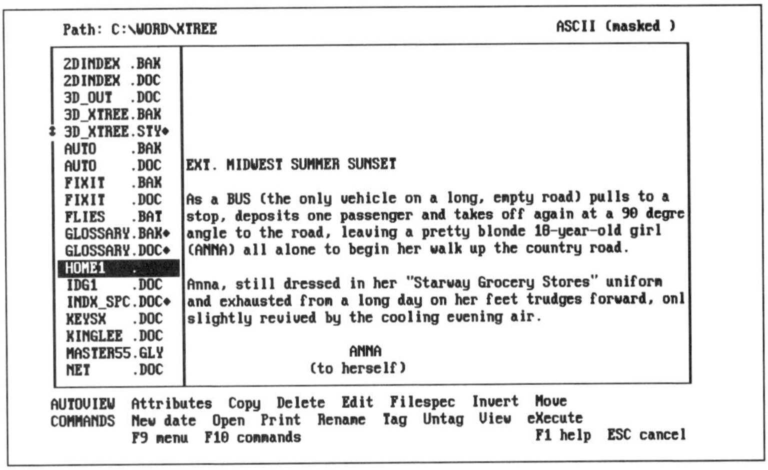

Figure 3-143: XTreeGold 2.5's AutoView screen lets you perform virtually all normal commands while in the View screen.

commands at the bottom of XTreeGold 2.5's screen include: Attributes, Copy, Delete, Edit, Filespec, Invert, Move, New date, Open, Print, Rename, Tag, Untag, View, and Execute. All of these commands can be accessed without leaving AutoView! F9 Menu and F10 Commands also work in AutoView. In short, being in AutoView doesn't limit your ability to act on a file.

XTreeGold 2.5 can display graphics files, in color if you wish. However, since displaying graphics files can take time to process, XTreeGold 2.5's AutoView first shows you data on the file (size, number of colors, and type of file). If you want to view the file, press V for View.

The XTreeMenu

If you *loved* the idea of XTreePro Gold's Application menu but found yourself hiding under the desk when it came time to actually figure out how to set up the menu, welcome to XTreeMenu — the revamped Application menu now appearing in XTreeGold and XTree Easy. You have only to ask (at installation) and XTree will search your hard disk and, all by itself, build a sophisticated menu system for you (like the one shown in Figure 3-144) in a matter of seconds.

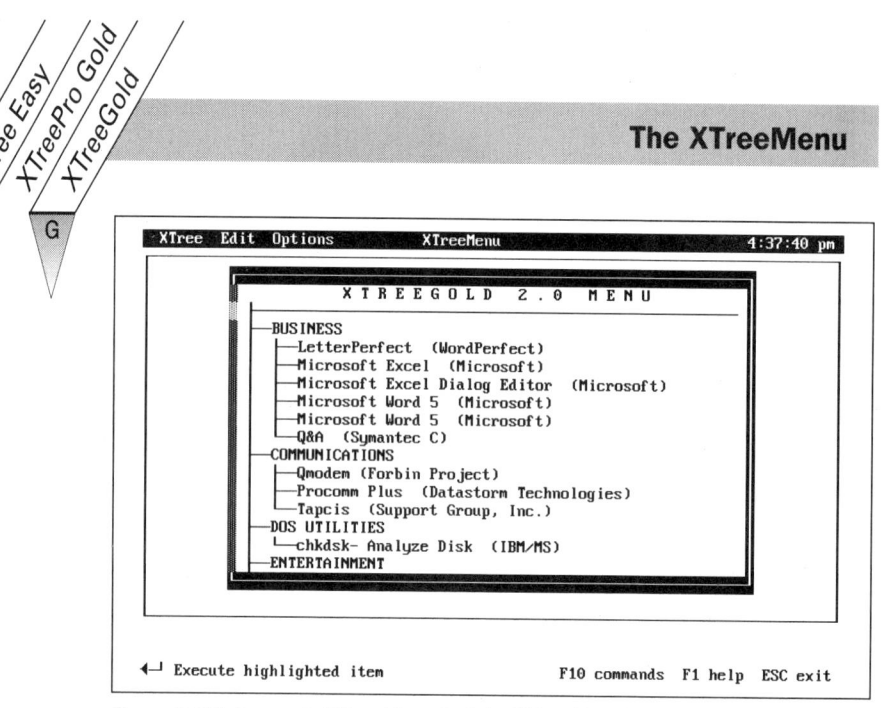

```
┌─XTree  Edit  Options          XTreeMenu                    4:37:40 pm
│
│              X T R E E G O L D   2 . 0   M E N U
│              ─────────────────────────────────────
│              ─BUSINESS
│                 ├─LetterPerfect  (WordPerfect)
│                 ├─Microsoft Excel  (Microsoft)
│                 ├─Microsoft Excel Dialog Editor   (Microsoft)
│                 ├─Microsoft Word 5  (Microsoft)
│                 ├─Microsoft Word 5  (Microsoft)
│                 └─Q&A  (Symantec C)
│              ─COMMUNICATIONS
│                 ├─Qmodem (Forbin Project)
│                 ├─Procomm Plus  (Datastorm Technologies)
│                 └─Tapcis  (Support Group, Inc.)
│              ─DOS UTILITIES
│                 └─chkdsk- Analyze Disk   (IBM/MS)
│              ─ENTERTAINMENT



  ↵  Execute highlighted item         F10 commands  F1 help  ESC exit
```

Figure 3-144: A sample XTreeMenu built by XTree Easy or XTreeGold during the XTree installation process.

Keep in mind that the menu builder is not omniscient. It will recognize over 700 programs but still may miss something on your system or mistake one program for another. (For instance, on my system a monitor-saver program was mistaken for a game called Mean Streets, since both programs use the same filename — MS.EXE.)

Accessing the XTreeMenu

Once the XTreeMenu has been built, you can pop it up from within XTree by using the F9 function key. As illustrated in Figure 3-144, XTree groups the programs it finds on your hard disk into grown-up categories such as "Business" and "Communications," making programs easier to locate. (If you don't like those category titles, you'll see how to rename them shortly.)

If you want to use a program on the menu, just highlight it with the cursor and press Enter. For instance, if you want to activate Excel, highlight it, press Enter, and after a few seconds, you'll be in Excel. At the conclusion of your Excel session, you'll be delivered right back to XTreeMenu.

Chapter 3: XTree for DOS Quick Reference Guide

```
XTree  Edit  Options          XTreeMenu                    4:39:30 pm

                         X T R E E G O L D   2 . 0   M E N U

               +─BUSINESS
                 ─COMMUNICATIONS
                    ├─Qmodem (Forbin Project)
                    ├─Procomm Plus (Datastorm Technologies)
                    └─Tapcis (Support Group, Inc.)
                 ─DOS UTILITIES
                    └─chkdsk- Analyze Disk  (IBM/MS)
                 ─ENTERTAINMENT
                    ├─Mean Streets  (Access Software)
                    └─Micro Spell
                 ─GRAPHICS
                    └─PageMaker  (Aldus)
                 ─HOME
                    └─Reminders!  (POP Computer Products)



  ↵  Execute highlighted item              F10 commands  F1 help  ESC exit
```

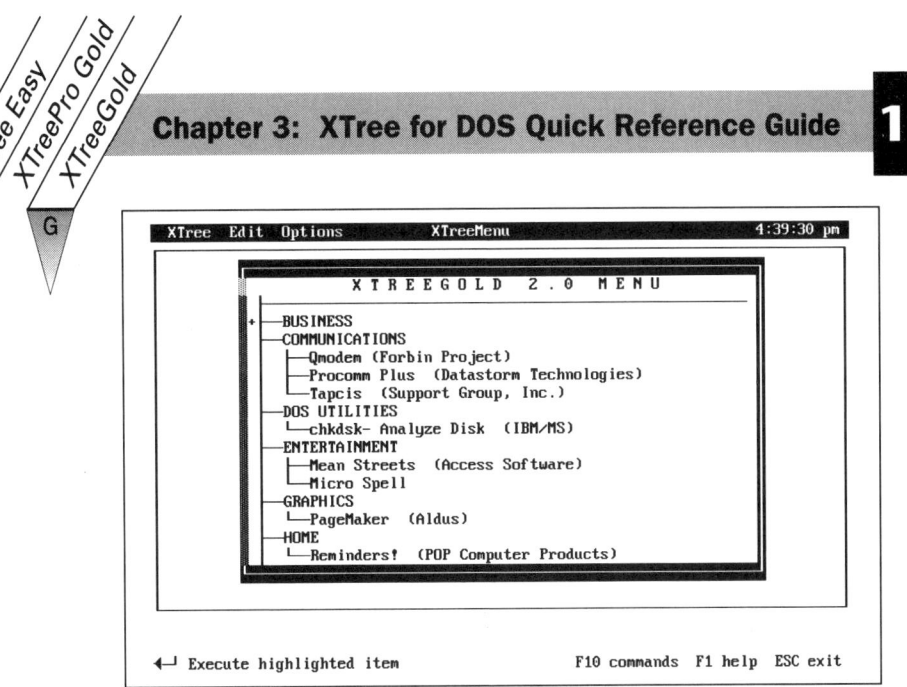

Figure 3-145: You can eliminate secondary headings from view by using the minus key.

Changing XTreeMenu's display

The old Applications Menu had a limit of 13 listings. Now, however, no such restrictions apply. You can have screenful after screenful of menu listings, if you wish. If you end up with *too* much of a good thing and your menu gets too long, you can collapse portions of the menu so that just the group titles, for instance, are visible.

In Figure 3-145 only the Business group title remains — all the sublistings are gone. This was accomplished simply by highlighting the group title (in this case Business) and pressing the minus key (–). The plus sign (+) to the left of Business tells you there's more.

To bring back the sublistings, just highlight the title and press the plus key (+) — or just press Enter.

Editing the XTreeMenu

Let's say there are a few things about the XTreeMenu you'd like to modify — delete a listing here, rename a group title there — that sort of thing. The first step is to highlight the menu listing you want to alter and then press F10. Pressing F10 (or clicking at the top of the screen with the mouse) activates the pull-down menu system for editing the XTreeMenu.

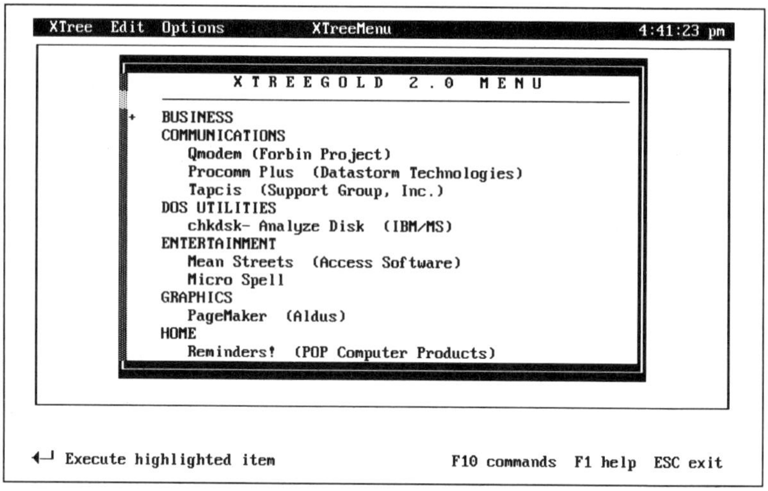

The XTreeMenu

```
 XTree  Edit  Options          XTreeMenu                    4:41:23 pm

                    X T R E E G O L D   2 . 0   M E N U
           • BUSINESS
             COMMUNICATIONS
                Qmodem  (Forbin Project)
                Procomm Plus  (Datastorm Technologies)
                Tapcis  (Support Group, Inc.)
             DOS UTILITIES
                chkdsk- Analyze Disk  (IBM/MS)
             ENTERTAINMENT
                Mean Streets  (Access Software)
                Micro Spell
             GRAPHICS
                PageMaker  (Aldus)
             HOME
                Reminders!  (POP Computer Products)


  ↵ Execute highlighted item               F10 commands  F1 help  ESC exit
```

Figure 3-146: XTreeMenu gets a designer look when the outline element is turned off.

Use the arrow keys to highlight the menu category you want and the options will appear underneath. Highlight the desired command and before you can say, "press Enter," you're on your way. (Alternately, you can press the letter that is highlighted in the word you wish to use.)

Take a deep breath and start with a simple but sort of dramatic change. As illustrated in Figures 3-144 and 3-145, the XTreeMenu is organized in a tree display (much like how the directories and subdirectories are laid out in XTree). You can, however, turn off XTreeMenu's tree, as shown in Figure 3-146, for an exciting change of pace.

To turn off the tree, press F10 to activate the menu bar and then press the right-arrow key to highlight Options. At this point you can press either Enter or simply G (for Graphics Toggle) and the tree display will vanish. Repeat this procedure to toggle the tree on.

More tools can be found under the Edit menu shown in Figure 3-147, which allow you to Add, Delete, Move, and Rename items in your XTreeMenu.

To delete rarely used (or sensitive) programs from the XTreeMenu, highlight the item you want to delete, press F10 (for the commands), use the arrow keys to move over and highlight

Chapter 3: XTree for DOS Quick Reference Guide

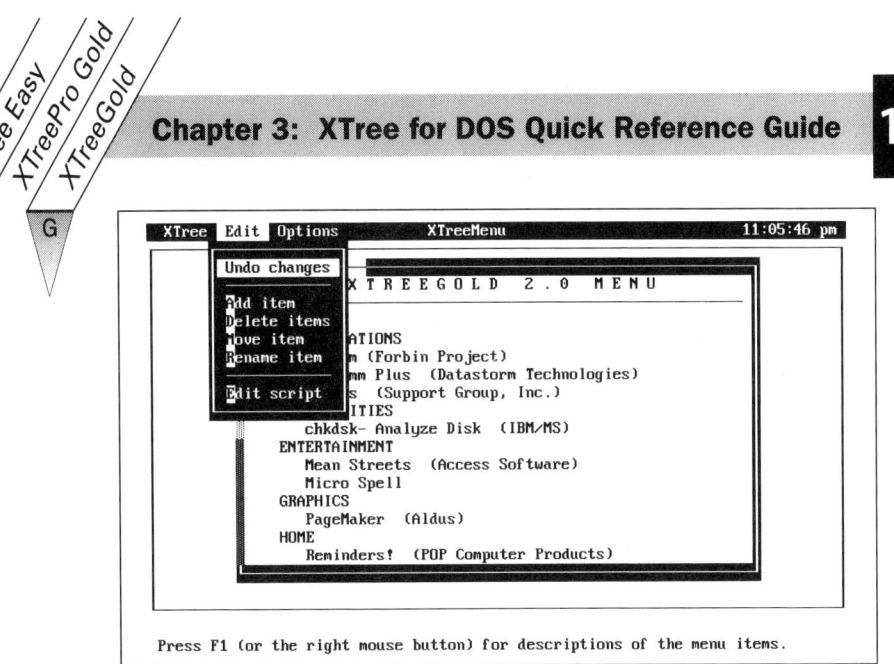

Figure 3-147: The pull-down menu offers easy access to the tools needed to edit the XTreeMenu.

Edit, then either press D or highlight the word Delete and press Enter. You'll be asked to verify that you want the item deleted; confirm your choice of deletion by pressing Enter.

NOTE: If you delete an item that has sublistings (items indented underneath it), the sublistings will be deleted as well.

If you make a mistake, immediately use the Undo changes command, also found under Edit, to reverse changes made to the menu. Be sure to use this before you exit XTreeMenu — otherwise it's too late.

The Move command enables you to change the assigned position of a listing. With this command you can customize XTreeMenu to your needs. The Move command, in addition to moving menu items up and down (with the up- and down-arrow keys), also allows you to indent (or outdent) items using the left- and right-arrow keys. To move an item, highlight it, press F10, highlight Edit, press M (for move), and move the item to its new home. Press Enter to lock the moved item into its new position.

When you use the Move command, you'll find that you cannot move an item from one group to another (from Entertainment to Business, for example), unless you outdent it first (use your left-arrow key to move the item to the left). Once you get the listing in the proper group, use the right-arrow key to indent the item to its

The XTreeMenu

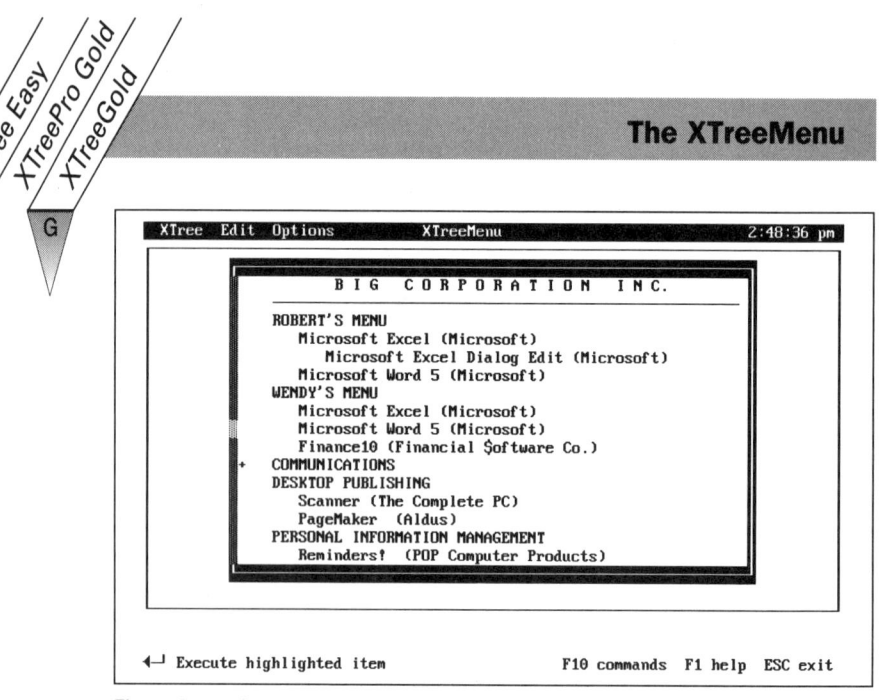

```
 XTree  Edit  Options              XTreeMenu                    2:48:36 pm
┌─────────────────────────────────────────────────────────────────────────┐
│                      B I G   C O R P O R A T I O N   I N C.             │
│              ─────────────────────────────────────────────              │
│              ROBERT'S MENU                                              │
│                  Microsoft Excel (Microsoft)                            │
│                      Microsoft Excel Dialog Edit (Microsoft)            │
│                  Microsoft Word 5 (Microsoft)                           │
│              WENDY'S MENU                                               │
│                  Microsoft Excel (Microsoft)                            │
│                  Microsoft Word 5 (Microsoft)                           │
│                  Finance10 (Financial $oftware Co.)                     │
│            + COMMUNICATIONS                                             │
│              DESKTOP PUBLISHING                                         │
│                  Scanner (The Complete PC)                              │
│                  PageMaker  (Aldus)                                     │
│              PERSONAL INFORMATION MANAGEMENT                            │
│                  Reminders! (POP Computer Products)                     │
│                                                                         │
└─────────────────────────────────────────────────────────────────────────┘
 ↵ Execute highlighted item                F10 commands  F1 help  ESC exit
```

Figure 3-148: A customized XTreeMenu screen.

correct position and then press Enter to complete the operation. If you want to rework the XTreeMenu, you'll quickly realize that editing listings via the pull-down menu is somewhat tiresome.

Fortunately, there's a secret shortcut: all highlighted key commands in the pull-down menu can be used whether you're in that pull-down menu or not. For instance, take a look at your menu and press G to turn the graphics toggle on and off. Want to move an item? Press M and move away. To expand or collapse the tree, press + or –. These shortcuts are quite the time and frustration savers.

Figure 3-148 shows one example of an edited XTreeMenu. You may also wish to replace the name XTreeMenu, shown at the top of the figure, with an appropriate company name. If you have other people using your computer, give them their own submenus (like "Robert" and "Wendy") to save time and frustration. You may add more indented levels as needed.

NOTE: Remember, using the History command when editing repetitive menus can save some keystrokes.

Editing XTreeMenu's instructions

Once you have edited the menu *display*, you must follow through by creating or editing the underlying instructions — the "script" — so that XTree will know what to do when you select your artfully

Chapter 3: XTree for DOS Quick Reference Guide

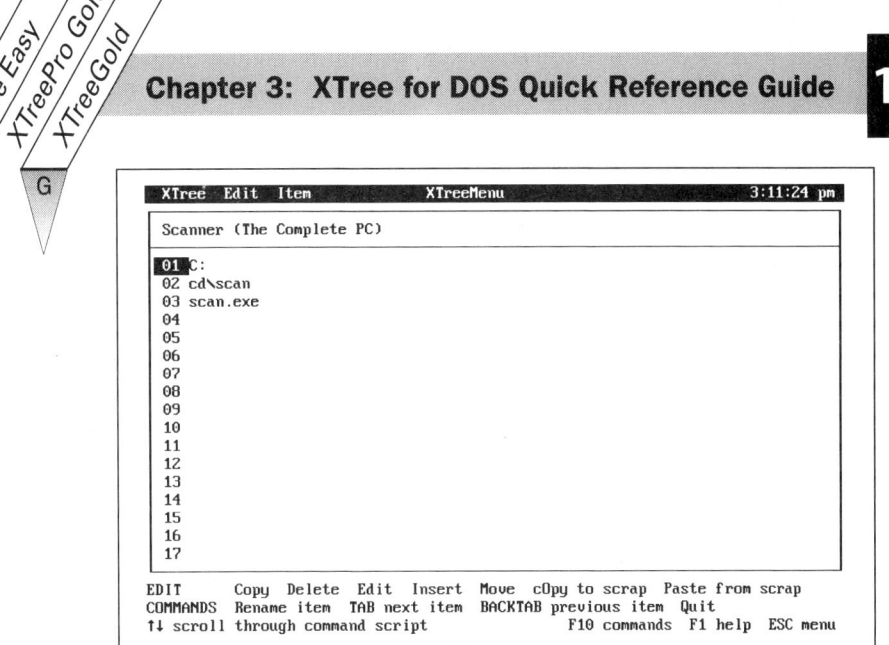

```
XTree  Edit  Item              XTreeMenu                    3:11:24 pm
Scanner (The Complete PC)
01 C:
02 cd\scan
03 scan.exe
04
05
06
07
08
09
10
11
12
13
14
15
16
17
EDIT        Copy  Delete  Edit  Insert  Move  cOpy to scrap  Paste from scrap
COMMANDS    Rename item  TAB next item  BACKTAB previous item  Quit
↑↓ scroll through command script              F10 commands  F1 help  ESC menu
```

Figure 3-149: Editing an XTreeMenu script for Scanner. All of the edit commands are listed at the bottom of the screen.

typed menu item. The computer needs to know all the boring details like the filename of the program and what directory it can be found in.

To edit a script, highlight the menu listing to be edited, press F10, and highlight Edit. Then highlight Edit Script and press Enter. (Or just press E for Edit.) You'll get a display something like that shown in Figure 3-149.

This figure shows the script for the highlighted menu item. If you've ever created a DOS batch file (like AUTOEXEC.BAT) you'll see that this is nothing more than a fancy, more convenient way to create a batch file. At this point, some of you may be experiencing that urge to crawl back under the desk. Others, familiar with the Application Menu, may be happy to see that several new options have been added here. The new options reduce the amount of typing required and make it possible to do things like copy a script from one menu listing to another.

Two of the fun new commands available for editing a script are the mysterious `Tab Next item` and `BACKTab previous item`. The word *item* refers to a menu listing (like Scanner). In this case, once you finish editing the Scanner script, you can use the Tab key to save your edits and move along to the next item on the menu — the PageMaker listing, in this example. To move backwards to the previous item, you hold down the Shift key while using the Tab key — this is called a *backtab* — and you'll then move up to the Desktop Publishing group title. The other handy additions are the Copy to scrap and Paste from scrap commands. *Scrap* does not mean thrown away (as in scrap heap). In computers, scrap is another name for a clipboard or temporary storage space.

In the menu back in Figure 3-139, both Robert and Wendy's menus contained Microsoft Word. While each menu listing needs its own script, chances are the scripts Robert and Wendy use to invoke Word will be nearly identical. With Copy and Paste you can take a script from one menu item and duplicate it into another. Then you can make whatever minor edits are necessary, rather than start from scratch each time.

To copy the script you are currently editing, press O (to Copy to scrap). Then use Tab or backtab (the Shift-Tab key combination) to display the other menu item's script screen and press P to Paste from scrap. The script will magically appear on-screen.

If you already have items in one script (script A), pasting script B into script A will wipe out script A. Paste with caution.

Once you are editing a script, there's yet another pull-down menu (accessed by pressing F10) waiting to help you out. As with most pull-down menus, this one offers basically the same choices as what you see at the bottom of the screen — with one important exception: the Undo command. The pull-down menu lists Undo, though you don't have to pull down the menu to use it: just press U.

The Configuration program for XTreeGold and XTree Easy will let you set XTreeMenu to automatically pop up whenever XTree is activated. Also, as a security measure, you can make it impossible for anyone to make changes to the menu (except you, of course). Finally, if you're the office guru, you can set up menus for your disciples and be free from concern about anyone accidentally changing anything.

Part II
XTree for Novell Networks

Chapter 4 201
    XTreeNet: Network File
    Management Made Easy

The 5th Wave
By Rich Tennant
"I THINK I'VE FOUND YOUR FILE, MARGARET! IT FEELS LIKE A SPREADSHEET! RIGHT?! RIGHT?!"

Chapter 4
XTreeNet: Network File Management Made Easy

In This Chapter
▶ What a network is and why it needs a special version of XTree
▶ The commands that are specific to XTreeNet

Introducing XTreeNet

In the beginning, there were individual, stand-alone computers (well, actually, there were rocks... but let's move on), and XTree was there to manage them. Then, over the course of time, someone said, "Hey, isn't there some way to connect these suckers so we can all share our data?" Lo and behold, the local area network (LAN) was born.

All of a sudden lots of computers were *networking* (talking to each other over cables). Instead of fifty computers with fifty copies of a database file, there was now one central computer (known as the *file server*) and one database file that everyone could share. As you might imagine, fifty people with computers can get themselves into a lot of trouble, so each network has a *system administrator* to make sure things stay on track.

The system administrator soon realized, however, that keeping track of files and updating programs on fifty computers was a daunting task (and fifty computers is not considered to be a very big network). To help the beleaguered system administrators of the world, XTreeNet (a special version of XTree made specifically for networks) burst forth to help manage LANs.

Who this chapter is for

If your computer is part of a network, but you are expected to manage only those files on your workstation's hard drive (if you have one), then you can continue to use XTree for DOS (or for Windows) and you can skip this chapter.

If, however, you're a LAN expert, you'll be interested to see how XTree has been adapted for use on a network. XTreeNet can make your duties much easier. Please don't give into the temptation to slap your old tried and true XTree (or XTree for Windows) onto the file server. This is not recommended. The differences between a stand-alone computer and a network of computers goes deeper than just the number of computers. The "non-Net" versions of XTree are just not prepared for the unique demands of a network.

What's so special about a LAN?

Because the main goal of a network is to have lots of people using the system at the same time, and since DOS can only handle one person at a time, multiuser operating environments have been created by various vendors. The most popular network operating environment (and the only one XTreeNet works with) is Novell's NetWare.

Although the idea of everyone on a network sharing and caring may give you the warm fuzzies, the bottom line is that file sharing is not always desired. There are two main reasons why most businesses don't really want all information equally available to every employee: confidentiality (for instance, only certain people should have access to payroll records) and security (whether by malice or ignorance, the ability to change a file on a computer includes the power to destroy).

Neither of these issues are relevant on a PC where the owner is the user/creator/owner of the work on the system. In a network, however, the system administrator is also in charge of doling out what are known as *user rights* (that is, who can do what, where, and when).

A network, therefore, needs a file-management program that not only copies, writes (saves), and deletes but also understands who has the *right* to copy, write, and delete.

Furthermore, because NetWare keeps track of what files and directories people create and use, a network file-management system must keep on top of that information as well; it can be more than embarrassing to find out you've just deleted a file while someone else was in the middle of using it. (In fact, in some states it's cause for immediate execution!) XTreeNet handles all these feats and more.

System administrators will be happy to know that XTreeNet can substantially replace SYSCON (the NetWare program that usually handles these tasks). XTreeNet goes beyond NetWare because it is also capable of directly connecting two computers on the network (known as *peer-to-peer communications*), as well as connecting and disconnecting from file servers, and more.

Understanding XTreeNet Concepts

If you are familiar with XTreePro Gold (see Chapter 3 for XTreePro Gold's command reference), consider yourself up and running on XTreeNet! The XTreePro Gold command set is what they started with when they put XTreeNet together. The differences between XTreePro Gold and XTreeNet have to do with XTreeNet's ability to recognize network file attributes (as described in Chapter 1 and later in this chapter) and user rights (when and where you can create, copy, delete, and so on). Use the XTreePro Gold commands in Chapter 3 as a starting place for XTreeNet.

This chapter contains the XTreeNet commands that are network-specific. So, if you want to copy a file, for example, you can look up the Copy command in Chapter 3 (since copying is a task common to both stand-alone PCs and networks). If, however, you want to log onto a network file server (clearly a network-specific activity), you'll find instructions for this command later in this chapter, in the "Attach/Detach" section.

Please note, because of the, er, uh, *robust* nature of the NetWare system, this is going to get a little technical — but if you're managing files on a network, you can take it.

Peer-to-peer file management

Although networks are designed so that each computer in the system can share data on a file server, peer-to-peer communication allows two computers on the system to connect directly. Thus someone (like a system administrator) can sit at one computer and *Map* to another computer in the system. (Much like XTreePro Gold lets you log to another drive, Map allows you to log to another computer and access all of its drives.)

Once you connect with the other computer, you can copy or delete (or whatever) files on that computer. Basically, this feature exacerbates the already sedentary lifestyle of system supervisors, allowing them to carry out network maintenance on other computers in the system without ever leaving their chairs.

The reason this is called *peer-to-peer* is that the two communicating computers are equals in the network (as opposed to one computer being a workstation and the other a file server — these two types are not equals). Logging onto a nonpeer machine (such as a file server) is possible via the Attach/Detach commands (coming up soon now).

The commands required to connect with another computer on the system while using XTreeNet are simple. Press Alt-M (for Map), press R (for Remote map), enter the workstation name and drive (CHRIS\C:, for example), and then press Enter. The disk drive you enter (in this case, CHRIS\C:) then appears as another *volume* (disk drive) on your own computer. Tedious updates, file transfers, and so on can be handled without endangering shoe leather.

The remote computer must first be running the host program, XTSERV, *before* you can map to that computer. (You can put XTSERV in AUTOEXEC.BAT files so it loads automatically.) Finally, you must either have supervisory rights or know Chris's password to have access to his computer.

Peer-to-peer remote control

Not only can you Map onto another computer in the system to copy and delete and stuff, you can actually take control of the other computer and use it as though you were sitting in front of it. If you're the one who provides help to other people on the system, this capability can be handy.

Press Alt-F7 to begin the remote control process. Figure 4-1 shows how your screen should look at this point. The remote control commands are listed at the bottom of the screen. You select Attach to connect to another computer; you

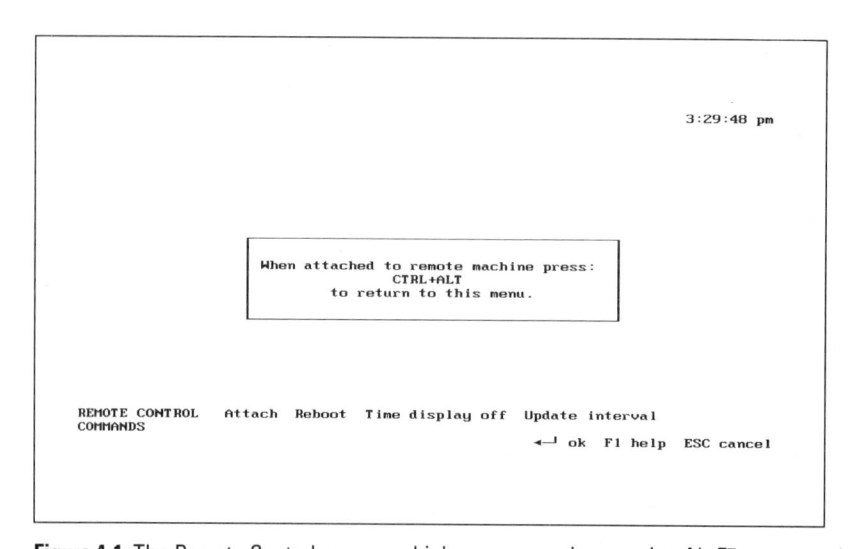

```
                                                           3:29:48 pm




                  ┌─────────────────────────────────────┐
                  │  When attached to remote machine press: │
                  │              CTRL+ALT                │
                  │         to return to this menu.      │
                  └─────────────────────────────────────┘




        REMOTE CONTROL    Attach  Reboot  Time display off  Update interval
        COMMANDS
                                               ←┘ ok   F1 help   ESC cancel
```

Figure 4-1: The Remote Control screen, which you access by pressing Alt-F7.

can now work on the remote machine as if it were your own. Press Ctrl-Alt to return to the Remote Control screen, where you can select Detach to disconnect from the other computer.

Directory information

You can use the Info display command (Alt-I) to toggle information in the Statistics and Information Box between current volume and directory statistics (the default), to current network directory and file information, or to network directory trustee information.

- **Statistics Mode:** This mode displays current volume statistics when the Directory window is active, and current directory statistics when the File window is active.
- **Information Mode:** This mode reveals some additional facts about the current directory (such as total files and size in bytes, effective and maximum rights, owner, and creation date) when the Directory window is active, and information about the current file (such as file flags, last modified and accessed dates, owner, creation date, and last archived date) when the File window is active.
- **Trustee Information Mode:** This mode shows current directory trustee information when any window is active. (A *trustee* is someone who has been given the right to create, use, and delete the current directory.)

Pick list

Any group of items available and known to XTreeNet can be displayed in *pick lists*. For example, when XTreeNet prompts you to indicate a particular drive or server (examples of the types of items you'll find in a pick list), you can simply press F2 to pop up the Pick List window. (You'll see the legend F2 display list at the bottom of your screen when pick lists are available.) At this point you can choose an item from the list by highlighting it with your cursor and pressing Enter.

Using XTreeNet Commands

The following commands are specific to XTreeNet. Remember to use XTreePro Gold commands from Chapter 3 for commands common to Pro Gold and XTreeNet.

Attach/Detach

Pressing Alt-A activates the Attach command for logging onto another file server.

Note: Attaching to a file server (one of the hubs of the network) and attaching to a remote computer (used by a coworker) are not interchangeable commands.

After activating Attach, you'll select from Attach, Detach, and Server list (to find out what's out there). As you go through the process of attaching to another computer, you'll be prompted for your user name and password.

Attributes (Directory)

You learned about attributes for *files* in Chapters 1 and 3. But NetWare also has *directory* attributes. From the Directory window of the current drive, you may modify directory rights by pressing A (for Attributes) and selecting from among the following choices (press the highlighted letter on your keyboard):

Creation Date	A directory's New Date command.
Flags	System, Hidden, Private (Private renders the contents of a directory invisible, unless you have Search rights.)
Owner	Each directory can be assigned to an owner (for tracking).
Rights mask	This is where the system administrator assigns various abilities to the users. Assigning any of the following rights establishes the maximum rights any user can have to a directory. (These rights apply to what can be done on a directory-wide basis.)
Read	Open and look at files.
Write	Open and save files.
Open	Read, save, and change attributes.
Create	Save a new file.
Delete	Remove the directory.
Parental	Create, rename, and delete subdirectories.
Search	List files and subdirectories.
Modify	Change file attributes.
Trustees	People can be designated as Trustees of a directory. No one has more rights to a directory than a Trustee does.

Attributes (File)

Basic file attributes (Read-only, Archive, System, and Hidden) are discussed in Chapters 1 and 3. In NetWare, because of the multiuser environment, many more attributes (also referred to as Flags) exist. From the File window, you may assign or modify one or more of the following file attributes, in either the Date or Flags category, by pressing A (for Attributes):

Dates

Accessed date	Shows the new date and time.
Creation date	Shows the creation date.

Flags

Read-only	Files with this attribute can be opened and read by all users, but not changed or saved.
Archive	Files with this attribute have been backed up.
System	Files with this flag have protected status.
Hidden	Files with this flag won't appear in DOS directories.
Network shareable	These files can be accessed by more than one user at a time (as long as the software was built to be shared).
Execute-only	Once they are set as Execute-only, COM or EXE files can't be copied, changed, renamed, or deleted.
Transactional	Marks the file for automatic transaction tracking by NetWare so that two people don't try to access a nonnetwork-aware program.
Indexed	A very technical flag that tells NetWare to build a special FAT entry for the file to speed up access. (Generally this is useful for very large files, but NetWare 386 automatically indexes very large files, so you don't have to manually set the flag.)
Modified date	Changes the date assigned by the network to the file at the time the file was saved.
Owner	Changes the owner name of files.
Archived date	Enables you to change the archived date stamp.

```
Path: XTREE\SYS:PUBLIC                                         3:18:25 pm
┌─<showall: >─
│ VIEWER   .EXE     75,907 r...n...  5-25-90 12:46:02 pm   FILE  *.*
│ VOLINFO  .EXE    142,235 r...n...  4-26-90  3:39:06 pm
│ VOLINFO  .HLP      8,521 ....n... 11-06-90  3:06:14 pm   NETWARE VOLUME
│ WANGTEK  .EXE     22,950 r...n... 12-08-89  3:19:46 pm   SYS
│ WBROLL   .EXE     20,688 r...n...  3-15-90 11:24:38 pm   Space    10,186,752
│ WBTRCALL .EXE     27,628 r...n...  3-22-90  3:51:06 pm
│ WHOAMI   .EXE     25,723 r...n...  5-18-90 11:05:04 am   FILE Information
│ WIND     .BAT        380 ........ 11-12-90 10:59:58 am   Current File
│ WIND     .MIS        380 ........ 11-12-90 10:59:58 am     WHOAMI  .EXE
│ WINSET   .BAT        414 ........ 11-12-90 10:54:26 am   Bytes         25,723
│ WINWORD  .           73 ....n... 10-18-90  1:20:34 pm   Flags    [r...n...]
│ WINWORD  .BAT        788 ........ 11-12-90 10:46:28 am   Last Modified
│ WORD     .           57 ....n... 10-17-90  6:58:10 am     5-18-90 11:05 am
│ WORD     .BAK        146 ........  1-23-91  5:25:04 pm   Owner
│ WORD     .BAT        525 ........  1-23-91  5:25:28 pm     SUPERVISOR
│ WORDTMS  .BAT        146 ........  1-23-91  5:25:22 pm   Accessed    2-12-91
│ XM       .BAK        999 ........ 11-15-90  7:03:30 am   Created     1-01-85
│▶XM       .BAT        466 ........ 11-19-90  8:26:02 am   Last Archived
│ XM$16    .BAT         16 ....n... 10-03-90  4:45:06 pm     No Date

FILE       Attributes  Copy   Delete  Edit   Filespec  Invert  Log volume  Move
COMMANDS   Open  Print Rename Tag     Untag  View      eXecute Quit
↵ tree  F7 autoview  F8 split     F9 menu  F10 commands     F1 help  ESC cancel
```

Figure 4-2: Flags assigned to files appear in the middle column of the Expanded file window.

Figure 4-2 shows a highlighted file, WHOAMI.EXE, in the Expanded file window. Note the eight dots next to the filename; the dots are place markers for each of the flags just described. In this example, WHOAMI.EXE has been assigned the Read-only and Network shareable attributes. All the details on WHOAMI.EXE are listed in the FILE Information window on the right.

> **WARNING:** Use the Execute-only flag with extreme caution. You may get a hot flash to set all your programs as execute-only to prevent deletion or for virus protection, but during normal use, many applications alter their own program files. So if you add the Execute-only flag to a file and the application can't revise itself, you may have just rendered the program useless. Furthermore, there is *no* way to remove this flag. Once a file is set to execute-only, it can never be changed. The only solution is to delete the file and reinstall it. So use it carefully!

Tag or untag a Branch

In XTreePro Gold you can tag a file or a directory (prior to carrying out a command on the files en masse). In XTreeNet you may also tag/untag a Branch (a directory and all its subdirectories) using the Ctrl-F7 and Ctrl-F8 key combinations.

Tag or untag by attributes

When you want to tag or untag by attributes in XTreeNet (with the Alt-T command), there are (as you may have surmised) more attributes available than there are in DOS:

Accessed date	Tags files that have been accessed within the dates you specify.
Creation date	Tags files with creation dates that fall within the dates you specify.
Flags	Tags those files that match the flag settings you enter.
Modified date	Tags those files changed between the dates you enter.
Owner	Tags files owned by a specified owner.
aRchived date	Tags files not backed up between the dates you enter.

Map

Map is NetWare's *path* command. It's different from DOS's path in two ways:

- Map is cumulative: In DOS's path, the last path statement *replaces* the previous path statement; in NetWare each path is *added* to the previous paths.
- A letter is assigned to each path.

If you want to access a directory or branch, it must be mapped first. To start, press Alt-M; you are then offered a choice between Delete (to remove a map), Remote (to add another computer as a volume), and S (to add a network volume). Figure 4-3 shows R, the mapped drive C: of the remote workstation BRK.

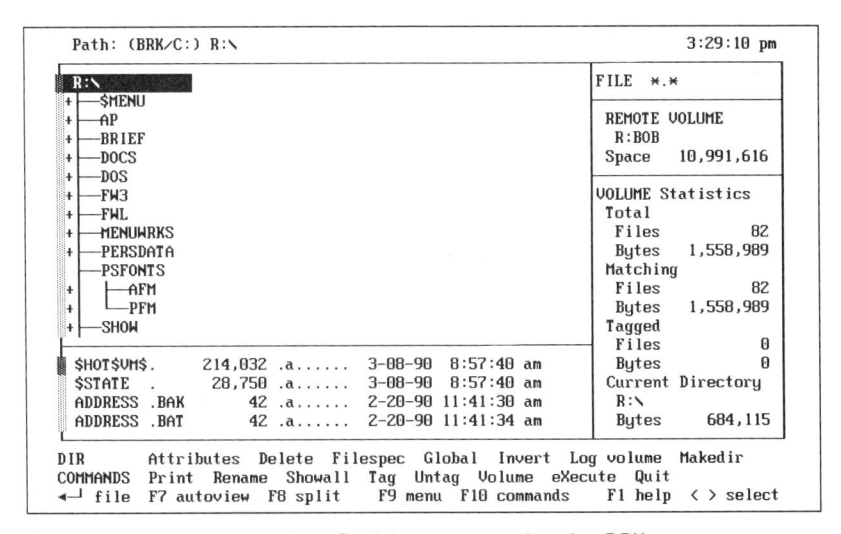

Figure 4-3: R is the mapped drive C: of the remote workstation BRK.

Volume

A *volume* is a disk. It can either be a hard disk or a floppy disk. The Volume command allows you to carry out a trio of terrific volume-wide tasks. Press V from the directory window and choose from the following options:

Available	Displays the amount of space available on the volume.
Format	Formats a floppy disk.
Label	Changes the name of the current volume, like "rename a Volume" in XTreePro Gold.
Wash	As in XTreeGold, Wash makes sure that deleted files are really deleted and cannot be "brought back" with fancy software.

Summary

- XTreeNet is basically XTreePro Gold plus some additional network-specific commands.
- System administrators should use XTreeNet because it not only is network-aware, but it also performs tasks that NetWare's SYSCON cannot.
- XTreeNet allows peer-to-peer communications as well as peer-to-peer remote control (attaching to file servers to make updates and user support more efficient).

Part III
XTree for Windows

Chapter 5 213
    Windows Concepts

Chapter 6 221
    XTree for Windows Basics

Chapter 7 233
    XTree for Windows Quick
    Reference Guide

The 5th Wave **By Rich Tennant**

"HEY DAD, IS IT ALRIGHT IF I WINDOW YOUR COMPUTER?"

Chapter 5
Windows Concepts

In This Chapter
- Taking the "pane" out of Windows
- Keyboard, mouse, and window maneuvers
- Activating, sizing, and closing windows
- Dialoging with Windows

Using Windows

You probably realize by now that, despite what they promised in the commercials, running Windows doesn't mean you can firmly plant your head in the sand when it comes to DOS. You still have to know about directories and wildcards and such — especially if you're using XTree for Windows. So, if you skipped Chapter 1 (the one about DOS), it would be wise to go back and read (or review) it now.

As with Chapter 1, this chapter doesn't provide an all-inclusive course in Windows. In fact, I'm making the dangerous assumption that you are already a fully functional, wild and crazy Windows user. Actually, that assumption is not so dangerous when you think about it because, after all, it wouldn't make much sense to get Windows for the sole purpose of running XTree for Windows. It's logical for me to assume, therefore, that you have *got* to be using Windows for something else already, right?

On-screen elements

This chapter runs *quickly* through basic Windows features so that we're all talking the same language. A sample Windows desktop labeled with the proper terminology is illustrated in Figure 5-1; three windows are open — Program Manager, Main, and Applications. Of these three windows, Main is the active window (the one currently in use).

Active Window: The active window on-screen is usually the one in the foreground and has a different color border than inactive windows.

Part III: XTree for Windows

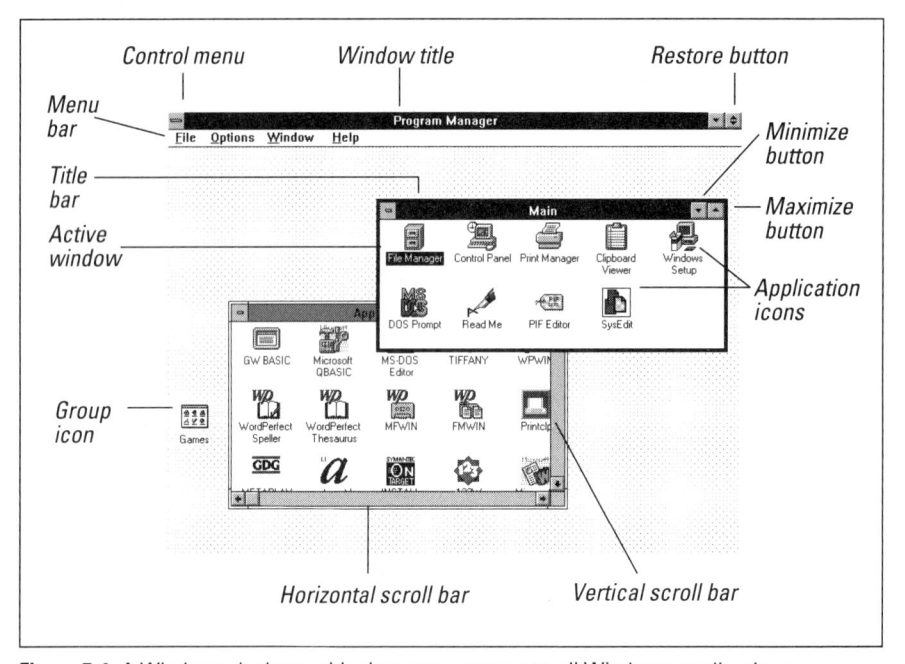

Figure 5-1: A Windows desktop with elements common to all Windows applications.

Application icon: Each program on your computer can be represented by an *icon,* a graphical element created to depict a particular program or type of program.

Title bar: Displays the name of the window.

Window title: Each open window has a title; for program windows, the title includes the name of the program and the open file.

Control menu: Commands on this menu let you shrink, enlarge, move, or close the active window.

Minimize button: Reduces a window to its icon. This is similar to the Mi*n*imize command in the window's Control menu.

Maximize button: Enlarges a window to its maximum size. This is similar to the Ma*x*imize command in the window's Control menu.

Restore button: Returns a window to its previous size and shape after you maximize it. This button appears only when a window is maximized.

Scroll bars: Horizontal and vertical scroll bars enable you to bring information not currently in view into the window. Scroll bars appear only when there is more information than the window can display.

Mouse moves

"It's all in the wrist," they say, about tennis, golf, and video games. Windows also gives you plenty of opportunity to build those all-important wrist muscles as you mouse your way through the Windows maze. Pointing to items on your Windows desktop is the *first* step to making something happen. The next step is to press the mouse button in one of the following ways:

Click: Press and release the mouse button.

Double-click: Same as a click except you do it twice (really fast).

Drag and drop: Requires a bit more effort, but it's worth it. Start by positioning the mouse pointer on an object, icon, or file, press and hold the mouse button while you move the mouse until the highlighted object is positioned where you want it — then release the button. This technique is useful for moving files in XTree from one directory to another, for moving program icons in Program Manager from one program group to another, and for moving objects or words in draw and word processing programs to other places in files.

Keyboard tactics

With few exceptions, you issue virtually all of your Windows commands with the mouse. Believe it or not, however, there are a few times when the keyboard might — just might — be faster and cleaner. The following key combinations are examples of that situation:

Ctrl+F6: Move to the next active window *within* the current application, or move from one open file to the next.

Ctrl+F4: Orders the computer to close an open file, but leaves you in the current program.

Ctrl+Esc: Pops up the Task List, a list of currently open applications, from which you can choose another application to switch to.

Alt+Tab: Cycles you through your currently open *application windows*.

Alt+F4: Terminates a currently running program. Use this shortcut to exit Windows, too.

Pressing Alt or F10 lets you access items on your program's main menu (see "Main menu and pull-down menus" later in this chapter). Even if you never use the keyboard commands just described, you should remember these warp-drive shortcuts:

■ When you press F10, the first menu on the menu bar highlights (usually the File menu); you must then either press Enter to drop down the File menu or use the left- and right-arrow keys to move to the menu item you want (you can also use the down-arrow key to drop down a highlighted menu item's menu). Once a menu drops down, you'll see the available commands, each with an underlined letter. At this point you don't need to press Alt — just press the underlined letter of the command you wish to activate.

- If you've got all the menu names memorized, you should use Alt. When you press Alt and the underlined letter of the menu item you want to access (use Alt-F to get into the File menu, for example), the corresponding menu drops down.
- Alt+spacebar accesses the Control menu (to size or close the window, or switch to the Task List) for the active window.

Discovering Windows Wonders

Not all windows are created equal. The following sections contain descriptions of some basic windows terms, types, and techniques.

Active and inactive windows

The active window is, simply, the window you are currently using. Or, more importantly, it's the window you *can* use. The main concept here is that you can't do anything in (or to) a window until it becomes the active window. There are two ways to figure out which window is the active window (not counting "you're currently using it"):

- The active window is the window on top (also known as the *foreground* window).
- The area around the active window's title — known as the *title bar* — is a different color or intensity than the title bars of the other (inactive) windows. (In Figure 5-1, the Main window, with the dark title bar, is *active*. The Applications window has a lighter color, which means it is *inactive*, and Program Manager's title bar always appears active.

To make an inactive window active, click any place on that window, or use one of the keyboard commands just described.

Closing a window

When you finish with a file or want to exit a program, you do so by *closing* the file or program window. One way to close a window is to double-click on the Control menu (see "Keyboard tactics" earlier for other examples).

Moving a window

If you find a window's location inconvenient, you can move the whole window to a new location on-screen: Position the mouse cursor on the window's title bar, press and hold the mouse button, and then drag the window to a new location and release the mouse button. (Keyboarders can open the Control menu by pressing Alt+spacebar and then use the Move command in conjunction with the arrow keys.)

Changing a window's size

You can stretch and squish a window to meet your needs using either the mouse or keyboard commands. Take the following steps to *resize* a window, using your mouse.

Steps: Sizing windows with the mouse

Step 1. Make the window you want to resize the active window.

Step 2. Position the mouse on a corner or border (you're in the right place when the mouse pointer changes to a two-headed arrow).

Step 3. Press and drag the window border (to change only that side) or a corner (to change the two adjoining sides) until the window is the size you want, then release the mouse button.

Sizing a window with the keyboard can take a little longer, but it's a breeze, too. The following steps show you how.

Steps: Sizing windows with the keyboard

Step 1. Make the window you want to resize the active window.

Step 2. From the Control menu, select Size.

Step 3. Use one arrow key to move a border and two arrow keys (the combination of the up-arrow and left-arrow keys, for instance) to move a corner.

Step 4. Press Enter when you are finished.

In both cases, pressing Esc before either releasing the mouse button or pressing Enter reverts the window to the size it was before you began.

Minimized programs on the desktop

If you want to keep a program open and available but don't want it in your face (or on your desktop) all the time, you can reduce the program to an *icon* — a small picture of itself — and reactivate the program at any time by double-clicking the icon.

To reduce an application to an icon, open the Control menu for that program and select Mi_n_imize or click the minimize button in the upper-right corner of the window.

Main menu and pull-down menus

The main menu is the horizontal series of words that appears under a program's title bar. When you select a menu item, *another* window drops down and offers commands. Figure 5-2 shows the XTree for Windows main menu with the File menu open.

Figure 5-2: The XTree for Windows File menu.

As always, to carry out a command you use one of the following options:

- Press the command's underlined letter.
- Click on the command with the mouse.
- Use the arrow keys to move down the list to the item and press Enter.

You can avoid the main menu in the first place by using the shortcut key offered to the right of the command. While memorizing shortcut keys may not be your first choice, these keys can save you a lot of time in the long run. In addition to the shortcut commands are a couple of other items on the right of some commands:

Arrows: Right-pointing arrows mean you'll get another drop-down menu with a few more choices when you highlight that command.

Ellipses: A set of three periods (. . .) means if you select that command, you'll be asked to type in some options.

When you see a check mark to the left of some commands, that tells you that the command in question is turned *on*. Selecting an option turns it on, and selecting the option again turns it off (and unchecks it).

Dialog boxes

The dialog box is a special kind of window that appears when the program needs more information from you. (It's like a genie asking, "What is your command, master?") For instance, when you want to open (or get) a file, a dialog box appears, asking you for the name of the file to retrieve — *you* have to type in an answer or select a file from a directory list. Sometimes you'll be asked to respond to a multiple-choice option. Figure 5-3 shows an example of an XTree for Windows dialog box. Let's look at the different *kinds* of choices offered.

For the moment, don't worry about what the specific choices mean (you'll get all that in Chapter 7). In addition to the traditional typing-in-an-answer sort of scenario, a dialog box can also contain circles, squares, and shaded buttons. Would you believe that even the *shape* and *size* of these things have a special meaning?

Options: In Figure 5-3 you can see circles to the left of some items. The items with circles next to them are called *options* and are selected by clicking on the circle next to the option. A circle option means you get to choose *one* and one only of the circle items. Every time you click one circle, a previously selected circle is automatically deselected.

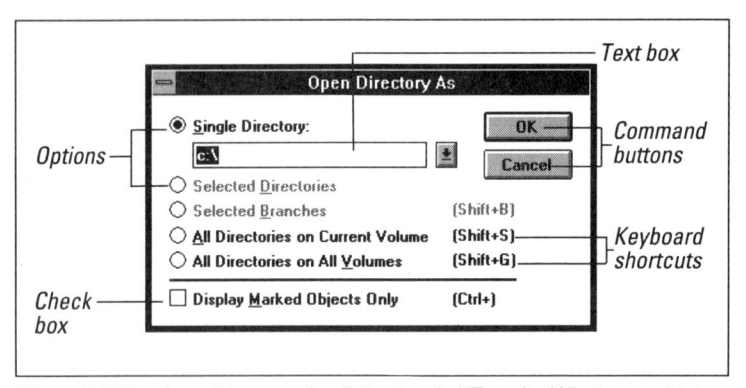

Figure 5-3: The Open Directory As dialog box in XTree for Windows, which appears when you select File ⇨ Open Directory As.

Check box: A square check box (such as the Display Marked Objects Only box in Figure 5-3) can be chosen in *addition* to the selected circle option. You can select as many or as few check boxes as you want.

Text box: This kind of box is the more traditional "you type in an answer" box. In Figure 5-3, C:\ is the text entered into the text box. If there is an downward-pointing arrow to the right of the text box, click on it to drop down a list of either your options or your past choices.

Command buttons: Every dialog box has at least two command buttons — OK and Cancel. If you've used Windows for more than ten minutes you know what these command buttons mean.

Keyboard shortcuts: In a dialog box, you can press Alt in combination with an option's underlined letter to select or deselect the option. In the example in Figure 5-3, pressing Alt-A selects All Directories on Current Volume. When you are finished with your selections, press Enter or choose OK — both choices have the same result. (And pressing Esc is the same thing as selecting Cancel.)

Summary

▶ A window must be made active (by simply clicking on it with a mouse) before you can act on anything contained in it.

▶ Use F10 as a shortcut to activate the current program's main menu.

▶ Dialog boxes let you make specific requests of Windows programs.

▶ Esc or Cancel will get you out of a current dialog box without making any changes.

Chapter 6
XTree for Windows Basics

In This Chapter
- Basic XTree for Windows terms and concepts
- Tree and Directory window basics
- Working with files, directories, and disks
- Using the Tool Palette
- New terms in XTree for Windows
- Tips on going from XTree for DOS to XTree for Windows

Welcome to XTree for Windows

The purpose of this chapter is to describe the concepts that are part of almost every command in XTree for Windows. Then, in the next chapter, I'll address the nitty gritty of specific tasks.

Special note to XTree for DOS users who are changing over to XTree for Windows: Just because you've been using XTree, don't think you already know everything. Although it may initially *look* like XTree for DOS, XTree for Windows is really something quite different — in both its approach and function. (To minimize culture shock and maximize productivity, don't miss "Going from XTree for DOS to XTree for Windows," in the second half of this chapter.)

Getting Started

When you first activate XTree for Windows, you'll see the familiar XTree logo while the program scans your hard drive (all of your hard drives if you have more than one), network drives (if any), and your floppy drives (if they contain disks). XTree for Windows saves time (and memory) by not counting the size and shape of every file and directory. It just collects enough information to get you started. Don't worry, when you need the detail, it'll appear. Once this process has been completed — and if you haven't changed the defaults — you'll get something like what is shown in Figure 6-1.

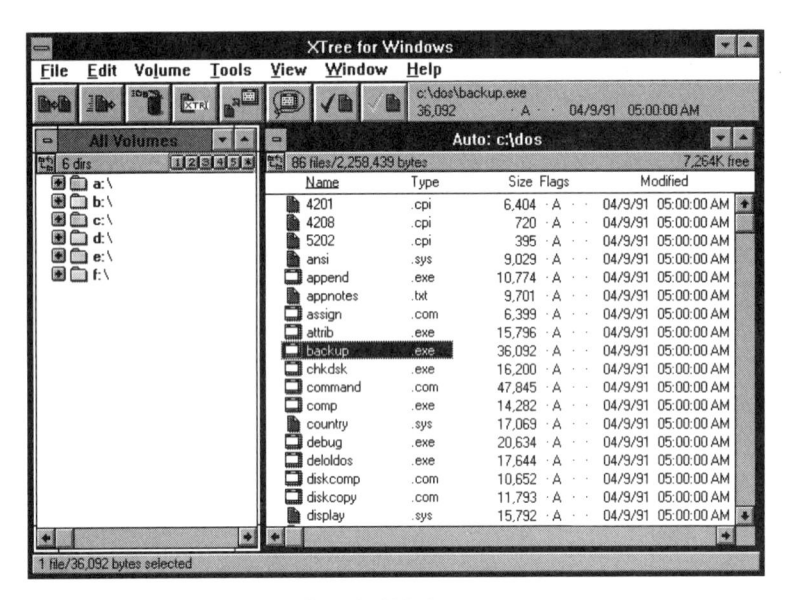

Figure 6-1: The initial default XTree for Windows screen.

The window you see on the left in Figure 6-1 is called the *Tree window;* in this figure, it is labeled *All Volumes.* The *Auto Directory window,* which shows the root directory, is on the right of the figure. (Note the icons in the shape of a file folder, indicating that you are looking at directories.) What the heck is a Tree window and an Auto Directory window? — I thought you'd never ask.

Understanding the Windows in XTree for Windows

There are a few basic varieties of windows in XTree for Windows:

Tree: The Tree window shows the *directory structure* of one or more drives. When more than one drive has been inventoried, the window title is All Volumes.

Directory: The Directory window shows the *files* and *subdirectories* of a selected directory or directories.

Auto Directory: The Auto Directory window is a special variety of a Directory window. The Auto Directory window is linked to the Tree window — highlight a directory name in the Tree window and the Auto Directory window displays its contents. As you move the highlight, the Auto Directory changes to reflect where you are. To open the Auto Directory, select File ➪ Open Auto Directory.

Chapter 6: XTree for Windows Basics

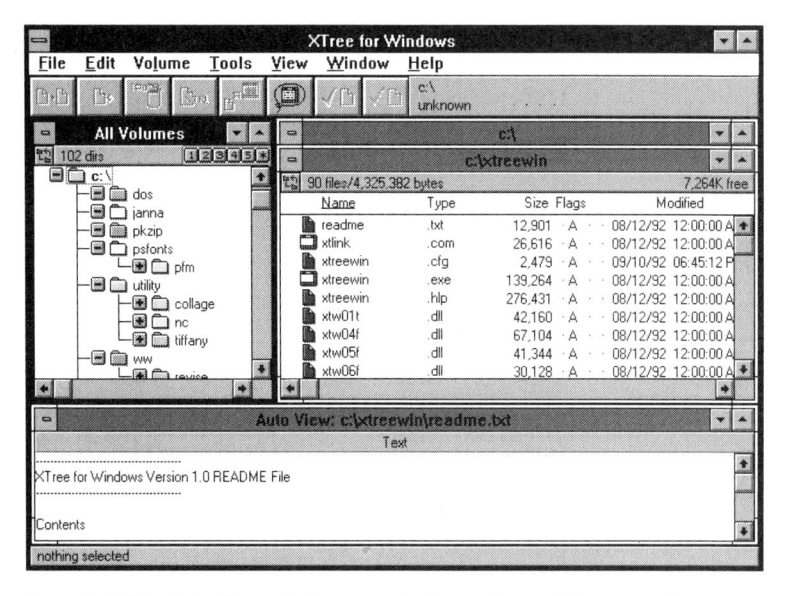

Figure 6-2: The Auto View window reveals the contents of the currently highlighted file in the open directory.

View: Shows one or more highlighted *files* in their native formats. To view a highlighted file, select Open Document View from the File menu.

Auto View: The Auto View window displays the contents of the current file in the active Directory window. When you select Open Auto View from the File menu, whatever file you highlight in the Directory window will be displayed (in its native format) in the Auto View window at the bottom of the screen. Highlight another file and the Auto View automatically pulls it up on screen. Figure 6-2 shows the XTree screen with the file C:\XTREEWIN\README.TXT open in the Auto View window.

Keep in mind that you are in Windows — you can open more trees, create new directories (although you can only have one each of the two Auto-type windows), move windows, maximize windows, minimize windows, close unneeded windows, and so forth. Have fun. Get crazy.

The Active Window

As discussed in the previous chapter, you must make a window *active* before you can do anything to its contents. There are several ways to make a window active. The two easiest ways are as follows:

- **Click on a window:** Position your mouse cursor anywhere on a window and click the button. This makes the window active.
- **Press Ctrl+F6:** This key combination cycles through all open windows. (Ctrl+Tab does the same thing.)

Tree and Directory window basics

As mentioned earlier, when you first get into XTree for Windows you'll see two windows — a Tree window and an Auto Directory window. (Your initial view can be customized via the File ➪ Preferences command.) The following sections describe how to navigate these windows.

Expanding the tree structure

If your Tree window is like the one shown in Figure 6-1, in which only the root is showing, the first thing you'll want to do is display the directories and subdirectories underneath the root. To get your Tree window to show its directories, just click on one of the number icons located in the upper-right corner of the window (1-5, or * for all); these represent the levels of directories and subdirectories on your system. If you select the * button, your display will resemble that shown in Figure 6-2, with all levels of directories showing in the Tree window.

Traveling the directory tree

You can now travel up and down the tree structure; your Auto Directory window automatically updates as you highlight different directories. Unfortunately, as you highlight each directory, there is a pause as XTree inventories the associated directory. You can bypass the continual updates by using the vertical scroll bar instead.

You can work with files in the Auto Directory window by making that window *active* — just click anywhere on the window or press Ctrl+F6.

Traveling in the Directory window

Once you're in a Directory window, you can *still* move up and down through the directories of your hard disk (aka the tree structure) with the mouse or the keyboard. Here are some ways to do both:

- To move down the directory structure (into a subdirectory) with your mouse, highlight a directory name and right-double-click.

- To move back up the directory structure using your mouse (from a subdirectory up to the parent directory), click the Move Up button located just below the Control menu icon.

- To move down the directory structure using your keyboard, press the up- or down-arrow key to move the highlight to a subdirectory name and press F11.

- To move back up the directory structure using your keyboard, press Shift+F11.

A special note to XTree for DOS converts: Though it is ingrained in your being to press Enter to cycle through XTree's various windows, if you start pressing Enter on directory and filenames in XTree for Windows you'll get very different results than what you're used to. As just noted, if you press Enter on a highlighted directory in the Tree window, a Directory window opens with the contents of the highlighted directory showing. If you press Enter while the cursor is positioned on a filename, XTree for Windows will try to launch the file, whether it's a program or not. So, please remember to use the proper commands to move between windows and travel up and down the tree.

Working with Files, Directories, and Disks

In Windows, files, directories, and disks and drives all appear as objects on the screen. To perform operations on files, directories, and drives, therefore, you must first highlight (or select) them. Just as a window must be *active* before you can use it, a file, directory, or drive must also be highlighted (or selected) before you can manipulate it. Further, it is imperative to have the right object highlighted *before* you attempt to carry out a particular command. If you highlight a directory name, for instance, commands specific to file operations will not be available.

For the most part, highlighting requires the minimal effort of clicking on the object (the filename or the directory name or whatever) of your intentions. Figure 6-3 shows an example of a maximized Directory window, in which some filenames are highlighted.

You can highlight one object at a time, several objects in sequential order, or a series of objects that are not sequential. There are lots of ways to highlight (or select) objects. Various mouse and keyboard methods follow.

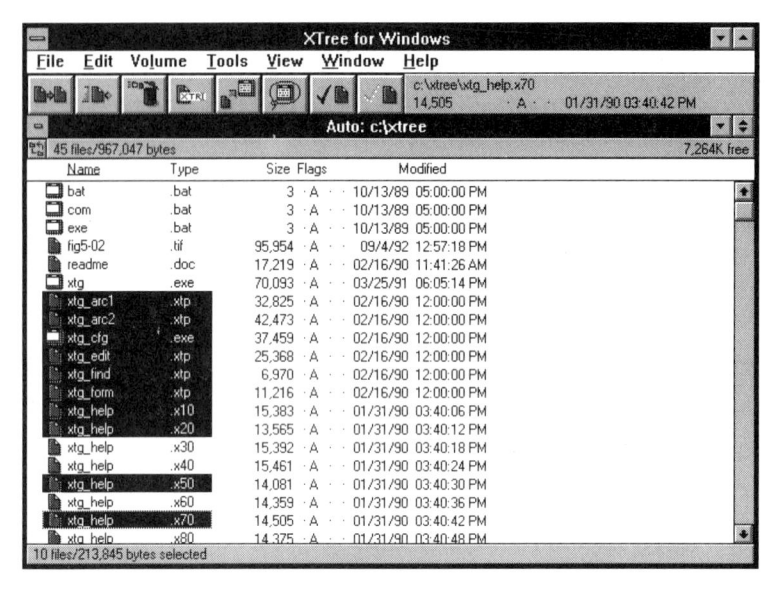

Figure 6-3: You must select objects, even nonsequentially if you wish, before you give an XTree for Windows command.

Highlighting objects with a mouse

- To highlight one object only, click on the object.

- To highlight sequential objects, click on the first object, move cursor to the last object in the list, and then Shift-click on the last object.

- To highlight nonsequential objects, right-click on the objects.

- To deselect highlighted objects, right-click on the selected object.

- To deselect all highlighted objects, click elsewhere in the window.

Highlighting objects with a keyboard

- To highlight one object only, move the cursor to the item.

- To highlight sequential objects, go to the first or last item, hold the Shift key down, and press the up- or down-arrow keys until all objects are highlighted.

- To highlight nonsequential objects, press Shift-F8 (turns on "add mode"). Position the cursor on the object and press the spacebar to select or deselect the object.

Chapter 6: XTree for Windows Basics

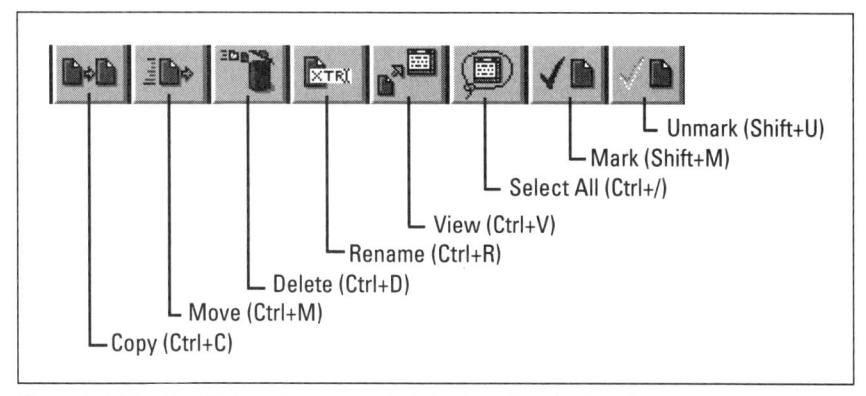

Figure 6-4 shows a row of tool palette icons with labels pointing to each:
- Copy (Ctrl+C)
- Move (Ctrl+M)
- Delete (Ctrl+D)
- Rename (Ctrl+R)
- View (Ctrl+V)
- Select All (Ctrl+/)
- Mark (Shift+M)
- Unmark (Shift+U)

Figure 6-4: The Tool Palette icons (and their keyboard equivalents).

Using the Tool Palette

After years of intensive double-blind consumer research, the scientists at XTree have converted oft-used XTree commands into easy-to-access icon buttons. And now, appearing for the first time above the Tree and Directory windows, is the fabulous Tool Palette. Folks, all you have to do is point to a picture and click!

The Tool Palette contains all the items that are in the Tools menu, plus more. Figure 6-4 shows the Tool Palette icons (and their keyboard equivalents).

Mark and Unmark aren't just a new way to highlight or deselect objects. Mark and Unmark are something different — which I'll cover in the next chapter.

The Tool Palette is designed to be simple to use. Highlight an object, then click on the appropriate Tool Palette icon to carry out the desired action (Copy or View, for instance). If you highlight a file called README.TXT, for example, and then click the Delete tool (the trash can), README.TXT will be deleted. You can also delete directories the same way. Naturally, whenever you delete or copy (or whatever), you must contend with a nagging dialog box that wants to know more or asks you "if you're sure."

Going from XTree for DOS to XTree for Windows

If you are moving from XTree for DOS to XTree for Windows, the first thing to understand is that, as an experienced XTree user, you are bringing a set of assumptions and thought patterns that will both help you learn *as well as* keep you from learning everything XTree for Windows has to offer. (Don't you just love paradoxes?)

XTree for Windows makes file and directory operations easy. Some examples of how XTree for Windows is different follow:

- You can compare as many directories, trees, or files as you wish. Open five or ten (or more) Directory windows with a single command.
- A new command combines what *were* the Filespec and Tag commands into *one* command.
- Want to work with a certain directory? Just *ask* for it — don't waste time traveling up or down a directory tree.
- Copy and move files and directories with *drag and drop* — pointing is the only skill required.
- Most-used commands are available from the spiffy new Tool Palette.
- You can easily combine files and directories in new windows for specific operations.

So, now begins the process of adjusting your thinking from two- to three-dimensional file management.

New Terms in XTree for Windows

Terminology alert! Lots of XTreeGold features have been renamed and reorganized. Most of the changes are intuitive, but a few changes require your attention. You should check out the documentation that came with your XTree for Windows software, which covers new terms in great detail. Alternatively, you can choose Help ⇨ XTreeGold Transition Tips from the menu bar in XTree for Windows. All commands are covered in the Help feature.

A window by any other name. . .

As you might expect, even the names of windows have changed.

- The Directory window in XTreeGold is now called the Tree window in XTree for Windows.
- The File window in XTreeGold is now called the Directory window in XTree for Windows.

Naturally, the names of windows are not the only changes you'll find in XTree for Windows.

New ways of doing things

Out with the old and in with the new. XTree for Windows does many things differently than the old, DOS-based XTrees.

- **Tagging files and directories is out, highlighting, or selecting, them is in.** New commands, called Mark and Unmark, do *not* replace Tag and Untag. Mark is a way to check-mark and gather objects from different directories to combine them altogether into a new Directory window.

- **Filespec is out, Directory Filter (and Select/Deselect) is in.** Press Shift+F to bring up the Directory Filter dialog box, which has a space for Filespeclike stuff. You'll be pleased to find the options in the Directory Filter dialog box let you go way beyond mere filespecs in requesting which files can be displayed.

  However, options in the Select/Deselect dialog box, which you access by choosing Edit ⇨ Select/Deselect (or Ctrl+Shift+/), is a big time-saver. If you used Filespec in XTree for DOS to show a certain group of files, and then pressed Ctrl-T to tag those files, now all you have to do is open the Select/Deselect dialog box, enter your file specifications, and XTree for Windows automatically highlights the files *for* you.

- **File Display is out, Toggle Directory is in.** Press Shift+T to cycle through adding the file size, attributes, and date and time saved (Toggle Directory works like the Alt-F key combination used to).

- **Make Directory is out, New Directory is in.** Press Ctrl+N in XTree for Windows, and you'll be making a new directory below the current one.

- **History is out, down-arrow buttons are in.** Instead of using the History command, each text box in pertinent dialog boxes automatically remembers the last few responses you've made. Now, whenever XTree for Windows asks you for a response, you can press the down-arrow button to the right of the appropriate text box to reveal your history, and then select one of your past responses.

- **Don't press Enter unless you mean it.** In previous versions of XTree, pressing Enter toggles the screen from the a Directory window to a File window and back. No more. Pressing Enter while the cursor is positioned on a directory name in XTree for Windows produces a new Directory window, which is great if that's what you want. But, if all you want is what *used to* happen when you pressed Enter (that is, you ended up in the list of files), then don't press Enter. Instead, click on the desired existing Directory window, or use Ctrl+F6 or Ctrl+Tab to move the cursor to the Directory window.

If you are in a Directory window and just want to travel up and down the directory tree, without creating any new windows, use the following mouse and keyboard maneuvers:

Navigating directories with the mouse

- To move down the Directory tree into a subdirectory, highlight a directory name and right-double-click.
- To move up the Directory tree into a parent directory, select the Move Up button, which is located just below the current window's Control menu.

Navigating directories with the keyboard

- To move down the Directory tree into a subdirectory, highlight a directory name and press the F11 function key.
- To move up the Directory tree into a parent directory, press Shift-F11.

Some things never change

Although the following four commands are now included on both the Tools menu and the Tool Palette, you can still access a few commands the same way as in previous versions of XTree. These commands will act upon whatever object (file, directory, disk) has been selected:

Copy	Ctrl+C
Move	Ctrl+M
Delete	Ctrl+D
Rename	Ctrl+R

Missing: The Commands that Didn't Make it

Remember the old adage, "Something got lost in translation"? Well, here are a few XTreeGold commands that didn't survive the trip to XTree for Windows. These are the features for which there are no replacement commands or *simple* workaround options:

Oops!

Compare

Edit

Invert

Chapter 6: XTree for Windows Basics

Merge Tags

Partial Untag

Print

Search for text in tagged files

Wash

If you can't remember what these commands did, they are each covered in Chapter 3. The missing commands are listed here so you won't drive yourself crazy trying to find them in XTree for Windows.

Summary

- Objects (filenames, directories, and drives) must be highlighted before they can be acted upon.
- There are three basic types of windows in XTree for Windows: Tree windows show the directory structure, Directory windows contain files and subdirectories, and View windows show the contents of highlighted files.
- The Tool Palette contains a collection of push-button commands providing access to the most-used commands.
- Users of XTree for DOS should remember that the Tag command has been replaced with on-screen highlighting. Filespec has been replaced by options in the Directory Filter and Select/Deselect dialog boxes. File Display has been replaced by the Toggle Directory command. You now make directories with the New Directory command. History is now accessed with the down-arrow buttons in text boxes. Enter no longer cycles you through directory and file windows.

The 5th Wave **By Rich Tennant**

"I'LL BE WITH YOU AS SOON AS I EXECUTE A FEW MORE COMMANDS."

Chapter 7
XTree for Windows Quick Reference Guide

In This Chapter
▶ Task-oriented topics for XTree for Windows
▶ Step-by-step instructions for each topic

Are you ready to learn how to make Silly Putty out of your hard disk to stretch, bounce, and reshape your files and directories to suit your whims? That's what XTree for Windows is all about.

Before I start, one thing bears repeating, as emphasized in Chapter 6: The key to most XTree for Windows commands is to first *highlight the object you want to work with*. The primary reason highlighting (also known as *selecting*) is important is because you *cannot* perform many functions *until* you've highlighted the item you want to manipulate.

The other reason highlighting is important is that XTree for Windows' responses depend on what you've highlighted. If you highlight a file and give the Copy command, XTree for Windows knows you're copying a file and provides you with file-type options; any irrelevant options are automatically unavailable, limiting your ability to make mistakes. If you highlight a directory, you get directory-relevant choices. The "highlight first" approach is how Windows applications are able to create a "true or false/multiple-choice" environment, rather than DOS's "essay question" purgatory.

Mouse and Keyboard Deliberations

All right, confess: Who *isn't* a sucker for a great shortcut? The sneaky approach always holds great appeal. Sometimes the quickest way to perform an action is through a keyboard command, and sometimes the mouse is quicker. But my advice is to find what works best for *you*. Throughout this Quick Reference Guide, variations on command options — how to accomplish tasks with either the mouse or the keyboard — are presented so that you can "find yourself." I must make this disclaimer, however: I've made no attempt to show every conceivable way to carry out every possible command; life is too short for such exercises in tedium. The point here is to give you what you need, with the least amount of chatter. So, to coin a phrase, let's get busy.

Arranging Your Windows

In order to move or rearrange the appearance of your XTree for Windows *desktop*, you need to become familiar with the Window menu, which offers several ways to reorganize your space and make it suit your way of doing things.

The Standard Region Layout

It is no mere coincidence that the Tree window is on the left side of your screen, the Directory window is on the right side, and View and Auto View windows appear across the bottom. The fact is, the desktop is split into regions, so that each time you open a new window, that window automatically groups itself with its own "kind" and order is maintained on your XTree for Windows desktop. This three-way schematic is called the Standard Region Layout.

The Auto Viewer Region Layout

The second layout scheme, the Auto Viewer Region Layout, kicks out the Tree Window and lets the Auto Viewer assume a respectable location on the right. (A Directory window occupies the coveted space on the left.) This setup is useful when you don't need to worry about moving files up and down a tree or copying to another drive. To select this layout, choose Window ➪ Region Layout ➪ Auto Viewer. Figure 7-1 shows an Auto Viewer Layout screen in XTree for Windows. If you open a Tree window while in this layout, XTree for Windows reverts back to the Standard Layout to make room for a Tree window.

Chapter 7: XTree for Windows Quick Reference Guide

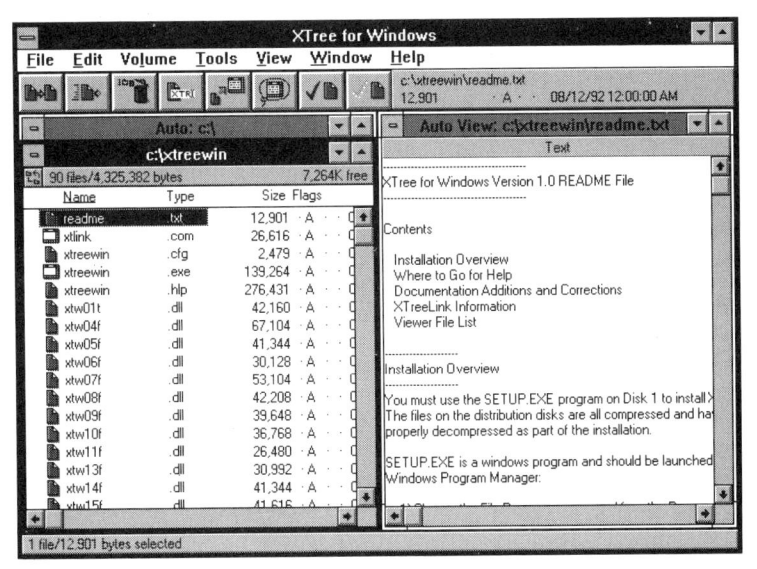

Figure 7-1: In the Auto Viewer Region Layout, the Directory window appears on the left and an Auto Viewer window appears on the right, displaying the contents of the file highlighted on the left.

Window Layout options

If you want to arrange the pattern in which new windows appear in a region, select Window ⇨ Window Layout. Three layout options are available — all are traditional Windows-type layouts you've seen before: Tile, Cascade, and Overlay.

Selecting one of these options affects only the active window region. So if you have three Directory windows open and you select Tile, the three windows will be stacked on top of each other; if you select Cascade, the contents of only the top window (the last window you open) will be visible, but you'll be able to see the title bars of the other open windows (clicking on a window's title bar brings it to the front of the stack); if you select Overlay, only the top window will be visible, period. To see windows that lay beneath the top window in Overlay mode, you have to close the window that's on top.

The Auto Arrange option

Auto Arrange is the border patrol for your XTree for Windows desktop. Auto Arrange is on the Window menu, also. By default, Auto Arrange is on (you can tell by the check mark beside it); XTree continually attends to desktop housekeeping by making sure new windows know their place. However, too much neatness can be annoying. If windows behave unexpectedly when you try to size or move them (if they resist a size or a move, for instance) you *may* want to turn Window ▷ Auto Arrange off by selecting it again (this removes the check mark).

The Arrange Now option

If you do turn Auto Arrange off, and you find yourself lost amongst your windows, choose Window ▷ Arrange Now to force the desktop to straighten itself up. Wouldn't it be great if you could just shout "Arrange now!" at your own office desk?

Attributes (File)

As you may recall from Chapter 1, "MS-DOS Concepts," there are four file attributes: Read-only, Archive, System, and Hidden. (If you don't remember what these terms mean, you may want to go back to Chapter 1 and refresh your memory.) If you attempt to delete, move, or rename a file that has a "read-only" attribute, XTree refuses to carry out the command and pops up a dialog box telling you that `Permission is Denied`. The only way to force XTree to do what you want in this situation is to first turn *off* the file's read-only attribute. Read-only files are usually set that way for a reason. Before you turn this attribute off, be sure it's safe to do so.

Figure 7-2 shows a list of files and, to the right of them, a series of four dots — these dots serve as place markers for the four "RASH" (**R**ead-only, **A**rchive, **S**ystem, and **H**idden) flags.

Making attributes visible

If your directory window doesn't show the attributes of files listed there (as shown in Figure 7-2), you can quickly turn them on by selecting View ▷ Directory Format ▷ Attribute Flags. (A shortcut is to press Shift+T, which will cycle through the various Directory formats until the attributes are displayed.)

Chapter 7: XTree for Windows Quick Reference Guide

Figure 7-2: Use View ⇨ Directory Format ⇨ Attribute Flags to reveal a file's attributes to the right of the file size.

Changing a file's attributes

Once you've selected file whose attributes you want to change, simply press Ctrl+A (or select Tools ⇨ Change Attributes), to pop up the Change Attributes dialog box. From here you can turn your favorite attributes on or off.

The Auto Directory Window

See The Directory Window

The Auto Directory window works *exactly* like a Directory window except in the following ways:

- The Auto Directory window automatically (whether it is the active window or not) updates its contents to display the files that are contained in the selected directory in the Tree window.

- You can have only one Auto Directory window open at a time.

- To open an Auto Directory window, press F3, or select File ⇨ Open Auto Directory.

The Auto View Window

See The View Window

The Auto View window works exactly like the View window except:

- The Auto View window automatically (whether it is the active window or not) updates its contents to display the text of the selected file in the current directory.

- You can have only one Auto View window open at a time.

- To open an Auto Directory window, press F7 or select File ⇨ Open Auto View.

Close

You can close any active window with a double-click on the Control menu icon. You can close more than one window at a time by selecting File ⇨ Close, as shown in Figure 7-3, and then selecting one of the options from the submenu that appears.

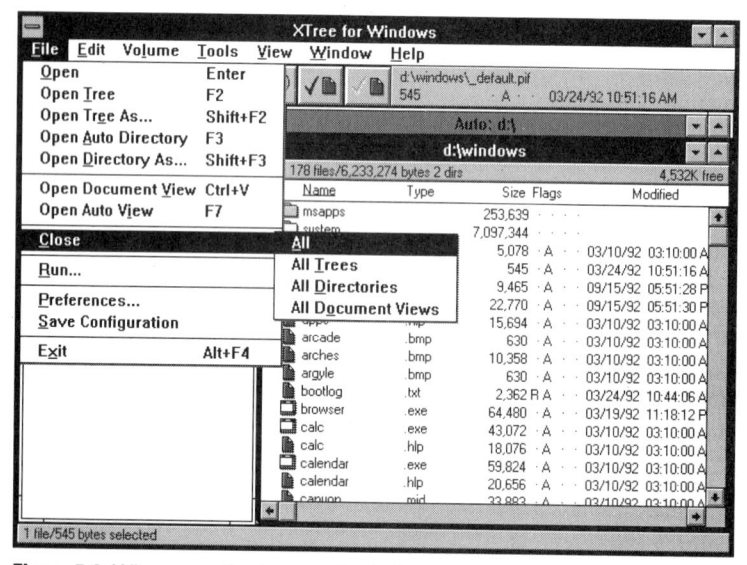

Figure 7-3: Why manually close each window when File ⇨ Close can close a bunch of them for you in a single keystroke?

Chapter 7: XTree for Windows Quick Reference Guide

> **NOTE:** You can exit XTree for Windows without closing your open windows. However, if you've opted (via File ➪ Preferences) to have XTree save your windows from session to session, you may want to close windows you've finished with so you won't have to wait while XTree jumps through hoops to rebuild them next time you use the program.

Configuration Options

> **CROSS REFERENCE:** *See* Preferences

Unlike previous versions of XTree for DOS, there is no configuration program, per se, in XTree for Windows. (Remember, Windows already knows about your printer, monitor, and so forth.) The closest XTree has to a configuration program is the File Preferences dialog box (accessed via File ➪ Preferences) and additional defaults that can be set during Copy and Move. To save preferences and defaults, select File ➪ Save Configuration.

Copy

The Copy command allows you to duplicate something — a file, a directory, or whatever, and end up with two of the original item. Having said that, however, remember that you cannot have two objects with the same name in the same location. If you do want two copies of something in the same directory, you'll have to rename one of them.

> **NOTE:** Sometimes what you *really* want to do is take something from point C and move it to point A. For that type of action, see the Move command.

Okay, let's jump into the wacky world of copying! The first step is, of course, to highlight the object to be copied. After you have highlighted the object of your desire, you must do *one* of the following to initiate the copy procedure:

- Click the Copy icon on the Tool Palette.
- Press Ctrl+C.
- Drag the object to be copied and drop it on the destination icon.
- Select Tools ➪ Copy from the main menu.

Once you have taken one of these steps, you'll see the Copy dialog box. If you select Options from this dialog box, it expands to include `Directory Options` and `File Options`, as shown in Figure 7-4.

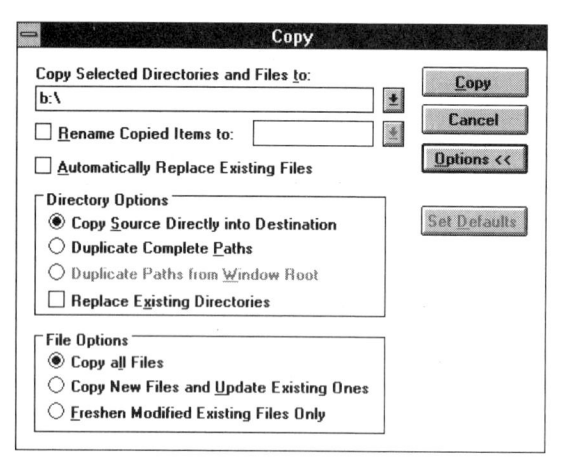

Figure 7-4: Once you've made your selections in the Copy dialog box, press Enter (or choose Copy) to initiate the actual copying.

Using the Copy dialog box options

The Copy dialog box contains several options for copying files and directories.

Selecting a destination

The text box at the top of the Copy dialog box, Copy Selected Directories and Files to:, is where you type in the destination of your copies. Normally, the last destination you used will appear in this text box. If you used the drag and drop method to copy files or directories, the text box will automatically reflect the destination you dropped the object on. Finally, the down-arrow button drops a list down that reveals the last several destinations you used. You can either type the destination for the copies into the text box (be sure to include the drive name, like C: or B:, or you'll get an invalid path complaint), or you can point to a directory or drive in one of your windows and highlight it (if the Copy dialog box is in the way, just move it aside).

Renaming while copying

If you want to simultaneously copy your object and give it a new name, check the Rename Copied Items to: box to enter the new name. (You can use wildcards here.)

Replacing exiting files

The option Automatically Replace Existing Files deals with the possibility that your destination already has a file with the same name as the one you're copying. By checking this box, you are saying "erase any and all files on the destination and replace with the file I'm copying." The safest thing to do is to leave the box unchecked — XTree will ask you on a file-by-file basis if you want to replace the file or not.

Selecting directory options

In the middle of the Copy dialog box is the Directory Options box. You can choose one of the first three items. The first two choices are familiar:

- Copy Source Directly into Destination: Copy just the files, no directories.
- Duplicate Complete Paths: Copy the files and their directories.

The third choice, Duplicate Paths from Windows Root, is available only if you've got a collapsed directory in a tree window. When you use this option, XTree pretends that the collapsed directory's visible root is actually the root and doesn't duplicate the whole path above it.

You can select the last item in this box, Replace Existing Directories, regardless of which of the first three you choose. If you turn this option on and there is a directory with the same name at the destination, XTree will wipe out the destination's original directory, including files and subdirectories, in favor of the directory being copied.

Selecting File Options

At the bottom of the Copy dialog box is the File Options box. By default, the Copy all Files option is selected. However, you shouldn't overlook these other available options:

- Copy New Files and Update Existing Ones: Selecting this option causes XTree to automatically compare the destination files with the source files, keeping the newer of the two.
- Freshen Modified Existing Files Only: If you select this option, XTree will *not* add any new files to the destination and will copy only those files that are updates to existing files. So if you've got LETTER.DOC and LETTER2.DOC selected for copying, XTree won't copy either file unless they already exist at the destination and the file in the destination directory is older.

Saving your selections

If you make any changes to the Copy dialog box, you can make those changes permanent by choosing Set Defaults.

Using the Preferences dialog box options

You can further streamline your copy operations by choosing File ⇨ Preferences, which opens the Preferences dialog box, shown in Figure 7-5. In this dialog box, you can make more permanent changes, including options under `Copying and Moving Operations`:

- `Set Archive Flag on Copies`
- `Copy Archive Flag on Copies`

Remember the archive attribute? (You know, the one that indicates whether a file has been backed up or not.) Well, when you copy a file, XTree can either turn it "on" on the copied file (`Set Archive Flag on Copies`) or *match* the archive bit from the source file (`Copy Archive Flag on Copies`). If you don't use the archive flag as an aid in backing up or as a filter, don't worry about this option.

Another option under `Copy and Move Operations` is `Dialogs on Drag and Drop`, which you can turn on or off. If you turn this option *off*, then when you use the drag and drop method for copying and moving files, XTree will carry out your command — no questions asked (using the current settings in the Copy dialog box).

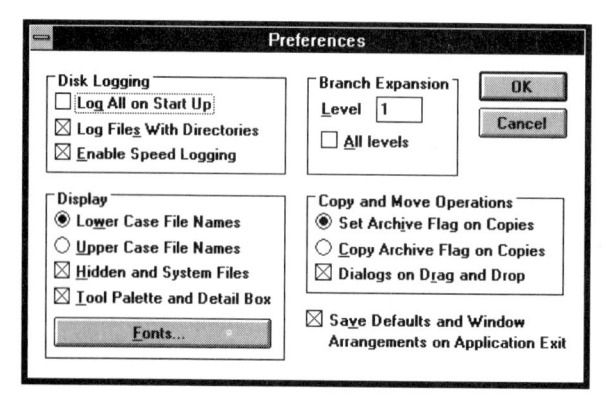

Figure 7-5: The Preferences dialog box lets you set the defaults on some of XTree for Windows' operations.

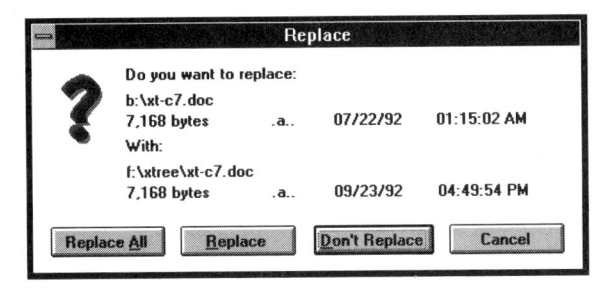

Chapter 7: XTree for Windows Quick Reference Guide

Figure 7-6: XTree warns you that a file with the same name as the one you're copying is about to be deleted in favor of the new file.

Getting messages from XTree

If you have not set your Preferences to `Replace Existing Files` in the Copy dialog box, and XTree encounters a file or directory at the destination with the same name as the one you're copying, you'll get what I call a "Yo, dude?" or a Replace message box (with a question mark on the left) like that shown in Figure 7-6.

Basically, the Replace box says "Yo, dude — do you realize what's happening?" In this case, "Do you want to replace this file or what?" The files in question are compared for size, attributes, and date and time saved. The command button options in this message box are self-explanatory.

If the destination disk (aka *volume*) is full, you get another "Yo, dude!" message box, like the one shown in Figure 7-7, which informs you that there is not enough space on the destination drive to perform the copy procedure.

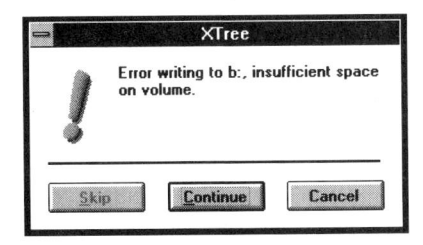

Figure 7-7: You'll get this message box if you attempt to copy files or directories to drives that don't have enough space on them.

At this point you can either select Cancel, replace the full disk with an empty one and continue (if you are copying to a floppy, for instance), or finally, you can select Skip (if you're copying more than one file) to pass over one file and go on to the next, perhaps smaller, one. (If the next file is smaller in size, it might fit on the destination disk.)

The Date and Time Stamp

When you save a file, DOS records the date and time the file was saved (or last modified). This information is called the *date and time stamp*.

If you wish to give a file (or files) a new date and time stamp, just select the object to be changed and press Ctrl+A (or select Tools ⇨ Change Attributes). The Change Attributes dialog box appears, from where you can change the date and time, among other things. You can either type in a new date and time or choose Now to transfer the current date and time to your selection.

Why change the date and time of a file? Well, since XTree can sort by date and time, as well as filter by date and time, this gives you another way of grouping files together for some sort of action.

Delete

Deleting obsolete files and directories from your hard disk is essential to maintaining a healthy drive. Extra files slow down performance, shorten hard disk life, and make it more difficult for you to find what you're looking for. The trick is to make hard disk housekeeping a part of your normal routine. To delete files and directories, select the object(s) to be deleted and use *one* of the following methods:

- Click the Delete icon on the Tool Palette.
- Press Ctrl+D.
- Press Delete on your keyboard.
- Select Tools ⇨ Delete from the main menu.

With any of these options, you'll see the Delete dialog box, as shown in Figure 7-8.

Select Delete or press Enter to continue the deletion process. Unless you "uncheck" the `Ask Before Each Deletion` box, you'll be prompted before each file is deleted, as shown in the message box in Figure 7-9.

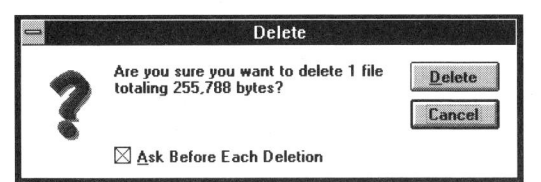

Chapter 7: XTree for Windows Quick Reference Guide

Figure 7-8: The Delete dialog box. Press Enter, D, or choose Delete to confirm your desire to delete.

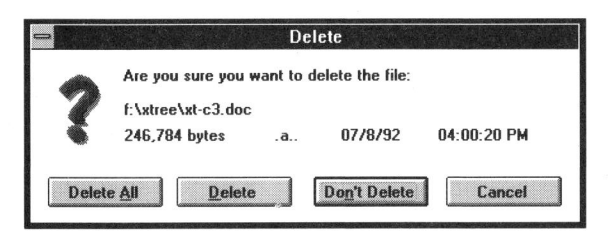

Figure 7-9: The file-by-file Delete confirmation message box.

> **WARNING:** If you select a *directory* for deletion, XTree asks you once if you want to nuke the whole thing (files, subdirectories, and all) — it *doesn't* ask for a confirmation on a file-by-file basis.

The Detail Box

Located to the right of the Tool Palette, the Detail Box shows statistics on the currently highlighted object in the active window. Information on files is automatically updated as you select and deselect them. If you select a directory name and the message UNKNOWN appears, press F4 to force XTree to calculate and display the amount of disk space that directory occupies.

The Detail Box, as well as the Tool Palette, can be hidden if you want to get some extra desktop space. Select File ⇨ Preferences and uncheck the Tool Palette and Detail Box option.

The Directory Window

> **NOTE:** The following describes how to open, select, and format the display of Directory windows. To perform operations such as Copy and Delete, refer to the section on that command in this chapter.

Normally, the Directory window appears on the right side of the XTree display, next to the Tree window. If you want to view more files, however, you can maximize the Directory window and let it completely take over the XTree desktop, as shown in Figure 7-10.

Opening a Directory window

To create a new Directory window for each and every selected directory (you can select and open more than one directory at a time), either press Enter after highlighting one or more directories or select File ⇨ Open. If you want to open just one directory, there are three methods:

- Highlight the directory you want to open and press Enter.
- Double-click on the directory.
- Highlight the directory and select File ⇨ Open.

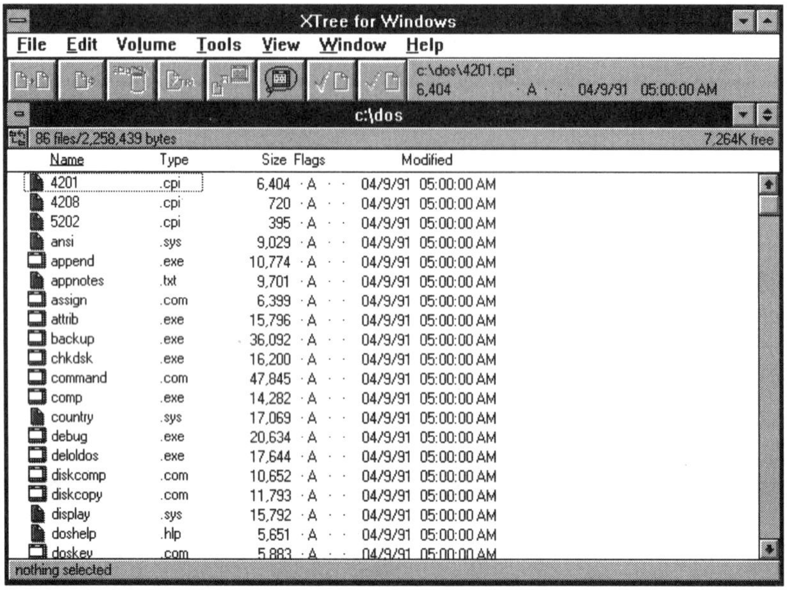

Figure 7-10: Maximizing a Directory window gives you a better view of the files inside.

Opening a custom Directory window

Another way to create a new Directory window by selecting File ⇨ Open Directory As or pressing Shift+F3. Use this command when:

- There is no existing directory name to enter or click on.

- You want to create your own collection of files and directories that might contain files from several different directories, or a branch, or several directories that are not from the same branch or the same drive.

When the Open Directory As dialog box appears, open an existing, single directory window by typing in the path (be sure to include the drive — such as C:) and then choosing OK, as shown in Figure 7-11. This option is handy when you know the name of the directory you want to open but don't want to search through your Directory tree to find it.

If you want to open a Custom Directory window and display the contents of more than one directory combined, choose one of the following options

- `Selected Directories`: Displays the contents of selected directories in the active window.

- `Selected Branches`: Displays the contents of all subdirectories under a selected directory.

- `All Directories on Current Volume`: Displays the contents of all directories on the current volume.

- `All Directories on All Volumes`: Displays the contents of all directories in all the volumes listed in the Directory tree.

You can further narrow your choice if you select the `Display Marked Objects Only` option first. (Naturally, you would have had to preselect and/or mark the directories or branches you want to bring together.) When you're finished with your selection, choose OK or press Enter to finish the job.

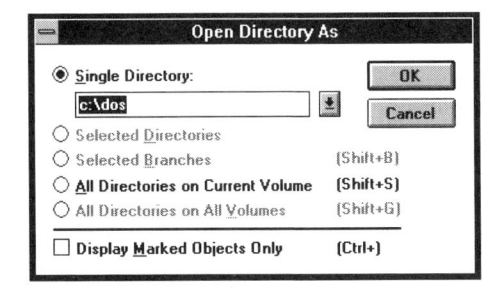

Figure 7-11: The Open Directory As dialog box.

Opening an Auto Directory window

The Auto Directory window works *exactly* like a Directory window *except* the Auto Directory window automatically — whether it is the active window or not — updates its contents to display the files contained in whatever directory is selected in the Tree window. You can open only one Auto Directory window; just press F3 or select File ➪ Open Auto Directory. After you've concluded your business in one directory locale, you may want to work with files located elsewhere. One option is to close the current Auto Directory window and open another. Another option is to move up or down the directory structure *within* the existing Auto Directory window.

Navigating a Directory window

You don't have to use a Tree window to move up and down the directory tree. It can get very tedious traveling up and down a hard disk one baby step at a time (especially if you have a macho-size hard disk). XTree knows that ('cause they've got macho disks, too). That's why they created the concept of Set Scope (View ➪ Set Scope).

Set Scope

As you can see in Figure 7-12, you can change the contents of the *current* window. To jump to a new directory, simply type in the name of the directory in the Directory text box (be sure the Directory option is selected) and choose OK.

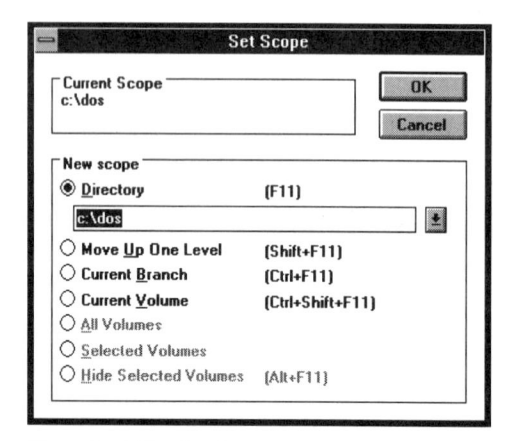

Figure 7-12: The Set Scope dialog box lets you specify the contents of the current window.

You'll warp to the specified directory. Or you can select other options to show a whole branch, drive, or all drives in the current window. Set Scope saves you the step of creating a new window and then closing windows that are no longer needed.

Using the Move Up button

The Move Up button is located just below the Control menu icon. Click on the Move Up button to move up a level in the directory structure so that the parent of the current subdirectory is displayed. (Keyboarders can press Shift-F11.)

Moving down to a subdirectory

Although there is no move down button, right-double-click on a directory name to move down a level to a subdirectory of the current directory. (You can also press F11 after highlighting the parent directory.)

Modifying your directory display

Getting to the right place is only half the fun. You have many choices about what will appear in your window and how it will be displayed. Other options on the View menu can assist you.

Directory Format

The Directory Format command determines what file information will be displayed in the Directory window. You can see a lot more than just a file's name. Select View ⇨ Directory Format or press Shift+D, and the Directory Format dialog box appears, as shown in Figure 7-13. In addition to having

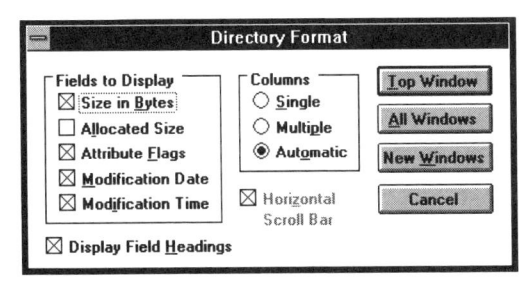

Figure 7-13: Select how much file information will be displayed in a Directory window with the Directory Format dialog box (Shift+D).

filenames showing, you can ask to see File size, Flags (aka *attributes*), and the date and time the file was last modified. Once you pick your options, select which windows will have this format — the <u>T</u>op Window (the active window), <u>A</u>ll Windows, or New <u>W</u>indows.

Directory Filter

Use the Directory Filter to limit the files displayed in the Directory window to those that match your criteria. You can use the File <u>N</u>ames text box to enter the name of a single file (if that's what you're looking for) or you can use what you learned about wildcards in Chapter 2 if you want to look at a certain group of files (*.DOC, for example, produces a directory display with files ending in DOC). But wait, there's more! You can also use combinations of filenames and "exclusionary" names to push the wildcard envelope. Here are some examples:

Filespec	Files displayed in Directory window
*.DOC *.BAT	All files either ending in DOC or BAT
−*.BAK	Every file except those ending in BAK
E*	Every file that begins with the letter E
A* −*.DOC	Files that begin with the letter A but don't end in DOC

XTree for DOS users: Use the Directory Filter like the Filespec command.

When you finish selecting the options in the Directory Filter dialog box — from the Include box, the Flags box, and the Modification Date/Time text boxes — you then get to choose which Directory Filter specifications will apply to the <u>T</u>op Window (the active window), <u>A</u>ll Windows, or just to New <u>W</u>indows that will be opened after the dialog box is closed.

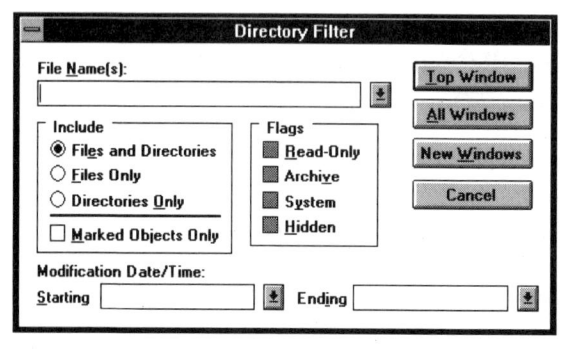

Figure 7-14: Select which file are displayed in a Directory window with the Directory Format dialog box (Shift+F).

Directory Sort Order

A third set of options, governing the order (by Name, Type, Size, and Date) and whether files are sorted in ascending or descending order will appear when your press Shift+O (or select View ➪ Directory Sort Order) and the Directory Sort Order dialog box appears, as shown in Figure 7-15. As usual, you can apply the sort order to the Top Window (active window), All Windows, or only New Windows.

There are two shortcuts you can use in relation to the Directory Format command:

- If you choose Display Field Headings in the Directory Format dialog box, then your Directory window will sport the headings Name, Type, Size, Flags, and Modified (aka date saved) above the files. Once those headings are displayed, you can click on a heading name to request a sort. For instance, if you click on the word Modified, the files would immediately re-sort themselves so that the oldest file would be at the top of the list. A right-click on Modified sorts the newest file to the top.

- Use the Shift+T key combination to activate the View ➪ Toggle Directory Format option, which cycles through the Fields to Display options in the Directory Format dialog box. (Try it, you'll like it.)

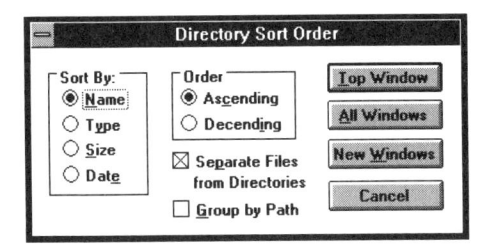

Figure 7-15: The Directory Sort Order dialog box.

The Edit Menu

See Find, View Window, Select/Deselect, and Mark/Unmark

Execute

See Open

Exit

When you've finished using XTree, you can exit the program selecting the File ⇨ Exit command or by pressing Alt+F4. You could, instead of actually leaving the program, use the Control menu and select Minimize to "freeze dry" XTree down to a handy icon. Clicking on the minimize button in the upper-right corner of your screen accomplishes the same thing.

Expand/Collapse Tree

When you first open a Tree window, the "tree" is usually no more than a stump — the name of a drive and that's it. To the left of the drive name a "+" sign icon indicates that there is at least one more directory under that tree. The puzzle of *why* the heck we want to expand or collapse a tree has baffled philosophers for generations. Finally, we have a few answers. First of all, expanding and collapsing a directory tree is another way of displaying only those items you want to see. A collapsed tree speeds up XTree (since it doesn't have to inventory everything), saves memory, and makes it easier for you to find things (since you don't have to spend as much time traveling up and down the whole tree). To reveal the hidden directories (also known as *expanding* the tree), you can take one of several approaches.

Using the level expansion buttons

The level expansion buttons are the little number icons (1-5) and the asterisk icon (*) in the upper-right corner of the Tree window. The number you click on will determine the number of directory levels that will be expanded — * means Expand All. Selecting the 5 icon, for example, expands the tree to five levels of subdirectories beneath the root.

Using the + or – icons

You can also expand a specific directory or drive by clicking on the plus (+) icon next to the drive letter or directory. You can do the same thing with the keyboard by highlighting a directory and pressing the + key. To completely expand a directory, either right-click on the + or highlight the directory or drive and type an asterisk (*). (If you do this while on the root, it'll expand the whole tree.) You can collapse the tree by doing much the same thing — except with

Chapter 7: XTree for Windows Quick Reference Guide

the minus (–) icon. Click the – icon to collapse the tree (or move your cursor to the directory and press – on your keyboard).

Using the View menu

You can perform the same tasks using the View menu when the Tree window is the active window. The following commands are available from the View menu that is shown in Figure 7-16.

- Expand Level — Expands one level down. Same as +.
- Expand Branch — Expands everything under the current level (if you were at the root, that would mean everything). Same as *.
- Expand Tree To — Gives you a dialog box that emulates the expansion buttons (you can choose how many levels, or all, that you want to expand).
- Expand All To — Does the same thing as Expand Volume (drive), except it includes all of the drives. (You can see all of the directories on all of the drives.)

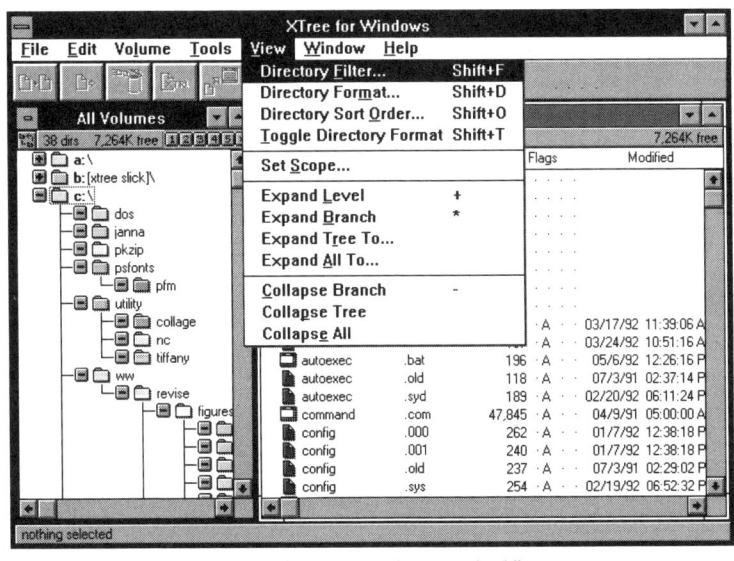

Figure 7-16: The Expand and Collapse options on the View menu.

- <u>C</u>ollapse Branch   Collapses the directory, one level at a time.
- Coll<u>a</u>pse Tree   Collapses the whole tree, as many levels as you want.
- Collaps<u>e</u> All   Collapse all trees on all drives.

The File Menu

See Open, Close, Run, Preferences, Configuration Options, and Exit

Find/Find Again

When you're in a Tree window, you can search for directories. When you're in a Directory window, you can search for both files *and* directories. If you're in a View window, you can search for text in the viewed file. Makes sense.

Finding files and directories

Whether you are in a Directory or a Tree window, highlight the first item in that window and then select <u>E</u>dit ⇨ <u>F</u>ind (or press F6). (XTree for Windows always searches from top to bottom in a file list or directory tree.) The Find dialog box appears, as shown in Figure 7-17, which is nearly identical to the Directory Filter dialog box.

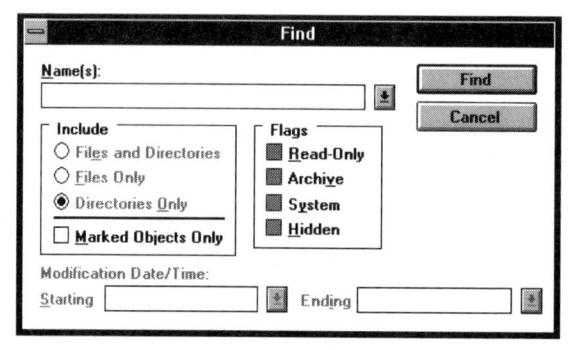

Figure 7-17: To find files or directories, press F6 to call up the Find dialog box.

Chapter 7: XTree for Windows Quick Reference Guide

If you are looking for a particular file, you can type its name in the File Name(s): box in the Find dialog box, and only that file will be displayed (if it's in the currently open directory).

If you want to see only files ending with DOC, for example, type the ***.DOC** filespec in the File Name(s): box to display only those files ending in DOC. (Here's your chance to use what you learned about wildcards in Chapter 1.) But wait, there's more! You can also use combinations of filenames and "exclusionary" names to push the wildcard envelope. Here are some examples:

Filespec	Files displayed in Directory window
*.DOC *.BAT	All files either ending in DOC or BAT
−*.BAT	Every file except those ending in BAK
E*	Every file that begins with the letter E
A* −*.DOC	Files that begin with the letter A but don't end in DOC

You can replay — and use — your previous text box answers by selecting the down-arrow icon to the right of the box. You can save yourself some typing if you find yourself repeating commands. When you're finished making choices, choose Find. (Select Cancel to void the operation.) The cursor outline will jump to the first occurrence that meets your specifications. Press Shift+F6 to search again (using the same specifications).

If you're looking for a file on a floppy disk, first highlight the drive designator where the floppy resides (A: or B:), and then proceed as just described.

Finding text in a View window

You can also use the Find feature to search for words or phrases in a file you've opened in the View window. Select Edit ⇨ Find (or press F6), and you'll get a simple dialog box asking for the word or phrase you want to find — be exact — and whether upper- or lowercase letters make a difference (they won't, unless you check the box). Select Find File (or press Enter), and XTree will highlight the text you're looking for and move that line to the top of the window. You can select Find Again to search for the same phrase again.

Formatting Floppy Disks

Floppy disks must be *formatted* before you can use them. Formatting allows DOS to lay down a magnetic system for recording and retrieving information — sort of like an "electronic honeycomb." These days, you can buy disks that have been preformatted. If you find formatting disks a chore, you can spend a little extra to have someone else do it for you.

How can you tell if it's formatted?

From the outside, an unformatted disk looks exactly like a formatted one. When you format an already formatted disk (called *reformatting*), you erase anything that might be stored on it. You can see why it's a good idea, if you're not sure, to verify that a floppy disk isn't already formatted and storing valuable information before you give that format command. You can determine whether the disk is or isn't formatted with XTree's File ⇨ Open Tree command (F2).

To use this command, put the suspect floppy in the drive, make sure you're in an All Volumes Tree window, and then highlight either drive A: (or drive B: as the case may be). Then select File ⇨ Open Tree. One of two things will happen next. You'll get a `Device Read Error` message, which you can interpret to mean that the disk is *not* formatted, or a tree will appear, showing the files and directories (if any) contained on the disk (meaning the disk is *already* formatted).

The difference between high-density and low-density floppies

Both 5 ¼- and 3 ½-inch floppy drives come in either low-density (also known as double-density) or high-density flavors. Density refers to, basically, how much information can be stored on the disk.)

A low-density drive can format only low-density disks. A high-density drive can, theoretically, format both high- and low-density disks. A word of caution: Some computers (mostly older computers) with high-density drives cannot format low-density disks very well — the low density disk may work fine in *your* high density drive computer but not on any other machine. You can experiment to see if a low-density disk you format on your high-density drive can be read in another machine, but you'd better keep copies of important files you transfer to low-density disks until you know the target computer can read them. The newer the computer, the better the chances are the low-density disk can be read by other high-density machines.

Formatting a floppy disk

Place the disk you want to format in the floppy drive and select Volume ⇨ Format Diskette. You'll have to tell XTree which drive (if you have more than one floppy drive) you want to use and whether you have a high-density or low-density drive. Then sit back and watch the fun happen.

Function Keys

Function keys, those keys on your keyboard labeled "F-something," are used by most programs to keep important commands down to the fewest number of keystrokes. A complete list of function key commands appears in Appendix A, "Shortcuts: Command Keys and Function Keys."

Launch

See Open

Logging Files and Directories

When XTree starts up, it performs a quick scan of the hard disk — checks out how many drives you've got (hard, floppy, network, and so on) and how much free space is available on your current drive. XTree performs only this quick scan (and not a thorough inventory of every file and directory) to save time and memory. That is why you will find, as you travel up and down the tree, the word UNKNOWN or a question mark next to certain objects. If you need to know the statistics on that object, highlight the object, press F4, and XTree calculates, and displays, the bottom-line numbers.

Setting logging options

If seeing UNKNOWN gives you the jitters, however, you can set it up so XTree collects the data on all the files and directories upon start-up. Select File ⇨ Preferences and in the Preferences dialog box, shown back in Figure 7-5, choose one or more of the following options from the Disk Logging box:

- Log All on Start Up: This option is checked on by default, so that all volumes (drives) and their directory structures are automatically scanned.

- Log Files with Directories: This option is usually not checked. If you do check it, it forces XTree to do the total inventory so you never see an UNKNOWN again.

- Enable Speed Logging: This option lets XTree use its own secret method to inventory the disk. The only reason to not select this option is if you're getting error messages when logging.

These are not mutually exclusive options; you may choose one or all.

In that same dialog box, the Branch Expansion box option is used to limit the number of levels to which the All Volumes tree is expanded. Usually, <u>A</u>ll Levels is selected.

Refreshing your display

When in a Tree or Directory window, you sometimes may find yourself in a situation where you want XTree to relog the window. XTree for Windows uses the word *refresh* for relog. You'd want to refresh your display in the following situations:

- When you rename an object, you have to ask XTree to refresh the window before you'll see that object in alphabetical order.

- When you replace one floppy disk with another, XTree needs to get acquainted with contents of the new disk by refreshing that Directory window.

As you might guess, there are several levels of refreshment, all available from the <u>W</u>indow menu:

- <u>W</u>indow ⇨ Refresh <u>S</u>election (Ctrl+F5)
- <u>W</u>indow ⇨ Refresh W<u>i</u>ndow (F5)
- <u>W</u>indow ⇨ Refresh A<u>l</u>l (Ctrl+Shift+F5)

Mark and Unmark

Mark is an exciting, unique-to-XTree for Windows feature. What is Mark? Well, it's a tool for identifying (via an on-screen check mark) objects that you want to gather together for some sort of action (such as comparing, backing up, or selecting). The cool thing about Mark's check mark is that it remains visible even when the window containing the mark is no longer active. (Highlighted objects are visible only in the active window.) Because such marks are always visible, you can be in one window and refer back, visually, to an inactive window to see what objects you've marked so far.

Figure 7-18 shows three open windows. The Tree window has two directories that have check marks. The C:\DOS window has several files that are marked also. Notice how the check marks are visible, even though E:\EXCEL is the active window.

Here is an example of what you can do with the Mark and Unmark feature: Select <u>F</u>ile ⇨ Open <u>D</u>irectory As and from the dialog box that appears, choose A<u>l</u>l `Directories on Current Volume,` and `Display` M`arked Objects Only,` and

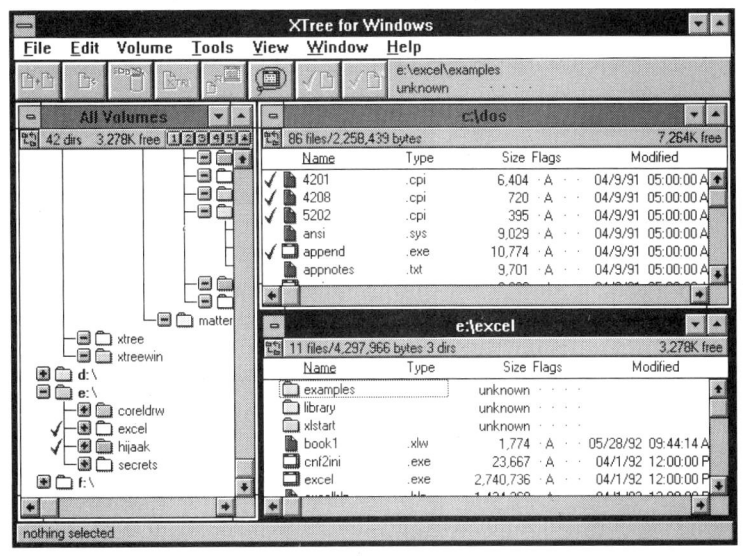

Chapter 7: XTree for Windows Quick Reference Guide

Figure 7-18: Marking files allows you to see files you've marked even when you're active in another directory.

then select OK. XTree then creates a branch window that contains all items that have been Marked — even the two directories, as shown in Figure 7-19. Now the Marked files and directories can be manipulated from one convenient location.

There are other ways to use Mark, too. For instance, in the Directory Filter dialog box, you can select Marked Objects Only, so that only those files and directories you have marked will be displayed in a Directory window.

> Marking is *not* a substitution for highlighting. Marked objects still have to be highlighted before you can carry out commands that require selecting.

Marking files and directories

Now that your mind is giddy with possibilities for putting this feature to use, let's find out how to use Mark. Before you can mark an object, you must first select it and then do one of the following:

- Select the Mark icon on the Tool Palette.
- Select Edit ⇨ Mark.
- Press Shift+M.

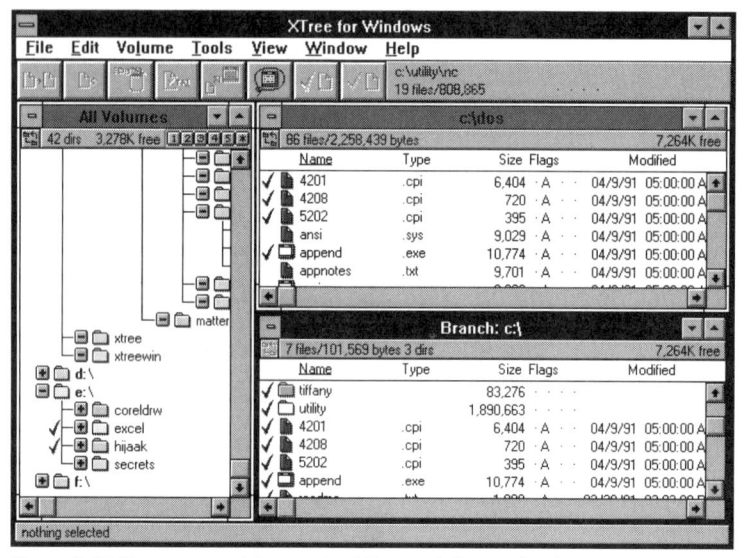

Figure 7-19: You can combine marked files and directories into one window for easy manipulation.

Unmarking files and directories

To Unmark an object, first select the object and then do one of the following:

- Select the Unmark icon on the Tool Palette.
- Select Edit ➪ Unmark.
- Press Shift+U.

Move

This section covers transporting files and directories from one location to another. If you want to move a window around on your screen, see "Arranging Your Windows."

Chapter 7: XTree for Windows Quick Reference Guide

The Move command is used to transport an object from one location to another. The first step is, of course, to highlight the object you want to move. Then you must do *one* of the following to initiate the Move procedure:

- Select the Move icon on the Tool Palette.
- Select Tools ➪ Move from the main menu.
- Press Ctrl+M.

After you've taken one of these actions, you'll get the Move dialog box, shown in Figure 7-20.

Choosing Move options

There are several options available to you in the Move dialog box that allow you to set parameters on what you are moving and where you want it to go.

Selecting a destination

The text box at the top of the Move dialog box, `Move Selected Directories and Files to:`, requests the destination of your highlighted object(s), including the drive name (such as C: or B:) and the path (such as \DOS). If this is not your first Move operation, the last destination you specified should be displayed. Select the down-arrow button to the right of the text box to drop down a list of the last several destinations you specified. For the example shown in Figure 7-20, I simply highlighted the proposed destination (in this case, the C:\FONTS directory) in the Tree window and XTree magically inserted the proper information in the destination box.

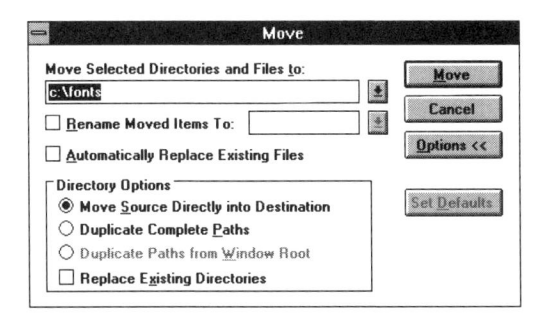

Figure 7-20: The Move dialog box.

Renaming while moving

If you want to simultaneously move and rename your objects, check the Rename Moved Items to: box and enter the new name. You can also use wildcards here.

Replacing files with the same name

If you check the Automatically Replace Existing Files option in the Move dialog box, you are telling XTree, "erase any and all files on the destination in favor of the file I'm moving." XTree will erase any files in the destination that have the same name as the ones you're moving. But the safest thing to do is to leave the box unchecked; XTree will ask you on a file-by-file basis if you want to replace a file or not.

Selecting Directory Options

The Directory Options box in the Move dialog box has several choices. The first two are familiar: Move Source Directly into Destination moves just the files, no directories; Duplicate Complete Paths moves the files and their directories. The third choice, Duplicate Paths from Window Root, is available only if you've got a collapsed directory in a Tree window. When you use this option, XTree pretends that the collapsed directory's visible root is actually the root and doesn't duplicate the whole path above it.

Finally, you have the option to Replace Existing Directories. If you select this option, and there is a directory with the same name as the one you are moving at the destination, XTree will wipe out the destination's existing directory, including its files and subdirectories, in favor of the directory being moved.

Setting defaults

If you make any changes to the Move dialog box, you can make those changes permanent by selecting Set Defaults. You can further streamline your Move operations by selecting File ➪ Preferences, which opens the Preferences dialog box (shown back in Figure 7-5), where you can make more permanent changes — including some aspects of copying and moving operations.

In the Preferences dialog box, you can choose Set Archive Flag on Copies or Copy Archive Flag on Copies. Remember the archive attribute? (You know, the one that indicates whether a file has been backed up or not.) Well, when you copy a file, XTree can either turn on the archive attribute on the copied file (Set Archive Flag on Copies) or match the archive bit from the source file (Copy Archive Flag on Copies). If you don't use the archive flag as an aid in backing up or as a filter, don't worry about this option.

Another option under Copy and Move Operations is Dialogs on D<u>r</u>ag and Drop, which you can turn on or off. If you turn this option *off*, then when you use the drag and drop method for copying and moving files, XTree will carry out your command — no questions asked (using the current settings in the Copy dialog box).

Getting messages from XTree

If you have not set your preferences to Replace E<u>x</u>isting Files in the Move dialog box, and XTree encounters a file or directory at the destination with the same name as the one you're moving, you'll get what I call a "Yo, dude?" or a Replace message box (with a question mark on the left) like that shown back in Figure 7-6.

Basically, the Replace box says "Yo, dude — do you realize what's happening?" In this case, "Do you want to replace this file or what?" The files in question are compared for size, attributes, and date and time saved. The command button options in this message box are self-explanatory.

If the destination disk (aka *volume*) is full, you get another "Yo, dude!" message box, like the one shown back in Figure 7-7, which informs you that there is not enough space on the destination drive to perform the copy procedure.

At this point you can either select Cancel, replace the full disk with an empty one and continue (if you are copying to a floppy, for instance), or finally, you can select <u>S</u>kip (if you're moving more than one file) to pass over one file and go on to the next, perhaps smaller, one. (If the next file is smaller in size, it might fit on the destination disk.)

The Move Up Button

The Move Up button is located just below the Control menu icon in both Tree and Directory windows. When you click on the Move Up button, the display changes to include additional directories or volumes, as detailed next.

Moving up in a Tree window

If you are viewing a tree that has been collapsed to a branch, XTree pretends that the top of that one branch is the root of the hard disk. If you press the Move Up button, the display would then include the parent to the branch as well as the branch. The Move Up button also reinstates any "missing drives" if not all volumes are currently displayed.

Moving up in a Directory window

In a Directory window, the Move Up button moves the display up one level. For example, if you are in the infamous C:\WP\LETTERS directory, clicking the Move Up button would take you out of the LETTERS directory and into the C:\WP directory (up one level from where you were).

Open

XTree for Windows Open commands are listed in the File menu, as shown in Figure 7-21. In general, you use Open commands for either activating a new window or launching a program.

Activating a new window

For information on opening windows, refer to the section in this chapter that covers the particular window you want to open ("The Tree Window," "The Directory Window," "The Auto Directory Window," "The View Window," and "The Auto View Window").

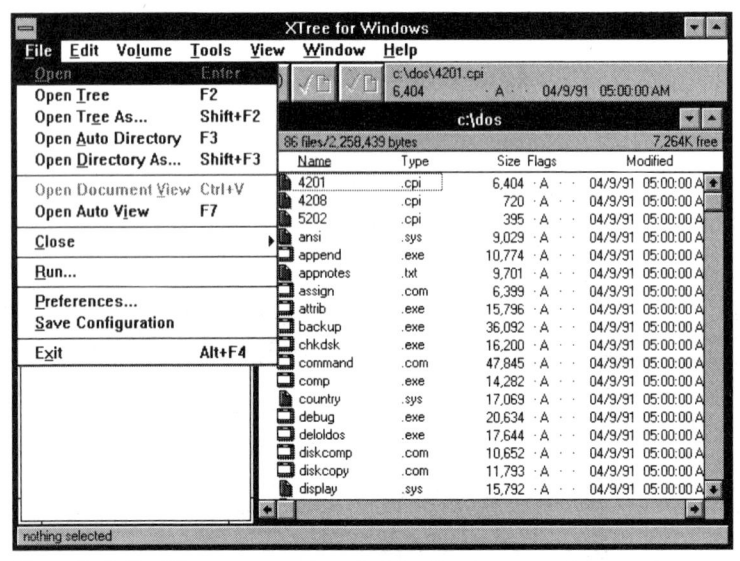

Figure 7-21: The File menu contains all of the Open commands.

Launching a program

You can start your favorite program, or a file ending in EXE, COM, or BAT, from an XTree Directory window by either double-clicking the filename, highlighting the filename and pressing Enter, or (if the application name is highlighted) selecting File ⇨ Open. You can even open a data file in the same way, launching the program that created that file simultaneously.

How can XTree know what program created which file? As discussed in Chapter 1, some filename extensions are unique to certain programs (Excel files end in XLS, files created by a word processor end in DOC, and so on). Because of that unique association between a file's extension and a program, you can tell XTree which file extensions belong to which program.

Most Windows applications are associated with a filename extension when you install them. However, Windows is not too good at guessing which DOS files go with which DOS programs. You'll have to set that up through Windows' clunky old File Manager. (The clunky way is to get into File Manager, find a filename with the extension you want to associate and highlight it, select File ⇨ Associate, choose Browse, and enter the appropriate information in the text box.)

With XTree for Windows, you can launch a program using the drag and drop method, also. This is handy if you give your filenames extensions other than the default provided by the program. For example, if you want to edit a WordPerfect file named LETTER.WP1, you can drag that file to the Directory window that contains the WP.EXE program file and drop LETTER.WP1 on top of WP.EXE. XTree then launches WordPerfect and loads LETTER.WP1 so you can work in it. When you exit WordPerfect, you return to XTree.

The Preferences Dialog Box

When you select File ⇨ Preferences, the Preferences dialog box appears, where you can make some permanent (until you change your mind) changes to the way XTree works. This dialog box was shown back in Figure 7-5. If you want to make your preferences permanent, be sure to select File ⇨ Save Configuration before you exit XTree.

Disk Logging

The following options are available in the Preferences dialog box:

- Log All on Start Up: This option is checked on by default, so that all volumes (drives) and their directory structures are automatically scanned.
- Log Files with Directories: This option is usually not checked. If you do check it, it forces XTree to do the total inventory so you never see an UNKNOWN again.
- Enable Speed Logging: This option lets XTree use its own secret method to inventory the disk. The only reason to not select this option is because you're getting error messages when logging.

TIP: These are not mutually exclusive options; you may choose one or all.

In that same dialog box, the Branch Expansion box option is used to limit the number of levels to which the All Volumes tree is expanded. Usually, All Levels is selected.

Copying and Moving Operations

Several preferences that affect the Copy and Move commands can be set in the Preferences dialog box.

Remember the archive attribute? (You know, the one that indicates whether a file has been backed up or not.) Well, when you copy a file, XTree can either turn on the archive attribute on the copied file (Set Archive Flag on Copies) or match the archive bit from the source file (Copy Archive Flag on Copies). If you don't use the archive flag as an aid in backing up or as a filter, don't worry about this option.

Another option under Copy and Move Operations is Dialogs on Drag and Drop, which you can turn on or off. If you turn this option *off*, then when you use the drag and drop method for copying and moving files, XTree will carry out your command — no questions asked (using the current settings in the Copy dialog box).

The Save Defaults and Window Arrangements on Application Exit option

If you check the Save Defaults and Window Arrangements on Application Exit box, XTree will remember to put *everything* — windows, check boxes, and options (but *not* selections) — back the way it was when you exited the program.

Rename

If you want to change a file, directory, or volume name, highlight the object to be changed and do *one* of the following:

- Select the Rename icon on the Tool Palette.
- Select Tools ⇨ Rename from the main menu.
- Press Ctrl+R.

You'll get a cute little dialog box that will ask you what you want to rename the object to. Just type your choice and choose Rename (or press Enter). Remember to refresh your screen by pressing Ctrl+F5 after a Rename operation. This gives XTree a chance to realphabetize the listings on the screen.

Rename while copying

When you are copying or moving an object, you are given the opportunity to rename the object on-the-fly. See Copy or Move for the details.

Renaming with care

If you change a directory name that is part of any batch file — including your AUTOEXEC.BAT file — you should change the directory name in the affected batch files. If you decide, for instance, to change your WordPerfect directory name from WORD_PRF to WP, WordPerfect may no longer work *unless* you adjust your path statement to reflect the new directory name. If your old path statement is the following:

```
PATH=C:\;C:\WORD-PERF;C:\DOS
```

then to accurately reflect the name change to your WordPerfect directory (WORD-PRF to WP), your new path statement should be:

```
PATH=C:\;C:\WP;C:\DOS
```

Rename a disk's volume label

Whenever you format a floppy disk, you can give that disk a name. This name is called a *label*. A *volume* is simply a disk, either a hard disk or a floppy disk. You may have seen the VOLUME HAS NO LABEL message, which just means you didn't name the disk when you formatted it. This has nothing to do with whether or not you put a sticker on the disk.

Naming the volume is useful, especially for floppy disks, because since the volume name appears in the Tree window, you'll know what disk is in your drive. (For example, a disk containing all your 1992 spreadsheet files might be called EXPENSES 92 — yes, spaces are allowed.)

A lot of people don't bother putting labels on their volumes. But if you want to label your volumes, XTree provides a very simple avenue for doing so. Put a disk in the floppy drive and highlight the drive designator (A: or B:). Select Volume ⇨ Label and when prompted to do so, type in the new name for your disk and press Enter. Voilà!

Run

See Open

The File ⇨ Run command lets you do two things:

- Type and carry out a command as *though* you were at the DOS system prompt. Select File ⇨ Run, type your favorite command, and press Enter. After the command is carried out, you'll be returned to XTree.

- Temporarily get out of XTree (though it's hard to imagine why anyone would *want* to) and get to your computer's system prompt. Select File ⇨ Run, type the word **COMMAND**, and press Enter. You'll see the system prompt. When you are finished, type **EXIT** and press Enter, and you'll be returned to XTree.

Selecting and Deselecting

As you know, before you can perform operations on files or directories or any combination thereof, you must first highlight the items to be acted upon. Even if that just means making a window active, its still the first step. Having convenient methods for selecting items, therefore, is important. There happen to be, conservatively speaking, a ba-zillion ways to highlight. Following my self-imposed mandate to keep information overload to a minimum, I'll cover the most popular selecting techniques. (Info junkies will find every single last selecting technique in the XTree for Windows *User's Guide*.)

Overall, there are two philosophic approaches to selecting:

- The "personal visit" method — you physically go to the object and select it with the mouse or with a keyboard command.

- The "long-distance" method — you either use the Tool Palette or choose Edit ⇨ Select/Deselect, and in the Select/Deselect dialog box enter the criteria for files to be selected; XTree then selects them for you.

Chapter 7: XTree for Windows Quick Reference Guide

Personal visit selection techniques

You can highlight one object at a time, several objects in sequential order, or a series of objects that are *not* sequential, as follows:

Highlighting objects with a mouse
- To highlight one object only, click on the object.
- To highlight sequential objects, click on first object, move cursor to last object in the list, and then Shift-click on last object.
- To highlight nonsequential objects, right-click on the objects.
- To deselect highlighted objects, right-click on the selected object.
- To deselect all highlighted objects, click elsewhere in the window.

Highlighting objects with a keyboard
- To highlight one object only, move the cursor to item.
- To highlight sequential objects, go to first or last item, hold the Shift key down and press the up- or down-arrow keys to highlight objects in sequential order.
- To highlight nonsequential objects, press Shift-F8 (turns on "add mode"). Position the cursor on the object and press the spacebar to select or deselect the object.

Long distance selection techniques

There are also methods for selecting files and directories from the Tool Palette and the Edit menu.

Highlighting objects with the Tool Palette
Clicking on the Select tool selects all files and directories in the active window. (To deselect all selected files, click somewhere else in the window.)

Highlighting objects from the Edit menu
- To highlight all files *and* directories in the active window, choose Edit ▷ Select All (or press Ctrl+/).

- To highlight only files (and not directories) in the window, choose Edit ⇨ Select All Files (or press Shift+/).

- To remove the highlight from selected objects in the active window, choose Edit ⇨ Deselect All (or press Ctrl+\).

Using the Select/Deselect dialog box

To select files with common extensions or similar filenames, choose Edit ⇨ Select/Deselect (or press Ctrl+Shift+/). The Select/Deselect dialog box appears, as shown in Figure 7-22 (this dialog box is similar to the Directory Filter dialog box). You can enter file specifications here, and XTree will automatically highlight (or unhighlight) according to your description.

If you want to see only files ending with DOC, for example, type the ***.DOC** filespec in the Name(s): box to display only those files ending in DOC. (Here's your chance to use what you learned about wildcards in Chapter 1.) But wait, there's more! You can also use combinations of filenames and "exclusionary" names to push the wildcard envelope. Here are some examples:

Filespec	Files displayed in Directory window
*.DOC *.BAT	All files either ending in DOC or BAT
–*.BAK	Every file except those ending in BAK
E*	Every file that begins with the letter E
A* –*.DOC	Files that begin with the letter A but don't end in DOC

You can replay — and use — your previous text box answers by selecting the down-arrow icon to the right of the box. You can save yourself some typing if you find yourself repeating commands. When you're finished making choices,

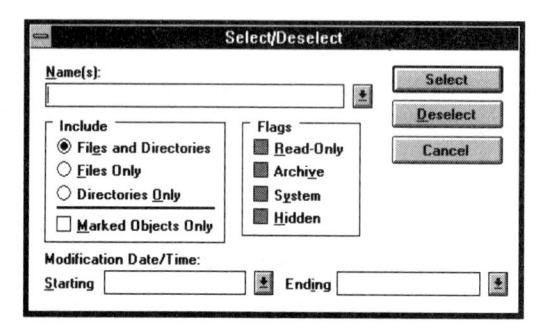

Figure 7-22: The Select/Deselect dialog box.

choose Find. (Select Cancel to void the operation.) The cursor outline will jump to the first occurrence that meets your specifications. Press Shift+F6 to search again (using the same specifications).

Keeping objects selected while moving between windows

Once you've selected something in one window, you can go to another window and return *without losing* your selections, as long as you exercise a little caution. As you may know, one way to deselect is by clicking any place outside of the filename region, such as on a date and time stamp. When you travel from window to window by clicking on the window (usually outside the filename region), you loose your selections. When you travel from window to window by clicking on the window's title bar, however, objects you've selected will remain selected.

> **TIP:** Selections are visible *only* in the active window. If you want to see your selections while in other windows, you'll need to mark the files as well.

Sort Order

Normally, files in a Directory window are displayed alphabetically, starting with A. You don't have to settle for that, if you don't want. Files can be displayed according to their name, extension (aka type), size, or date, either in an ascending or descending order. Guess who is in control of the sort order — that's right, it's *you*. Select View ⇨ Directory Sort Order (or press Shift+O) to pop up the Directory Sort Order dialog box and make your choices. The Directory Sort Order dialog box was shown back in Figure 7-15.

Alternatively, selecting View ⇨ Toggle Directory Format (press Shift+T) cycles the file list in an active Directory window through three variations: the filename only; the name plus the file's size and attributes; and the name, size, attributes, and date and time stamp. Try it, you'll like it.

If you choose Display Field Headings in the Directory Format dialog box, then your Directory window will sport the headings `Name`, `Type`, `Size`, `Flags`, and `Modified` (aka date saved) above the files. Once those headings are displayed, you can click on a heading name to request a sort. For instance, if you click on the word `Modified`, the files would immediately re-sort themselves so that the oldest file would be at the top of the list. A right-click on `Modified` sorts the newest file to the top.

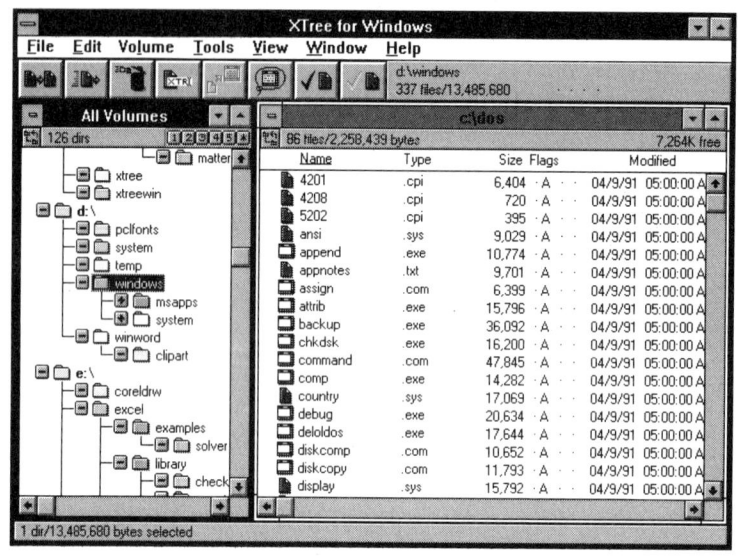

Figure 7-23: Status lines provide a variety of information about file size and available disk space.

Statistics

Statistics on highlighted objects are available in the Detail Box (next to the Tool Palette) and the Status Line (at the bottom of the screen). If you see the word UNKNOWN at the bottom of the screen, instead of the size of the file or directory in bytes, pressing F4 forces XTree to calculate and display the amount of disk space that object occupies. Statistics on selected objects are available on the Status Line at the bottom of the active window. Statistics on the current directory are available to the right of the Move Up button, as shown in Figure 7-23.

The Tool Palette

See Copy, Move, Delete, Rename, Select and Deselect, Mark and Unmark

As discussed in Chapter 6, "XTree for Windows Basics," the Tool Palette is, for the most part, another version of the Tool menu; you can use Copy, Move, Delete, Rename, Select and Deselect, and Mark and Unmark by simply clicking a Tool Palette icon. Figure 7-24 points out the names of the Tool Palette icons and gives their keyboard equivalents. The Tool Palette is designed to be simple to use. You

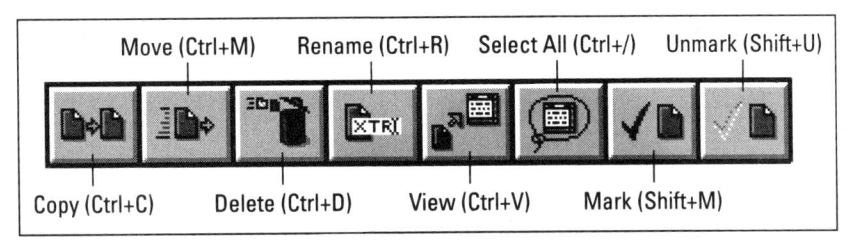

Chapter 7: XTree for Windows Quick Reference Guide

Figure 7-24: The Tool Palette and its icons.

highlight the object you want to manipulate and then click on the appropriate Tool Palette icon to carry out the desired action.

If you highlight a file called README.TXT, for example, and then click the Delete tool (the trash can), your file will be deleted. You can also delete directories the same way.

If you don't want the Tool Palette, it, along with the Detail box, can be removed from the screen to get a little more desktop space. You can also remove the Detail Box by selecting File ⇨ Preferences and unchecking the `Tool Palette and Detail Box` option.

The Tools Menu

See Copy, Move, Delete, Rename, Attributes (File), and The Directory Window

The Tree Window

A Tree window displays the tree structure of one or more volumes, branches, or directories. Usually, when you first get into XTree, an All Volumes Tree window opens, which shows all the disk drives on your system. The following description covers opening and altering the display of the tree structure. To Copy, Move, and Expand or Collapse directories, see those sections.

Opening a tree

Select File ➪ Open Tree (or press F2) to create a new tree for each and every selected directory or file. XTree makes a tree from a file's directory. If nothing is selected, a new All Volumes Tree appears.

Opening combination trees

Select File ➪ Open Tree As (or press Shift+F2) to open the Open Tree As dialog box and open a new Tree window. The new tree in this window either reflects your request in the text box (you enter the path of the root of the tree to be displayed) *or* collects all of your current selections (drives, directories, and files) into one new Tree window. However, you can modify this by checking as many boxes under `Combined Trees` as you need. In Figure 7-25, for example, drives B: and C: have been selected and can be combined into one new Tree.

Using Set Scope

Another way to change what is being displayed in a Tree window, *without* opening a new window, is to select View ➪ Set Scope, which brings up the Set Scope dialog box, shown back in Figure 7-12. You can type in the root of the tree you want to see displayed.

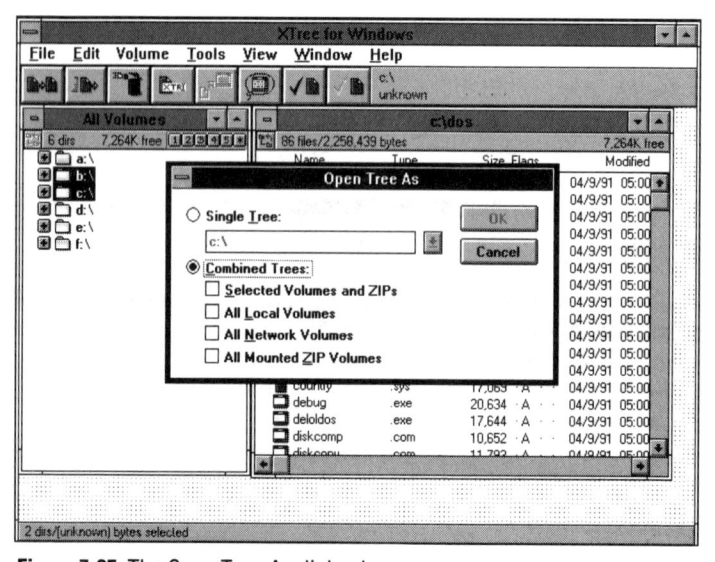

Figure 7-25: The Open Tree As dialog box.

Chapter 7: XTree for Windows Quick Reference Guide 275

Unknown and ?

See Log

If you select an object and the message UNKNOWN appears in the Detail Box or the Status Line, press F4 to force XTree to calculate and display the amount of disk space that directory occupies. This action results in a "size in bytes" message, so at least you'll know how many bytes are in that unlogged directory. (XTree for Windows does not log every file in every directory automatically upon start-up unless you select otherwise in the Preferences dialog box.)

The View Menu

See The Directory Window, The Tree Window, and The View Window

The View Window

The View window lets you view (naturally enough) the contents of a file in its *native format,* or how the file would look if you opened it in the application that it was created in. XTree comes with over fifty viewers (covering the most popular applications). Viewing a file does not harm or alter it in any way.

Viewing files

To open a View window showing a file in its native format, highlight the file to be viewed and do *one* of the following:

- Right-double-click on the filename.
- Select the View icon on the Tool Palette.
- Select File ➪ Open Document View from the main menu.
- Press Ctrl+V.

What happens next may take a second, but after XTree determines the type of file you want to view, a message box appears on-screen to let you know that the file is being converted for viewing. Finally, a window appears, containing your file. Once the View window is on-screen, you can close the Directory window to make more room for the View window.

At this point it's possible (but not probable) that you may want to change how XTree has interpreted your file. You have *limited* control over how the file appears. The View menu expands at this point, and you can choose from among the following options:

- Normal View: This is what you see by default — XTree's best interpretation of your file in its native format.
- Plain Text View: You can select this option to view your file in ASCII format (only letters and numbers).
- Character Dump View: If the file is mostly not ASCII, like a program or a graphics file, then XTree lets it all hang out in a character dump — which will probably look like garbage.
- Hexadecimal Dump View: Usually, program and other technical files are displayed in hexadecimal. (You have to be a real computer nerd to be dealing with Hex dumps.)

What you can do with the file once its in a View window, other than scroll through it with the scroll bar, depends on whether it is a graphics file (pictures) or a text file (words and numbers).

Viewing graphics files

Figure 7-26 shows a graphics file in the View window and an open View window. When you're in a View window, the View menu changes to include some new options:

- Zoom In: This option lets you move in up to six levels closer on the image.
- Zoom Out: This option, basically, undoes a Zoom In.
- Fit in Window: This option will force the whole image to fit into whatever size and shape window you create. (This is where you get to make Silly Putty out of your images.)

Viewing text files

When you open a text file in a View window, you can apply the Word Wrap feature, which displays files in an 80-column format. Another useful feature is the ability to find text within a file, using the Find dialog box shown in Figure 7-27.

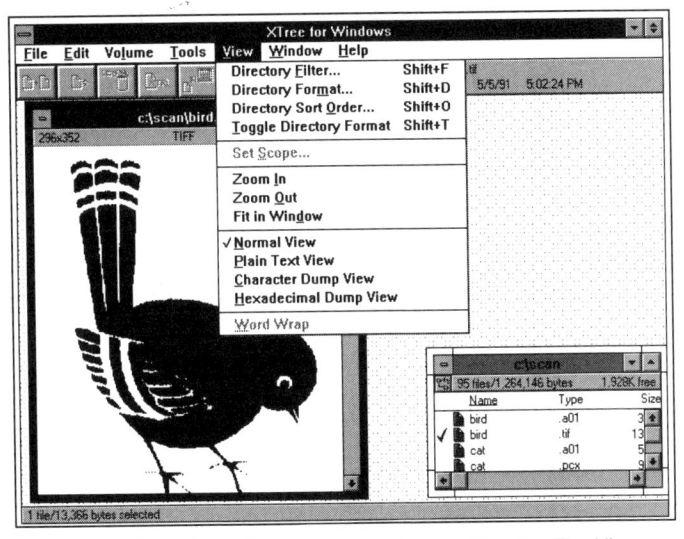

Chapter 7: XTree for Windows Quick Reference Guide

Figure 7-26: The View window, open with a graphics file. The View menu has expanded to include zooming options.

While a window containing a text file is active, pressing F6 (or selecting Edit ⇨ Find) brings up the Find dialog box. From here you could type in any text you want to find (the exact phrase or word) and specify whether upper- or lowercase letters make a difference (they won't, unless you check the box). Press Enter, and when XTree finds the text you're searching for, it goes to the place in the file, highlights the word or phrase, and makes it visible on-screen. You can choose Find Again to search for the same word or phrase again. You can also select Edit ⇨ Go To and specify which line you want to look at (if you happen to know each line by heart).

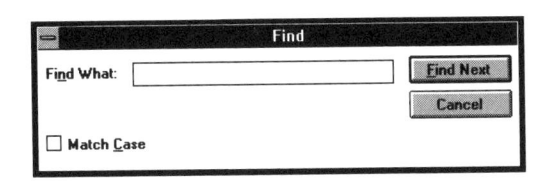

Figure 7-27: The Find dialog box.

The Volume Menu

See Rename, Format, and Chapter 9, "Archiving with XTreePro Gold, XTreeGold, and XTree for Windows"

The Window Menu

See "Arranging Your Windows" and Log

Part IV
XTree Extras

Chapter 8 281
Hard Disk Management in
a Nutshell

Chapter 9 297
Archiving with XTreePro Gold,
XTreeGold, and XTree for Windows

Chapter 10 317
Linking Computers with XTreeLink

The 5th Wave By Rich Tennant

"I ALWAYS BACK UP EVERYTHING."

Chapter 8
Hard Disk Management in a Nutshell

In This Chapter
- Hard disk optimization
- Configuring your system properly
- Strategies and techniques for maintaining hard disk performance
- Step-by-step back-up instructions for all versions of XTree

There's a saying that anything that can fit in a nutshell belongs there. At the risk of proving that axiom, I've broken hard disk management down into two basic categories: *maintenance* and *operation*.

Maintenance includes all the tasks that ensure efficient functionality and increased longevity of the hard disk. Operation includes those functions that structure data and programs and make them easy for you to access. There are five key guidelines for hard disk maintenance:

- Keep related files together. Keep WordPerfect files in the appropriate WordPerfect directory, Lotus 1-2-3 files in the appropriate Lotus directory, and so forth.
- Delete files and directories when they become obsolete.
- Back up your hard disk regularly.
- Be aware of the amount of free space on your drive.
- Make the most of, or *optimize,* your hard disk (explained in the next section).

If you own XTree, you already have the ability to easily perform all these tasks except the last one, optimizing your hard disk, which requires some special action and some additional software. Read on.

Hard Disk Optimization

Overall, this section on hard disk optimization describes maintenance tasks that safeguard the health of your hard disk. Hard disk optimization means specifically one thing: Do whatever you can to make sure the hard disk isn't working any harder than necessary. More work equals more wear and tear and leads to a shorter hard disk life. When you make things easy on the hard disk, the by-product is not only longer life, but faster *access time*. Granted, access time is measured usually in seconds or portions thereof, but every time you open a file and save a file, you sit through access time. Anytime you see your hard disk light go on, that's access time. Over the years, it all adds up in wasted time and in hard disk wear and tear.

Taking advantage of free options

The methods you can use to optimize your hard disk fall into two basic categories: what you can do for free and what costs money. Let's start with the free stuff.

Using CHKDSK

Your hard disk already contains a program called CHKDSK (aka *check disk*). You should run this program at least once a month. CHKDSK does two things:

- It gives you a bottom line total of all files stored on the disk and the amount of available space and memory.
- It searches for hard disk errors (called *lost and cross-linked clusters*).

A *cluster* is just a piece of a file. A lost cluster is a piece of a file that has become disconnected from the rest of the file. Everybody gets lost clusters now and then. It's not a big deal. Clusters get separated from the rest of their file when you don't exit a program properly and DOS doesn't have a chance to put things away neatly. A *cross-linked cluster* is a lost cluster that has become embedded in another file. This is slightly more serious, but it's not necessarily a big problem *if* you have no more than a half dozen cross-linked clusters. If you run CHKDSK once a month, you can prevent lost and cross-linked clusters from accumulating.

Fortunately, running CHKDSK is a simple procedure. Just take the following steps:

Steps: Running CHKDSK

Step 1. Make sure you exit any currently running programs.

Step 2. At the system prompt, type **CHKDSK** and press Enter.

Chapter 8: Hard Disk Management in a Nutshell

Step 3. If you *do* have cross-linked clusters, the computer can fix them for you by collecting them together for disposal. All you have to do is type **CHKDSK /F** and press Enter.

The /F option switch says "fix it" to DOS. DOS takes all your lost and cross-linked clusters and puts them in files with a CHK extension, which you can then delete.

If, after you run CHKDSK, you find you have more than half a dozen cross-linked clusters, do not try to fix them by running CHKDSK /F. If things are really messed up, the fix may be worse than the problem. Excessive cross-linked clusters can be a symptom of impending computer failure. If you have lots of cross-linked clusters, backup your system on a fresh set of floppies. Then run CHKDSK /F.

Using efficient directory strategies

The way you structure directories on your hard disk has a definite effect on hard disk performance and longevity. There are four key points for directory creation:

- **Keep programs and data in separate directories.** Make a directory for each of your programs and subdirectories for the data belonging to each program.

- **Keep your root as empty as possible.** Your root is your entryway, not your storage area. All that really needs to be in the root are your special files (COMMAND.COM, CONFIG.SYS, AUTOEXEC.BAT, and the two hidden files), plus of course directories. If you find you've got a lot of files in your root, be sure to back everything up before you start moving and deleting things.

- **Make many small directories (vs. a few large ones).** Know how many files are in a directory and make more directories when they get too full. One hundred files to a directory, at the most, is recommended — 200 files is equivalent to clogging your arteries!

- **Keep directory names simple.** The longer the name, the harder it is to type. Life is difficult enough — make it easy on yourself when you can.

> **POP QUIZ #8**
>
> Here are some true-or-false questions:
>
> 1. The root should not be used as a storage area.
> 2. Give directories long and complex names.
> 3. Keep the file count under 200 in each directory.
>
> For the answers, see Appendix F.

Configuring your system properly

The contents of your CONFIG.SYS and AUTOEXEC.BAT files can affect your hard disk performance. If you don't know how to view and edit CONFIG.SYS and AUTOEXEC.BAT, see "View" and "Editing with 1Word," both in Chapter 3, "XTree for DOS Quick Reference Guide." However, *before* you begin experimenting with these two key files, be sure to back them up *first*. Although you should already have a CONFIG.SYS and an AUTOEXEC.BAT on your computer, you might want to compare them to the following example files, which reflect the suggested *minimum* setup for running XTree.

A sample CONFIG.SYS file

```
FILES=20
BUFFERS=30
DEVICE=\DOS\ANSI.SYS
```

The FILES and BUFFERS lines affect memory and directory-access speed. If your files and buffers numbers are greater than in this example, that's OK. ANSI.SYS is a DOS file that handles your screen display, among other things.

A sample AUTOEXEC.BAT file

```
PROMPT $P $G
PATH C:\;C:\DOS;C:\WP;C:\XTGOLD
```

The PROMPT command in this example ensures that your system prompt always tells you what directory you are in. The PATH statement tells your operating system where to look for your program files. Let me explain this concept.

Let's assume you're in your WP directory. If you type **XTGOLD** and press Enter to start XTreeGold, it won't start. XTreeGold is not stored in the WP directory; XTGOLD is stored in your XTGOLD directory. You should, therefore, be told by DOS that the XTGOLD you entered from the WP directory is a `BAD COMMAND OR FILE NAME`.

If you include `;C\XTGOLD` in your PATH statement, however, DOS will find XTreeGold when it searches the yellow-brick road (that is, the PATH statement, which DOS checks whenever you issue a command to start a program). DOS searches for XTGOLD in each of the directories specified by the PATH statement. If your PATH looks like the one in the previous example, DOS would first look in the root for XTGOLD, then in the DOS directory, then in the WP directory, and finally in the XTGOLD directory. Since XTGOLD is stored in the XTGOLD directory, DOS is able to launch the program. All this hunting and searching takes place in the blink of an eye.

Here's another example. Your WordPerfect program is stored in a directory called WP. All your data and work files are stored in a directory called LETTERS. Usually, when you want to work with files in this directory, you go to the LETTERS directory to get to the files stored there. *Then* you type **WP** and press Enter to run your WordPerfect software. But WordPerfect is not stored in the LETTERS directory. If you have put WP in your PATH statement, DOS can track down the program and crank it up.

You don't have to include the location of every piece of software on your hard disk in your PATH statement. If you have a game you play infrequently, for instance, you don't need to include it in the PATH. If you have a program you use often and want to run it from any directory, then you should include the program's directory in your PATH statement.

> The amount of information you can put in your PATH statement is finite. Put only those directories you frequently use *throughout your hard disk* in the PATH statement.

Shelling out cash for optimization

So much for the free stuff. What follows in this section are programs you purchase to make your life easier. Refer to Appendix D, "Where to Go from Here," for more information on the companies and programs listed here.

Other backup programs

All versions of XTree have the capability to back up your hard disk. There are, however, programs made specifically for that task. The advantage of buying one of these programs is that they are usually faster and require less mental effort. Fifth Generation Systems' Fastback and Symantec's Norton Backup are two programs dedicated to this procedure. Central Point Software's PC Tools is another program that performs several hard disk maintenance operations, including backup. Another (expensive) alternative is the purchase of a piece of hardware called a *tape backup unit.* Such devices make backing up a truly mindless, fast process. If you need to make daily system backups, have a large hard disk, or like to spend your money on cool stuff, this device is highly recommended.

Disk defraggers

When DOS saves your files, it puts them in the next available space on your hard disk. Later, when you add to an existing file, DOS is generally forced to put that new piece of the file in some other place on the hard disk. Whenever you call up (or save) a file, DOS must search through the drive to collect all the pieces — your file is to-be-continued all over the drive. This, of course, increases access time and promotes wear and tear on the drive. A *disk defragger* goes through the drive and puts all the pieces of each file next to each other. Two simple programs, Gazelle Systems' OPTune and Golden Bow Systems' VOPT, are designed specifically to handle this chore, although both Symantec's Norton Utilities and Fifth Generation Systems' Mace Utilities include a disk defragging feature along with their other functions.

Disk scrubbers

After you've owned a hard disk for a while, entropy — and evil electromagnetic fluctuations — start to take their toll on your disk's magnetic fields. Really. This isn't "Lost In Space" double-talk. The only cure for this problem is to reformat the hard disk. Of course, formatting has the unfortunate side effect of *erasing* everything on the disk. Most people don't have the time or inclination to spend a day backing up, formatting, and restoring their data all for the sake of strengthening their magnetic fields.

What a disk scrubber does is reformat and test your hard disk *without* disturbing (erasing) the data on it. Gibson Research's SpinRite II and Prime Solutions' Disk Technician handle this unique job. Regular reformatting will extend the life of your hard disk, perhaps indefinitely. SpinRite II and Disk Technician (as well as OPTune) also check to make sure your hard disk is set to the proper *interleave* (a problem found mostly in older hard disks). Proper interleave can seriously increase disk performance. And save you-know-what (wear and tear).

Cache programs

Most computers, these days, come with *at least* one megabyte of memory and a cache program. A cache program works on the theory that you are likely to keep using the commands you frequently use. The cache program keeps track of the most recently employed commands. If you do repeat a command, the cache already knows how to proceed, instead of having to ask the hard disk for the instructions. If you didn't get a cache program with your computer, Multisoft's PC-Kwik is the program to try.

Unerase and disaster recovery

Although disaster recovery isn't exactly part of hard disk optimization, any chapter on hard disks would be incomplete without *some* mention of this important topic. A disaster is when you delete something by mistake. A disaster is when you accidentally reformat your hard disk. There are even more (technical) things that can go wrong, but let's not dwell on the subject of disasters.

If you have DOS version 5.0 or XTreeGold, you can use Unerase or XTreeGold's Oops! command, respectively, to recover from a simple accidental deletion. However, suffice it to say that Peter Norton's Advanced Utilities and the Mace Utilities can save the day in almost all major catastrophes. The Norton and Mace products also do defragging (as does PC Tools).

The ideal wish list

In addition to XTree, of course, you should have either Norton or Mace Utilities and SpinRite II. Next, you should have a backup program. And PC-Kwik for caching if your computer didn't come with a cache program. (Norton Utilities also comes with a cache program.) Go to your local friendly computer or software store and look at the boxes, talk to the professionals, and make a selection.

The point of all these programs is not so much to save you money by making your hard disk last a long, long time. If you buy *everything,* you'll be spending as much as the cost of a new 80MB hard disk. The point is to put off and reduce the tragedy of a hard disk crash. The loss of data is the critical issue here. On the other hand, prolonging the life of your drive might actually save you thousands of dollars. The death of a drive often precipitates the rationalization of the purchase of a whole new computer system.

When you are considering the purchase of any software, be sure to note the system requirements on the box before shelling out cash. You'll need to know how much memory your computer has as well as what version of DOS you own.

Your version of DOS

It's easy to determine which version of DOS is installed in your computer. At any system prompt, type **VER** and press Enter, and whatever version of DOS that you are running will be displayed. If you have version 2.0 or 2.11 of MS-DOS and are toying with the idea of upgrading to 3.1 or higher, go for it if any of these reasons apply:

- You want to use software that requires a higher version of DOS.
- You need to take advantage of the memory-saving capabilities in DOS 5.
- You want to exchange work with someone who has a higher version of DOS.
- Your laptop has a higher version of DOS than your desktop.
- You want to repartition your hard disk.

If any of these cases is true for you, it is wise to upgrade. If you do upgrade, a low-level and high-level format of your hard disk *may* be required (that means you need to backup everything, reformat your hard drive, and restore your system). If this makes you squeamish, look for a friend, consultant, or computer store you feel comfortable dealing with to help you out.

Some older computers may also require a chip upgrade to accommodate the new DOS. Some software also requires adjustments in the CONFIG.SYS to accommodate the new DOS. Translation: Upgrading DOS is not recommended as a fun thing to do.

Step-by-Step Hard Disk Maintenance

This next section is devoted to the commands needed to perform the two things you *must* do to maintain your hard disk (and your sanity):

1. Back up your files.
2. Delete what you don't need.

If these two lessons are all you get from this book, we'll both sleep easier at night.

Backing up your hard disk

One of the greatest conveniences of a hard disk — that all your programs and files are in one place — is also the most dangerous aspect of a hard disk — everything *is* in one place! To soften the blow of a hard disk failure (an *inevitable* hard disk failure), you should duplicate (back up) the contents of your hard disk onto a set of floppy disks at least once a month. In addition, every day you should back up any file you edit or create. Although your word processor may be programmed to make backup files as you work (those files with that BAK extension), these files don't count as a backup because both the original file and the backup are in the same place. The point of backing up is to avoid dependence on one device as the guardian of *all* your data. Unfortunately, learning to back up regularly is a lesson most people learn the hard way. When you do experience the sheer terror of a hard disk failure (without a backup to save you) you, too, will become a staunch, born-again backer-upper.

There are several different backup strategies. You'll probably end up using all of them in various combinations.

The daily backup

The first backup strategy is the simple, daily backup. At the end of the day you have to remember only which files you created or edited that day and copy them onto a floppy disk. To backup only a few files, you can use XTree's Copy command.

The system backup

A system backup copies your data, your programs, and your directory structure setup onto a big stack of floppy disks. You may wonder why you should copy the programs when your master program disks are sitting safely in their boxes. What you're backing up is the program and whatever hard-fought customizations have been performed by you or your brother-in-law. A system backup once a month is recommended. Further, you should have two complete copies of your computer system that you rotate. In January, say, use one set of backup disks. In February, use the second. In March, use the first set of disks again, and so forth. If you're using a database, a point-of-sale system, a complex accounting system, or any kind of software that updates dozens of individual files every day, you probably need to do a system backup once a day.

The incremental backups

In between your daily backups and your monthly system backups are *incremental* backups — when you backup everything that hasn't been backed up since the last system backup. This is an interim, just-to-be-sure backup.

Prepare your floppies

Since a full system backup requires a slew of floppies, the first step is to determine the number of floppies you'll need. Get into XTree and check the disk statistics for the total bytes that occupy your hard disk.

If you have files and programs totaling 18,000,000 bytes on your hard disk, and you use high-density 5¼-inch floppy disks (which hold 1,200,000 bytes each),then you'll need at least 15 floppy disks. (Divide 18,000,000 by 1,200,000.) If you have low-density 5¼-inch disks, which hold 360,000 bytes each, you'll need at least 50 floppy disks. (High-density 3½-inch disks hold 1,400,000 bytes, and low-density 3½-inch disks hold 720,000 bytes.)

If you calculate that you need seven disks to backup your system, you should also be prepared with a few extra disks, because XTree will not fill each disk. For example, if you have a 2,500-byte file to be copied but only 2,000 bytes of disk space left over on your backup disk, XTree determines that the 2,500-byte file won't fit and asks you to put a new floppy disk in the drive. That 2,000 bytes of disk space is then just left blank.

Also, XTree cannot backup a file if it is larger than a floppy disk. If you have a disk with a 360,000-byte capacity and a file that is 425,000 bytes big, XTree cannot copy that file onto your disk (and you should explore some of the other backup-specific software available). Once you've determined how many disks you need, you must then format them (see "Formatting Floppy Disks" in Chapter 3 and Chapter 7).

Deleting obsolete files

Every now and then, you should do some housecleaning on your hard disk. Take a look at the files on your disk. Anything growing mold? If a file is obsolete, either delete it or copy it to a floppy disk if you think you may want to use it again someday. In addition to these familiar files, however, there may be some additional junk files that have accumulated on your hard disk. Junk files are created in a few ways:

- Some programs deposit stray files on your disk when you quit by either rebooting or turning off your computer without exiting properly. In Microsoft Word, for example, these junk files end with TMP; in WordStar they end with $?$.
- Word processors create BAK files that you may want to delete to keep directories clean and save space.

Hard Disk Maintenance with XTree for DOS

Use these XTree for DOS operations to maintain a healthy hard disk. You can basically back up everything in five easy steps.

Steps: Backing up with XTree for DOS

Step 1. Get into XTree and, from the Directory window, press S to execute the Showall command and enter a Showall file window.

Step 2. Press Ctrl-T to tag all files.

Step 3. Press Alt-C to copy all tagged files and the directory structure.

Step 4. Press Enter to maintain the same name for all the files.

Step 5. When XTree prompts you, type the name of the destination drive (your floppy drive) and press Enter. XTree then starts the backup process. As floppy disks fill up, XTree prompts you to feed the computer another formatted floppy disk.

Keeping track of your backups

After you've finished your system backup, there's one last small task: While your files are still tagged, press Ctrl-A (for attribute), then type –A and press Enter. This turns *off* the archive flag on each of the tagged files. Any file you create or edit from this point forward will automatically have its archive flag

Chapter 8: Hard Disk Management in a Nutshell

turned *on*. You can use these turned-on archive flags as signals when it comes time to do an incremental backup. Only those files with their archive flags turned on need to be backed up — you'll see how to do that next.

Making incremental backups

An incremental backup (backing up any files that have been created or edited since the last backup) should be performed between system backups. If you've done a system backup and you turned off the archive bit on the backed up files (as instructed in the previous section), you can perform an incremental backup as follows.

Steps: Making an incremental backup

Step 1. Get into XTree and, from the Directory window, press S to execute the Showall command and enter a Showall file window.

Step 2. Press Alt-T (to tag by attributes).

Step 3. Type **+A** and press Enter to tag all files that have their archive flag turned on. (These are the files that have changed since your last system backup.)

Step 4. Press Alt-C to copy all tagged files (and preserve your directory structure).

Step 5. Press Enter to maintain the same names of the files.

Step 6. When XTree prompts you, type the name of the destination drive and press Enter.

Step 7. After you finish backing up (while your files are still tagged), press Ctrl-A, type **–A**, and press Enter to turn off the archive flag.

Backing up by date

You can use XTree's ability to sort files by date to isolate files created or updated during any period of time (weekly, or since last Tuesday, for example).

Steps: Backing up recently created or edited files

Step 1. Get into XTree and, from the Directory window, press S to execute the Showall command and enter a Showall file window.

Step 2. Press Alt-F-F to change the file display to include the date and time each file was last saved.

Step 3. Press Alt-S-D to sort the files by date and time.

Step 4. Look at the date and time next to the filenames and tag those files within the range of dates you want.

Step 5. Press Ctrl-C to copy all tagged files, or use Alt-C to copy the files and their directory structures.

Step 6. Press Enter to maintain the names of the files.

Step 7. When XTree prompts you, type the name of the destination drive and press Enter.

Removing duplicate files

To get rid of duplicate files, get into XTree, and from the Directory window, press S (for Showall). All files will be displayed in alphabetical order. Files with the same names will, therefore, be listed next to each other. To help you decide which files to keep and which to tag for deletion, you can use one of the following methods:

- Highlight a file and look at its directory path (displayed at the top of the screen). This will tell you where the file is stored, which may be a deciding factor.

- Press Alt-F-F to change the file display to include the size and the date and time the file was last saved. Whichever is the newer or the bigger *may* be the one to keep.

- View the files contents. Just highlight the file and press V to view the contents of the file.

Once you've tagged all the files you want to delete, press Ctrl-D to delete them.

> **WARNING:** Remember not to delete any of the following files from the root: AUTOEXEC.BAT, CONFIG.SYS, COMMAND.COM, IBMBIO.SYS, and IBMDOS.COM.

Removing BAK and TMP files

You can take the following steps to remove useless BAK and TMP files.

Steps: Removing BAK and TMP files

Step 1. Get into XTree and from the Directory Window press F for Filespec. Type ***.BAK** (or ***.TMP**, or any other filespec) and press Enter.

Step 2. Press S (for SHOWALL). All files with the *.BAK filespec you entered will be displayed.

Step 3. Use the Ctrl-T key combination to tag all files.

Step 4. Use the Ctrl-D key combination to delete them.

Remember, when you have deleted all the tagged files, XTree will report NO FILES! in the File window. When you change your Filespec back to *.*, you'll see the rest of your files.

Retiring old files

You can take rarely used files off your hard disk and store them on floppies. If you want to remove files that have common extensions (such as DOC, WK1, DBF, or whatever extension your software generates), have XTree list those files by extension. You can examine the list of files, using View, and then tag those files you want to copy to a floppy and delete from your hard disk. To remove files that have common extensions, take these steps.

Steps: Storing old files on floppies

Step 1. Get into XTree and, from the Directory window, press F for Filespec. Type the filespec that applies to your files (***.DOC**, ***.XLS**, ***.DBF**, or whatever) and press Enter.

Step 2. Press S to enter a Showall file window. All files with the filespec you specify will be displayed.

Step 3. Decide which files to archive. You can press V to view a file's contents.

Step 4. Tag each file that you want removed from the hard disk and copied to a floppy.

Step 5. When you finish tagging files, press Ctrl-C to copy all tagged files.

Step 6. When XTree prompts you, type the name of the destination drive and press Enter.

Step 7. After you finish backing up (while your files are still tagged), press Ctrl-A, type **−A**, and press Enter to turn off the archive flag.

Step 8. When you finish copying, press Ctrl-D to delete the tagged files from your hard disk.

Hard Disk Maintenance with XTree for Windows

Use these XTree for Windows operations to maintain a healthy hard disk. You can basically back up everything in four easy steps.

Steps: Backing up with XTree for Windows

Step 1. Get into XTree for Windows. From the Tree window, highlight the icon of the drive you wish to backup (make sure the tree structure is collapsed, with only the root showing).

Step 2. Press Ctrl+C (or select the Copy tool) and the Copy dialog box will appear.

Step 3. Type the name of the destination drive and press Enter. XTree begins backing up your system.

Step 4. As your floppy disks fill, XTree prompts you to feed the computer more formatted floppy disks.

Making incremental backups and backing up by date

When you give the Copy command in XTree for Windows, you can check the option `Copy New Files and Update Existing Ones` (an incremental backup in disguise). You can narrow your choices to certain dates or attributes by selecting View ⇨ Directory Filter, and in the Directory Filter dialog box, select an attribute and specify a date and time. Then proceed with the backup, as just described.

Removing duplicate files

To get rid of duplicate files, take the following steps.

Steps: Removing duplicate files

Step 1. Get into XTree for Windows and select View ⇨ Directory Filter.

Step 2. In the Directory Filter dialog box, select the Files Only option and then press Enter.

Step 3. Highlight the icon of the drive that contains the duplicates and then select File ⇨ Open Directory As.

Chapter 8: Hard Disk Management in a Nutshell

Step 4. Select All Directories on Current Volume and choose OK. At this point all files on the selected drive will then be displayed in alphabetical order. Files with the same names will, therefore, be listed next to each other. To help you decide which files to keep and which to select for deletion, you can use one of the following methods:

- Highlight a file and look at its directory path (displayed in the Detail Box). This will tell you where the file is stored, which may be a deciding factor.
- Compare the size of the files and note the date and time they were last saved. Whichever is the newer or the bigger *may* be the one to keep. (If this information is not being displayed, press Shift+D to open the Directory Format dialog box and choose the items to include in the display.)
- View the file's contents. Just highlight the file and press Ctrl+V to view the contents of the file.

Step 5. Once you've tagged all the files you want to delete, press Ctrl+D to delete them.

> **NOTE:** When you are finished with this task, you may want the Directory window to again show both files and directories. To return your display to the way it was, select View ⇨ Directory Filter to open the Directory Filter dialog box (or press Shift+F), choose Files and Directories, and press Enter.

Removing BAK and TMP files

You can take the following steps to remove useless BAK and TMP files.

Steps: Removing BAK and TMP files

Step 1. Get into XTree for Windows and select View ⇨ Directory Filter. In the Directory Filter dialog box, select the Files Only option and press Enter.

Step 2. Highlight the icon of the drive that contains the BAK and TMP files and then select File ⇨ Open Directory As. Select the option All Directories on Current Volume and choose OK. All the files on the drive will be displayed (in alphabetical order).

Step 3. Select Edit ⇨ Select/Deselect (Ctrl+Shift+/), type the ***.BAK** and ***.TMP** file specifications in the text box, and choose OK. This will cause all the files with those filespecs to be selected.

Step 4. Press Ctrl+D to delete the selected files.

WARNING: Remember not to delete any of the following files from the root: AUTOEXEC.BAT, CONFIG.SYS, COMMAND.COM, IBMBIO.SYS, and IBMDOS.COM.

Retiring old files

You can take rarely used files off your hard disk and store them on floppies. If you want to remove files that have common extensions (such as DOC, WK1, DBF, or whatever extension your software generates), have XTree list those files by extension. You can examine the list of files, using View or Auto View, and then tag those files you want to copy to a floppy and delete from your hard disk. To remove files that have common extensions, take these steps.

Steps: Storing old files on floppies

Step 1. Get into XTree for Windows and select View ⇨ Directory Filter (or press Shift+F). In the Directory Filter dialog box, select the Files Only option and then press Enter.

Step 2. Highlight the icon of the drive that contains the duplicates and then select File ⇨ Open Directory As. Select the option All Directories on Current Volume and choose OK. All the files containing the extension(s) you requested will be displayed in the new window.

Step 3. Select the files to be stored on the floppy. If you can't remember what's in a file, you can highlight the file and press Ctrl+V to view it's contents.

Step 4. When you finish selecting, press Ctrl+C to copy all selected files.

Step 5. When the Copy dialog box appears, type in the name of the destination floppy drive and press Enter.

Step 6. When you finish copying, press Ctrl+D to delete the selected files from your hard disk.

Summary

▶ The key to hard disk maintenance is vigilance — delete unneeded files and keep directories lean.

▶ A number of programs are available to prolong the life of your hard disk.

▶ Devising a regular back-up system is critical.

▶ All versions of XTree make backing up your system painless.

Chapter 9
Archiving with XTreePro Gold, XTreeGold, and XTree for Windows

In This Chapter
- How archiving and zipping can make file storage easier
- How to decide when to archive files
- Step-by-step instructions for creating, modifying, and extracting archived files

Only XTreePro Gold, XTreeGold, and XTree for Windows have built-in archiving powers — and the options among the programs vary. However, before we get into the specific commands, it might be best to explain what the heck *archiving* (also known as *zipping*) is, in the first place.

Archiving Basics

In normal English, the word *archives* refers to either the place where public documents are stored or to the documents themselves. In computers, *file archiving* has little to do with the public but a lot to do with storing.

You probably already participate in an annual archiving ritual for your noncomputer files — you collect the year's invoices or correspondence in a box, label the box with the date, and put the box away on some high shelf (throwing your back out in the process).

The process of archiving lets you do something similar with your computer files (with no danger to your back). When you archive a group of files, two things happen:

1. The selected files are *compressed* (not unlike freeze-drying) so they actually take up less space — usually at least 50 percent less space.
2. The compressed versions of the files are collected into one megafile.

NOTE: Creating an archive file does not in any way harm, delete, or otherwise disturb the files you have selected to archive. The archiving utility automatically creates duplicates of your files while compressing and packing them. After you've created the archive file, you have two sets of files — the original and the compressed, packed version.

Once you have created an archive file, you can copy it to a floppy disk (more compressed files will fit on a floppy than noncompressed files), give it to a friend, or whatever. Archived files are also handy for simplified (and speedy) transmission over a modem, if you're into that sort of thing.

If you ever need to access one of the files included in an archived file (or if you get an archived file from a friend), you must go through the unarchive process to reconstitute your files (kind of like adding water to your freeze-dried coffee).

While this may sound like a lot of work, remember that XTree is going to do everything for you. All you have to do is select the files you want to have archived (or unarchived).

Deciding When to Archive

Here's a typical archiving scenario.

Let's say that some time ago you wrote a bunch of letters to a Mr. Mike Brady. At this point, however, your business with Mr. Brady is concluded and there is no reason why those obsolete letters should be allowed to take up disk space. You decide to store them on a floppy disk as a group (kind of like putting them in a box). In other words, you decide to archive the files.

First, as always, you invoke XTree. Then you tag (or select) the letters to Mr. Brady. Finally, you give the command to archive the files (this command is covered in detail later in this chapter).

At this point, XTree copies, compresses, and packs the tagged (or selected) files. Because of the compression, the size of the resulting archive file will actually be smaller than the sum total of the selected files.

Chapter 9: Archiving with XTree

Once the archive file is created, you can delete the original, individual letters from your hard disk and copy (or move) the archive file to a floppy disk.

A postscript to this process comes one day, three months down the road. You suddenly realize you need to use one or more of those letters in the archive file. To access the individual files packed into the archive file, you need to first *extract* (unpack) them. As you extract the files, they'll be automatically restored to their original size.

Whew!

This is just one example of archiving. Don't be afraid to get creative. You could, for example, archive files and keep them on the hard disk as a method of organization. Or, if you're dealing with limited space, archiving is a way to keep little-used files handy without paying a hefty disk-space price.

Okay, let's get down to specifics. Check out the instructions for the XTree program you have.

Archiving with XTreePro Gold

Let's try this in a real-life example, step by step, using a bunch of Lotus 1-2-3 spreadsheet files.

Creating an archive file

I created spreadsheets named JAN90.WK1, FEB90.WK1, and so forth, for an entire year. I'm finally getting around to taking these files off my hard disk and I want to archive the files together in a single 1990 Arc file.

First, I need to tag the files I want to archive. I use the filespec *.WK1 to isolate the spreadsheet files so that I can then tag them as a group. (See Chapter 3 for details on tagging files.) Once I've tagged the files, I can issue the archive command, Ctrl-F5, to initiate the archiving process. As you can see in Figure 9-1, all the WK1 files in the Lotus directory are tagged. I type the name 1990, press Enter, and then get a request for more information, namely which archive format to use and whether I want to use a password.

> **NOTE:** When XTreePro Gold receives the archive command, it asks for a name for the archive file. *Do not* add an extension to the filename; XTreePro Gold automatically adds the ARC extension, which designates the file as archived.

```
Path: C:\LOTUS                                         2:44:11 pm

APR90     .WK1♦                          FILE  *.WK1
AUG90     .WK1♦
DEC90     .WK1♦                          DISK  C:POWER USER
FEB90     .WK1♦                          Available
JAN90     .WK1♦                             Bytes      2,088,960
JUL90     .WK1♦
JUN90     .WK1♦                          DIRECTORY Stats
MAR90     .WK1♦                          Total
MAY90     .WK1♦                             Files             36
NOV90     .WK1♦                             Bytes      1,026,979
OCT90     .WK1♦                          Matching
SEP90     .WK1♦                             Files             12
                                            Bytes         81,340
                                         Tagged
                                            Files             13
                                            Bytes         94,949
                                         Current File
                                            SEP90     .WK1
                                            Bytes          8,377

Archive all tagged files
to:
Enter archive file name        ↑ history  ↵ ok  F1 help  ESC cancel
```

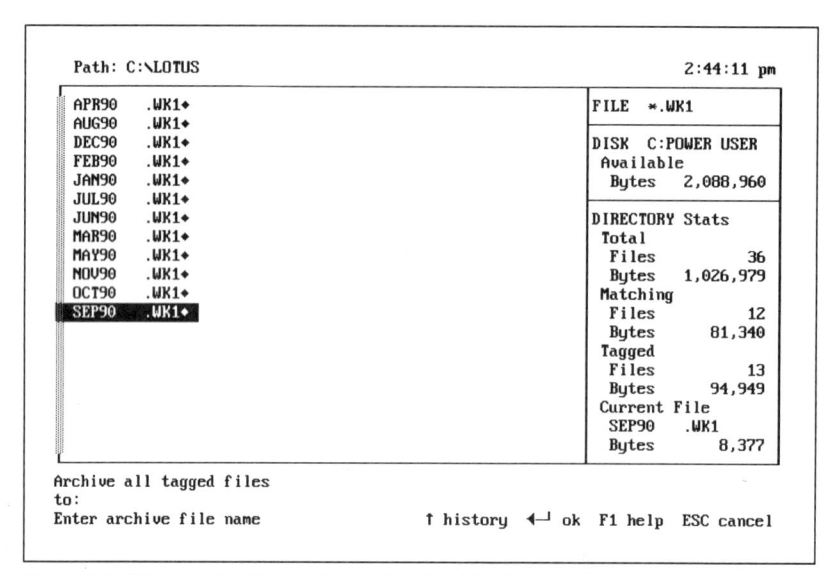

Figure 9-1: After tagging files and pressing Ctrl-F5, XTreePro Gold asks you to name the archive file.

Selecting an archive format

Believe it or not, there are a *number* of archiving schemes. XTreePro Gold offers two choices. Each of the two types has advantages and disadvantages.

Take a look at Figure 9-2. After choosing a filename for the archive file and pressing Enter, the options shown at the bottom of the screen appear. The default compatibility format that appears is always XTree. XTreePro Gold's own archive format preserves the directory structure of the files being archived. When the files are restored, the path will also be restored (if needed). The disadvantage is that if you wish to exchange the file with a co-worker, they must also own XTreePro Gold to be able to extract the archived files. As shown in Figure 9-2, I chose PKarc, which is the other available archiving format in XTreePro Gold. This format is widely available (even to non-XTreePro Gold users), which means that if you give an Arc file to someone, they can probably extract the files whether they own XTreePro Gold or not.

To switch from the default compatibility format (XTree) to PKarc, I pressed C for compatibility. This command acts as a toggle between the two file formats, the default and PKarc.

Chapter 9: Archiving with XTree

```
       Path: C:\LOTUS                                    2:44:53 pm
                                              ┌─────────────────────────
          APR90    .WK1◆                      │ FILE  *.WK1
          AUG90    .WK1◆                      │
          DEC90    .WK1◆                      │ DISK  C:POWER USER
          FEB90    .WK1◆                      │ Available
          JAN90    .WK1◆                      │   Bytes      2,105,344
          JUL90    .WK1◆                      │
          JUN90    .WK1◆                      │ DIRECTORY Stats
          MAR90    .WK1◆                      │ Total
          MAY90    .WK1◆                      │   Files            35
          NOV90    .WK1◆                      │   Bytes     1,000,917
          OCT90    .WK1◆                      │ Matching
          SEP90    .WK1◆                      │   Files            12
                                              │   Bytes        81,340
                                              │ Tagged
                                              │   Files            13
                                              │   Bytes        94,949
                                              │ Current File
                                              │   SEP90    .WK1
                                              │   Bytes         8,377

       ARCHIVE file: C:\LOTUS\1990.ARC
                  Compatibility (PKarc)  Encryption (off)  method (archive)
                                                 ↵ ok   F1 help   ESC cancel
```

Figure 9-2: After naming the archive file, XTreePro Gold offers several options at the bottom of the screen.

Applying data encryption

Applying data encryption to your archive file increases the file's security. When you create a basic Arc file, *anyone* can extract the contents of your file by using a compatible program. Encryption allows you to add a password to your Arc file. Then, only people with your password can open the file. A password can be up to 32 characters long. (However, don't outsmart yourself with bizarre and difficult-to-remember passwords. If you forget the password, you're out of luck.)

By default, encryption is turned off in XTreePro Gold. If you press E, however, the legend Encryption at the bottom of the screen toggles to (on). For now, let's leave encryption off. (Even if you decide not to encrypt a file, XTreePro Gold asks for a password anyway. If you're not using the Encryption option, just ignore the question by pressing Enter whenever XTreePro Gold asks you for a password.)

> **NOTE:** The options along the bottom of the screen are available for your use if the first letter of the option is capitalized. For example, the option next to Encryption is method. When you create a new archive, method is unavailable (that's why the *m* is a lowercase letter). When the *m* is capitalized, you can use this option when adding files to an already existing Arc file. I'll get into the method option later.

After setting the format to PKarc and leaving encryption off, just press Enter to finally, actually create the Arc file. After XTreePro Gold finishes the archiving process, you can delete the original files, because they've all been neatly packed in the archive file.

Opening an archive

Looking inside a compressed file is called *opening an archive.* Opening an archive is not the same thing as removing a file from an archive. (Before you can remove a file from an archive, however, you have to open it. Removing files from archives is called *extracting.* See the next section for how to extract a file.)

Let's take a look at the 1990.ARC file, which is now in the Lotus directory shown in Figure 9-3, to make sure everything is there. To look inside an Arc file, all you have to do is highlight the file and press Alt-F5.

Figure 9-4 shows the contents of 1990.ARC. As you can see, the listing looks a lot like a full file display, with one important addition: the percentage of compression that resulted from the archiving. This lets you know how much space you've saved on your drive by archiving the files. Also, the Statistics box on the right is now solely focused on the highlighted Arc file, APR90.WK1. You can see

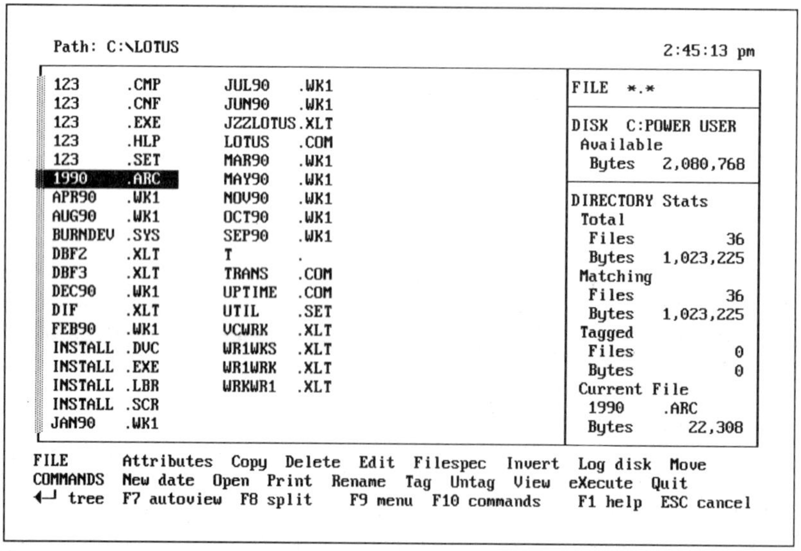

```
Path: C:\LOTUS                                              2:45:13 pm

  123      .CMP      JUL90    .WK1          FILE   *.*
  123      .CNF      JUN90    .WK1
  123      .EXE      JZZLOTUS .XLT          DISK  C:POWER USER
  123      .HLP      LOTUS    .COM          Available
  123      .SET      MAR90    .WK1            Bytes     2,080,768
  1990     .ARC      MAY90    .WK1
  APR90    .WK1      NOV90    .WK1          DIRECTORY Stats
  AUG90    .WK1      OCT90    .WK1          Total
  BURNDEV  .SYS      SEP90    .WK1            Files            36
  DBF2     .XLT      T        .                Bytes     1,023,225
  DBF3     .XLT      TRANS    .COM          Matching
  DEC90    .WK1      UPTIME   .COM            Files            36
  DIF      .XLT      UTIL     .SET            Bytes     1,023,225
  FEB90    .WK1      VCWRK    .XLT          Tagged
  INSTALL  .DUC      WR1WKS   .XLT            Files             0
  INSTALL  .EXE      WR1WRK   .XLT            Bytes             0
  INSTALL  .LBR      WRKWR1   .XLT          Current File
  INSTALL  .SCR                                1990     .ARC
  JAN90    .WK1                                Bytes        22,308

  FILE         Attributes  Copy   Delete  Edit   Filespec  Invert  Log disk  Move
  COMMANDS     New date    Open   Print   Rename Tag       Untag   View      eXecute  Quit
  ↵ tree   F7 autoview   F8 split      F9 menu   F10 commands      F1 help  ESC cancel
```

Figure 9-3: Once an archive file has been created, it appears in the File window next to the other files.

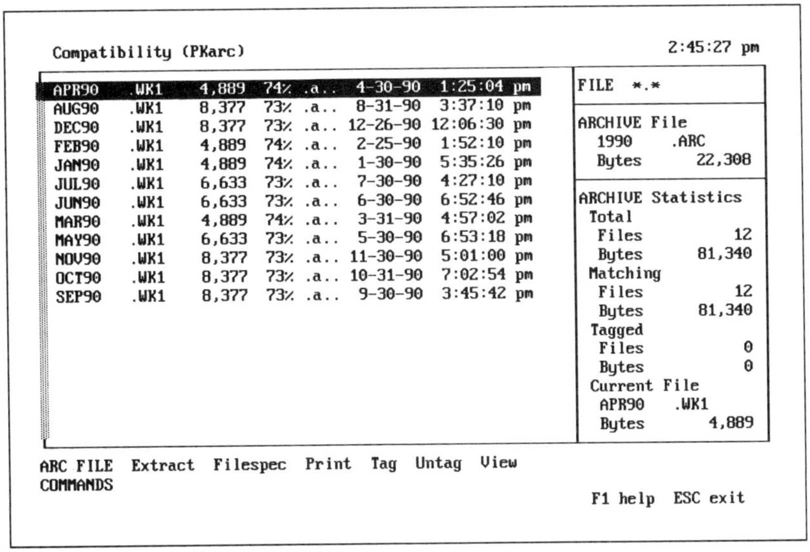

Chapter 9: Archiving with XTree

```
 Compatibility (PKarc)                                    2:45:27 pm
 APR90    .WK1    4,889   74%  .a..  4-30-90   1:25:04 pm  FILE  *.*
 AUG90    .WK1    8,377   73%  .a..  8-31-90   3:37:10 pm
 DEC90    .WK1    8,377   73%  .a.. 12-26-90  12:06:30 pm  ARCHIVE File
 FEB90    .WK1    4,889   74%  .a..  2-25-90   1:52:10 pm   1990       .ARC
 JAN90    .WK1    4,889   74%  .a..  1-30-90   5:35:26 pm   Bytes     22,308
 JUL90    .WK1    6,633   73%  .a..  7-30-90   4:27:10 pm
 JUN90    .WK1    6,633   73%  .a..  6-30-90   6:52:46 pm  ARCHIVE Statistics
 MAR90    .WK1    4,889   74%  .a..  3-31-90   4:57:02 pm   Total
 MAY90    .WK1    6,633   73%  .a..  5-30-90   6:53:18 pm    Files         12
 NOV90    .WK1    8,377   73%  .a.. 11-30-90   5:01:00 pm    Bytes     81,340
 OCT90    .WK1    8,377   73%  .a.. 10-31-90   7:02:54 pm   Matching
 SEP90    .WK1    8,377   73%  .a..  9-30-90   3:45:42 pm    Files         12
                                                            Bytes     81,340
                                                           Tagged
                                                            Files          0
                                                            Bytes          0
                                                           Current File
                                                            APR90    .WK1
                                                            Bytes      4,889

 ARC FILE   Extract  Filespec  Print  Tag  Untag  View
 COMMANDS
                                                          F1 help  ESC exit
```

Figure 9-4: The archive open command, Alt-F5, creates an archive file window to display the contents of an archive file.

in the figure that the total size of 1990.ARC is 22,308 bytes. However, the total size of the files in the archive file, when extracted, is 81,340 bytes. That's quite a savings, space-wise.

When you highlight an Arc file like this, you'll see some familiar command options along the bottom of the screen: Filespec, Print, Tag, Untag, and View; all these work as you might expect. In addition, however, there is a new command, Extract, which copies and uncompresses a file (or files) from the archive.

Extracting a file from an archive

If you want to extract a single file from an open archive file, first press T to tag it and then press E to extract it. Remember the terminology: Looking inside a compressed file is called opening an archive; removing files from an archive is called extracting. If you want to extract all the files, press Ctrl-T to tag all files and then Ctrl-E to extract all tagged files. From this point on, the process works just like copying or moving. XTreePro Gold asks you for a destination and whether you wish to replace existing files.

Modifying an existing Arc file

After you create an Arc file (and copy it to a floppy disk), you don't necessarily *have* to delete the source files from your hard disk. You can continue using them. Then, when it's time to back up again, you can just *update* or *freshen* the existing Arc file. (Updating and freshening are quicker than creating the Arc file from scratch.)

In the current example, let's say I've made changes to some of the spreadsheet files but can't remember which ones. Also, I've created another worksheet file (TOTAL90.WK1) that needs to be included in 1990.ARC. What I need to do is add the new file (TOTAL90.WK1) and make sure I have the most current version of the other files (JAN-DEC.WK1) in 1990.ARC.

First, I'll tag the files that were originally archived as well as the new file. I just press Ctrl-F5 (just like when creating a new archive). When XTree asks for the name of the archive file, I type the name of the Arc file I want to modify (1990 in this example) and press Enter.

At the bottom of the screen shown in Figure 9-5, the word `compatibility` is shown in lowercase type, indicating that option is not currently available. Remember, you specify compatibility only when you create the Arc file — since 1990.ARC has already been created as a PKarc file, its compatibility is not an issue. As a consolation prize, however, the Method option is now available.

```
Path: C:\LOTUS                                          2:46:51 pm

    123      .CMP    JUL90    .WK1◆     FILE  *.*
    123      .CNF    JUN90    .WK1◆
    123      .EXE    JZZLOTUS .XLT      DISK  C:POWER USER
    123      .HLP    LOTUS    .COM      Available
    123      .SET    MAR90    .WK1◆       Bytes    2,080,768
    1990     .ARC    MAY90    .WK1◆
    APR90    .WK1◆   NOV90    .WK1◆     DIRECTORY Stats
    AUG90    .WK1◆   OCT90    .WK1◆     Total
    BURNDEV  .SYS    SEP90    .WK1◆       Files             36
    DBF2     .XLT    TOTAL9   .WK1◆       Bytes      1,023,225
    DBF3     .XLT    TRANS    .COM      Matching
    DEC90    .WK1◆   UPTIME   .COM        Files             36
    DIF      .XLT    UTIL     .SET        Bytes      1,023,225
    FEB90    .WK1◆   VCWRK    .XLT      Tagged
    INSTALL  .DVC    WR1WKS   .XLT        Files             13
    INSTALL  .EXE    WR1WRK   .XLT        Bytes         94,949
    INSTALL  .LBR    WRKWR1   .XLT      Current File
    INSTALL  .SCR                         1990         .ARC
    JAN90    .WK1◆                        Bytes         22,308

ARCHIVE file: C:\LOTUS\1990.ARC
              compatibility (PKarc)  Encryption (off)  Method (update)
                                         ↵ ok   F1 help   ESC cancel
```

Figure 9-5: You can add tagged files to an archive with Ctrl-F5. As always, options appear at the bottom of the screen.

Chapter 9: Archiving with XTree

There are three ways, or methods, of altering an existing compressed file. The three methods are shown at the bottom of the screen when you create an Arc file or modify an existing compressed file.

- **Update:** Updating compares any tagged files with those of the same name in an Arc file. If a tagged file is newer, then it replaces the older file in the Arc file. If a tagged file is not in the Arc file, it is then added to the Arc file.

- **Freshen:** Freshening compares the dates of tagged files to the dates of files with the same name in the Arc file and then replaces the newer files as needed. No additional files are added to the Arc file.

- **Archive:** Archiving means all tagged files will be added to the Arc file. No questions asked.

To cycle through Update, Freshen, and Archive, press M. In the current example, I select Update and then press Enter.

NOTE: If the Arc command doesn't work, it's possible that your version of XTreePro Gold does not have the Arc module. Contact XTree Company about either getting the Arc module or just upgrading to XTreeGold. See Appendix D, "Where to Go from Here," for information about contacting XTree.

Archiving with XTreeGold

The major difference between XTreeGold and XTreePro Gold is that XTreeGold incorporates an additional archiving scheme. Going beyond the venerable (a nice way of saying *outmoded*) Arc method of archiving files, Gold employs the newer Zip method. The differences between Arc and Zip have to do with efficiency and compatibility with other versions of XTree. If you don't specify which of the two methods you want to use — Arc or Zip — XTreeGold assumes you want to use the Zip format — which is the recommended way to go.

No matter how a file is archived (be it Arc, Zip, or even XTree's own archiving scheme), XTreeGold can recognize and handle the situation appropriately.

Creating a Zip (or Arc) file

For this example, consider the series of reports I created in Microsoft Word entitled JAN.DOC, FEB.DOC, and so on, shown in Figure 9-6. As always, I'm a little behind in my file maintenance activities. However, the day has finally arrived to store the files together in a single 1991 Zip file.

```
Path: C:\WORD\REPORTS                                  7:20:30 am
 APR      .DOC♦                          FILE  *.*
 AUG      .DOC♦
 DEC      .DOC♦                          DISK  C:POWER USER
 FEB      .DOC♦                          Available
 JAN      .DOC♦                            Bytes    16,670,720
 JUL      .DOC♦
 JUN      .DOC♦                          DIRECTORY Stats
 MAR      .DOC♦                          Total
 MAY      .DOC♦                            Files            12
 NOV      .DOC♦                            Bytes        24,064
 OCT      .DOC♦                          Matching
 SEP      .DOC♦                            Files            12
                                           Bytes        24,064
                                         Tagged
                                           Files            12
                                           Bytes        24,064
                                         Current File
                                          APR      .DOC
                                           Bytes         2,048

COMPRESS all tagged files
   to:
Enter path and file name        ↑ history  ↵ ok  F1 help  ESC cancel
```

Figure 9-6: Tagging document files before zipping.

First, I tag the files I want to zip together. Then I press Ctrl-F5 to begin the archiving process. XTreeGold prompts me to name the new Zip file; in reality, Gold is asking for more than just a filename — *how* you name such files affects the type of archive files Gold creates.

If you type in a filename *without* an extension (such as REPORTS), XTreeGold assumes that you want to create a Zip file. If you type in a filename with the ARC extension (such as REPORTS.ARC), XTreeGold uses the Arc method to archive the file.

If you have XTreeGold 2.5, you can also type in a filename with an EXE extension (such as REPORTS.EXE) and XTreeGold will create a special kind of Zip file — a self-extracting Zip file. A self-extracting Zip file can reconstitute itself whenever you type the filename (such as REPORTS) at the system prompt and press Enter. This is especially helpful if you're giving the file to someone who may not have (or know how to use) an unzip program. The disadvantage to this is that a "self-extracting" engine must be placed in the archive file which, naturally, makes the file larger than a regular Zip file. You're trading size for simplicity. (It's always something.)

For this example, however, I wanted to make a nice, normal Zip file. When XTreeGold asked me to name the archive file, I typed REPORTS and pressed Enter. What a surprise! Gold presented all those darned options, shown at the bottom of Figure 9-7.

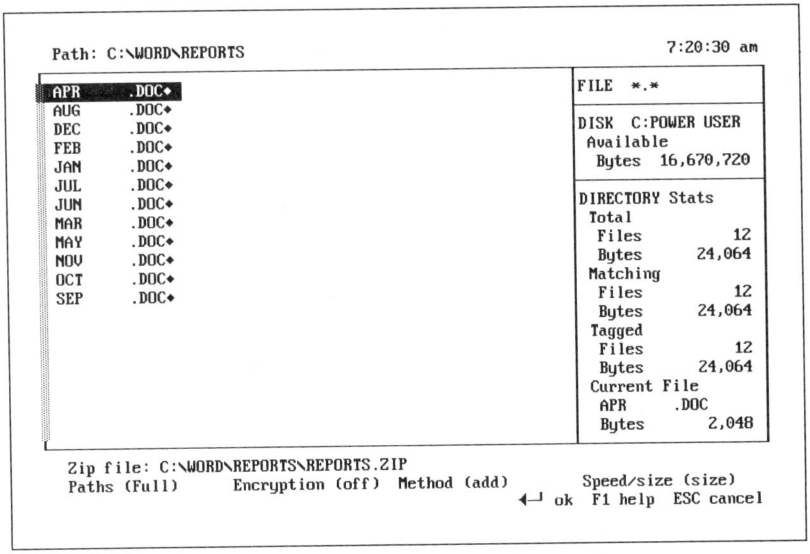

```
Path: C:\WORD\REPORTS                          7:20:30 am

APR      .DOC♦           FILE  *.*
AUG      .DOC♦
DEC      .DOC♦           DISK  C:POWER USER
FEB      .DOC♦           Available
JAN      .DOC♦             Bytes   16,670,720
JUL      .DOC♦
JUN      .DOC♦           DIRECTORY Stats
MAR      .DOC♦           Total
MAY      .DOC♦             Files              12
NOV      .DOC♦             Bytes          24,064
OCT      .DOC♦           Matching
SEP      .DOC♦             Files              12
                           Bytes          24,064
                         Tagged
                           Files              12
                           Bytes          24,064
                         Current File
                           APR       .DOC
                           Bytes           2,048

Zip file: C:\WORD\REPORTS\REPORTS.ZIP
Paths (Full)     Encryption (off)  Method (add)    Speed/size (size)
                                              ↵ ok   F1 help  ESC cancel
```

Figure 9-7: The options at the bottom of the screen reflect the Zip process.

Paths

There are two variations of the Paths options. You may select either Paths (Full) or Paths (None). The Paths (Full) option tells Gold to not only archive the files, but also keep track of which directory the files are in. Later, when you restore the files, you can choose to use this information to re-create the paths (this is especially helpful if you are reconstituting a crashed disk). You'll have to judge for yourself whether this option is for you or not. In any case, the default is Paths (Full); you can press P to change the option to (None).

Encryption

The Encryption option adds a level of security to your archive file. Normally, when you create an archive file, *anyone* can extract the contents as long as they use the correct program. Encryption allows you to add a password to your compressed file. Then, only those with the right password can access it. A password can be up to 32 characters long. (However, don't outsmart yourself with bizarre and difficult-to-type passwords. If you forget the password, you're out of luck.) This option is off by default, and you'll see Encryption (off) at the bottom of the screen. Press E to toggle this option to Encryption (on).

Method

The Method option is used when you are *adding* files to an existing archive file. When you are creating a new archive, `method` is in lowercase, which means it is not an option (you can press M, but nothing will happen. (More on Method later.)

Speed/size

Even *within* the compression methods there are different levels of compression. You can request a higher rate of compression (more bytes into less space), but the smaller size file takes longer for XTreeGold to create (we're talking a difference of seconds, not minutes). If you want the smallest archive size possible, select Size. If you just want it *now*, select Speed. Press S to toggle between speed and size.

After specifying all the available options, press Enter to finally, actually create a Zip file. After XTreeGold is finished, the name of the Zip file appears on-screen. As you can see in Figure 9-8, REPORTS.ZIP appears along with my other files. I can now delete my original files because they've all been neatly packed in the archive file "suitcase."

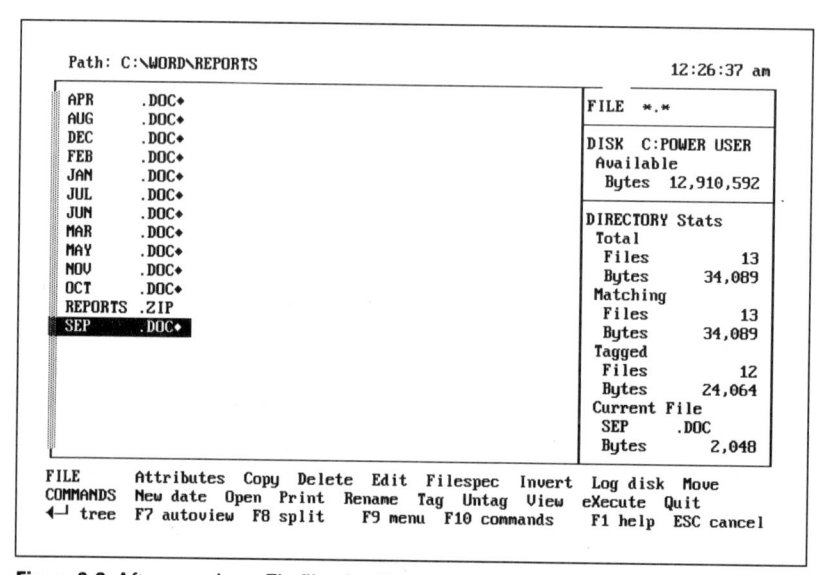

```
Path: C:\WORD\REPORTS                                          12:26:37 am
  APR      .DOC•
  AUG      .DOC•                         FILE  *.*
  DEC      .DOC•
  FEB      .DOC•                         DISK  C:POWER USER
  JAN      .DOC•                         Available
  JUL      .DOC•                           Bytes    12,910,592
  JUN      .DOC•
  MAR      .DOC•                         DIRECTORY Stats
  MAY      .DOC•                         Total
  NOV      .DOC•                           Files            13
  OCT      .DOC•                           Bytes        34,089
  REPORTS  .ZIP                          Matching
  SEP      .DOC•                           Files            13
                                           Bytes        34,089
                                         Tagged
                                           Files            12
                                           Bytes        24,064
                                         Current File
                                           SEP      .DOC
                                           Bytes         2,048

FILE       Attributes  Copy  Delete  Edit  Filespec  Invert  Log disk  Move
COMMANDS   New date    Open  Print   Rename  Tag  Untag  View  eXecute  Quit
  ↵ tree   F7 autoview  F8 split    F9 menu  F10 commands   F1 help  ESC cancel
```

Figure 9-8: After creating a Zip file, the file appears in the Directory window along with all the files that constitute it.

Opening an archived file

Looking inside a compressed file is called *opening an archive.* Opening an archive is not the same thing as removing a file from an archive. (Before you can remove a file from an archive, however, you have to open it. Removing files from archives is called *extracting.* See the next section for how to extract a file.)

To make sure all the Word documents are indeed in my newly created REPORTS.ZIP file, I highlight the file and press Alt-F5. Figure 9-9 shows the results. Notice the `No Files!` message in the Small file window. This appears because when you create an archive file using `Paths (Full)`, the location of the files is preserved as well. In this example, the cursor is highlighting the root directory, in which no files exist.

To see the files in the archive, you can either highlight the \WORD\REPORTS directory or use the Branch command, located at the bottom of the screen in Figure 9-9, to show all files in the current branch in one list. The files are all there, as you can see in Figure 9-10.

Though the screen in Figure 9-10 looks a lot like a full file display, there is one important addition: the percentage of compression is shown in the middle of the file statistics list. The Statistics box on the right now deals solely with the

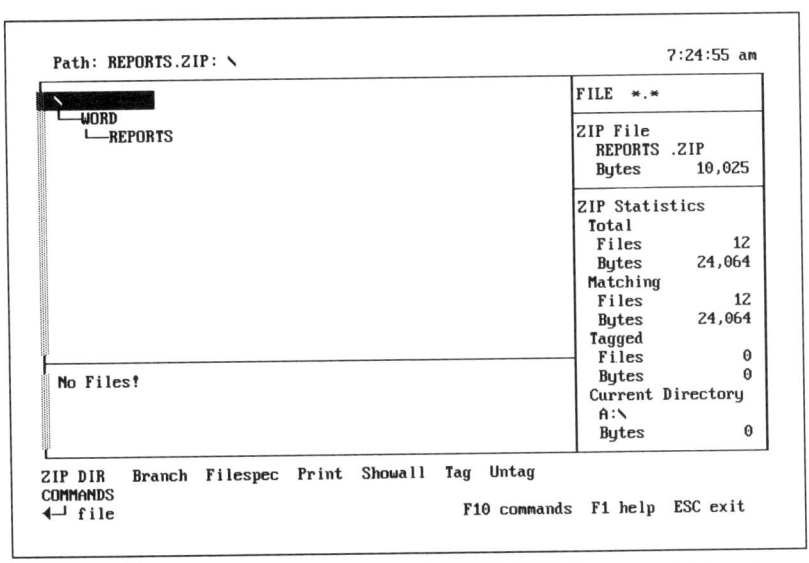

```
Path: REPORTS.ZIP: \                                  7:24:55 am
 \                                            ┌─────────────────────┐
  └─WORD                                      │FILE  *.*            │
      └─REPORTS                               │                     │
                                              │ZIP File             │
                                              │  REPORTS .ZIP       │
                                              │  Bytes      10,025  │
                                              │                     │
                                              │ZIP Statistics       │
                                              │ Total               │
                                              │  Files          12  │
                                              │  Bytes      24,064  │
                                              │ Matching            │
                                              │  Files          12  │
                                              │  Bytes      24,064  │
                                              │ Tagged              │
                                              │  Files           0  │
   No Files!                                  │  Bytes           0  │
                                              │Current Directory    │
                                              │ A:\                 │
                                              │  Bytes           0  │
                                              └─────────────────────┘
 ZIP DIR   Branch  Filespec  Print  Showall  Tag  Untag
 COMMANDS
   ↵ file                                     F10 commands  F1 help  ESC exit
```

Figure 9-9: The zipped files appear in the \WORD\REPORTS directory, which is why the `No files!` message appears when the cursor is highlighting the root directory.

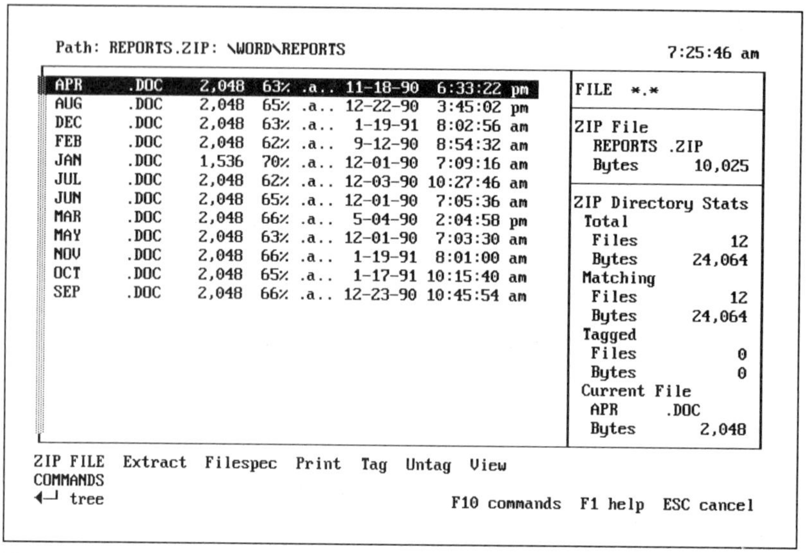

```
Path: REPORTS.ZIP: \WORD\REPORTS                          7:25:46 am

 APR     .DOC   2,048  63%  .a..  11-18-90   6:33:22 pm   FILE    *.*
 AUG     .DOC   2,048  65%  .a..  12-22-90   3:45:02 pm
 DEC     .DOC   2,048  63%  .a..   1-19-91   8:02:56 am   ZIP File
 FEB     .DOC   2,048  62%  .a..   9-12-90   8:54:32 am     REPORTS .ZIP
 JAN     .DOC   1,536  70%  .a..  12-01-90   7:09:16 am     Bytes       10,025
 JUL     .DOC   2,048  62%  .a..  12-03-90  10:27:46 am
 JUN     .DOC   2,048  65%  .a..  12-01-90   7:05:36 am   ZIP Directory Stats
 MAR     .DOC   2,048  66%  .a..   5-04-90   2:04:58 pm     Total
 MAY     .DOC   2,048  63%  .a..  12-01-90   7:03:30 am       Files         12
 NOV     .DOC   2,048  66%  .a..   1-19-91   8:01:00 am       Bytes     24,064
 OCT     .DOC   2,048  65%  .a..   1-17-91  10:15:40 am     Matching
 SEP     .DOC   2,048  66%  .a..  12-23-90  10:45:54 am       Files         12
                                                             Bytes     24,064
                                                           Tagged
                                                             Files          0
                                                             Bytes          0
                                                           Current File
                                                             APR      .DOC
                                                             Bytes      2,048

 ZIP FILE    Extract  Filespec  Print  Tag  Untag  View
 COMMANDS
 ┘  tree                                   F10 commands  F1 help  ESC cancel
```

Figure 9-10: Alt-F5 opens a Zip display window that shows the zipped files and their compression ratios.

current Zip file. You can see that the size of the REPORTS.ZIP file is 10,025 bytes. However, the total size of the files in the Zip file (when extracted) is 24,064 bytes. That's quite a savings, space-wise.

When you are looking at a zipped file like this, some familiar commands are available: Filespec, Print, Tag, Untag, and View (and F10). These options work as expected on the currently open, compressed file. In addition, however, there is a new command, Extract. The Extract command is used for copying and uncompressing a file (or files) from an archive.

Extracting a file from an archive

To extract a file from an open archive file, first press T to tag the file and then press E to extract it. If you want to extract all the archived files, press Ctrl-T to tag all the files and then press Ctrl-E to extract all the tagged files. From this point on, the process works just like copying or moving any file or group of files. XTreeGold first requests a destination for the extracted or restored file and asks if you wish to replace an existing file in that location.

Modifying an existing compressed file

After you create a Zip file (and copy it to a floppy disk), you don't necessarily *have* to delete the source files from your hard disk. You can continue using them. Then, when it's time to back up again, you can *update* or *freshen* the existing Zip file. (Updating and freshening are quicker than creating another archive file from scratch.)

In the running example, I made changes to some of the spreadsheet files, but I can't remember which files. I want to be sure REPORTS.ZIP has current versions of the other files. First, I tag the files that were originally compressed (you can also tag any new files you wish to add to the compressed file at this point). Then I used the traditional Ctrl-F5 key combination, just as though I were creating a new archive file. XTreeGold asks for the name of the file I want to compress next, so I type the name of the file (REPORTS.ZIP in this example) and press Enter. The result of these actions is shown in Figure 9-11. At the bottom of the screen in this figure are our old pals `Paths`, `Encryption`, `Method`, and `Speed/size`. However, now Method is available.

There are three ways, or methods, to alter an existing compressed file. The three methods are shown at the bottom of the screen when you create a Zip file or modify an existing compressed file.

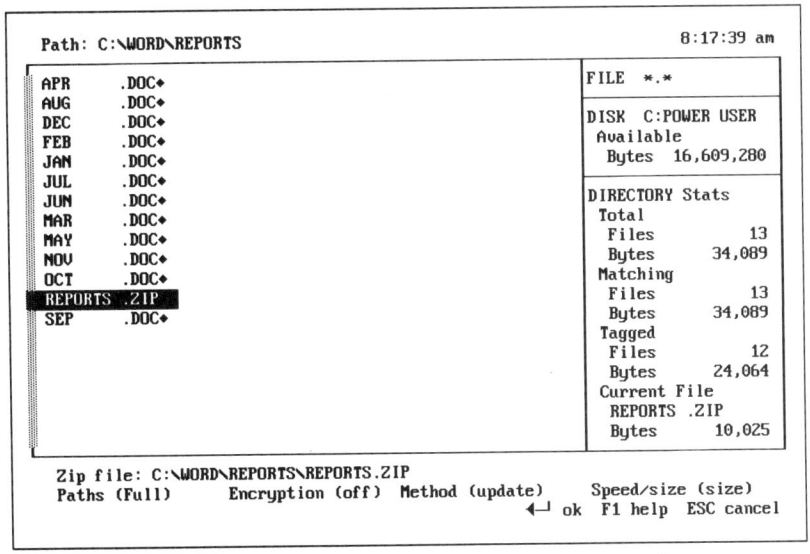

Figure 9-11: The new Zip file appears in the list of files used to create it.

- **Update:** Updating compares any tagged files with those of the same name in a Zip file. If a tagged file is newer, then it replaces the older file in the Zip file. If a tagged file is not in the Arc file, it is then added to the Zip file.
- **Freshen:** Freshening compares the dates of tagged files to the dates of files with the same name in the Zip file and then replaces the newer files as needed. No additional files are added to the Zip file.
- **Add:** Adding means all tagged files will be added to the Arc file. No questions asked.

Press M to cycle through Update, Freshen, and Add. When you have selected the method you want to use, press Enter and XTreeGold will archive away.

Archiving with XTree For Windows

The main difference between archiving files in XTreeGold, XTreePro Gold, and XTree for Windows is that XTree for Windows does not use Arc at all, only Zip.

Creating and working with Zip files in XTree for Windows is simple. In fact, if you understand how to copy a group of files, you're 90 percent there. There are two ways to create a Zip file in XTree for Windows: a shortcut, and a longer method that provides some customization options.

Using the shortcut

Select the files you want to Zip and then press Ctrl+C (yes, the Copy command) or choose the Copy icon on the Tool Palette. (If you haven't learned the Copy command, folks, now is a good time to head for Chapter 7, "XTree for Windows Quick Reference Guide.") Anyway, after you invoke the Copy command, XTree for Windows presents the Copy dialog box, shown in Figure 9-12.

Here's the trick. When you type a filename ending with the ZIP extension (such as 1992.ZIP) in the Copy Selected Directories and Files to: text box, XTree for Windows assumes you want to create an archive-type file. XTree for Windows then asks for confirmation that you want to create a Zip file. Choose Yes and XTree complies with your wishes, creating a new Zip file that contains the selected files. That's it!

Chapter 9: Archiving with XTree

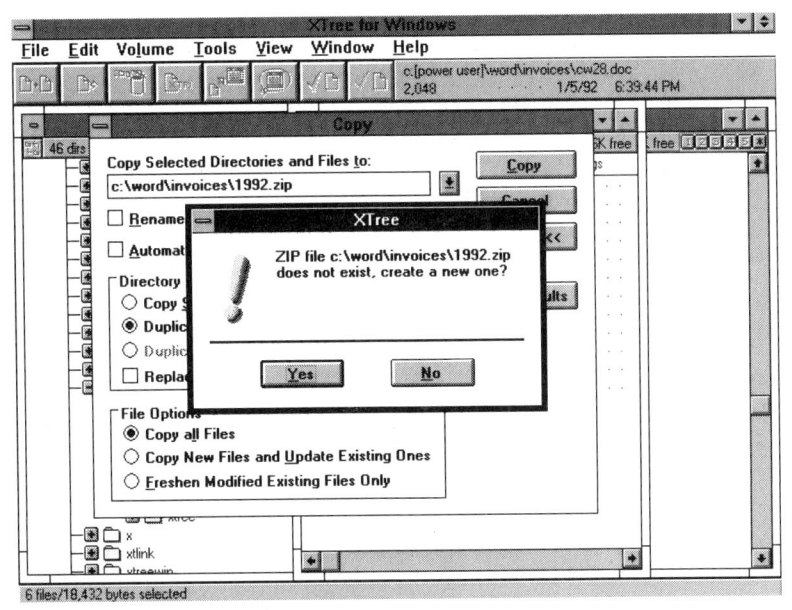

Figure 9-12: After specifying a Zip file as a destination for your selected files, XTree for Windows confirms that you really want to create a Zip file.

Zipping the long way

The long way to create a Zip file requires an extra step, but this method allows you to customize your archive file. The first step is to create an empty Zip shell. (This is like getting an empty box in which to store your files.)

Create the empty Zip shell by selecting Volume ⇨ New ZIP (or press Ctrl+Z) from a Directory window. The New ZIP dialog box appears and from here you enter a name for the new Zip file (but don't specify an extension). Though you can press Enter at this point to begin the Zip process, you can first select Options to see those customization opportunities I promised you. The customization features are shown in Figure 9-13 and explained next.

Compression Options: You have two compression options, Optimize for Size and Optimize for Speed. The real choice is between "slow and small" and "fast and big." Creating a Zip file requires a lot of calculating on the part of the Zip utility. The smaller you want the final zipped file to be, the more calculations and the longer it takes. We're not talking hours vs. minutes here — unless you've got some monster files. Sometimes space is critical, sometimes time is worth more. Make your choice and move on. (A sound philosophy in any situation.)

Part IV: XTree Extras

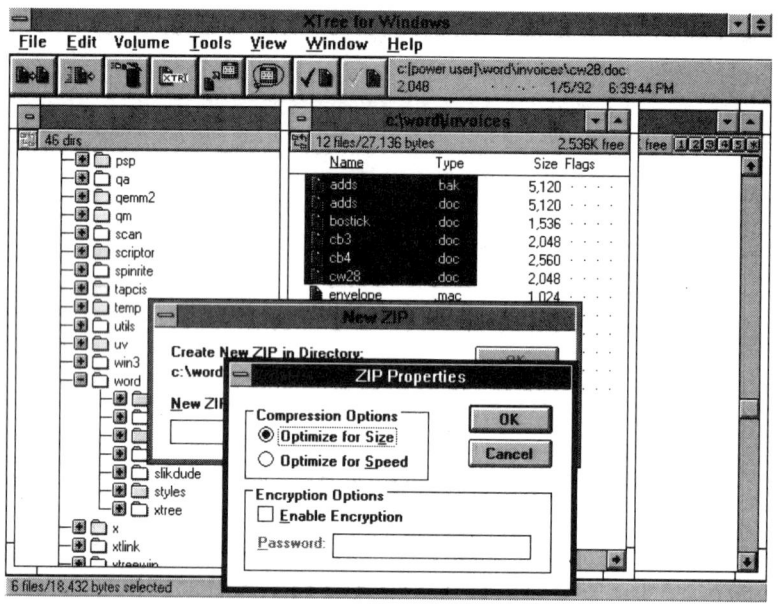

Figure 9-13: Select Volume ⇨ New ZIP to create an empty Zip shell.

Encryption Options: Encryption adds a level of security to your archive file. Normally, when you create an archive file, *anyone* can extract the contents as long as they use the correct program. Encryption allows you to add a password to your compressed file. Then, only those with the right password can have access it. (However, don't outsmart yourself with bizarre and difficult-to-type passwords. If you forget the password, you're out of luck.) By default, encryption is turned off.

Once you've selected your customization options, choose OK and the Zip file will appear in the Directory window. If the File Size display is turned on, you'll see that the file contains 0 bytes. Remember, you're just creating the empty box to put the zipped files into.

Next, select the files you want to put into the empty Zip file. Press Ctrl+C or choose Tools ⇨ Copy to open the Copy dialog box. Type in the name of the Zip file you just created in the Copy dialog box and choose Copy — the files will be copied, compressed, and put into the Zip file.

Amending Zip file properties

If you're kicking yourself now because you realize you should have given your Zip file a password when you created it (or if you created the Zip file using the shortcut and you now want to customize it), relax. You can still apply the customization options, retroactively.

Just select the Zip file that you want to customize, and then select Volume ⇨ ZIP Properties (or press Ctrl+Z) to pop up the ZIP Properties dialog box, where you can create a password as well as select the compression and encryption options.

When is a Zip file like a drive?

Always.

Granted, you can copy, delete, move, and see the Zip file listed in the appropriate Directory window just like any other file. However, be aware that XTree for Windows treats archived files like a "Volume" (that is, as another drive). As a result, there are some additional Zip tricks you can use that you might not have otherwise considered possible with an ordinary file.

Using File ⇨ Open to view Zip files

You can highlight a Zip file and select File ⇨ Open to see what's inside. A Directory window opens to display the files contained within the Zip file. These files can be copied, deleted, and viewed just like the other files. However, you can't edit or launch a file until it has been copied from the Zip file.

If you copy a file into a Zip file window, that new file will be automatically compressed. If you copy a file *from* a Zip file, that file will automatically be decompressed. When you copy files into your Zip file, remember all the normal rules of the Copy command apply. For instance, you can't have two files in the same place with the same name. Also, you can specify Freshen Modified Existing Files Only (copy only those files that are updates to existing files), or Copy New Files and Update Existing Ones (which automatically compares the destination files with the source files, keeping the newer of the two) to make sure you've got the most current version in your Zip file.

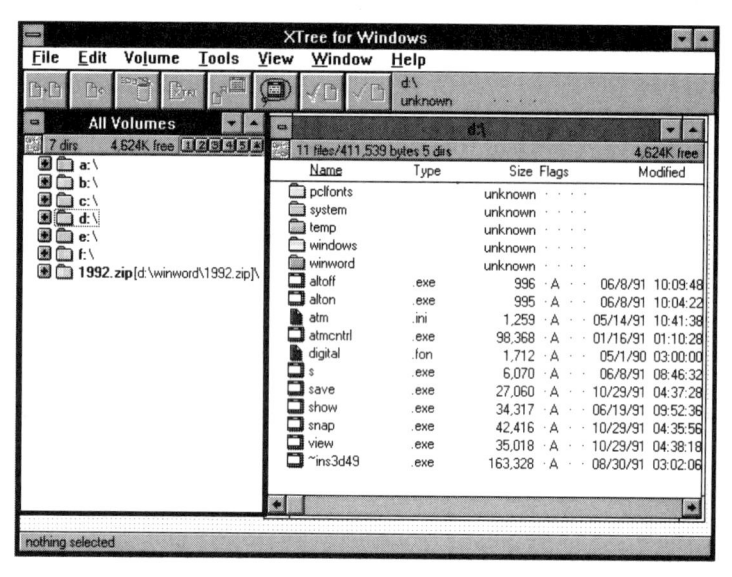

Figure 9-14: The last item in the Tree window on the left is actually a Zip file. You can treat it like a volume, as shown in the Directory window on the right.

Mounting Zip files

Since XTree for Windows thinks your Zip file is a volume, you can add the Zip file to your tree structure by first highlighting the Zip file and then selecting Volume ⇨ Mount ZIP. The file will be added to the *bottom* of the tree structure, as shown in Figure 9-14. To remove the Zip file from the tree, highlight the Zip file and then select Volume ⇨ Unmount ZIP.

Summary

▶ Once files have been tagged (or highlighted) they may collected together into a single archived file (like clothes in a suitcase) for easy storage or transport.

▶ Opening an archive file lets you see the files stored within.

▶ If you want to use a file in an archive, you must first open the archive and then extract (or remove) the file.

Chapter 10
Linking Computers with XTreeLink

In This Chapter
▶ How to get two computers to talk to each other using XTreeLink
▶ Transferring data from one computer to another
▶ Running a remote computer from a local keyboard

XTreeLink, a brand-new program that is being included in the XTree for Windows and XTreeGold packages, runs completely independently of XTree for Windows or XTreeGold. With XTreeLink, and the appropriate connecting cable, you can connect two computers (a laptop and a desktop, for instance) and send files (and commands) back and forth across the cable. In fact, when the two computers are connected, they become one giant computer, controlled from one keyboard. This is a huge boon to people who have two computers with incompatible drive types (for example, a desktop with a 5¼-inch drive and a laptop with a 3½-inch drive). Or when you want to transfer a lot of files from one computer to another (and doing so via floppy would be tedious at best). Or when a file is too big to fit on a floppy. Frankly, there are 101 fun ways to use XTreeLink.

When XTreeLink is running, you are free to perform any operations you want on either computer, including (but not limited to):

- Loading XTree on one computer and then logging the other computer's drives so you can copy, delete, make a directory, or use any other XTree command on that computer.
- Carrying out any MS-DOS commands at the DOS prompt.
- Running a program or a batch file located on the other computer (though this operation can be painfully slow).

Although a desktop-to-laptop connection is used as the example throughout this chapter, you are not limited to that configuration. *Any* two computers (two desktops, two laptops, and so on) can be linked as long as they are both running MS-DOS (version 3.1 or higher).

Once the two computers are linked, you perform operations on the *local* computer, which is the "command central" for linking operations. The *remote* computer is the machine being accessed.

> **NOTE:** Either the desktop or the laptop can be used as the local or remote computer. Generally, it's more common to use the more powerful computer as the local computer.

Preparing Computers for Linking

In order for XTreeLink to do it's job, the two computers must be hooked up via a special cable (plugged into the back of both machines). Step one is to get the special cable. There are three options here:

- Shell out some bucks and order the cable via the order form that came in the XTreeLink package. (If you can't find the order form, call XTree Co.)
- If you own Traveling Software's LapLink, Fifth Generation's Brooklyn Bridge, or Rupp Brothers' FastLynx, you already own the cable. Huzzah!
- Make your own cable following the specifications in the XTreeLink manual. (If you can make your own cable, you don't need any help from me.)

Assuming you are going to buy a cable, you'll be confronted with another question: Do you want a *serial* or a *parallel* cable? The technical differences between serial and parallel cables are not the issue here. What *is* important is what's going on in the back of your two computers.

For instance, generally your printer cable connects to the spot in the back of the computer where a parallel cable is plugged in. (This spot is called the *parallel port.*) If you look at your computer, you may see `LPT`, `Printer`, or something like that where the printer cable is plugged in.

The spot where the serial cable plugs in is called the *serial port.* This port is usually identified by a `COM` label. The serial port may have a modem or a mouse hooked up to it. Often, computers have more than one serial port (the second is labeled `COM2`).

If you don't have any unused ports, decide which port is easier to get to. Then place your order. (Also, while you're looking at the back of your computer, you may notice a lot of dust back there. Now's a good time to clean up your computer's environment.) When your cable arrives, connect it to the appropriate ports.

> **NOTE:** If you want to spend even more money, you can buy a *switcher box* — which allows two devices to share one port. If you plan to use XTreeLink frequently, this alternative allows you to have a permanent setup.

Preparing the XTreeLink Installation

Part of what XTreeLink does is trick DOS into thinking your computer has more drives than it actually does. In fact, it tricks your computer into thinking that the laptop's drives are actually part of the desktop, or vice versa. Before XTreeLink can play out its deception, however, you have to make sure DOS is prepared to deal with the extra drives (DOS insists on being told about these things beforehand). The next section will help you determine if you need to make changes to your CONFIG.SYS file before you attempt any linking.

Counting your drives

You can perform a simple test to find out whether changes to the CONFIG.SYS file on your local computer are necessary. From a DOS prompt, type **LASTDRIVE** and press Enter. The computer will reply with the message LASTDRIVE=letter. The standard reply is the letter *E,* which as Vanna White could tell you, is the fifth letter of the alphabet. This means that DOS is prepared to acknowledge the existence of five drives.

If your local computer and your remote computer combined have no more than a total of five drives (including floppy drives), you *don't* have to modify the CONFIG.SYS file on your local computer. Lucky you! Just skip ahead to "Installing XTreeLink," the next section in this chapter.

If, however, the total number of drives you *wish to access* is six or more, you'll need to modify your CONFIG.SYS file to let DOS know you want to access some additional drives. If you only want to access five of those drives, you don't have to modify CONFIG.SYS. If you don't remember how to edit your CONFIG.SYS file, see "Editing with 1Word," in Chapter 3, "XTree for DOS Quick Reference Guide."

Modifying CONFIG.SYS with XTreeGold

If you have XTreeGold, you can edit your CONFIG.SYS file with 1Word, XTree's text editor. Simply highlight CONFIG.SYS, located in your root directory, and press E for edit. The 1Word text editor pops up and you can then make modifications to CONFIG.SYS.

Once you are there, go to the bottom of the file and on a separate line, type **LASTDRIVE=*letter*** (use a letter of the alphabet the allows for the number of drives you wish to use — LASTDRIVE=G allows for seven drives). Next, save the file, exit 1Word, and then exit XTreeGold. From a DOS prompt, reboot your computer to make the changes take effect.

Modifying CONFIG.SYS with XTree for Windows

If you have XTree for Windows, you can call up CONFIG.SYS in the Windows text editor, Notepad. Notepad is located, by default, in the Accessories program group in Program Manager. Double-click the Notepad icon to start the text editor. Select File ⇨ Open and type **C:\CONFIG.SYS** in the File Name: text box and press Enter.

Once you are there, go to the bottom of the file and on a separate line, type **LASTDRIVE=***letter* (use a letter of the alphabet that allows for the number of drives you wish to use — LASTDRIVE=G allows for seven drives). Next, select File ⇨ Exit, and answer Yes to the message box asking if you want to save changes to the file. Next, exit Windows, making sure to properly quit any currently running programs first. From a DOS prompt, reboot your computer to make the changes take effect.

Installing XTreeLink

If you've survived the cable installation and any necessary editing of CONFIG.SYS, you'll be happy to know that the rest is easy. The first step is to copy XTreeLink onto the hard disks of both computers. If you've got XTreeGold or XTree for Windows on both computers, it makes sense to copy the XTreeLink program file into the directory that contains XTree (just to keep the universe in order). If you don't have XTree on one of your computers, the next best place to put XTreeLink is in the root directory (because everyone has one of those). You must repeat this process on both computers.

> **NOTE:** If the XTreeLink floppy fits in your B: drive, be sure to substitute B: for A: in these steps.

Steps: Installing XTreeLink on the host and remote computers

Step 1. Put the XTreeLink disk in the appropriate floppy drive (either A: or B:).

Step 2. Depending on the state of your software, use one of the following options:

- If you have XTree for Windows, XTreeLink will automatically be installed in the directory that contains XTree for Windows (generally, XTREEWIN).

- If you don't have a copy of XTreeGold or XTree for Windows on one of the computers you'll be connecting, copy XTreeLink into the root directory of that computer by typing **COPY A:XTLINK.COM **.

Running XTreeLink

OK. Your cables are hooked up, your CONFIG is properly SYS'd, and the XTreeLink program is installed on the hard disk of both of your computers. Only one more thing to do before you can actually start using the program: decide which of the two computers is the local computer and which is the remote. Personally, I'd choose the computer that has the most comfortable chair in front of it. You can use your own criteria.

Activating the remote computer

If the computers are connected via a *serial* cable, type **XTLINK S** and press Enter at the system prompt of the remote computer. If the computers are connected via a *parallel* cable, type **XTLINK P** at the system prompt and press Enter. P stands for parallel and S stands for serial; XTree needs to know which kind of cable is being used. Once you've entered these commands, your remote computer will indicate that it's "waiting" to be contacted by the local computer, as illustrated in Figure 10-1. As long as you see Waiting at the bottom of the screen, the two computers are not yet in communication.

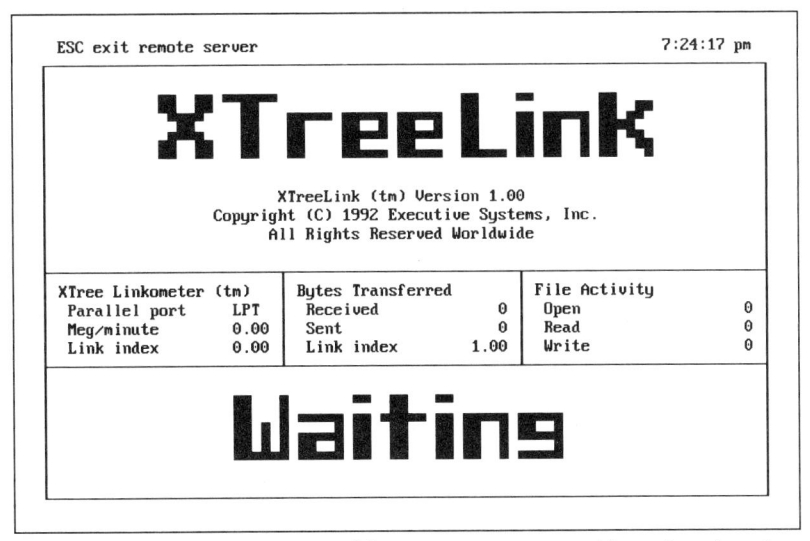

```
ESC exit remote server                                    7:24:17 pm

                        XTreeLink
                   XTreeLink (tm) Version 1.00
                Copyright (C) 1992 Executive Systems, Inc.
                      All Rights Reserved Worldwide

  XTree Linkometer (tm)  | Bytes Transferred    | File Activity
  Parallel port    LPT   | Received         0   | Open          0
  Meg/minute      0.00   | Sent             0   | Read          0
  Link index      0.00   | Link index    1.00   | Write         0

                          Waiting
```

Figure 10-1: The XTreeLink screen of the remote computer, waiting to hear from the local (or main) computer.

Activating the local computer

If the computers are connected via a *serial* cable, at the keyboard of the local computer, type **XTLINK S L** at the system prompt and press Enter. If the computers are connected via a *parallel* cable, type **XTLINK P L** at the system prompt and press Enter. The L switch in these examples stands for the local computer. At this point two things will happen:

1. The local computer will display a message listing the mapped drive letters. A drive is considered mapped when DOS assigns it a letter. (If the last drive on your local computer is drive C:, the remote computer's hard disk would be "mapped" as drive D: — the next available letter.)

2. The remote computer screen will confirm the connection has been established, as shown in Figure 10-2.

NOTE: Your laptop's floppy drive will *not* be recognized by XTreeLink unless, when you invoke XTreeLink, you specifically request to have it mapped. (Including the floppy drive on the remote is considered to be an option.)

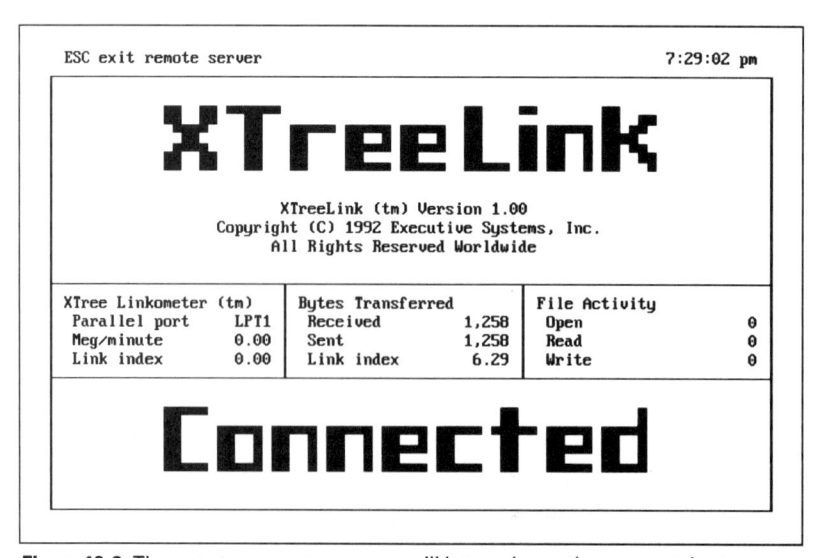

```
ESC exit remote server                                    7:29:02 pm

                        XTreeLink
                      XTreeLink (tm) Version 1.00
                   Copyright (C) 1992 Executive Systems, Inc.
                         All Rights Reserved Worldwide

   XTree Linkometer (tm)  | Bytes Transferred    | File Activity
   Parallel port    LPT1  | Received     1,258   | Open        0
   Meg/minute       0.00  | Sent         1,258   | Read        0
   Link index       0.00  | Link index    6.29   | Write       0

                          Connected
```

Figure 10-2: The remote computer screen will let you know the moment the two computers are "connected."

Using XTreeLink

Once XTreeLink is running, doubtless the first thing you'll want to do (after you've alerted the media) is to run XTree.

Running XTreeGold with XTreeLink

Once you load XTreeGold, you can log onto any of the mapped drives. Figure 10-3 shows XTreeGold logged onto the D: drive of a laptop. You can now copy, move, print, view, and so on.

Running XTree for Windows with XTreeLink

Once you've invoked Windows and XTree for Windows, an All Volumes Tree window appears on-screen. In the example in Figure 10-4, this window shows the remote computer's hard disk drive as D:. Once you see the remote's drives, you can proceed as if those drives are local. You can copy, move, print, and view files on the remote, as well as run programs stored on that computer's hard drive.

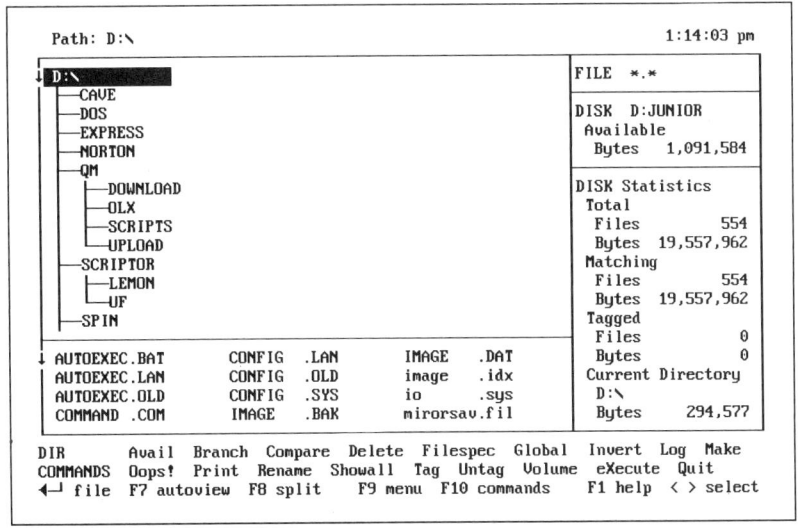

```
Path: D:\                                               1:14:03 pm
┌─────────────────────────────────────────┬──────────────────────┐
│↓ D:\                                    │ FILE  *.*            │
│ ├─CAVE                                  │                      │
│ ├─DOS                                   │ DISK  D:JUNIOR       │
│ ├─EXPRESS                               │ Available            │
│ ├─NORTON                                │   Bytes    1,091,584 │
│ ├─QM                                    │                      │
│ │ ├─DOWNLOAD                            │ DISK Statistics      │
│ │ ├─OLX                                 │ Total                │
│ │ ├─SCRIPTS                             │   Files          554 │
│ │ └─UPLOAD                              │   Bytes   19,557,962 │
│ ├─SCRIPTOR                              │ Matching             │
│ │ ├─LEMON                               │   Files          554 │
│ │ └─UF                                  │   Bytes   19,557,962 │
│ └─SPIN                                  │ Tagged               │
│                                         │   Files            0 │
│↓ AUTOEXEC.BAT   CONFIG  .LAN  IMAGE .DAT│   Bytes            0 │
│  AUTOEXEC.LAN   CONFIG  .OLD  image .idx│ Current Directory    │
│  AUTOEXEC.OLD   CONFIG  .SYS  io    .sys│ D:\                  │
│  COMMAND .COM   IMAGE   .BAK  mirorsav.fil│ Bytes      294,577 │
├─────────────────────────────────────────┴──────────────────────┤
│ DIR      Avail  Branch  Compare  Delete  Filespec  Global  Invert  Log  Make │
│ COMMANDS Oops!  Print   Rename   Showall Tag       Untag   Volume  eXecute Quit│
│ ←┘ file  F7 autoview  F8 split    F9 menu   F10 commands    F1 help  < > select│
└────────────────────────────────────────────────────────────────┘
```

Figure 10-3: Once the two computers are talking, you can log onto the remote computer's hard drive (in this case drive D:) and perform XTreeGold commands.

Part IV: XTree Extras

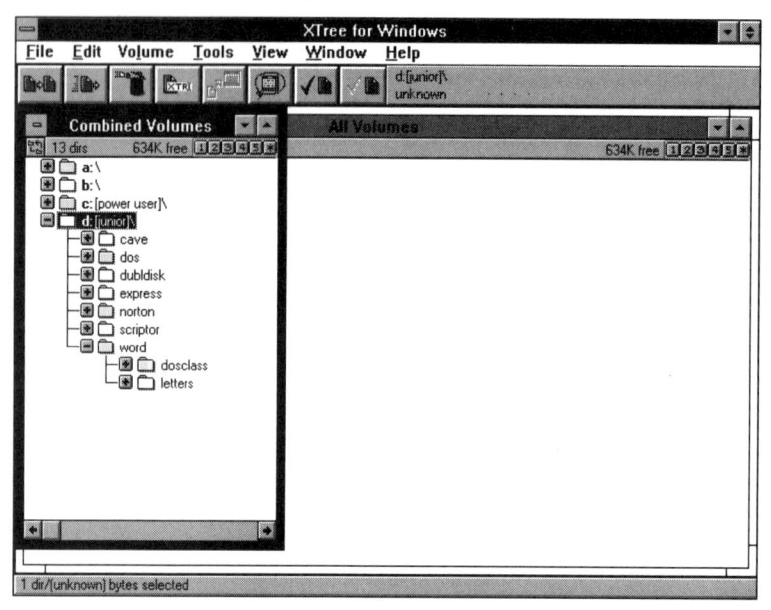

Figure 10-4: XTree for Windows recognizes a remote computer's hard disk — drive 0: in this case.

When you log onto your remote computer, the remote computer screen will report that it is Transferring, and the "XTree Linkometer" will display a dizzying amount of data to prove it, as shown in Figure 10-5.

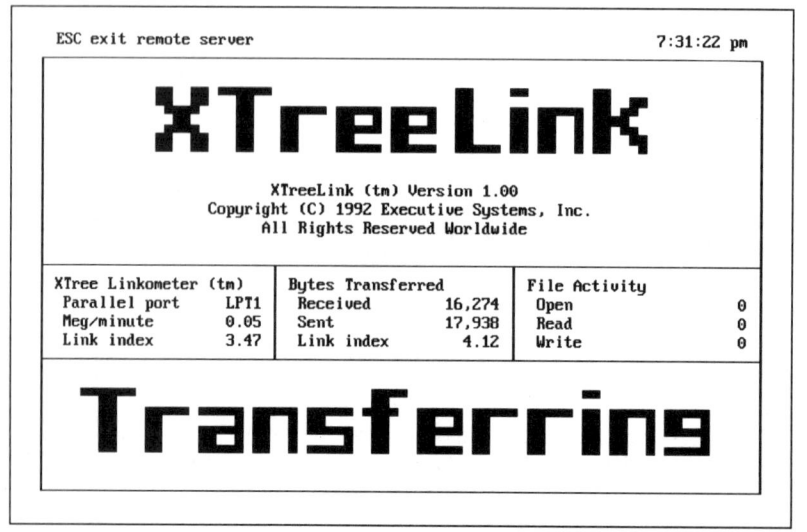

Figure 10-5: When information is passed between local and remote computers, Transferring appears on the remote, and statistics describing the data stream are calculated.

Using XTreeLink option switches

If you type **XTLINK** and press Enter, you'll get a list of all the various options available, with a brief explanation. I've already described three option switches (P, S, and L). More switches and their usage are detailed as follows:

XTLINK M   M stands for Map. This command shows a list of the mapped drive letters (so you can see what remote drive has been assigned which letter, if you need reminders).

XTLINK RF   When invoking XTreeLink on the local drive, this command sequence means to map all drives (including floppy drives) on the remote computer.

XTLINK P L RF   The command sequence in this example means that XTreeLink should look for a parallel connection, that the command is being issued from the local computer, and that XTreeLink should map all "Removable and Fixed" drives on remote computer. Note: RF has to come *after* the P and L options.

XTLINK P L R   The command sequence in this example means that XTreeLink should look for a parallel connection, that the command is being issued from the local computer, and that XTreeLink should map only the removable (floppy) drives on the remote computer. Note: R has to come *after* the P and L option switches.

Exiting XTreeLink

When you are finished with XTreeLink, you can disconnect from the remote computer by pressing Esc.

On the local computer, you must type **XTLINK U** and press Enter at the system prompt. The U switch stands for Unload, which removes the program from memory. Do not try to remove XTreeLink from memory while in a command shell or Windows. (Yanking a program out of memory cannot be done safely if another program is also in memory.)

Summary

▶ When two computers are linked via XTreeLink, one computer is called the *local* computer (this is the one you type on and look at), the other computer is called the *remote* computer.

▶ Once XTreeLink is running, the remote computer's drives are mapped onto the local computer, creating one computer with lots of drives.

▶ Any command you give at the DOS prompt on the local computer (including running programs, launching batch files, and so on) can be carried out on either the local or remote computer.

Part V
Appendixes

Appendix A 329
Shortcuts: Command Keys and Function Keys

Appendix B 345
Laptop Configuration

Appendix C 355
Insider Info from XTree Tech Support

Appendix D 367
Where to Go from Here

Appendix E 370
An Unapologetic History of XTree

Appendix F 375
Pop Quiz Answers

The 5th Wave   By Rich Tennant

"NAAAH - HE'S NOT THAT SMART. HE WON'T BACK UP HIS HARD DISK, FORGETS TO CONSISTENTLY NAME HIS FILES, AND DROOLS ALL OVER THE KEYBOARD."

Appendix A
Shortcuts: Command Keys and Function Keys

On the following pages you'll find the most-often used shortcuts for each version of XTree. In the section for each program, tables of the most popular command keys, for both Directory and File windows, are followed by a table of function key commands. I provide these shortcuts as cheat sheets — quick refreshers. All these commands have been detailed in the chapters in this book, but if you come across something you don't recall, use the Index and Table of Contents to point you in the right direction.

Keep in mind that in XTree for DOS, *where* you are in the program is as important as what you press. For instance, pressing F can mean File specification or Format, depending on whether you're in the Directory window or the View window. In XTree for Windows, what you *highlight* determines what commands are available (highlight a file for file commands, a directory for directory commands).

The cheat sheets are set up as follows:

First, the title of the table tells you whether the commands work from the Directory window or the File window. Second, the *Action* column, on the left, describes the function of the accompanying command, which you'll find in the column on the right, labeled *Key*. Depending on the action you are carrying out, you'll either use the *key* alone, Ctrl-*key,* or Alt-*key*.

Following the command key list for each version of XTree is the function key table for that same version. The first column lists the function key, the second column gives the explanation, including whether you have to be doing a specific operation for the command to be active.

XTree Shortcuts

XTree Directory Window Commands

Action	Key
Display available free space	A
Delete current directory	D
Change the current filespec	F
Change the File display	Alt-F
Log a new disk	L
Make a directory	M
Print files, paths, or the tree	P
Rename the current directory	R
Open Showall file window	S
Show all tagged files	Ctrl-S
Change the sort criteria	Alt-S
Tag all files in directory	T
Tag all files on disk	Ctrl-T
Tag by attribute	Alt-T
Untag all files in directory	U
Untag all files on disk	Ctrl-U
Untag by attribute	Alt-U
Name a disk volume label	V
Execute or run programs	X

XTree File Window Commands

Action	Key
Change a file's attributes	A
Change a tagged file's attributes	Ctrl-A
Copy the current file	C
Copy tagged files	Ctrl-C
Copy tagged files and paths to another disk	Alt-C
Delete current file	D
Delete tagged files	Ctrl-D
Change the current filespec	F
Change the File display	Alt-F
Log a new disk	L
Move the current file	M
Move all tagged files	Ctrl-M
Print the current file	P
Print all tagged files	Ctrl-P
Rename the current file	R
Rename all tagged files	Ctrl-R
Change the sort criteria	Alt-S
Tag the current file	T
Tag all displayed files	Ctrl-T
Tag files by attribute	Alt-T
Untag the current file	U
Untag all displayed files	Ctrl-U
Untag files by attribute	Alt-U
View a file's contents	V
Execute or run programs	X
Runs program using least memory	Alt-X

Appendix A: Shortcuts

XTree Function Keys

Function key	Action
F1	Quit XTree.
F2	Get Help.
F3	Cancel a command.
F4	Makes the Directory and File Commands disappear from the bottom of the screen.
F5	Keep filespec. Normally, if you log another drive, the filespec defaults back to *.*. If you set a filespec, press F5, and then log another drive, the filespec will not default back to *.*. This is useful when hunting through several disks for a file.
F10	Locks the Alt key. This is an alternative to holding down the Alt key. Press and release F10 to remain in Alt mode. You may peruse the Alt menu without the physical exertion of holding down the Alt key.

XTreePro Shortcuts

XTreePro Directory Window Commands

Action	Key	Action	Key
Display available free space	A	Release a disk	Alt-R
Delete current directory	D	Open Showall file window	S
Edit a file	Alt-E	Show all tagged files	Ctrl-S
Change the current filespec	F	Change the sort criteria	Alt-S
Change the File display	Alt-F	Tag all files in directory	T
View files on logged disks in a Global file window	G	Tag all files on disk	Ctrl-T
		Tag files by attribute	Alt-T
View tagged files on logged disks in a Global file window	Ctrl-G	Untag all files in directory	U
		Untag all files on disk	Ctrl-U
Log a new disk	L	Untag by attribute	Alt-U
Log a new disk/release logged disks	Alt-L	Name a disk volume label	V
Make a directory	M	Execute or run programs	X
Print files, paths, or the tree	P	Run program/release disk	Alt-X
Exit program	Q		
Exit to the current directory	Alt-Q		

XTreePro File Window Commands

Action	Key	Action	Key
Change a file's attributes	A	Print all tagged files	Ctrl-P
Change tagged file's attributes	Ctrl-A	Exit program	Q
Copy the current file	C	Exit to the current directory	Alt-Q
Copy tagged files	Ctrl-C	Rename the current file	R
Copy tagged files and paths to another disk	Alt-C	Rename all tagged files	Ctrl-R
		Release a disk	Alt-R
Delete current file	D	Change the sort criteria	Alt-S
Delete tagged files	Ctrl-D	Tag the current file	T
Edit the current file	E	Tag all displayed files	Ctrl-T
Change the current filespec	F	Tag files by attribute	Alt-T
Change the File display	Alt-F	Untag the current file	U
Log a new disk	L	Untag all displayed files	Ctrl-U
Log a new disk/release logged disks	Alt-L	Untag files by attribute	Alt-U
		View a file's contents	V
Move the current file	M	Execute or run programs	X
Move all tagged files	Ctrl-M	Reduce XTree to 7K on launch	Alt-X
Print the current file	P		

XTreePro Function Keys

Function key	Action
F1	Get Help.
F2	Open the Destination directory window. When in Copy or Move mode, press F2 to pop up the Destination window. This allows you to merely point to where you want to copy or move your files to.
F9	Ctrl lock. An alternative to holding down the Ctrl key. Press and release F9 to remain in the Ctrl menu. You may peruse the Ctrl menu without the physical exertion of holding down the Alt key.
F10	Locks the Alt key. This is an alternative to holding down the Alt key. Press and release F10 to remain in Alt mode. You may peruse the Alt menu without the physical exertion of holding down the Alt key.

Appendix A: Shortcuts

XTreePro Gold Shortcuts

XTreePro Gold Directory Window Commands

Action	Key
Display available free space	A
Delete current directory	D
Edit a file	Alt-E
Change the current filespec	F
Change the File display	Alt-F
Show files on logged disks in Global file window	G
Show tagged files on logged disks in Global file window	Ctrl-G
Graft directory	Alt-G
Hide/unhide a directory	Alt-H
Reverse tags on files in a directory	I
Reverse tags on files on a disk	Alt-I
Log a new disk	L
Switch to logged disk	Ctrl-L
Log a new disk/unlog the current disk	Alt-L
Make a directory	M
Print files, paths, or the tree	P
Prune a directory	Alt-P

Action	Key
Exit XTreePro Gold	Q
Exit to the current directory	Alt-Q
Rename the current directory	R
Release a disk	Alt-R
Open Showall file window	S
Show all tagged files	Ctrl-S
Change the sort criteria	Alt-S
Tag all files in directory	T
Tag all files on disk	Ctrl-T
Tag by attribute	Alt-T
Untag all files in directory	U
Untag all files on disk	Ctrl-U
Untag by attribute	Alt-U
Name a disk volume label	V
Wash a hard disk	W
Execute or run programs	X
Reduce XTreePro Gold to 7K on launch	Alt-X
Quit XTreePro Gold and save structure	Z

XTreePro Gold File Window Commands

Action	Key
Change a file's attributes	A
Change a tagged file's attributes	Ctrl-A
Copy the current file	C
Copy tagged files	Ctrl-C

Action	Key
Copy tagged files and paths to another disk	Alt-C
Delete current file	D
Delete tagged files	Ctrl-D
Edit the current file	E

(continued)

XTreePro Gold File Window Commands (continued)

Action	Key	Action	Key
Change the current filespec	F	Exit to the current directory	Alt-Q
Change the File display	Alt-F	Rename the current file	R
Reverse tags on one file	I	Rename all tagged files	Ctrl-R
Reverse tags on all files	Ctrl-I	Release a disk	Alt-R
Log a new disk	L	Search tagged files for text	Ctrl-S
Switch to logged disk	Ctrl-L	Change the sort criteria	Alt-S
Log new disk/unlog current disks	Alt-L	Tag the current file	T
Move the current file	M	Tag all displayed files	Ctrl-T
Move all tagged files	Ctrl-M	Tag files by attribute	Alt-T
Change the date on current file	N	Untag the current file	U
Change the date on tagged files	Ctrl-N	Untag all displayed files	Ctrl-U
Launch program associated with a file	O	Untag files by attribute	Alt-U
		View the current file's contents	V
Reduce XTreePro Gold to 7K on launch of program with associated file	Alt-O	View a tagged file's contents	Ctrl-V
		Execute or run programs	X
Print the current file	P	Reduce XTree to 7K on launch	Alt-X
Print all tagged files	Ctrl-P	Quit XTreePro Gold and save structure	Z
Exit program	Q		

XTreePro Gold Function Keys

Function key	Action
F1	Get Help.
F2	Open the Destination directory window. When in Copy, Move, or Graft mode, press F2 to pop up the Destination window. This allows you to merely point to where you want to copy or move your files to.
F2	Update the screen when in a Showall tagged files window; press F2 to redisplay the screen and eliminate those items that have been untagged since Ctrl-S was invoked.
Alt-F2	Formats a floppy disk.
F3	When entering text, displays last response.

(continued)

Appendix A: Shortcuts

XTreePro Gold Function Keys (continued)

Function key	Action
Alt-F3	Relogs the current directory.
F4	Menu toggle. Cycles through the standard Ctrl and Alt menus. Press F4 once and the Ctrl menu will be displayed. Press it again and the Alt menu will be displayed. Press it a third time and you'll cycle back to the standard menu.
F5	Collapses or expands directories two levels below the current directory.
Alt-F5	Opens an Arc file (see Chapter 9).
Ctrl-F5	Archives tagged files (see Chapter 9).
F6	Collapses or expands directories below the current directory.
Ctrl-F6	Merges tags between two file windows.
F7	Autoview. For viewing the contents of a file.
F8	Splits/unsplits the display into two directories.
Alt-F8	Untags all tagged files that have been operated on.
Ctrl-F8	Same as Alt-F8.
F9	Pops up the Application Menu.
Alt-F9	Toggles between the 25-line and 51-line modes for EGA and VGA systems.
F10	Pops up the Quick Reference Help Window.
Alt-F10	Starts the Configuration program.

XTree Easy Shortcuts

XTree Easy Directory Window Commands

Action	Key	Action	Key
Display available free space	A	Print files, paths, or the tree	P
Delete current directory	D	Exit XTree Easy	Q
Edit a file	Alt-E	Exit to the current directory	Alt-Q
Change the current filespec	F	Rename the current directory	R
Change the File display	Alt-F	Open Showall file window	S
Log a new disk	L	Show all tagged files	Ctrl-S
Make a directory	M	Change the sort criteria	Alt-S

(continued)

XTree Easy Directory Window Commands (continued)

Action	Key	Action	Key
Tag all files in directory	T	Untag by attribute	Alt-U
Tag all files on disk	Ctrl-T	Name a disk volume label	V
Tag by attribute	Alt-T	Execute or run programs	X
Untag all files in directory	U	Quit XTreePro Gold and save structure	Z
Untag all files on disk	Ctrl-U		

XTree Easy File Window Commands

Action	Key	Action	Key
Change a file's attributes	A	Print all tagged files	Ctrl-P
Change a tagged file's attributes	Ctrl-A	Exit program	Q
Copy the current file	C	Exit to the current directory	Alt-Q
Copy tagged files	Ctrl-C	Rename the current file	R
Copy tagged files and paths to another disk	Alt-C	Rename all tagged files	Ctrl-R
		Change the sort criteria	Alt-S
Delete current file	D	Tag the current file	T
Delete tagged files	Ctrl-D	Tag all displayed files	Ctrl-T
Edit the current file	E	Tag files by attribute	Alt-T
Change the current filespec	F	Untag the current file	U
Change the File display	Alt-F	Untag all displayed files	Ctrl-U
Log a new disk	L	Untag files by attribute	Alt-U
Move the current file	M	View the current file's contents	V
Move all tagged files	Ctrl-M	Execute or run programs	X
Move tagged files/paths to another disk/directory	Alt-M	Quit XTree Easy and save structure	Z
Print the current file	P		

Appendix A: Shortcuts

XTree Easy Function Keys

Function key	Action
F1	Get Help.
F2	Open the Destination directory window. When in Copy or Move mode, press F2 to pop up the Destination window. This allows you to merely point to where you want to copy or move your files to.
F2	Update the screen when in a Showall tagged files window; press F2 to redisplay the screen and eliminate those items that have been untagged since Ctrl-S was invoked.
Alt-F2	Formats a floppy disk.
F3	When entering text, displays last response.
Alt-F3	Relogs the current directory.
F4	Menu toggle. Cycles through the standard Ctrl and Alt menus. Press F4 once and the Ctrl menu will be displayed. Press it again, and the Alt menu will be displayed. Press it a third time and you'll cycle back to the standard menu.
Alt-F4	Compare directory (available in a File window).
F6	Collapses or expands directories below the current directory.
F9	Pops up the Application Menu.
Alt-F9	Toggles between the 25-line and 51-line modes for EGA and VGA systems.
F10	Activates the pull-down menus for currently available commands.
Alt-F10	Starts the Configuration program.

XTreeGold Shortcuts

XTreeGold Directory Window Commands

Action	Key	Action	Key
Display available free space	A	Edit a file	Alt-E
Display the current branch	B	Change the current filespec	F
Display tagged files in branch	Ctrl-B	Change the File display	Alt-F
Compare the current directory to another	C	Show files on logged disks in Global file window	G
Delete current directory	D	Show tagged files on logged disks in Global file window	Ctrl-G

(continued)

XTreeGold Directory Window Commands (continued)

Action	Key	Action	Key
Graft directory	Alt-G	Open Showall file window	S
Hide/unhide a directory	Alt-H	Show all tagged files	Ctrl-S
Reverse tags on files in a directory	I	Change the sort criteria	Alt-S
Reverse tags on files on a disk	Alt-I	Tag all files in directory	T
Log a new disk	L	Tag all files on disk	Ctrl-T
Switch to logged disk	Ctrl-L	Tag by attribute	Alt-T
Log a new disk/unlog the current disk	Alt-L	Untag all files in directory	U
		Untag all files on disk	Ctrl-U
Make a directory	M	Untag by attribute	Alt-U
Undelete files with Oops!	O	Name a disk volume label	V
Print files, paths, or the tree	P	Wash a hard disk	W
Prune a directory	Alt-P	Execute or run programs	X
Exit XTreePro Gold	Q	Reduce XTreePro Gold to 7K on launch	Alt-X
Exit to the current directory	Alt-Q		
Rename the current directory	R	Quit XTreePro Gold and save structure	Z
Release a disk	Alt-R		

XTreeGold File Window Commands

Action	Key	Action	Key
Change a file's attributes	A	Change the File display	Alt-F
Change a tagged file's attributes	Ctrl-A	Reverse tags on one file	I
Copy the current file	C	Reverse tags on all files	Ctrl-I
Copy tagged files	Ctrl-C	Log a new disk	L
Copy tagged files and paths to another disk	Alt-C	Switch to logged disk	Ctrl-L
		Various other logging options	Alt-L
Delete current file	D	Move the current file	M
Delete tagged files	Ctrl-D	Move all tagged files	Ctrl-M
Edit the current file	E	Move tagged files/paths to another disk/directory	Alt-M
Change the current filespec	F		

(continued)

XTreeGold File Window Commands (continued)

Action	Key	Action	Key
Change the date on current file	**N**	Change the sort criteria	**Alt-S**
Change the date on tagged files	**Ctrl-N**	Tag the current file	**T**
Launch program associated with a file	**O**	Tag all displayed files	**Ctrl-T**
		Tag files by attribute	**Alt-T**
Reduce XTreeGold to 7K on launch of program with associated file	**Alt-O**	Untag the current file	**U**
		Untag all displayed files	**Ctrl-U**
Print the current file	**P**	Untag files by attribute	**Alt-U**
Print all tagged files	**Ctrl-P**	View the current file's contents	**V**
Exit program	**Q**	View a tagged file's contents	**Ctrl-V**
Exit to the current directory	**Alt-Q**	Execute or run programs	**X**
Rename the current file	**R**	Reduce XTree to 7K on launch	**Alt-X**
Rename all tagged files	**Ctrl-R**	Quit XTreePro Gold and save structure	**Z**
Search tagged files for text	**Ctrl-S**		

XTreeGold Function Keys

Function key	Action
F1	Get Help.
F2	Open the Destination directory window. When in Copy, Move, Compare, or Graft mode, press F2 to pop up the Destination window. This allows you to merely point to where you want to copy or move your files to.
F2	Update the screen when in a Showall tagged files window; press F2 to redisplay the screen and eliminate those items that have been untagged since Ctrl-S was invoked.
Alt-F2	Formats a floppy disk.
F3	When entering text, displays last response.
Alt-F3	Relogs the current directory.
F4	Menu toggle. Cycles through the standard Ctrl and Alt menus. Press F4 once and the Ctrl menu will be displayed. Press it again and the Alt menu will be displayed. Press it again and you'll cycle back to the standard menu.
Alt-F4	Compare directory (available in a File window).

(continued)

XTreeGold Function Keys (continued)

Function key	Action
F5	Collapses or expands directories two levels below the current directory.
Alt-F5	Opens an archive file (when you're in a File window).
Ctrl-F5	Archives tagged files (when you're in a File window).
F6	Collapses or expands directories below the current directory.
Ctrl-F6	Merges tags between two file windows.
F7	Autoview. For viewing the contents of a file.
F8	Splits/unsplits the display into two directories.
Alt-F8	Untags all tagged files that have been operated on.
Ctrl-F8	Same as Alt-F8.
F9	Pops up the XTreeMenu.
Alt-F9	Toggles between the 25-line and 51-line modes for EGA and VGA systems.
F10	Activates the pull-down menus for currently available commands.
Alt-F10	Starts the Configuration program.

XTreeNet Shortcuts

You may not have access to all these commands unless you have the necessary rights.

XTreeNet Directory Window Commands

Action	Key	Action	Key
Display available free space	A	Show tagged files on logged disks in Global file window	Ctrl-G
Attach/detach to a remote computer	Alt-A	Graft directory	Alt-G
Delete current directory	D	Reverse tags on files in a directory	I
Edit a file	Alt-E	Reverse tags on files on a disk	Ctrl-I
Change the current filespec	F	Display various information modes	Alt-I
Change the File display	Alt-F	Log a volume or new disk	L
Show files on logged disks in Global file window	G	Switch to logged disk	Ctrl-L

(continued)

Appendix A: Shortcuts

XTreeNet Directory Window Commands (continued)

Action	Key	Action	Key
Log a new disk/unlog the current disk	Alt-L	Show all tagged files	Ctrl-S
		Change the sort criteria	Alt-S
Make a directory	M	Tag all files in directory	T
Map a drive	Alt-M	Tag all files on disk	Ctrl-T
Print files, paths, or the tree	P	Tag by attribute	Alt-T
Prune a directory	Alt-P	Untag all files in directory	U
Exit XTreeNet	Q	Untag all files on disk	Ctrl-U
Exit to the current directory	Alt-Q	Untag by attribute	Alt-U
Rename the current directory	R	Name a disk volume label	V
Release a disk	Alt-R	Execute or run programs	X
Open Showall file window	S	Reduce XTreeNet to 7K on launch	Alt-X

XTreeNet File Window Commands

Action	Key	Action	Key
Change a file's attributes	A	Switch to logged disk	Ctrl-L
Change a tagged file's attributes	Ctrl-A	Log new disk/unlog current disks	Alt-L
Attach/detach from a remote computer	Alt-A	Move the current file	M
		Move all tagged files	Ctrl-M
Copy the current file	C	Map a new drive	Alt-M
Copy tagged files	Ctrl-C	Change the date on current file	N
Copy tagged files or paths to another disk	Alt-C	Change the date on tagged files	Ctrl-N
Delete current file	D	Launch program associated with a file	O
Delete tagged files	Ctrl-D	Reduce XTreeNet to 7K on launch of program with associated file	Alt-O
Edit the current file	E		
Change the current filespec	F		
Change the File display	Alt-F	Print the current file	P
Reverse tags on one file	I	Print all tagged files	Ctrl-P
Reverse tags on all files	Ctrl-I	Exit program	Q
Log a new disk	L	Exit to the current directory	Alt-Q

(continued)

XTreeNet File Window Commands (continued)

Action	Key	Action	Key
Rename the current file	R	Untag the current file	U
Rename all tagged files	Ctrl-R	Untag all displayed files	Ctrl-U
Release a disk	Alt-R	Untag files by attribute	Alt-U
Search tagged files for text	Ctrl-S	View the current file's contents	V
Change the sort criteria	Alt-S	View a tagged file's contents	Ctrl-V
Tag the current file	T	Execute or run programs	X
Tag all displayed files	Ctrl-T	Reduce XTreeNet to 7K on launch	Alt-X
Tag files by attribute	Alt-T	Quit XTreeNet and save structure	Z

XTreeNet Function Keys

Function key	Action
F1	Get Help.
F2	Open the Destination directory window or Pick list. When in Copy, Move, or Graft mode, press F2 to pop up the Destination window. This allows you to merely point to where you want to copy or move your files to.
F2	Update the screen when in a Showall tagged files window; press F2 to redisplay the screen and eliminate those items that have been untagged since Ctrl-S was invoked.
Alt-F2	Formats a floppy disk.
Alt-F3	Relogs the current directory.
F4	Menu toggle. Cycles through the standard Ctrl and Alt menus. Press F4 once and the Ctrl menu will be displayed. Press it again and the Alt menu will be displayed. Press it again and you'll cycle back to the standard menu.
Alt-F5	Opens an Arc file (see Chapter 9).
Ctrl-F5	Archives tagged files (see Chapter 9).
Ctrl-F6	Merges tags between two file windows.
F7	Autoview. Can see the contents of a file.
Ctrl-F7	Tag branch.
F8	Splits/unsplits the display into two directories.
Ctrl-F8	Untag branch.
F9	Pops up the Application Menu.

(continued)

Appendix A: Shortcuts

XTreeNet Function Keys (continued)

Function key	Action
Alt-F9	Toggles between 25-line and 51-line modes for EGA and VGA systems.
Ctrl-F9	From a File window, updates tags (untags files that have been operated on).
F10	Pops up the Quick Reference Help windows.
Alt-F10	Starts the Configuration program.

XTree for Windows Shortcuts

Action	Key
Change a file's attributes	Ctrl+A
Calculate statistics	F4
Collapse a branch	- (hyphen key)
Copy a file or directory	Ctrl+C
Delete a file or directory	Ctrl+D
Deselect all files or directories	Ctrl+\
Open the Directory Filter dialog box	Shift+F
Open the Directory Format dialog box	Shift+D
Toggle the file display	Shift+T
Open the Directory Sort Order dialog box	Shift+O
Exit XTree for Windows	Alt+F4
Expand a branch	* (asterisk key)
Expand a directory level	+ (plus key)
Open the Find dialog box	F6
Find the same text again	Shift+F6
Get Help	F1
Make a new directory	Ctrl+N
Mark a file or directory	Shift+M

Action	Key
Move a file or directory	Ctrl+M
Open a highlighted file or directory	Enter
Open an Auto Directory window	F3
Open an Auto View window	F7
Open the Open Directory As dialog box	Shift+F3
Open Directory window with all selected directories on the current volume	Shift+S
Open Directory window with all selected directories on all volumes containing marked objects only	Ctrl+Shift+G
Open Directory window with all selected directories on all volumes	Shift+G
Open Directory window with all selected directories on the current volume containing marked objects only	Ctrl+Shift+S
Open Directory window with selected branches containing marked objects only	Ctrl+Shift+B
Open Directory window with selected branches	Shift+B
Open a document view	Ctrl+V

(continued)

XTree for Windows Shortcuts (continued)

Action	Key
Open a Tree window	**F2**
Open the Open Tree As dialog box	**Shift+F2**
Refresh all windows	**Ctrl+Shift+F5**
Refresh the current selection	**Ctrl+F5**
Refresh the current window	**F5**
Rename a file or directory	**Ctrl+R**
Select all items in the active window	**Ctrl+/**

Action	Key
Select files only	**Shift+/**
Open the Select/Deselect dialog box	**Ctrl+Shift+/**
Set Scope on the current branch or directory	**F11**
Set Scope on the current volume	**Ctrl+Shift+F11**
Set Scope/Move up one level	**Shift+F11**
Unmark files or directories	**Shift+U**
Create a new Zip file	**Ctrl+Z**

Appendix B
Laptop Configuration

More and more people have two computers: a desktop for home or office use and a laptop for computing on the go. Doubtless this is a practice all computer manufacturers encourage. However, a lot of laptops have less storage and less memory than their desktop sisters (or brothers). Of course, you'll want to have XTree on your "to-go" computer, but with space at a premium, you may feel as though you have to leave XTree at home. Hey, maybe not!

You may have noticed that all versions of the XTree programs are composed of a number of modules. You can actually run the program without all the modules. So if you need to conserve disk space, what follows here is what you can leave at home, and how you can run XTree in memory-lean mode. (See "Memory Management," in Chapter 3, for RAM-saving tips.) The numbers next to the files, of course, indicate how much disk space that file takes up on your computer.

XTree Modules

XTREE.EXE (43K)   This file is required to run XTree.

Files that are used for installation and configuration, which can later be deleted from your system, are as follows:

XTREEINS.EXE (43K)   The Installation program. Once you have installed and configured your program, you no longer need this file.

XTREEINS.DAT (21K)   This is an information file for XTREEINS.EXE. Once you've configured your system, you no longer need this file.

READ.ME (13K)   This is a file that contains stuff that didn't make it into the manual. After you've read it or printed it, you may delete this file.

XTreePro Modules

XTPRO.COM (48K)   This file is required to run XTreePro.

Files that are used for installation and configuration, which can later be deleted from your system, are as follows:

README.DOC (11K)   This file contains information that didn't make it to the manual. After you've read it or printed it out, you may delete this file.

XTPROCFG.EXE (22K)   The Configuration program. Once you've configured your program, you no longer need this file, unless you want to make changes to your configuration.

XTPRO.X01 (25K)   If you want to use 1Word, the text editor, you'll need this file. Otherwise, you can do without this file.

The following files compose Pro's Help system. If you can do without Help, you can do without these files:

XTPRO.X02 (4K)   **XTPRO.X30** (13K)

XTPRO.X10 (15K)   **XTPRO.X40** (14K)

XTPRO.X20 (15K)   **XTPRO.X50** (14K)

XTPRO.PIF (3K)   This file allows XTreePro to work with Microsoft Windows version 2.*x*.

XTreePro Gold Modules

Naturally, Gold comes with the most files. You only really need these first three:

XTG.EXE (70K)   This file is required to run XTree.

XTGOLD.COM (1K)

XTGOLD.CFG (less than 1K)   Configuration settings.

Files that are used for installation and configuration, which can later be deleted from your system, as well as Help files, are as follows:

XTG_CFG.EXE (38K)   The Configuration program. Once you have configured your program, you no longer need this file.

Appendix B: Laptop Configuration

The following files are part of the Help system. If you don't need Help, you can live without these:

XTG_HELP.XTP (6K)   **XTG_HELP.X50** (14K)
XTG_HELP.X10 (15K)   **XTG_HELP.X60** (14K)
XTG_HELP.X20 (14K)   **XTG_HELP.X70** (14K)
XTG_HELP.X30 (14K)   **XTG_HELP.X80** (14K)
XTG_HELP.X40 (14K)   **XTG_HELP.X90** (8K)

The following files control various features and functions. If you don't need the feature or function, you can delete the file.

XTG_ARC1.XTP (33K)	Archive Manager compression module.
XTG_ARC2.XTP (43K)	Archive Manager open module.
XTG_EDIT.XTP (25K)	Internal text editor.
XTG_FIND.XTP (7K)	Search file module.
XTG_FORM.XTP (11K)	Format diskette module.
XTG_HEXX.XTP (15K)	View Hex editor module.
XTG_MENU.BIN (17K)	Application Menu module.
XTG_MENU.XTP (19K)	Application Menu module.
XTG_MOVE.XTP (5K)	Graft module.
XTG_QREF.XTP (11K)	Quick Reference module.
XTG_VIEW.XTP (28K)	View file module.
XTG_WASH.XTP (7K)	Wash disk module.
XTG_WBAT.XTP (8K)	Write batch file module.

The following files help the View system work. Select the modules for the types of files you will be viewing. Delete the ones you don't need.

XTG_VWKS.XTP (64K)	View 1-2-3 file module.
XTG_VDBF.XTP (53K)	View dBASE file module.
XTG_VDET.XTP (9K)	Word processor auto file-type detect.
XTG_V_TO.XTP (31K)	Word processor conversion utility (for all formats).
XTG_V_MW.XTP (31K)	View Microsoft Word file module.
XTG_V_MM.XTP (27K)	View MultiMate file module.

XTG_V_LM.XTP (56K)	View Lotus Manuscript file module.
XTG_VWP4.XTP (23K)	View WordPerfect 4 file module.
XTG_VWP5.XTP (27K)	View WordPerfect 5 file module.
XTG_V_DC.XTP (30K)	View DCA file module.
XTG_V_WS.XTP (35K)	View WordStar file module.

The following files are needed if you want to use the Open and associate command to start BAT, COM, and EXE files. (However, they are so small in size that you may as well keep them on your system.)

BAT.BAT	Association batch file for BAT files.
COM.BAT	Association batch file for COM files.
EXE.BAT	Association batch file for EXE files.

Additional miscellaneous files:

README.DOC (19K)	Addendum to the manual.
XTGOLD.HST	History file. (A new one is created as you use the program.)

The size of the the history file (XTGOLD.HST) varies depending on how much you use features that record history. All HST files are automatically created by XTree whenever you use a command that records your response. So even if you erase an HST file, a new one will be created or the old one will have commands added to it when you use the program.

XTGOLD.PIF	Required to run Gold under Windows (very small file). Call XTree Tech Support for the latest info on PIF files for Windows 3.0.

XTree Easy Modules

You must keep the following two files on your system for XTree Easy to work:

XTREE.COM (1K)	The XTree Easy program and loader file.
XTR.EXE (75K)	The auxiliary program file.

Appendix B: Laptop Configuration

Files that are used for installation and configuration, which can later be deleted from your system, as well as Help files, are as follows:

XTR_CFG.EXE (24K) — The Configuration program. Once you have configured your program, you no longer need this file.

XTR_HELP.XTR (6K) — Part of the Help system. If you don't need Help, you can live without this and all of the Help system files.

XTR_HELP.PD0 (10K) — Help text files.

XTR_HELP.X10 *through* **XTR_HELP XD0** (14K each) — These files are part of the Help system. The exact number of these Help files varies as the programmers add material in later revisions, but they're always called XTR_HELP.X-something, and they run 14K to 15K apiece.

The following files control various features and functions. If you don't need the feature or function, you can delete the file.

XTR_EDIT.XTR (25K) — 1Word text editor module.

XTR_FORM.XTR (12K) — Format diskette module.

XTR_MENU.XTR (6K) — Application Menu module.

XTR_VIEW.XTR (39K) — View file module.

These files are needed to run Easy under Windows:

README.WIN (9K) — Helpful information for running Easy in Windows.

XTREE.PIF — Files required to run Easy under Windows.

XTREE.ICO — The XTree Easy icon for Windows.

Miscellaneous files, optional as well, are as follows:

README.DOC (17K) — Addendum to the manual.

XTREE.HST — History file. (A new one is created as you use the program.)

NOTE: The size of the the history file (XTGOLD.HST) varies depending on how much you use features that record history. All HST files are automatically created by XTree whenever you use a command that records your response. So even if you erase an HST file, a new one will be created or the old one will have commands added to it when you use the program.

XTreeGold Modules

You must keep the following three files on your system for XTreeGold to work:

XTGOLD.COM (1K)   The XTreeGold program and loader.

XTG.EXE (80K)   The auxiliary program file.

XTGOLD.CFG (less than 1K)   The configuration file.

Files that are used for installation and configuration, which can later be deleted from your system, as well as Help files, are as follows:

XTG_CFG.EXE (40K)   The Configuration program. Once you have configured your program, you no longer need this file.

XTG_HELP.XTP (6K)   This and the following files are part of the Help system. If you don't need Help, you can live without all of the Help system files.

XTG_HELP.PD0 (10K)   **XTG_HELP.X70** (15K)

XTG_HELP.X10 (14K)   **XTG_HELP.X80** (14K)

XTG_HELP.X20 (14K)   **XTG_HELP.X90** (14K)

XTG_HELP.X30 (15K)   **XTG_HELP.XA0** (15K)

XTG_HELP.X40 (14K)   **XTG_HELP.XB0** (14K)

XTG_HELP.X50 (15K)   **XTG_HELP.XC0** (15K)

XTG_HELP.X60 (15K)   **XTG_HELP.XD0** (8K)

The following files control various features and functions. If you don't need the feature or function, you can delete the file.

XTG_EDIT.XTP (25K)   1Word text editor module.

XTG_FIND.XTP (8K)   Search file module.

XTG_FORM.XTP (12K)   Format disk module.

XTG_HEXX.XTP (15K)   View Hex editor module.

XTG_MENU.XTP (6K)   Application Menu module.

XTG_MOVE.XTP (5K)   Graft module.

XTG_OOPS.XTP (23K)   Undelete module.

XTG_VIEW.XTP (39K)   View file module.

XTG_V_TO.XTP (26K)   Word processor conversion utility (for all formats).

XTG_WASH.XTP (7K)   Wash disk module (Alt-W).

Appendix B: Laptop Configuration

XTG_WBAT.XTP (9K)	Write batch file module.
XTG_ARC1.XTP (32K)	Archive Manager PKarc compression module.
XTG_ARC2.XTP (42K)	Archive Manager PKarc open module.
XTG_AZIP.XTP (14K)	Archive Manager loader.
XTG_ZIP1.XTP (32K)	Archive Manager Zip compression module.
XTG_ZIP2.XTP (52K)	Archive Manager Zip open module.

The following files are used with the View system. Delete the ones you don't need.

XTG_VDBF.XTP (72K)	View Database file module.
XTG_VWKS.XTP (85K)	View Spreadsheet file module.
XTG_VFFT.XTP (20K)	View FFT files.
XTG_VMSR.XTP (28K)	View Microsoft RTF and MS Word 3.0, 3.1, 4.0, and 5.0.
XTG_VPFS XTP (32K)	PFS: First Choice 1.0, 2.0, and Write Version C.
XTG_VWP4.XTP (20K)	WordPerfect 4.0.
XTG_VWP5.XTP (29K)	WordPerfect 5.0.
XTG_VWS2.XTP (26K)	WordStar 2000.
XTG_V_DC.XTP (27K)	View DCA file module.
XTG_V_EN.XTP (22K)	Enable 1.0, 2.0, 2.15.
XTG_V_LM.XTP (50K)	Lotus Manuscript 2.0, 2.1.
XTG_V_MM.XTP (26K)	MultiMate 3.3 and 4 and Advantage I, II, 3.6, and 3.7.
XTG_V_MW.XTP (29K)	Microsoft Windows Write 3.0.
XTG_V_QA.XTP (20K)	Q&A Write.
XTG_V_WS.XTP (31K)	WordStar.
XTG_V_XY.XTP (27K)	XyWrite.
XTG_VFRM.XTP (21K)	Framework III 1.0 and 1.1.
XTG_VIBM.XTP (20K)	IBM Writing Assistant.
XTG_VOFF.XTP (24K)	Office Writer 4.0, 5.0, 6.0, and 6.1.
XTG_VRAP.XTP (18K)	RapidFile (Memo) 1.0, 1.2.
XTG_VSAM.XTP (24K)	Samna Word IV and Word IV Plus.
XTG_VVK2.XTP (16K)	Volkswriter Deluxe 2.2.
XTG_VVK3.XTP (28K)	Volkswriter 3 and 4.
XTG_VWNG.XTP (16K)	Wang PC Version 3.

Information on running XTreeGold under Windows:

README.WIN (9K)   Helpful information for running Gold in Windows.

XTGOLD.PIF   File required to run XTreeGold under Windows.

XTGOLDF.PIF   File required to run XTreeGold under Windows.

Miscellaneous files, optional as well, are as follows:

README.DOC (17K)   Addendum to the manual.

XTGOLD.HST   History file. (A new one is created as you use the program.)

> **NOTE:** The size of the the history file (XTGOLD.HST) varies depending on how much you use features that record history. All HST files are automatically created by XTree whenever you use a command that records your response. So even if you erase an HST file, a new one will be created or the old one will have commands added to it when you use the program.

The following files are needed only if you want to use the Open (and Associate) command to start BAT, COM, and EXE files. (However, they are so small in size you may as well leave them on your system.)

BAT.BAT   Association batch file for BAT files.

COM.BAT   Association batch file for COM files.

EXE.BAT   Association batch file for EXE files.

XTree for Windows Modules

All files are needed to run XTree for Windows except the following, which are mostly file viewers that you may delete if you don't need them. (Back up the viewers if you think you might need them later. Otherwise, you must run Setup again to re-create them.) You can also delete the Help file if you don't need or use XTree for Windows' Help.

Word Processor viewers

Following is a list of word processor file viewers that may be deleted if you no longer need them. (Back up the viewers if you might need them later. Otherwise, you must run Setup again to recreate them.)

XTW33F.DLL (61K)   Ami Professional.

XTW28F.DLL (35K)   Enable.

XTW29F.DLL (31K)   Framework III, IV.

Appendix B: Laptop Configuration

XTW32F.DLL (30K)	Final Form Text.
XTW15F.DLL (42K)	IBM DisplayWrite DCA, RFT.
XTW13F.DLL (31K)	IBM Writing Assistant.
XTW37F.DLL (42K)	Legacy.
XTW24F.DLL (61K)	Lotus Manuscript.
XTW52F.DLL (39K)	MacWrite II.
XTW51F.DLL (42K)	MacWrite.
XTW05F.DLL (41K)	MS Word for DOS.
XTW53F.DLL (48K)	MS Word for Mac 3.0.
XTW54F.DLL (67K)	MS Word for Mac 4.0.
XTW44F.DLL (78K)	MS Word for Windows.
XTW39F.DLL (40K)	MS Works for DOS.
XTW43F.DLL (35K)	MS Write 3.0.
XTW10F.DLL (37K)	Multimate.
XTW16F.DLL (35K)	OfficeWriter.
XTW08F.DLL (42K)	PFS\Professional Write.
XTW23F.DLL (31K)	Q&A Write.
XTW25F.DLL (32K)	Rapid File 1.*x*.
XTW19F.DLL (66K)	Rich text format.
XTW22F.DLL (33K)	Samna Word\HP AdvanceWrite+.
XTW11F.DLL (26K)	Volkswriter Deluxe.
XTW14F.DLL (41K)	Volkswriter\Total Word.
XTW06F.DLL (30K)	WordPerfect 4.*x*.
XTW07F.DLL (53K)	WordPerfect 5.*x*.
XTW59F.DLL (31K)	WordPerfect for Mac 1.0.
XTW60F.DLL (42K)	WordPerfect for Mac 2.0.
XTW04F.DLL (67K)	WordStar.
XTW09F.DLL (40K)	Wordstar 2000.
XTW17F.DLL (57K)	XyWrite III.
XTW502F.DLL (61K)	TIFF.
XTW519F.DLL (41K)	WordPerfect bitmap.
XTW606F.DLL (111K)	WordPerfect vector.

Graphic viewers

Following is a list of graphics file viewers that may be deleted if you no longer need them. (Back up the viewers if you might need them later. Otherwise, you must run Setup again to recreate them.)

XTW518F.DLL (41K)	GEM Image.
XTW512F.DLL (57K)	GIF.
XTW601F.DLL (106K)	Lotus 1-2-3 PIC.
XTW508F.DLL (40K)	MacPaint.
XTW609F.DLL (123K)	Micrografx Designer\Charisma.
XTW605F.DLL (84K)	Micrografx Draw.
XTW507F.DLL (40K)	MS Paint.
XTW517F.DLL (41K)	MS Windows 3.x Icon.
XTW501F.DLL (42K)	Paintbrush.
XTW505F.DLL (40K)	PC Paint\Pictor.

Spreadsheet viewers

The module for spreadsheet viewers is the same for all products.

XTWWKSS.DLL (98K)   All formats

Database viewers

The module for database viewers is the same for all products.

XTWDBFL.DLL (54K)   All formats

Other files

XTREEWIN.HLP (276K)	Help file.
XTLINK.COM (27K)	XTreeLink program.

Happy camping!

Appendix C
Insider Info from XTree Tech Support

The Most Commonly Asked Questions about XTree for DOS

Technical support Q&A straight from the XTree tech support team! Here are the most commonly asked questions (and the answers, of course) about XTree, XTreePro, XTreePro Gold, XTreeGold, and there's even a section on XTreeNet. Although most of these questions are explored in depth elsewhere in this book, maybe you can get a quick answer to *your* burning question right here! (Or maybe get an answer to a question you didn't know you had.) You may want to browse through *all* of the questions because there are some questions that can apply to more than one program.

XTree Questions

How do I install XTree to my hard drive?

You can even *use* XTree to *install* XTree. Just take the following steps.

Steps: Using XTree to install XTree

Step 1. Put your XTree master disk in your floppy drive (let's assume it's the A: drive).

Step 2. Type **A:** and press Enter to log onto the A: drive.

Step 3. Type **XTREE** and press Enter.

Step 4. Once you see the XTree screen, press L (for log) and then C (for your hard drive — or D or E or whatever the letter is for the hard drive you want to install XTree on).

Step 5. Press M (for Make directory), type **XTREE**, and press Enter.

Step 6. Press L and then A to get back to your floppy.

Step 7. Press Enter to get into the Small file window.

Step 8. Now press Ctrl-T to tag all the files (a diamond will appear next to the filenames) and Ctrl-C to copy all tagged files.

Step 9. Finally, type **C:\XTREE** and press Enter when you're asked for the destination path.

After the files have been copied, you can exit XTree. Type **C:** and press Enter to get back to your hard disk. (Make sure you edit your AUTOEXEC.BAT file to include XTree in your path statement — see "Batch Files," in Chapter 3.)

I have an 80MB hard drive with 4300 files, and XTree doesn't log all of my files.

The original XTree can only read in 2500 files. The easiest thing to do is upgrade to one of the more powerful programs. However, you can use the DOS SUBST command and log only *parts* of your directory tree. (See Chapter 3, "XTree for DOS Quick Reference Section" for details.)

How can I find my serial number?

Finding your serial number is a test of skill and manual dexterity — sort of the "video game" portion of XTree. First, get XTree up and running. Press L for Log drive then put one finger on the C key and one on the F1 key. Right after you press C, press F1 as fast as you can to freeze the logo screen, where this elusive number is displayed.

XTreePro Questions

I get an error message on-screen when I first load XTreePro.

It's probably because you have recently upgraded to a higher version of DOS. You need to run the Configuration program (XTPROCFG.EXE) and change the disk logging method under option 1 to standard. (See "Configuration Options," in Chapter 3.)

Appendix C: Insider Info from XTree Tech Support

When I try to edit a file I get this message:
```
Can't find file XTPRO.X01
```

One of two things are going on here. You either deleted that file somehow, or you have moved (or renamed) the XTPRO directory. If you did the first, get out your original disk and reinstall XTPRO.X01. If you did the latter, simply run the Configuration program (XTPROCFG.EXE) and change the program path under option 1. ("See Configuration Options," in Chapter 3.)

After starting XTreePro, I run out of memory when I try to run other programs.

Hold the Ctrl and Alt key down at the same time to see what version you have. It's probably version 1.0; if so, call XTree to receive version 1.1 — that will solve your problem. If you have version 1.1, then try executing your program by pressing Alt-X instead of X (this will reduce XTreePro to its smallest size).

XTreePro Gold Questions

How do I collapse Pro Gold to a 7K wedge?

First, make sure you start Pro Gold using the command XTGOLD.COM, not XTG.EXE. Then, instead of pressing X to execute a program, press Alt-X. (Or press Alt-O instead of O to open a file.) Also, the `Memory utilization` options in the Configuration program (located on page 3 of `Modify configuration items`) can be set to `All Memory` (collapse) or `Available Memory` (no collapse). (See "Configuration Options," in Chapter 3.)

How do I use the instant logging feature?

Let's say you have drives C:, D:, and E: logged in a split window with 100 files tagged. It's midnight and you want to go to sleep but don't want to lose your work. Press Alt-Z to quit, and the next time you start Pro Gold, you'll be right back where you left off!

How do I find a file on my hard disk that contains the word *cash*?

Go into Showall mode (or Global for all drives) and press Ctrl-T to tag all files. Now, press Enter to search all tagged files and type **cash**. Gold will untag all files that do not contain the word *cash*. After Gold finishes, press Esc and then

Ctrl-S to get a list of all the remaining tagged files (those files containing the word *cash*). You can use the View command to find the specific file you want.

Does XTreePro Gold support VGA? A mouse?
Yes, it supports both.

How can I see two directories at the same time?
Use the split window command (F8) to split the display in two. Each side of the display operates independently so that you may view two directories, two drives, or any other combination you wish.

Can I log onto my CD-ROM drive?
But of course!

I know Pro Gold can edit my ASCII files, but can it edit in Hex mode?
Yes. View the file in Hex mode and press E for edit.

What is the difference between Prune and Graft?
Prune allows you to quickly delete an entire branch from your directory tree. Because Prune is such a powerful feature, Pro Gold double-checks your action before files are deleted. Graft is a feature that lets you quickly move an entire branch of a directory tree, including all subdirectories, to a different location on the tree.

What does the Wash disk command do?
Wash disk makes all deleted files unrecoverable. Technically, it zeroes out (writes over) everywhere on the disk where there are no viable files.

Does XTreePro Gold run under DOS 4.0 and 5.0?
Yes. Starting with DOS 4.0/4.01, disk partitions larger than 32MB could finally be recognized. XTreePro Gold, as well as other XTree products, can read a disk past the 32MB boundary. The only limit is the number of files and directories a user has on the disk.

Appendix C: Insider Info from XTree Tech Support

Does XTreePro Gold run under OS/2?

No. We do not have a version yet that will run under the OS/2 operating system. However, XTree *will* run under the DOS portion of OS/2 (the DOS compatibility box).

How much memory does XTreePro Gold use?

Pro Gold requires 256K of RAM in order to function properly. When running other programs from Pro Gold, Pro Gold's memory usage can shrink down to only 7K to 8K of memory, thus allowing large programs to run. Memory usage also depends on the number of files and directories on disk. Each file or directory entry will occupy 32 bytes of computer memory, so the more files you have, the more computer memory you will use (remember, 1K is 1024 bytes).

How large a file can I edit with the 1Word text editor?

A user may edit text files up to 64K with 1Word. If the user has another editor that can edit files greater than 64K, or prefers it over 1Word, the user can configure XTreePro Gold to use that editor instead.

Will XTreePro Gold run under DESQView?

Yes, as long as you give it enough memory. We suggest 425K.

Will XTreePro Gold run under Windows?

For a program to run properly under Microsoft Windows, a special set of instructions about that program must be created for Windows. These instructions are saved in a file with a PIF extension. A PIF file (for example, XTGOLD.PIF) is provided on your disk to run under version 2.*x* of Windows (the latest version when XTreePro Gold was released). Call tech support for a PIF file for version 3.1.

How do I return to a previously logged drive without relogging?

Use the + or − key to cycle through all logged drives.

XTreeGold 2.0 Questions

The XTreeMenu is a bit tedious to edit; is there an easier way?
You bet! All the commands used by the menu system are hot keys. To Add an item press A, to Delete press D, to Move press M, to Rename press R, and so on.

I used to use the + or − keys to switch between drives with XTreePro Gold, and I don't like using the < or > instead. Is there a way to switch back to my old ways?
Yes. When you start XTreeGold, use the undocumented /XT command switch. In other words, start the program by typing **XTGOLD /XT** and pressing Enter.

Where are the pull-down menus?
Everywhere! To invoke the pull-downs, either press F10 or use the mouse and click on the top row of the screen. Even if you don't normally use pull-down menus, there are some occasions when they come in handy. For example, while viewing or autoviewing, you can change the view mode, set bookmarks, and gather text more easily using the pull-down menus.

Is there any way to easily find duplicate files on my computer?
There are a number of ways, but a new, simpler way is available in XTreeGold. Open a Showall file window by pressing S. Then press Alt-F4 to invoke the Showall/Global Compare facility. Press D for duplicates and all the files that appear more than once will be listed.

Can I Graft across drives?
Not directly, but the Branch command and the Alt-Move command can accomplish the same thing. Highlight the parent of the branch you want to Graft. Press Ctrl-T, press Alt-M, and then enter a destination. From there select partial branch paths for the Source Paths prompt.

I run out of memory when I try to run some of my programs.
Make sure you start XTreeGold with XTGOLD.COM and not XTG.EXE. Then press Alt-X instead of X to execute a program.

How do I switch between windows in split windows mode?

Use the Tab key, or point with the mouse.

When I try to view files created in my word processor, I see garbage instead of the document.

If you find yourself looking at garbage while in View, press F to produce a formatted view.

My mouse doesn't work.

In order to conserve memory, XTreeGold does not have its own mouse driver — it just knows how to use the mouse driver already loaded in memory. The first step is to make sure your mouse is functioning properly in other programs. If it isn't, then find MOUSE.COM (or MOUSE.SYS) and make sure it is properly installed before entering XTree.

XTreeGold 2.5 Questions

Why can't I view my WPG (WordPerfect graphics) files?

XTreeGold's WPG viewer works with bitmap-type WordPerfect graphics, but the samples that come with WordPerfect are of the vector type. To achieve the bitmap variety, you can either use the Screen Grab command (GRAB.COM in WordPerfect), which will make a snapshot of the current screen, or the GRAPHCNV program included with WordPerfect, which takes other graphic formats and creates bitmapped files (but not the WPG samples!) CompuServe also has a large selection of WPG bitmapped files.

Why can't I view my AutoCAD drawing files?

XTreeGold's AutoCAD viewer needs approximately 300K to successfully bring up a drawing file. A quick way to see how much memory you actually have while in XTreeGold is to press X and check out the Available Memory box. If the number displayed is lower than 300K, exclusively log the drive containing the drawings (first level) and log only the directory with the files. Also, you can start XTreeGold with the switch \XM, which will display a number in the Available Bytes box that indicates the number of files and directories you can still read in. Bring this number up to around 8500 for the desired memory.

After I run XTreeGold, Windows doesn't run!

In XTreeGold version 2.5, a file named VGA.DRV has the same name as a Windows file, which Windows looks for when starting up. If you are in the XTGOLD directory when you try to invoke Windows, Windows will try to use XTree's VGA.DRV and then simply kick out to DOS. In XTreeGold 2.51, the problem is fixed; the file is now called XTG_VGA.DRV.

When I press F1, I get a missing overlay message.

If you have Norton's AntiVirus program loaded in memory, pressing F1 at the main directory will produce the missing overlay message. To work around this problem, use NAV_.SYS instead of NAV$.SYS for the Norton program.

My XTreeMenu won't execute programs.

If you highlight an item in XTreeMenu and when you press Enter (or double-click with the mouse) nothing happens at all, not even a screen flicker, then the problem probably lies with the XTGTEMP variable. Check this variable by typing **SET** at the DOSprompt and making sure XTGTEMP points to a valid location.

I cannot execute C:\XTGOLD\XTG.EXE.

If you are using EMM386.SYS, PC-CACHE, or a few other such programs, you will get an error message when you try to execute XTreeGold 2.5. XTGOLD.ZIP is on the XTree BBS and on CompuServe and contains a new version of XTGOLD.COM that solves this problem. The old XTGOLD.COM is over 1000 bytes while the new one is 954 bytes. This problem is also fixed in XTreeGold version 2.51.

Entering XTG doesn't load XTreeGold version 2.5.

XTGOLD.COM is the correct command to use to start XTreeGold. This command allows the user to collapse XTreeGold to a 7K wedge and prevents relogging of the drive upon return from executing a program from within XTreeGold. If you must use XTG, specify the /ZS switch.

Appendix C: Insider Info from XTree Tech Support

How do I restore the paths that were in my self-extracting Zip file?

If you specify Paths (Full) when you create a self-extracting Zip file, you must add the command-line switch -d (or /d) at the end of the line when you decompress to keep the paths intact.

What does the ** attribute mean when I use Oops!?

The ** attribute on a file in the list of deleted files shown when you invoke the Oops! command simply means "undelete me first!" as it has the best chance of being recovered.

After installing XTree Gold 2.5, my car won't start!

Ahem, user, have you read the manual yet?

Questions for All Versions

What's the difference between a Showall and a Global file window?

A Showall file window lists all files on the *currently* logged drive whereas a Global file window lists all files on *all* logged drives.

Can I print to a file?

Yes. Start up your XTree product with a redirection. For example, type **XTGOLD > *filename* /ps**. The /ps specifies standard output.

How can I print to LPT2:?

Use the same technique for printing to a file but use the term LPT2: instead of a filename.

Can I rename my XT*xxxx*.COM to X.COM for easier access?

You can, but if you later want to configure your XTree product, you will run into some problems. Instead, make a batch file called X.BAT that calls up your program.

I want the directory from which I started XTree to be the highlighted directory when XTree comes up.

You can create a batch file to do this. In the X.BAT example from the previous question, the batch file would be: C:\XTREE\XTREE, which would start XTree from the current directory, without going to C:\XTREE first.

How can I quit XTree and be in the highlighted directory when I exit to DOS?

Press Alt-Q when you quit, and you'll end up with the highlighted directory at the system prompt.

How do I create a new text file with XTree products?

In all products except the original XTree, simply highlight the directory where you want the new file to be located and press E for edit. When prompted, type in the name you want to call your new file and press Enter. You can then create your document.

XTreeNet Questions

Greg just got fired(!). Is there an easy way to find all of his files?

Enter a Showall or a Global file window and press Alt-T to tag by attribute. Now press O (for owner) and type in Greg's name.

Appendix C: Insider Info from XTree Tech Support

When I've logged two volumes and go to log a third, I run out of memory. Is there a way to find out how many more files I can read in?

If you start XTreeNet with a /XM option switch there will be a number located just above the available bytes number in the upper-right corner of the screen, indicating the number of files and directories you can still read in. You can increase this number by releasing branches from memory with the minus (–) key (highlight the branch, first).

What is the easiest way to find the owner of a directory or file?

Press Alt-I to go into Information mode. The Statistics box on the right side of the screen will change and allow you to get detailed information on each file and directory.

Mail directories in Novell are always some number that doesn't mean anything to me. Is there a way in XTreeNet to easily see who these directories belong to?

If you press Alt-I twice the Statistics box changes to show Trustee information. Now you can scroll through the mail directories to find out.

How do I log my entire volume instead of just the first level of directories?

While in the Directory window, press the asterisk (*) key. XTreeNet will log from the cursor down. You can press Alt-L, which causes XTreeNet to automatically read the whole volume.

Can I set up a default configuration for users who don't do any configuring for themselves?

Yes. When you save a configuration, press C for Change path and then enter the path to your XTreeNet program.

Can I add trustees while in XTreeNet?

Yes. You can add, delete, and modify trustees by highlighting the appropriate directory and pressing A for Attributes and then T for Trustees.

I set the X attribute to a file in XTreeNet and I can't remove it.

Once it is set, the X attribute is an unchangeable attribute in Novell NetWare. You can reinstall the affected program to remove this attribute.

typing **SET** at the DOS prompt and making sure XTGTEMP points to a valid location.

Appendix D
Where to Go from Here

Just in case you become intrigued by DOS (well, stranger things have happened), or some of the products mentioned in this book sound like they might lighten your load, here's a list of where you can find what.

Company names are given as a point of reference. Most of these products are available (at a discount) from your local friendly computer store.

The books are available in most bookstores, in the larger computer superstores, and directly from IDG Books (800-762-2974).

The XTree Company

You can contact XTree Company's technical support directly if you have questions about their products. To get the most out of your technical support experience, call when you are in front of your computer with your program running. If you decide to get a newer version of XTree, it is cheaper to upgrade directly through XTree Company than to rush down to your local retail outlet. (Call 800-333-6561.)

If you have a version of XTreePro Gold that doesn't have the Archive module, simply fill out and return your warranty registration card and you'll receive the current version of Gold (including the Archive module) within a couple of weeks.

You can discover the version number of your copy of Pro or Gold by simultaneously pressing Ctrl and Alt. In the original version of XTree, the version number is displayed when you call up the program. The makers of XTree can be contacted by phone, fax, or mail.

Mailing Address for XTree

XTree Company
4115 Broad Street, Building 1
San Luis Obispo, CA 93401-7993

Technical Support for XTree

Phone: 805-541-0604
Fax: 805-541-8053
XTree BBS: 805-546-9150
CompuServe Address: 75300,226
XTree Company Technical Support Forum on CompuServe: GO XTREE

Recommended Software

Disk Technician
Prime Solutions
1940 Garnet Avenue
San Diego, CA 92109
800-847-5000

PC-Kwik
Multisoft Corporation
15100 S.W. Koll Parkway
Beaverton, OR 97006
800-234-KWIK

Fastback
Mace Utilities
Fifth Generation Systems
10049 N. Reiger Road
Baton Rouge, LA 70809
Sales: 800-873-4384
Technical support: 504-291-7283

Norton Utilities
Symantec
10201 Torre Avenue
Cupertino, CA 95014
Customer service: 408-252-3570

OPTune
Gazelle Systems
42 N. University Avenue #10
Provo, UT 84601
800-233-0383

PC Tools
Central Point Software
15220 N.W. Greenbrier Parkway #200
Beaverton, OR 87006
Sales: 503-690-8090
Technical support: 503-690-8080

SpinRite II
Gibson Research
22991 LaCadena
Laguna Hills, CA 92653
Sales: 714-830-2200
Technical support: 714-830-2500

VOPT
Golden Bow Systems
P.O. Box 3039
San Diego, CA 92103
Sales: 800-284-3269
Technical support: 619-298-9349

Books on MS-DOS, Windows, Hard Disks, and PC Systems

The following books are published by IDG Books Worldwide and can be ordered directly by calling 800-762-2974.

DOS For Dummies
By Dan Gookin

DOS 5 Complete Handbook
By John Socha and Clint Hicks

You Can Do It with DOS
By Chris Van Buren

Windows For Dummies
By Andy Rathbone

Windows 3.1 Secrets
By Brian Livingston

You Can Do It with Windows
By Chris Van Buren

Hard Disk Secrets
By John Goodman

PCs For Dummies
By Dan Gookin and Andy Rathbone

PC Secrets
By Caroline M. Halliday

Appendix E
An Unapologetic History of XTree

By Jeff Johnson, Co-creator of XTree

I'd like to tell you that we had it all planned. That in 1983, the creative geniuses at Executive Systems Inc. (ESI) sat down and, probing the depths of our programming and engineering knowledge, peered into the future and said, "Ah-ha! Hard disks." Then in a round-the-clock hacker frenzy of pepperoni pizzas and Classic Cokes, created XTree.

I'd like to say that.

I'd like to tell you it's going to be a movie and Tom Cruise is playing me.

But, like many great products and inventions, what you now know as XTree just sorta happened while we were involved in other projects. Think of it as a hi-tech version of Woody Allen's statement that life is what happens to you while you're out doing something else.

It was 1983, a critical, pivotal year for the computer industry, and for me. Saying 1983 to someone who really knows the computer industry is like saying 1929 to a stock broker, or 1960 to a Yankees fan.

At the end of 1983, three important events took place: MS-DOS began its ascent as the dominant computer operating system, replacing CP/M; IBM's PCjr, a computer recently cited by an industry magazine as arguably (IBM's) biggest failure of the 1980s, was pronounced D.O.A. by everyone in the computer industry; and ESI gave me a try as an independent contractor. After a month, they hired me as a full-time employee, and I've been part of the company ever since. At the time, ESI was writing the BIOS and utilities for the Epson QX-10.

Nineteen eighty-four rolled in and Epson asked Henry Hernandez, one of ESI's founders, if we could design utilities for their new PC DOS computers. Now, Henry is this great big bear of a guy. Lovable, fun to work with and for, and not one to let a little thing like not knowing any better get in the way, he said "Sure."

Appendix E: An Unapologetic History of XTree

So we got the job and everybody (I mean everybody) at ESI was involved in the project: Dale Sinor, Tom Smith, and Henry (the owners); Ken Broomfield and me (the full-time programmers); and Claire Johnson (who did everything to run the company) put in 16-hour days. Three weeks and no sleep later, we delivered half a dozen utilities to Epson. They thanked us and gave us more work — a lot more work.

A couple of months later we had hundreds of floppy disks and several hard disks cram-packed with files and no idea where anything was. We had no way to manage all the files — and there hangs the tale.

You see *nobody* had a way of managing files. At least not any reasonably easy way. There just weren't any utilities to do it. There was a utility for CP/M written by a friend of ours, Mike Karas, that we had been using, and some command-line-oriented programs, but none of them addressed the concept of managing a directory structure. You know, paths and stuff like that.

Which made us all say, "Hmmmm?"

So we thought about it. We talked about it. We shouted over it. We threatened one another with ancient Klingon curses. In other words, we sat down like adults and reasoned the thing out.

We discussed different kinds of tree structures, recursive processing, and other technical stuff. Drawings and diagrams came and went like the kitchen trash.

Among the subjects discussed were *how* the program would represent the DOS directory structure on-screen, and *what* the screen might look like. I drew a picture of this outline on a white board. It looked like a tree that needed water. It was a swell picture but no one thought it could be done. Impossible, they said.

Famous last words.

I went home on a Friday, programmed like mad until Sunday, and showed it to Henry on Monday. A week later we decided to try out the tree display in a backup program we were writing for Epson. They liked it. And we had the beginnings of a product.

In December of 1984, we began really working on what you now know as XTree. Our feature list was huge, and a lot of these features didn't make it into the original version of XTree but were added later in XTreePro and XTreePro Gold. I was working full time on the program, Ken worked on it between other tasks, and everyone else chipped in as needed. When enough of the program was written so it could be used, we used it ourselves. We felt that if other people were going to rely on the program, it had to be rock solid for everyday use, easy to learn, and a cinch to operate.

If it's not yet obvious, I don't want you to think that I'm some kind of mad genius and created XTree all by myself. Far from it. Whenever you're trying to do something that's never been done before, lots of people are involved.

That's the way it was with XTree. Dale made sure it had plenty of whiz-bang features. Henry made sure we didn't write any bad code. Tom made sure the user interface was consistent. (His unrelenting efforts to maintain consistency in the interface really weren't appreciated until the hundreds of reviews and millions of users began expressing their pleasure at how easy XTree is to use. Of course, back then, every time we thought XTree was ready, Tom had just one more small revision. Right.) Finally, there was Ken, bug catcher supreme.

All that was left was a name.

Arletta, my wife, gets credit for that one. We had been throwing names around the office for months and no one could agree on anything. One night, late at night, very late at night, she suggested, "XTree." You know, like "X-Tree, X-Tree read all about it!"

Pretty stupid, I thought, but jotted it down.

When I mentioned it to everyone at the office the next day, they said, "Pretty stupid," and before you knew it we had a name — XTree.

Okay, we've got a name, we've got a program, we've also got a problem; how do we get it into the stores so people like you can buy it and we can make ba-zillions of dollars? At the time, we had two choices: We could either publish it ourselves or find someone who knew more about software publishing than we did — and in early 1985 there weren't a lot of people to choose from.

On March 1, 1985, we made the decision to publish XTree ourselves. Which is when Dale took charge and in a moment of sheer insanity vowed to have XTree ready to sell at the West Coast Computer Faire in San Francisco on April 1, 1985. Dale promised to have XTree packaged; the manual completed, written, and printed; and all the hundreds other details required to bring a product to market . . . ready in 30 days. As this was a seemingly impossible task, we thought April Fools' Day was an appropriate choice for our premiere.

What we didn't know was Dale had an ace up his sleeve . . . Michael Cahlin, president of Cahlin/Williams Communications.

In the next four weeks, Cahlin had the product packaged; the cover designed and printed; press materials created and in the hands of the industry's most influential reviewers and syndicated columnists; the first XTree brochure, *XTree Read All About It,* written, produced, and printed; and, along with Dale Sinor and Judy Mason, had XTree's booth at the West Coast Computer Faire set up. (Rumor

Appendix E: An Unapologetic History of XTree

has it that when Cahlin hired Bob Cabeen to actually design the first XTree package, he gave Bob only seven days to create it. When Bob protested, Cahlin is alleged to have said, "Look, Bob, God created the Universe in six days — all I want is a package design." When Bob came through in five days, the rumor continues, he replied, "Show *that* to God!")

Of course, Dale had his own miracles to perform. Two days before the show, he went to the typesetters to pick up the final proofs for the manual and discovered the typesetter had been evicted and was ducking everyone. Dale finally tracked him down, but the guy would only exchange the proofs for cash — something we weren't exactly knee-deep in. While the countdown to the West Coast Computer Faire continued, Dale found the cash, got the proofs, rushed them to the printer, then to the bindery, and waited for them, refusing to let them out of his sight. He left Los Angeles at 1:30 a.m. Four hours later, he pulled into Moscone Center in San Francisco, carried the boxes of manuals, software cases, cover inserts, and brochures inside, and calmly began assembling the booth. The show opened at 9 a.m.

And so it goes.

It's ironic that the original XTree was officially introduced on April 1, 1985. The West Coast Computer Faire, at the time, was one of the most popular computer shows in the country. I hate to sound like your father, but this was back in the old days when computer shows were a far cry from the slick conventions you see today. These were *end*-user shows, and there were so many silicon-type bargains at these shows that they made the 24 bucks the Indians sold Manhattan for seem a bit high.

We sold XTree version 1.0 for only $39.95 at that show, and we were literally selling it from the front of the booth while frantically putting the software packages together in the back! (And now they're a bonafide collectors item.) We shared a ten-by-ten booth with a small software publisher, who, as fate would have it, almost published the original XTree. The president's name was Pete Ryan, and knowing a good thing when he saw one, he became XTree's product manager six months later and eventually worked his way up to marketing vice president and chief wheeler-dealer.

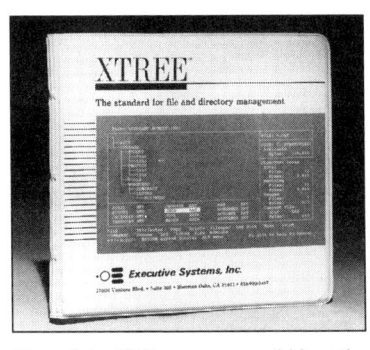

The original XTree, as we sold it at the West Coast Computer Faire in 1985. (photograph by Nora Hernandez)

Within weeks after the show, XTree was in the hands of John Dvorak, Jerry Pournelle, and all those other demigods of hi-tech who decide the fate of products. Dvorak, et al., loved the product, and positive reviews appeared one after another. Near as I can figure, XTree was quite simply the right product, at the right price, at the right time: inexpensive software that solved a common problem and was easy to use. A rare beast in those days, or any days. In November 1985, *PC Magazine* gave XTree their prestigious Editors Choice Award. (XTreePro, released in 1987, received the same award, as did XTreePro Gold in 1990.) Other reviews and awards followed, and following them were orders from distributors and retailers.

. . . And the rest is software history.

XTreePro, XTreePro Gold, XTreeGold, XTree Easy, and XTree for Windows were developed as more and more features were added. Gold is now translated into Dutch, French, German, Italian, and Spanish, to name a few. With more than three million copies in use, all versions of XTree are well-recognized industry standards for disk management. And that impossible tree structure has been copied by almost everyone who has made a hard disk management system since.

As for the future, the XTree program will continue to grow and expand its capabilities as it has in the past. Our main concern is answering the needs of our customers. We read your letters. We listen to your concerns. And we appreciate your support.

This time we have it all planned.

Right.

Jeff Johnson

P.S.: To my wife Arletta and our children, Tari, Dan, and Arynn, for putting up with my long workdays: I love you.

Appendix F
Pop Quiz Answers

POP QUIZ #1

What are the three things DOS can mean?

1. Disk Operating System.
2. A place on a disk for storing DOS files.
3. You are not in a program (as in "go to DOS").

POP QUIZ #2

What does the colon mean in "A:" and "C:"?

It means "drive." As in the A: drive and the C: drive — which is how I refer to them in this book.

POP QUIZ #3

What is the purpose of directories?

Directories are storage areas for files and programs.

POP QUIZ #4

What are the two things the system prompt tells you?

1. The computer is ready for a command.
2. The current disk and directory.

POP QUIZ #6

What do these filenames mean?

*.TXT

Any file that ends in TXT.

*.DOC

Any file that begins with L and ends with DOC.

CHAP?.DOC

Any file that begins with CHAP and has one character after CHAP and ends in DOC. (This would include chap1.doc and chap9.doc, but not chap11.doc.)

.

All files.

Appendix F: Pop Quiz Answers

POP QUIZ #7

1. If you can't delete a file, what does that tell you about the file's attributes?

The file has been set to be read-only.

2. Is it okay to delete system files?

Never.

3. Which one of the attributes would tell you whether you've backed up the file or not?

The archive flag.

4. Do all computers have the same CONFIG.SYS and AUTOEXEC.BAT files?

All computers should have CONFIG.SYS and AUTOEXEC.BAT files, but the contents of each CONFIG.SYS and AUTOEXEC.BAT files are different on different computers.

POP QUIZ #8

True or false?

The root should not be used as a storage area.

True. The root should only be used as the entryway or gateway to the rest of your computer system.

Give directories long and complex names.

False. The less you have to type, the better.

Keep the file count under 200 in each directory.

True. Having too many large directories inhibits your performance — and the machine's!

Index

* (asterisk)
  ** attribute with Oops!, 363
  star-dot-star filespec, 32
  Tree window icon, 252
  as wildcard, 19
\ (backslash)
  highlighting using, 269–270
  in system prompt, 15
^ (carat) in XTree for DOS command area, 28
: (colon) in drive names, 12
... (ellipses)
  on Windows menus, 219
  on XTree for DOS menus, 154
> (greater-than symbol) in system prompt, 15
– (minus sign)
  collapsing XTreeMenu display, 193
  cycling through logged drives, 359, 360
  exclusionary filespecs, 109
  Tree window icon, 252–253
  turning attributes off, 42–43
  unlogging directories, 131
% (percent sign) in batch file variables, 47–48
. (period) in filenames, 16, 17
+ (plus sign)
  collapsed directories, 91
  collapsed XTreeMenu display, 193
  cycling through logged drives, 359, 360
  key combinations in this book, 5
  logging directories, 131
  Tree window icon, 252–253
  turning attributes on, 42–43
+/– (plus/minus prompt), 173
? (question mark)
  for Extended Statistics window access, 173
  as wildcard, 20
1Word, 94–99
  creating new files, 99, 364
  editing files, 96–98
  keyboard commands, 95–96
  limitations, 94–95
  maximum file size, 359
  printing from, 151–152
7K Wedge, 135, 357, 362

— A —

Accessed date attribute, 207, 209
Across drives option, 57
activating. See starting programs; turning on and off
active window
  Microsoft Windows, 213, 216
  XTree for DOS, 169–170
  XTree for Windows, 224
addresses of drives, 11–12
  See also names/naming
All option (Scope), 57
Alt key combinations. See shortcuts

American Standard Code for Information Interchange files. See ASCII files
answers to pop quiz, 375–377
Application Menu, 38–41
  accessing from pull-down menus, 153
  activating menu items, 38
  editing the menu, 39–41
  overview, 38
  system management using, 41
applications. See programs
Arc files
  creating, 299–302, 305–308
  encryption, 301–302, 307
  extracting archived files, 303, 310
  modifying, 304–305, 311–312
  opening, 302–303, 309–310
  See also archiving
archive attribute, 20
  XTree for DOS, 42–43
  XTree for Windows, 236–237, 242
  XTreeNet, 207
Archived date attribute, 207, 209
archiving, 297–316
  Archive module missing, 367
  basics, 297–298
  defined, 297–298
  when to archive, 298–299
  with XTree for Windows, 312–316
    encryption option, 314
    long method, 313–314
    modifying Zip file properties, 315
    mounting Zip files, 316
    opening Zip files, 315
    shortcut, 312
    treating Zip files like drives, 315–316
  with XTreeGold, 305–312
    creating archive files, 305–308
    encryption option, 307
    extracting archived files, 310
    method option, 308
    modifying archive files, 311–312
    opening archives, 309–310
    path options, 307
    speed/size option, 308
  with XTreePro Gold, 299–305
    creating archive files, 299–302
    encryption option, 301–302
    extracting archived files, 303
    format selection, 300–301
    modifying archived files, 304–305
    opening archives, 302–303
Arrange Now command, 236
arrow keys
  in 1Word, 96
  for filespec history, 110, 111
  in Windows, 219

ASCII files, 18
   saving viewed files as, 188–189
associating data files with programs, 147–148
asterisk (*)
   ** attribute with Oops!, 363
   star-dot-star filespec, 32
   Tree window icon, 252
   as wildcard, 19
Attach command, 204, 206
Attribute Flags command, 236–237
Attributes command
   XTree for DOS, 42–43
   XTreeNet directories, 206
   XTreeNet files, 207–208, 209
attributes of files, 20–21
   ** attribute with Oops!, 363
   changing, 42–43, 161–162, 237
   displaying, 41–42, 236–237
   tagging files by, 180–181, 209
   XTree for DOS, 41–43, 161–162, 180–181
   XTree for Windows, 236–237
   XTreeNet, 206–208, 209
Audible error indicator configuration, 65
Auto Arrange command, 235–236
Auto Directory window, 222
   basics, 224
   Directory window vs., 237, 248
   opening, 248
   See also Directory window
Auto View window, 223, 238
   View window vs., 238
Auto Viewer command, 234
Auto Viewer Region Layout, 234–235
AutoCAD files, 361
AUTOEXEC.BAT file
   editing with 1Word, 96–98
   overview, 22
   renaming directories and, 86, 267
   sample, 284–285
AutoView command, 190–191
Avail command, 44

— B —

backing up
   commercial programs for, 285
   daily backup, 288
   by date, 291–292, 294
   incremental backups, 289, 291, 294
   keeping track, 290–291
   overview, 288–289
   preparing floppies, 289
   system backup, 289
   with XTree for DOS, 290–292
   with XTree for Windows, 294
backslash (\)
   highlighting using, 269–270
   in system prompt, 15
Backspace key in 1Word, 94, 95
BACKTAB previous item command, 197–198
BACKUP command, 23
BAK extension, 17
   deleting BAK files, 292–293, 295–296
BAT extension, 17
   See also batch files
batch files, 44–48
   associating data files with programs, 147–148
   creating, 45–46

DOS variables, 46–47
   overview, 44–45
   XTree variables, 48
bold type in this book, 5
books, reference, 369
Branch command, 49
   Showall command vs., 49
Branch log option, 131
Branch tagging in XTreeNet, 208
Broomfield, Ken, 371

— C —

Cabeen, Bob, 373
cables for XTreeLink, 318
cache programs, 286
Cahlin, Michael, 372
Cahlin/Williams Communications, 372
Cancel command, 49–50
   Quit command vs., 49
canceling commands, 49–50, 136
Can't find file XTPRO.X01 message, 357
Can't Update Parent Directory message, 73, 89, 142
car won't start, 363
carat (^) in XTree for DOS command area, 28
Cascade command, 235
case of DOS commands, 9
CD-ROM drives, 358
Central Point Software, 285, 368
Change Attributes command, 237, 244
character, 17
Character Dump View option, 276
check boxes, 220
CHKDSK command, 23, 282–283
click, 215
Close command, 238–239
closing. *See* exiting
cluster, 282
Collapse commands, 254
collapsing
   directory tree, 90–92, 252–254
   XTreeMenu display, 193
colon (:) in drive names, 12
COM extension, 17
COM port, 318
command buttons in dialog boxes, 220
COMMAND.COM file, 21
command keys. *See* keyboard commands
Command shell
   activating, 51
   Execute command, 32, 51, 100–102
   History command, 53–55, 126–127
   overview, 32, 51
   using, 52–53
   XTree for DOS, 32, 51–55
commands
   canceling in XTree for DOS, 49–50, 136
   case of DOS commands, 9
   conventions in this book, 5–6
   editing typographical errors, 127
   XTree for DOS Quick Reference Guide, 35–198
   XTree for Windows Quick Reference Guide, 233–278
   See also DOS commands; XTree for DOS commands; XTree for Windows commands; *specific DOS and XTree commands*
common questions. *See* questions commonly asked
Compare command, 55–58

Index

compressing files. *See* archiving
CompuServe, 368
computers, laptop. *See* laptop configuration
computers, linking. *See* XTreeLink
CONFIG.SYS file
   modifying with XTree for Windows, 320
   modifying with XTreeGold, 319
   overview, 21
   sample, 284
   SUBST command and, 174–175
   for XTreeLink, 319–320
configuration
   AUTOEXEC.BAT sample, 284–285
   CONFIG.SYS sample, 284
   defined, 58
   Edit command for your word processor, 99
   for hidden directories, 163
   for hidden files, 162
   laptop configuration for XTree versions, 345–354
   logging instructions, 133
   XTree for DOS options, 58–65
   XTree for Windows options, 239
   XTreeNet default configuration, 365
   See also laptop configuration
Control menu (Windows), 214
Copy Archive Flag on Copies option, 242, 266
Copy command
   Copy dialog box options, 240–242
   copying directories, 72–73, 87–88
   copying files, 65–75
   getting messages from XTree for Windows, 243–244
   Move command vs., 65
   Preferences dialog box options, 242–243
   XTree for DOS, 65–75, 87–88
   XTree for Windows, 230, 239–244
COPY CON command, 45–46
Copy dialog box options, 240–242
Copy icon, 239
Copy New Files and Update Existing Ones option, 241
Copy Source Directly into Destination option, 241
copying directories
   directory options, 241
   duplicating directory structure, 72–73, 87–88
   getting messages from XTree for Windows, 243–244
   grafting directories, 73–74
   in XTree for Windows, 239–244
copying files, 22, 65–75
   Destination window for, 74–75
   directory options, 241
   directory structure duplication, 72–73
   file options, 241
   getting messages from XTree for Windows, 243–244
   multiple files, 69–72
   to other directories, 68–69
   to other drives, 66–68
   renaming during, 66, 240
   replacing files, 67–68, 241
   in XTree for Windows, 239–244
   as Zip files, 312
copying scripts in XTreeMenu, 198
Create directory attribute, 206
Creation date attribute
   XTreeNet directories, 206
   XTreeNet files, 207, 209
cross reference icon, 5
cross-linked cluster, 282
Ctrl key combinations. *See* shortcuts
current drive, 12
Custom Directory window, 247
customer support, 367, 368

— D —

daily backup, 288
date
   backing up by, 291–292, 294
   date and time stamp, 76–77, 244
   sorting files by, 76–77, 167, 168
Date & time sort criteria, 167, 168
date and time stamp, 76–77, 244
DATE command, 76
Dates attributes (XTreeNet), 207–208
defraggers, 285–286
Del key in 1Word, 95
Delete command, 230
   deleting directories, 80, 86–87, 244–245
   deleting files, 78–80, 244–245
   XTree for DOS, 78–80, 86–87, 230
   XTree for Windows, 230, 244–245
Delete directory attribute, 206
Delete icon, 244
deleting
   Application Menu items, 40–41
   attributes and, 80
   BAK and TMP files, 292–293, 295–296
   COMMAND.COM file, 21
   Delete command, 78–80
   directories, 80–81, 86–87, 88–89, 244–245
   duplicate files, 292, 294–295
   files, 78–80, 244–245
   files from Command shell, 51
   files from floppy drive, 78–79
   files unrecoverably, 81–82, 164, 210
   multiple files, 79–80
   obsolete files, 290
   pruning directories, 81, 88–89
   turning off file attributes, 42–43
   undeleting files, 145–146
   XTreeMenu items, 194–195
Department of Defense 5220.22-M specification, 82, 164
Deselect command, 270
desktop-to-laptop connection. *See* XTreeLink
DESQView, XTreePro Gold with, 359
Destination window
   copying using, 74–75
   moving using, 142
Detach command, 205, 206
Detail Box, 245
dialog boxes, 219–220
Dialogs on Drag and Drop option, 242, 266
DIR Empty message, 82–83
DIR Not Logged message, 82–83
directories, 12–14, 84–94
   collapsing the directory tree, 90–92
   comparing, 55–58
   copying, 239–244
   copying files between, 68–69
   creating, 14, 84–85
   deleting, 80–81, 86–87, 88–89, 244–245
   DOS directory, 10
   duplicating structure when copying, 72–73, 87–88
   finding, 112, 254–255
   finding owner, 365
   grafting, 73–74, 89, 141–142, 360
   hiding and unhiding, 93–94, 162–163
   highlighting in XTree for DOS, 29
   Inverted Tree Hierarchical Structure, 12–13
   logging, 131–132
   logging single directory at startup, 134, 174–177
   management strategies, 283
   managing, 84–94

marking and unmarking, 258–260
maximum files per directory, 14
moving, 73–74, 89, 141–142
Novell mail directories, 365
overview, 12–14
path, 13
printing list of, 148
pruning, 81, 88–89
renaming, 85–86, 158, 267
replacing when moving, 262
restoring collapsed directories, 90–92
splitting and unsplitting windows, 169–171, 358
starting XTree with specific directory highlighted, 364
subdirectories, 15
substituting as drives, 174–177
tagging all files in, 178–179
XTree for Windows basics, 225–226
See also tagging directories
Directory Filter, 250, 259
Directory Format command, 236–237, 249–250
Directory Format dialog box, 249–250
  Attribute Flags option, 236–237
Directory Sort Order command, 251, 271
DIRECTORY Stats window, 172
Directory window (XTree for DOS), 27, 94
  Auto Directory window vs., 237
  comparing directories from, 56–57
  mouse usage, 137
  shortcuts, 330, 331, 333, 335–336, 337–338
  splitting and unsplitting, 169–171
  XTree for Windows version of, 228
Directory window (XTree for Windows), 222, 245–251
  Auto Directory window vs., 237, 248
  basics, 225
  custom windows, 247
  Directory Filter, 250
  Directory Format, 249–250
  Directory Sort Order, 251
  modifying display, 249–251
  Move Up button, 263, 264
  navigating, 248–249
  opening, 246
Directory window (XTreeNet) shortcuts, 340–341
disaster recovery programs, 286–287
disk cache programs, 286
Disk drive log option, 131
disk drives. *See* drives; floppy drives; hard disks
disk scrubbers, 286
DISK Statistics window, 28, 171
Disk Technician, 286, 368
DISK window, 28
diskettes. *See* floppy disks
displaying
  all files in current directory and child directories, 49
  all files in current drive, 165
  all tagged files in current directory and child directories, 49
  all tagged files in current drive, 165, 181
  attributes of files, 41–42, 236–237
  AutoCAD files, 361
  AutoView command, 190–191
  collapsing/restoring directory tree, 90–92
  current date and time, 76–77
  date and time before changing, 76
  disk space available, 44, 210
  EGA configuration, 65
  file contents, 184–191, 275–277, 361

File display command, 41–42, 103–104
files by date and/or time, 76–77
filespecs too long for window, 110
hidden files, 161–162
hiding and unhiding directories, 93–94, 162–163
history in Command shell, 53–55
Showall command for, 165–166
splitting and unsplitting windows, 169–171, 358
VGA configuration, 65
View command, 184–189
WPG files, 361
DOC extension, 17
DoD washing option, 82, 164
DOS 5 Complete Handbook, 369
DOS, 9–23
  batch files, 44–48
  case of commands, 9
  command conventions in this book, 6
  date and time stamp, 76–77
  directories, 12–14
  drives, 11–12
  exiting to DOS, 11
  file extensions, 17–18
  filename rules, 16–17
  knowledge required, 1
  meanings of, 10–11
  MS-DOS acronym explained, 10
  programs vs., 11
  system prompt, 14–15
  upgrading, 287–288
  version determination, 287–288
  wildcards, 18–20
  XTreePro Gold with DOS 4.0 and 5.0, 358
DOS commands
  BACKUP, 23
  case of, 9
  CHKDSK, 23, 282–283
  COPY CON, 45–46
  DATE, 76
  FORMAT, 23, 117
  LH XTGOLD, 135
  LOADHIGH XTGOLD, 135
  SUBST, 174–177
  TIME, 76
  VER, 23, 287–288
DOS directory, 10
DOS For Dummies, 369
DOS shell. *See* Command shell
double-click, 215
drag and drop, 215
drives
  copying files between, 66–68
  current drive, 12
  defined, 11
  finding directories and files, 112–115
  names of, 11–12
  overview, 11–12
  relogging, 51, 129
  substituting directories as, 174–177
  Zip files as, 315–316
  See also floppy drives; hard disks; logging
Duplicate Complete Paths option, 241, 262
Duplicate directory comparison criterion, 57
Duplicate Paths from Window Root option, 262
duplicating. *See* copying
Dvorak, John, 373

Index

— E —

Edit command
 for 1Word, 94–99
 for your word processor, 99
 See also 1Word
Edit menu
 Deselect command, 270
 Find command, 254–255
 Mark command, 258–260
 Select commands, 269–271
 Unmark command, 260
editing
 Application Menu, 39–41
 creating new text files, 364
 files with 1Word, 94–99
  creating new files, 99, 364
  editing files, 96–98
  keyboard commands, 95–96
  limitations, 94–95
  maximum file size, 359
  printing, 151–152
 in Hex mode, 358
 typographical errors in commands, 127
 XTreeMenu display, 193–196
 XTreeMenu instructions, 196–198
Editors Choice Award, 374
EGA configuration, 65
ellipses (...)
 on Windows menus, 219
 on XTree for DOS menus, 154
EMM386.SYS, XTreeGold conflict with, 362
Enable Speed Logging option, 257, 266
encrypting archive files, 301–302, 307, 314
Enter key, Windows vs. DOS XTree usage, 225, 229
erasing. *See* deleting
error messages
 Can't find file XTPRO.X01, 357
 Can't Update Parent Directory, 73, 89, 142
 DIR Empty, 82–83
 DIR Not Logged, 82–83
 Error writing to *drive*, 243–244
 insufficient memory, 102, 148
 missing overlay, 362
 No Files!, 106, 143–144
 No Files Match, 83
 starting XTreePro, 356
 UNKNOWN, 275
Error writing to *drive* message, 243–244
Esc key
 in 1Word, 95–96
 canceling commands, 49
 returning to Directory window, 94
exclusionary filespecs, 109
EXE extension, 17
Execute command, 32, 51, 100–102
Execute-only attribute, 207, 208, 366
executing programs. *See* starting programs
Executive Systems Inc., 370
Exit command, 252
exiting
 Alt-Z for, 132, 156–157
 to another directory, 156
 canceling vs. quitting, 49
 closing windows, 216, 238–239
 to DOS, 11
 saving snapshot of screen, 132, 156–157

saving windows, 239
XTree for Windows, 252
XTree for Windows temporarily, 268
XTreeLink, 325
Expand commands, 253
Expanded file window, 27, 105
Ext sort criteria, 167, 168
Extended Statistics window, 172–173
extensions. *See* file extensions
extracting archived files, 303, 310

— F —

F keys. *See* function keys
Fastback, 285, 368
Fifth Generation Systems, 285, 286, 368
figures in XTree for DOS Quick Reference Guide, 37
file compression. *See* archiving
File display command, 103–104
 displaying attributes, 41–42
 XTree for Windows change, 229
file extensions
 associating with programs, 147–148
 Filespec command, 31–32
 guidelines, 18
 overview, 17–18
 sorting files by, 167, 168
File menu
 Close command, 238–239
 Exit command, 252
 Open Auto Directory command, 237, 248
 Open Auto View command, 238
 Open command, 246, 264–265, 315
 Open Directory As command, 247
 Open Document View command, 275–277
 Open Tree As command, 274
 Open Tree command, 274
 Preferences command, 239, 245, 262–263, 265–266
 Run command, 268
 Save Configuration command, 239, 265
file server, 201
File specification. *See* Filespec command
file transfers. *See* XTreeLink
File windows
 comparing directories from, 57–58
 Expanded file window, 27, 105
 Global file window, 110, 115, 119–121, 169, 363
 mouse usage, 137
 shortcuts, 330, 332, 333–334, 336, 338–339, 341–342
 Showall file window, 165–166, 169, 363
 Small file window, 27, 105
 splitting and unsplitting, 169–171
 XTree for Windows version of, 228
filenames
 conventions in this book, 6
 renaming when copying, 66
 renaming when moving, 138–139
 rules, 16–17
 wildcards, 18–20
files
 archiving, 297–316
 ASCII files, 18, 188–189
 associating with programs, 147–148
 attributes, 20–21
  XTree for DOS, 41–43, 161–162, 180–181
  XTree for Windows, 236–237
  XTreeNet, 206–208, 209
 batch files, 44–48

copying, 22, 65–75, 239–244
creating new text files, 364
defined, 15
deleting, 78–80, 244–245
   BAK and TMP files, 292–293, 295–296
   from Command shell, 51
   duplicate files, 292, 294–295
   from floppy drive, 78–79
   obsolete files, 290
   unrecoverably, 81–82, 164, 210
displaying contents, 184–191, 275–277, 361
duplicate files, 292, 294–295, 360
editing with 1Word, 94–99
file extensions, 17–18
finding, 112–115, 254–255, 364
finding owner, 365
graphics file viewing, 276, 277
hiding and unhiding, 161–162
highlighting in XTree for DOS, 29–30
marking and unmarking, 258–260
maximum for XTreePro, 61
maximum per directory, 14
moving, 138–141
naming rules, 16–17
operating system files, 21
overview, 15–17
peer-to-peer file management, 203–204
printing, 149–152, 189
printing list of, 148
printing to a file, 363
renaming using Rename command, 157–158, 267
renaming when copying, 66, 267
renaming when moving, 138–139
renaming XT*xxxx*.COM file, 364
sizes of XTree files, 345–354
storing old files on floppies, 293, 296
temporary, 292–293, 295–296
viewing contents, 184–191, 275–277
XTree for Windows basics, 225–226
XTree modules, 345–354
   XTree, 345
   XTree Easy, 348–349
   XTree for Windows, 352–354
   XTreeGold, 350–352
   XTreePro, 346
   XTreePro Gold, 346–348
See also tagging files; *specific files by name*
Filespec command, 31–32, 106–112
   basics, 106–108
   default, 106
   Directory Filter and, 250
   displaying lengthy filespecs, 110
   exclusionary specifications, 109
   Global file window with, 110
   History command with, 110, 111, 126
   inverting, 111–112, 129
   multiple filespecs, 108–110
   No Files Match message, 83
   No Files! message, 106
   preselecting filespecs at startup, 109, 133–134
   Showall command with, 165
   star-dot-star filespec, 32
   tagging files using, 70–71, 179–180
   wildcards with, 106–107
   XTree for Windows change, 229
Find command, 254–255
Find dialog box, 254–255

finding
   directories, 112, 254–255
   directory owner, 365
   duplicate files, 360
   file owner, 365
   files in XTreePro Gold, 357–358
   files on current disk, 112–113, 254–255
   files on floppies, 113–114, 255
   text, 114–115, 188, 255
   in XTree for DOS, 112–115
   XTreeNet files for an owner, 364
Fit in Window option, 276
Flags attributes
   XTreeNet directories, 206
   XTreeNet files, 207–208, 209
floppy disks
   batch file for formatting, 45–46
   deleting files unrecoverably, 81–82, 164
   determining if formatted, 116, 256
   finding files, 113–114, 255
   formatting, 116–119, 210, 255–256
   high-density vs. low-density, 116–117, 256
   preparing for backups, 289
   space available on, 44
   storing old files on, 293, 296
   tagging all files, 179
   washing, 81–82, 358
   XTree for Windows basics, 225–226
floppy drives
   copying files between drives, 66–68
   current drive, 12
   deleting files from, 78–79
   high-density vs. low-density, 116–117
   names of, 11–12
   overview, 11–12
   See also drives
FORMAT command, 23, 117
Format command, XTreeNet, 210
Format Diskette command, 256
formatting disks
   batch file for formatting floppies, 45–46
   determining if formatted, 116, 256
   floppy disks, 116–119, 210
   high-density vs. low-density, 116–117, 256
   XTree for Windows, 255–256
Freshen Modified Existing Files Only option, 241
freshening archived files, 305, 312
fun meter, 1
function keys, 329–344
   Alt-F2 (format), 117–119
   Alt-F7 (remote control), 204–205
   Alt-F8 (partial untag), 183
   Ctrl-F7 (tag branch), 208
   Ctrl-F8 (untag branch), 208
   described, 256
   F1 (Help), 32, 96, 122–124
   F2 (display list), 205
   F2 (Help), 32, 121–122
   F2 (open tree), 274
   F2 (select path or point), 74–75, 142
   F2 (Wash Disk options), 82
   F3 (cancel), 49–50
   F4 (disk space used), 275
   F5 (collapse/restore two directory levels), 91–92
   F6 (collapse/restore all directory levels), 92
   F6 (find), 254–255
   F8 (split window), 358

Index

F10 (pull-down menus), 153, 193, 360
F10 (Quick Reference), 124–126
Shift-F2 (open tree as), 274
Shift-F8 (add mode), 226
Windows (Microsoft), 215–216
XTree, 331
XTree Easy, 337
  in XTree for DOS, 119
  XTree for Windows, 343–344
  XTreeGold, 339–340
  XTreeNet, 342–343
  XTreePro, 332
  XTreePro Gold, 334–335

— G —

Gather command, 188, 189
Gazelle Systems, 286, 368
Gibson Research, 286, 368
Global command, 119–121
Global file window, 119–121
  finding text over several drives, 115
  multiple filespecs with, 110
  Showall file window vs., 363
  sorting by path, 169
GLOBAL Statistics window, 172, 173
Golden Bow Systems, 286, 368
Goodman, John, 369
Gookin, Dan, 369
Graft command, 73–74, 89, 121, 141–142
  Prune command vs., 358
grafting directories, 73–74, 89, 141–142
  across drives, 360
  pruning vs., 358
  relogging after, 73, 89, 142
greater-than symbol (>) in system prompt, 15
guidelines. See rules and guidelines

— H —

Halliday, Caroline M., 369
hard disk management, 281–296
  backing up, 285, 288–289, 290–292, 294
  commercial programs, 285–288
  configuring your system, 284–285
  deleting BAK and TMP files, 292–293, 295–296
  deleting duplicate files, 292, 294–295
  deleting obsolete files, 290
  directory strategies, 283
  optimization, 282–288
  overview, 281
  step-by-step maintenance, 288–290
  with XTree for DOS, 290–293
  with XTree for Windows, 294–296
Hard Disk Secrets, 369
hard disks
  backing up, 285, 288–289, 290–292, 294
  cache programs, 286
  copying files between drives, 66–68
  current drive, 12
  defraggers, 285–286
  deleting files unrecoverably, 81–82, 164
  deleting obsolete files, 290
  disk scrubbers, 286
  finding directories and files, 112–115
  installing XTree on, 355–356
  laptop configuration for XTree versions, 345–354
  managing, 281–296

names of, 11–12
overview, 11–12
space available on, 44, 210
space requirements of XTree files, 345–354
tagging all files, 179
washing, 81–82
XTree for Windows basics, 225–226
See also drives
headers, printing, 151
Help
  Help command, 121–124
  Quick Reference, 124–126
  XTree for DOS, 32
Hernandez, Henry, 370
Hexadecimal Dump View option, 276
Hicks, Clinton, 369
hidden attribute, 21
  XTree for DOS, 42–43, 161–162
  XTree for Windows, 236–237
  XTreeNet directories, 206
  XTreeNet files, 207
Hide command, 93–94, 162–163
hiding
  Detail Box, 245
  directories, 93–94, 162–163
  files, 161–162
hierarchical structure, 13
high memory, loading XTreeGold into, 135
high-density floppies, 116–117, 256
  See also floppy disks
highlighting
  destination directory for copying, 74–75
  directories in XTree for DOS, 29
  files in XTree for DOS, 29–30
  keyboard usage in XTree for Windows, 269
  marking vs., 259
  mouse usage, 137, 269
  tagging files using, 70
  XTree for Windows basics, 225–226
History command, 126–128
  for Command shell, 53–55, 126–127
  editing typographical errors in commands, 127
  for filespecs, 110, 111, 126
  labels for entries, 128
  moving using, 143
  for page length when printing, 151
  permanent history entries, 127–128
  for renaming, 160
  XTree for Windows change, 229
history of XTree, 370–374

— I —

IBMBIO.COM file, 21
IBMDOS.COM file, 21
icons
  in margins of this book, 5
  Tool Palette, 227, 272–273
    Copy icon, 239
    Delete icon, 244
    illustrated, 273
    Mark icon, 259
    Move icon, 260
    Rename icon, 267
    Select icon, 269
    Unmark icon, 260
    View icon, 275

Tree window expand/collapse icons, 252–253
Windows application icons, 214
for XTree for DOS versions, 36–37
Identical dates directory comparison criterion, 57
Identical directory comparison criterion, 56
IDG Books, 367, 369
illustrations in XTree for DOS Quick Reference Guide, 37
incremental backups, 289, 291, 294
Indexed attribute, 207
Info display command, 205
Information Mode (XTreeNet), 205
Initial directory configuration, 63
Insert key, for permanent history entries, 127–128
installing
    XTree on hard disk, 355–356
    XTreeLink, 320
Instant Log command, 132, 357
insufficient memory message, 102, 148
Invert command, 128–129
    for filespecs, 111–112, 129, 181–182
inverted filespecs, 111–112
Inverted Tree Hierarchical Structure, 12–13
IO.SYS file, 21
italic type in this book, 5

— J —

Johnson, Arletta, 372, 374
Johnson, Arynn, 374
Johnson, Claire, 371
Johnson, Dan, 374
Johnson, Jeff, 370
Johnson, Tari, 374

— K —

Karas, Mike, 371
keyboard commands, 329–344
    in 1Word, 95–96
    conventions in this book, 5
    directory navigation in XTree for Windows, 230
    for highlighting in XTree for Windows, 226
    mouse vs., 233–234
    sizing windows, 217–218
    Windows (Microsoft), 215–216
    Windows dialog box shortcuts, 220
    XTree, 330–331
    XTree Easy, 335–337
    XTree for Windows, 343–344
    XTreeGold, 337–340
    XTreeNet, 340–343
    XTreePro, 331–332
    XTreePro Gold, 333–335
keyboard locking, 161

— L —

L XTreeLink option switch, 322, 325
Label command, 210
labels
    for history entries, 128
    renaming volume labels, 159
    XTreeNet label command, 210
LANs. *See* local area networks (LANs)
laptop configuration, 345–354
    XTree Easy modules, 348–349
    XTree for Windows modules, 352–354
    XTree modules, 345

XTreeGold modules, 350–352
XTreePro Gold modules, 346–348
XTreePro modules, 346
laptop-to-desktop connection. *See* XTreeLink
LASTDRIVE statement, 175
    for XTreeLink, 319–320
launching programs. *See* starting programs
level expansion buttons, 252
LH XTGOLD command, 135
lists
    pick lists (XTreeNet), 205
    printing for directories and files, 148
Livingston, Brian, 369
LOADHIGH XTGOLD command, 135
local area networks (LANs), 202
    See also XTreeNet
Log All on Start Up option, 257, 266
Log command, 129–134
Log Files with Directories option, 257, 266
logging
    command line switches for, 133–134
    cumulatively, 130
    cycling through logged drives, 130, 359, 360
    defined, 129
    DIR Not Logged message, 82–83
    directories, 131–132
    entire volume in XTreeNet, 365
    grafting directories and, 73, 89, 142
    Instant Log command, 132, 357
    logging options, 131–132, 257–258
    maximum files in XTreeNet, 365
    multiple drives at startup, 134
    preferences for, 257, 266
    refreshing the display, 131, 258
    releasing from memory, 130–131
    relogging drives, 51, 129
    single directory at startup, 134, 174–177
    unformatted floppies and, 116
    in XTree for DOS, 129–134
    in XTree for Windows, 257–258, 266
lost clusters, 282
low-density floppies, 116–117, 256
    See also floppy disks
LPT2, printing to, 363
LPT port, 318

— M —

M XTreeLink option switch, 325
Mace Utilities, 286, 287, 368
Main menu (Windows), 218–219
Make command, 84–85
    XTree for Windows change, 229
managing your system, 41
Map command, 209
    file management, 203–204
    remote control, 204–205
margin icons in this book, 5
Mark command, 258–260
marking
    files and directories, 259–260
    highlighting vs., 259
    how to use, 258–259
    unmarking, 260
Mason, Judy, 372
Matching paths option, 57
Maximize button (Windows), 214

Index

media, 118
memory, 134–135
    7K Wedge, 135, 357, 362
    DIR Not Logged message and, 83
    Execute command and, 102, 148
    insufficient memory message, 102, 148
    laptop configuration for XTree versions, 345–354
    loading XTreeGold into high memory, 135
    managing, 134–135
    Open command and, 148
    releasing logged drives, 130–131
    XTreeGold 2.0 and memory shortages, 360
    XTreePro 1.0 and memory shortages, 357
    XTreePro Gold requirement, 359
menus (Windows), 218–219
menus (XTree for DOS)
    Application Menu, 38–41, 153
    command menu, 136–137
    configuration menus, 59–65
    ellipses on, 154
    pull-down menus, 152–155, 360
    XTreeMenu, 191–198
    See also specific menus by name
Microsoft Disk Operating System (MS-DOS). *See* DOS
Microsoft Windows. *See* Windows (Microsoft)
Minimize button (Windows), 214
minus sign (–)
    collapsing XTreeMenu display, 193
    cycling through logged drives, 359, 360
    exclusionary filespecs, 109
    Tree window icon, 252–253
    turning attributes off, 42–43
    unlogging directories, 131
missing overlay message, 362
Modified date attribute, 207, 209
Modify directory attribute, 206
modifying archived files, 304–305, 311–312, 315
modules. *See* laptop configuration
Mount ZIP command, 316
mouse (XTree for DOS), 37, 136–137
    executing programs, 53
    menu navigation, 153
mouse (XTree for Windows)
    click, 215
    command menu usage, 136–137
    directory navigation, 230
    double-click, 215
    drag and drop, 215
    highlighting items, 226
    keyboard vs., 233–234
    not working with XTreeGold, 361
    sizing windows, 217–218
    Windows basics, 215
Move command
    Copy command vs., 65
    directory options, 262
    getting messages from XTree for Windows, 263
    Preferences dialog box options, 262–263
    setting defaults, 262
    XTree for DOS, 138–143
    XTree for Windows, 230, 260–263
Move Source Directly into Destination option, 262
Move Up button, 249, 263–264
moving
    cycling through logged drives, 130, 359, 360
    default settings, 262–263
    destination selection, 261
    Destination window for, 142
    directory options, 262
    files, 138–141
    getting messages from XTree for Windows, 263
    grafting directories, 73–74, 89, 141–142
    History command and, 143
    multiple files, 140–141
    renaming files during, 138–139, 262
    replacing files, 139–140
    in XTree for DOS, 138–143
    in XTree for Windows, 260–263
    XTreeMenu items, 195–196
    See also navigating
MS-DOS. *See* DOS
MSDOS.SYS file, 21
multiple files
    copying, 69–72
    deleting, 79–80
    moving, 140–141
multiple filespecs, 108–110
Multisoft Corp., 286, 368

— N —

Name sort criteria, 167, 168
names/naming
    DOS directory, 10
    drive names, 11–12
    filename conventions in this book, 6
    filename rules, 16–17
    History command and renaming, 160
    renaming
        directories, 85–86, 158, 267
        files using Rename command, 157–158, 267
        files when copying, 66, 241, 267
        files when moving, 138–139, 263
        volume labels, 159, 210, 267–268
        XT*xxxx*.COM file, 364
    sorting files by name, 167, 168
    wildcards, 18–20
navigating
    between split windows, 361
    between windows, 29
    cycling through logged drives, 130, 359, 360
    directories in XTree for Windows, 230, 248–249
    moving windows, 217
NetWare, 202, 203
Network shareable attribute, 207
networking, 201
networks. *See* local area networks (LANs); XTreeNet
New ZIP command, 313
Newdate command, 76–77
Newer directory comparison criterion, 56
Newest dates directory comparison criterion, 57
No Files Match message, 83
No Files! message, 106, 143–144
Normal View option, 276
Norton Utilities, 286, 287, 368
note icon, 5
notebook computer configuration. *See* laptop configuration
Novell mail directories, 365
number icons, 252

— O —

obsolete files, deleting, 290
Official XTree MS-DOS, Windows, and Hard Disk Management Companion, The
    conventions used, 4–6
    how to use, 2–4, 36–37

icons in margins, 5
purpose, 6
Older directory comparison criterion, 56
Oldest dates directory comparison criterion, 57
One level log option, 131
Oops! command, 145–146, 363
Open Auto Directory command, 237, 248
Open Auto View command, 238
Open command
    associating data files with programs, 147–148
    XTree for Windows, 246, 264–265, 315
    for Zip files, 315
Open Directory As command, 247
Open directory attribute, 206
Open Document View command, 275–277
Open Tree As command, 274
Open Tree command, 274
opening applications. *See* starting programs
opening archive files, 302–303, 309–310, 315
operating system
    described, 10
    files, 21
    See also DOS
optimizing your hard disk, 282–288
OPTune, 286, 368
OS/2, XTreePro Gold with, 359
Overlay command, 235
Owner attribute
    finding XTreeNet files for an owner, 364
    XTreeNet directories, 206
    XTreeNet files, 207, 209, 364

— P —

P XTreeLink option switch, 321, 322, 325
page length when printing, 150–151
parallel port, 318
Parental directory attribute, 206
path
    defined, 13
    Map command, 203–205, 209
    renaming directories and, 86, 267
    restoring paths from Zip file, 363
    sorting files by, 169
Path sort criteria, 169
PC Magazine, 374
PC Secrets, 369
PC Tools, 285, 368
PC-CACHE, 362
PC-DOS. *See* DOS
PC-Kwik, 286, 287, 368
PCs For Dummies, 369
peer-to-peer file management, 203–204
peer-to-peer remote control, 204–205
percent sign (%) in batch file variables, 47–48
period (.) in filenames, 16, 17
Pick List window, 205
PIF files, 359
PKarc. *See* Arc files; archiving
PKzip. *See* archiving; Zip files
Plain Text View option, 276
plus sign (+)
    collapsed directories, 91
    collapsed XTreeMenu display, 193
    cycling through logged drives, 359, 360
    key combinations in this book, 5
    logging directories, 131
    Tree window icon, 252–253
    turning attributes on, 42–43

plus/minus prompt (+/–), 173
pop quiz answers, 375–377
portable computer configuration. *See* laptop configuration
Pournelle, Jerry, 373
Preferences command, 239, 245, 262–263, 265–266
Preferences dialog box, 265–266
    copy options, 242–243, 266
    disk logging, 266
    hiding Tool Palette and Detail Box, 245
    move options, 262–263, 266
    Save Defaults and Window Arrangements on Application Exit option, 266
Prime Solutions, 286, 368
Print command, 148–151
printing
    from 1Word, 151–152
    to a file, 363
    files, 149–152, 189
    headers, 151
    History command and, 151
    list of files and directories, 148
    to LPT2, 363
    page length for, 150–151
private attribute, 206
programs
    adding to Application Menu, 39–41
    backup software, 285
    cache programs, 286
    deleting from Application Menu, 40–41
    deleting from XTreeMenu, 194–195
    disaster recovery programs, 286–287
    disk defraggers, 285–286
    disk scrubbers, 286
    DOS vs., 11
    minimizing in Windows, 218
    recommended software, 368
    starting from Application Menu, 38
    starting in XTree for DOS Command shell, 32
    utility collections, 287
prompt
    overview, 14–15
    reaching from XTree for Windows, 268
Prune command, 81, 88–89
    Graft command vs., 358
pruning directories, 81, 88–89
    grafting vs., 358
pull-down menus
    Windows, 218–219
    XTree for DOS, 152–155
    XTreeGold, 360
punctuation marks. *See* signs and symbols; *specific punctuation marks by name*

— Q —

question mark (?)
    for Extended Statistics window access, 173
    as wildcard, 20
questions commonly asked, 355–366
    all versions, 363–364
    XTree, 355–356
    XTreeGold, 360–363
    XTreeNet, 364–366
    XTreePro, 356–357
    XTreePro Gold, 357–359
Quick Reference, 124–126
quick reference guides
    XTree for DOS, 35–198
    XTree for Windows, 233–278

Index

Quit command, 156–157
  Cancel command vs., 49
quitting. *See* exiting
quiz answers, 375–377

— R —

RAM. *See* memory
Rathbone, Andy, 369
Read directory attribute, 206
READ.ME files, printing, 149
read-only attribute, 20
  XTree for DOS, 42–43
  XTree for Windows, 236–237
  XTreeNet, 207
reference books, 369
Refresh commands, 258
Refresh log option, 131
Region Layout menu, 234
Release command, 83
remote control over LANs, 204–205
removing. *See* deleting
Rename command
  XTree for DOS, 85–86, 157–160
  XTree for Windows, 230, 267–268
renaming
  directories, 85–86, 158, 267
  files using Rename command, 157–158, 267
  files when copying, 66, 241, 267
  files when moving, 138–139, 262
  History command and, 160
  path statement and, 86, 267
  volume labels, 159, 210, 267–268
  XT*xxxx*.COM file, 364
  See also names/naming
Replace Existing Directories option, 262
replacing directories, 262
replacing files
  when copying, 67–68, 241
  when moving, 139–140
Restore button (Windows), 214
restoring
  collapsed directory tree, 90–92
  undeleting files, 145–146
  unerase programs, 286–287
  unhiding directories, 93–94, 163
retiring old files, 293, 296
RF XTreeLink option switch, 325
Rights mask directory attribute, 206
rules and guidelines
  asterisk wildcard usage, 19
  file extensions, 18
  filenames, 16–17
Run command, 268
running programs. *See* starting programs
Ryan, Pete, 373

— S —

S XTreeLink option switch, 321, 322
Save Configuration command, 239, 265
Save Defaults and Window Arrangements on Application Exit option, 266
saving viewed files as ASCII files, 188–189
Scope directory comparison criterion, 57
screen illustrations, 37
scripts, XTreeMenu, 196–198
Scroll bars (Windows), 214
Search directory attribute, 206
searching. *See* finding

security, 160–164
  hiding directories, 93–94, 162–163
  hiding files, 161–162
  locking keyboards, 161
  for networks, 202, 210
  Wash command, 210
  Wash Disk command, 81–82, 164, 358
  for XTreeMenu, 198
Select All command, 269
Select All Files command, 270
Select/Deselect dialog box, 270–271
selecting. *See* highlighting; tagging directories; tagging files
serial number of XTree, 356
serial port, 318
Set Archive Flag on Copies option, 242, 266
Set Scope command, 248–249, 274
shell. *See* Command shell
shortcuts, 329–344
  XTree, 330–331
  XTree Easy, 335–337
  XTree for Windows, 343–344
  XTreeGold, 337–340
  XTreeNet, 340–343
  XTreePro, 331–332
  XTreePro Gold, 333–335
Showall command, 165–166
  Branch command vs., 49
  tagged files and, 165, 181
Showall file window, 165–166
  Global file window vs., 363
  sorting by path, 169
SHOWALL Statistics window, 172, 173
showing. *See* displaying
signs and symbols
  forbidden in filenames, 17
  wildcards, 18–20
  See also specific signs and symbols by name
Sinor, Dale, 371, 372
Six passes washing option, 82, 164
Size sort criteria, 167, 168
sizing windows, 217–218
Skip Quit command configuration, 65
Small file window, 27, 105
Smith, Tom, 371
Socha, John, 369
software. *See* programs
Sort Criteria command, 166–169
sort order
  by date, 76–77, 167, 168
  Directory Sort Order command, 251
  by extension, 167, 168
  by path, 169
  by size, 167, 168
  Sort Criteria command, 166–169
  by time, 76–77, 167, 168
  unsorted, 168
  in XTree for Windows, 271
  XTreePro configuration, 60
speed/size option for archiving, 308, 313
SpinRite II, 286, 287, 368
Split command, 169–171, 358
Standard Region Layout, 234
star-dot-star filespec, 32
starting programs
  activating the Command shell, 51
  activating XTreeMenu, 192
  from Application Menu, 38
  associating data files with programs, 147–148
  from DOS Command shell, 32, 51, 100–102
  Edit command for your word processor, 99
  Execute command usage, 32, 51, 100–102

using mouse, 53
using Run command, 268
using XTreeLink, 317
Windows from XTreeGold directory, 362
XTree for DOS configuration programs, 59, 60, 62
in XTree for Windows, 265
XTreeLink, 321–322
XTreeMenu not executing programs, 362
starting XTree
   error message when starting XTreePro, 356
   loading XTreeGold into high memory, 135
   logging multiple drives, 134
   logging single directory, 134, 174–177
   preselecting filespecs, 109, 133–134
   with specific directory highlighted, 364
   with XTreeMenu displayed, 198
statistics, 171–173
   DIRECTORY Stats window, 172
   DISK Statistics window, 28, 171
   Extended Statistics window, 172–173
   GLOBAL Statistics window, 172, 173
   SHOWALL Statistics window, 172, 173
   XTree for Windows, 272
   XTreeNet, 205
Statistics Mode (XTreeNet), 205
storing old files on floppies, 293, 296
subdirectories, 15
   See also directories
SUBST command, 174–177
support, 367, 368
switcher box, 318
Symantec, 285, 286, 287, 368
symbols. *See* signs and symbols; *specific symbols by name*
SYSCON (NetWare program), 202
system administrator, 201, 202
system attribute, 21
   XTree for DOS, 42–43
   XTree for Windows, 236–237
   XTreeNet directories, 206
   XTreeNet files, 207
system backup, 289
system management, 41
system prompt
   overview, 14–15
   reaching from XTree for Windows, 268

— T —

Tab next item command, 197–198
Tag command, 177–183
tagging directories
   Branches in XTreeNet, 208
   mouse usage, 137
   untagging in XTree for DOS, 31
   in XTree for DOS, 30–31
   See also highlighting
tagging files, 177–183
   all files in a directory, 178–179
   by attributes, 180–181, 209
   in compared directories, 56–57
   copying multiple files, 69–72
   deleting multiple files, 79–80
   displaying contents of tagged files, 189
   Filespec command and, 70–71
   Global command with, 121

hiding and unhiding tagged files, 162
inverting tags, 181–182
mouse usage, 137
Showall command and, 165, 181
untagging in XTree for DOS, 31, 177–180, 182–183
whole disk, 179
in XTree for DOS, 30–31, 70–71
See also highlighting
tape backup unit, 285
technical support, 367, 368
temporary files, 292–293, 295–296
text
   creating new text files, 364
   editing with 1Word, 94–99
   finding, 114–115, 188, 255
   saving viewed files as ASCII files, 188–189
   viewing file contents, 184–191, 276–277
text boxes, 220
Tile command, 235
time
   date and time stamp, 76–77
   sorting files by, 76–77, 167, 168
TIME command, 76
tip icon, 5
Title bar (Windows), 214
TMP files, deleting, 292–293, 295–296
Toggle Directory Format command, 271
toggling. *See* turning on and off
Tool Palette, 227, 272–273
   Copy icon, 239
   Delete icon, 244
   illustrated, 273
   Mark icon, 259
   Move icon, 260
   Rename icon, 267
   Select icon, 269
   Unmark icon, 260
   View icon, 275
Tool Palette and Detail Box option, 245
Tools menu
   Change Attributes command, 237, 244
   Copy command, 230, 239–244
   Delete command, 230, 244–245
   Move command, 230, 260–263
   Rename command, 230, 267–268
Transactional attribute, 207
transferring files. *See* XTreeLink
Tree only log option, 131–132
tree structure, 12–13
   moving up, 263–264
   XTreeMenu, 194
Tree window, 222, 273–274
   basics, 224
   expanding and collapsing the tree, 252–254
   level expansion buttons, 252
   Move Up button, 263
trustee, 205
Trustee Information Mode (XTreeNet), 205
Trustees directory attribute, 206, 366
turning on and off
   file attributes, 42–43
   XTreeMenu tree display, 194
TXT extension, 17–18

Index

— U —

U XTreeLink option switch, 325
unapologetic history of XTree, 370–374
undeleting files
    deleting files unrecoverably, 81–82, 164, 210
    Oops! command, 145–146
unerase programs, 286–287
Unhide command, unhiding directories, 93–94
unhiding directories, 93–94, 163
Unique directory comparison criterion, 56, 57
UNKNOWN message, 275
unloading XTreeLink, 325
unlogging directories, 131–132
Unmark command, 260
Unsorted sort criteria, 168
Unsplit command, 169–171
Untag command, 177–180, 182–183
untagging files and directories, 177–180, 182–183
    all files in a directory, 178–179
    filespecs for, 179–180
    by network attributes, 209
    partially untagging files, 182–183
    updating Showall file window, 166
    whole disk, 179
    XTree for DOS, 31
updating archived files, 305, 312
upgrading DOS version, 287–288
upgrading XTree version, 367
user rights, 202
utility collections, 287

— V —

Van Buren, Chris, 369
variables
    DOS batch file variables, 46–47
    XTree batch file variables, 48
VER command, 23, 287–288
versions of XTree, 25, 35–37
    upgrading, 367
VGA configuration, 65
View command, 184–189
    AutoView command, 190–191
    garbage displayed, 361
    See also displaying
View menu
    Collapse commands, 254
    Directory Format command, 236–237, 249–250
    Directory Sort Order command, 251, 271
    Expand commands, 253
    Set Scope command, 248–249, 274
    Toggle Directory Format command, 271
    viewing and zooming options, 276
View window, 223, 275–277
    Auto View window vs., 238
viewing. *See* displaying
volume, defined, 210
Volume command, 210
volume labels, renaming, 159, 210, 267–268
Volume menu
    Format Diskette command, 256
    Mount ZIP command, 316
    New ZIP command, 313
VOPT, 286, 368

— W —

warning icon, 5
Wash command, 210
Wash Disk command, 81–82, 164, 358
wetware, 14
wildcards, 18–20
    with Filespec command, 106–107
Window Layout commands, 235
Window menu
    Arrange Now command, 236
    Auto Arrange command, 235–236
    Refresh commands, 258
    Region Layout command, 234
    Window Layout commands, 235
Windows 3.1 Secrets, 369
Windows (Microsoft), 213–220
    active window, 213, 216
    closing windows, 216
    dialog boxes, 219–220
    DOS knowledge required, 213
    keyboard commands, 215–216
    menus, 218–219
    minimizing programs, 218
    mouse usage, 215
    moving windows, 217
    screen elements, 213–214
    sizing windows, 217–218
    starting from XTreeGold directory, 362
    XTreePro Gold with, 359
windows (XTree for DOS), 26–28
    active window, 169–170
    comparing directories, 55–58
    Destination window, 74–75, 142
    DIRECTORY Stats window, 172
    Directory window, 27, 94, 137
    DISK Statistics window, 28, 171
    DISK window, 28
    Expanded file window, 27, 105
    Extended Statistics window, 172–173
    Global file window, 110, 115, 119–121, 169, 363
    GLOBAL Statistics window, 172, 173
    mouse usage, 137
    moving between windows, 29, 361
    Showall file window, 165–166, 169, 363
    SHOWALL Statistics window, 172, 173
    Small file window, 27, 105
    splitting and unsplitting, 169–171, 358
windows (XTree for Windows), 222–223
    activating new window, 264
    active window, 224
    Arrange Now command, 236
    arranging, 234–236
    Auto Arrange command, 235–236
    Auto Directory window, 222, 237
    Auto View window, 223, 238
    Auto Viewer Region Layout, 234–235
    Custom Directory window, 247
    Directory window, 222, 225, 245–251
    layout options, 235
    maintaining selections when moving between windows, 271
    Standard Region Layout, 234
    Tree window, 222, 252–254, 273–274
    View window, 223, 275–277
windows (XTreeNet), Pick List window, 205
Windows For Dummies, 369
word processors, starting with Edit command, 99

WordPerfect graphics files, 361
words. *See* text
WPG files, 361
Write directory attribute, 206

— X —

X attribute, 207, 208, 366
X command, 32, 51, 100–102
XTG.EXE program, 362
XTG_CFG program, 62–65
XTLINK program. *See* XTreeLink
XTPROCFG program, 60–61
XTR_CFG program, 62–65
XTree
    canceling commands, 49–50
    Command shell with, 52
    configuring, 59–60
    Editors Choice Award, 374
    finding files on floppies, 113
    formatting floppies, 117
    Help, 121–122
    icon, 36–37
    installing on hard disk, 355–356
    keyboard commands and function keys, 330–331
    laptop configuration, 345
    maximum files readable, 356
    printing files, 150
    questions commonly asked, 355–356, 363–364
    quitting, 156
    replacing files when copying, 67
    serial number, 356
    shortcuts, 330–331
    Sort Criteria options, 167
    SUBST command with, 176
    version number, 367
    viewing file contents, 184–185
    See also XTree for DOS
XTree Company, 367
    mailing address, 368
    technical support, 367, 368
    upgrading XTree directly, 367
XTree Easy
    canceling commands, 50
    Command shell with, 52–53
    configuring, 61–65
    finding files on floppies, 114
    formatting floppies, 117–119
    Help, 122–123
    History command and, 54–55
    icon, 36–37
    keyboard commands and function keys, 335–337
    laptop configuration, 348–349
    multiple filespecs with, 108–110
    printing files, 150–151
    quitting, 156
    replacing files when copying, 68
    shortcuts, 335–337
    Sort Criteria options, 167–169
    viewing file contents, 186
    See also XTree for DOS
XTree for DOS
    backing up with, 290–292
    basics, 25–33
    batch file variables, 48
    command area, 28
    Command shell, 32
    configuration options, 58–65

    display screen, 26–28
    finding words, files, and directories, 112–115
    hard disk management, 290–293
    Help, 32, 121–126
    highlighting directories, 29
    highlighting files, 29–30
    key combination convention in this book, 5
    mouse usage, 37, 136–137
    moving between windows, 29
    quick reference guide, 35–198
    tagging files and directories, 30–31
    untagging files and directories, 31
    versions, 25, 35–37
    windows, 26–28
    XTree for Windows vs., 225, 227–231
    See also specific versions of XTree
XTree for DOS commands
    Attributes, 42–43
    AutoView, 190–191
    Avail, 44
    Branch, 49
    Cancel, 49–50
    Compare, 55–58
    Copy, 65–75, 87–88
    Delete, 78–80, 86–87
    Edit, 94–99
    Execute, 32, 51, 100–102
    File display, 41–42, 103–104
    Filespec, 31–32, 70–71, 83, 106–112, 126, 129, 133–134, 165
    Gather, 188, 189
    Global, 119–121
    Graft, 73–74, 89, 121, 141–142, 358
    Help, 121–124
    Hide, 93–94, 162–163
    History, 53–55, 110, 111, 126–128, 143, 151, 160
    Instant Log, 132, 357
    Invert, 111–112, 128–129, 181–182
    Log, 129–134
    Make, 84–85
    missing from XTree for Windows, 230–231
    Move, 65, 138–143
    Newdate, 76–77
    Oops!, 145–146, 363
    Open, 147–148
    Print, 148–151
    Prune, 81, 88–89, 358
    Quit, 49, 156–157
    Release, 83
    Rename, 85–86, 157–160
    Showall, 49, 165–166
    Sort Criteria, 166–169
    Split, 169–171
    Tag, 177–183
    Unhide, 93–94
    Unsplit, 169–171
    Untag, 177–180, 182–183
    View, 184–189
    Wash Disk, 81–82, 164, 358
    See also specific commands
XTree for Windows
    active window, 224
    archiving with, 312–316
    arranging windows, 234–236
    backing up with, 294
    basics, 221–231
    CONFIG.SYS modification using, 320
    exiting, 252

Index

exiting temporarily, 268
hard disk management, 294–296
initial screen, 221–222
key combination convention in this book, 5
keyboard commands and function keys, 343–344
laptop configuration, 352–354
new terms, 228
quick reference guide, 233–278
selecting and deselecting, 268–271
shortcuts, 343–344
sort order, 271
starting programs, 265
statistics, 272
Tool Palette, 227
windows in, 222–223
XTree for DOS vs., 225, 227–231
XTreeLink with, 323–324
See also specific menus and commands
XTree for Windows commands
  Arrange Now, 236
  Auto Arrange, 235–236
  Auto Viewer, 234
  Cascade, 235
  Change Attributes, 237, 244
  Close, 238–239
  Collapse commands, 254
  Copy, 230, 239–244
  Delete, 230, 244–245
  Deselect, 270
  Directory Format, 236–237, 249–250
  Directory Sort Order, 251, 271
  Exit, 252
  Expand commands, 253
  Find, 254–255
  Format Diskette, 256
  Mark, 258–260
  Mount ZIP, 316
  Move, 230, 260–263
  New ZIP, 313
  Open, 246, 264–265, 315
  Open Auto Directory, 237, 248
  Open Auto View, 238
  Open Directory As, 247
  Open Document View, 275–277
  Open Tree, 274
  Open Tree As, 274
  Overlay, 235
  Preferences, 239, 245, 262–263, 265–266
  Refresh commands, 258
  Rename, 230, 267–268
  Run, 268
  Save Configuration, 239, 265
  Select commands, 269–271
  Set Scope, 248–249, 274
  Tile, 235
  Toggle Directory Format, 271
  Unmark, 260
  Window Layout commands, 235
  XTree for DOS commands missing, 230–231
XTree version modules. *See* laptop configuration
XTreeGold
  7K Wedge, 362
  archiving with, 305–312
  AutoCAD files with, 361
  AutoView command, 190–191
  canceling commands, 50
  command line switches for logging, 133–134
  Command shell with, 52–53
  CONFIG.SYS modification using, 319

configuring, 61–65
configuring logging instructions, 133
cycling through logged drives, 360
EMM386.SYS conflict, 362
finding duplicate files, 360
finding files on floppies, 114
finding text, 114–115
formatting floppies, 117–119
grafting across drives, 360
Help, 122–124
History command and, 54–55
icon, 36–37
Instant Log command, 132
inverting filespecs, 111–112, 129
keyboard commands and function keys, 337–340
laptop configuration, 350–352
loading into high memory, 135
logging directories, 131–132
logging drives cumulatively, 130
memory management, 134–135
memory shortages, 360
missing overlay message, 362
mouse not working, 361
moving among logged drives, 130, 360
moving between split windows, 361
multiple filespecs, 108–110
Newdate command, 76–77
PC-CACHE conflict, 362
preselecting filespecs at startup, 109, 133–134
printing files, 150–151
pull-down menus, 360
questions commonly asked, 360–364
quitting, 156–157
replacing files when copying, 68
shortcuts, 337–340
Sort Criteria options, 167–169
starting Windows from XTreeGold directory, 362
version number, 367
View shows garbage, 361
viewing file contents, 186–187
WPG files and, 361
XTreeLink with, 323
XTreeMenu, 191–198, 360, 362
See also XTree for DOS
XTREEINS program, 59–60
XTreeLink, 317–326
  activating local computer, 322
  activating remote computer, 321
  cables for, 318
  CONFIG.SYS file for, 319–320
  exiting, 325
  installing, 320
  LASTDRIVE statement for, 319–320
  option switches, 325
  preparing computers for linking, 318
  preparing for installation, 319–320
  running, 321–322
  unloading, 325
  using, 323–325
  XTree for Windows with, 323–324
  XTreeGold with, 323
XTreeMenu, 191–198
  accessing, 192
  collapsing and expanding, 193
  deleting items, 194–195
  editing menu display, 193–196
  editing menu instructions, 196–198
  hot keys, 360
  moving items, 195–196
  not executing programs, 362

popping up at startup, 198
turning off tree display, 194
XTreeNet, 201–210
  benefits of, 202
  default configuration, 365
  finding owner of files or directories, 365
  Information Mode, 205
  keyboard commands and function keys, 340–343
  logging entire volume, 365
  maximum files loggable, 365
  Novell mail directories, 365
  peer-to-peer file management, 203–204
  peer-to-peer remote control, 204–205
  questions commonly asked, 363–364, 364–366
  shortcuts, 340–343
  Statistics Mode, 205
  trustee changes, 366
  Trustee Information Mode, 205
  who needs it, 201–202
  XTreePro Gold vs., 203
XTreeNet commands
  Attach, 204, 206
  Attributes (directory), 206
  Attributes (file), 207–208
  Available, 210
  Detach, 205, 206
  Format, 210
  Info display, 205
  Label, 210
  Map, 203–205, 209
  Volume, 210
  Wash, 210
XTreePro
  canceling commands, 50
  Can't find file XTPRO.X01 message, 357
  Command shell with, 52–53
  configuring, 60–61
  Editors Choice Award, 374
  error message when starting, 356
  finding files on floppies, 113
  formatting floppies, 117
  Help, 122–124
  History command and, 53–54
  icon, 36–37
  keyboard commands and function keys, 331–332
  laptop configuration, 346
  logging drives cumulatively, 130
  memory management, 134–135
  memory shortages with version 1.1, 357
  moving among logged drives, 130
  multiple filespecs with, 108
  printing files, 150–151
  questions commonly asked, 356–357, 363–364
  quitting, 156–157
  releasing logged drives, 130–131
  replacing files when copying, 68
  shortcuts, 331–332
  Sort Criteria options, 167–169
  SUBST command with, 176
  version number, 367
  viewing file contents, 185–186
  See also XTree for DOS
XTreePro Gold
  7K Wedge, 135, 357
  Application Menu, 38–41
  Archive module missing, 367
  archiving with, 299–305
  AutoView command, 190
  canceling commands, 50
  CD-ROM drives, 358

  Command shell with, 52–53
  configuring, 61–65
  DESQView with, 359
  DOS 4.0 and 5.0 with, 358
  Editors Choice Award, 374
  finding files, 357–358
  finding files on floppies, 114
  finding text, 114–115
  formatting floppies, 117–119
  Help, 122–123
  Hex mode editing, 358
  History command and, 54–55
  icon, 36–37
  Instant Log command, 132, 357
  inverting filespecs, 111–112, 129
  keyboard commands and function keys, 333–335
  laptop configuration, 346–348
  logging directories, 131
  logging drives cumulatively, 130
  memory management, 134–135
  memory required, 359
  mouse support, 358
  moving among logged drives, 130
  multiple filespecs, 108–110
  Newdate command, 76–77
  OS/2 with, 359
  printing files, 150–151
  questions commonly asked, 357–359, 363–364
  Quick Reference, 124–126
  quitting, 156–157
  releasing logged drives, 130–131
  replacing files when copying, 68
  shortcuts, 333–335
  Sort Criteria options, 167–169
  split window command, 358
  SUBST command with, 177
  version number, 367
  VGA support, 358
  viewing file contents, 186–187
  Windows (Microsoft) with, 359
  XTreeNet vs., 203
  See also XTree for DOS
XTSERV program, 204

— Y —

You Can Do It with DOS, 369
You Can Do It with Windows, 369

— Z —

Zip files
  copying files as, 312
  creating, 305–308, 312–314
  encryption, 307, 314
  extracting files, 310
  modifying, 311–312, 315
  mounting, 316
  opening, 309–310, 315
  path options, 307
  restoring paths from, 363
  speed/size options, 308, 313
  treating like drives, 315–316
  See also archiving
zipping. See archiving
zippy exit, 132, 156–157
Zoom In option, 276
Zoom Out option, 276
zooming viewed files, 190, 276

VALUABLE COUPONS
FOR BONUS SOFTWARE

SAVE OVER $500!

On the following pages you'll find money-saving coupons for numerous software programs and utilities that will help you get the most out of your PC.

There's also a special offer on the new
XTree for Windows
— get it for just **$69.95** —
$29 off the
list price!

Turn the page for more details...
Money-saving coupons — just another way
IDG Books offers you *value!*

IDG BOOKS

XTree for Windows for just $69.95!

That's giant savings for windows shoppers.

Take advantage of this special offer on XTree® for Windows™ and get the best in file management at no risk—we offer a 60-day money back guarantee. **XTree for Windows regularly sells for $99.00 SRP.**

Whether you know XTree from DOS, UNIX, or NetWare, you're expecting a lot from XTree for Windows. And you'll get it. XTree provides the power, ease of use, and versatility, but now comes wrapped in a new, streamlined, intuitive Windows interface.

The August,'92 issue of *PC Computing* hailed XTree for Windows as a program **"loaded with file-management muscle."** In acknowledging XTree's expertise in file management, the reviewer said, **"Pick one thing and do it well. XTree Company must have taken that advice to heart in creating XTree for Windows...it's the most powerful Windows file manger to date."**

The September,'92 issue of *Windows Magazine* agreed, stating **"XTree offers the smartest, most intuitive technique for ZIP file management I have ever seen."** The article also noted that while many multifunction packages have to compromise somewhere, XTree didn't.

XTree for Windows is fast. Like other XTree products, *you can instantly copy, delete, move, rename, and view files and directories with a single keystroke or mouse click.* Plus, the tool palette provides button access to frequently used commands. And the drag-and-drop control lets you visually copy and move files and directories with the click of a mouse. You can access all files, directories and archived volumes (zipped files) *all from one screen!*

XTree for Windows supports the industry-standard ZIP format for fast, compatible file compression and can easily create and extract files from ZIP archives, which can save up to 50% of your disk space. Adding to or extracting from ZIP files is as simple as dragging and dropping with a mouse or using the copy command. *You can even view files that are compressed in ZIP archives without extracting them!*

A new feature in the XTree line up is XTreeLink, and it is included in XTree for Windows! This feature lets you *connect two computers with a serial or parallel transfer cable and then seamlessly work with and manage files on both*– as though the files were all on the same computer.

XTree for Windows goes beyond being amazingly powerful by allowing users to instantly launch into application programs or data. Other features include:

- Virtually no memory limitations, so you can log or display as many files as you have.
- A convenient tool palette with graphical icons delivers mouse button access to frequently used commands allowing you to execute commands without having to use the pull-down menus.
- Network support, compatible with any DOS-based Novell or NetBIOS network supported by Windows.
- Background processing so that long operations can be worked on in the background while you operate other programs.

Who should get XTree for Windows? Well, if you use Windows on a regular basis, you owe it to yourself to take a look at this exciting product. While we've changed the long-time DOS interface to provide greater flexibility and follow Windows conventions, we're sure you'll like the new approach.

Order today! Call: **1-800-395-8733**

offer #130

XTREE COMPANY

4115 Broad Street, Bldg 1, San Luis Obispo, CA 93401-7993

Limited offer. Shipping and applicable sales tax will be added to all orders. Offer available in U.S. and Canada only. All prices are in U.S. dollars.

SitBack®

The Only Backup Program That Provides <u>Unattended</u>, <u>Background</u> Operation in Both DOS And Windows

100% Protection....100% Security
Up-To-The-Minute Backups

Regularly $99.00 Special Price $49.95

The Problem
If you're like most people, you know how important it is to regularly back up your hard disk. But like most people, you probably don't. Why? Because backup is a chore. It's non-productive and traditional backup software - although fast - requires too much effort, making backup easy to ignore.

Even if you backup once a week or month, all of the files you have created or changed since your last backup are still exposed. These files are usually the most important at the time, and if lost, causes the greatest productivity loss.

The Solution
Is SitBack, a memory resident backup program that keeps your most recently created and changed files backed up automatically, in the background, without lifting a finger or exiting the programs you are working with.

You remain 100% productive and at the same time 100% protected.

It is perfect for professionals who have more important things to worry about than the usual hassle involved with other backup programs, but who's data is critical and time sensitive.

SitBack is the perfect program for those who want more protection than nightly or periodic backups. It assures that backups are done and up-to-the-minute.

How It Works
SitBack works unattended by backing up newly created and changed files throughout the day, each time your computer is idle for an amount of time you specify or you can schedule backups at specific times of the day or week.

Either way, SitBack provides up-to-the-minute protection of your most valuable asset - information, keeping your hard disk, workstation or server currently backed up automatically and in the background.

Easy To Use/Setup
SitBack is easy to install and setup. Choose which drives, directories or files to backup, how frequently and to where. The rest is left to SitBack. You probably won't even know it's working.

Major Uses
You'll find a use for SitBack in virtually all PC environments from standalone to workstation to server backup applications. It's also the perfect companion to complement your existing backup practices and procedures.

- ◆ Hard disk to floppy, floptical, optical, Bernoulli and Syquest drives.
- ◆ Workstation to server
- ◆ Server to server or workstation
- ◆ Hard disk to hard disk

Network Compatible
SitBack is certified and approved by Novell Inc. and works with all leading peer-to-peer or server based net-bios networks.

Comparable feature set available in the SitBack For DOS

20 And 100 User Network License Available - Includes Both SitBack For DOS and Windows

---

SitBack Technologies, Inc. - 9290 Bond, Suite 104 - Overland Park, KS 66214 - 913-894-0808 - Fax 913-894-0250

Get Control of Your Finances!

Get Finance10®

**To Order, call
1-800-332-2983**

Outside the U.S.
1-213-658-7731

ONLY $39.95!

Finally, an easy-to-use software program that helps you make "cents" out of complex financial information.

Finance 10 is a collection of ten, easy-to-use financial calculators that puts you in complete control of financial information. Complicated financial calculations are made *in seconds,* while input data is checked automatically for tax law limitations and other special considerations.

With **Finance** 10 you can quickly estimate the affordable price for property. Evaluate whether it makes sense to lease or purchase a car of finance a house. Compare financial benefits of a pension plan. Determine sums for tax returns and financial statements. Calculate bank balances at the end of a series of deposits, and much, much more. **Finance** 10 even prints customized reports in seconds!

Only **Finance** 10 has two modes of operation. Use it as a stand alone application or as a handy pop-up utility (using a thrifty 8K of RAM)! Great for consultants working on laptops.

No accounting or computer experience is required. Simply choose the calculator you need, enter the facts you know, and *ba-bing,* **Finance** 10 does the rest! No other financial software is as fast, comprehensive, or easy to learn.

Only **Finance** 10 includes all of the following calculators:
❶ Bond Yield to Maturity; ❷ Depreciation; ❸ Financial Manager Rate of Return; ❹ Individual Retirement Account (IRA); ❺ Internal Rate of Return; ❻ Lease vs. Purchase Analysis; ❼ Loan Amortization Schedule; ❽ Personal Financial Statement; ❾ Present Value/Future Value; ❿ Statistics.

Special Offer: Normally, **Finance** 10 retails for $69.95. But you can get yours for only $39.95 (and save $30!), just by mentioning *The Official XTree Companion.* Want more? **Finance** 10 even has a 30-day NO RISK money-back guarantee. No other financial software offers this unbelievable combination of price, value, support and savings.

FINANCIAL $OFTWARE COMPANY

P.O. Box 481290 • Los Angeles 90048

To order by mail, please send your name, company, address, phone number, VISA or MC credit card number expiration date, and signature (or send certified check or money order) to The Financial Software Company. Price is $39.95 + $8.00 shipping and handling per copy. (CA residents add $3.30 sales tax per copy. Canadian orders add $2.00 per copy. Overseas add $10.00 per copy.) The entire ten program package requires DOS 3.0 or later and 130K RAM (8K in pop-up mode).

Why stick with second-rate communications software when upgrading is this easy?

Did you know that the best communications software is not Crosstalk, Procomm or Smartcom? It's HyperACCESS/5 from Hilgraeve.

Seeing is believing. So we're making a very special offer to owners of Crosstalk™, Relay™, Smartcom™, Mirror™, Procomm, Telix and Qmodem. For a limited time, you can step up to HyperACCESS/5, normally $199, for only

$49.95

There's NO RISK. If within 60 days you're not completely satisfied, return HyperACCESS/5 for a full refund.

Some programs lack important features like: Zmodem, PC-to-PC power, strong script language, or terminal emulators you need. Others may have what you need, but are slow, awkward or unreliable. HyperACCESS/5 gives you everything you need, with the speed, agility, and reliability you deserve!

Guaranteed results in 10 minutes or less

We guarantee you can install and make your first call in 10 minutes or less. HyperACCESS/5 is Hardware Aware™ —it adapts itself to your PC and 70 specific modems, plus generic types—so you can place and answer calls *immediately*. And its slick Sliding Windows™ interface is more than intuitive, it's obvious!

HyperProtocol sends files faster

HyperACCESS/5's HyperProtocol has on-the-fly compression and lets you

> "A must-have for those interested in telecommunications..." John C. Dvorak - PC Magazine, 12/12/89
>
> "A new standard in performance of communications software has arrived, and its name is HyperACCESS/5." PCResource, 8/90
>
> "The graphics and user interface are top notch and visually impressive." InfoWorld, 6/11/90
>
> "...makes all other communications software positively obsolete...enough goodies to keep a super-power-user interested and busy for a long time." REMark, 6/90

transfer files through your modem at up to 5 times the modem's speed. And now that we've put HyperProtocol in the public domain, you can get the same fast transfers when you call BBSs or friends with other comm software.

Automating communications is a breeze

HyperACCESS/5's Discerning Learning™ watches you, learning not just your keystrokes, but your intentions. Quickly, easily, and without writing scripts, you can automate every facet of your communications, even entire calls!

Upgrade to the experts' choice now!

The computer industry's top software evaluators have unanimously chosen HyperACCESS/5. Isn't it worth $49.95 to find out why?

PC MAGAZINE   **TOP RATED**   **Software Digest RATINGS REPORT**

Editor's Choice   **Best Overall**   **Best Overall**
July 1988 & May 1987   April 1990   September 1986

Attention Procomm, Crosstalk and Smartcom owners!

Step up to HyperACCESS/5 for DOS for only $49.95 risk-free. Proof of ownership is required.

TO ORDER:

CALL TOLL-FREE: 800-826-2760, 8am-6pm EST
OR BY FAX: 313-243-0645. See info below.
OR BY MAIL: See info below.

Hilgraeve Inc.

To order by mail or fax, please send your name, company, address, phone number, credit card number, expiration date, and signature (or send certified check or money order) to Hilgraeve Inc., HyperACCESS/5 Upgrade, 111 Conant Ave., Suite A, Monroe, MI 48161. Price is $49.95 plus $6.00 shipping. Offer good in US and Canada only. Limited time offer. Limit of one per customer.

DECIDE ON DYSAN
AND YOU'LL SAVE MORE THAN DATA

International Data Group publishes 150 magazines in 51 countries.

Dysan's teamed up with the world's largest technology publishing group to bring you over $200 in savings on top-selling IDG computer magazines and books. Plus you could be one of 20,000 instant winners in Dysan's "Win and Save" Sweepstakes. So look for one million specially marked boxes to start your savings today.

Dysan 100. 3 1/2" & 5 1/4" pre-formatted flexible disks for IBM PC-compatibles. Always 100% tested to be 100% error free over the entire disk surface. Get more quality from the 100% better brand. Dysan.

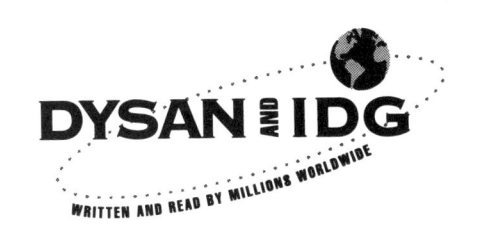

DYSAN AND IDG
WRITTEN AND READ BY MILLIONS WORLDWIDE

Make This Year's Taxes Easy-- With TurboTax!

7 Million Returns Prepared With TurboTax Last Year!

$40 Savings for "The Official XTree Companion" Readers!

Now available for DOS and Windows™

Discover the New EasyStep™ system. Introducing EasyStep, a revolutionary new tax preparation system that leads you through your tax return from start to finish, guides you every step of the way, and completes the return for you -- automatically. More than just an interview or a tutorial, EasyStep is a whole new way to do your taxes. And only TurboTax has it.

Even tough tax returns are easy... with EasyStep. Now people with complicated tax returns, who never thought they could do their own taxes, are using EasyStep. EasyStep breaks up the tax preparation process into short, concise steps. From importing your data from Quicken®, to an interview that shows you exactly where each figure belongs, to checking your return, to printing an IRS approved form you just sign and file; each step is clear and easy.

Go straight to the forms -- it's still easy, fast and accurate. If you don't need the extra help our new EasyStep system provides, just go straight to the forms. TurboTax helps you determine which forms you need, and saves you time by automatically doing all the tedious calculations for you. And, you can get help if you need it -- from EasyStep, or the IRS instructions.

TurboTax is simply the best way to do your taxes -- with everything you need to do your taxes quickly and accurately. TurboTax includes over 90 forms, schedules, and worksheets, complete IRS instructions, tax help in plain English, itemizations, "Which Forms" function, and new EasyStep.

You can print an IRS approved form on most printers, or file electronically for a small transmission fee. Just sign it and mail it in!

Nine out of ten people who try TurboTax use it again. TurboTax is, by far, America's best selling tax software. Once taxpayers try TurboTax they can't believe they ever did taxes without it. And research shows that 9 out of 10 TurboTax customers intend to keep using it next year.

Loaded with features. TurboTax contains a wealth of powerful features such as tax savings suggestions, a final review, and audit flags to make sure your return is accurate and complete.

Backed by America's #1 tax preparation software company. TurboTax is supported by the strongest development and technical support team in the industry. And we stand behind our products with a 30-day money-back guarantee.

Order Today!
See Reverse Side For Order Form

TurboTax®

ChipSoft

© 1992/1993 ChipSoft, Inc. TurboTax® is a registered trademark of ChipSoft, Inc. EasyStep™ is a trademark of ChipSoft, Inc. All other trademarks are the sole property of their respective owners.

SAVINGS CERTIFICATE

For "The Official XTree Companion" Readers!

TurboTax®

Save up to $40.00 when you buy both Federal and State packages!

Don't Forget Your State Tax Return!

You'll save plenty of time doing your Federal tax return with TurboTax. But what about your state return? All you have to do is "Go To State" and all applicable data will flow over to your state tax package. In just a few minutes you can have a completed state income tax return. That is... *if* you have a TurboTax Personal/State Package!

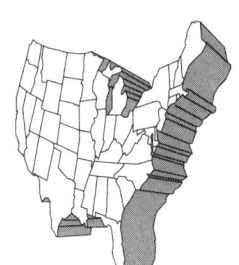

Our Personal/State packages allow you to prepare your state tax return quickly and easily. Our state packages contain all the commonly used state forms and assist you in their preparation. Order today and get your taxes done fast!

Federal Tax Software

		Qty	Total
TurboTax for DOS	$49.95		
TurboTax for Windows	$49.95		

State Tax Software (please specify state)

			Qty	Total
❑ DOS	state	$39.95		
❑ Windows	state	$39.95		

SALES TAX: California residents add 7.25% sales tax. Minnesota residents add 6.5% sales tax.

DOS state version available for all states having income tax. Windows state versions available for CA, CT, DC, IL, MA, MD, MI, MN, NC, NJ, NY, OH, OR, PA & VA.

TurboTax for DOS requires IBM® PC, AT, PS/1, PS/2 or compatible; 640K RAM; 512K RAM free memory; DOS 3.0 or higher; and hard disk. Mouse support included.

TurboTax for Windows requires IBM® PC, AT, PS/2 or compatible; 2mb RAM; Windows 3.0 or higher; and hard disk.

Subtotal	
Sales Tax	
Shipping	$7.00
Grand Total	

Please choose:
❑ 3½" disks -or-
❑ 5¼" disks

Backed By A 30-Day Money Back Guarantee!

Name_____
Address_____ (no P.O. Boxes, please)
City_____ State____ Zip_____
Daytime Phone (____)_____ (in case there's a question about your order)
❑ Check Enclosed (payable to "ChipSoft")
❑ MasterCard ❑ VISA ❑ AmEx ❑ Discover
Card#_____ Exp. Date_____
Signature_____

Please bill my credit card immediately to expedite delivery when products are released in October ("HeadStart" version which contains preliminary forms) and January ("Final" version which contains IRS approved, fileable forms).

Mail Your Order To:

**ChipSoft, Inc.
P.O. Box 85709
San Diego, CA 92186-5709**

Credit Card Telephone Orders:

1-619-453-8722

Offer Good Through April 15, 1993.
Not Valid With Any Other Offer. **Ext. 3914**

❑ Please check here if you want only the Final version. Otherwise, we will ship both the HeadStart and Final versions.

Try PackRat at no risk for $195 and stop sweating the details.

This award-winning Personal Information Manager (PIM) for Windows handles the details so you can concentrate on the more important things that only YOU can do. PackRat flexibly manages your:

- phone book
- calendar
- to-do's
- hard disk files
- projects
- autodialing
- reminders
- finances
- time tracking
- billing
- free-form notes
- and more!

Seamlessly exchange information with:

- Word for Windows
- WordPerfect for Windows
- Ami Pro
- files containing CompuServe forum messages
- Excel
- WinFax Pro
- Da Vinci eMAIL

The experts are raving about PackRat:

- Editors' Choice Award
- Buyers Assurance Seal
- Win 100 Award
- Computer Currents Class of 1991

So stop sweating the details and put PackRat to work for you. And right now it's easier than ever because you can save $200 on this award-winning PIM -- and at no risk. Try PackRat for 60 days. Keep it only if you're satisfied.

Limit one per customer. Offer good only in the United States and its territories. Use reservation number IDG-93 when ordering.

Only $195

Call 1-800-PACKRAT
(1-800-722-5728)
ORDER TODAY

KEEPING YOUR BUSINESS YOUR OWN!

FASTLOCK PLUS is two software programs in one package, *FastLock 2.0* and *FastLock Plus*. *FastLock 2.0* offers the easiest solution to hard disk security. It is a program you run each time you choose to password protect your hard drive. It can **lock any size hard disk**, offers **dual passwords** (master and default), **floppy boot protection**, **hard disk parking** and **an alarm**. For those that like the quick and easy route *FastLock 2.0* is simple, powerful and perfect.

If your security needs are more complex try our "*Plus Module*". It consists of a simple **one-time installation** process and you never have to run the program again. Each time you boot up, the computer will ask for a **log-on and password**. It also comes complete with **detailed audit trail** capabilities and has a **Windows and DOS compatible screen-blanker and keyboard lock**.

Special Offer!!
$49.95
Plus shipping & handling
Regularly $84.95

RUPP TECHNOLOGY COORPORATION 3228 EAST INDIAN SCHOOL ROAD, PHOENIX, AZ 85018
To order call or fax and mention IDG:
800-852-7877 or 602-224-9922 (Fax) 602-224-0898

Vopt

T.M.

Is your disk running slower than when it was new? That's fragmentation buildup!

File fragmentation is the unavoidable result of the way DOS stores disk files, by writing file segments wherever it can find space on the disk. As you process files — adding, editing and deleting records — fragments are scattered across your disk.

File fragmentation slows down your system and shortens the life of your hard drive. Files must be accessed sequentially even when they're not stored in proper order on the disk so, over time, applications run slower as fragmentation builds up.

If disaster strikes your system, file fragmentation can even be dangerous to your data — intact files can usually be recovered after a disk crash, but fragmented files may be lost forever.

Vopt is the quickest, safest way to clean up your disk and keep it as fast and efficient as when it was new. Vopt gets rid of a whole day's fragmentation in just seconds, so you can run it automatically every day to keep your files intact and compact.

Vopt is available in computer stores everywhere at $60 and up. Now you can order the complete Vopt package for only $40.00, 1/3 off the regular price! Mail this coupon today to

GOLDEN BOW SYSTEMS

PO BOX 3039

SAN DIEGO

CA 92163-1039

Multi-user Site Licenses are available at reduced prices.

For more information about Vopt and our other fine products, call (800)284-3269 or fax (619) 298-9950.

Vopt NOW
to keep your disk as fast as new

- **SIMPLE MENU-DRIVEN OPERATION**
- **RUNS AUTOMATICALLY IN SECONDS**
- **HANDLES DISKS UP TO 1000 MEGABYTES**
- **ORGANIZES DISK FILES INTO CONTIGUOUS CLUSTERS FOR EFFICIENT ACCESS**
- **COMPACTS DISK CONTENTS FOR OPTIMAL STORAGE UTILIZATION**
- **SAFE FOR PROTECTED AND HIDDEN FILES**
- **SAFE FOR YOUR DATA**
- **WORKS WITH YOUR SYSTEM**
  - *All popular hard disks – MFM, RLL, ESDI, SCSI, IDE, removable media drives, Device Drivers*
  - *All popular disk formats – PC-DOS, MS-DOS, DR DOS, PC/MOS, Vfeature Deluxe, Speedstor, Disk Manager*

OPTIONS
- *Automatic correction of lost or unreadable disk clusters*
- *Data verification during optimization*
- *Suppression of optimization display*
- *Extra Speed*
- *File spacing*

EXTRAS
- *Disk cluster map*
- *Disk maintenance – recover file data from bad clusters, mark them for future avoidance.*
- *AUTOEXEC program scheduler*
- *Diskette media and alignment tests*
- *PrintScreen turbocharger*
- *Hard disk seek timing plotter*
- *System benchmarks*
- *Resident program monitor*

YES! Send me Vopt at the bargain price of just $40*!

____ Charge my VISA or MasterCard account   ____ Check enclosed

Card number_____-_____-_____-_____ Expires_____

Name on card_____ Signature _____

SHIP TO_____ Phone _____

COMPANY_____

STREET ADDRESS_____

_____

CITY_____STATE/ZIP_____COUNTRY_____

* Export orders add $5 for air mail shipping. California orders add sales tax. Void where prohibited.

I prefer a 3.5" ____   5.25" ____ diskette.

8/92

Vopt is a trademark of Golden Bow Systems.

Two Special Offers from PC-Kwik Corporation

DOS Users!
Triple the Speed of Your Computer

▶ Speeds up your disk drives
▶ Speeds up your screen
▶ Speeds up your keyboard
▶ Speeds up your printers

PC-Kwik Power Pak

PC-Kwik Power Pak is an integrated package of utilities which work together to improve the overall performance of your computer by three to nine times, whether it's an AT or a 486. It's like getting a newer, faster computer for a fraction of the cost.

Make your purchase now, and we'll send you PC-Kwik Power Pak for $59.95! Top performance has never been so easy.

$59.95

Windows Users!
Faster, Easier, Better Windows Today

▶ Fast and easy program launching
▶ System performance monitoring
▶ Disk testing and optimization
▶ File compression and storage

WinMaster

WinMaster, the essential everyday tool set, lets you take control of Windows and make it work the way that **suits you** best. WinMaster's easy-to-use tools **are** the best way to make a great system better. Designed to be useful in minutes, you can start being more productive right away.

Make your purchase now, and we'll send you WinMaster for $59.95!

$59.95

PC-Kwik CORPORATION

15100 S.W. Koll Parkway
Beaverton, OR 97006-6026

ORDER CODE 0CQ

WATS: 800-274-5945
tel: 503-644-5644
fax: 503-646-8267

---

① Product	② Ship & Hand.	③ TOTAL
☐ **WinMaster** $59.95	USA/Can. $6.50	
☐ **Power Pak** $59.95	Int'l $20.00	
	+ $	= $

Shipping Information:

Name _____
Company _____
Address One _____
Address Two _____
City, State/Province Zip+4/Postal Code _____
Country _____
Day Phone _____ Fax _____

④ Disk Size:
☐ 3.5"
☐ 5.25"

⑤ Payment Information:
☐ Check ☐ Visa ☐ MasterCard ☐ AmEx
Card #: _____ Exp: __/__
Sig: _____

Coupon may accompany personal or business check payable in US funds as alternative method of payment. Must order direct from PC-Kwik Corporation in the US. Not good with any other offer. Limit one copy of each product per customer. Please allow 2 - 4 weeks for delivery. Offer expires December 31, 1993.

International Data Group (IDG) and IDG Books Worldwide, Inc., an affiliate of IDG based in San Mateo, CA, are committed to directing the power of business and industry toward improving the environment.

▲▼▲

This book was printed on recycled paper and can be recycled.

World Class Information

Look to IDG Books for information on your specific microcomputer needs, with books bearing the endorsements of *PC World, InfoWorld,* and *Macworld*. Use the order form at the back of the book to request a catalog of our current selections or to order directly. Following is a portion of our list:

Hard Disk SECRETS
by John M. Goodman, Ph.D.

From hard disk fundamentals to more advanced technical topics — it's all here! Learn how hard disks really work, why they die, and how you can prolong their life. Hundreds of expert tips, techniques, and insights help you maximize your hard disk's efficiency.

$34.95/$44.95 Canada, includes one 5 1/4" disk of free hard disk tune-up software

ISBN: 1-878058-64-9

Windows 3.1 SECRETS

by Brian Livingston

Windows expert Brian Livingston reveals the secret power of Windows 3.1 and 3.0 — includes over 40 programs of the best in Windows shareware.

$39.95/$52.95 Canada, includes three 5 1/4" disks

ISBN: 1-878058-43-6

PC SECRETS

by Caroline Halliday

A comprehensive and valuable guide to optimizing your PC's performance — includes two disks loaded with over 20 software utilities.

$39.95/$52.95 Canada, includes two 5 1/4" disks of PC-Tune-Up utilities

ISBN: 1-878058-49-5

PC World DOS 5 Complete Handbook
by John Socha & Clint Hicks

This book includes a Special Edition of the Norton Commander disk management software — the ultimate combination that lets DOS Versions 2–5 work for you.

$34.95/$44.95 Canada, includes one 5 1/4" disk with Special Edition of Norton Commander software

ISBN: 1-878058-13-4

PC World Excel 4 for Windows Handbook

by John Walkenbach & David Maguiness

Complete tutorial and reference to the ins and outs of the latest version of Excel — includes a 32-page Quick Reference Answer booklet.

$29.95/$39.95 Canada

ISBN: 1-878058-46-0

DOS For Dummies

by Dan Gookin

Teaches DOS to even the most reluctant computer user with humor and style. This year's most popular computer book!

$16.95/$21.95 Canada

Recommended by *The New York Times*.

ISBN: 1-878058-25-8

COMPUTER BOOK SERIES FROM IDG

Windows For Dummies

by Andy Rathbone

A light-hearted "…For Dummies" approach that clears up Windows confusion — covers the basics from installation nightmares to troubleshooting problems.

$16.95/$21.95 Canada

ISBN: 1-878058-61-4

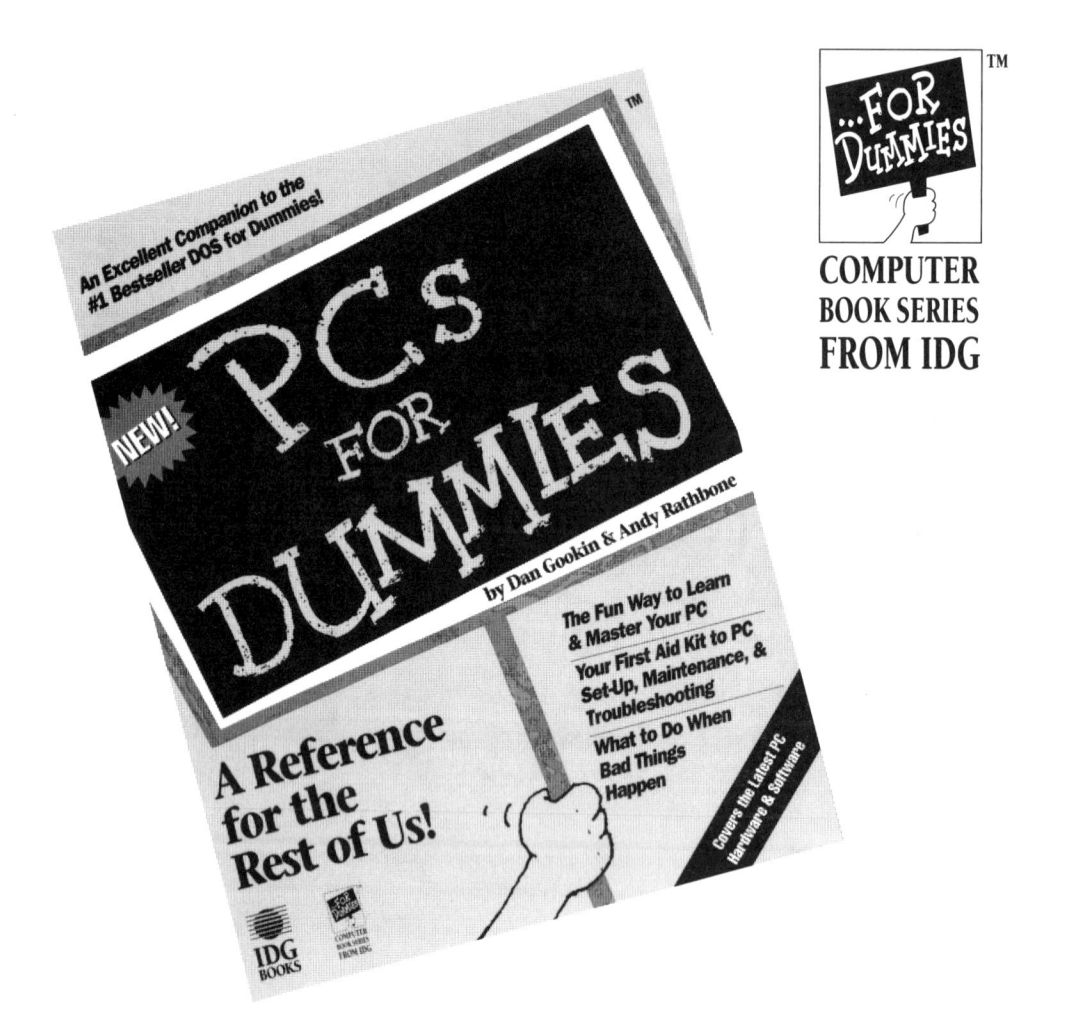

PCs For Dummies

by Dan Gookin, author of the #1 bestseller DOS For Dummies, & Andy Rathbone

The non-nerd's guide to PC configuration, upgrading, and repair. System hardware, and popular peripherals explained — for the computer phobic!

$16.95/$21.95 Canada

ISBN: 1-878058-51-7

IDG Books Worldwide Registration Card
The Official XTree Companion, 3rd Edition

Fill this out — and hear about updates to this book and other IDG Books Worldwide products!

Name _____

Company/Title _____

Address _____

City/State/Zip _____

What is the single most important reason you bought this book? _____

_____

Where did you buy this book?
- ❏ Bookstore (Name: _____)
- ❏ Electronics/Software store (Name: _____)
- ❏ Advertisement (If magazine, which? _____)
- ❏ Mail order (Name of catalog/mail order house: _____)
- ❏ Other: _____

How did you hear about this book?
- ❏ Book review in: _____
- ❏ Advertisement in: _____
- ❏ Catalog
- ❏ Found in store
- ❏ Other: _____

How many computer books do you purchase a year?
- ❏ 1   ❏ 6-10
- ❏ 2-5   ❏ More than 10

What are your primary software applications?
_____
_____
_____

How would you rate the overall content of this book?
- ❏ Very good   ❏ Satisfactory
- ❏ Good   ❏ Poor

Why? _____

What chapters did you find most valuable? _____

What chapters did you find least valuable? _____

What kind of chapter or topic would you add to future editions of this book? _____

_____

Please give us any additional comments. _____

_____

Thank you for your help!

❏ I liked this book! By checking this box, I give you permission to use my name and quote me in future IDG Books Worldwide promotional materials. Daytime phone number_____ .

❏ FREE! Send me a copy of your computer book and book/disk catalog.

Fold Here

Place
stamp
here

IDG Books Worldwide, Inc.
155 Bovet Road
Suite 610
San Mateo, CA 94402

Attn: Reader Response / XTree, 3rd Edition

IDG BOOKS

Order Form

Order Center: (800) 762-2974 (7 a.m.–5 p.m., PST, weekdays)
or (415) 312-0650
Order Center FAX: (415) 358-1260

Quantity	Title & ISBN	Price	Total

Shipping & Handling Charges

Subtotal	U.S.	Canada & International	International Air Mail
Up to $20.00	Add $3.00	Add $4.00	Add $10.00
$20.01–40.00	$4.00	$5.00	$20.00
$40.01–60.00	$5.00	$6.00	$25.00
$60.01–80.00	$6.00	$8.00	$35.00
Over $80.00	$7.00	$10.00	$50.00

In U.S. and Canada, shipping is UPS ground or equivalent. For Rush shipping call (800) 762-2974.

Subtotal _____
CA residents add applicable sales tax _____
IN residents add 5% sales tax _____
Canadian residents add 7% GST tax _____
Shipping _____
TOTAL _____

Ship to:

Name _____
Company _____
Address _____
City/State/Zip _____
Daytime phone _____

Payment: ☐ Check to IDG Books   ☐ Visa   ☐ MasterCard   ☐ American Express

Card # _____   Expires _____

Please send this order form to: IDG Books, 155 Bovet Road, Suite 610, San Mateo, CA 94402.
Allow up to 3 weeks for delivery. Thank you!

BK=100192

Fold Here

Place stamp here

IDG Books Worldwide, Inc.
155 Bovet Road
Suite 610
San Mateo, CA 94402

Attn: Order Center / XTree, 3rd Edition